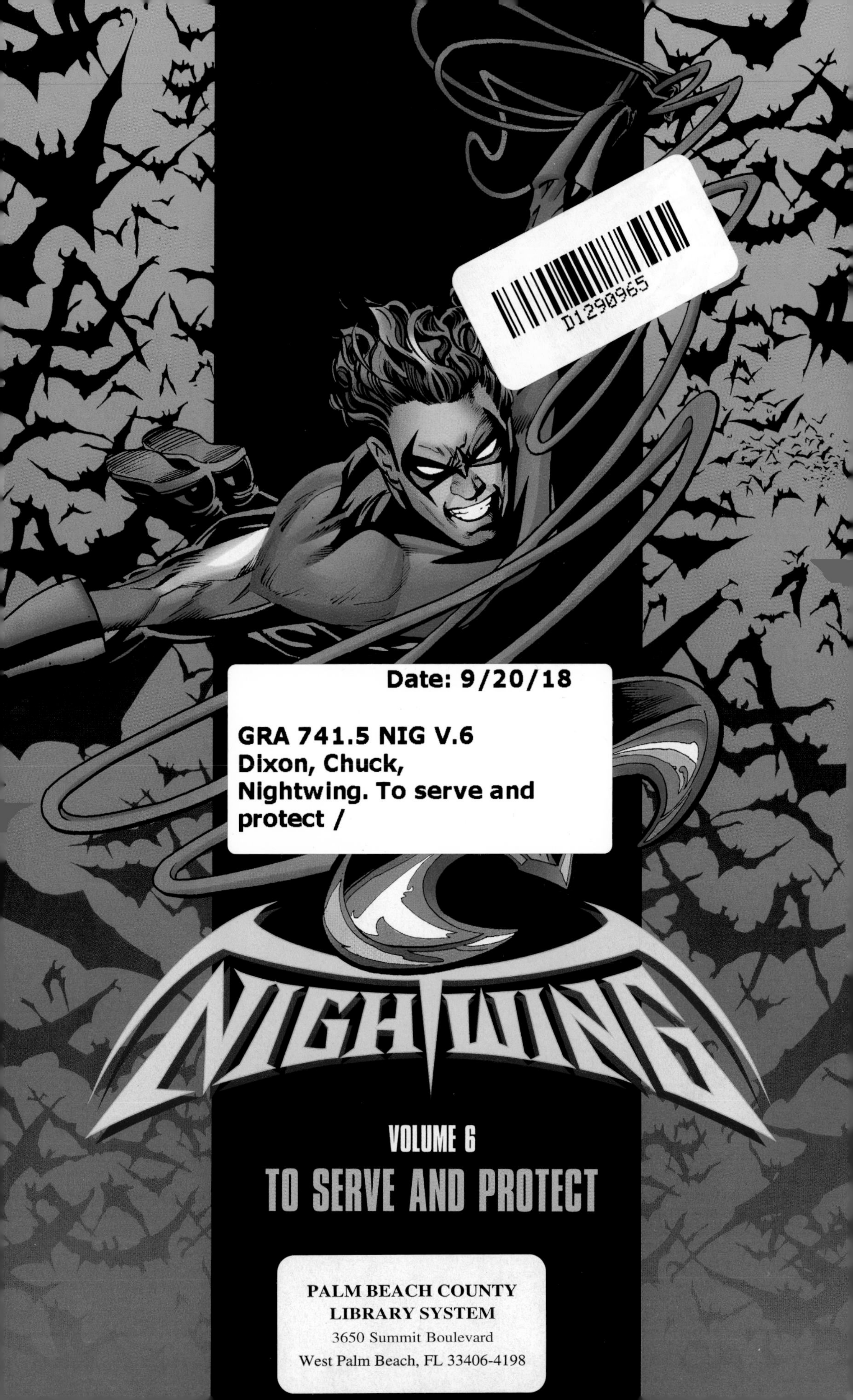
NIGHTWING
VOLUME 6
TO SERVE AND PROTECT

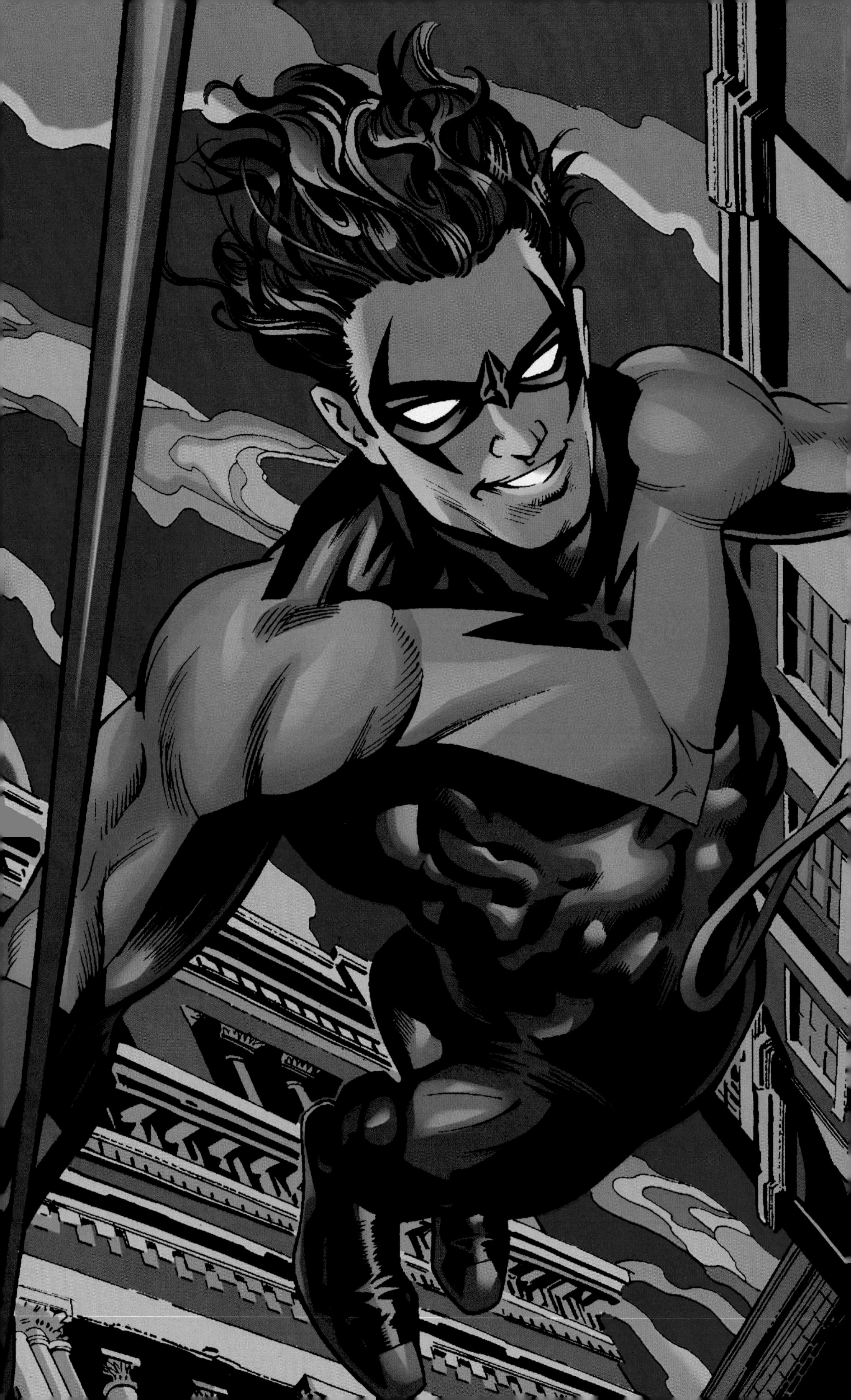

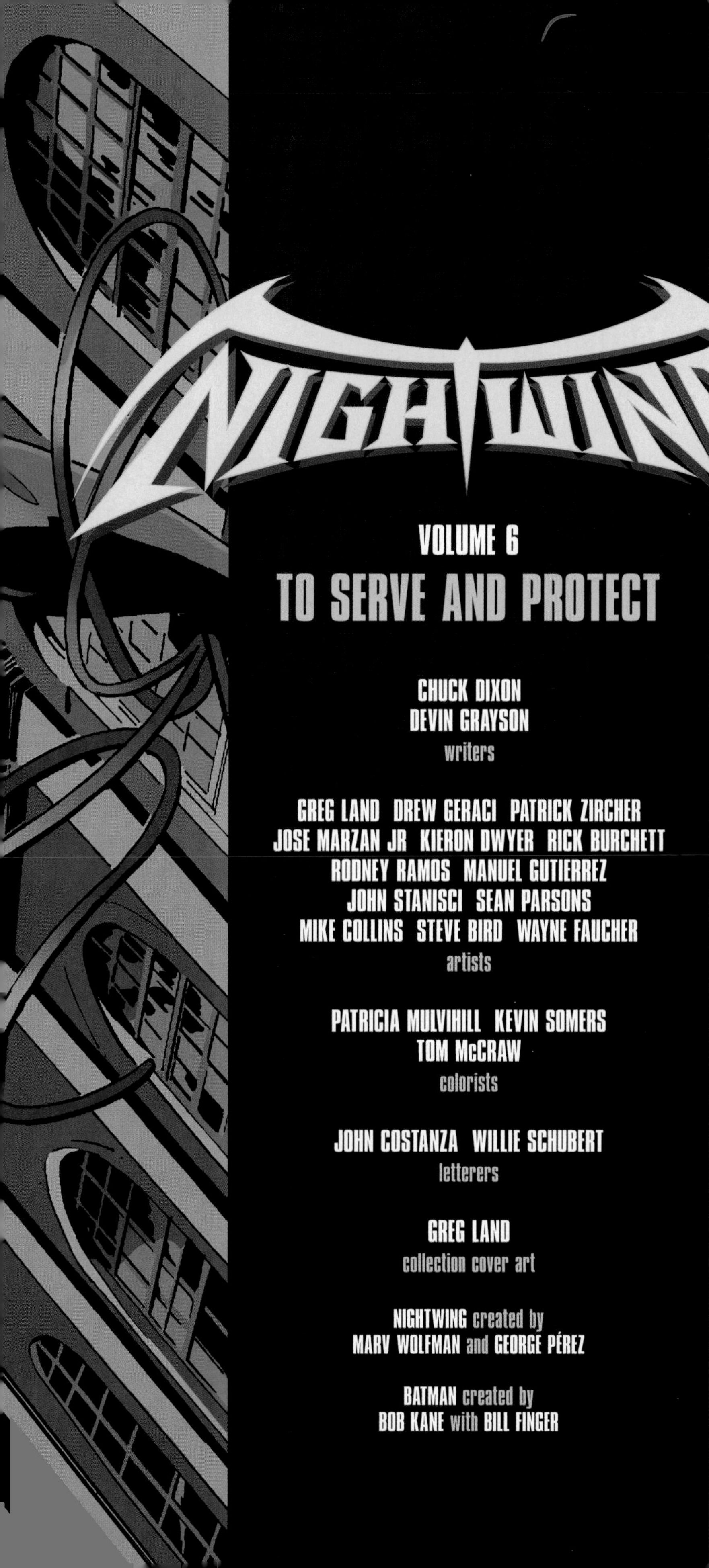

NIGHTWING

VOLUME 6
TO SERVE AND PROTECT

CHUCK DIXON
DEVIN GRAYSON
writers

GREG LAND DREW GERACI PATRICK ZIRCHER
JOSE MARZAN JR KIERON DWYER RICK BURCHETT
RODNEY RAMOS MANUEL GUTIERREZ
JOHN STANISCI SEAN PARSONS
MIKE COLLINS STEVE BIRD WAYNE FAUCHER
artists

PATRICIA MULVIHILL KEVIN SOMERS
TOM McCRAW
colorists

JOHN COSTANZA WILLIE SCHUBERT
letterers

GREG LAND
collection cover art

NIGHTWING created by
MARV WOLFMAN and GEORGE PÉREZ

BATMAN created by
BOB KANE with BILL FINGER

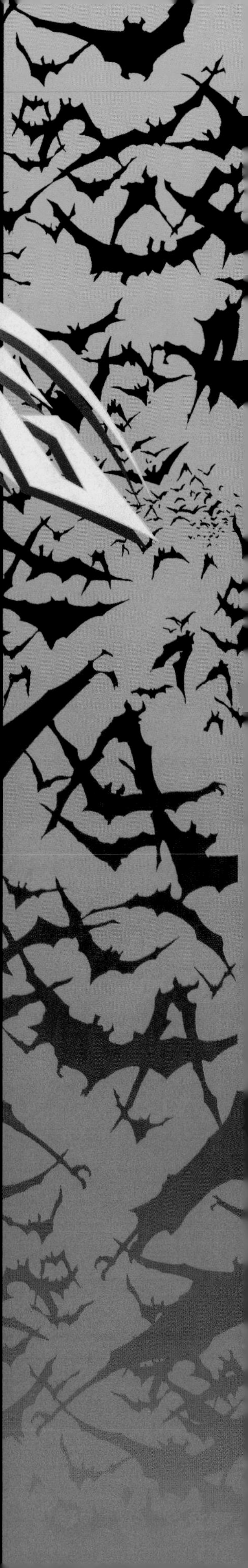

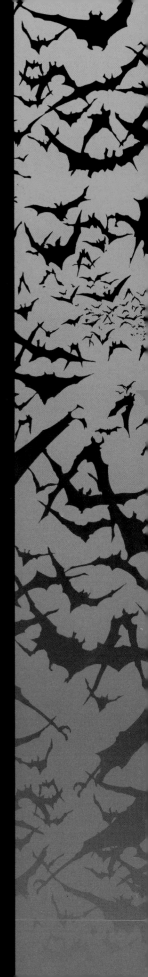

TABLE OF CONTENTS

MATT IDELSON
BOB SCHRECK   Editors – Original Series
JOSEPH ILLIDGE
MICHAEL WRIGHT   Associate Editors – Original Series
JEB WOODARD   Group Editor – Collected Editions
PAUL SANTOS   Editor – Collected Edition
STEVE COOK   Design Director – Books
CURTIS KING JR.   Publication Design

BOB HARRAS   Senior VP – Editor-in-Chief, DC Comics

DIANE NELSON   President
DAN DiDIO   Publisher
JIM LEE   Publisher
GEOFF JOHNS   President & Chief Creative Officer
AMIT DESAI   Executive VP – Business & Marketing Strategy,
                    Direct to Consumer & Global Franchise Management
SAM ADES   Senior VP – Direct to Consumer
BOBBIE CHASE   VP – Talent Development
MARK CHIARELLO   Senior VP – Art, Design & Collected Editions
JOHN CUNNINGHAM   Senior VP – Sales & Trade Marketing
ANNE DePIES   Senior VP – Business Strategy, Finance & Administration
DON FALLETTI   VP – Manufacturing Operations
LAWRENCE GANEM   VP – Editorial Administration & Talent Relations
ALISON GILL   Senior VP – Manufacturing & Operations
HANK KANALZ   Senior VP – Editorial Strategy & Administration
JAY KOGAN   VP – Legal Affairs
THOMAS LOFTUS   VP – Business Affairs
JACK MAHAN   VP – Business Affairs
NICK J. NAPOLITANO VP – Manufacturing Administration
EDDIE SCANNELL   VP – Consumer Marketing
COURTNEY SIMMONS   Senior VP – Publicity & Communications
JIM (SKI) SOKOLOWSKI VP – Comic Book Specialty Sales & Trade Marketing

NIGHTWING VOLUME 6: TO SERVE AND PROTECT

DC Comics, 2900 West Alameda Ave., Burbank, CA 91505
Printed by Vanguard Graphics, LLC, Ithaca, NY, USA. 6/9/17. First Printing.
ISBN: 978-1-4012-7081-0

Library of Congress Cataloging-in-Publication Data is available.

MIX
Paper from
responsible sources
FSC® C016956

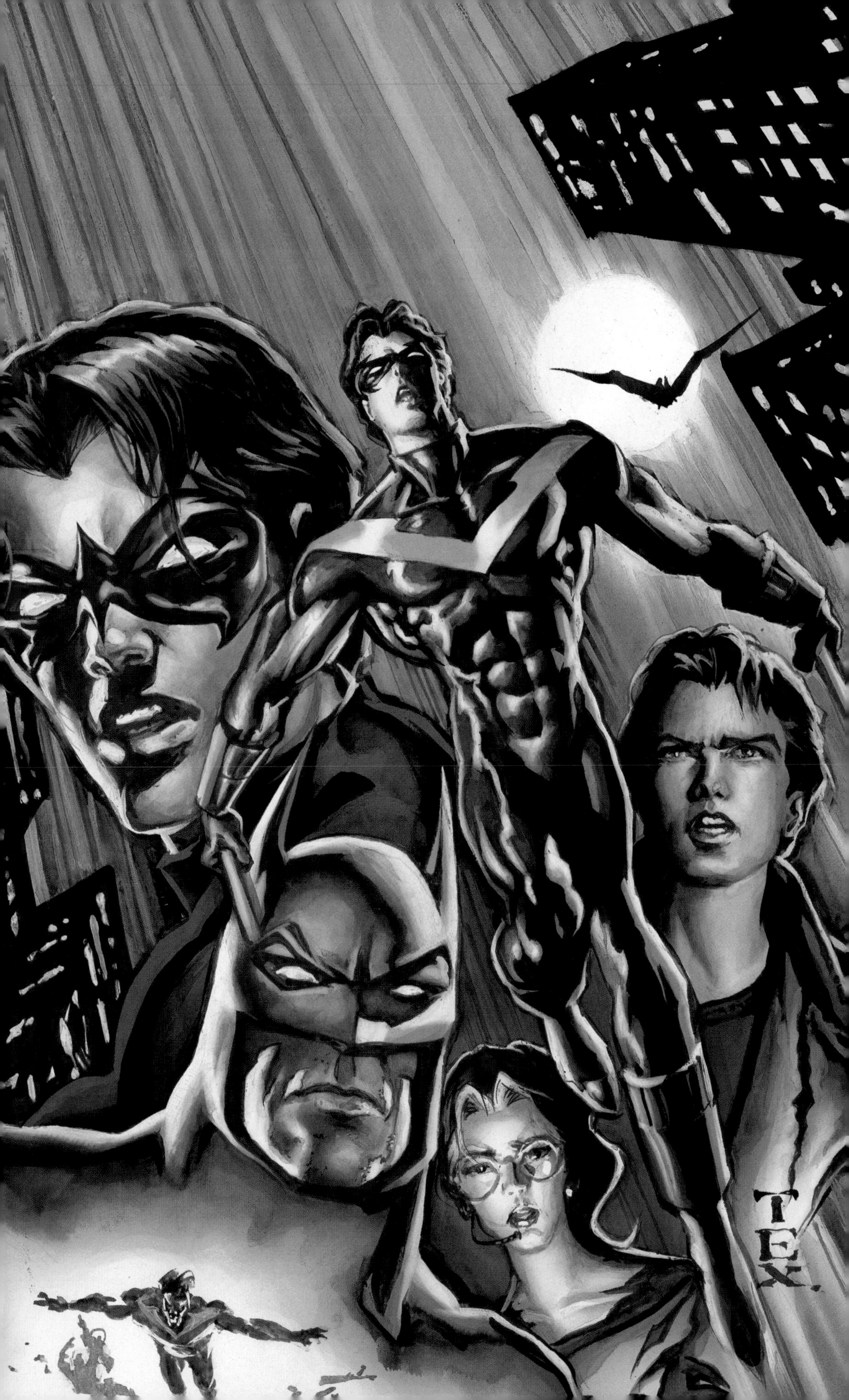
TEX.

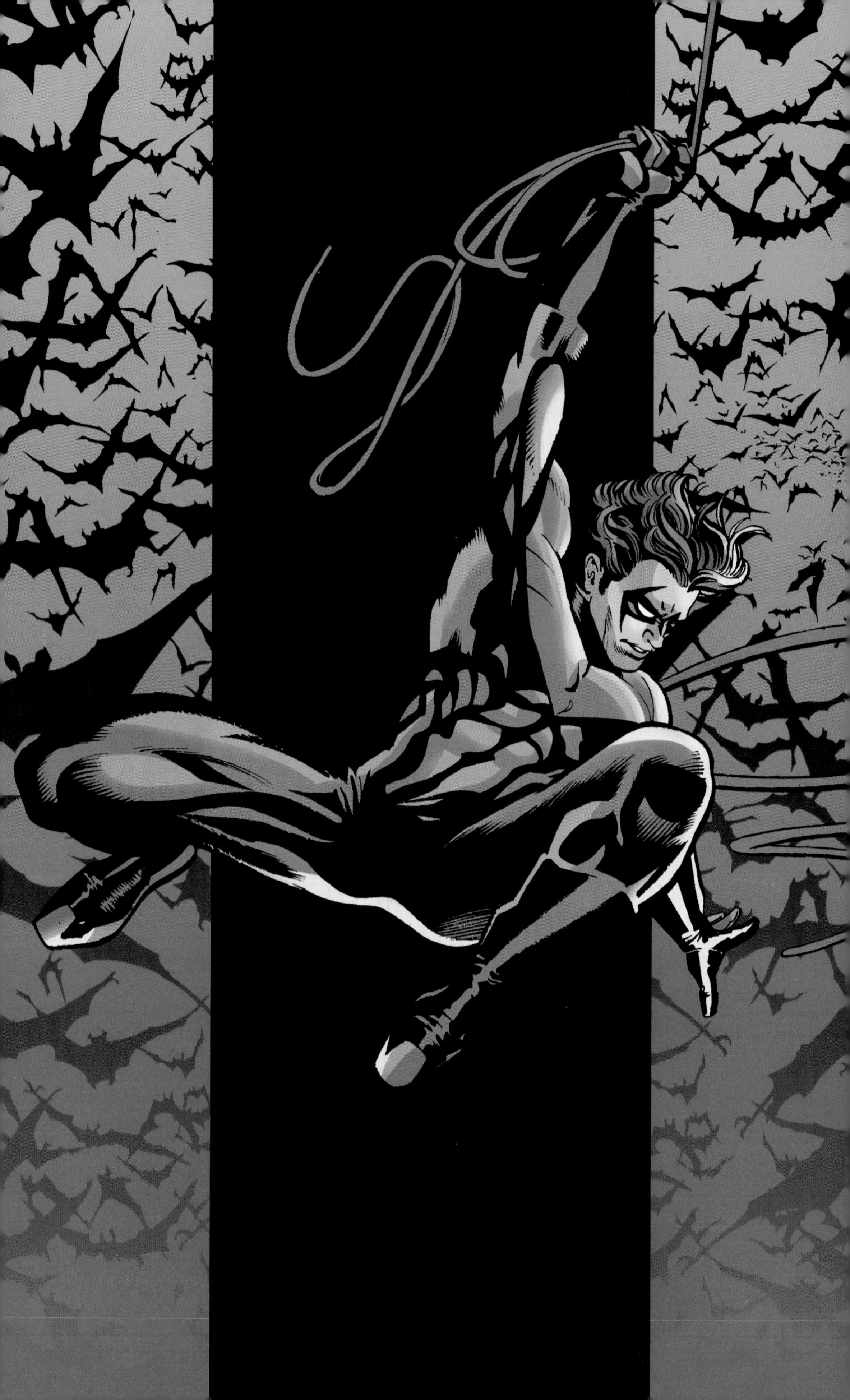

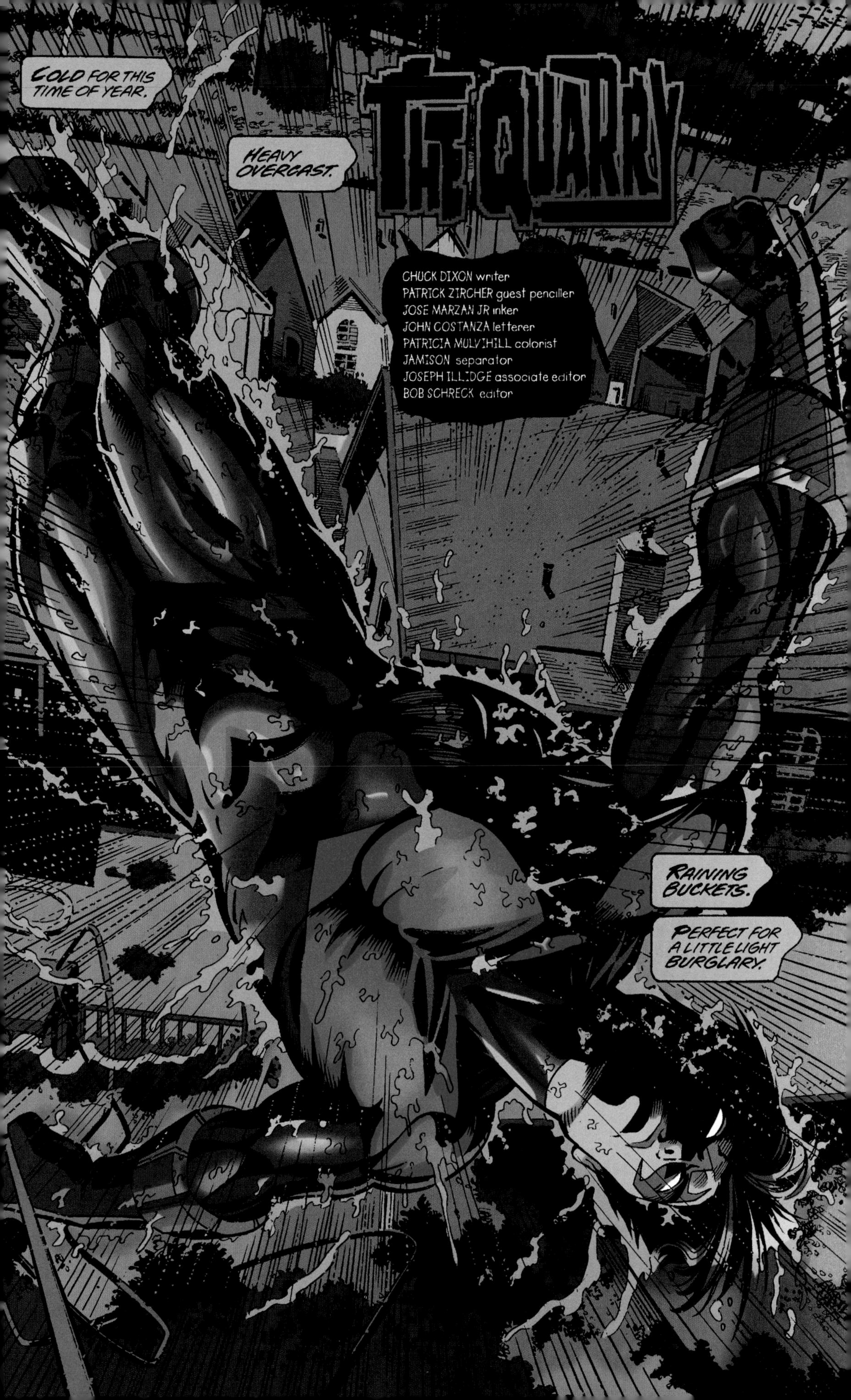

COLD FOR THIS TIME OF YEAR.
HEAVY OVERCAST.
THE QUARRY
CHUCK DIXON writer
PATRICK ZIRCHER guest penciller
JOSE MARZAN JR inker
JOHN COSTANZA letterer
PATRICIA MULVIHILL colorist
JAMISON separator
JOSEPH ILLIDGE associate editor
BOB SCHRECK editor
RAINING BUCKETS.
PERFECT FOR A LITTLE LIGHT BURGLARY.

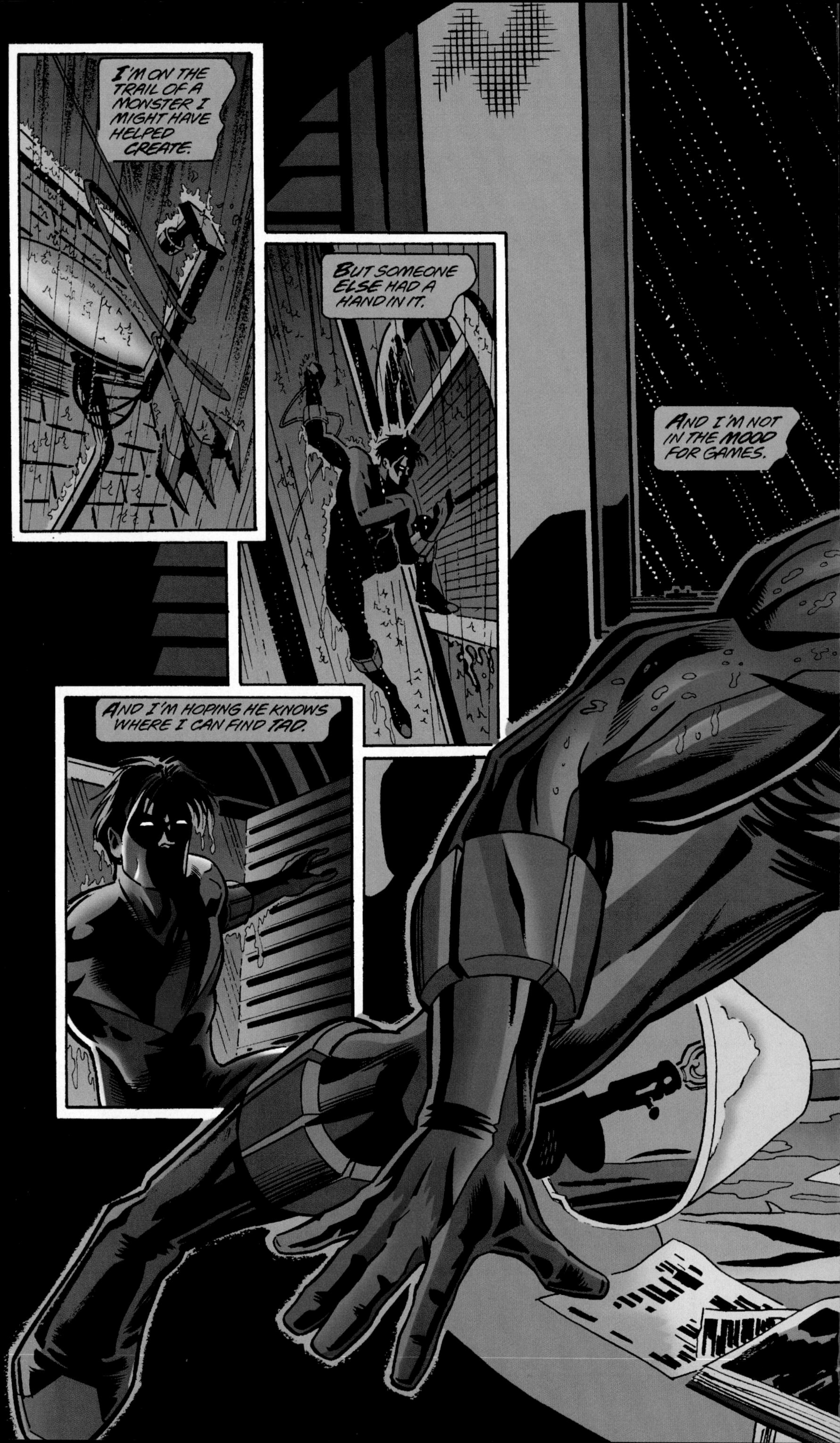
I'M ON THE TRAIL OF A MONSTER I MIGHT HAVE HELPED CREATE.
BUT SOMEONE ELSE HAD A HAND IN IT.
AND I'M HOPING HE KNOWS WHERE I CAN FIND TAD.
AND I'M NOT IN THE MOOD FOR GAMES.

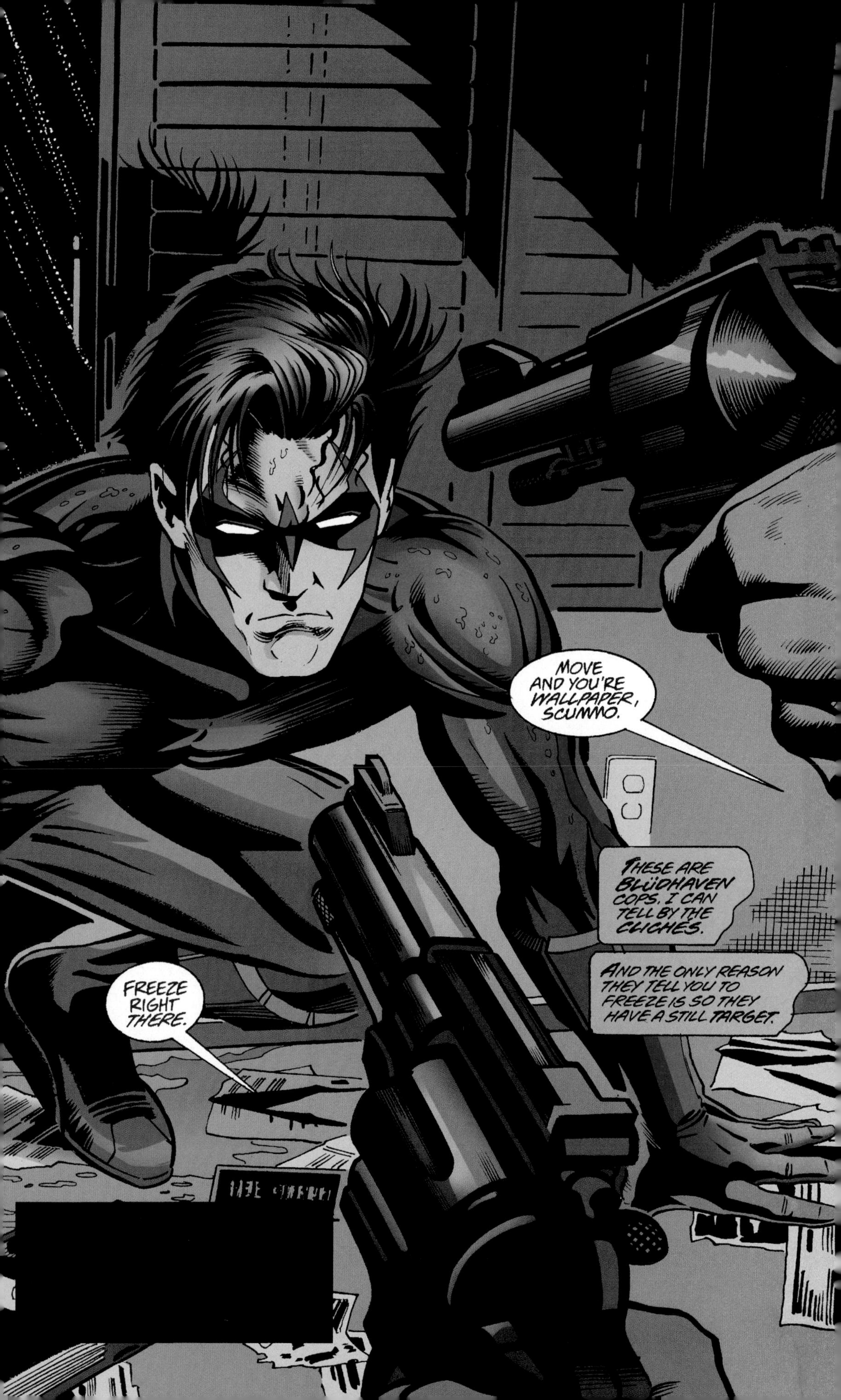

MOVE AND YOU'RE WALLPAPER, SCUMMO.
FREEZE RIGHT THERE.
THESE ARE BLÜDHAVEN COPS. I CAN TELL BY THE CLICHES.
AND THE ONLY REASON THEY TELL YOU TO FREEZE IS SO THEY HAVE A STILL TARGET.
[redacted]

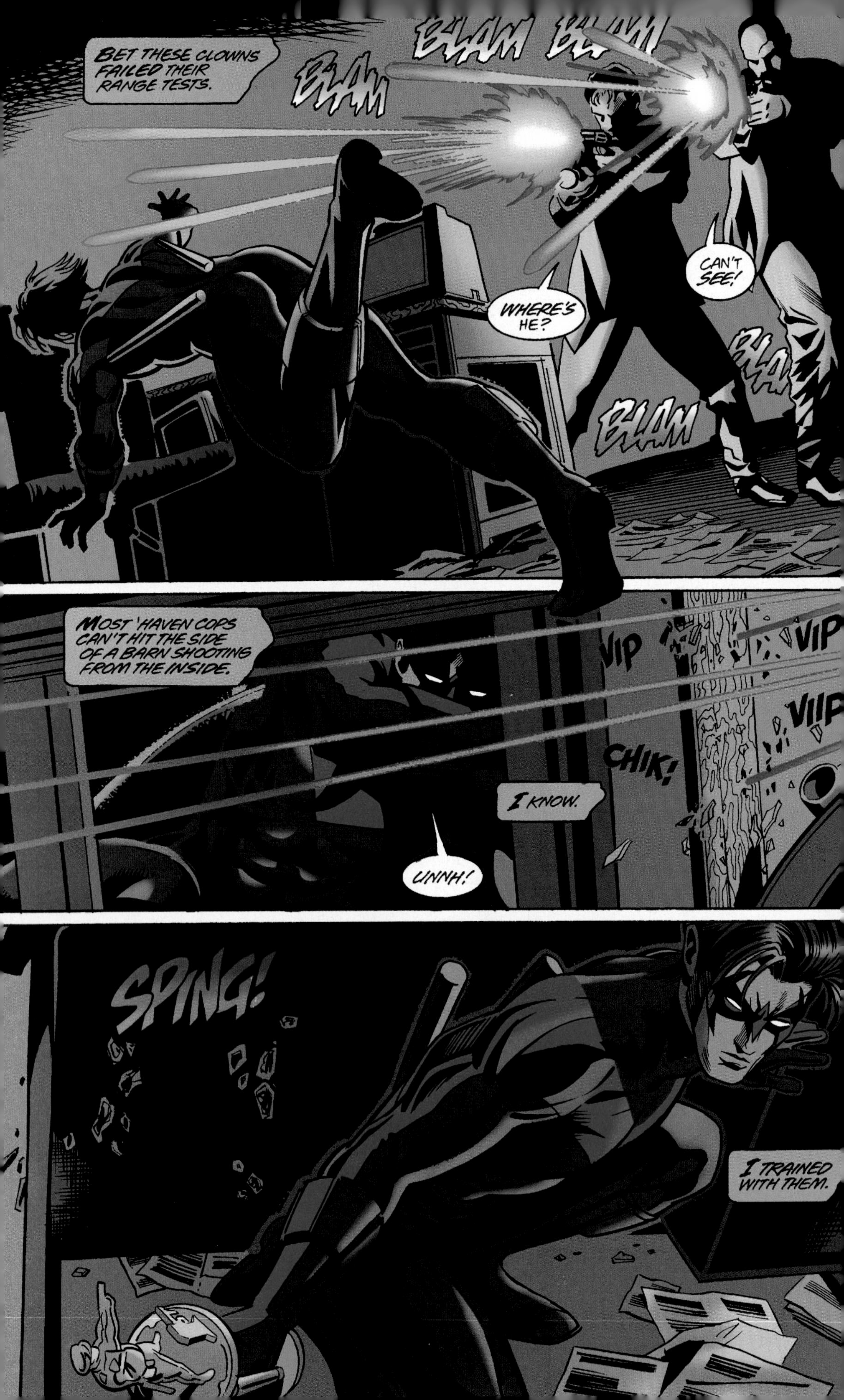

BET THESE CLOWNS FAILED THEIR RANGE TESTS.
BLAM
BLAM BLAM
WHERE'S HE?
CAN'T SEE!
BLAM
BLAM
MOST 'HAVEN COPS CAN'T HIT THE SIDE OF A BARN SHOOTING FROM THE INSIDE.
VIP
VIP
VIP
CHIK!
I KNOW.
UNNH!
SPING!
I TRAINED WITH THEM.

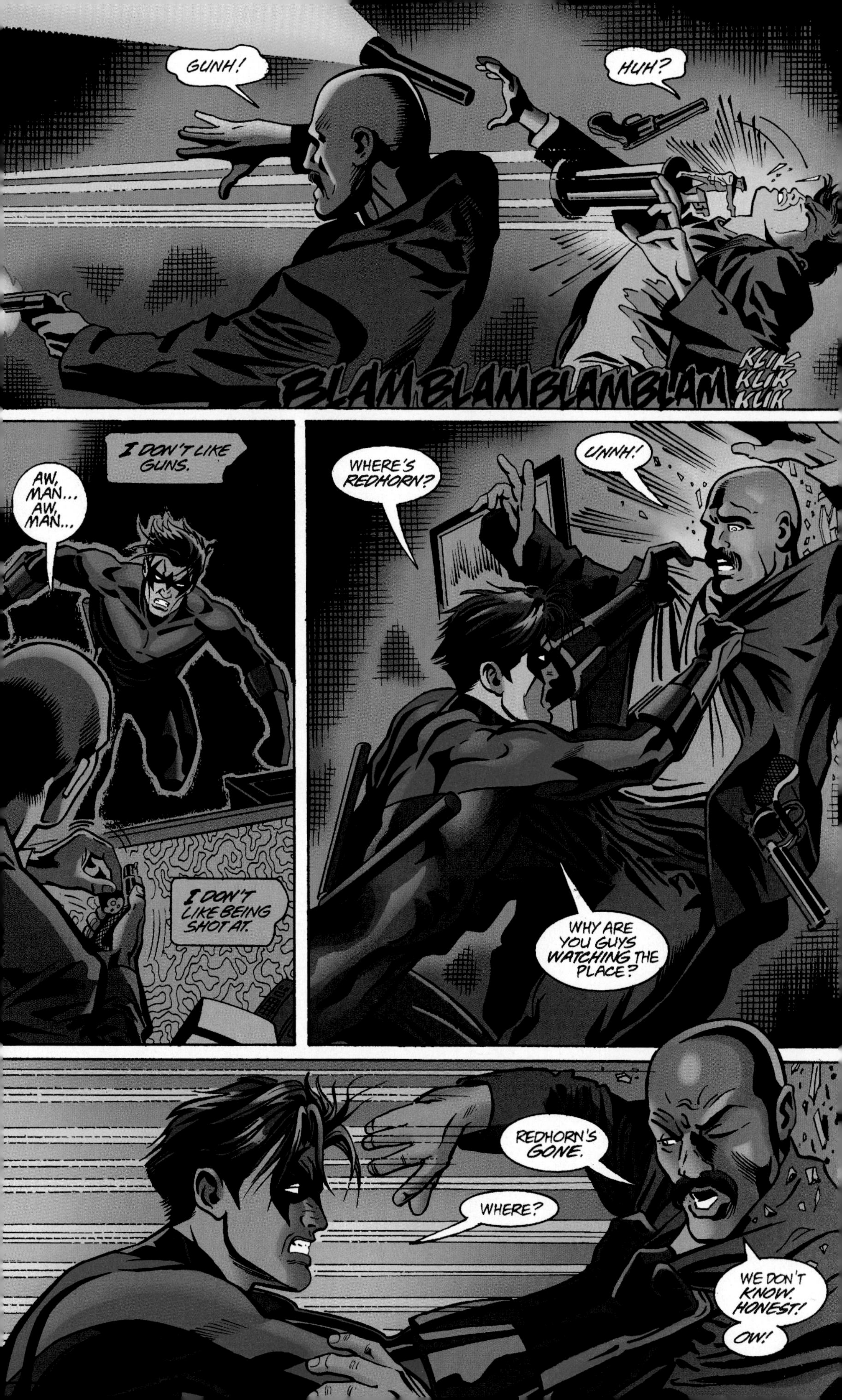
GUNH!
HUH?
BLAMBLAMBLAMBLAM
KLIK KLIK KLIK
I DON'T LIKE GUNS.
AW, MAN... AW, MAN...
I DON'T LIKE BEING SHOT AT.
WHERE'S REDHORN?
UNNH!
WHY ARE YOU GUYS WATCHING THE PLACE?
REDHORN'S GONE.
WHERE?
WE DON'T KNOW. HONEST!
OW!

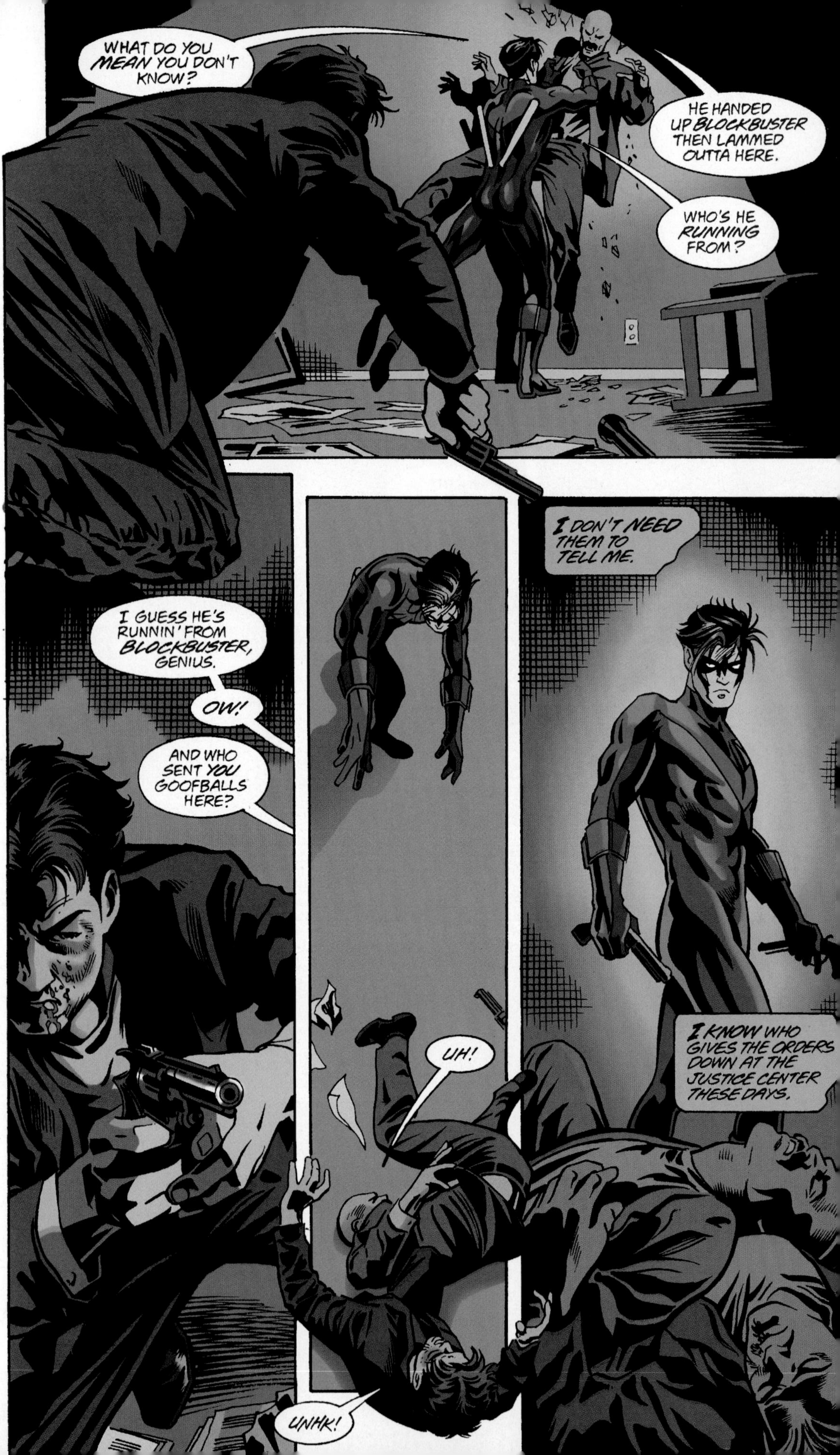
WHAT DO YOU MEAN YOU DON'T KNOW?
HE HANDED UP BLOCKBUSTER THEN LAMMED OUTTA HERE.
WHO'S HE RUNNING FROM?
I GUESS HE'S RUNNIN' FROM BLOCKBUSTER, GENIUS.
OW!
AND WHO SENT YOU GOOFBALLS HERE?
UH!
UNHK!
I DON'T NEED THEM TO TELL ME.
I KNOW WHO GIVES THE ORDERS DOWN AT THE JUSTICE CENTER THESE DAYS.

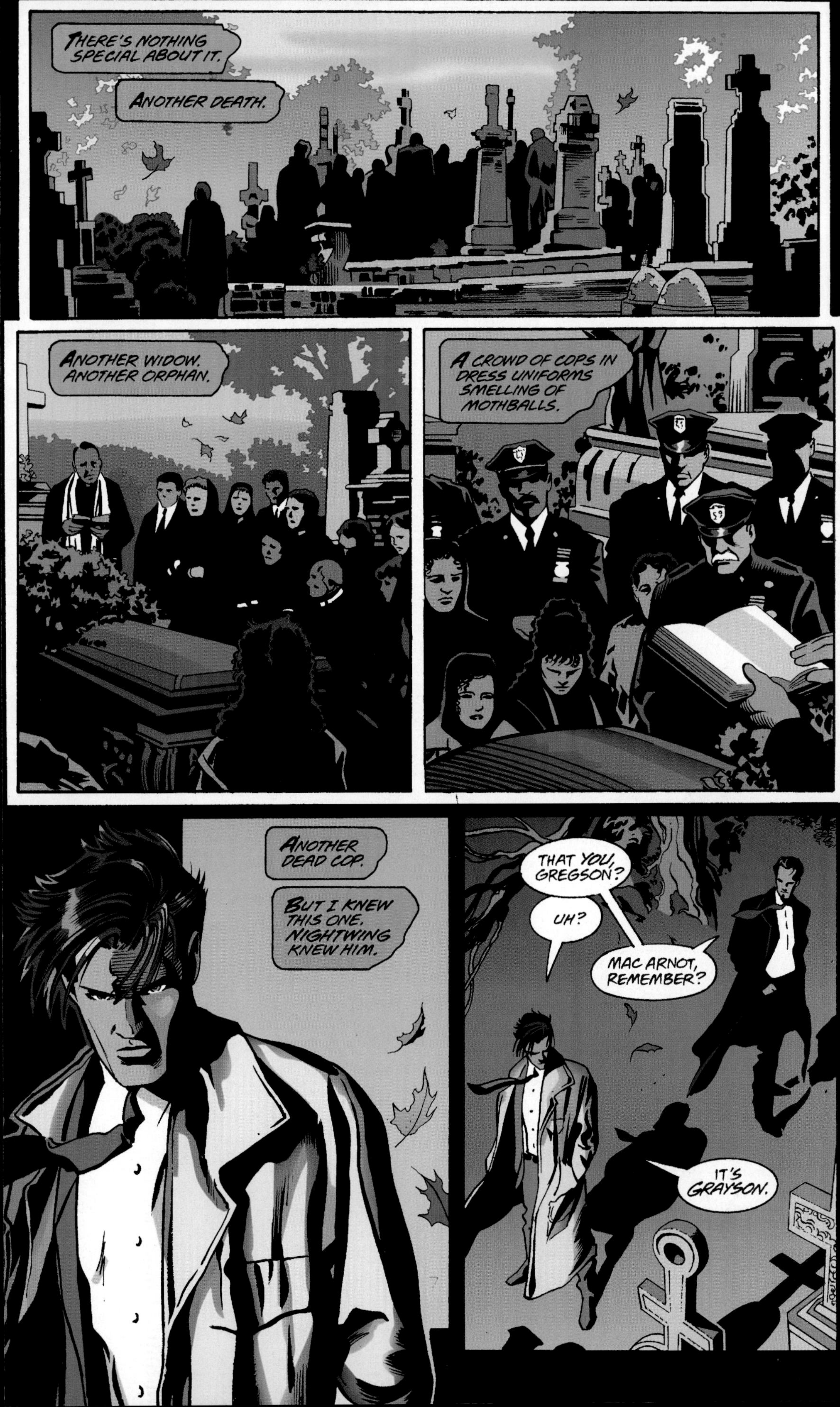
THERE'S NOTHING SPECIAL ABOUT IT.
ANOTHER DEATH.
ANOTHER WIDOW. ANOTHER ORPHAN.
A CROWD OF COPS IN DRESS UNIFORMS SMELLING OF MOTHBALLS.
ANOTHER DEAD COP.
BUT I KNEW THIS ONE. NIGHTWING KNEW HIM.
THAT YOU, GREGSON?
UH?
MAC ARNOT, REMEMBER?
IT'S GRAYSON.

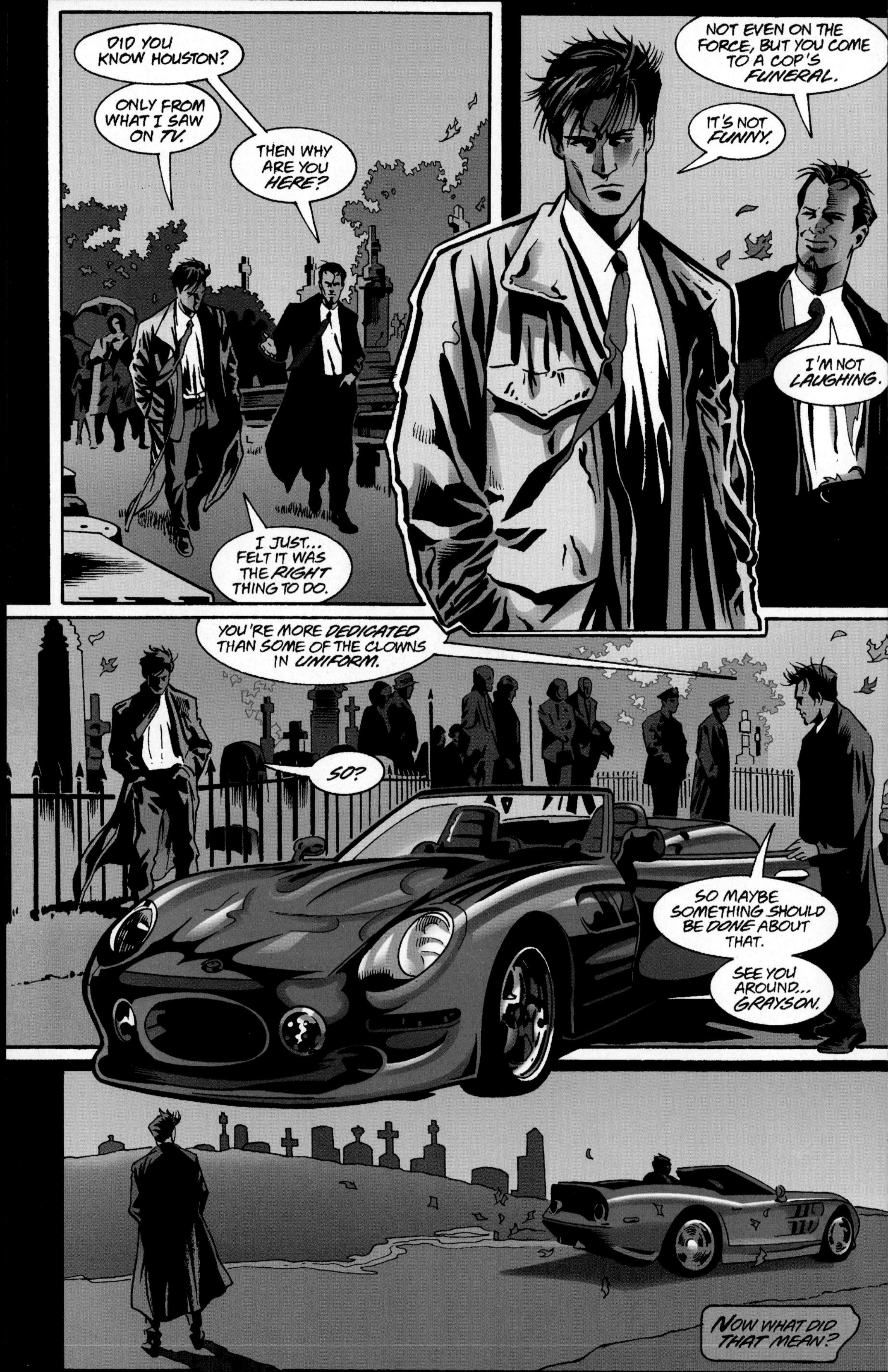
DID YOU KNOW HOUSTON?
ONLY FROM WHAT I SAW ON TV.
THEN WHY ARE YOU HERE?
I JUST... FELT IT WAS THE RIGHT THING TO DO.
NOT EVEN ON THE FORCE, BUT YOU COME TO A COP'S FUNERAL.
IT'S NOT FUNNY.
I'M NOT LAUGHING.
YOU'RE MORE DEDICATED THAN SOME OF THE CLOWNS IN UNIFORM.
SO?
SO MAYBE SOMETHING SHOULD BE DONE ABOUT THAT.
SEE YOU AROUND... GRAYSON.
NOW WHAT DID THAT MEAN?

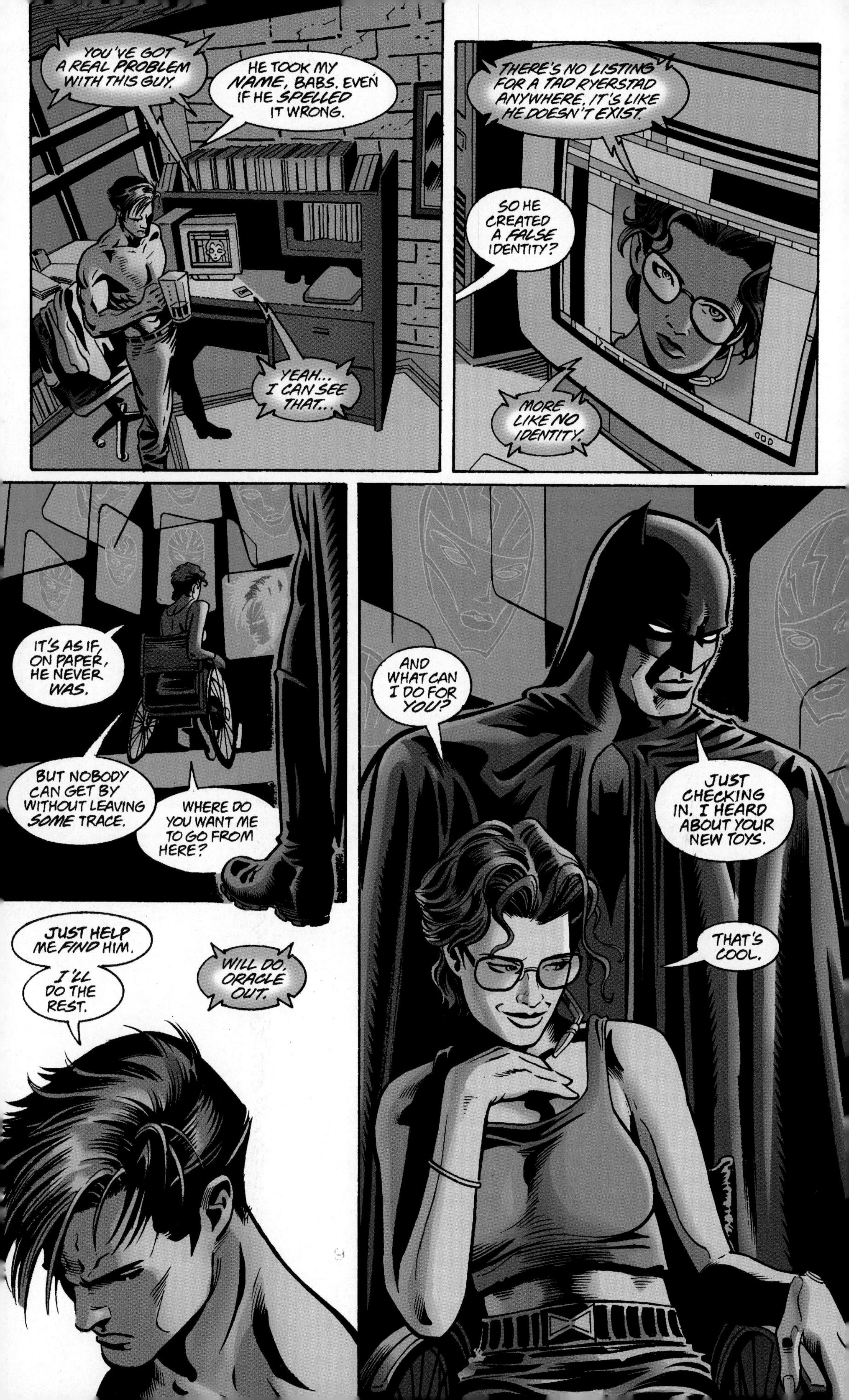

YOU'VE GOT A REAL PROBLEM WITH THIS GUY.
HE TOOK MY NAME, BABS. EVEN IF HE SPELLED IT WRONG.
YEAH... I CAN SEE THAT...
THERE'S NO LISTING FOR A TAD RYERSTAD ANYWHERE. IT'S LIKE HE DOESN'T EXIST.
SO HE CREATED A FALSE IDENTITY?
MORE LIKE NO IDENTITY.
IT'S AS IF, ON PAPER, HE NEVER WAS.
BUT NOBODY CAN GET BY WITHOUT LEAVING SOME TRACE.
WHERE DO YOU WANT ME TO GO FROM HERE?
JUST HELP ME FIND HIM.
I'LL DO THE REST.
WILL DO. ORACLE OUT.
AND WHAT CAN I DO FOR YOU?
JUST CHECKING IN. I HEARD ABOUT YOUR NEW TOYS.
THAT'S COOL.

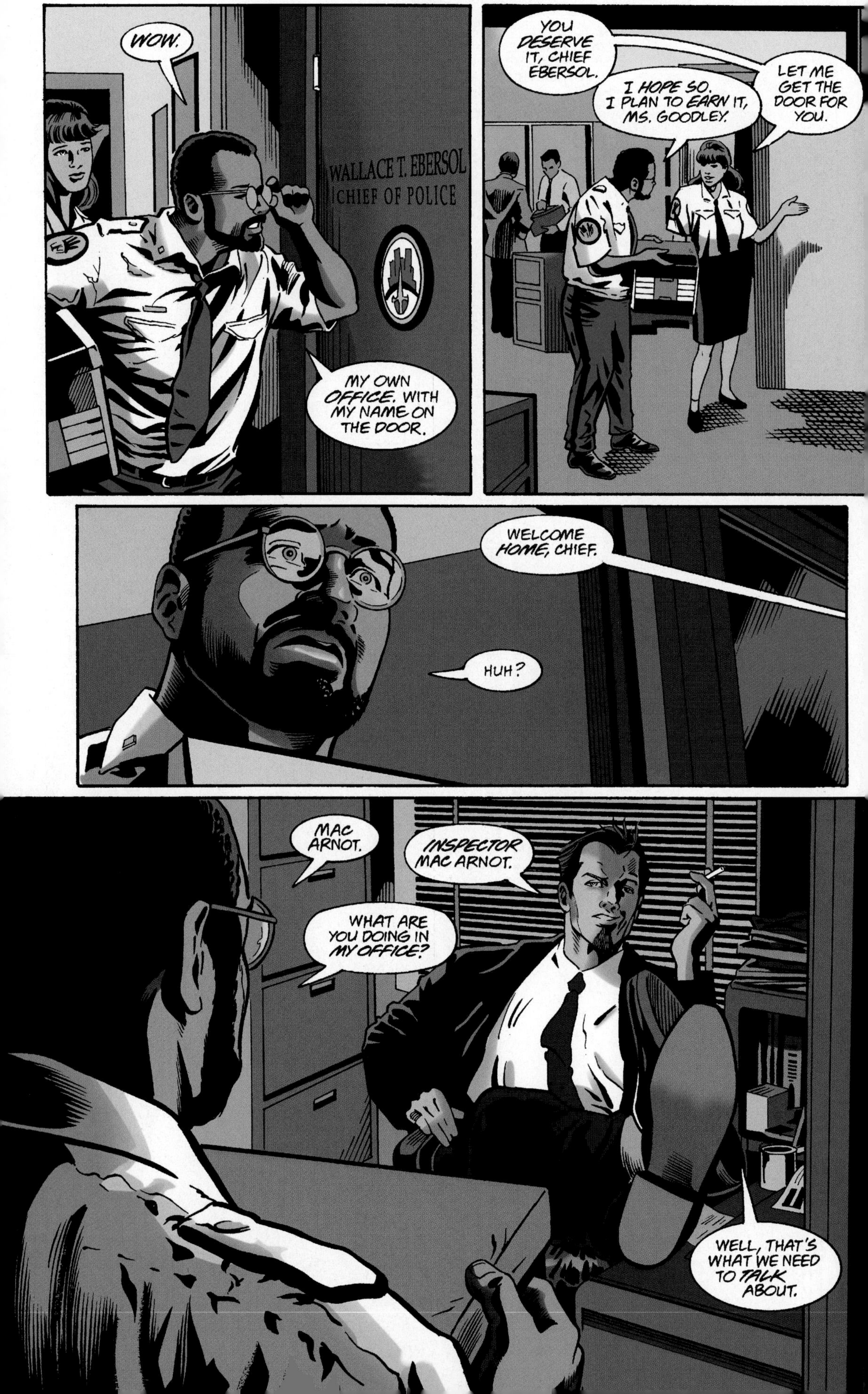
WOW.
WALLACE T. EBERSOL
CHIEF OF POLICE
MY OWN OFFICE. WITH MY NAME ON THE DOOR.
YOU DESERVE IT, CHIEF EBERSOL.
I HOPE SO. I PLAN TO EARN IT, MS. GOODLEY.
LET ME GET THE DOOR FOR YOU.
WELCOME HOME, CHIEF.
HUH?
MAC ARNOT.
INSPECTOR MAC ARNOT.
WHAT ARE YOU DOING IN MY OFFICE?
WELL, THAT'S WHAT WE NEED TO TALK ABOUT.

SEE, BEFORE CHIEF REDHORN TOOK OFF FOR THE BOON-DOCKS HE APPOINTED *ME* INSPECTOR.

BEFORE HE APPOINTED *YOU* CHIEF.

I DON'T SEE WHAT *THAT* HAS TO DO WITH--

IT'S LIKE THIS-- BLÜDHAVEN HAS *TWO* POLICE DEPARTMENTS.

TWO?

THE ONE THE PUBLIC SEES AND THE ONE THEY *DON'T* SEE.

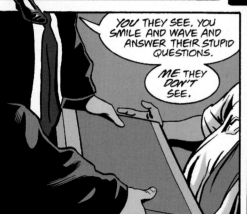

YOU THEY SEE. YOU SMILE AND WAVE AND ANSWER THEIR STUPID QUESTIONS.

ME THEY *DON'T* SEE.

SO I'LL BE RUNNING THINGS UNTIL REDHORN GETS BACK. *IF* HE GETS BACK.

JUST A SECOND. BLÜDHAVEN P.D. DOESN'T *HAVE* AN *"INSPECTOR"* POST.

SURE THEY DO. I'M REPLACING THE *LAST* ONE.

SOAMES.

NOW YOU'RE GETTING IT.

NICE KIDS.

OH. I SEE.

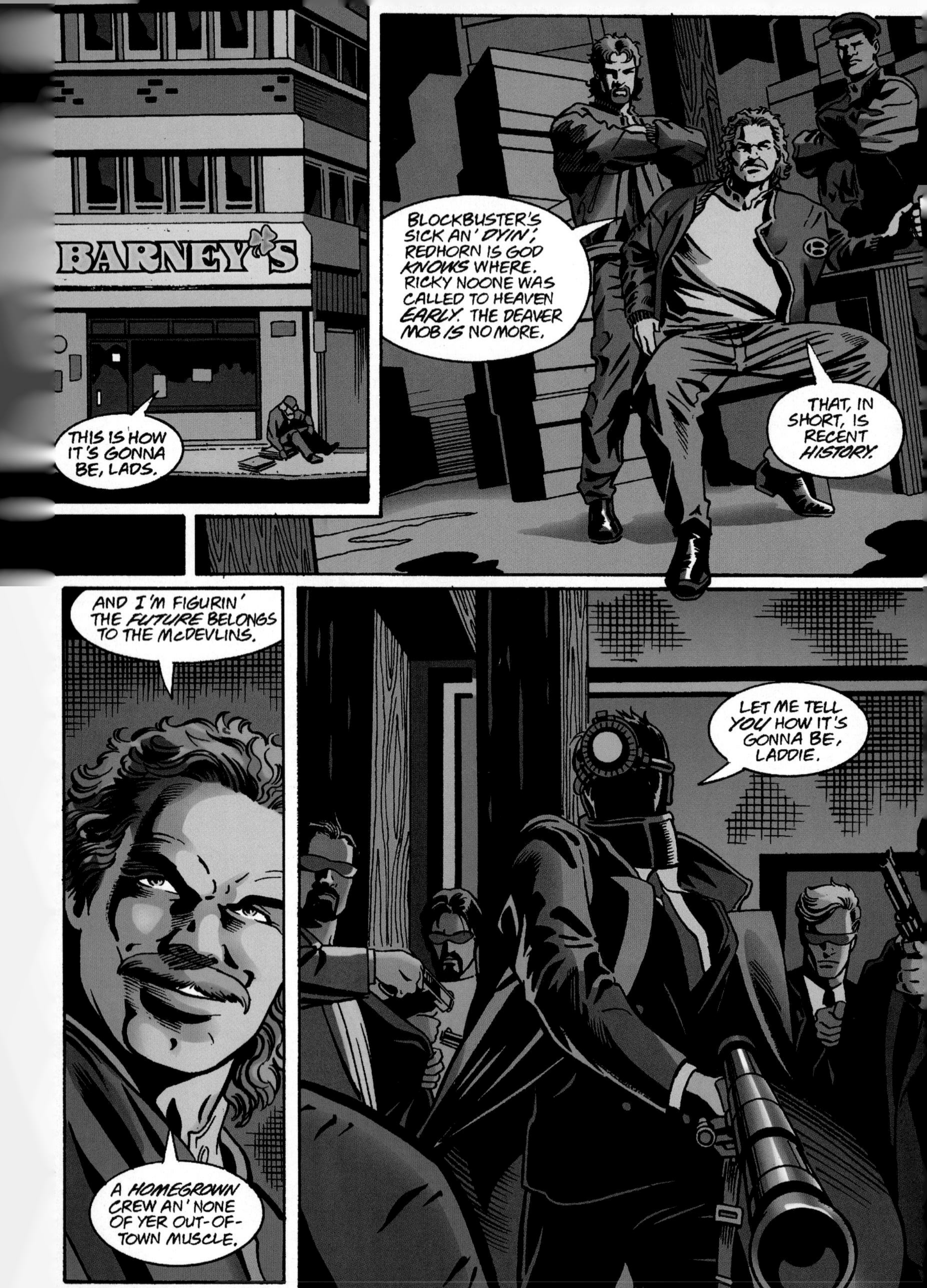
THIS IS HOW IT'S GONNA BE, LADS.
BLOCKBUSTER'S SICK AN' DYIN'; REDHORN IS GOD KNOWS WHERE. RICKY NOONE WAS CALLED TO HEAVEN EARLY. THE DEAVER MOB IS NO MORE.
THAT, IN SHORT, IS RECENT HISTORY.
AND I'M FIGURIN' THE FUTURE BELONGS TO THE McDEVLINS.
A HOMEGROWN CREW AN' NONE OF YER OUT-OF-TOWN MUSCLE.
LET ME TELL YOU HOW IT'S GONNA BE, LADDIE.

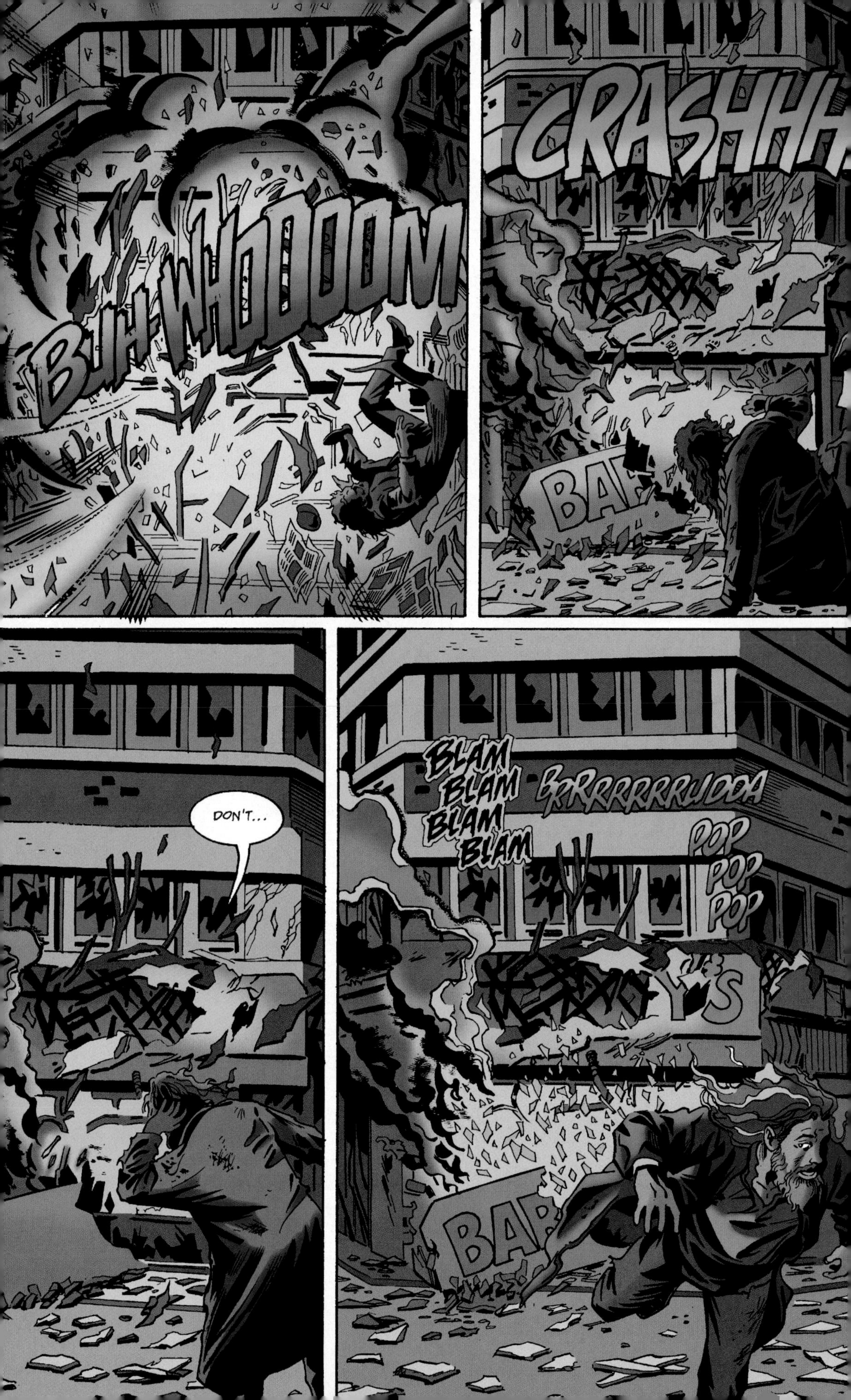
BUH-WHOOOM
CRASHHH
BA
DON'T...
BLAM
BLAM
BLAM
BLAM
BRRRRRRRUDDA
POP
POP
POP
Y'S
BA

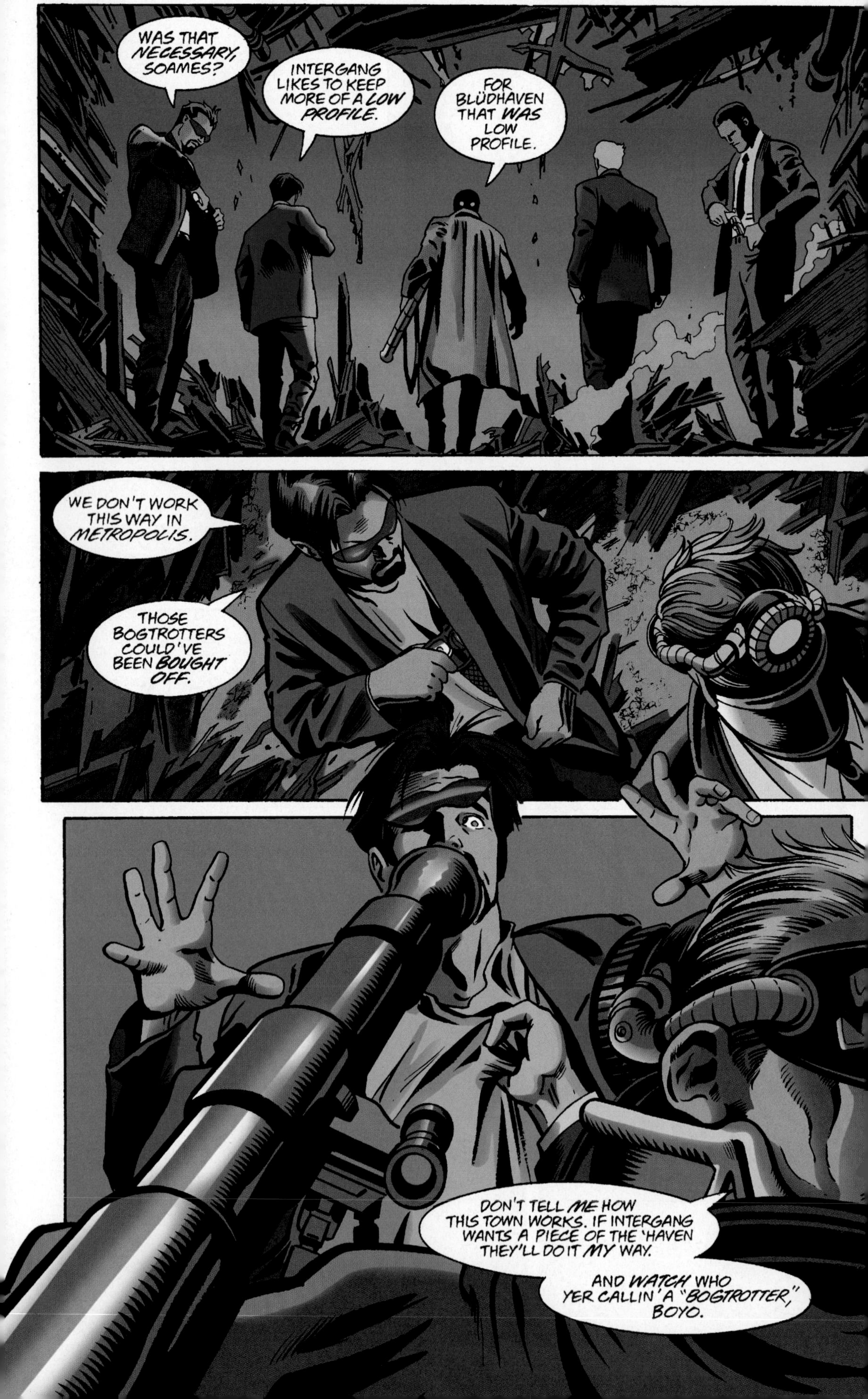
WAS THAT NECESSARY, SOAMES?
INTERGANG LIKES TO KEEP MORE OF A LOW PROFILE.
FOR BLÜDHAVEN THAT WAS LOW PROFILE.
WE DON'T WORK THIS WAY IN METROPOLIS.
THOSE BOGTROTTERS COULD'VE BEEN BOUGHT OFF.
DON'T TELL ME HOW THIS TOWN WORKS. IF INTERGANG WANTS A PIECE OF THE 'HAVEN THEY'LL DO IT MY WAY.
AND WATCH WHO YER CALLIN' A "BOGTROTTER," BOYO.

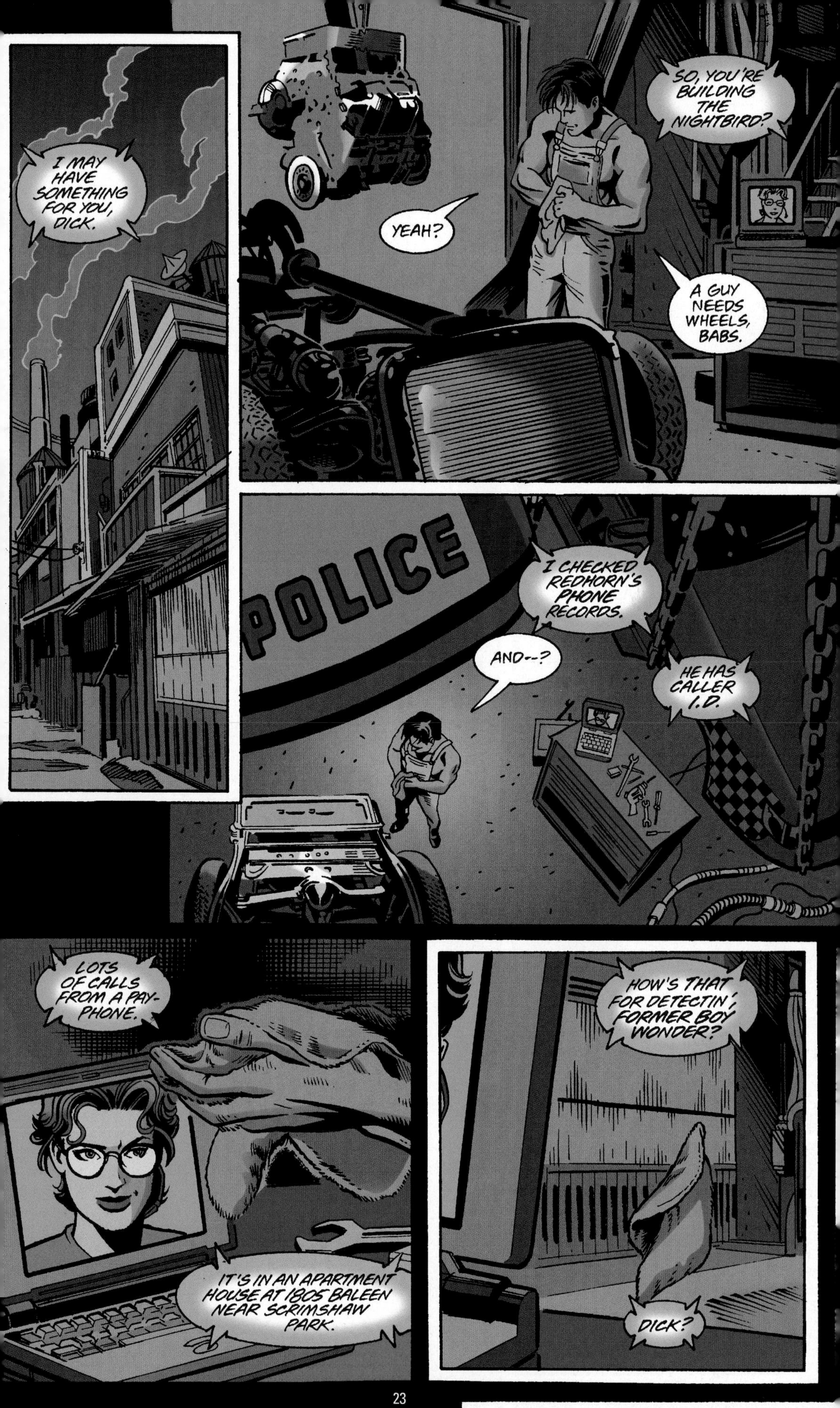
I MAY HAVE SOMETHING FOR YOU, DICK.
YEAH?
SO, YOU'RE BUILDING THE NIGHTBIRD?
A GUY NEEDS WHEELS, BABS.
POLICE
I CHECKED REDHORN'S PHONE RECORDS.
AND--?
HE HAS CALLER I.D.
LOTS OF CALLS FROM A PAY-PHONE.
IT'S IN AN APARTMENT HOUSE AT 1805 BALEEN NEAR SCRIMSHAW PARK.
HOW'S THAT FOR DETECTIN', FORMER BOY WONDER?
DICK?

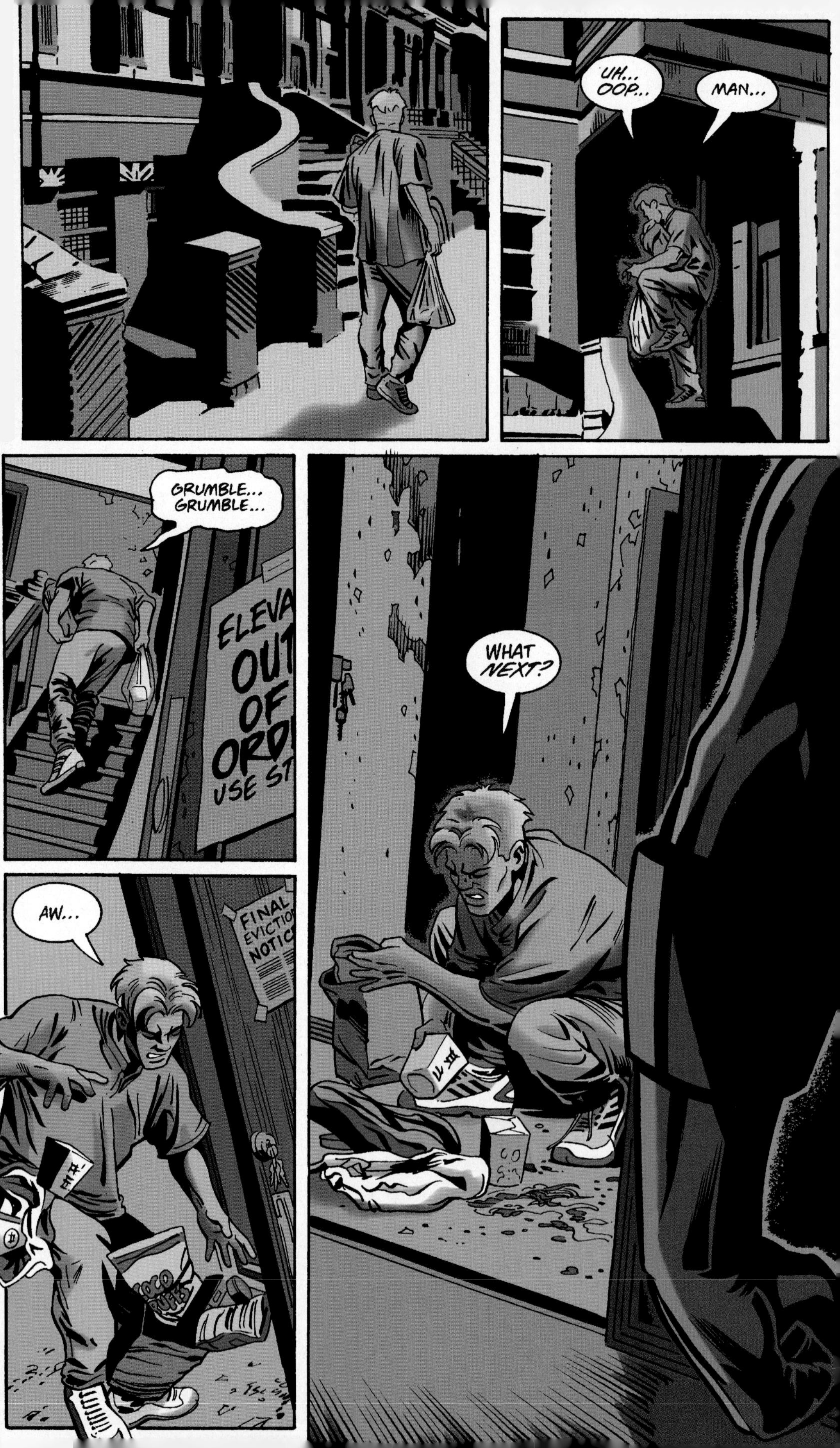
UH... OOP...
MAN...
GRUMBLE... GRUMBLE...
ELEVA
OUT
OF
ORD
USE ST
WHAT NEXT?
AW...
FINAL
EVICTIO
NOTIC

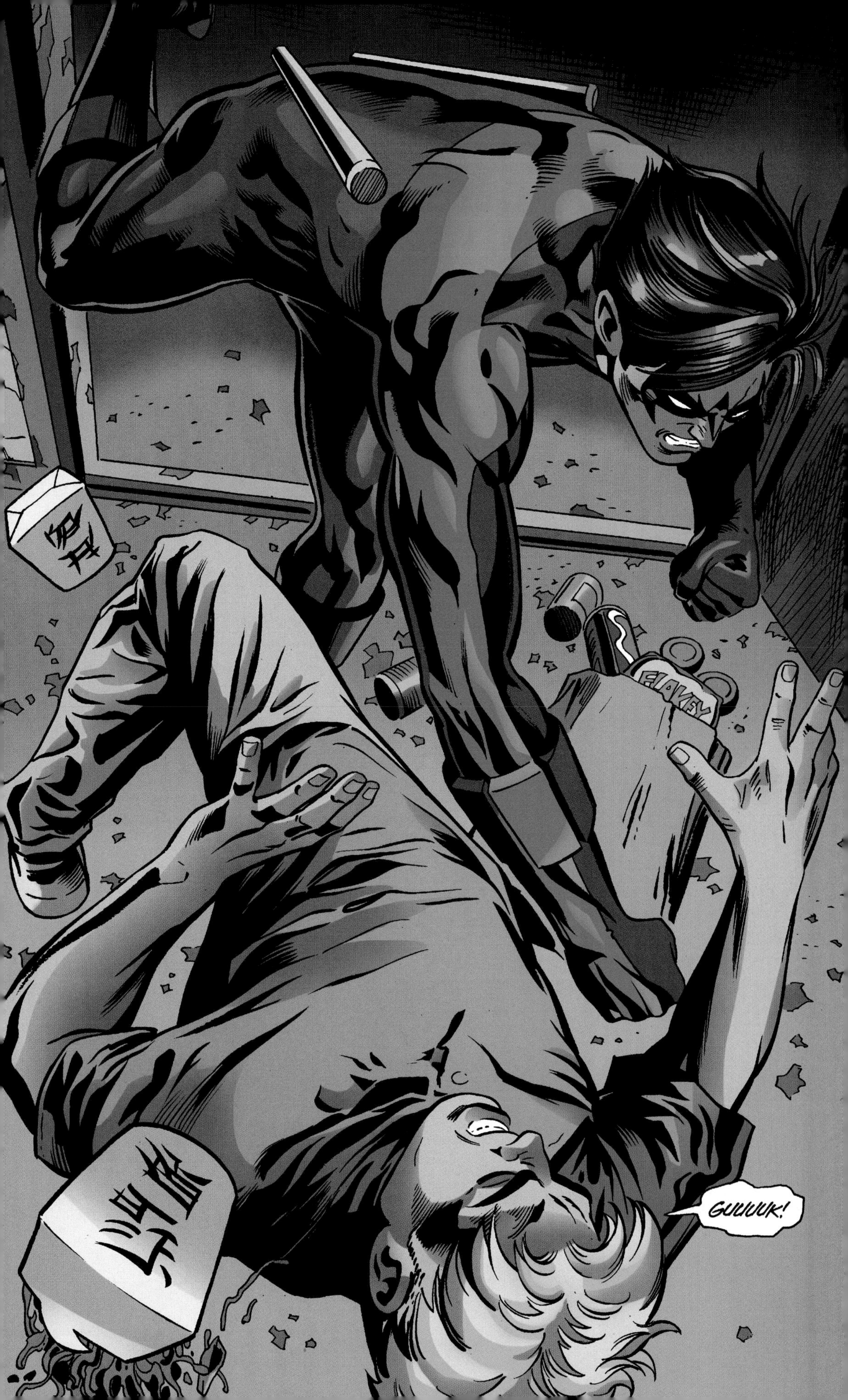
FLAKEY
GUUUUK!

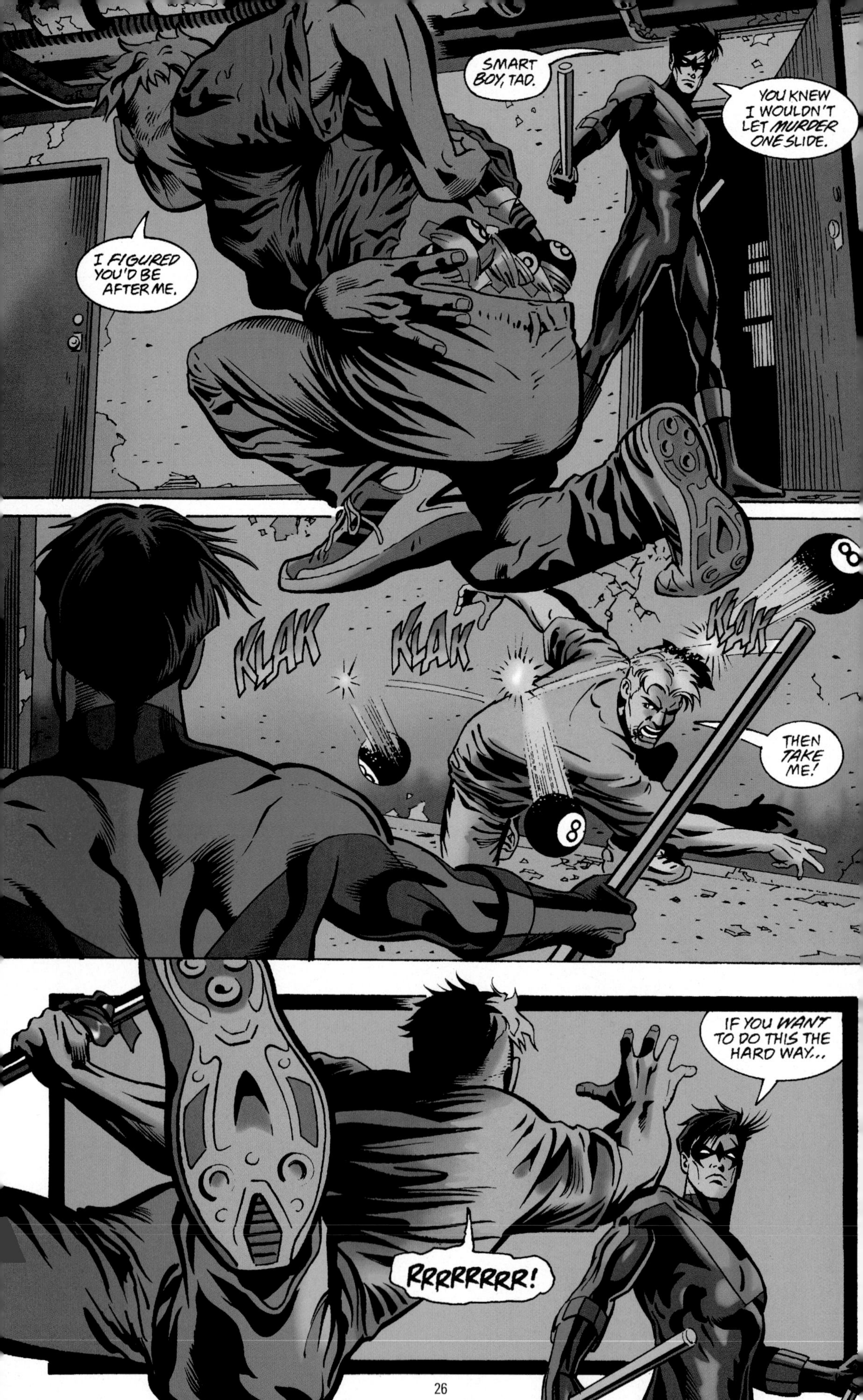
SMART BOY, TAD.
YOU KNEW I WOULDN'T LET MURDER ONE SLIDE.
I FIGURED YOU'D BE AFTER ME.
KLAK
KLAK
KLAK
THEN TAKE ME!
IF YOU WANT TO DO THIS THE HARD WAY...
RRRRRRRR!

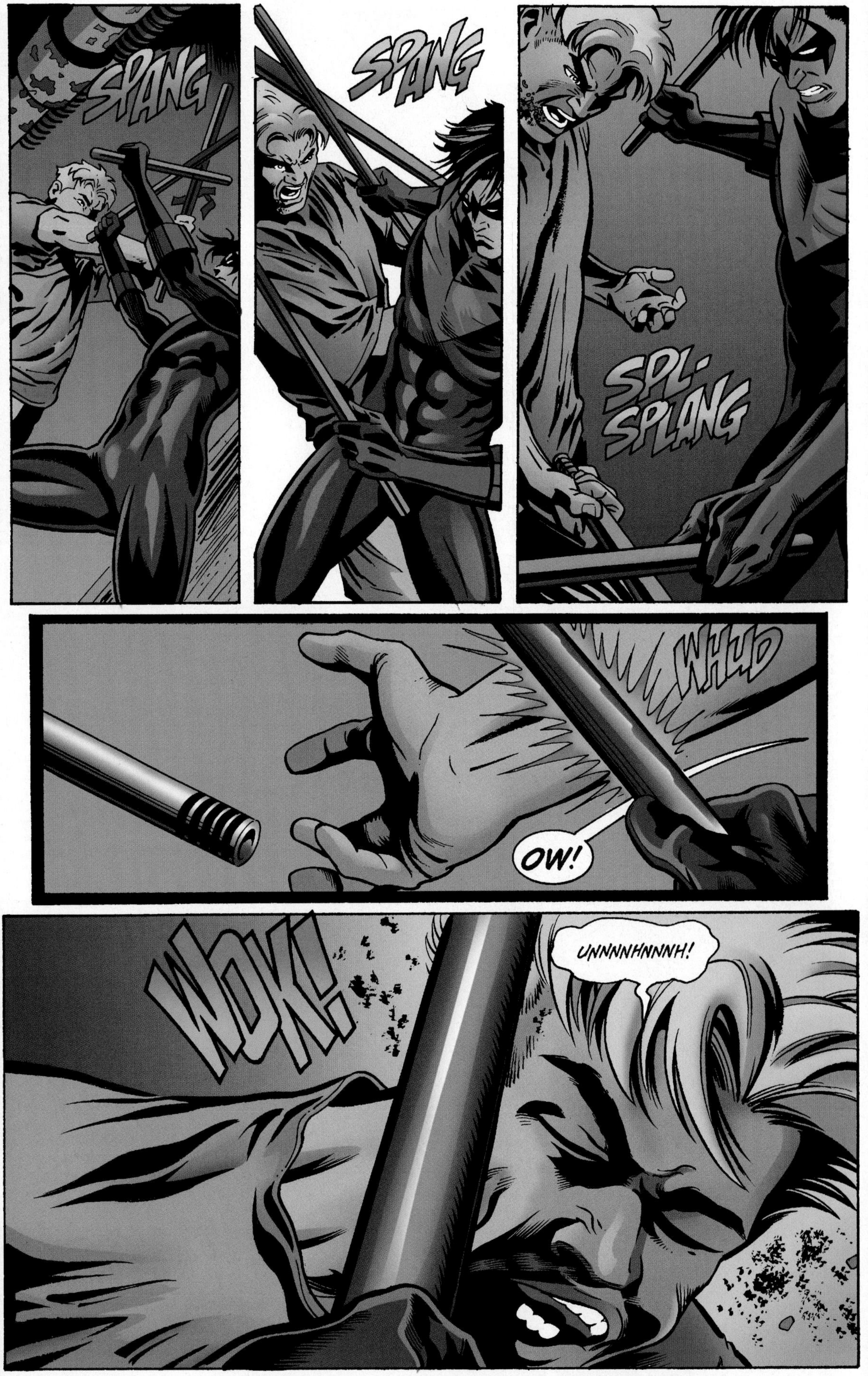
SPANG
SPANG
SPL-SPLANG
WHUD
OW!
WOK!
UNNNNHNNNH!

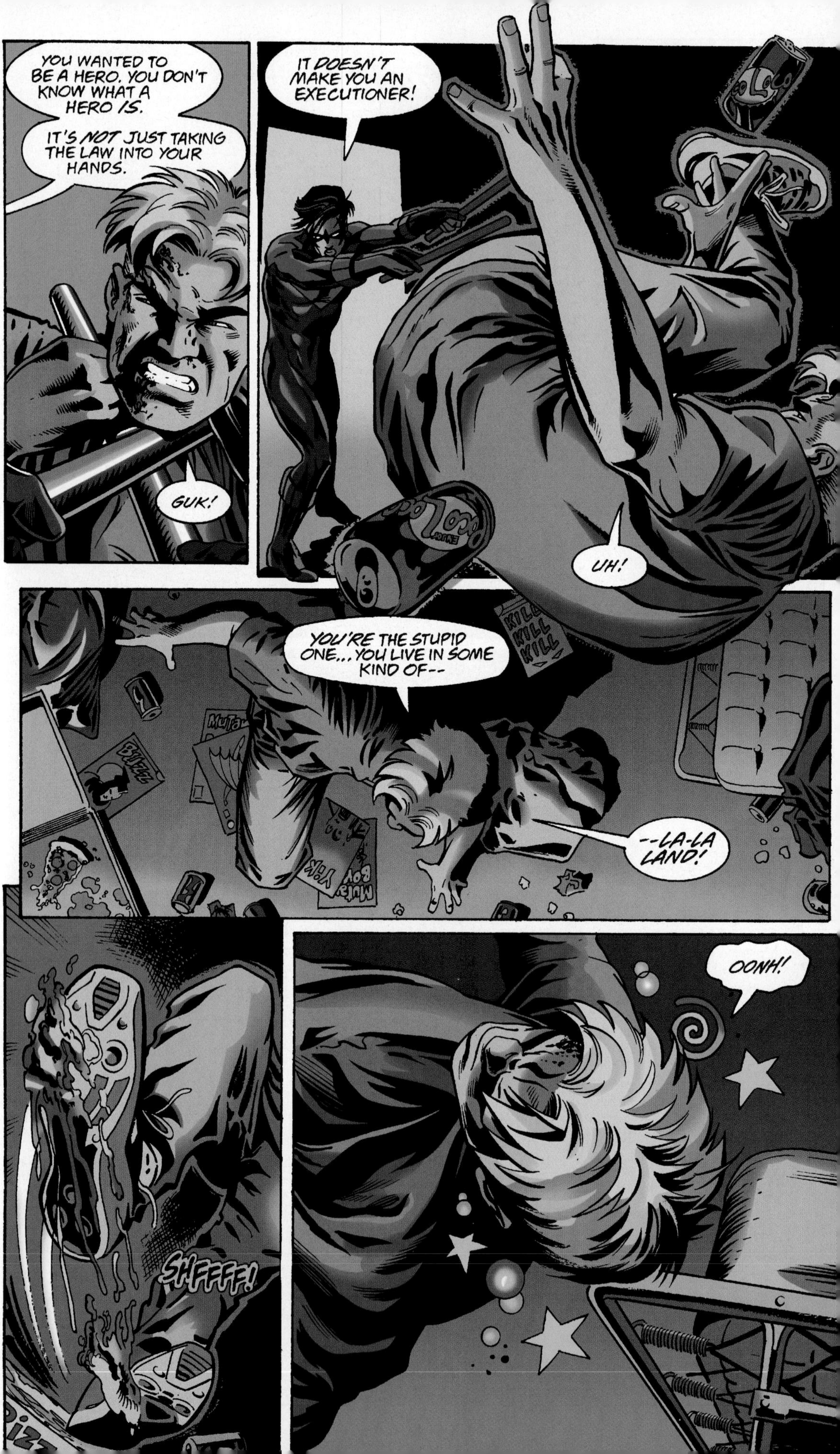
YOU WANTED TO BE A HERO. YOU DON'T KNOW WHAT A HERO IS.
IT'S NOT JUST TAKING THE LAW INTO YOUR HANDS.
IT DOESN'T MAKE YOU AN EXECUTIONER!
GUK!
UH!
YOU'RE THE STUPID ONE... YOU LIVE IN SOME KIND OF--
--LA-LA LAND!
KILL KILL KILL
OONH!
SHFFFF!

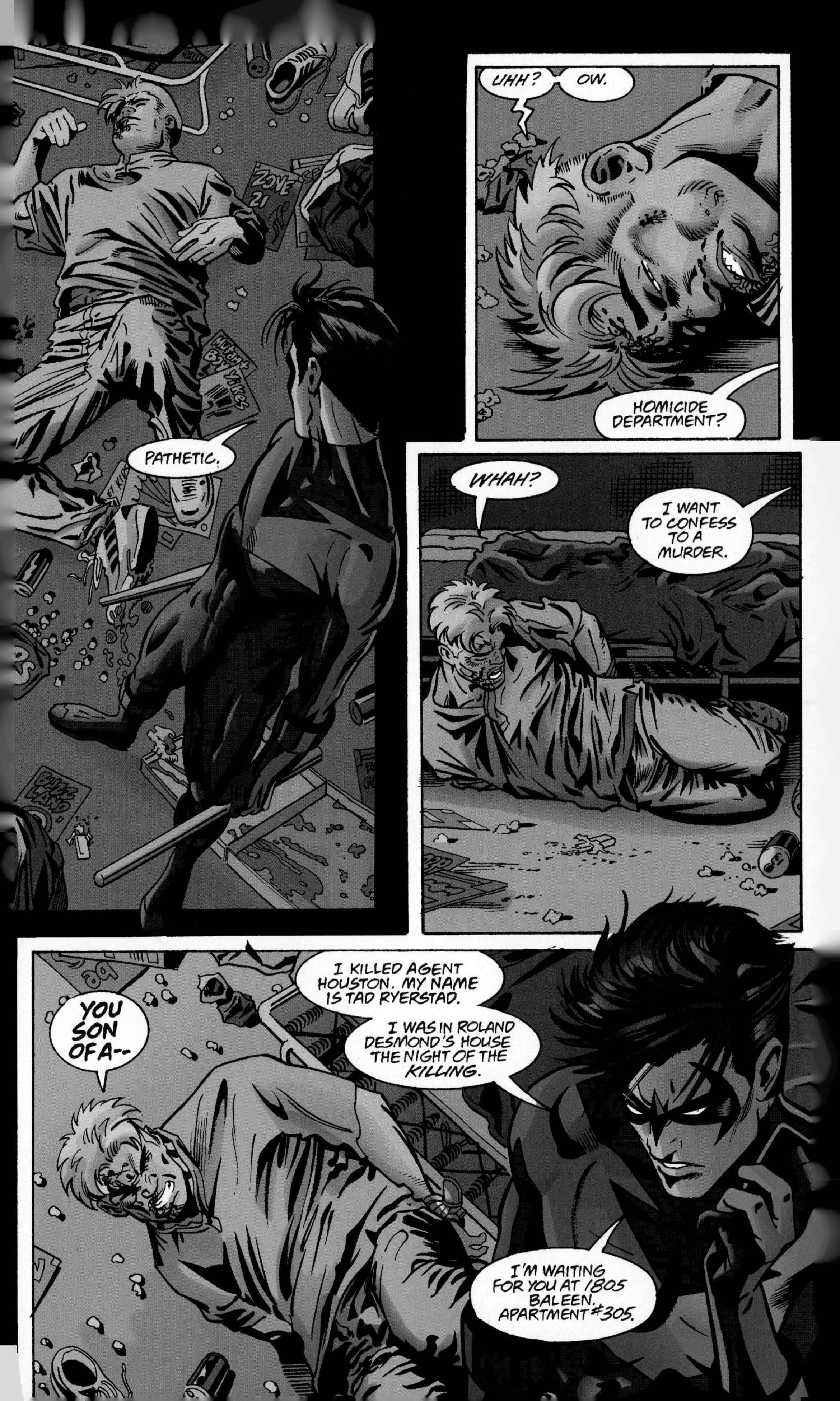
PATHETIC.
UHH?
OW.
HOMICIDE DEPARTMENT?
WHAH?
I WANT TO CONFESS TO A MURDER.
I KILLED AGENT HOUSTON. MY NAME IS TAD RYERSTAD.
I WAS IN ROLAND DESMOND'S HOUSE THE NIGHT OF THE KILLING.
YOU SON OF A--
I'M WAITING FOR YOU AT 1805 BALEEN. APARTMENT #305.

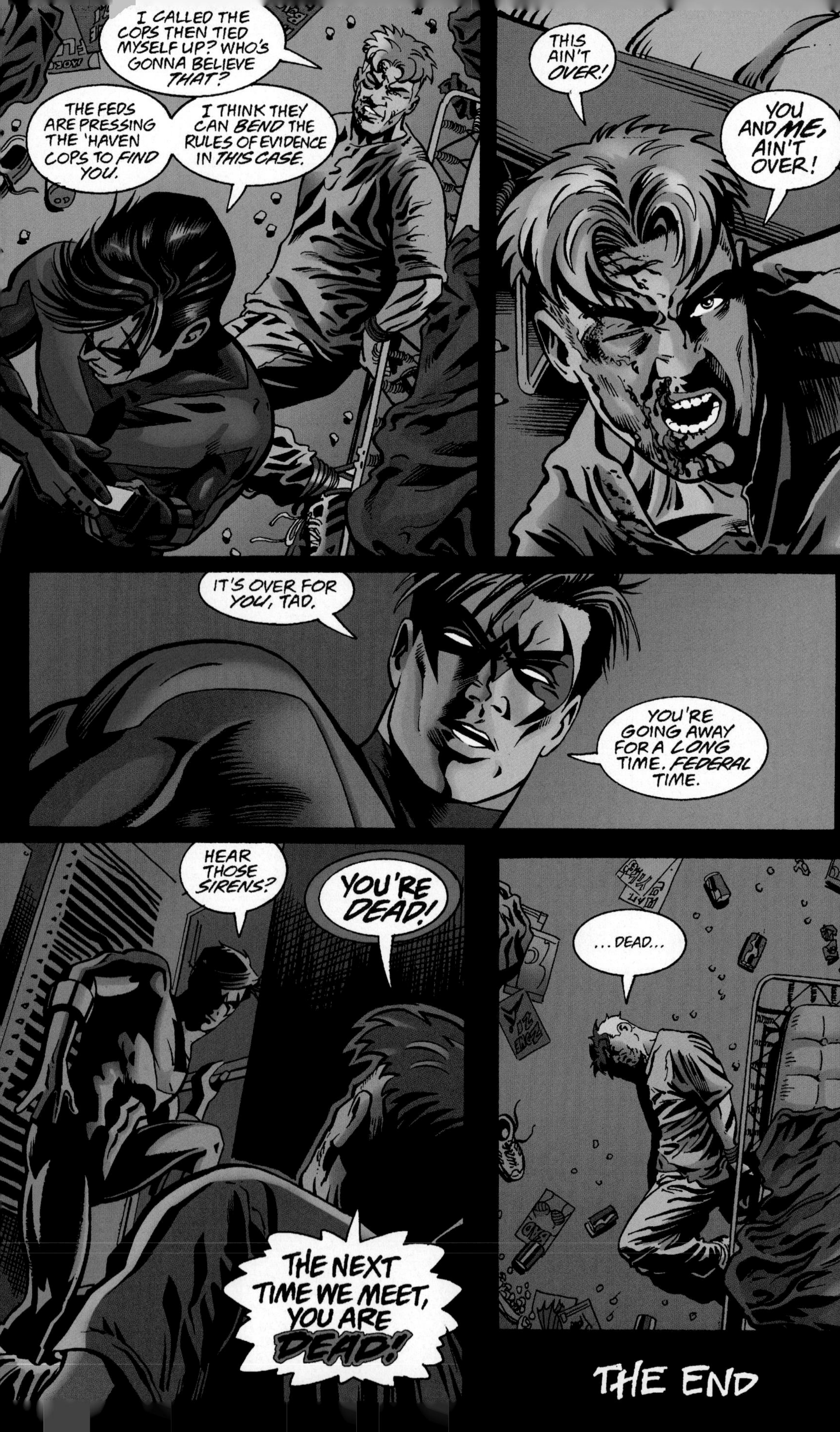
I CALLED THE COPS THEN TIED MYSELF UP? WHO'S GONNA BELIEVE THAT?
THE FEDS ARE PRESSING THE 'HAVEN COPS TO FIND YOU.
I THINK THEY CAN BEND THE RULES OF EVIDENCE IN THIS CASE.
THIS AIN'T OVER!
YOU AND ME, AIN'T OVER!
IT'S OVER FOR YOU, TAD.
YOU'RE GOING AWAY FOR A LONG TIME. FEDERAL TIME.
HEAR THOSE SIRENS?
YOU'RE DEAD!
THE NEXT TIME WE MEET, YOU ARE DEAD!
...DEAD...
THE END

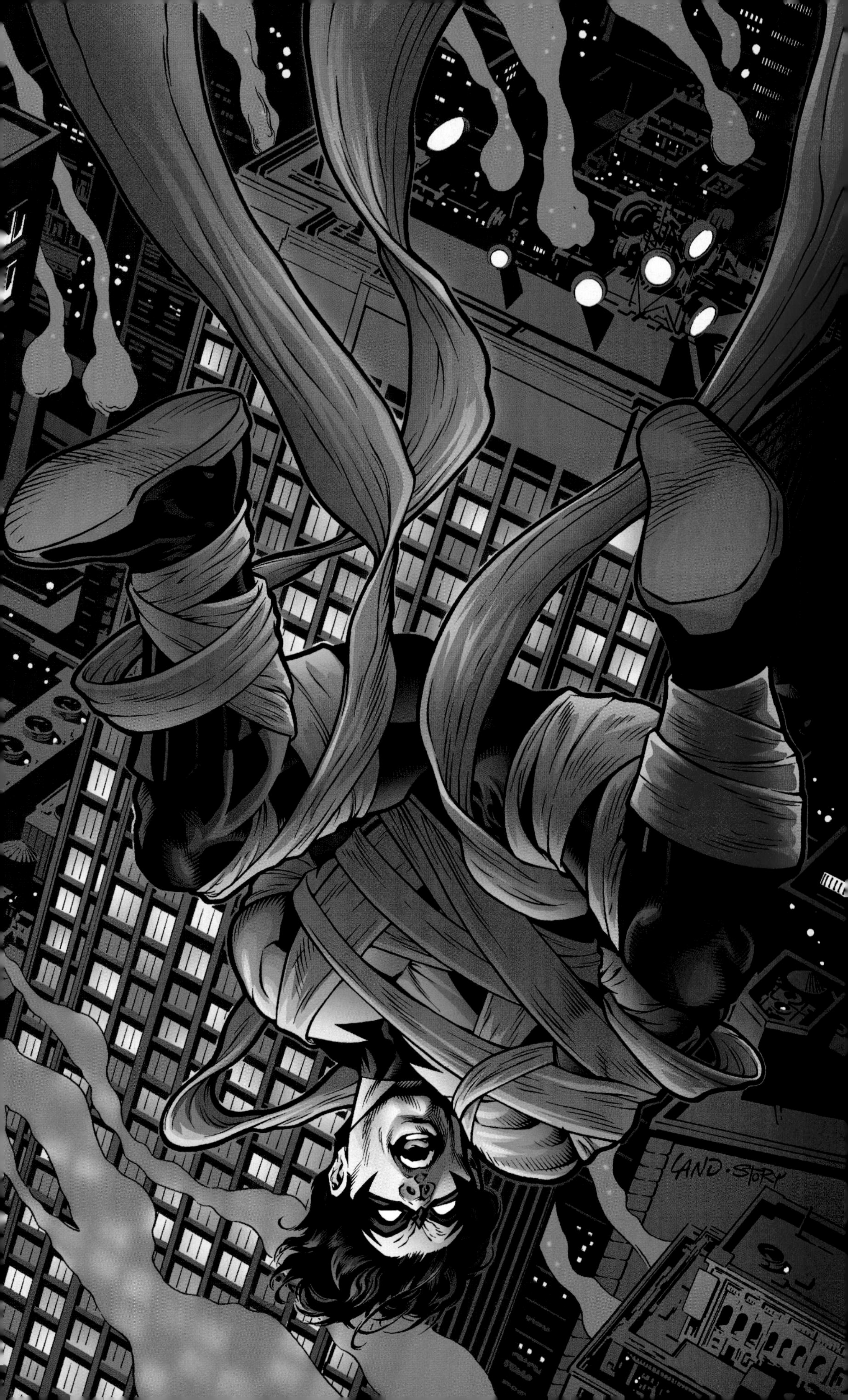
LAND · STORY

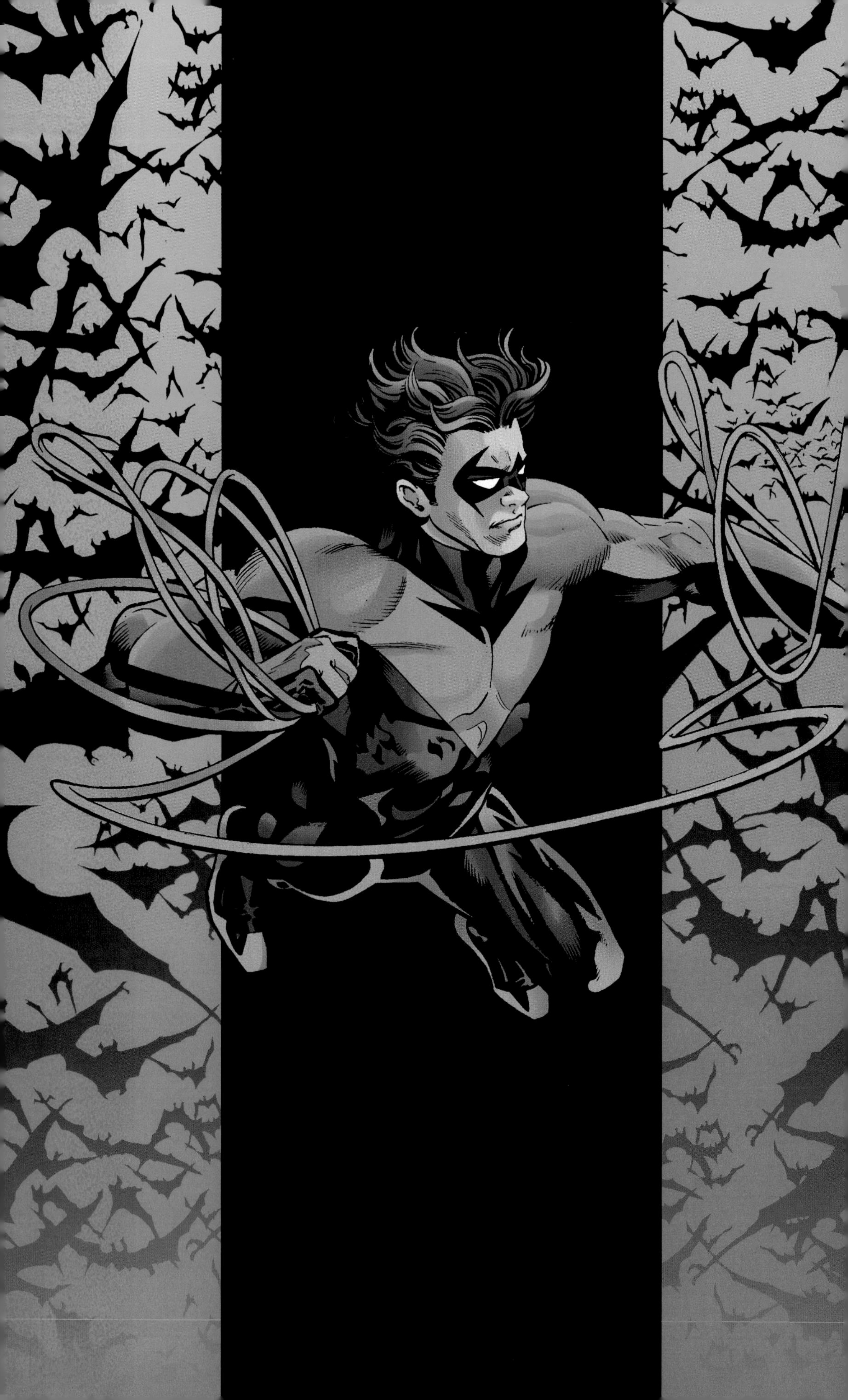

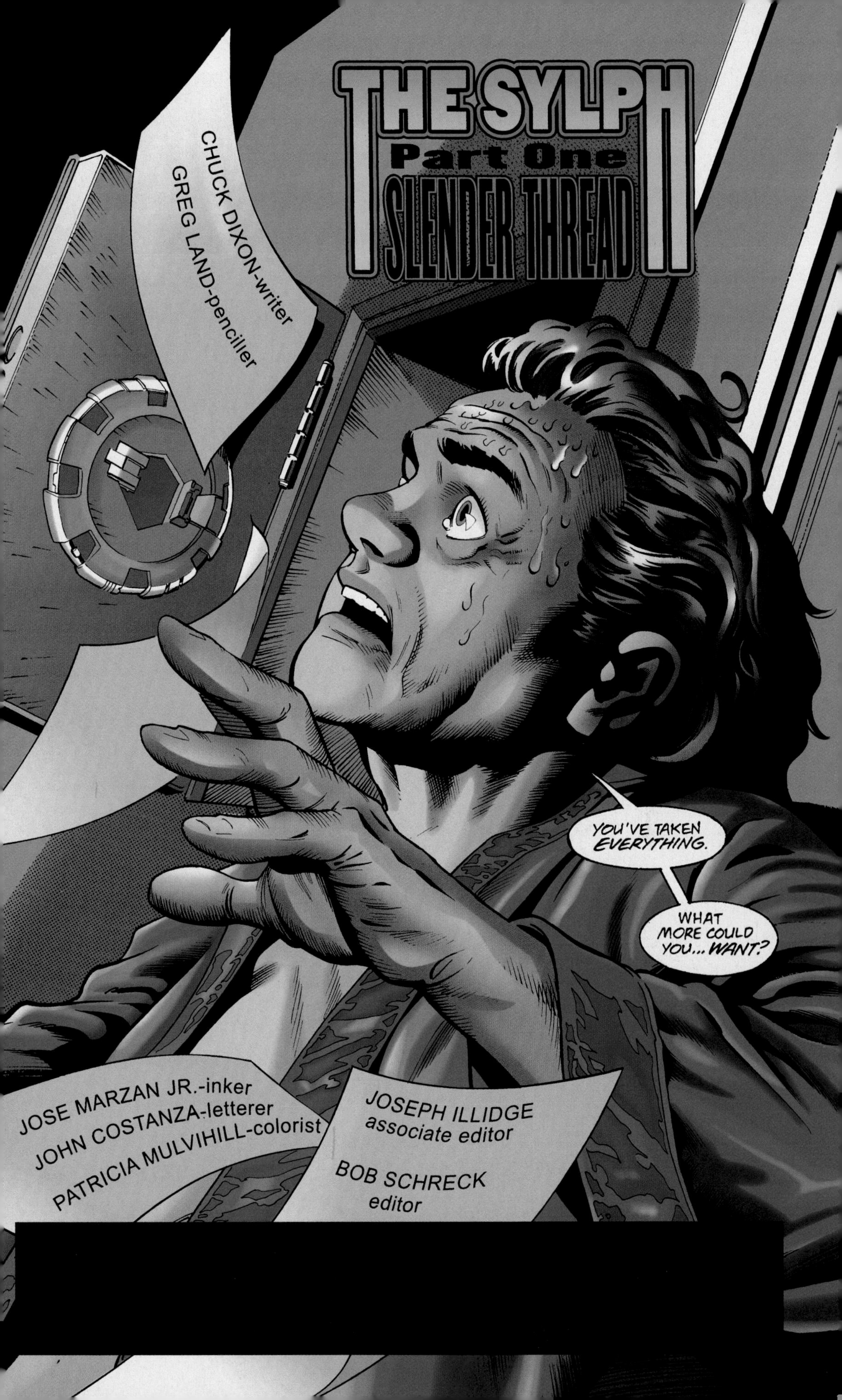
THE SYLPH
Part One
SLENDER THREAD
CHUCK DIXON-writer
GREG LAND-penciller
YOU'VE TAKEN EVERYTHING.
WHAT MORE COULD YOU... WANT?
JOSE MARZAN JR.-inker
JOHN COSTANZA-letterer
PATRICIA MULVIHILL-colorist
JOSEPH ILLIDGE
associate editor
BOB SCHRECK
editor
[redacted]

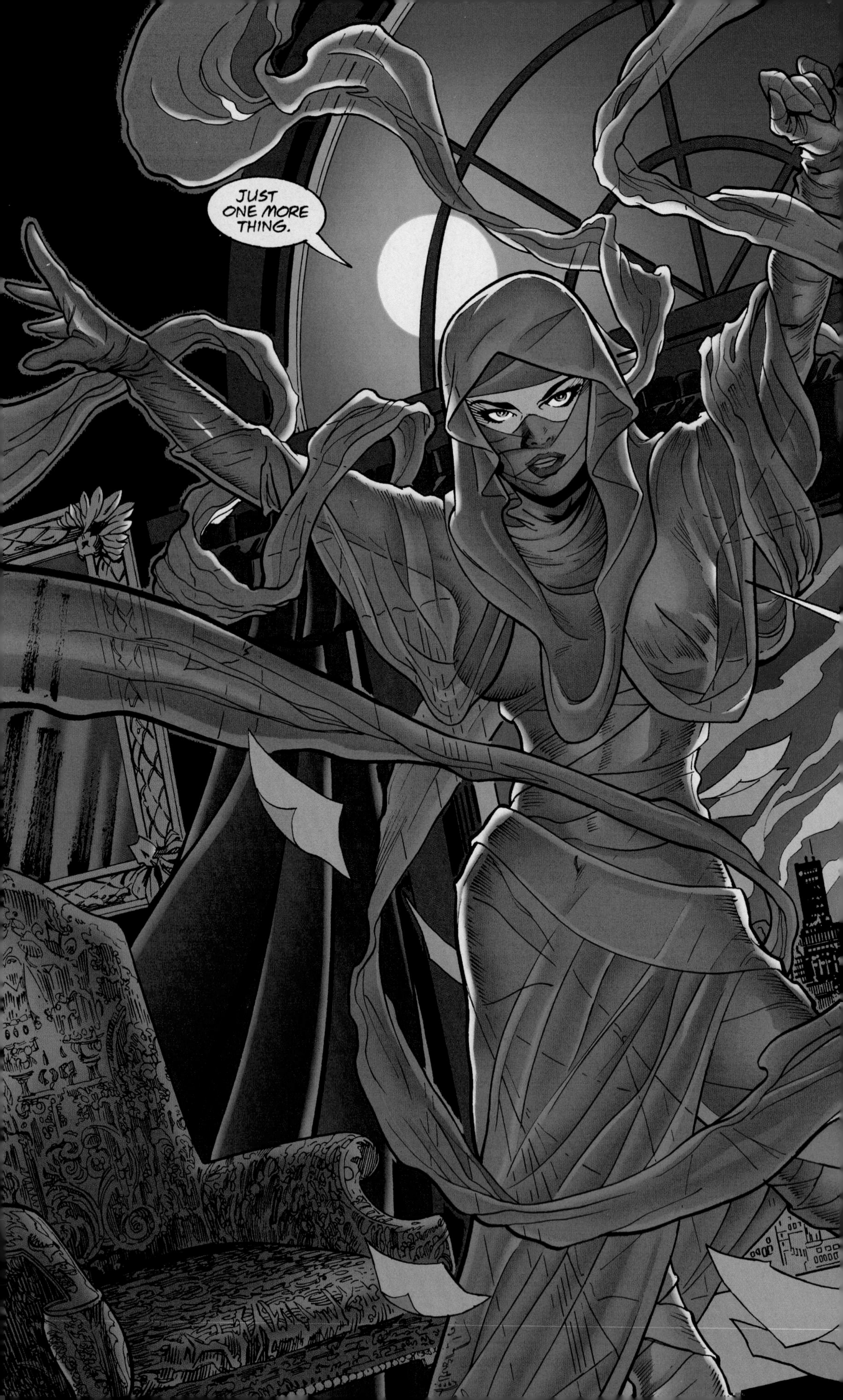
JUST ONE MORE THING.

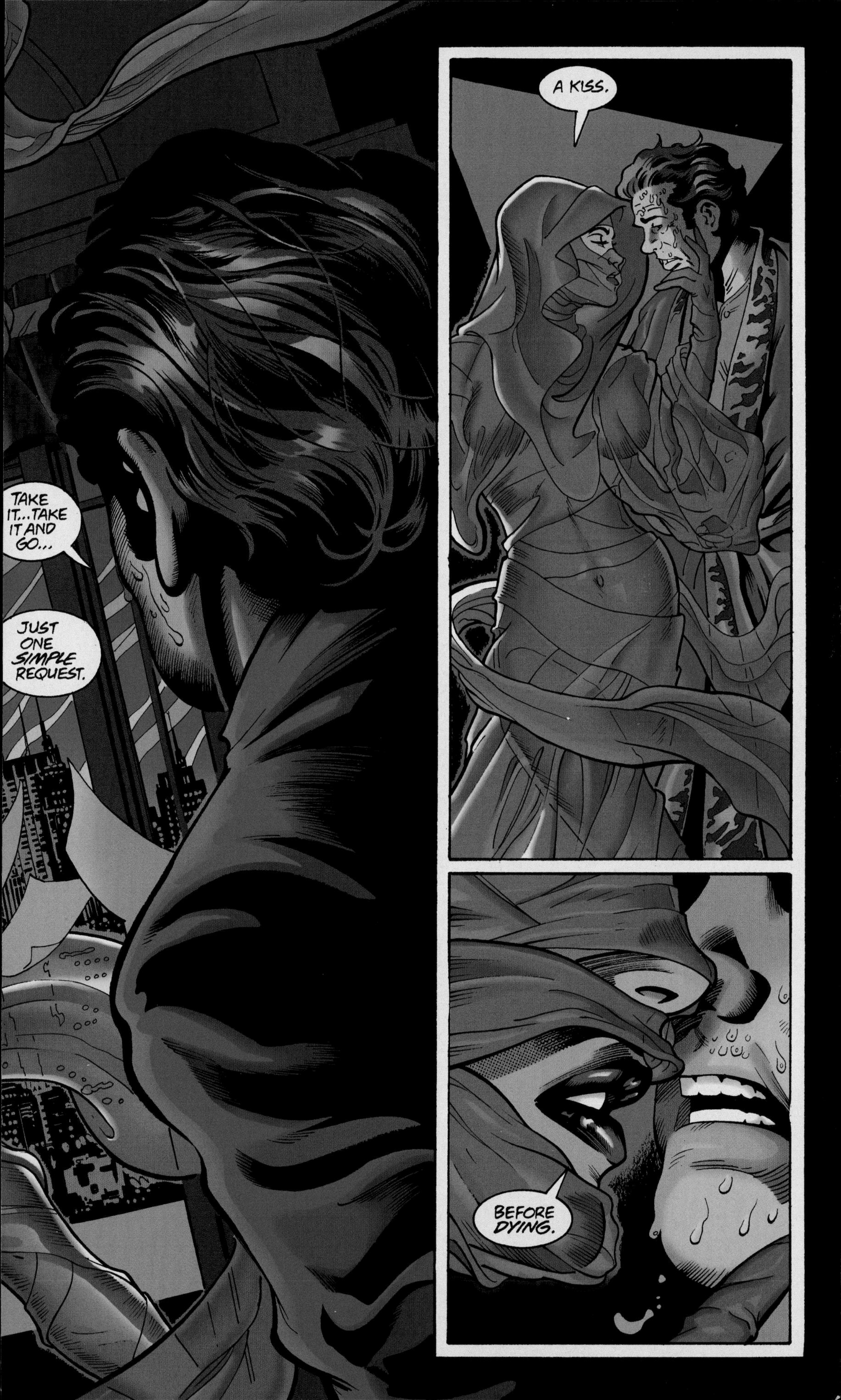
TAKE IT...TAKE IT AND GO...
JUST ONE SIMPLE REQUEST.
A KISS.
BEFORE DYING.

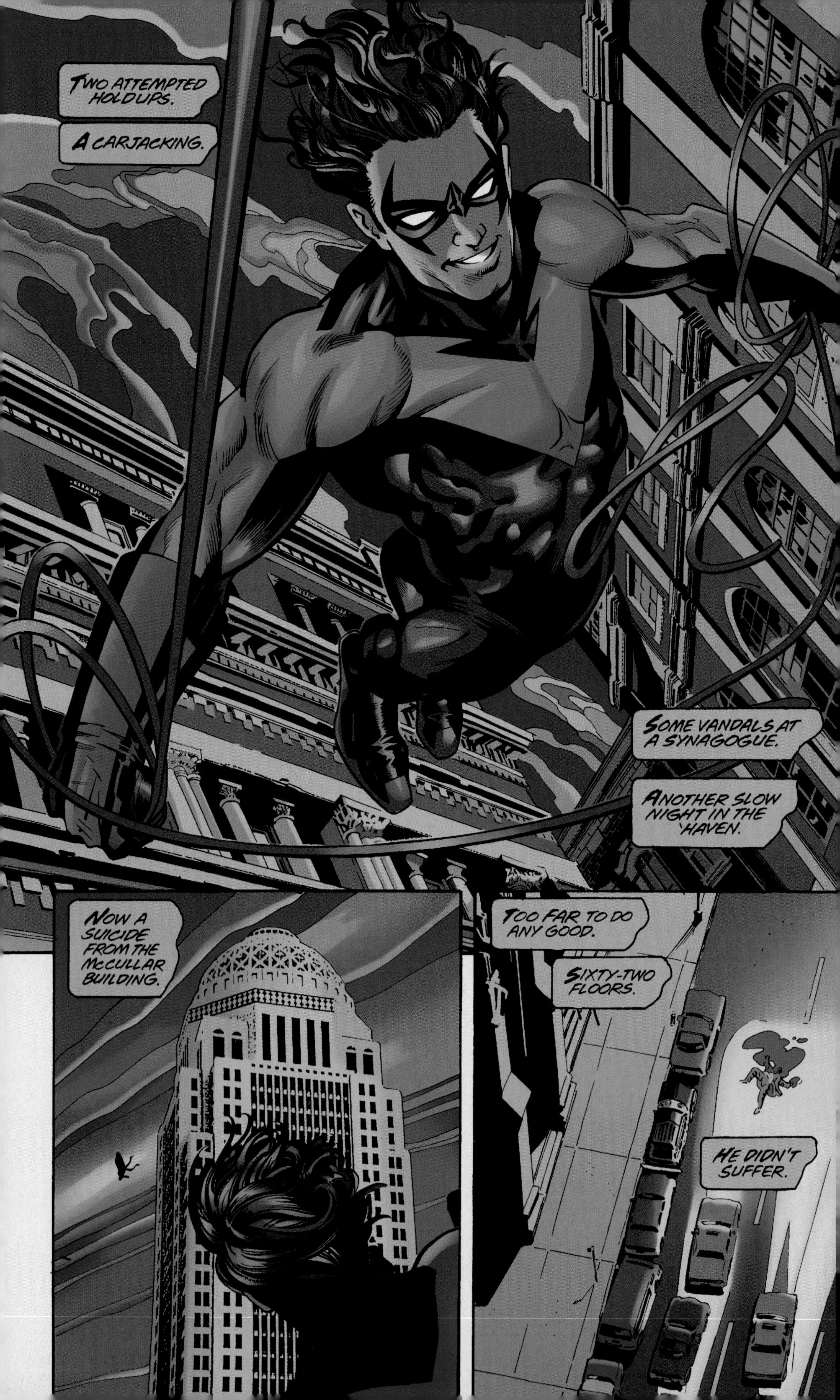
TWO ATTEMPTED HOLDUPS.
A CARJACKING.
SOME VANDALS AT A SYNAGOGUE.
ANOTHER SLOW NIGHT IN THE 'HAVEN.
NOW A SUICIDE FROM THE McCULLAR BUILDING.
TOO FAR TO DO ANY GOOD.
SIXTY-TWO FLOORS.
HE DIDN'T SUFFER.

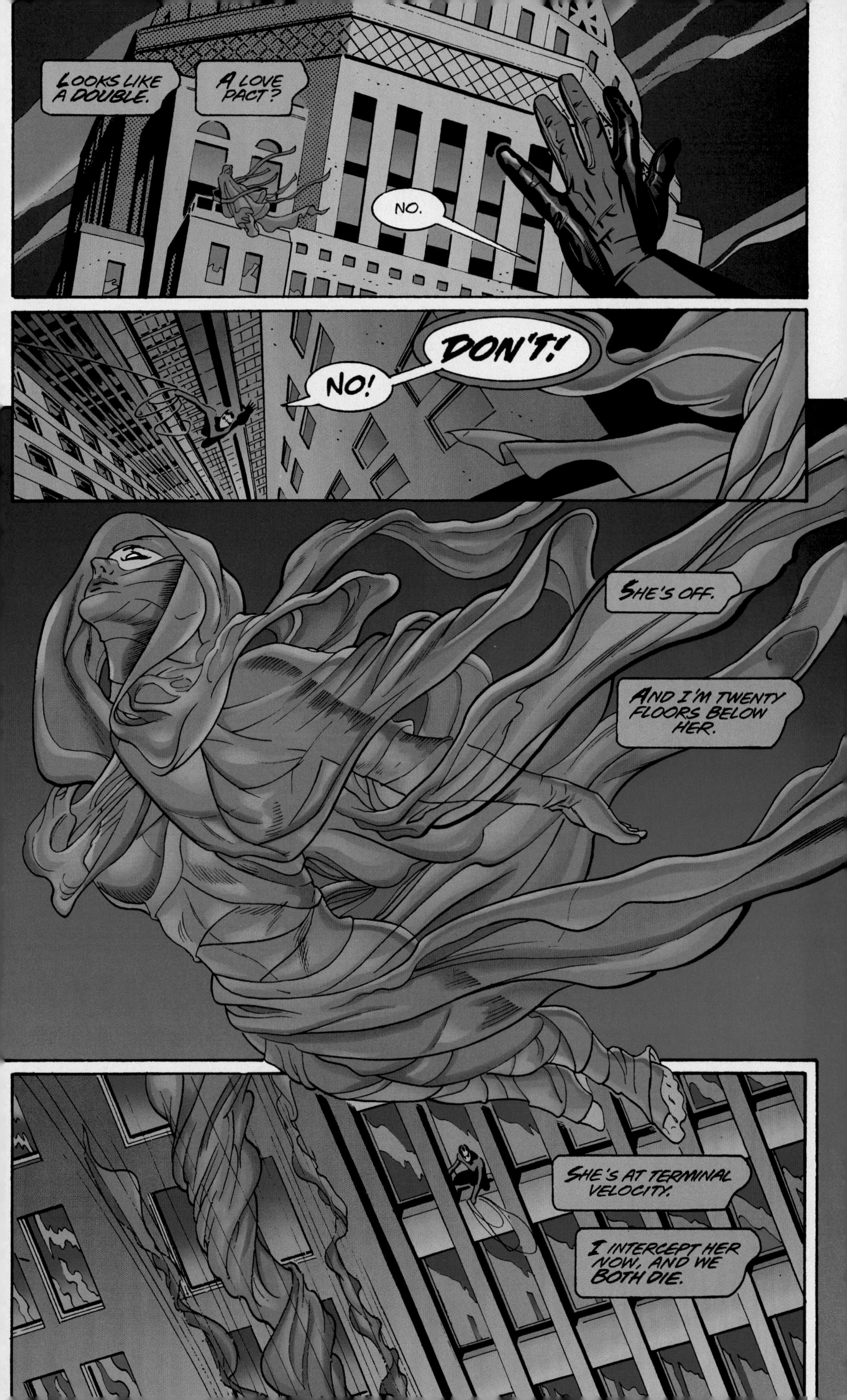
LOOKS LIKE A DOUBLE.
A LOVE PACT?
NO.
NO!
DON'T!
SHE'S OFF.
AND I'M TWENTY FLOORS BELOW HER.
SHE'S AT TERMINAL VELOCITY.
I INTERCEPT HER NOW, AND WE BOTH DIE.

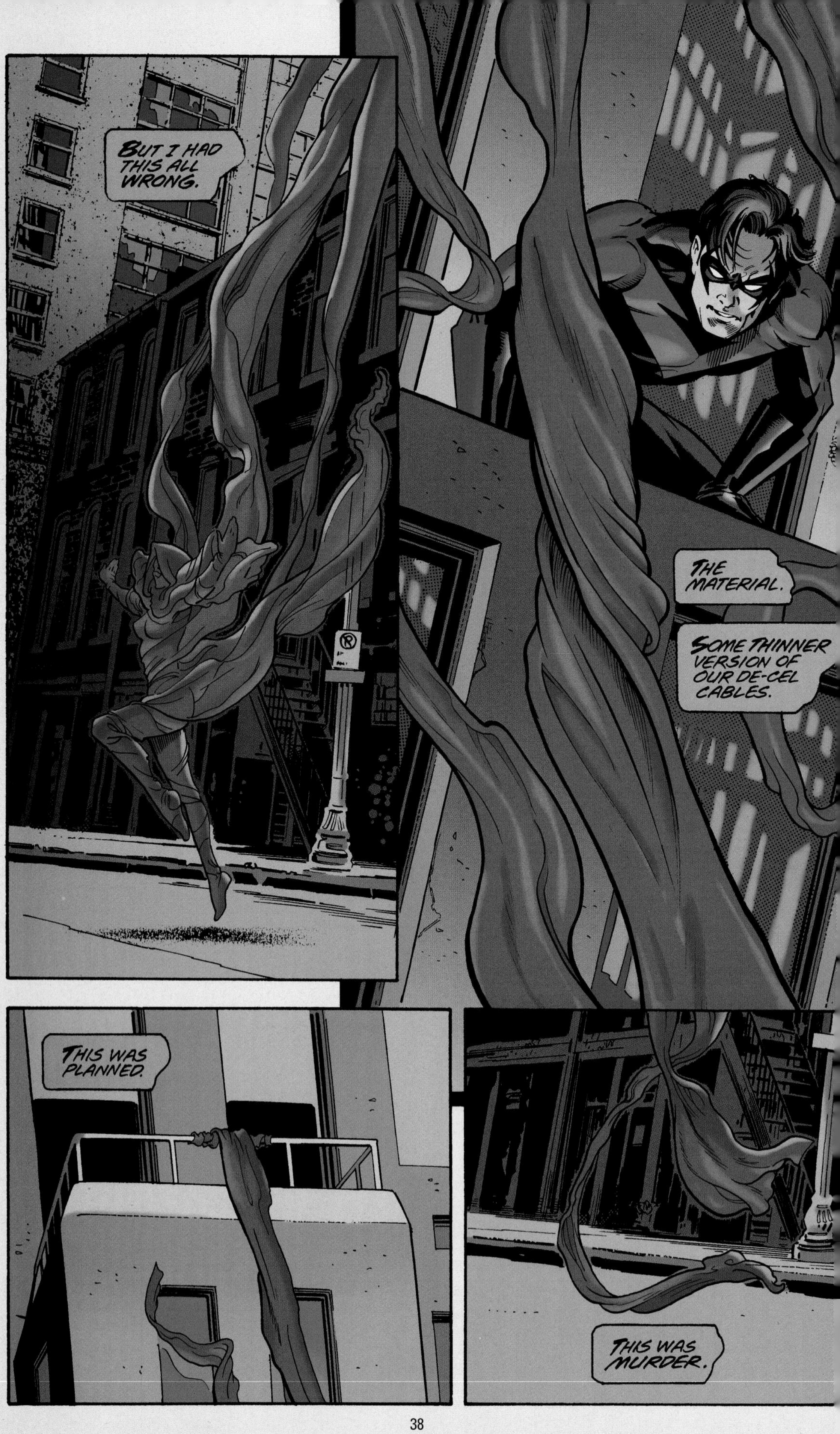
BUT I HAD THIS ALL WRONG.
THE MATERIAL.
SOME THINNER VERSION OF OUR DE-CEL CABLES.
THIS WAS PLANNED.
THIS WAS MURDER.

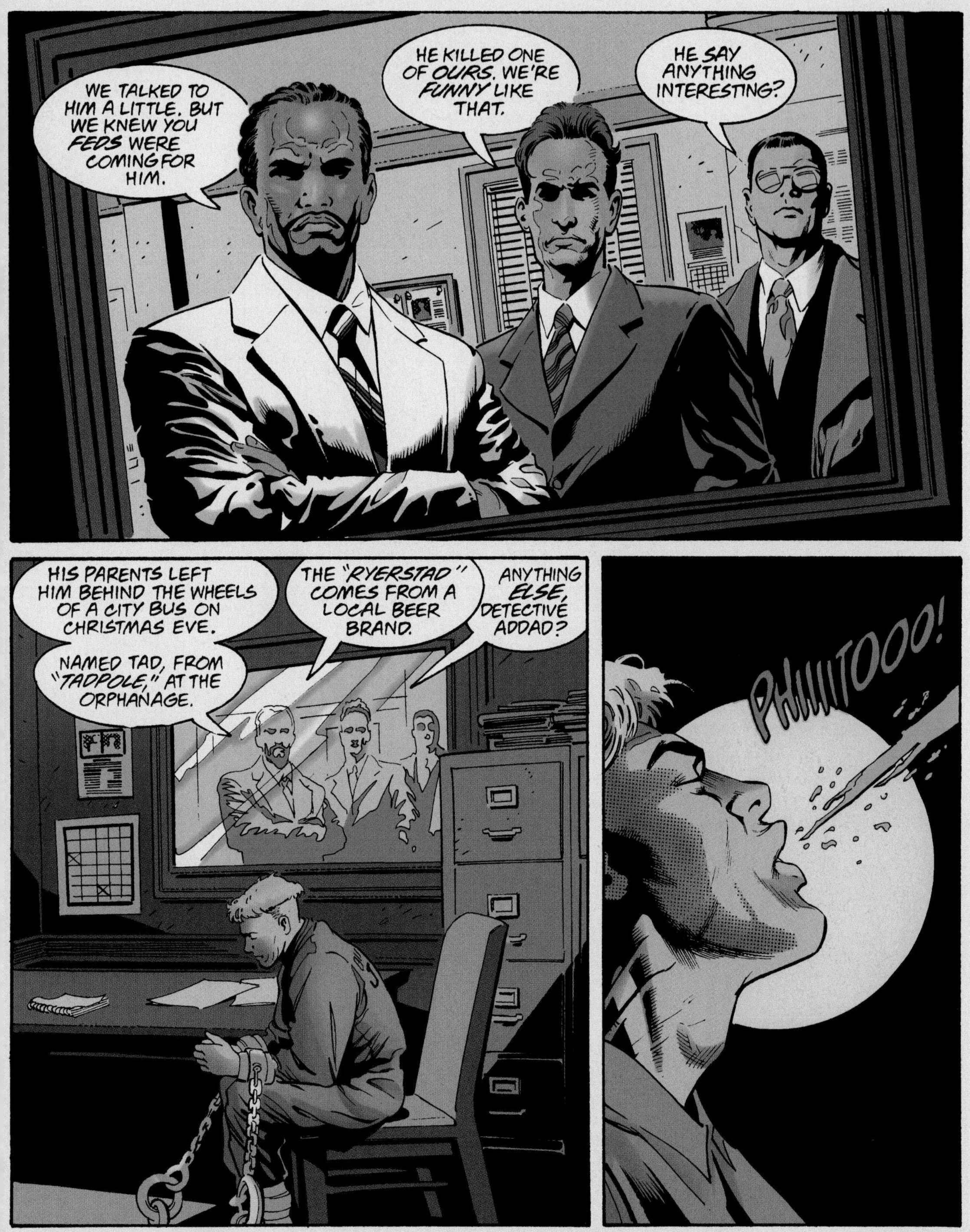
WE TALKED TO HIM A LITTLE. BUT WE KNEW YOU FEDS WERE COMING FOR HIM.
HE KILLED ONE OF OURS. WE'RE FUNNY LIKE THAT.
HE SAY ANYTHING INTERESTING?
HIS PARENTS LEFT HIM BEHIND THE WHEELS OF A CITY BUS ON CHRISTMAS EVE.
NAMED TAD, FROM "TADPOLE," AT THE ORPHANAGE.
THE "RYERSTAD" COMES FROM A LOCAL BEER BRAND.
ANYTHING ELSE, DETECTIVE ADDAD?
PHHHTOOO!
YOU GOT YOUR WORK CUT OUT FOR YOU.

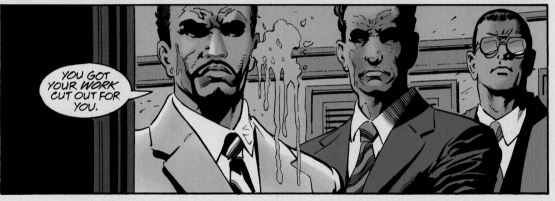

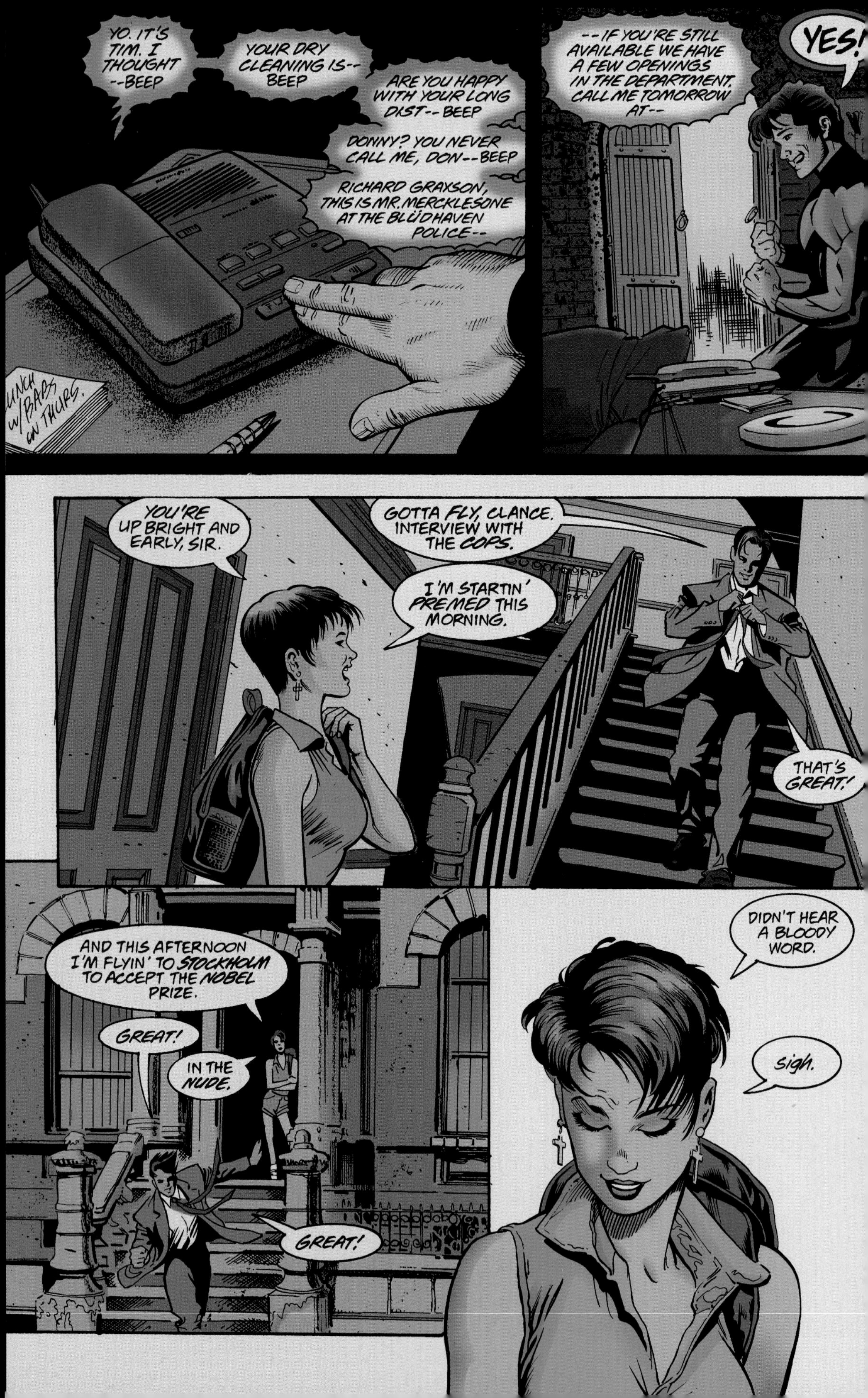
YO. IT'S TIM. I THOUGHT --BEEP
YOUR DRY CLEANING IS-- BEEP
ARE YOU HAPPY WITH YOUR LONG DIST--BEEP
DONNY? YOU NEVER CALL ME, DON--BEEP
RICHARD GRAYSON, THIS IS MR. MERCKLESONE AT THE BLÜDHAVEN POLICE--
LUNCH W/BABS ON THURS.
--IF YOU'RE STILL AVAILABLE WE HAVE A FEW OPENINGS IN THE DEPARTMENT. CALL ME TOMORROW AT--
YES!
YOU'RE UP BRIGHT AND EARLY, SIR.
GOTTA FLY, CLANCE. INTERVIEW WITH THE COPS.
I'M STARTIN' PREMED THIS MORNING.
THAT'S GREAT!
AND THIS AFTERNOON I'M FLYIN' TO STOCKHOLM TO ACCEPT THE NOBEL PRIZE.
GREAT!
IN THE NUDE.
GREAT!
DIDN'T HEAR A BLOODY WORD.
sigh.

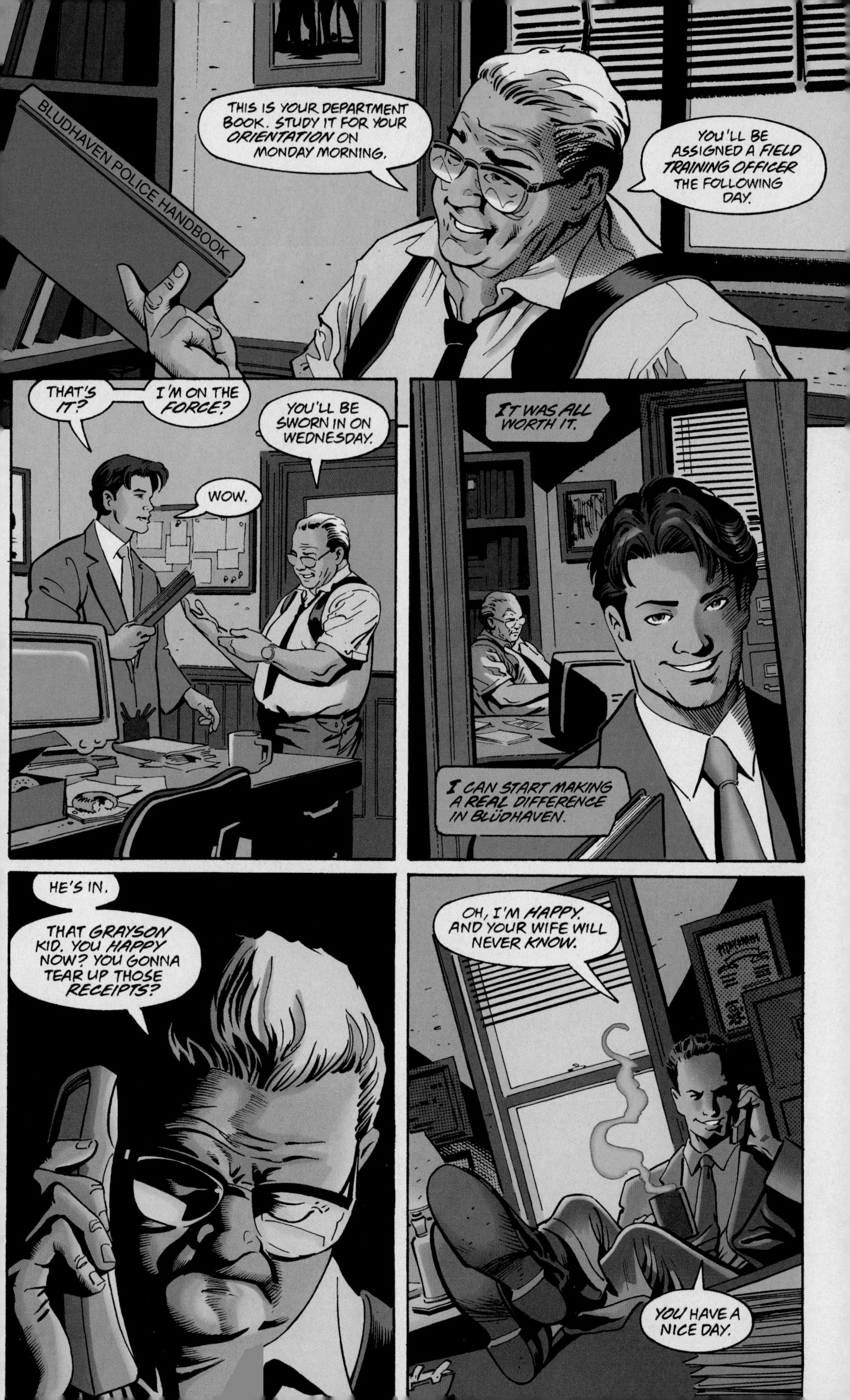
BLUDHAVEN POLICE HANDBOOK
THIS IS YOUR DEPARTMENT BOOK. STUDY IT FOR YOUR ORIENTATION ON MONDAY MORNING.
YOU'LL BE ASSIGNED A FIELD TRAINING OFFICER THE FOLLOWING DAY.
THAT'S IT?
I'M ON THE FORCE?
YOU'LL BE SWORN IN ON WEDNESDAY.
WOW.
IT WAS ALL WORTH IT.
I CAN START MAKING A REAL DIFFERENCE IN BLÜDHAVEN.
HE'S IN.
THAT GRAYSON KID. YOU HAPPY NOW? YOU GONNA TEAR UP THOSE RECEIPTS?
OH, I'M HAPPY. AND YOUR WIFE WILL NEVER KNOW.
YOU HAVE A NICE DAY.

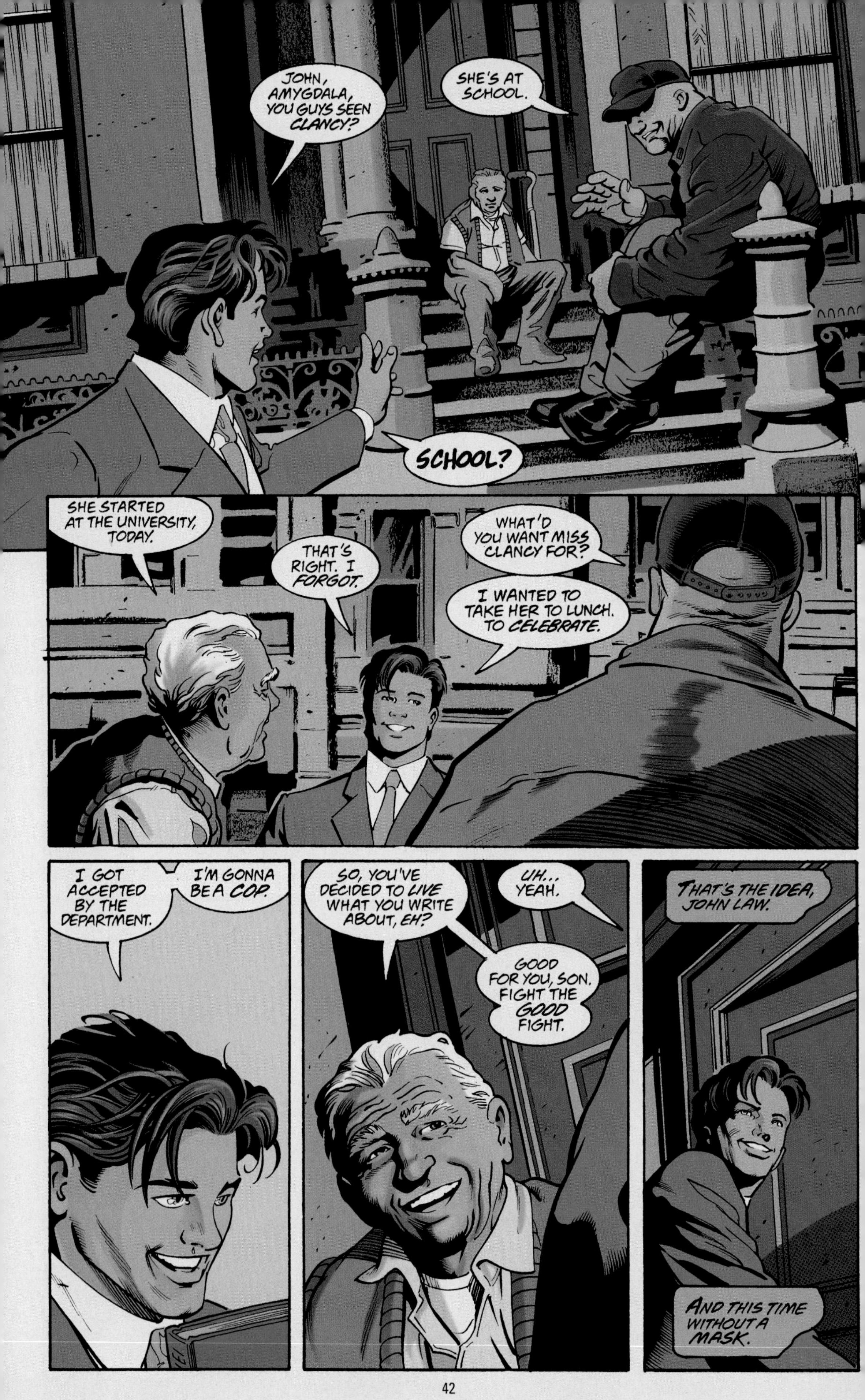
JOHN, AMYGDALA, YOU GUYS SEEN CLANCY?
SHE'S AT SCHOOL.
SCHOOL?
SHE STARTED AT THE UNIVERSITY, TODAY.
THAT'S RIGHT. I FORGOT.
WHAT'D YOU WANT MISS CLANCY FOR?
I WANTED TO TAKE HER TO LUNCH. TO CELEBRATE.
I GOT ACCEPTED BY THE DEPARTMENT.
I'M GONNA BE A COP.
SO, YOU'VE DECIDED TO LIVE WHAT YOU WRITE ABOUT, EH?
UH... YEAH.
GOOD FOR YOU, SON. FIGHT THE GOOD FIGHT.
THAT'S THE IDEA, JOHN LAW.
AND THIS TIME WITHOUT A MASK.

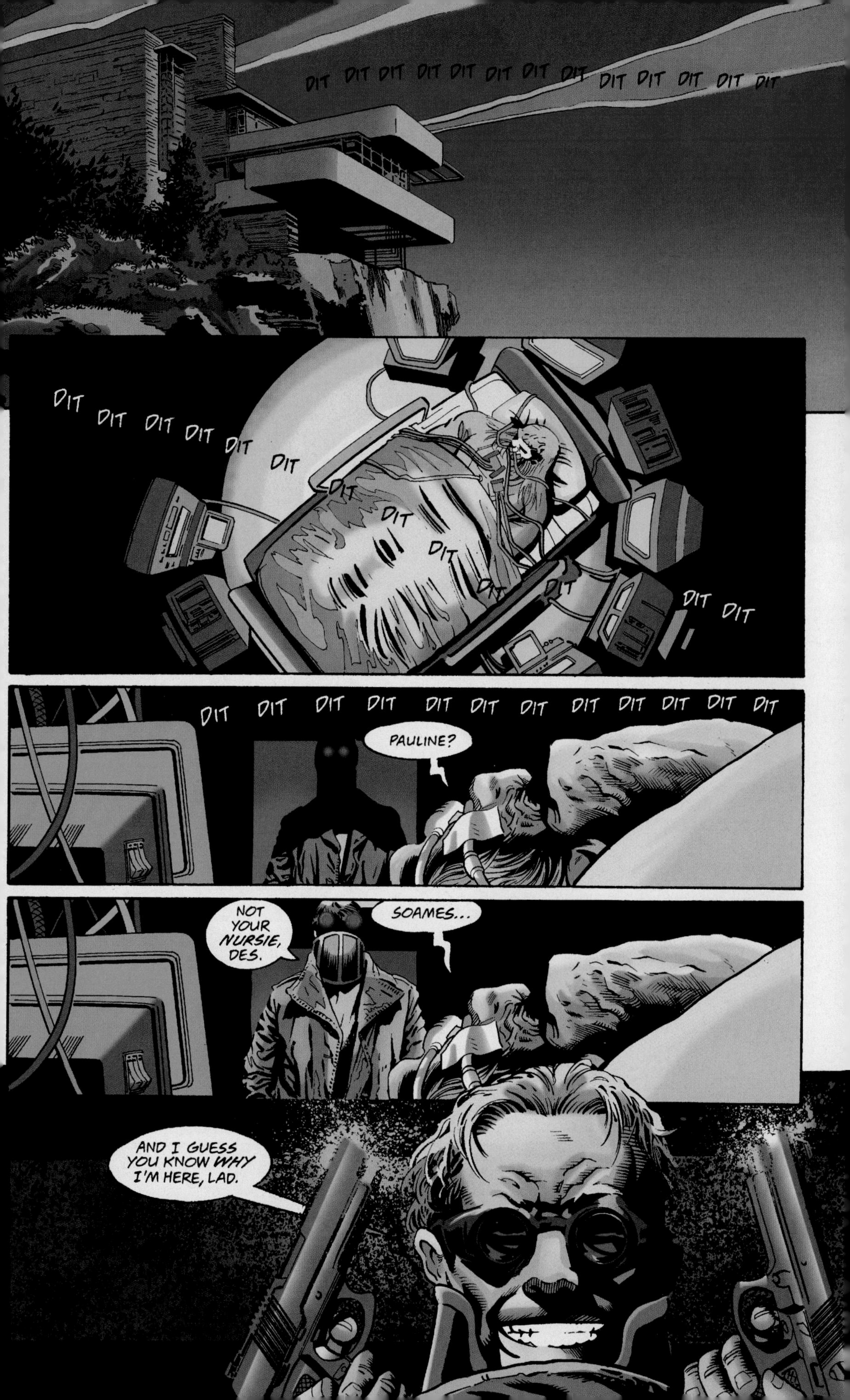
DIT DIT DIT DIT DIT DIT DIT DIT DIT DIT DIT DIT DIT
DIT DIT DIT DIT DIT DIT DIT DIT DIT DIT DIT DIT
DIT DIT DIT DIT DIT DIT DIT DIT DIT DIT DIT DIT
PAULINE?
NOT YOUR NURSIE, DES.
SOAMES...
AND I GUESS YOU KNOW WHY I'M HERE, LAD.

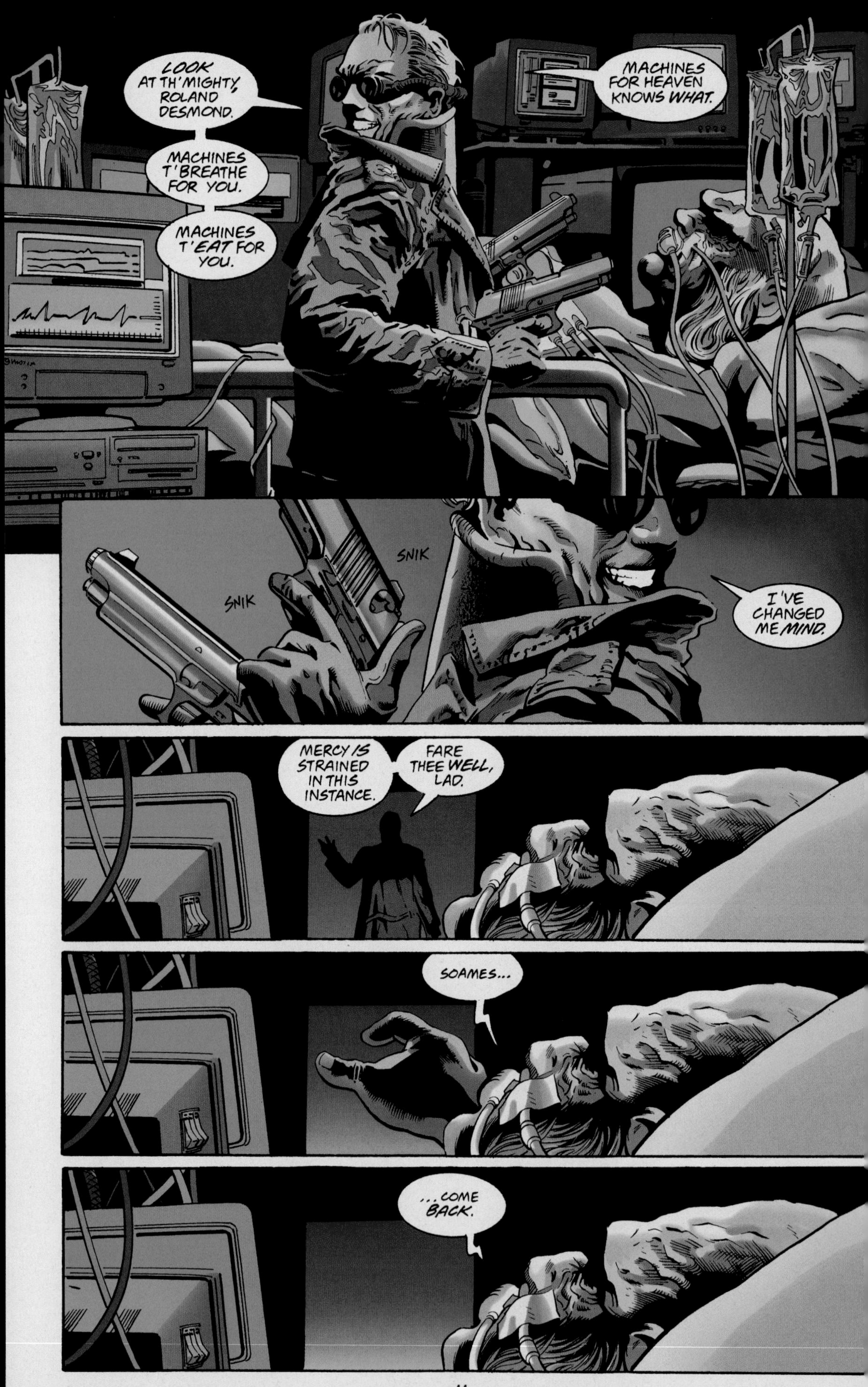
LOOK AT TH' MIGHTY, ROLAND DESMOND.
MACHINES T' BREATHE FOR YOU.
MACHINES T' EAT FOR YOU.
MACHINES FOR HEAVEN KNOWS WHAT.
SNIK
SNIK
I'VE CHANGED ME MIND.
MERCY IS STRAINED IN THIS INSTANCE.
FARE THEE WELL, LAD.
SOAMES...
...COME BACK.

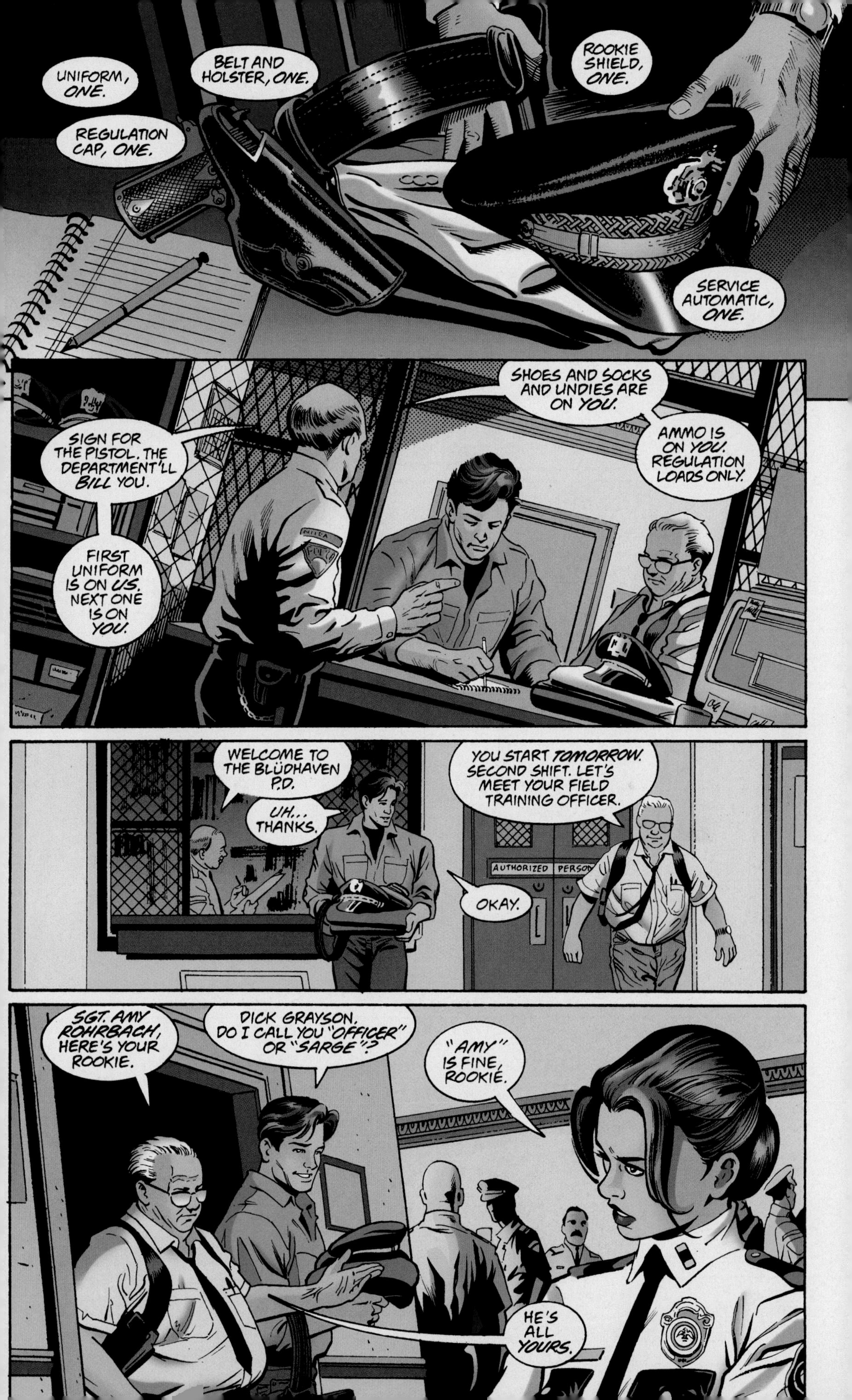
UNIFORM, ONE.
BELT AND HOLSTER, ONE.
ROOKIE SHIELD, ONE.
REGULATION CAP, ONE.
SERVICE AUTOMATIC, ONE.
SHOES AND SOCKS AND UNDIES ARE ON YOU.
SIGN FOR THE PISTOL. THE DEPARTMENT'LL BILL YOU.
AMMO IS ON YOU. REGULATION LOADS ONLY.
FIRST UNIFORM IS ON US. NEXT ONE IS ON YOU.
WELCOME TO THE BLÜDHAVEN P.D.
UH... THANKS.
YOU START TOMORROW. SECOND SHIFT. LET'S MEET YOUR FIELD TRAINING OFFICER.
OKAY.
AUTHORIZED PERSON
SGT. AMY ROHRBACH, HERE'S YOUR ROOKIE.
DICK GRAYSON. DO I CALL YOU "OFFICER" OR "SARGE"?
"AMY" IS FINE, ROOKIE.
HE'S ALL YOURS.

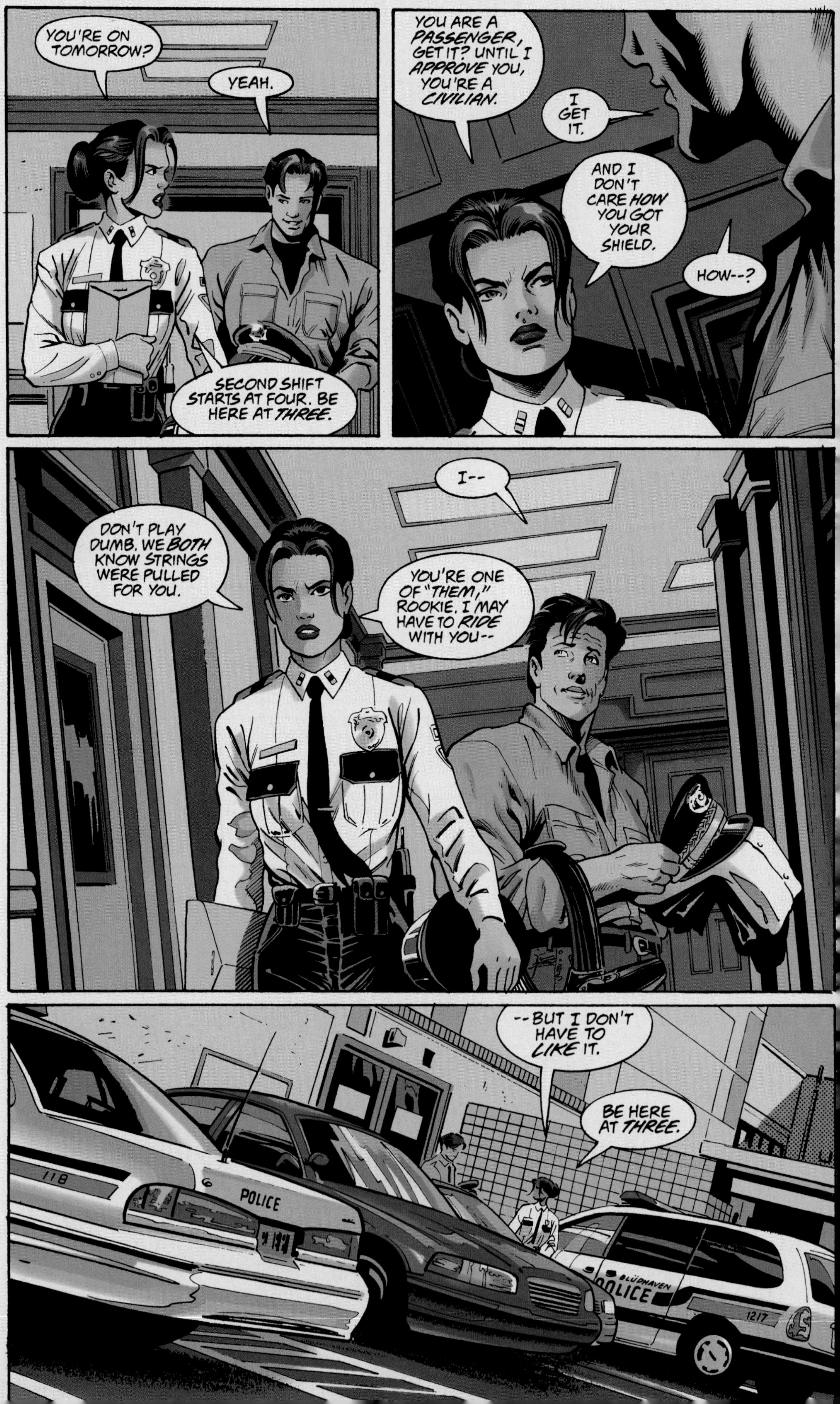
YOU'RE ON TOMORROW?
YEAH.
SECOND SHIFT STARTS AT FOUR. BE HERE AT *THREE*.
YOU ARE A *PASSENGER*, GET IT? UNTIL I *APPROVE* YOU, YOU'RE A *CIVILIAN*.
I GET IT.
AND I DON'T CARE *HOW* YOU GOT YOUR SHIELD.
HOW--?
DON'T PLAY DUMB. WE *BOTH* KNOW STRINGS WERE PULLED FOR YOU.
I--
YOU'RE ONE OF "*THEM*," ROOKIE. I MAY HAVE TO *RIDE* WITH YOU--
--BUT I DON'T HAVE TO *LIKE* IT.
BE HERE AT *THREE*.
118
POLICE
BLÜDHAVEN POLICE
1217

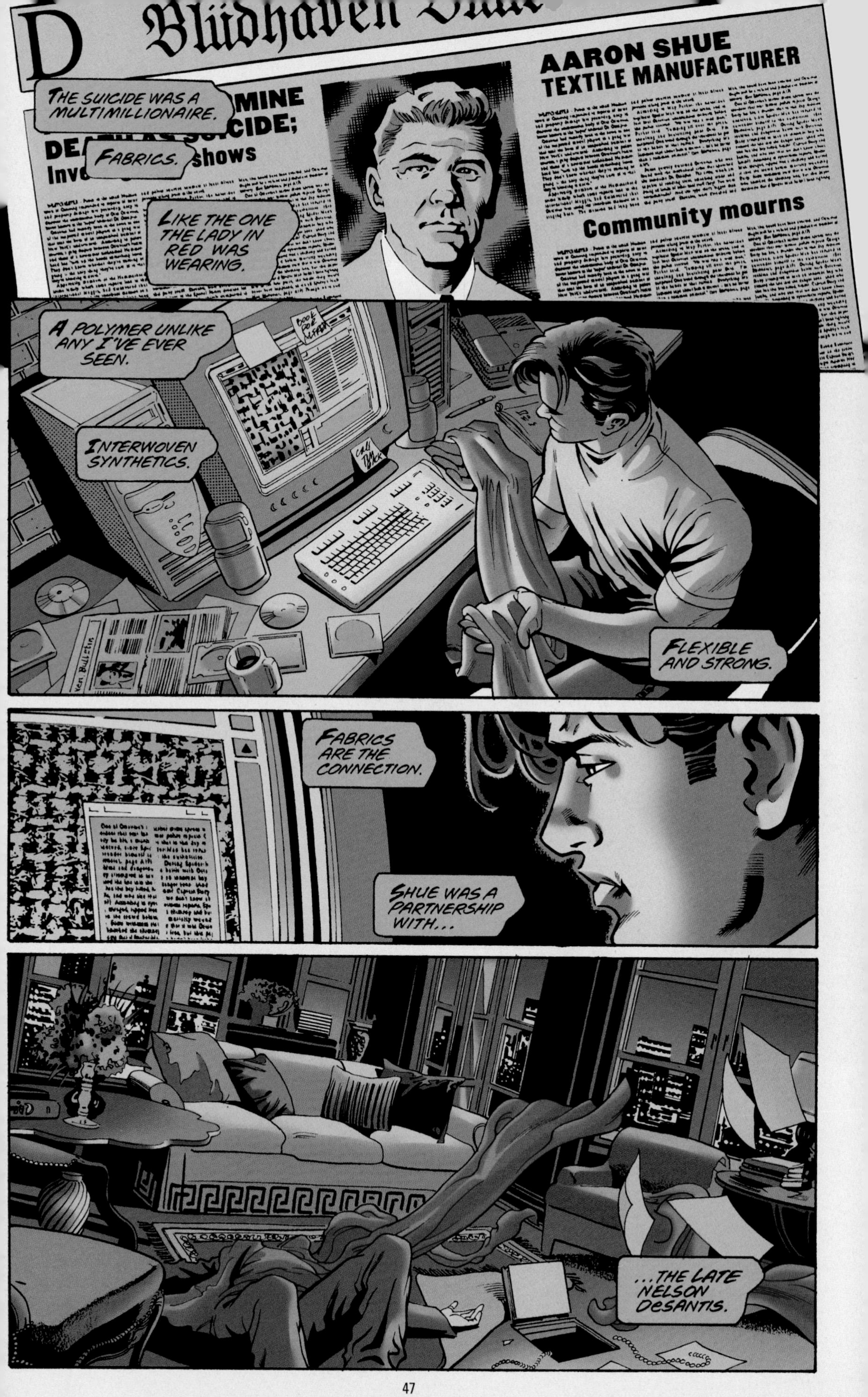

Blüdhaven
AARON SHUE
TEXTILE MANUFACTURER
MINE
CIDE;
DE
shows
Inve
Community mourns
THE SUICIDE WAS A MULTIMILLIONAIRE.
FABRICS.
LIKE THE ONE THE LADY IN RED WAS WEARING.
A POLYMER UNLIKE ANY I'VE EVER SEEN.
INTERWOVEN SYNTHETICS.
FLEXIBLE AND STRONG.
FABRICS ARE THE CONNECTION.
SHUE WAS A PARTNERSHIP WITH...
...THE LATE NELSON DeSANTIS.

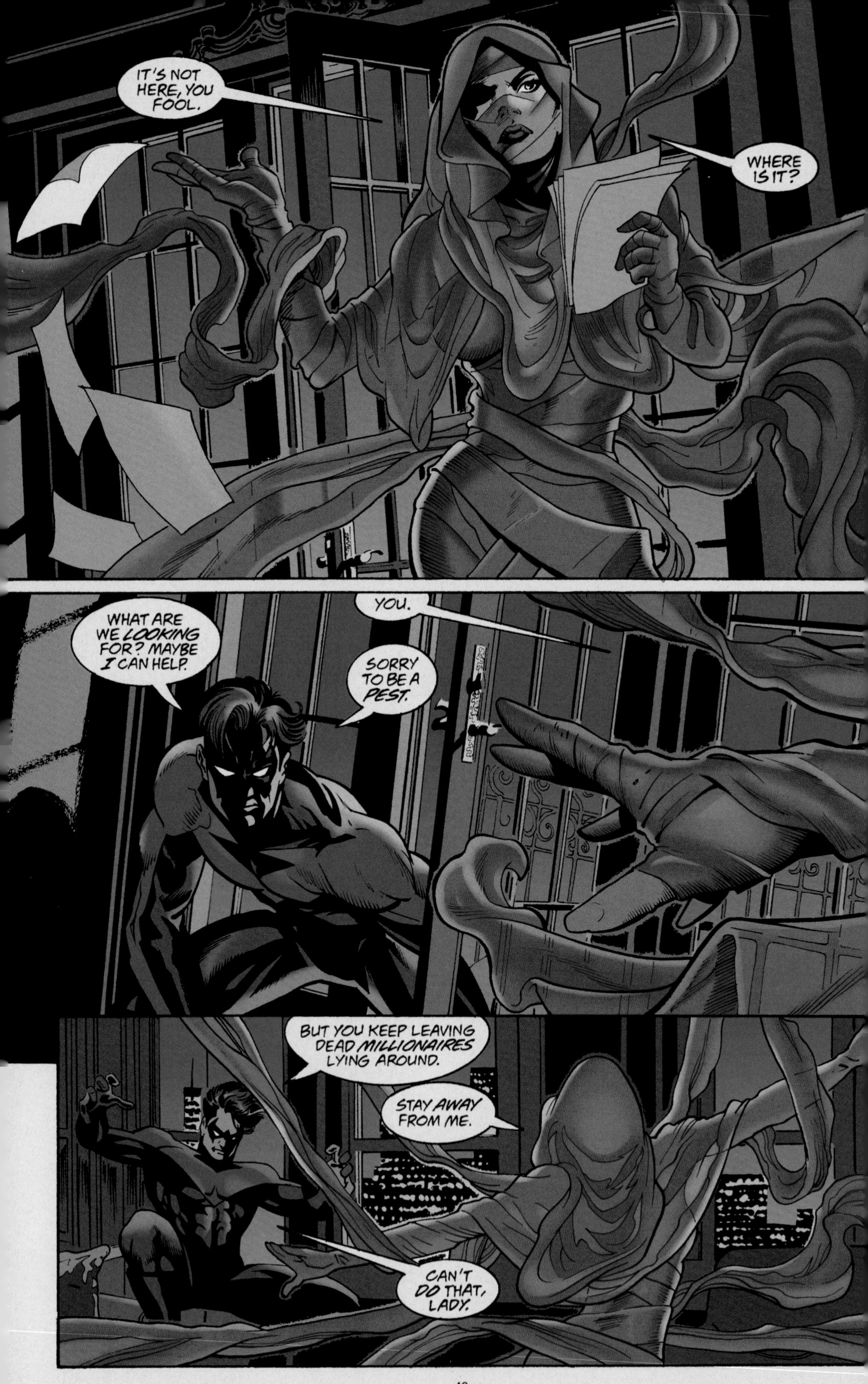
IT'S NOT HERE, YOU FOOL.
WHERE IS IT?
WHAT ARE WE LOOKING FOR? MAYBE I CAN HELP.
YOU.
SORRY TO BE A PEST.
BUT YOU KEEP LEAVING DEAD MILLIONAIRES LYING AROUND.
STAY AWAY FROM ME.
CAN'T DO THAT, LADY.

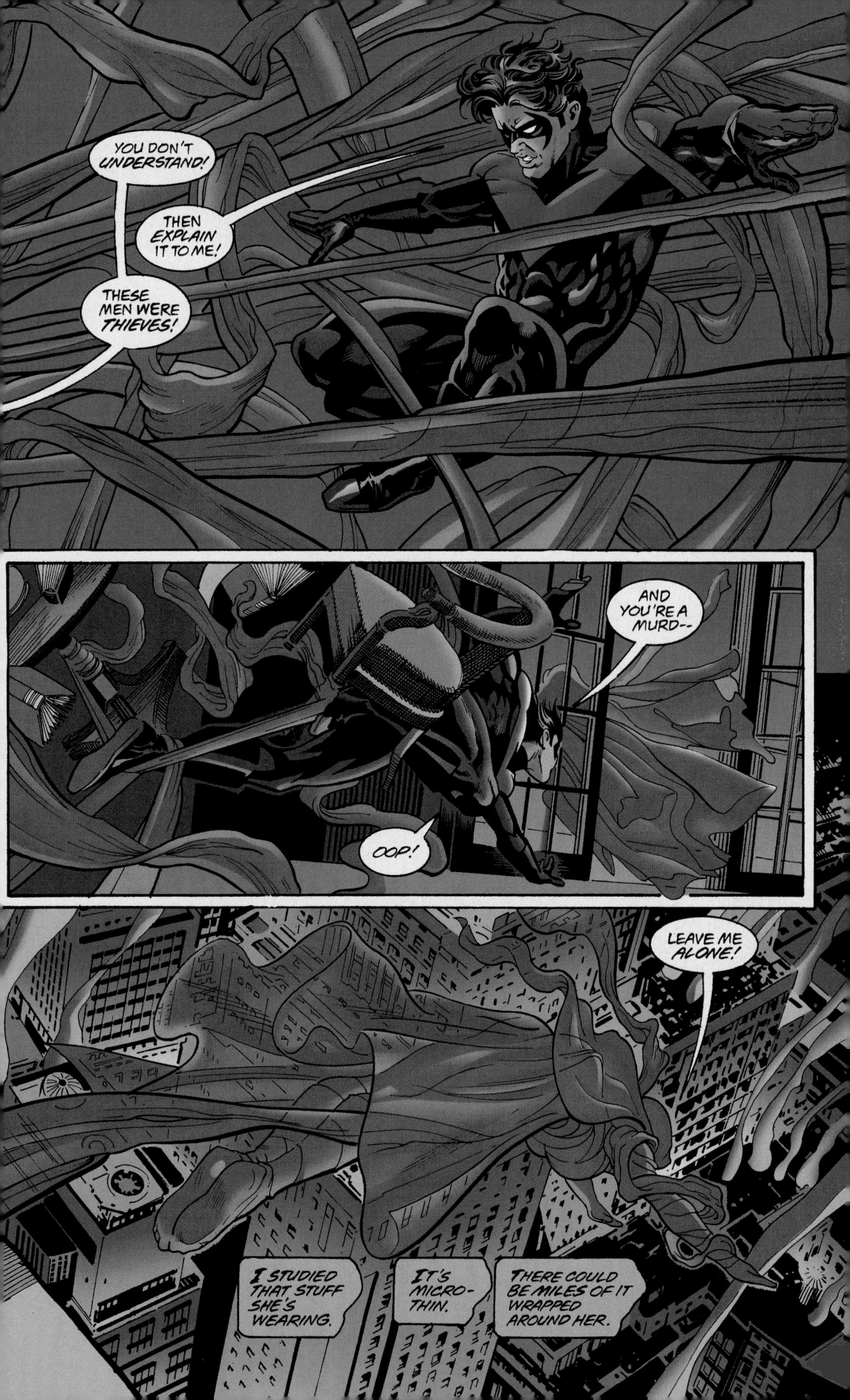
YOU DON'T UNDERSTAND!
THEN EXPLAIN IT TO ME!
THESE MEN WERE THIEVES!
AND YOU'RE A MURD--
OOP!
LEAVE ME ALONE!
I STUDIED THAT STUFF SHE'S WEARING.
IT'S MICRO-THIN.
THERE COULD BE MILES OF IT WRAPPED AROUND HER.

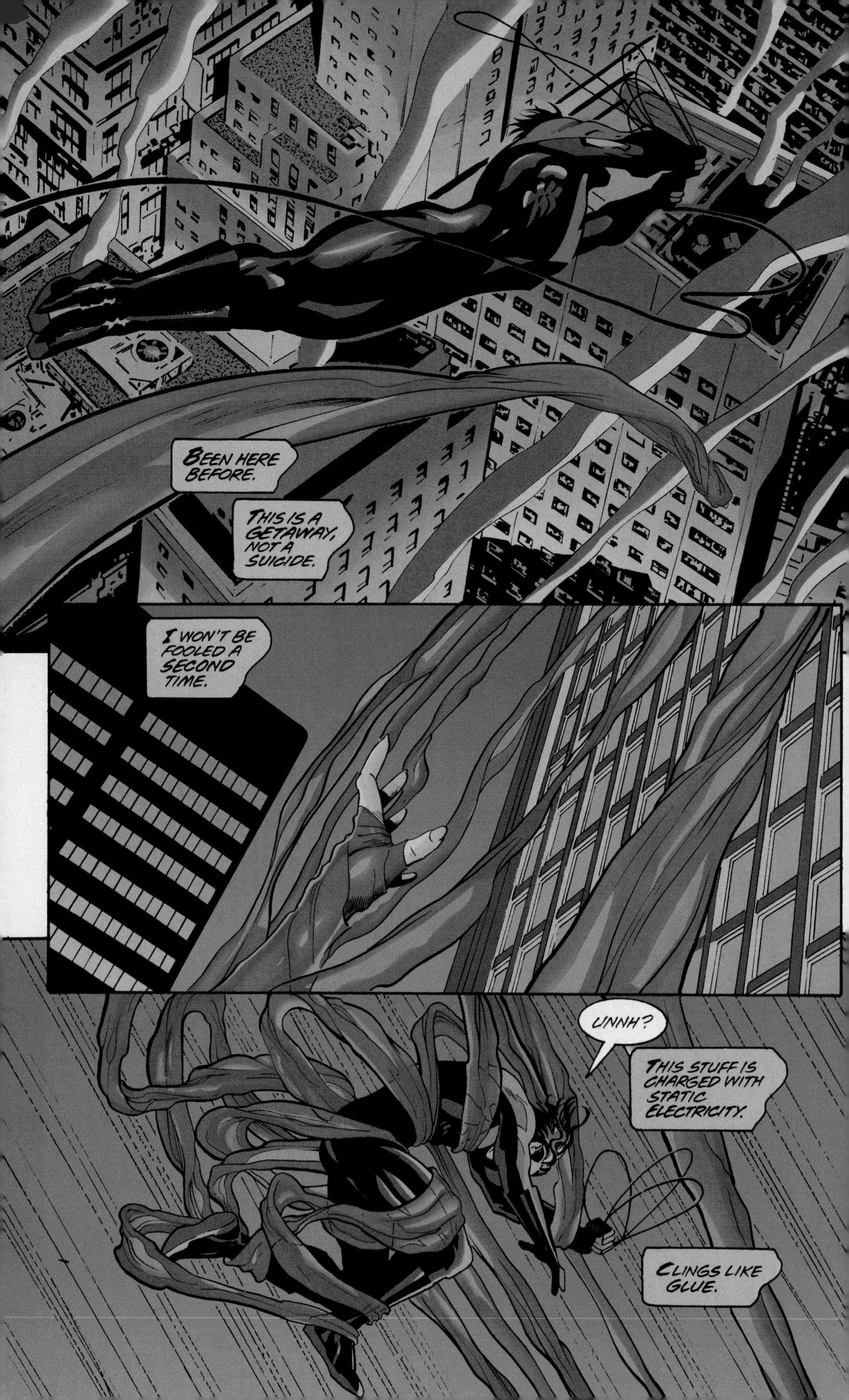
BEEN HERE BEFORE.
THIS IS A GETAWAY, NOT A SUICIDE.
I WON'T BE FOOLED A SECOND TIME.
UNNH?
THIS STUFF IS CHARGED WITH STATIC ELECTRICITY.
CLINGS LIKE GLUE.

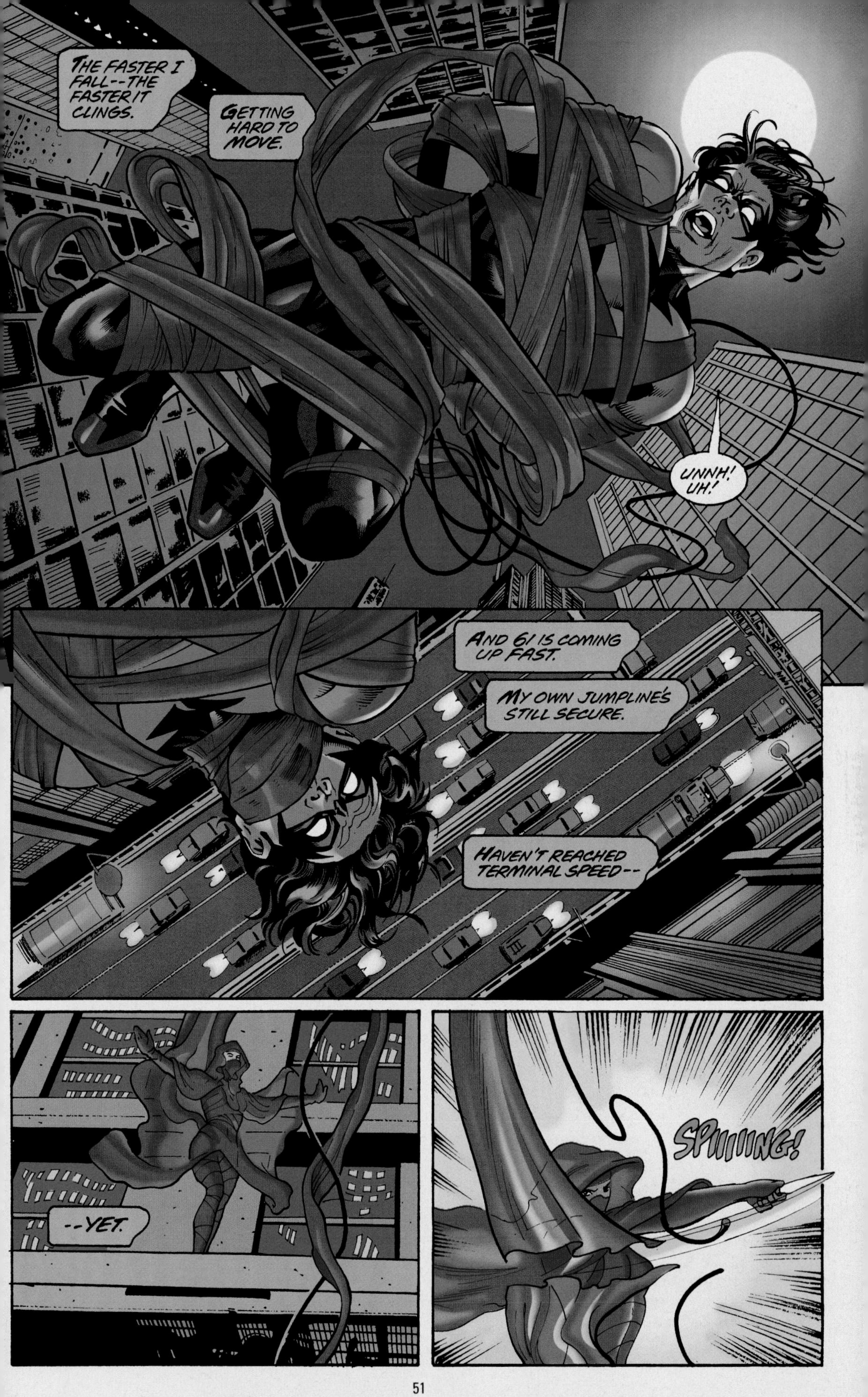
THE FASTER I FALL--THE FASTER IT CLINGS.
GETTING HARD TO MOVE.
UNNH! UH!
AND 61 IS COMING UP FAST.
MY OWN JUMPLINE'S STILL SECURE.
HAVEN'T REACHED TERMINAL SPEED--
--YET.
SPIIIIING!

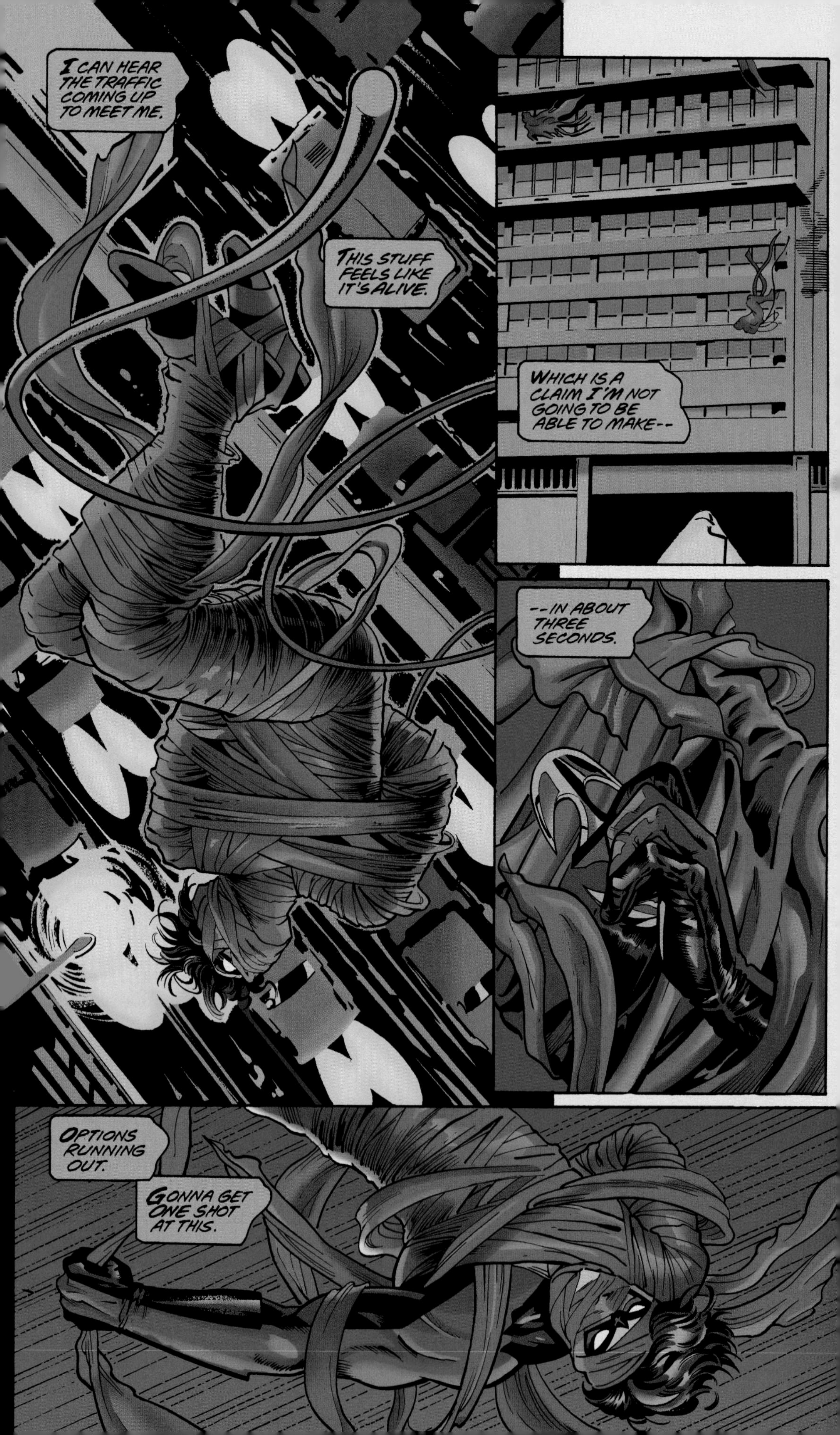
I CAN HEAR THE TRAFFIC COMING UP TO MEET ME.
THIS STUFF FEELS LIKE IT'S ALIVE.
WHICH IS A CLAIM I'M NOT GOING TO BE ABLE TO MAKE--
--IN ABOUT THREE SECONDS.
OPTIONS RUNNING OUT.
GONNA GET ONE SHOT AT THIS.

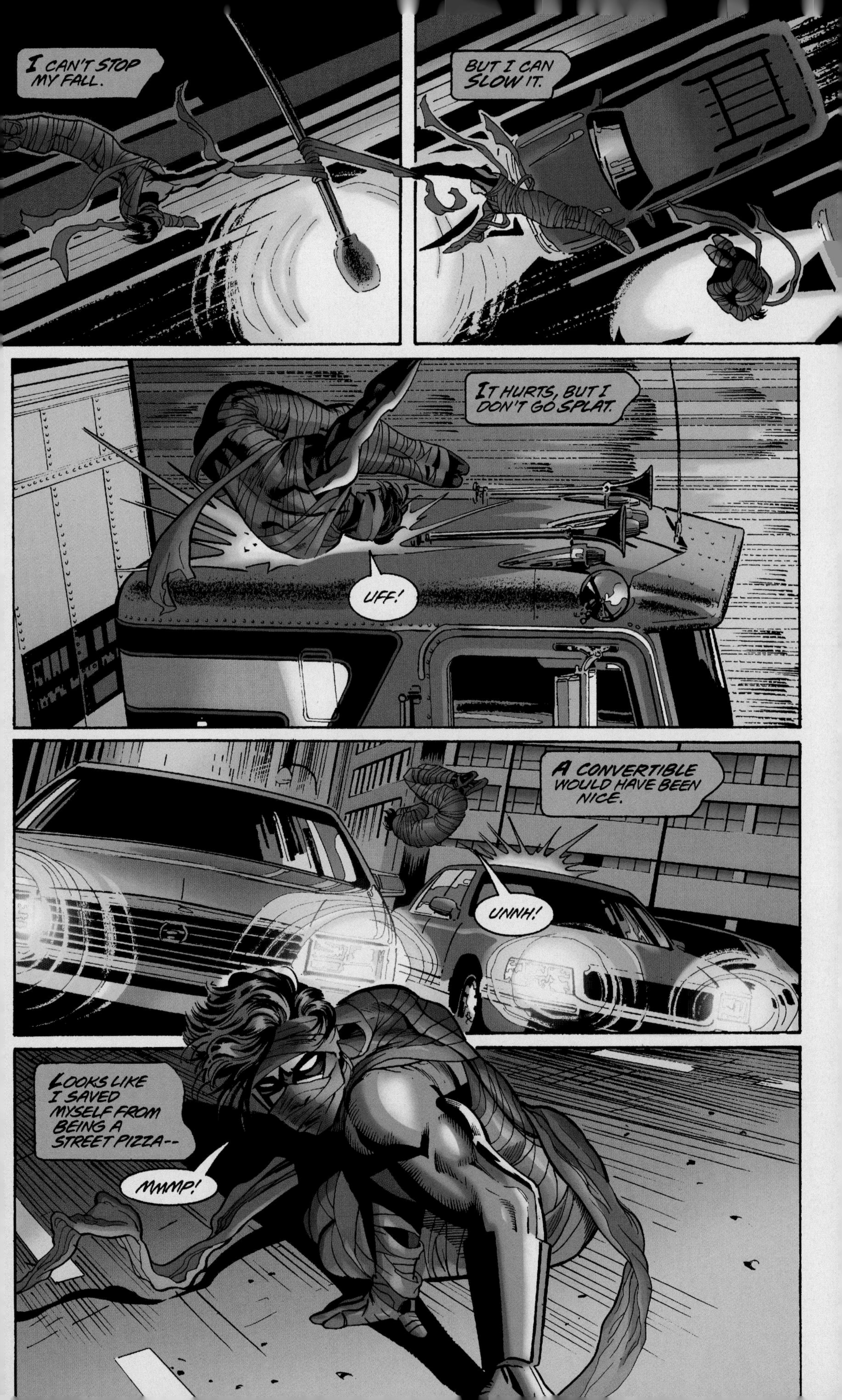

I CAN'T STOP MY FALL.
BUT I CAN SLOW IT.
IT HURTS, BUT I DON'T GO SPLAT.
UFF!
A CONVERTIBLE WOULD HAVE BEEN NICE.
UNNH!
LOOKS LIKE I SAVED MYSELF FROM BEING A STREET PIZZA--
MMMP!

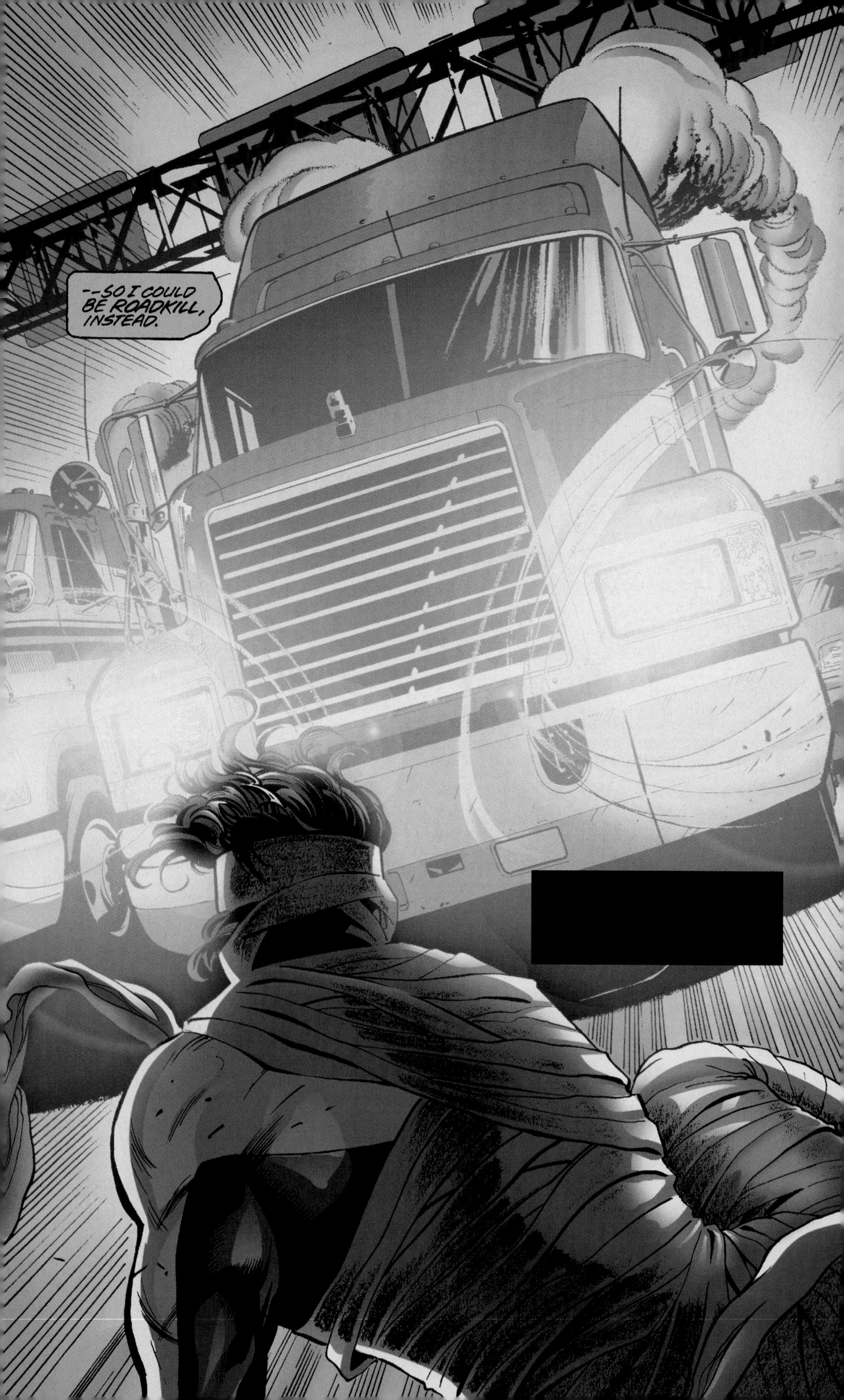
--SO I COULD BE ROADKILL, INSTEAD.
[redacted]

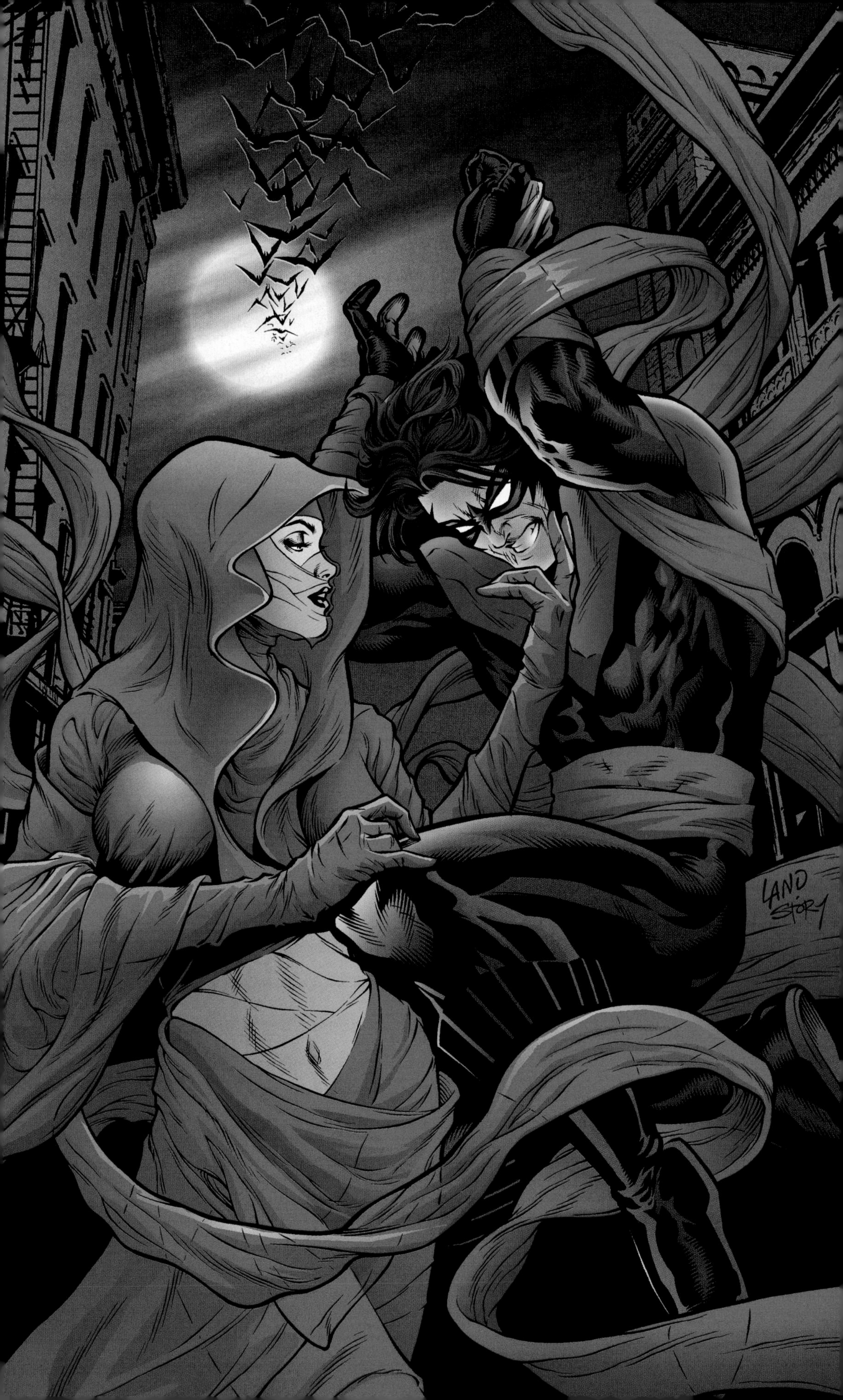
LAND
STORY

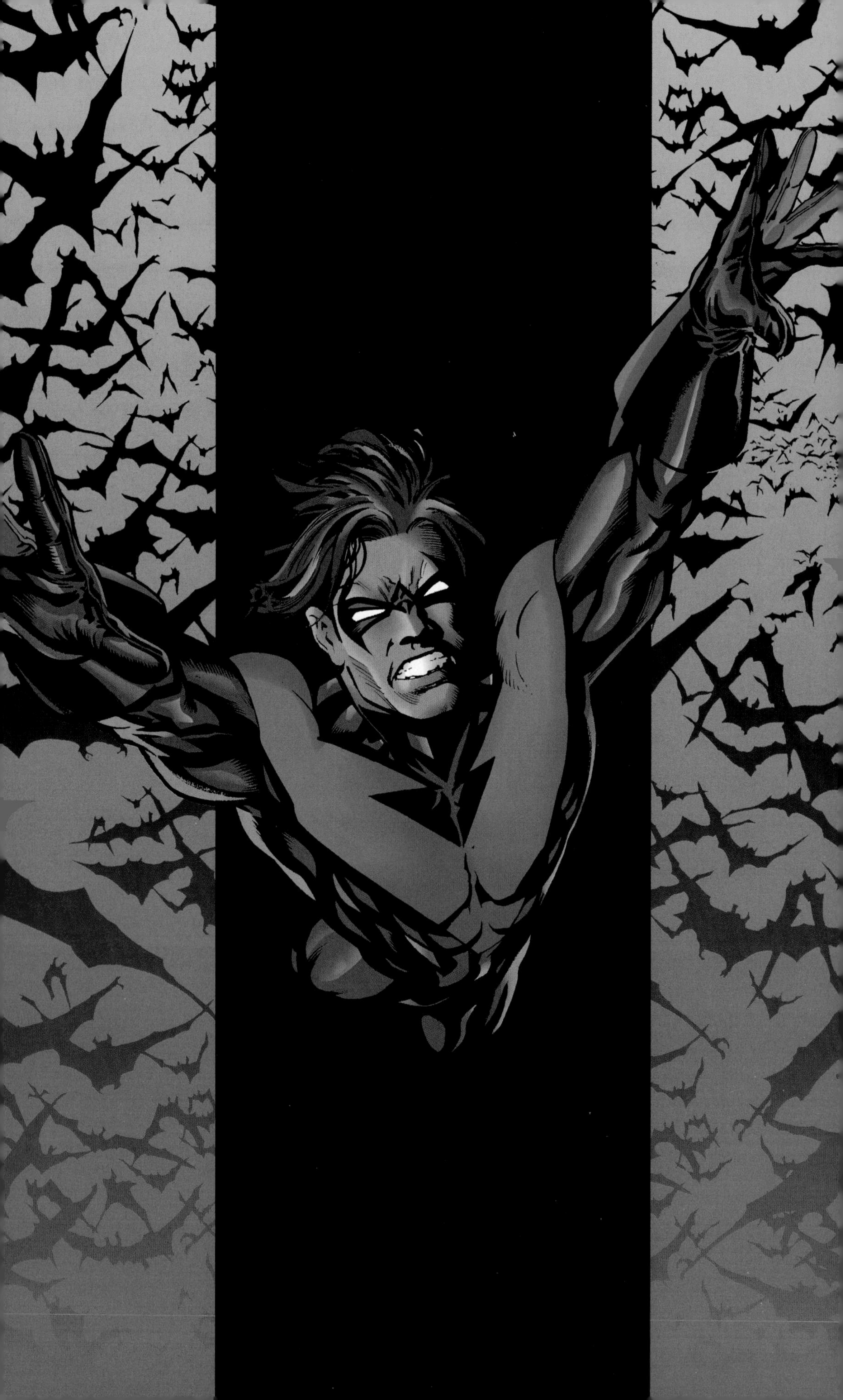

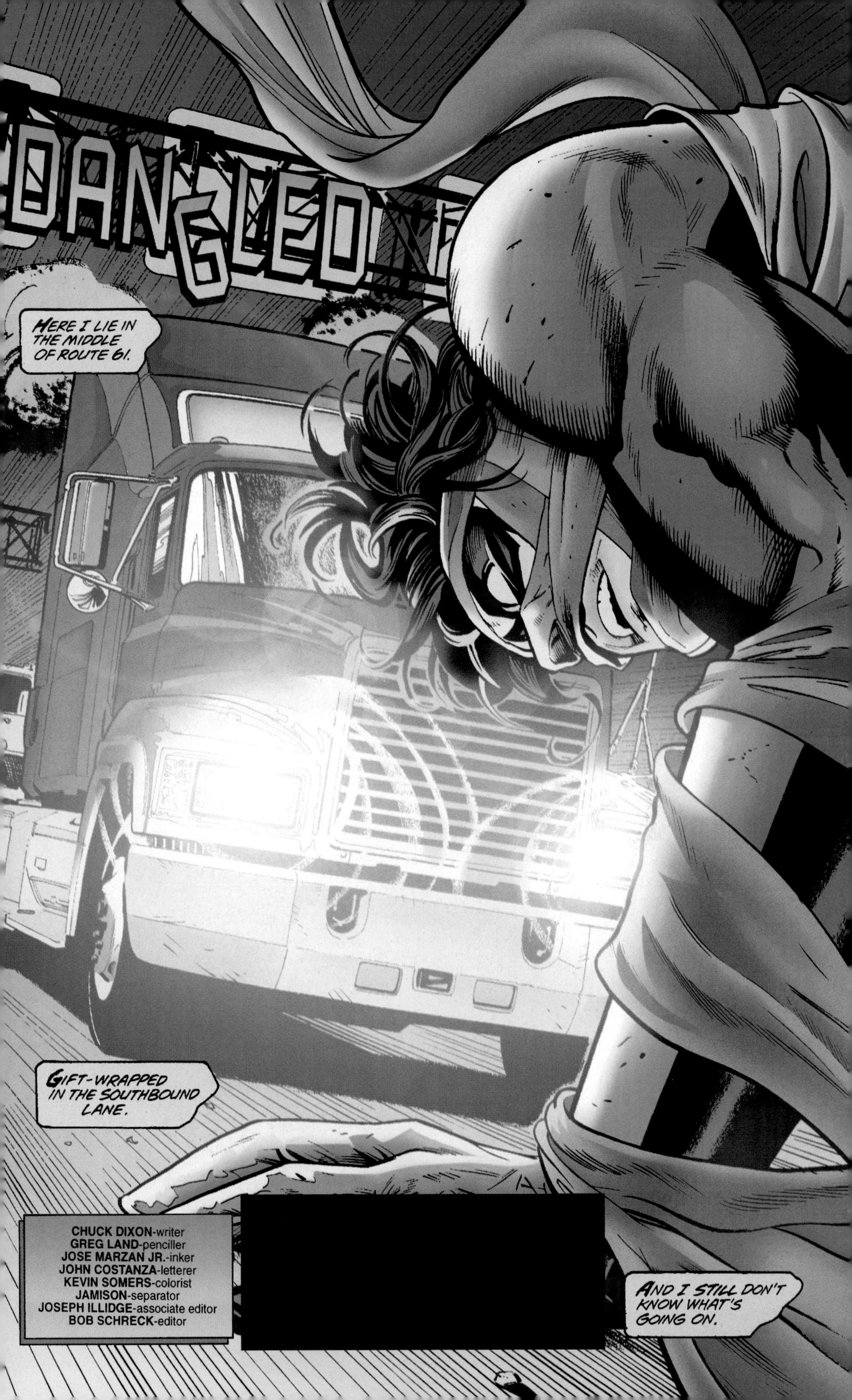
HERE I LIE IN THE MIDDLE OF ROUTE 61.
GIFT-WRAPPED IN THE SOUTHBOUND LANE.
CHUCK DIXON-writer
GREG LAND-penciller
JOSE MARZAN JR.-inker
JOHN COSTANZA-letterer
KEVIN SOMERS-colorist
JAMISON-separator
JOSEPH ILLIDGE-associate editor
BOB SCHRECK-editor
[redacted]
AND I STILL DON'T KNOW WHAT'S GOING ON.

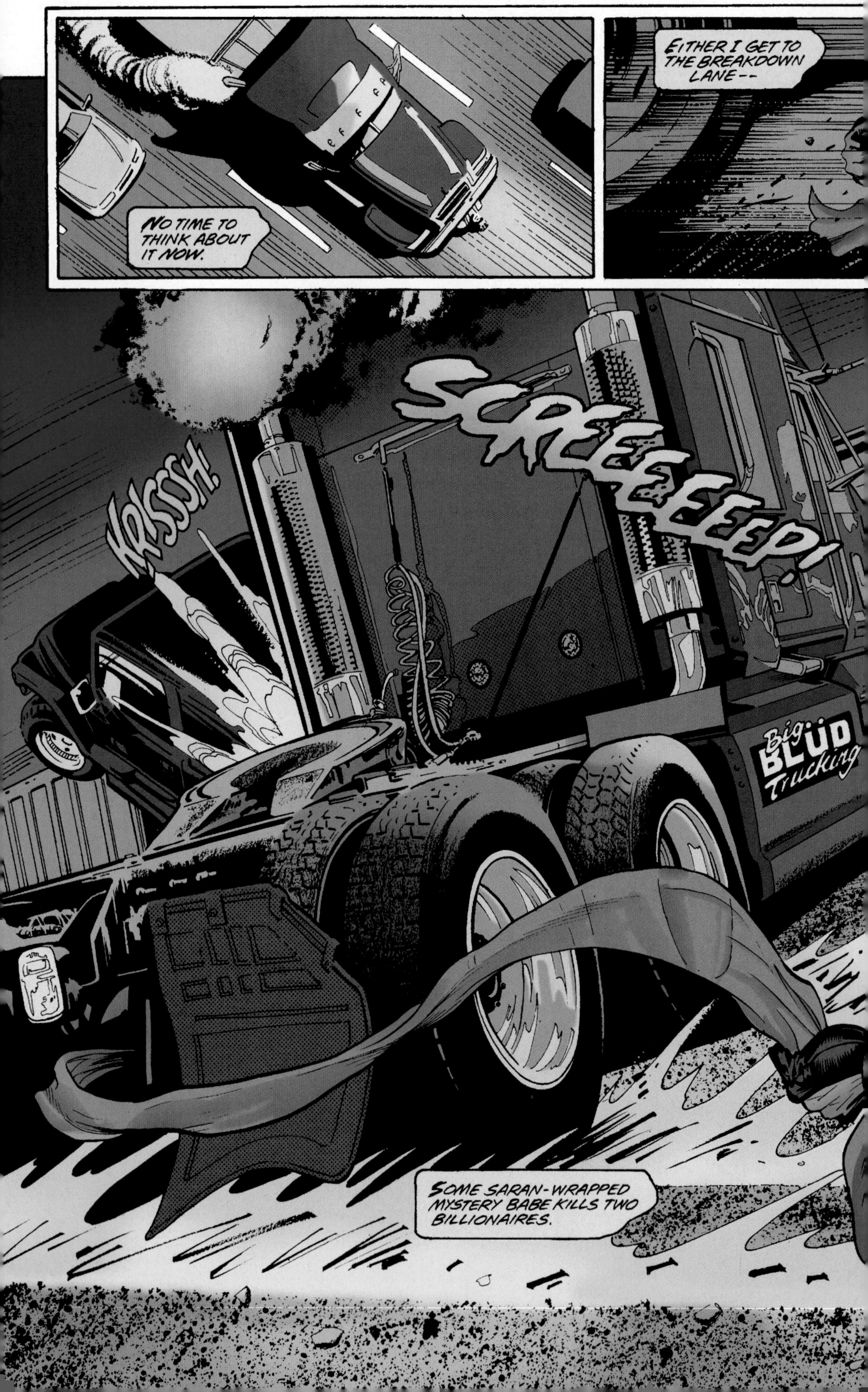
NO TIME TO THINK ABOUT IT NOW.
EITHER I GET TO THE BREAKDOWN LANE--
SCREEEEEEEP!
KRSSSH!
Big BLÜD Trucking
SOME SARAN-WRAPPED MYSTERY BABE KILLS TWO BILLIONAIRES.

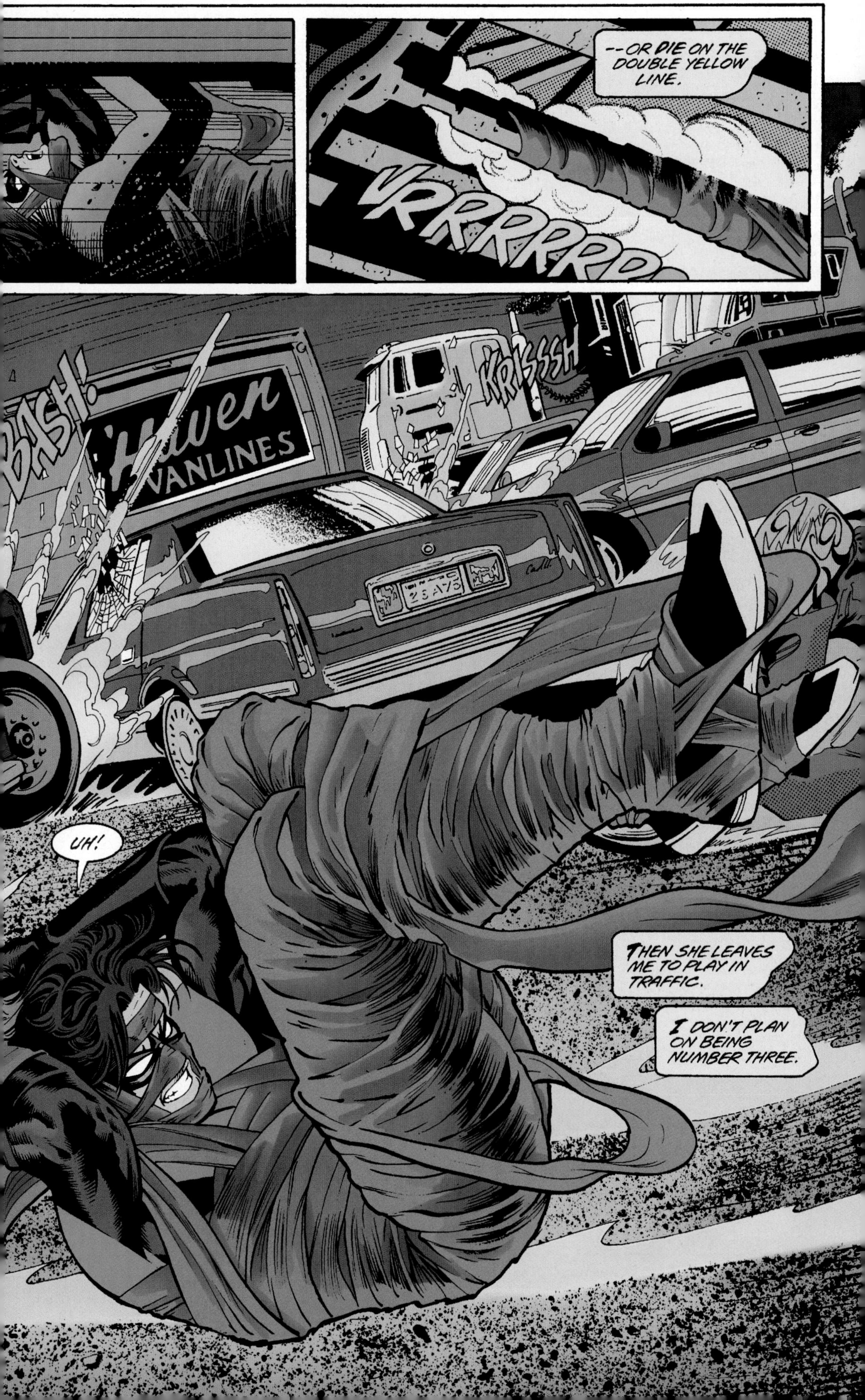
--OR DIE ON THE DOUBLE YELLOW LINE.
URRRRRRR
BASH!
HAVEN VANLINES
KRISSSH
UH!
THEN SHE LEAVES ME TO PLAY IN TRAFFIC.
I DON'T PLAN ON BEING NUMBER THREE.

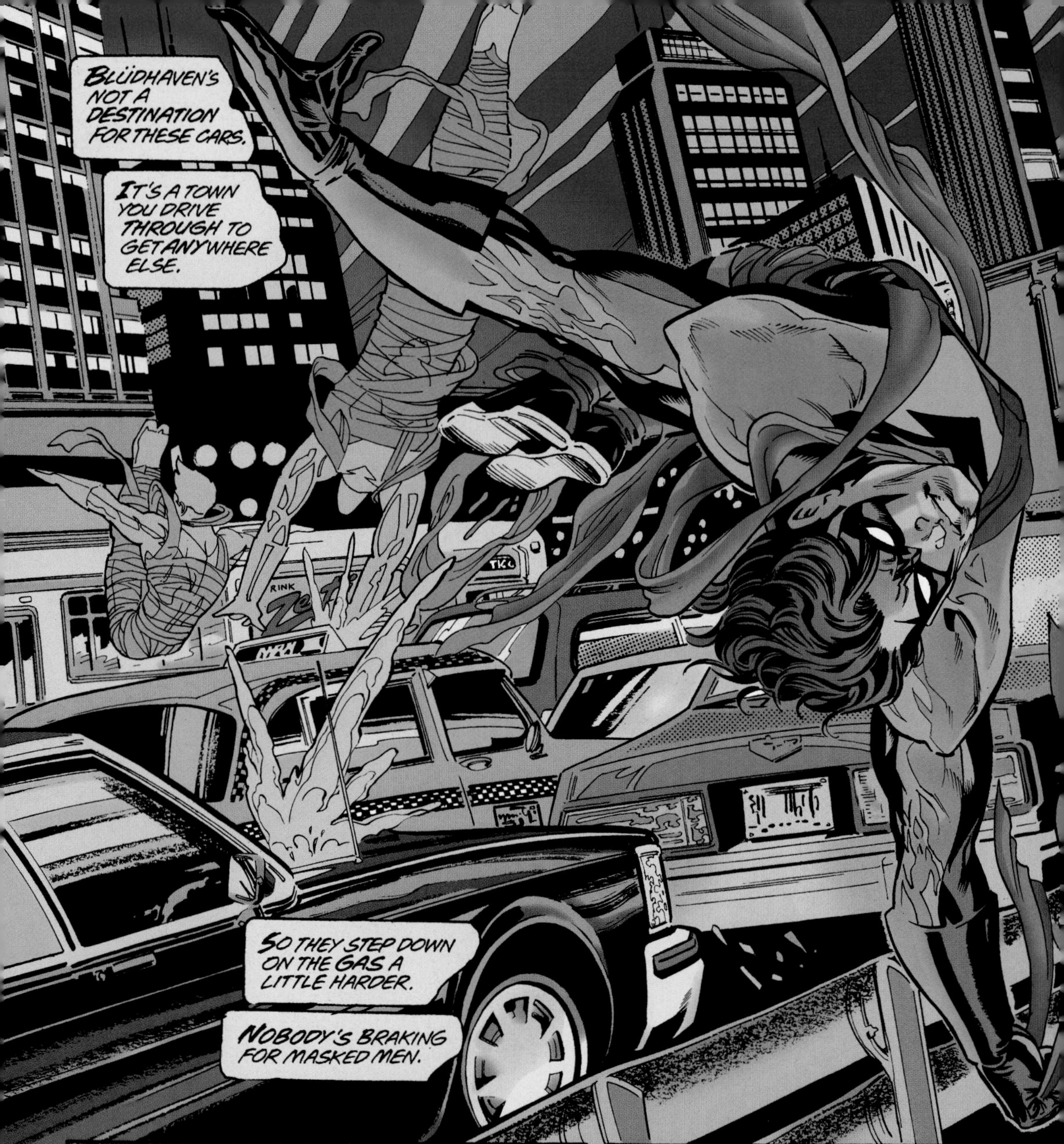
BLÜDHAVEN'S NOT A DESTINATION FOR THESE CARS.
IT'S A TOWN YOU DRIVE THROUGH TO GET ANYWHERE ELSE.
SO THEY STEP DOWN ON THE GAS A LITTLE HARDER.
NOBODY'S BRAKING FOR MASKED MEN.

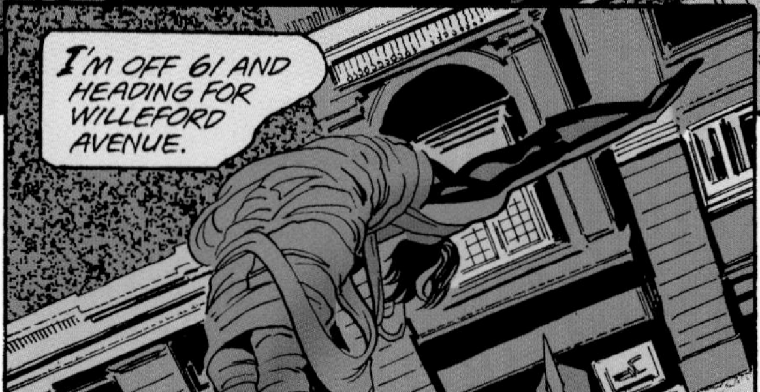
I'M OFF 61 AND HEADING FOR WILLEFORD AVENUE.
Chocolatz

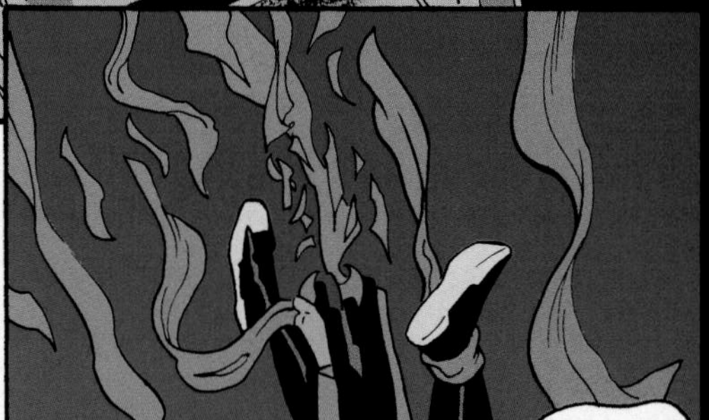
UNNH!
HAVE TO GET THIS KILLER FABRIC OFF.

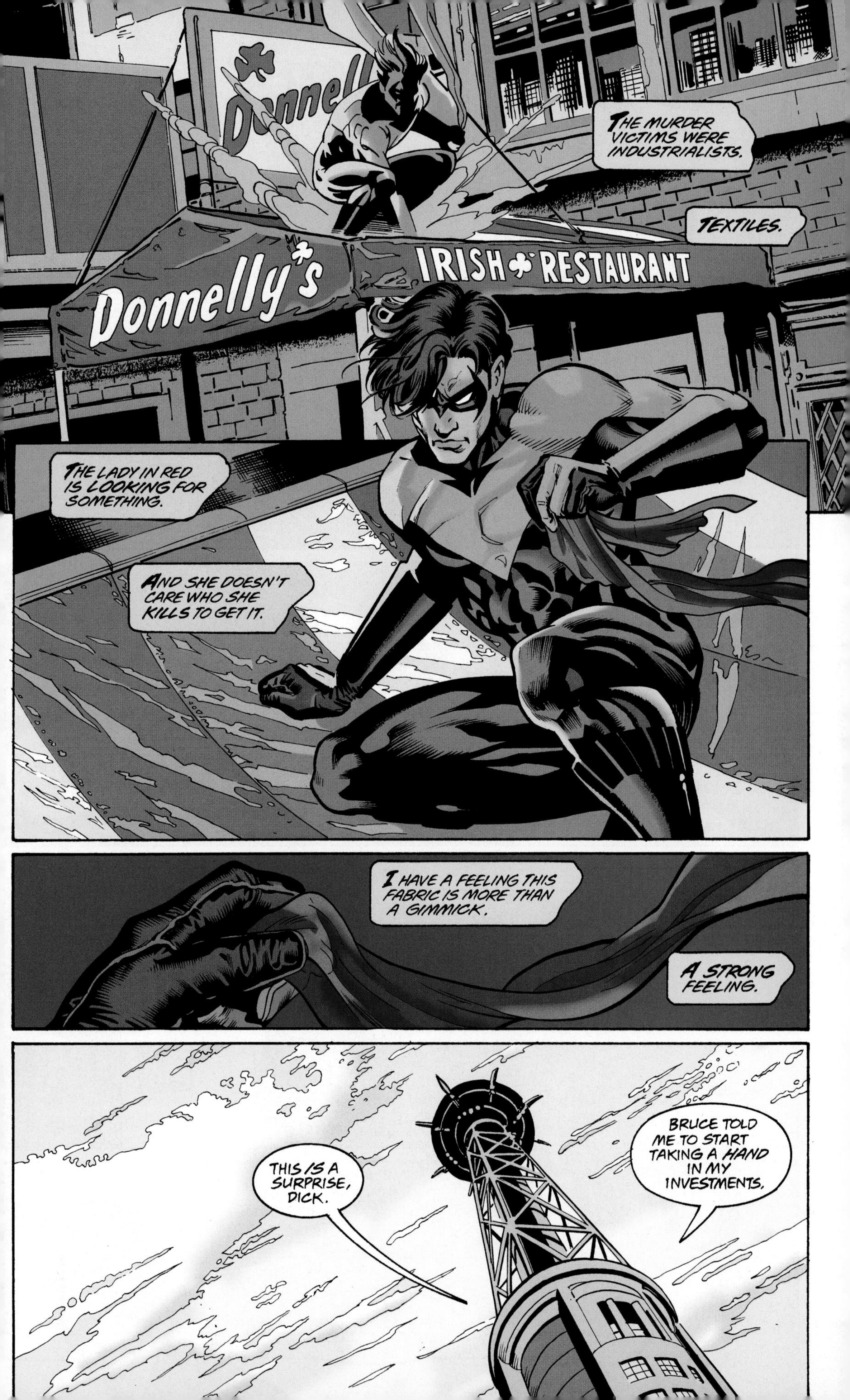
THE MURDER VICTIMS WERE INDUSTRIALISTS.
TEXTILES.
Donnelly's
Donnelly's IRISH RESTAURANT
THE LADY IN RED IS LOOKING FOR SOMETHING.
AND SHE DOESN'T CARE WHO SHE KILLS TO GET IT.
I HAVE A FEELING THIS FABRIC IS MORE THAN A GIMMICK.
A STRONG FEELING.
THIS IS A SURPRISE, DICK.
BRUCE TOLD ME TO START TAKING A HAND IN MY INVESTMENTS.

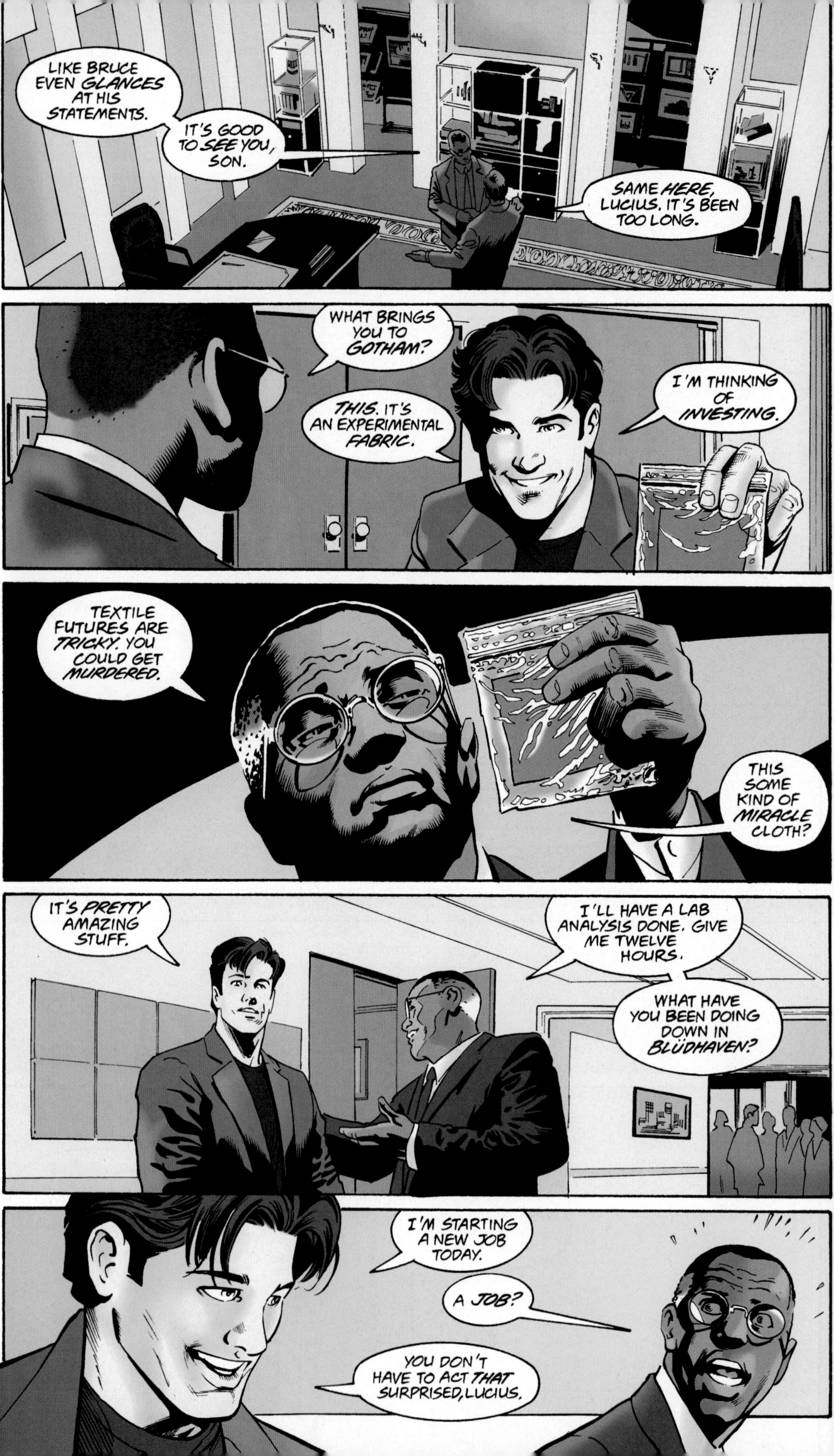
LIKE BRUCE EVEN GLANCES AT HIS STATEMENTS.
IT'S GOOD TO SEE YOU, SON.
SAME HERE, LUCIUS. IT'S BEEN TOO LONG.
WHAT BRINGS YOU TO GOTHAM?
THIS. IT'S AN EXPERIMENTAL FABRIC.
I'M THINKING OF INVESTING.
TEXTILE FUTURES ARE TRICKY. YOU COULD GET MURDERED.
THIS SOME KIND OF MIRACLE CLOTH?
IT'S PRETTY AMAZING STUFF.
I'LL HAVE A LAB ANALYSIS DONE. GIVE ME TWELVE HOURS.
WHAT HAVE YOU BEEN DOING DOWN IN BLÜDHAVEN?
I'M STARTING A NEW JOB TODAY.
A JOB?
YOU DON'T HAVE TO ACT THAT SURPRISED, LUCIUS.

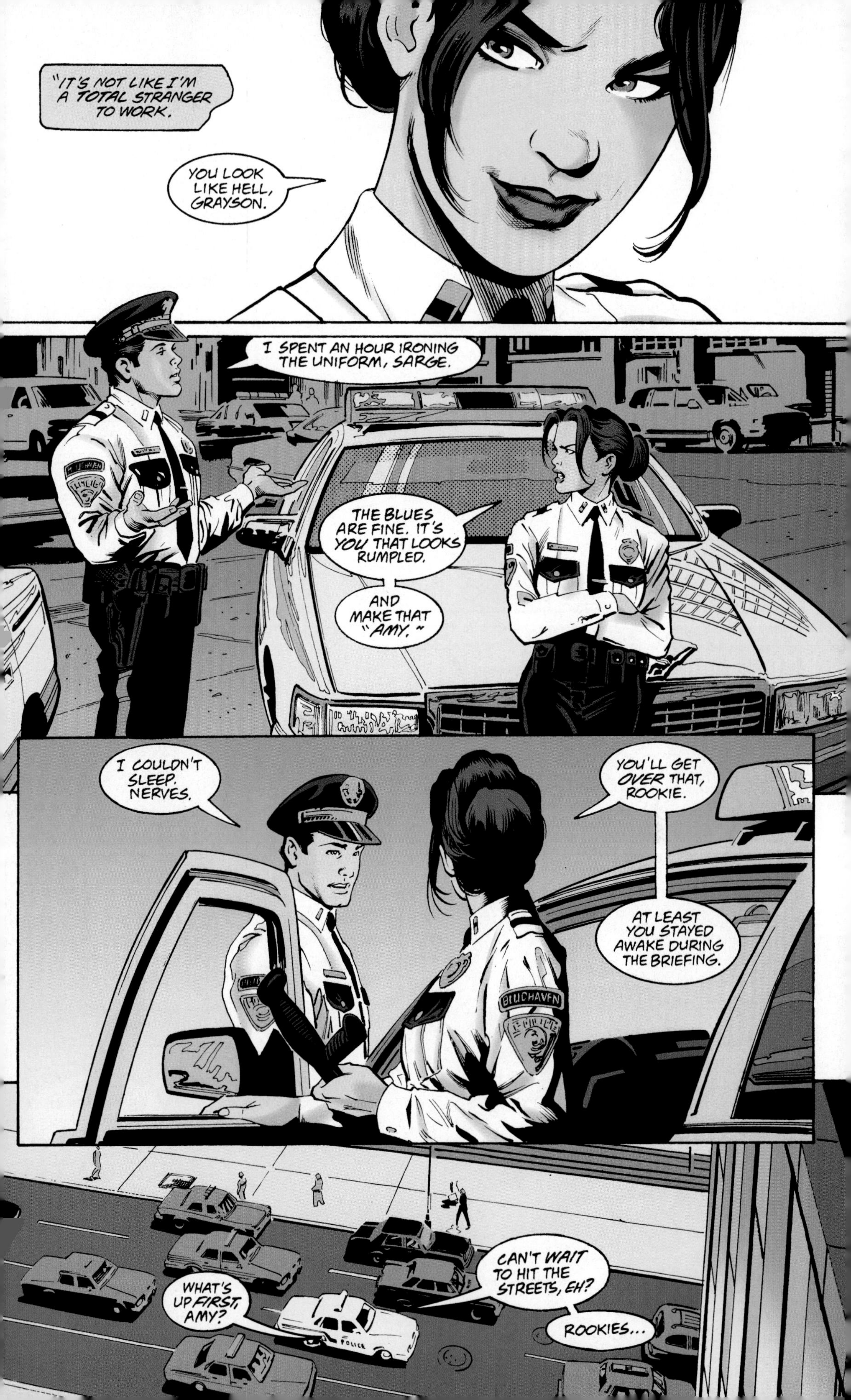
"IT'S NOT LIKE I'M A TOTAL STRANGER TO WORK.
YOU LOOK LIKE HELL, GRAYSON.
I SPENT AN HOUR IRONING THE UNIFORM, SARGE.
THE BLUES ARE FINE. IT'S YOU THAT LOOKS RUMPLED.
AND MAKE THAT "AMY."
I COULDN'T SLEEP. NERVES.
YOU'LL GET OVER THAT, ROOKIE.
AT LEAST YOU STAYED AWAKE DURING THE BRIEFING.
WHAT'S UP FIRST, AMY?
CAN'T WAIT TO HIT THE STREETS, EH?
ROOKIES...

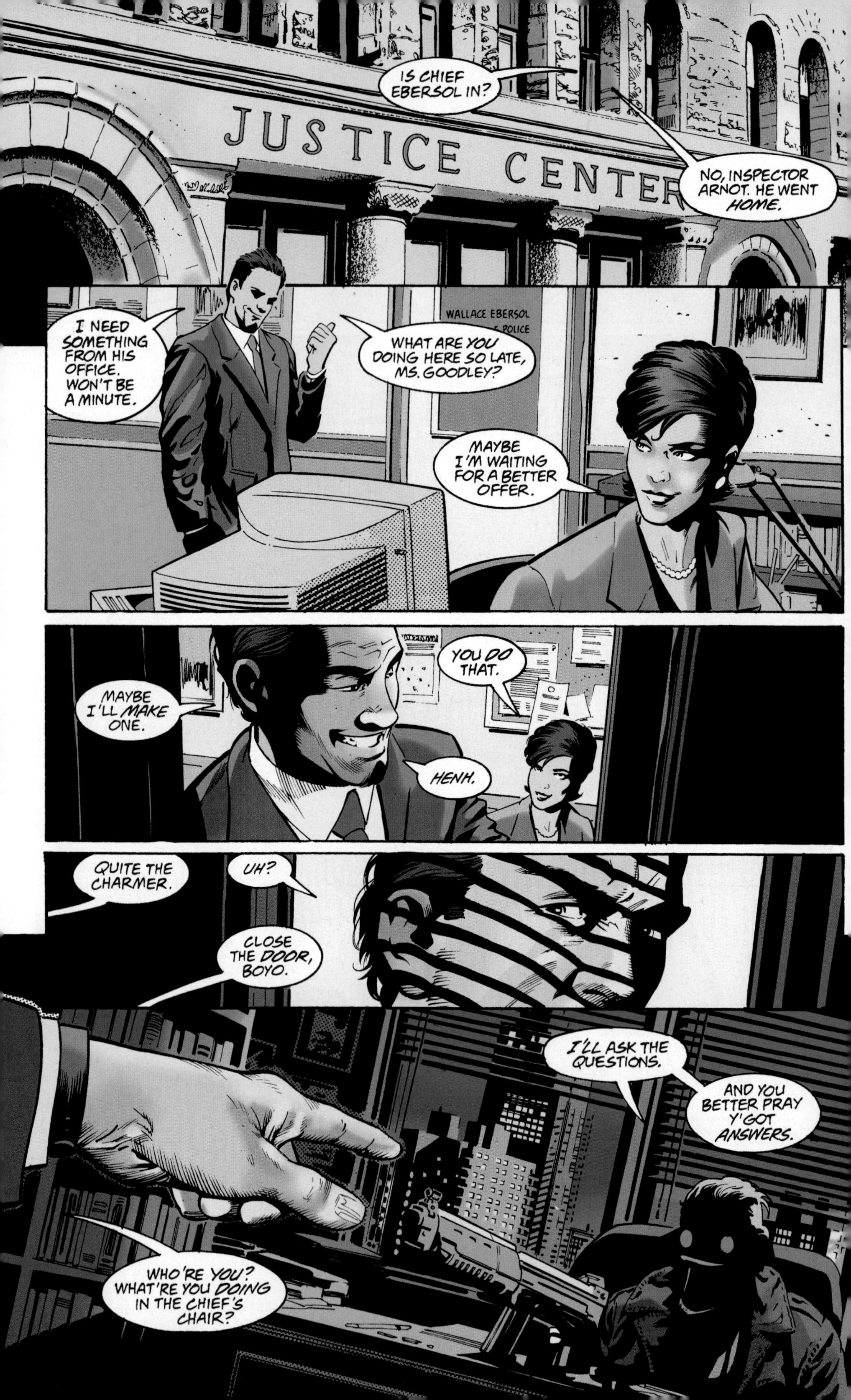
JUSTICE CENTER
IS CHIEF EBERSOL IN?
NO, INSPECTOR ARNOT. HE WENT HOME.
WALLACE EBERSOL
I NEED SOMETHING FROM HIS OFFICE. WON'T BE A MINUTE.
WHAT ARE YOU DOING HERE SO LATE, MS. GOODLEY?
MAYBE I'M WAITING FOR A BETTER OFFER.
MAYBE I'LL MAKE ONE.
YOU DO THAT.
HENH.
QUITE THE CHARMER.
UH?
CLOSE THE DOOR, BOYO.
I'LL ASK THE QUESTIONS.
AND YOU BETTER PRAY Y'GOT ANSWERS.
WHO'RE YOU? WHAT'RE YOU DOING IN THE CHIEF'S CHAIR?

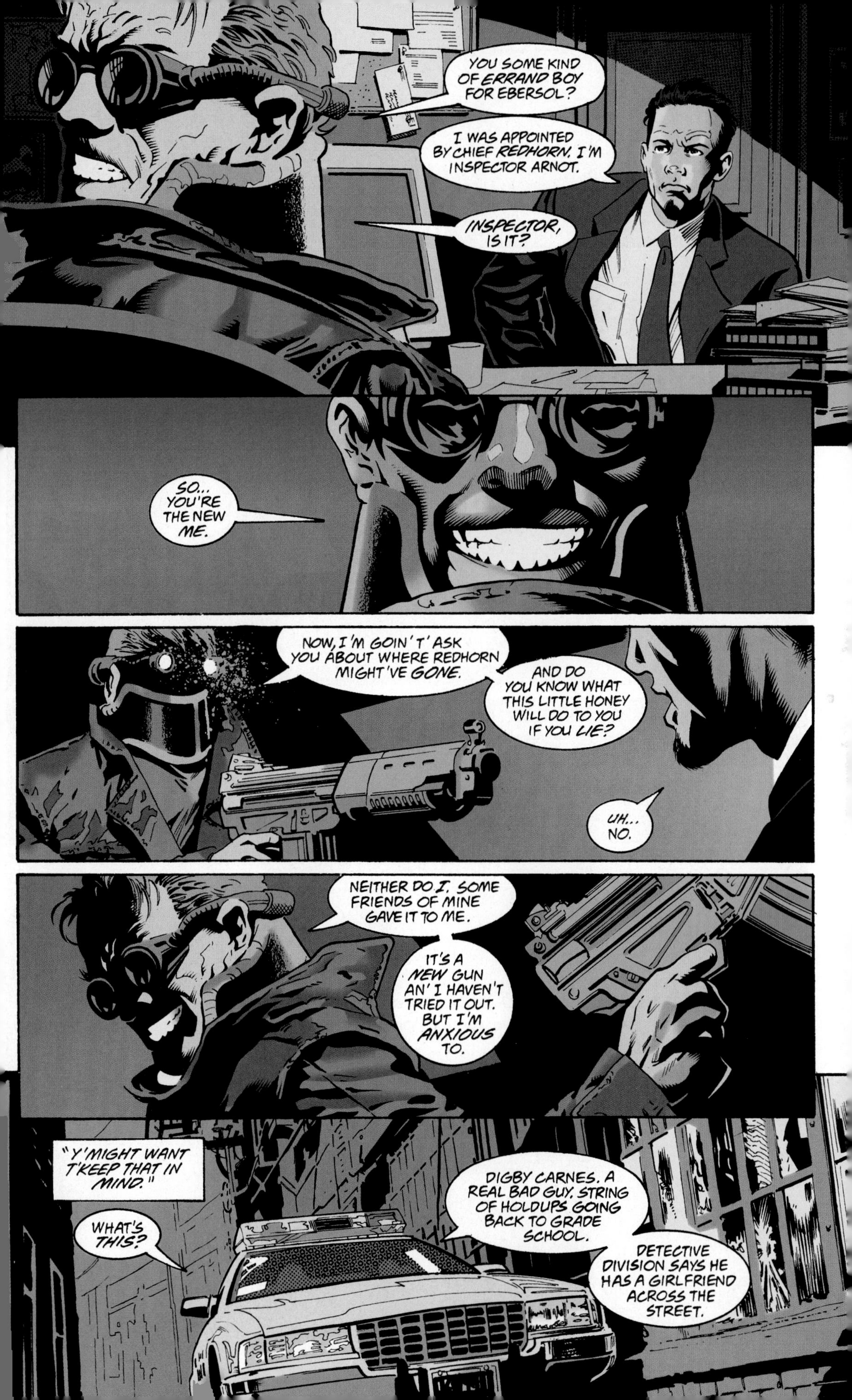
YOU SOME KIND OF ERRAND BOY FOR EBERSOL?
I WAS APPOINTED BY CHIEF REDHORN. I'M INSPECTOR ARNOT.
INSPECTOR, IS IT?
SO... YOU'RE THE NEW ME.
NOW, I'M GOIN' T' ASK YOU ABOUT WHERE REDHORN MIGHT'VE GONE.
AND DO YOU KNOW WHAT THIS LITTLE HONEY WILL DO TO YOU IF YOU LIE?
UH... NO.
NEITHER DO I. SOME FRIENDS OF MINE GAVE IT TO ME.
IT'S A NEW GUN AN' I HAVEN'T TRIED IT OUT. BUT I'M ANXIOUS TO.
"Y'MIGHT WANT T'KEEP THAT IN MIND."
WHAT'S THIS?
DIGBY CARNES. A REAL BAD GUY. STRING OF HOLDUPS GOING BACK TO GRADE SCHOOL.
DETECTIVE DIVISION SAYS HE HAS A GIRLFRIEND ACROSS THE STREET.

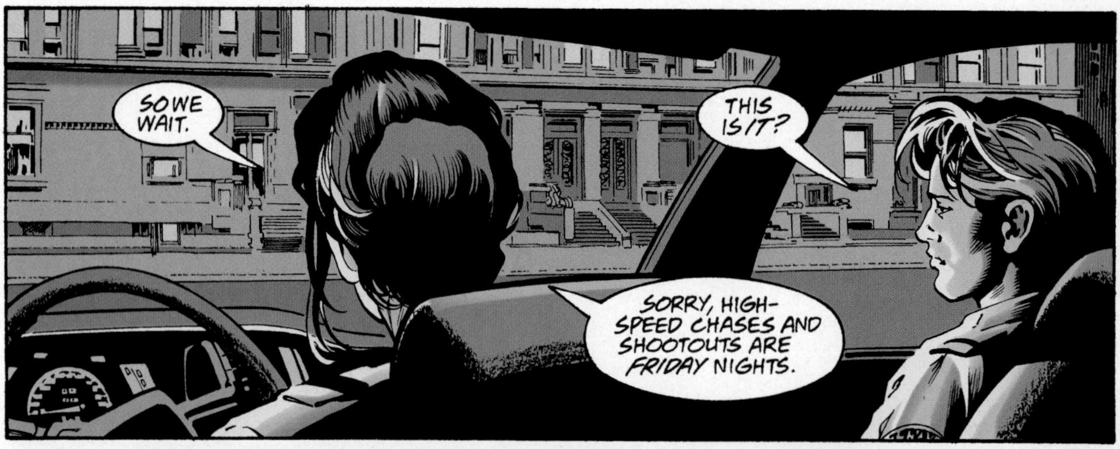
SO WE WAIT.
THIS IS IT?
SORRY, HIGH-SPEED CHASES AND SHOOTOUTS ARE FRIDAY NIGHTS.

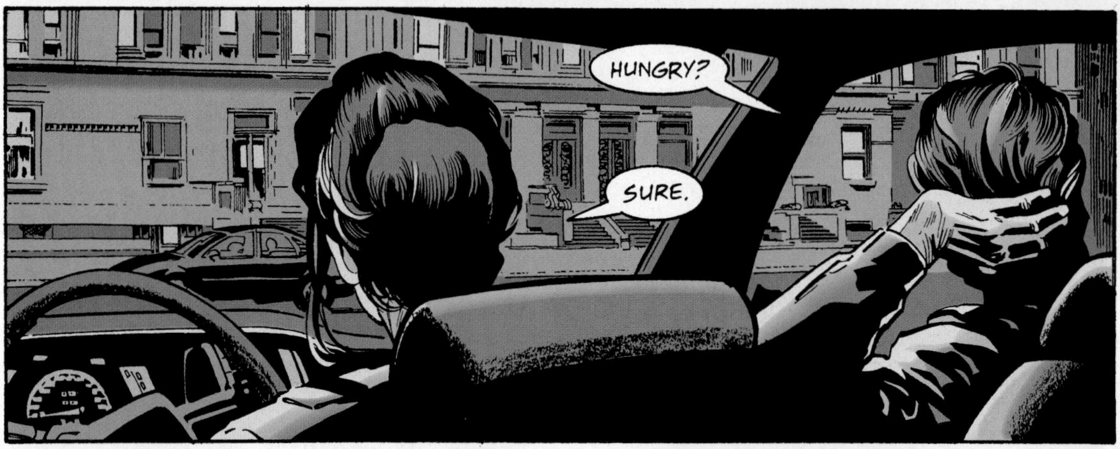
HUNGRY?
SURE.

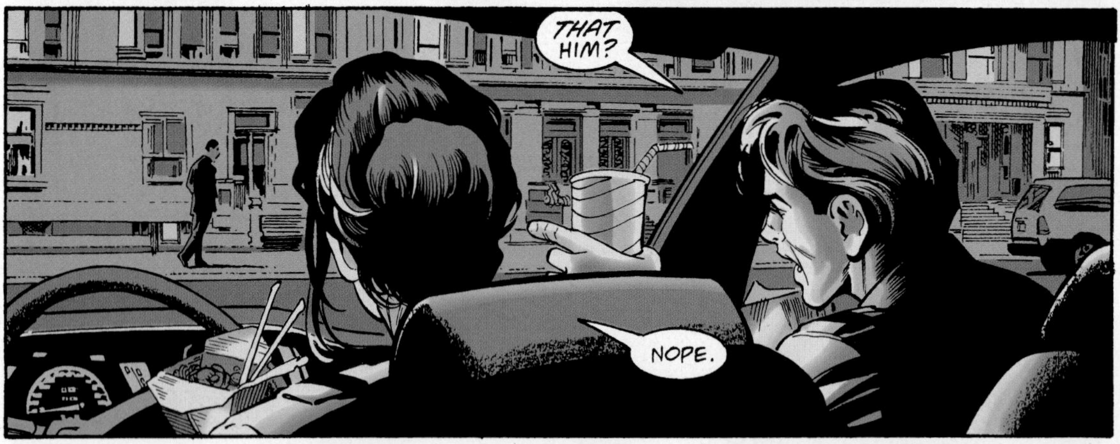
THAT HIM?
NOPE.

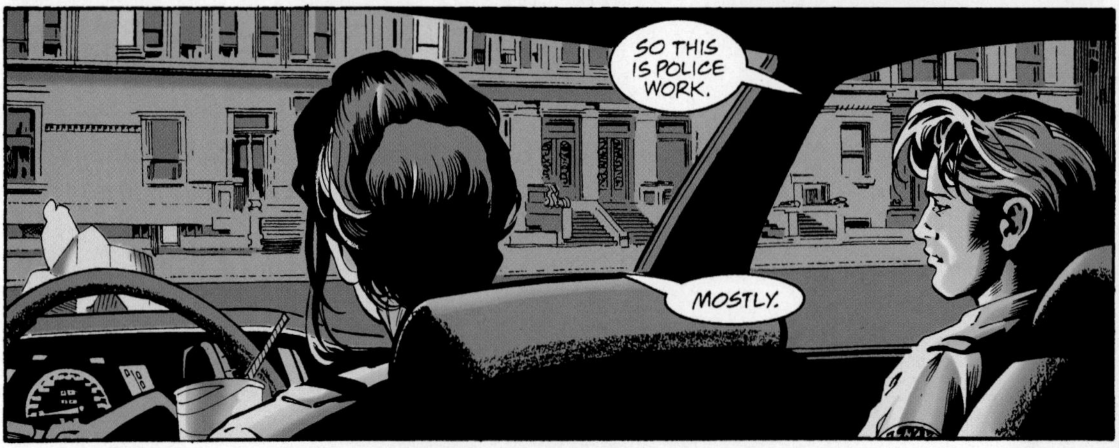
SO THIS IS POLICE WORK.
MOSTLY.

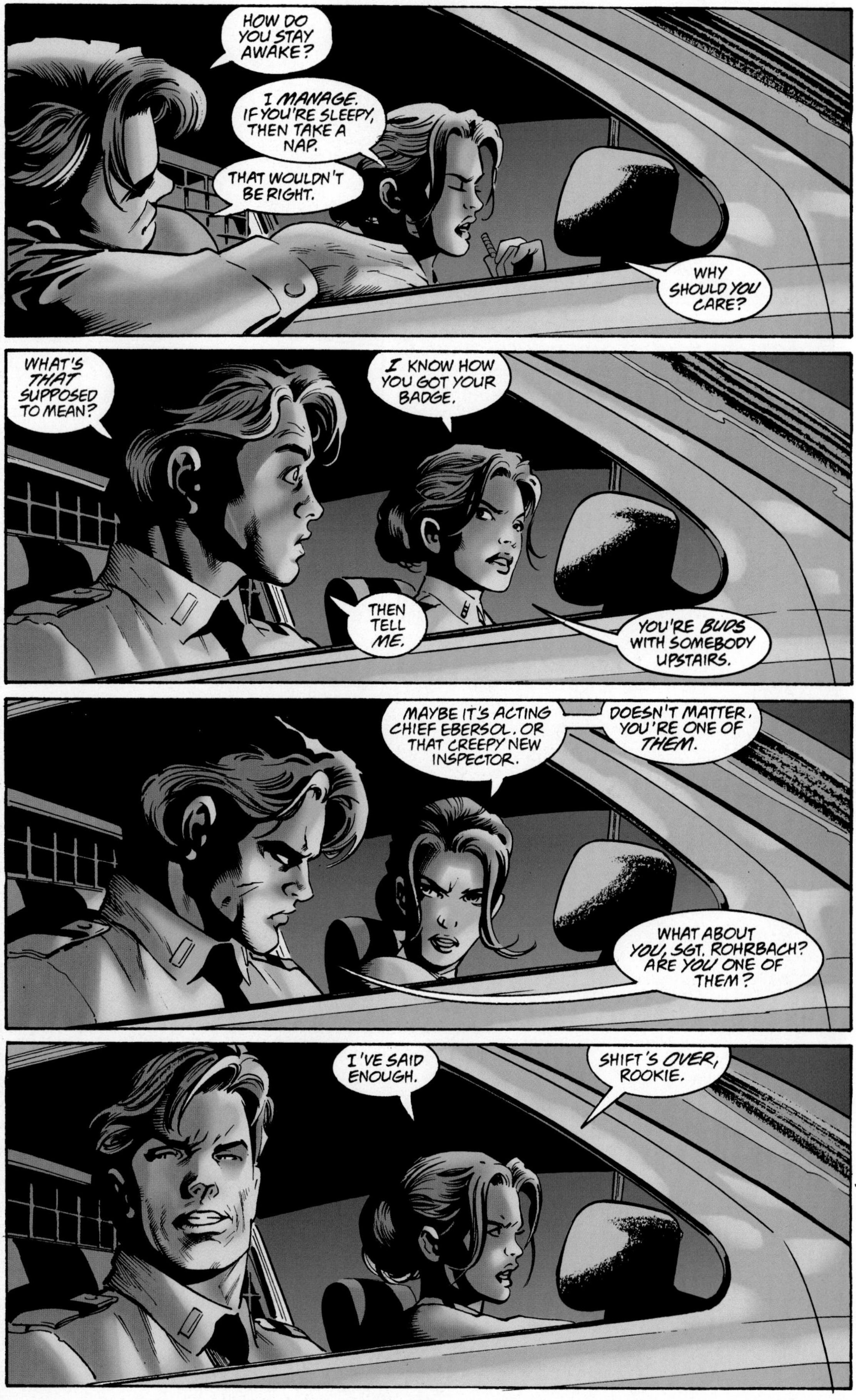
HOW DO YOU STAY AWAKE?
I MANAGE. IF YOU'RE SLEEPY, THEN TAKE A NAP.
THAT WOULDN'T BE RIGHT.
WHY SHOULD YOU CARE?
WHAT'S THAT SUPPOSED TO MEAN?
I KNOW HOW YOU GOT YOUR BADGE.
THEN TELL ME.
YOU'RE BUDS WITH SOMEBODY UPSTAIRS.
MAYBE IT'S ACTING CHIEF EBERSOL. OR THAT CREEPY NEW INSPECTOR.
DOESN'T MATTER. YOU'RE ONE OF THEM.
WHAT ABOUT YOU, SGT. ROHRBACH? ARE YOU ONE OF THEM?
I'VE SAID ENOUGH.
SHIFT'S OVER, ROOKIE.

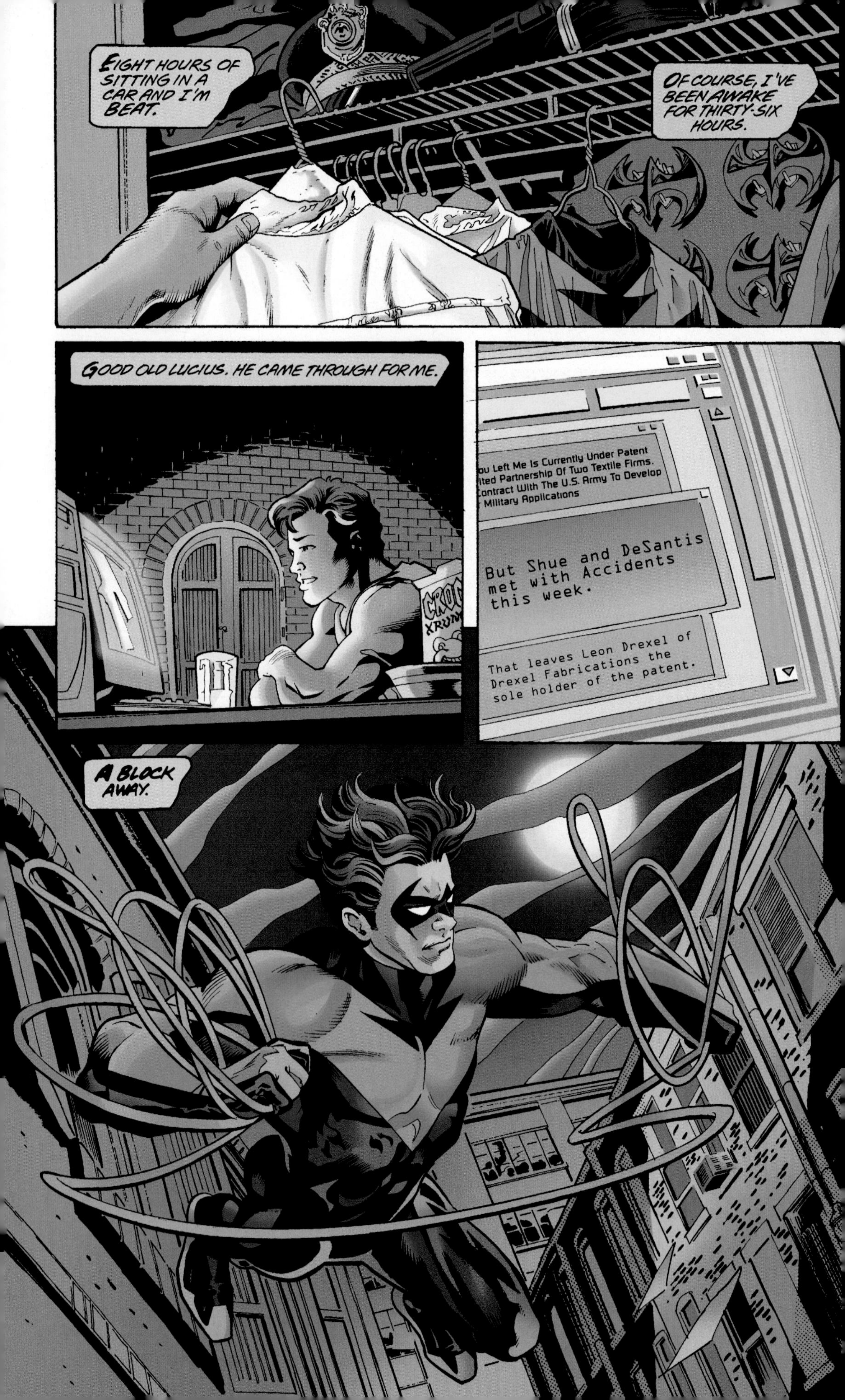
EIGHT HOURS OF SITTING IN A CAR AND I'M BEAT.
OF COURSE, I'VE BEEN AWAKE FOR THIRTY-SIX HOURS.
GOOD OLD LUCIUS. HE CAME THROUGH FOR ME.
ou Left Me Is Currently Under Patent
ited Partnership Of Two Textile Firms.
Contract With The U.S. Army To Develop
Military Applications
But Shue and DeSantis met with Accidents this week.
That leaves Leon Drexel of Drexel Fabrications the sole holder of the patent.
A BLOCK AWAY.

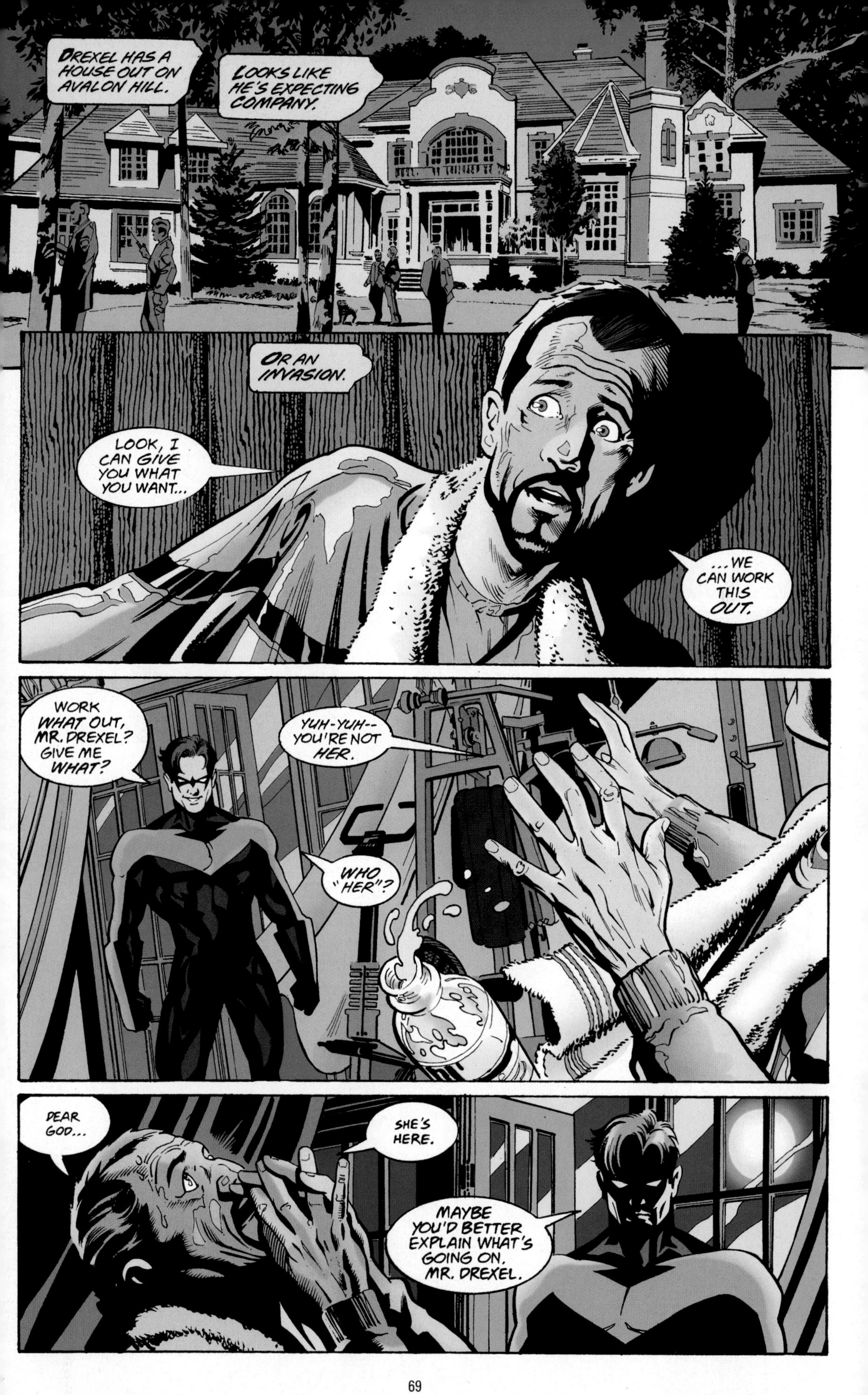
DREXEL HAS A HOUSE OUT ON AVALON HILL.
LOOKS LIKE HE'S EXPECTING COMPANY.
OR AN INVASION.
LOOK, I CAN GIVE YOU WHAT YOU WANT...
...WE CAN WORK THIS OUT.
WORK WHAT OUT, MR. DREXEL? GIVE ME WHAT?
YUH-YUH-- YOU'RE NOT HER.
WHO "HER"?
DEAR GOD...
SHE'S HERE.
MAYBE YOU'D BETTER EXPLAIN WHAT'S GOING ON, MR. DREXEL.

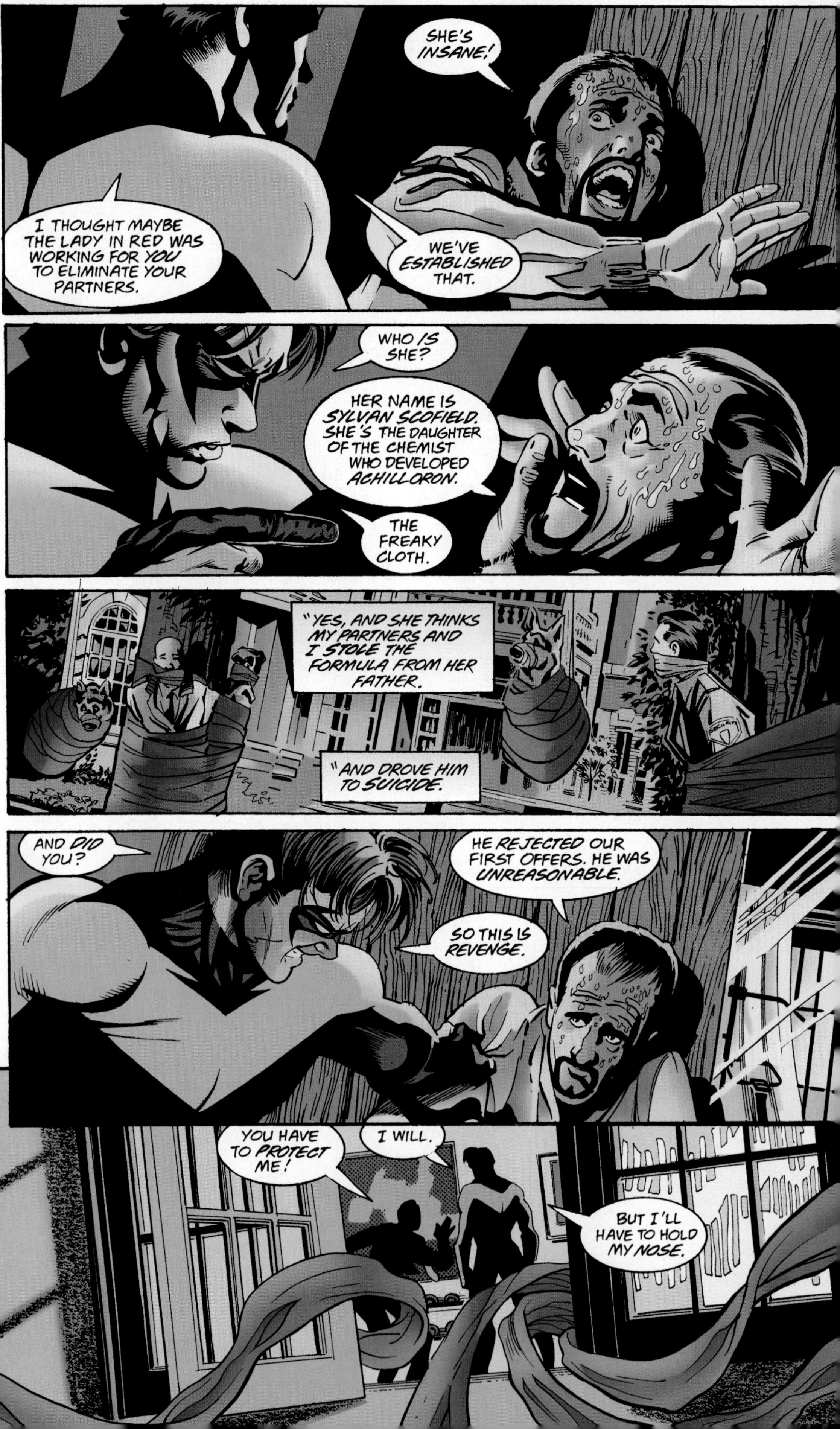
SHE'S INSANE!
I THOUGHT MAYBE THE LADY IN RED WAS WORKING FOR YOU TO ELIMINATE YOUR PARTNERS.
WE'VE ESTABLISHED THAT.
WHO IS SHE?
HER NAME IS SYLVAN SCOFIELD. SHE'S THE DAUGHTER OF THE CHEMIST WHO DEVELOPED ACHILLORON.
THE FREAKY CLOTH.
"YES, AND SHE THINKS MY PARTNERS AND I STOLE THE FORMULA FROM HER FATHER.
"AND DROVE HIM TO SUICIDE.
AND DID YOU?
HE REJECTED OUR FIRST OFFERS. HE WAS UNREASONABLE.
SO THIS IS REVENGE.
YOU HAVE TO PROTECT ME!
I WILL.
BUT I'LL HAVE TO HOLD MY NOSE.

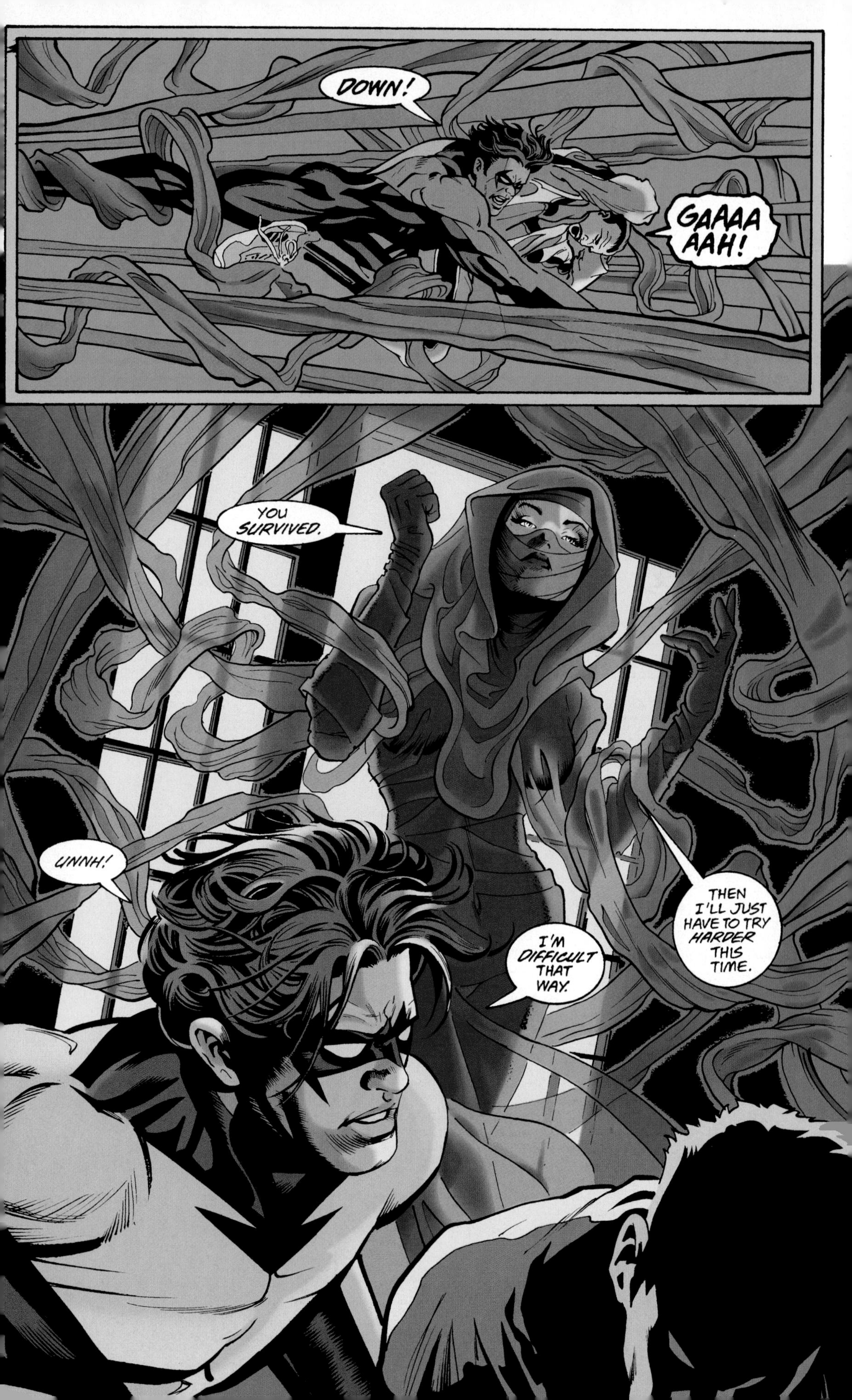
DOWN!
GAAAA AAH!
YOU SURVIVED.
UNNH!
I'M DIFFICULT THAT WAY.
THEN I'LL JUST HAVE TO TRY HARDER THIS TIME.

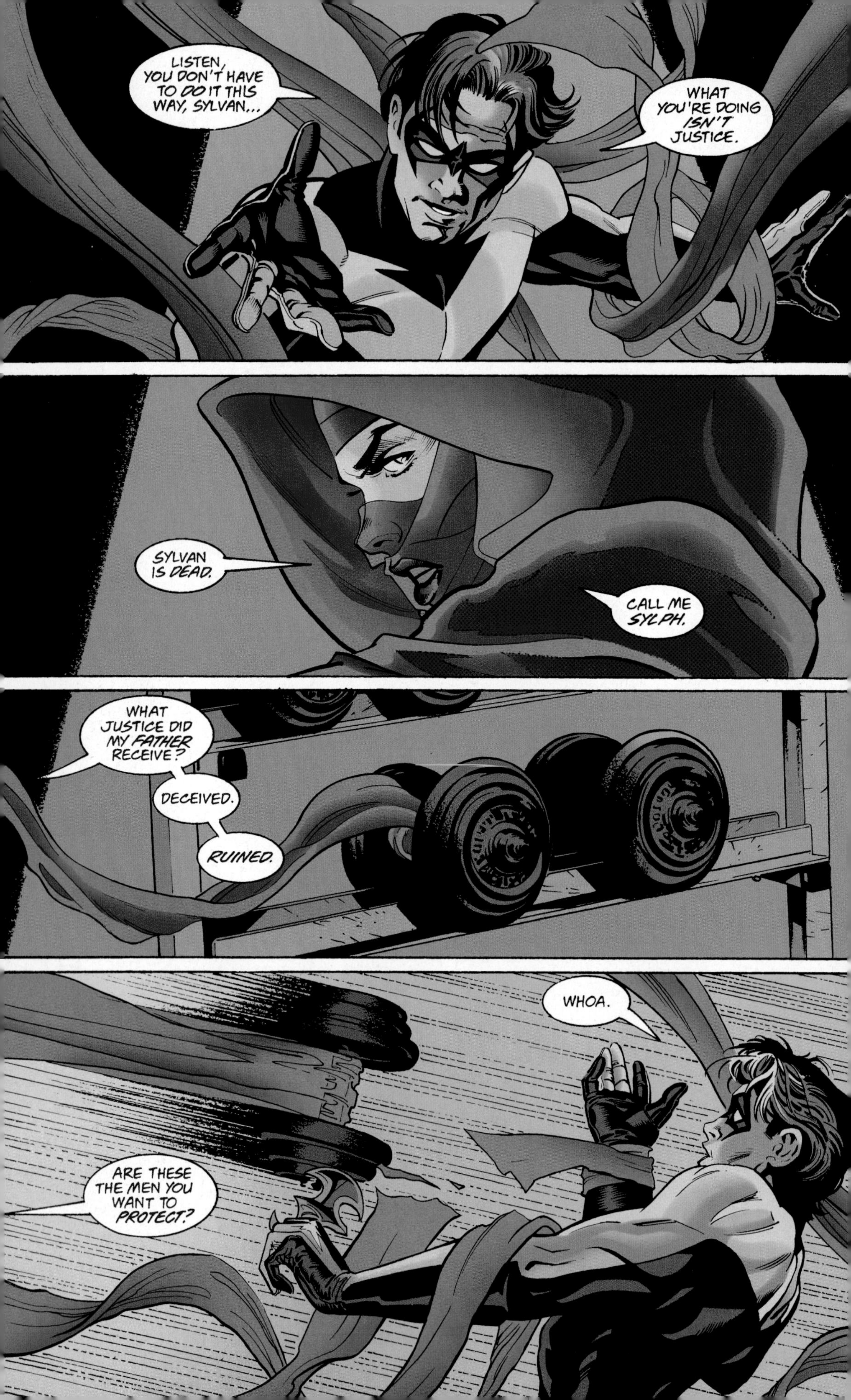
LISTEN, YOU DON'T HAVE TO DO IT THIS WAY, SYLVAN...
WHAT YOU'RE DOING ISN'T JUSTICE.
SYLVAN IS DEAD.
CALL ME SYLPH.
WHAT JUSTICE DID MY FATHER RECEIVE?
DECEIVED.
RUINED.
WHOA.
ARE THESE THE MEN YOU WANT TO PROTECT?

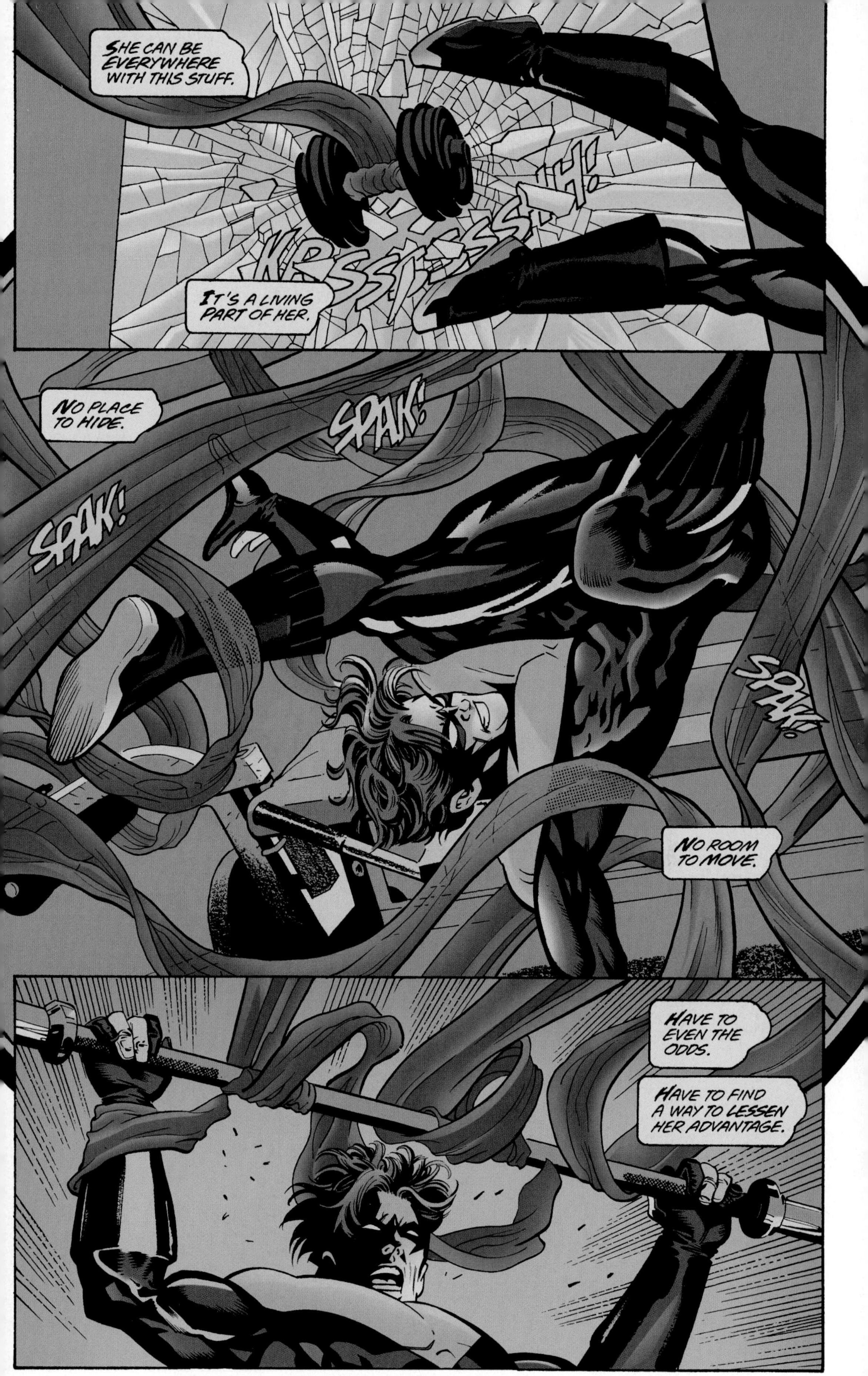
SHE CAN BE EVERYWHERE WITH THIS STUFF.
KRSSSHSSSHH!
IT'S A LIVING PART OF HER.
NO PLACE TO HIDE.
SPAK!
SPAK!
SPAK!
NO ROOM TO MOVE.
HAVE TO EVEN THE ODDS.
HAVE TO FIND A WAY TO LESSEN HER ADVANTAGE.

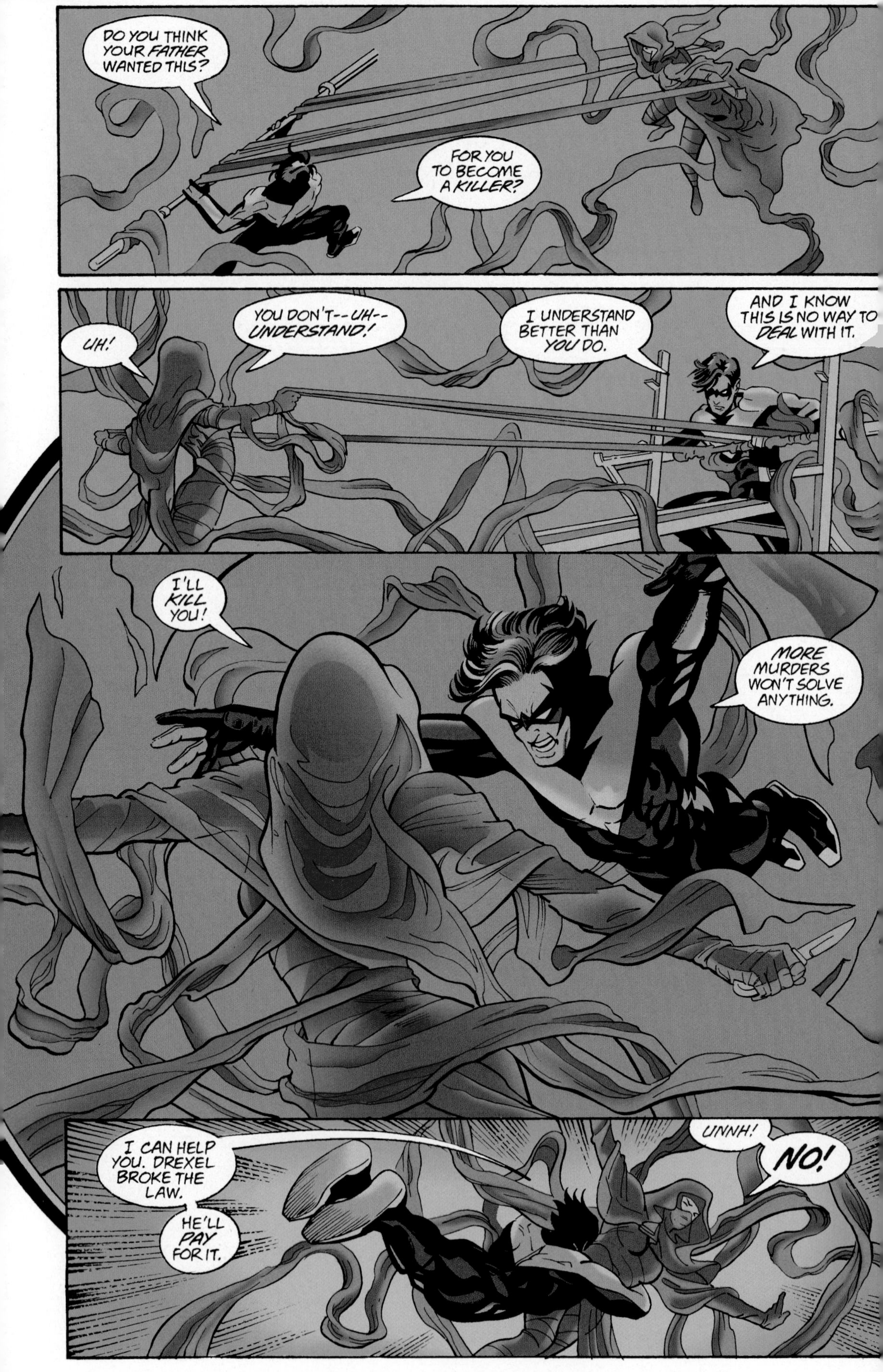
DO YOU THINK YOUR FATHER WANTED THIS?
FOR YOU TO BECOME A KILLER?
UH!
YOU DON'T--UH--UNDERSTAND!
I UNDERSTAND BETTER THAN YOU DO.
AND I KNOW THIS IS NO WAY TO DEAL WITH IT.
I'LL KILL YOU!
MORE MURDERS WON'T SOLVE ANYTHING.
I CAN HELP YOU. DREXEL BROKE THE LAW.
HE'LL PAY FOR IT.
UNNH!
NO!

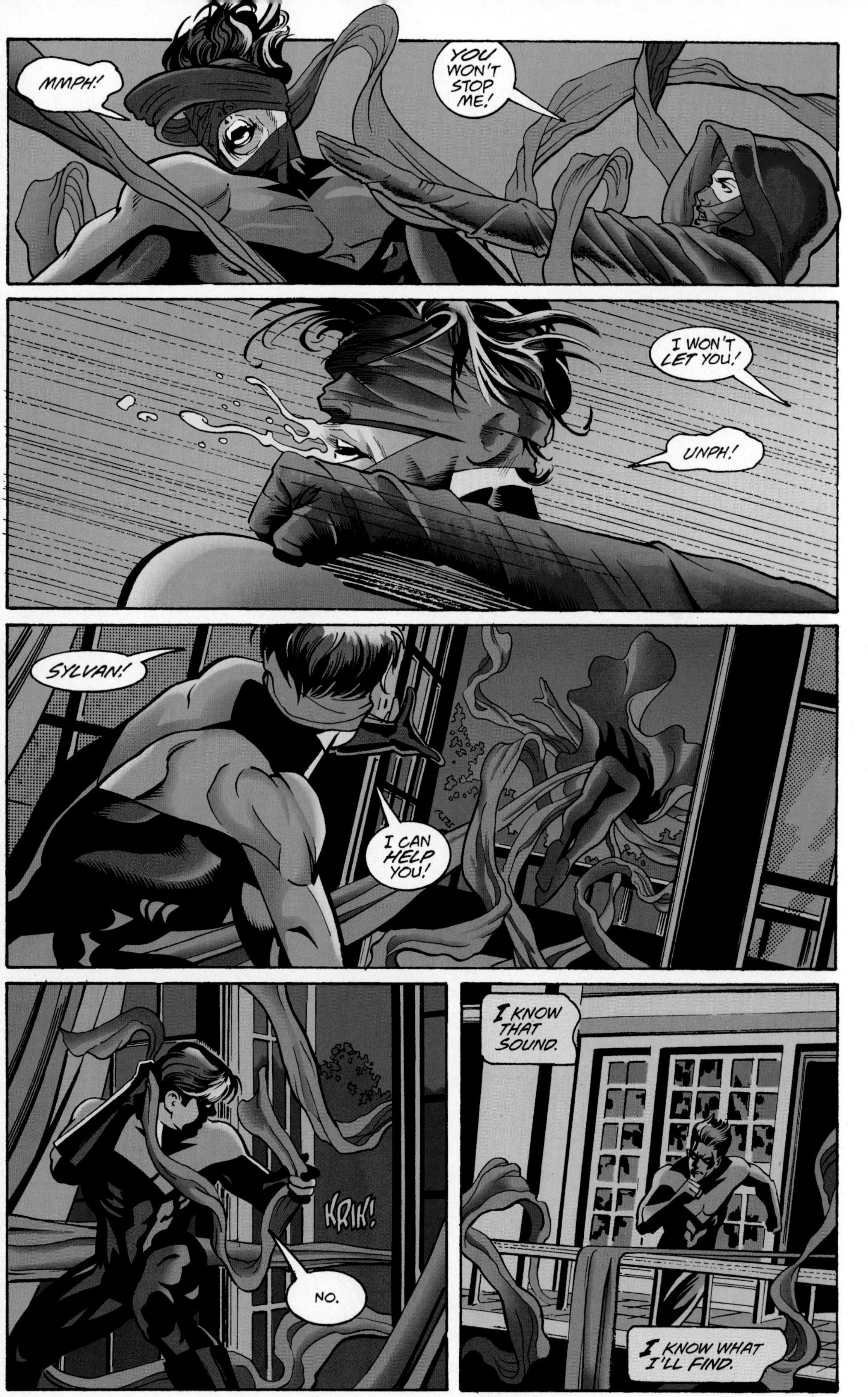
MMPH!
YOU WON'T STOP ME!
I WON'T LET YOU!
UNPH!
SYLVAN!
I CAN HELP YOU!
KRIK!
NO.
I KNOW THAT SOUND.
I KNOW WHAT I'LL FIND.

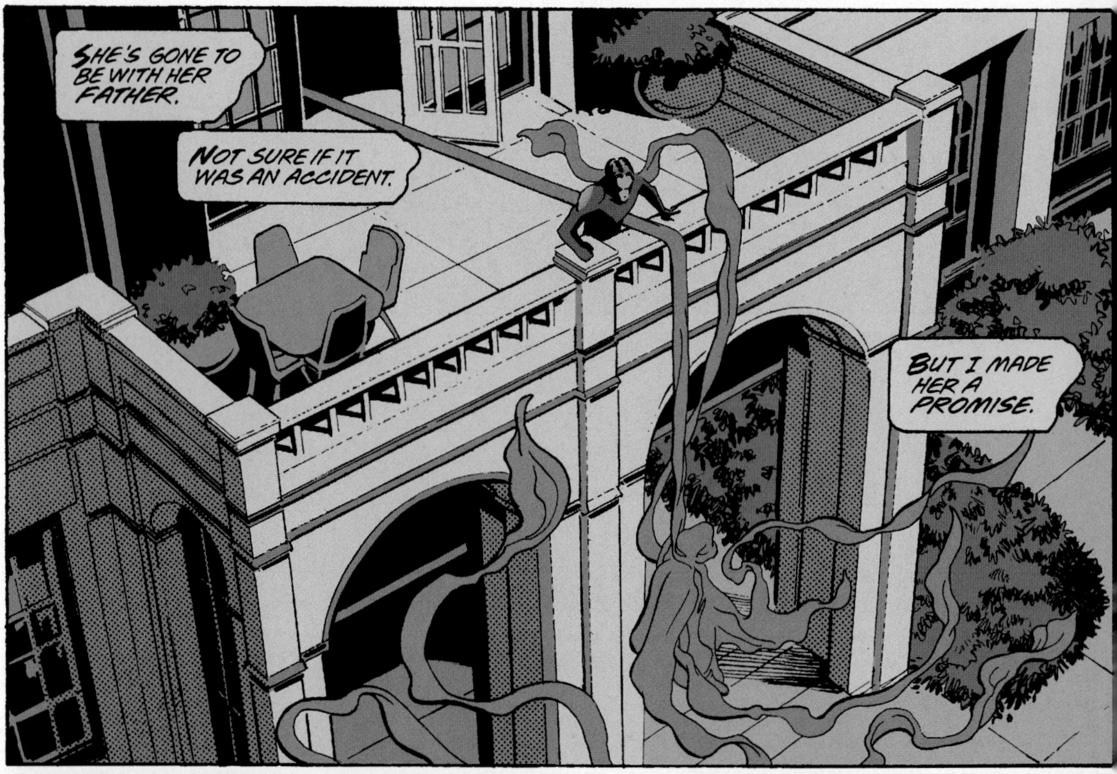
SHE'S GONE TO BE WITH HER FATHER.
NOT SURE IF IT WAS AN ACCIDENT.
BUT I MADE HER A PROMISE.

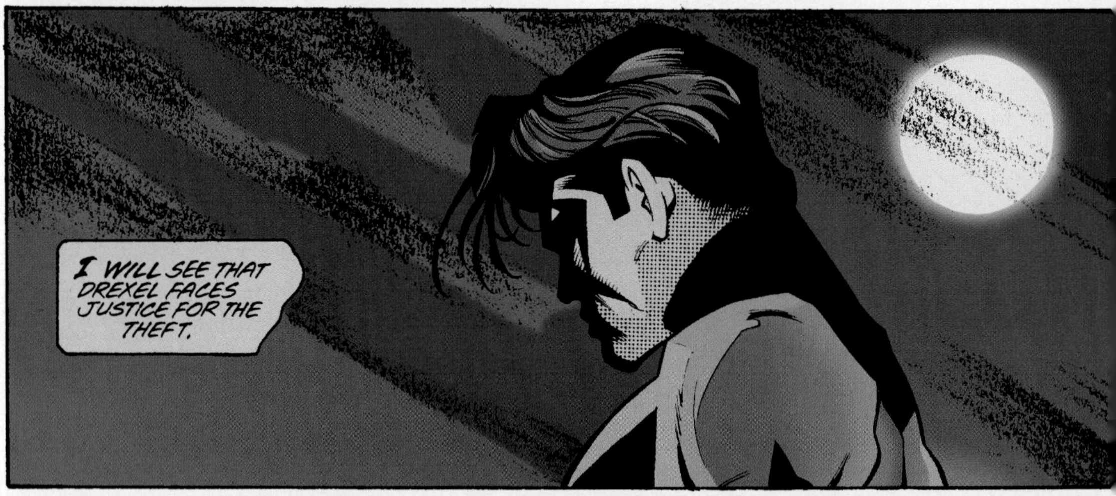
I WILL SEE THAT DREXEL FACES JUSTICE FOR THE THEFT.

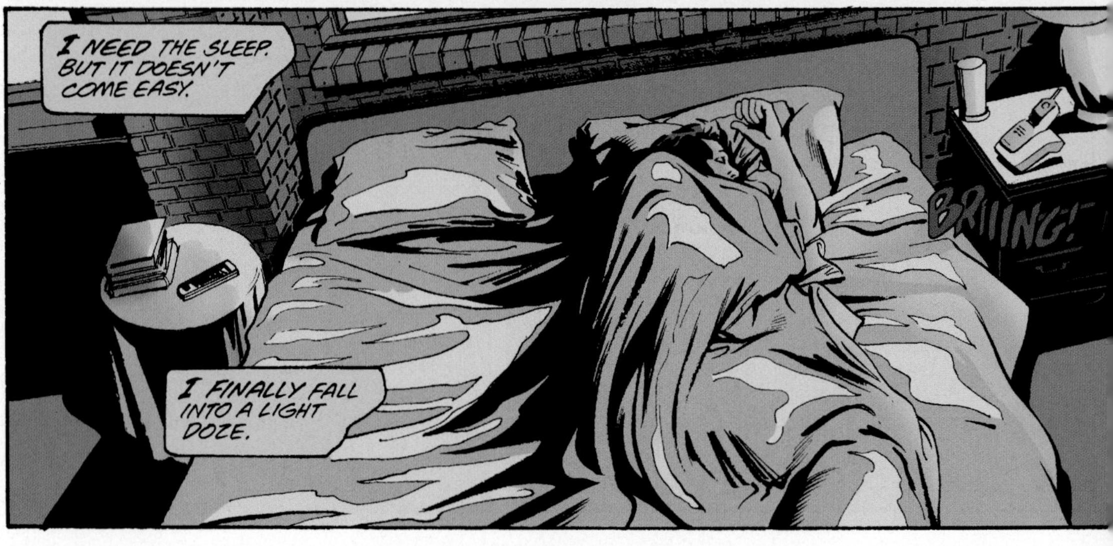
I NEED THE SLEEP. BUT IT DOESN'T COME EASY.
BRIIING!
I FINALLY FALL INTO A LIGHT DOZE.

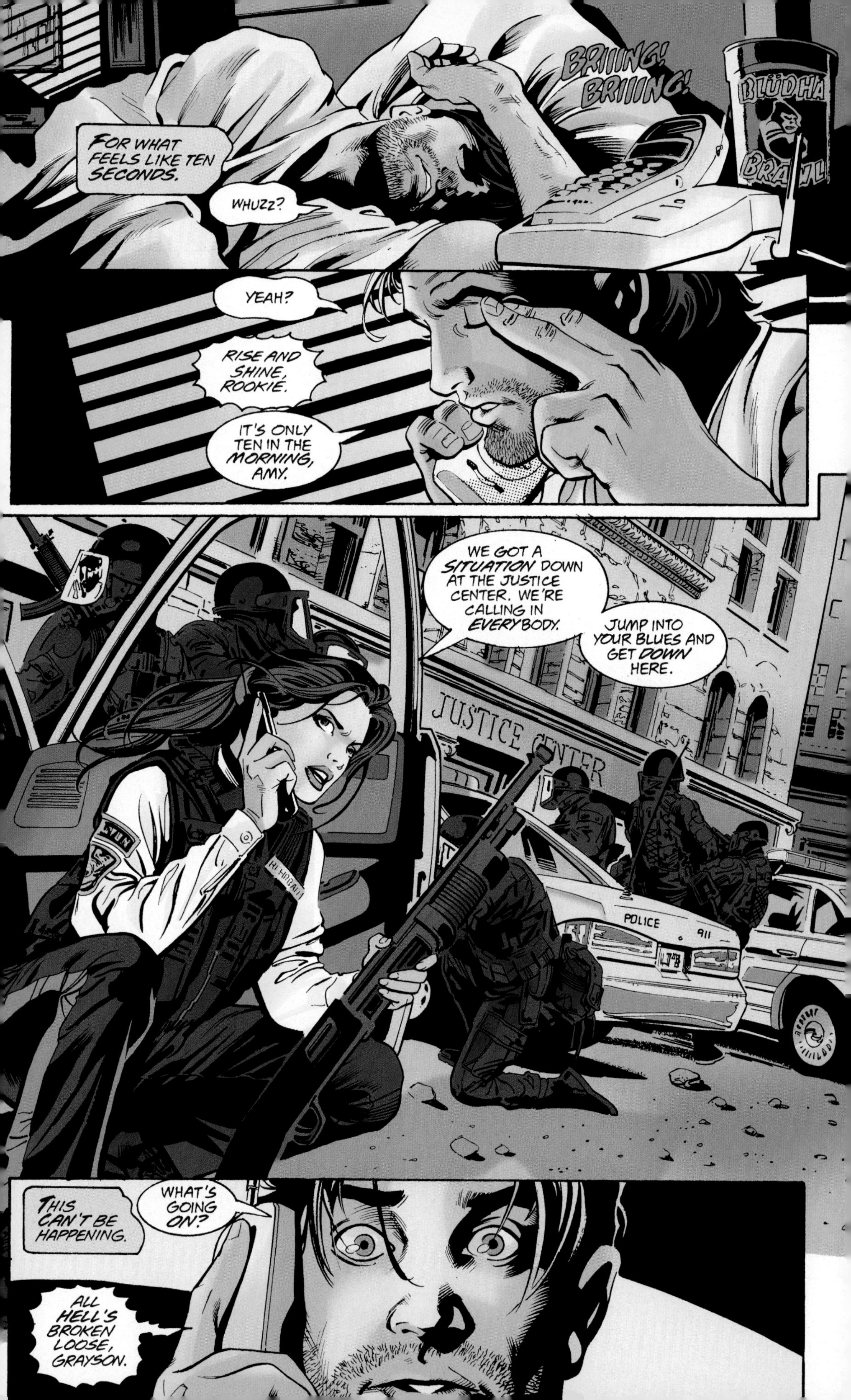
BRIIING! BRIIING!
BLÜDHA
BRAWL
FOR WHAT FEELS LIKE TEN SECONDS.
WHUZZ?
YEAH?
RISE AND SHINE, ROOKIE.
IT'S ONLY TEN IN THE MORNING, AMY.
WE GOT A SITUATION DOWN AT THE JUSTICE CENTER. WE'RE CALLING IN EVERYBODY.
JUMP INTO YOUR BLUES AND GET DOWN HERE.
JUSTICE CENTER
POLICE 911
THIS CAN'T BE HAPPENING.
WHAT'S GOING ON?
ALL HELL'S BROKEN LOOSE, GRAYSON.

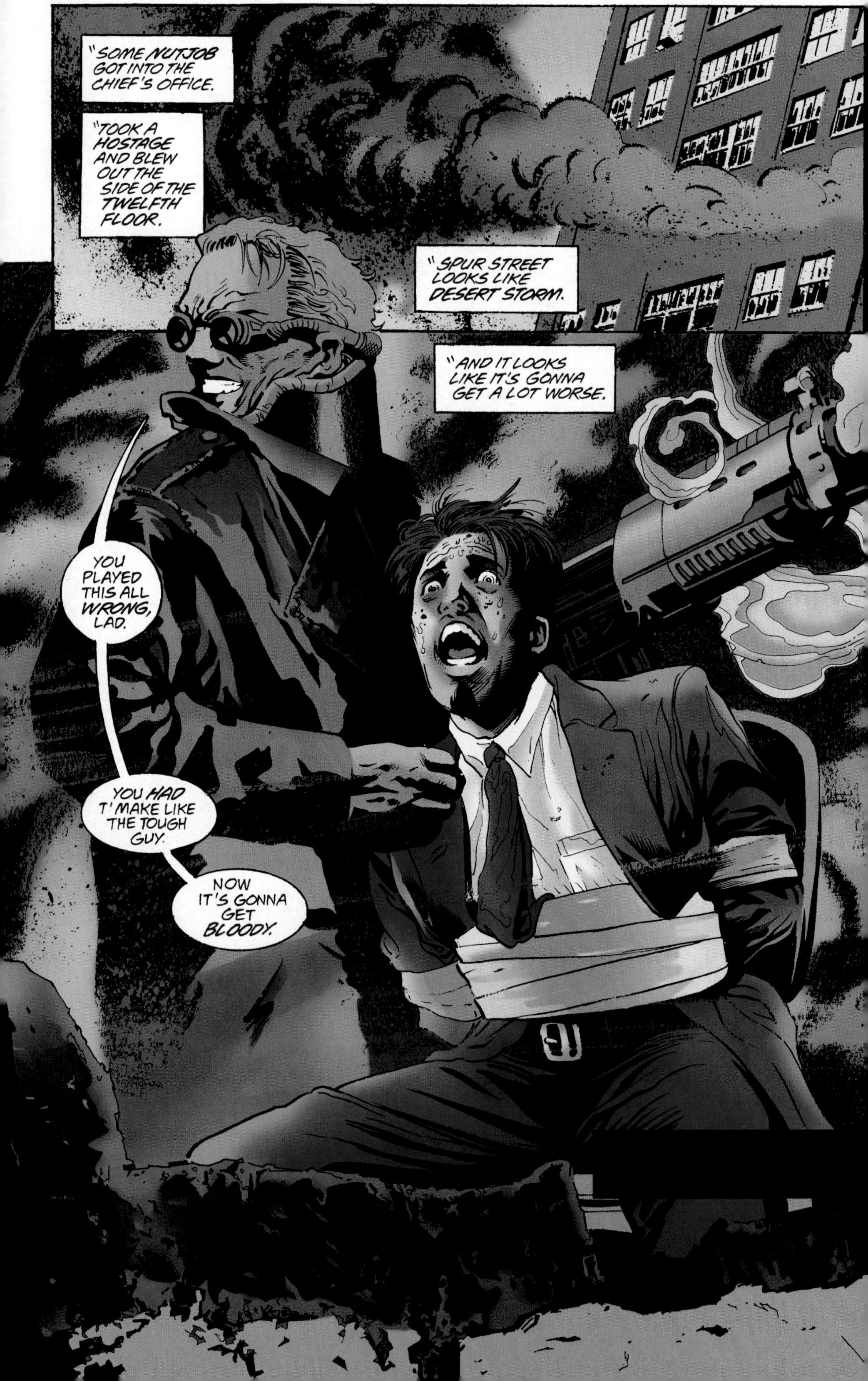
"SOME NUTJOB GOT INTO THE CHIEF'S OFFICE.
"TOOK A HOSTAGE AND BLEW OUT THE SIDE OF THE TWELFTH FLOOR.
"SPUR STREET LOOKS LIKE DESERT STORM.
"AND IT LOOKS LIKE IT'S GONNA GET A LOT WORSE.
YOU PLAYED THIS ALL WRONG, LAD.
YOU HAD T'MAKE LIKE THE TOUGH GUY.
NOW IT'S GONNA GET BLOODY.

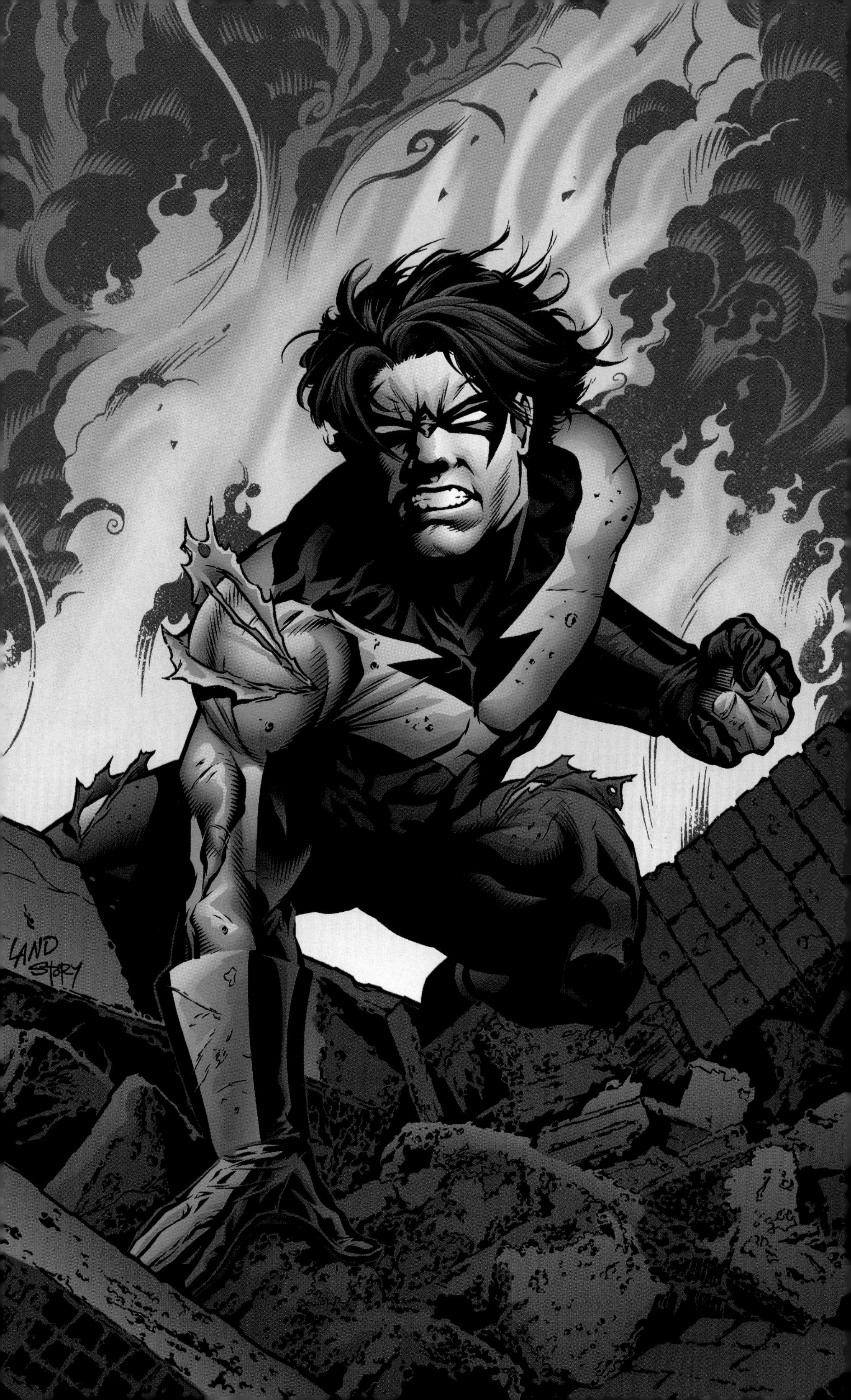
LAND
STORY

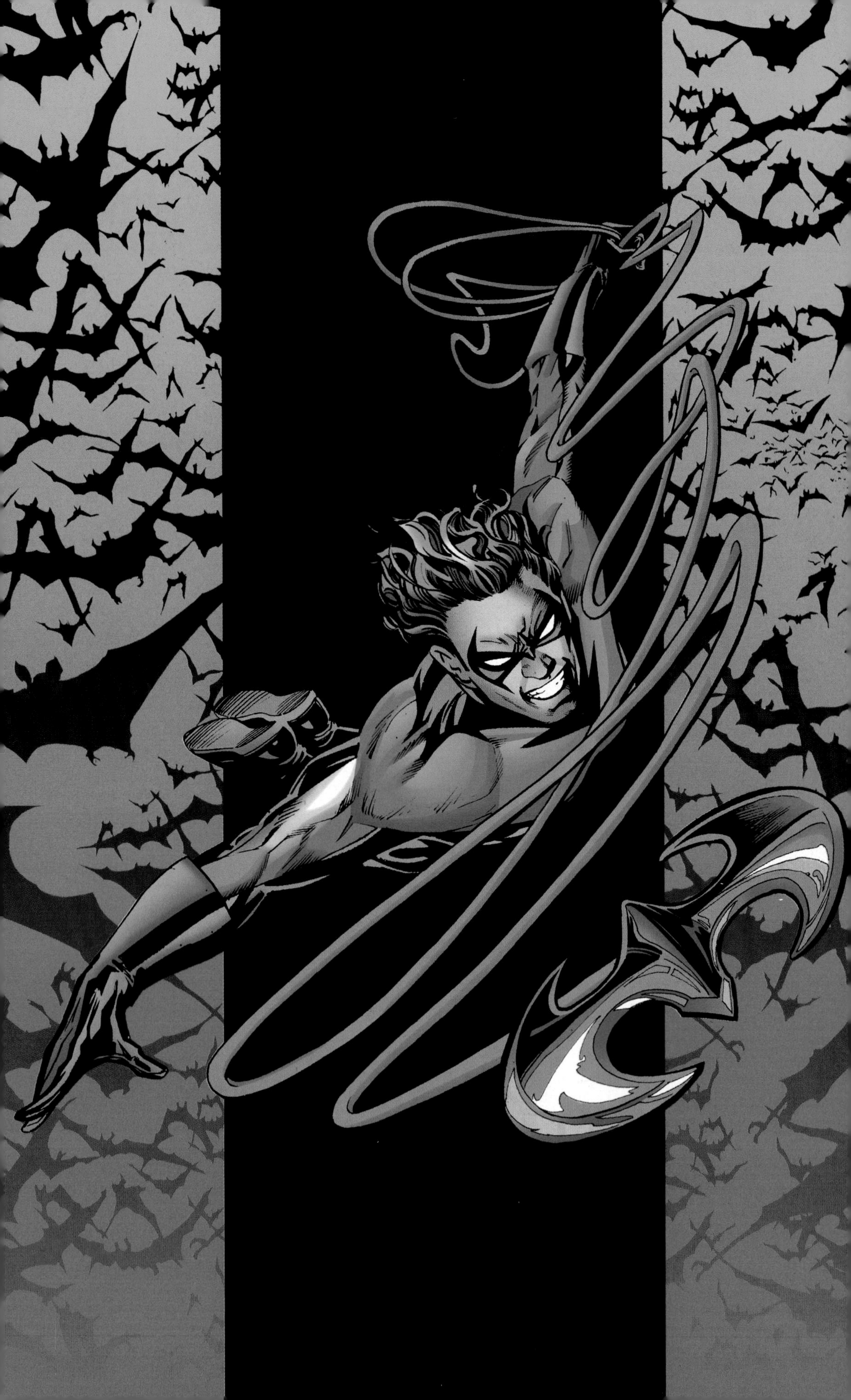

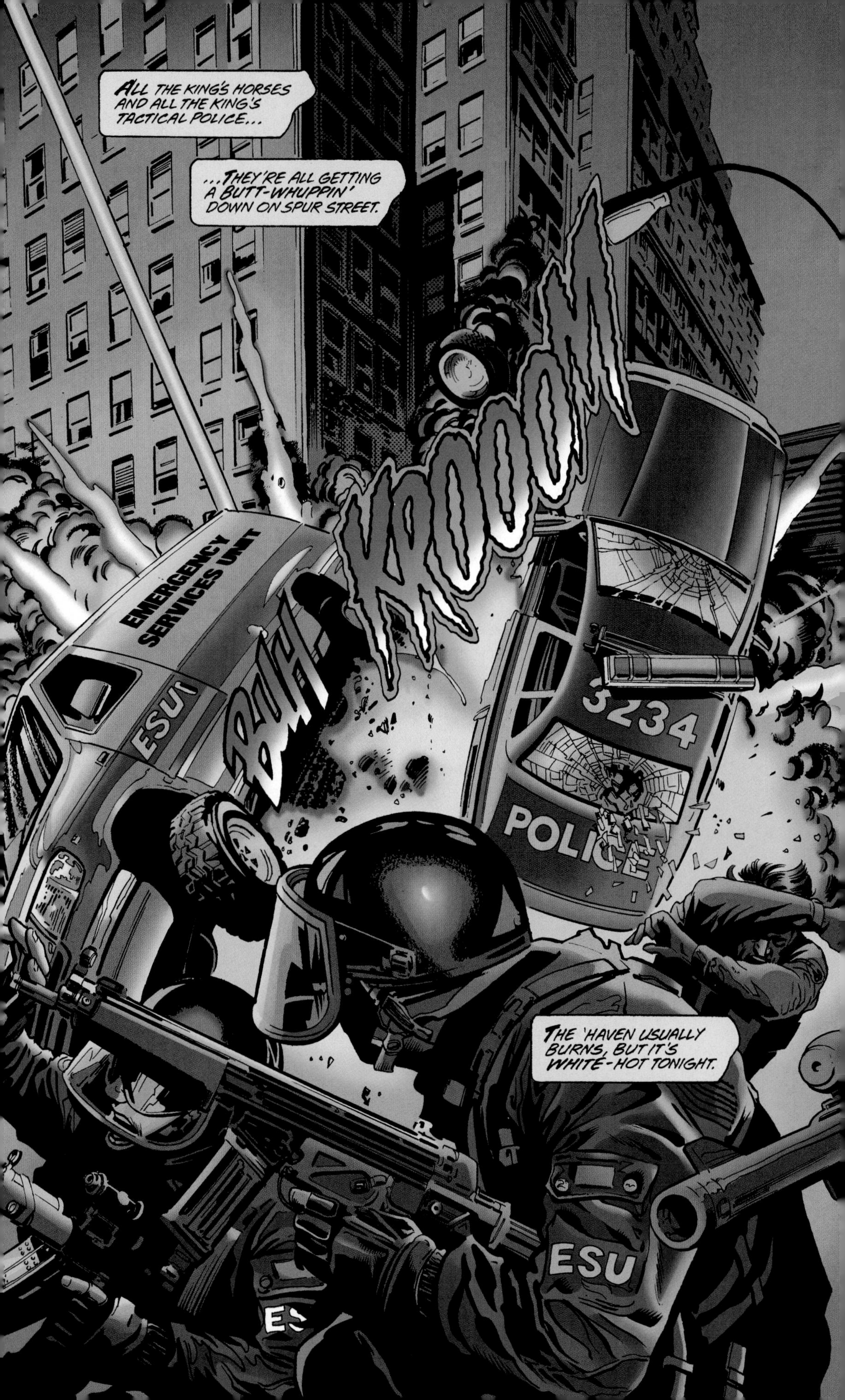
ALL THE KING'S HORSES AND ALL THE KING'S TACTICAL POLICE...
...THEY'RE ALL GETTING A BUTT-WHUPPIN' DOWN ON SPUR STREET.
EMERGENCY SERVICES UNIT
ESU
BUH-KROOOM
3234
POLICE
THE 'HAVEN USUALLY BURNS, BUT IT'S WHITE-HOT TONIGHT.
ESU
ES

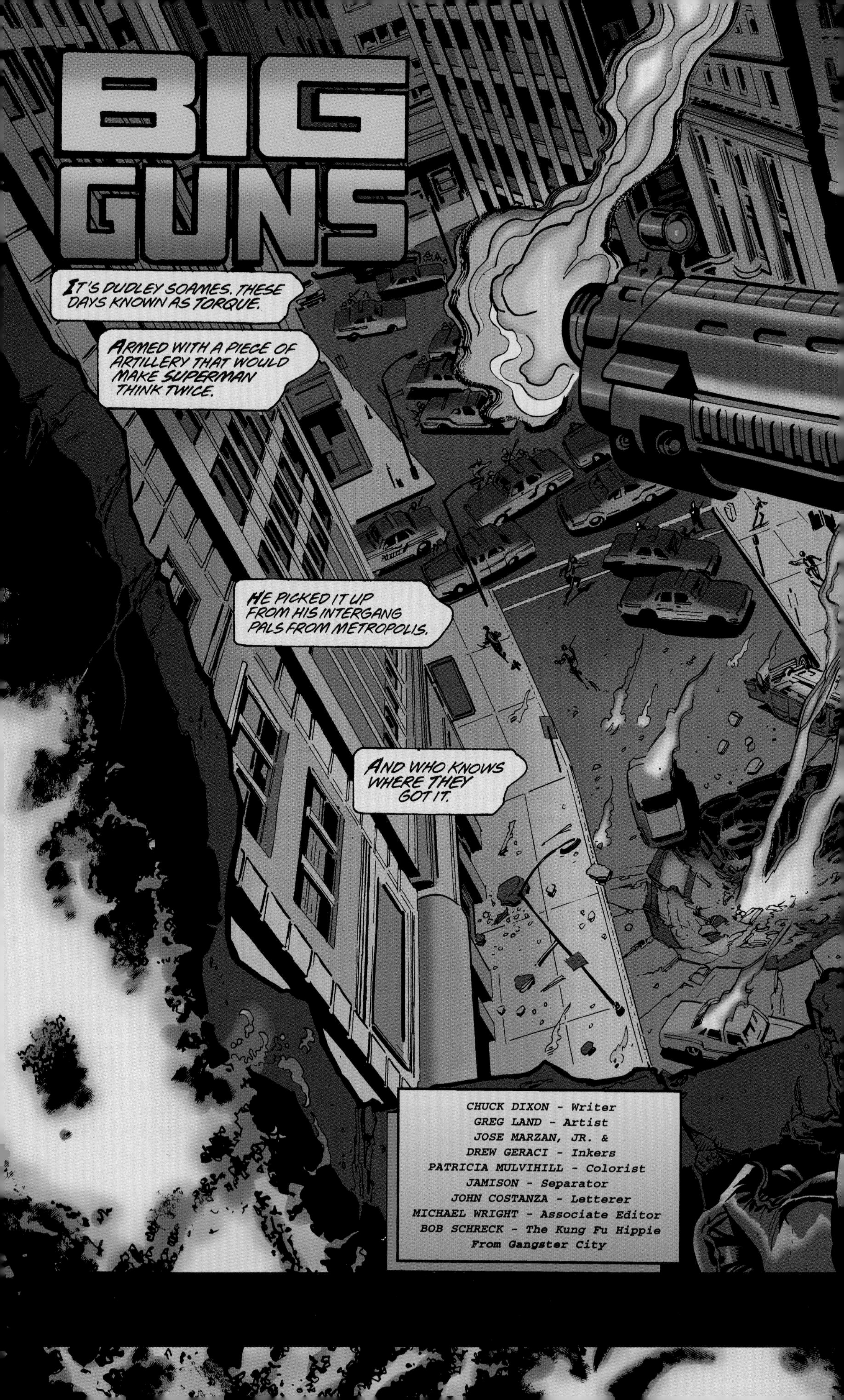
BIG GUNS
IT'S DUDLEY SOAMES. THESE DAYS KNOWN AS TORQUE.
ARMED WITH A PIECE OF ARTILLERY THAT WOULD MAKE SUPERMAN THINK TWICE.
HE PICKED IT UP FROM HIS INTERGANG PALS FROM METROPOLIS.
AND WHO KNOWS WHERE THEY GOT IT.
CHUCK DIXON - Writer
GREG LAND - Artist
JOSE MARZAN, JR. &
DREW GERACI - Inkers
PATRICIA MULVIHILL - Colorist
JAMISON - Separator
JOHN COSTANZA - Letterer
MICHAEL WRIGHT - Associate Editor
BOB SCHRECK - The Kung Fu Hippie From Gangster City

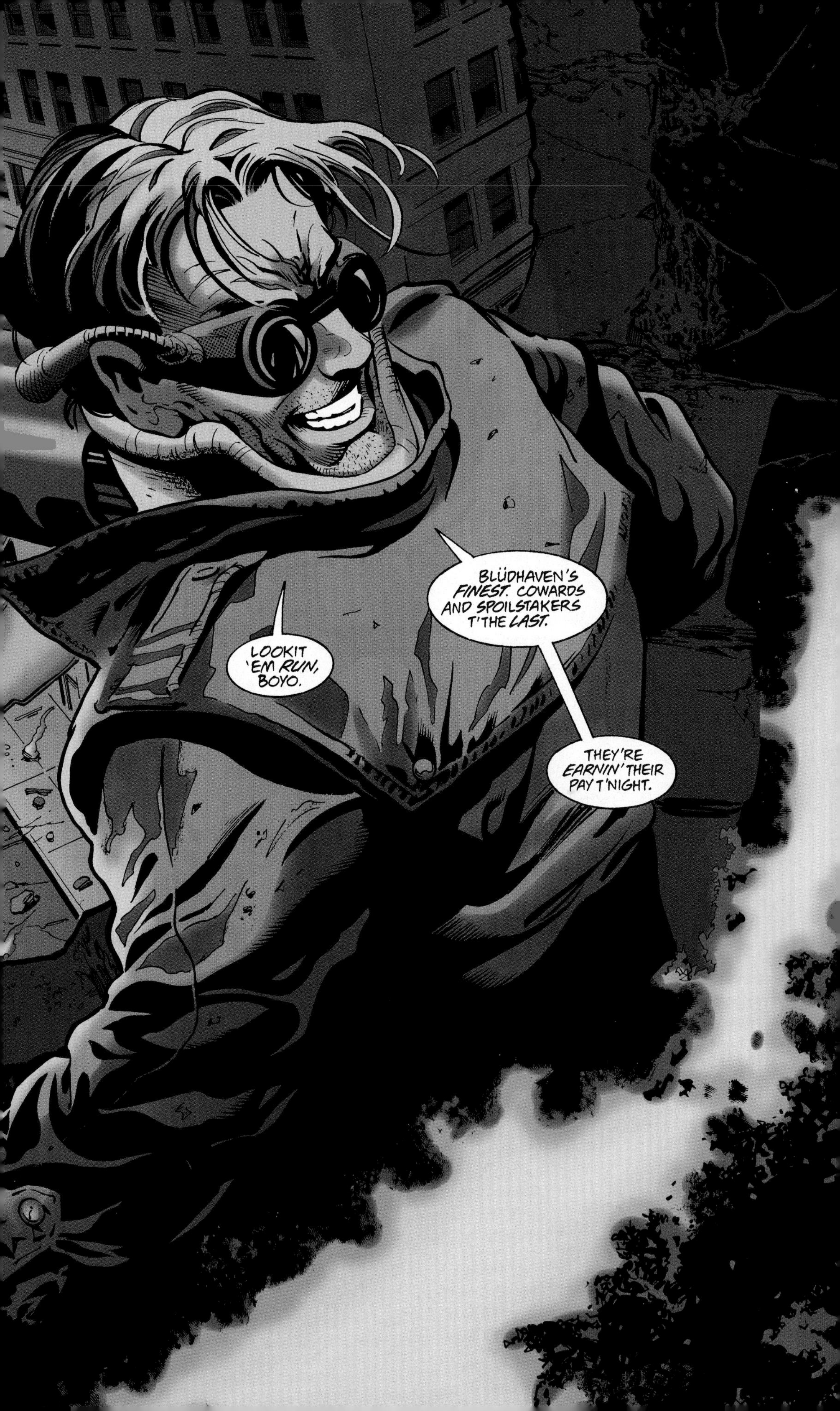
LOOKIT 'EM *RUN*, BOYO.
BLÜDHAVEN'S *FINEST*. COWARDS AND SPOILSTAKERS T'THE *LAST*.
THEY'RE *EARNIN'* THEIR PAY T'NIGHT.

SO THE RUMORS OF SOAMES STARTING AN INTERGANG FRANCHISE IN THE 'HAVEN ARE TRUE.

IT'S T'LAUGH, IT IS.

AN' YOU AN' ME WITH A FRONT ROW SEAT, INSPECTOR ARNOT.

BUT THEY DON'T KNOW WHAT THEY'VE BOUGHT INTO.

THEY DON'T KNOW WHICH WAY T'JUMP.

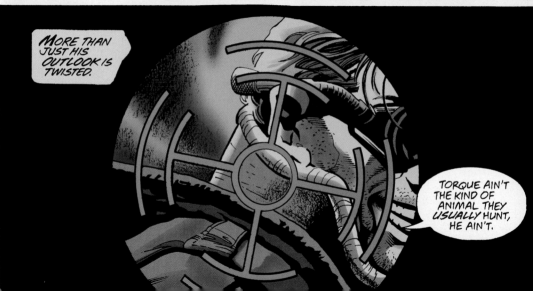

MORE THAN JUST HIS OUTLOOK IS TWISTED.

TORQUE AIN'T THE KIND OF ANIMAL THEY USUALLY HUNT, HE AIN'T.

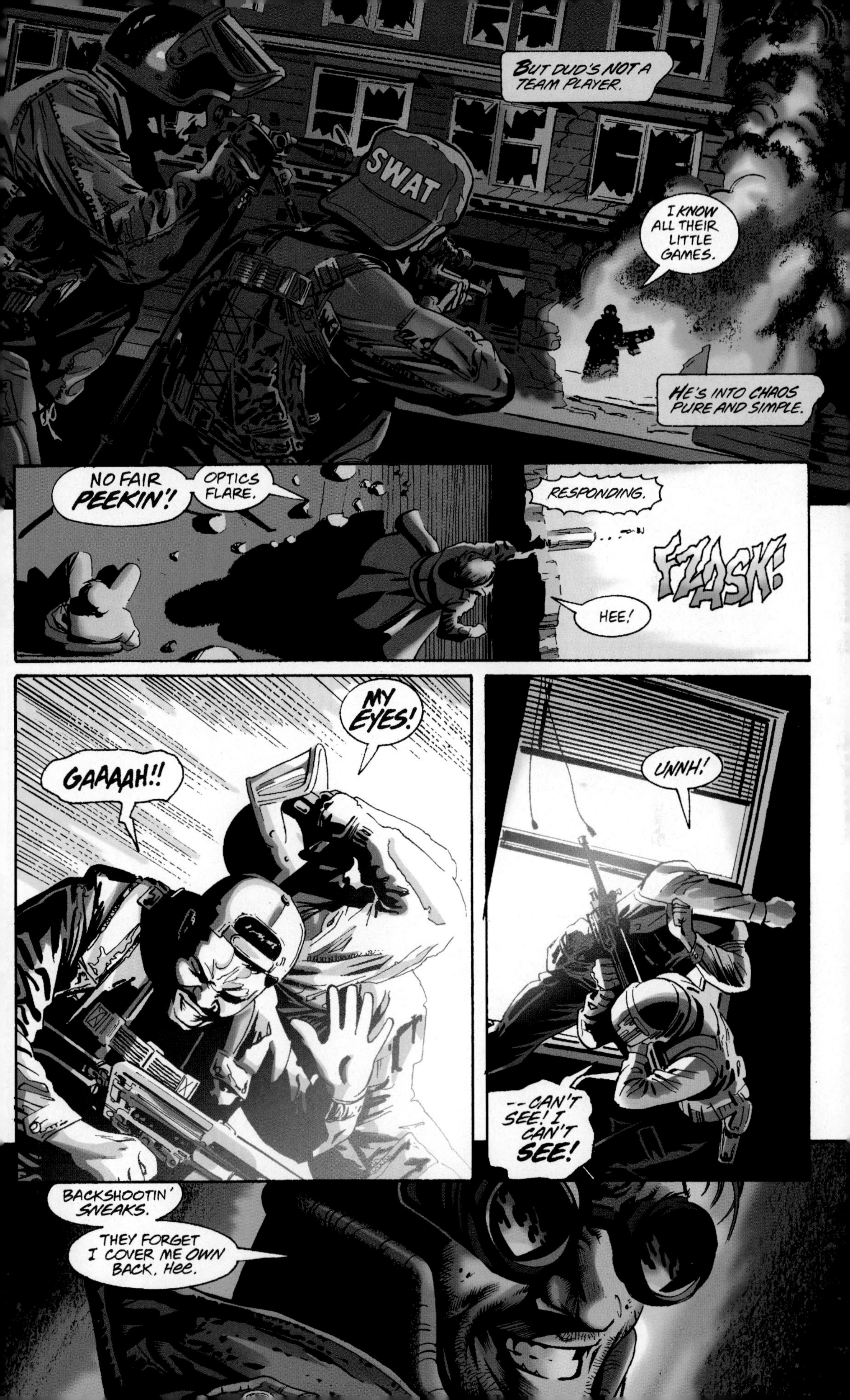
BUT DUD'S NOT A TEAM PLAYER.
I KNOW ALL THEIR LITTLE GAMES.
HE'S INTO CHAOS PURE AND SIMPLE.
NO FAIR PEEKIN'!
OPTICS FLARE.
RESPONDING.
FZASK!
HEE!
MY EYES!
GAAAAH!!
UNNH!
--CAN'T SEE! I CAN'T SEE!
BACKSHOOTIN' SNEAKS.
THEY FORGET I COVER ME OWN BACK. Hee.

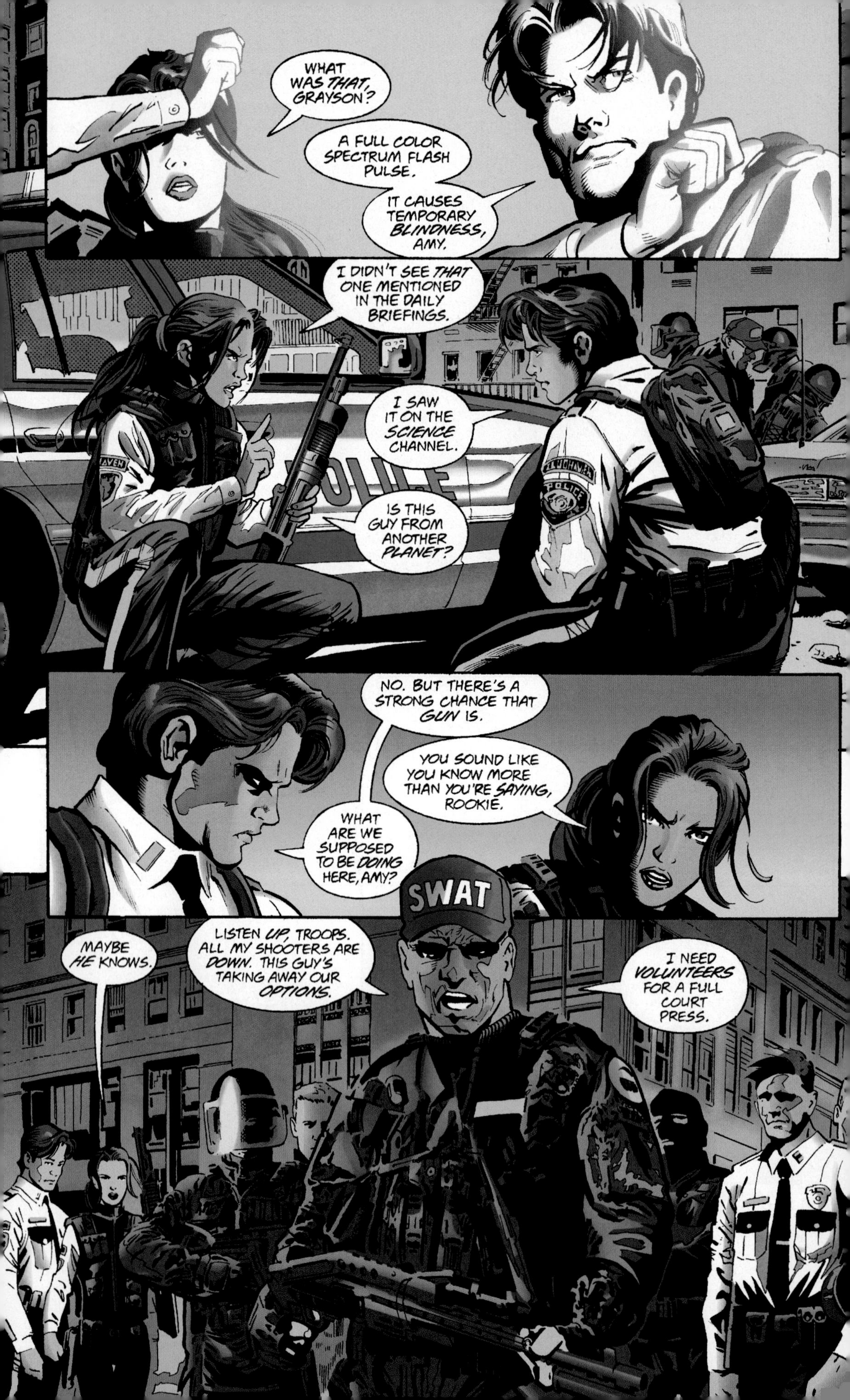
WHAT WAS THAT, GRAYSON?
A FULL COLOR SPECTRUM FLASH PULSE.
IT CAUSES TEMPORARY BLINDNESS, AMY.
I DIDN'T SEE THAT ONE MENTIONED IN THE DAILY BRIEFINGS.
I SAW IT ON THE SCIENCE CHANNEL.
IS THIS GUY FROM ANOTHER PLANET?
POLICE
NO. BUT THERE'S A STRONG CHANCE THAT GUN IS.
YOU SOUND LIKE YOU KNOW MORE THAN YOU'RE SAYING, ROOKIE.
WHAT ARE WE SUPPOSED TO BE DOING HERE, AMY?
SWAT
MAYBE HE KNOWS.
LISTEN UP, TROOPS. ALL MY SHOOTERS ARE DOWN. THIS GUY'S TAKING AWAY OUR OPTIONS.
I NEED VOLUNTEERS FOR A FULL COURT PRESS.

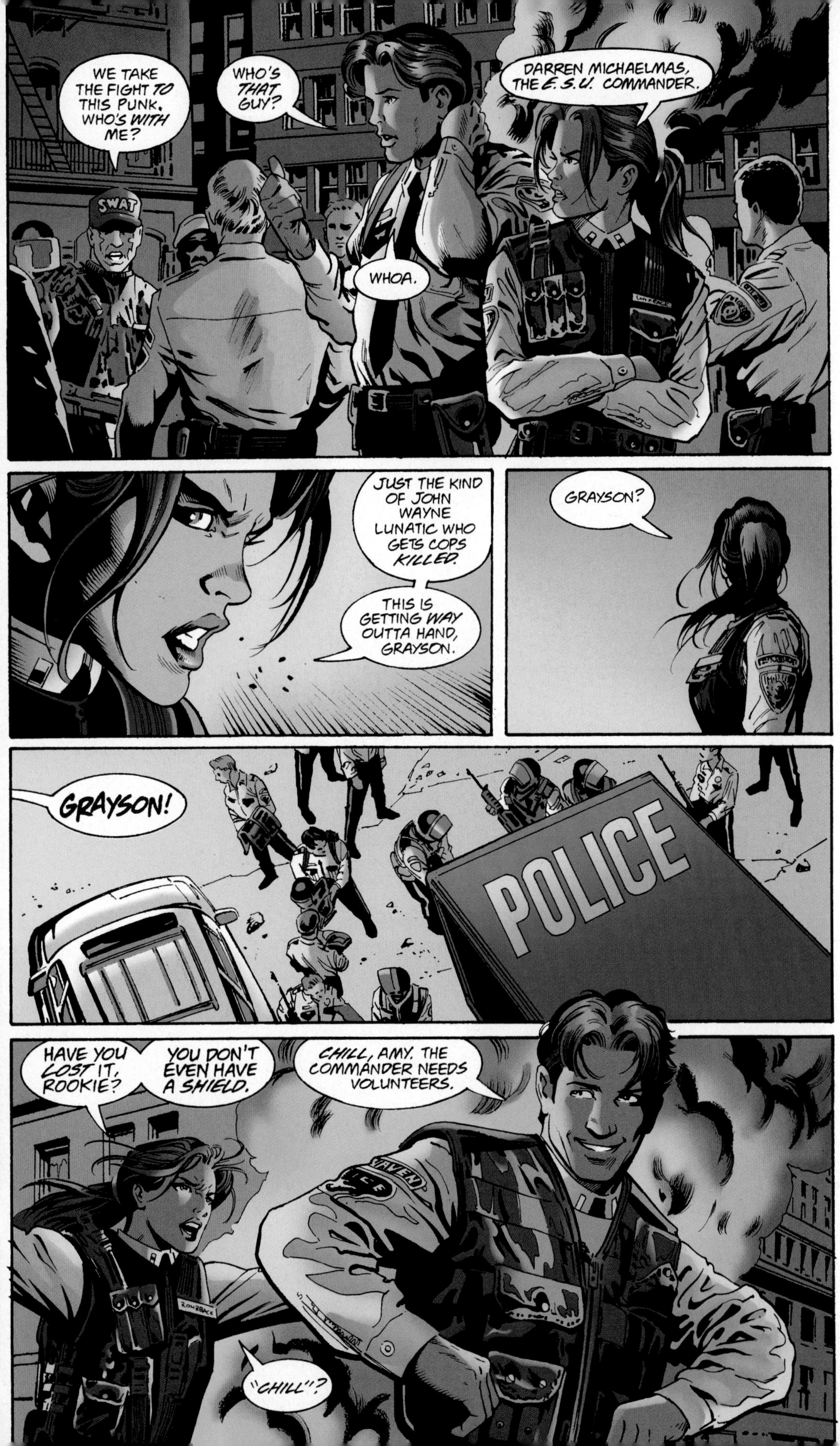

WE TAKE THE FIGHT TO THIS PUNK. WHO'S WITH ME?
WHO'S THAT GUY?
DARREN MICHAELMAS, THE E.S.U. COMMANDER.
WHOA.
JUST THE KIND OF JOHN WAYNE LUNATIC WHO GETS COPS KILLED.
THIS IS GETTING WAY OUTTA HAND, GRAYSON.
GRAYSON?
GRAYSON!
POLICE
HAVE YOU LOST IT, ROOKIE?
YOU DON'T EVEN HAVE A SHIELD.
CHILL, AMY. THE COMMANDER NEEDS VOLUNTEERS.
"CHILL"?

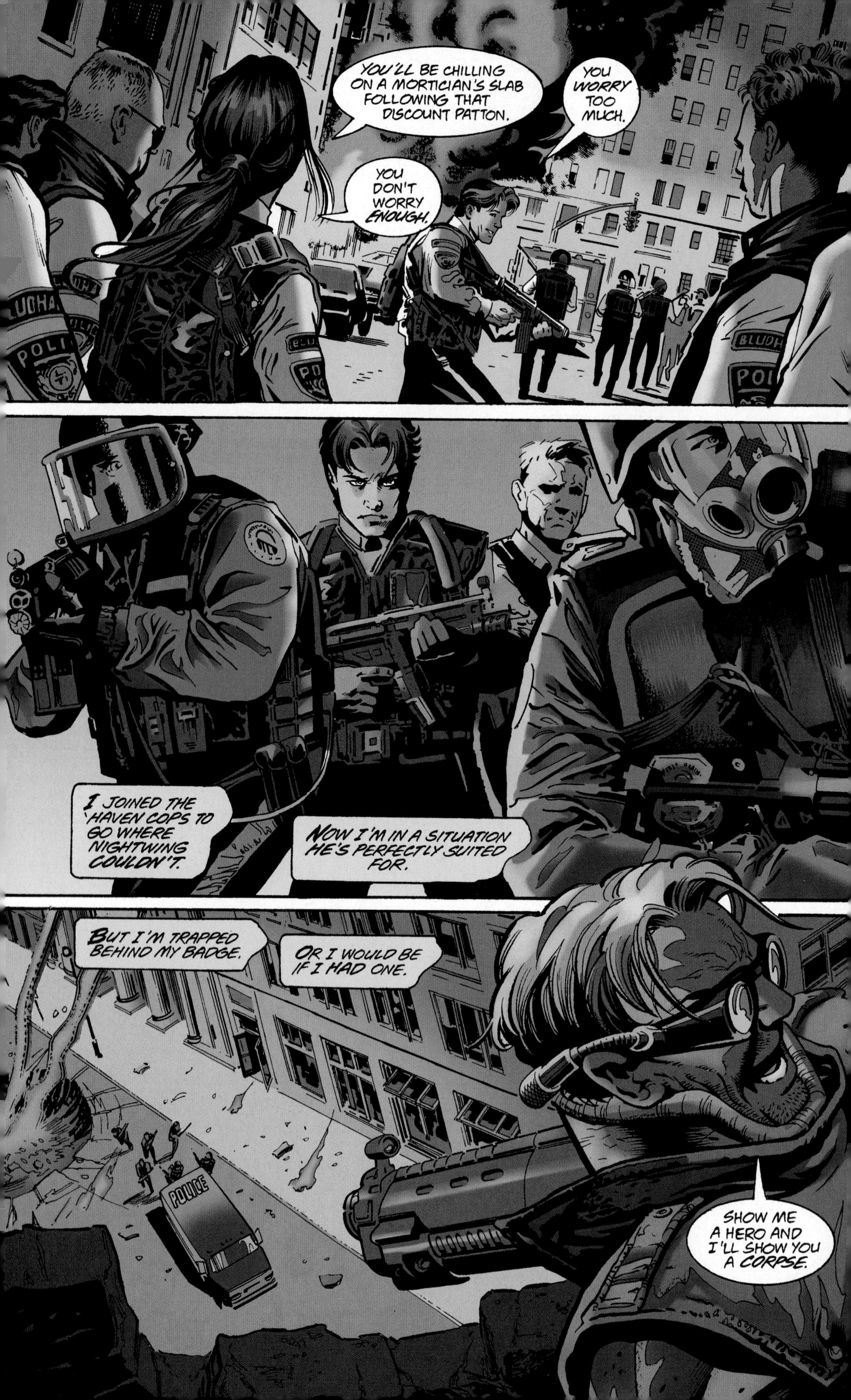

YOU'LL BE CHILLING ON A MORTICIAN'S SLAB FOLLOWING THAT DISCOUNT PATTON.
YOU WORRY TOO MUCH.
YOU DON'T WORRY ENOUGH.
BLUDHAVEN POLICE
I JOINED THE 'HAVEN COPS TO GO WHERE NIGHTWING COULDN'T.
NOW I'M IN A SITUATION HE'S PERFECTLY SUITED FOR.
BUT I'M TRAPPED BEHIND MY BADGE.
OR I WOULD BE IF I HAD ONE.
POLICE
SHOW ME A HERO AND I'LL SHOW YOU A CORPSE.

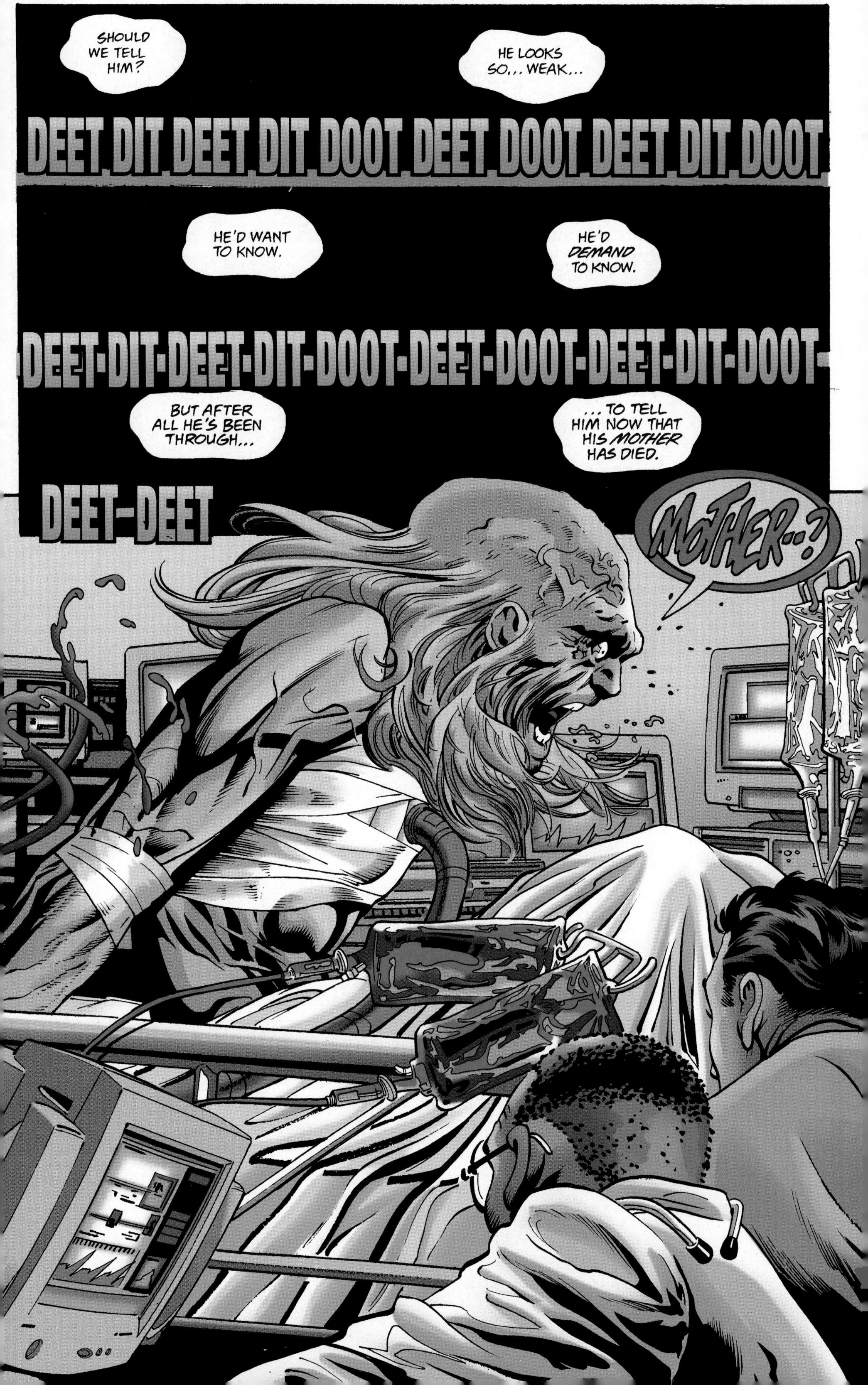

SHOULD WE TELL HIM?
HE LOOKS SO... WEAK...
DEET DIT DEET DIT DOOT DEET DOOT DEET DIT DOOT
HE'D WANT TO KNOW.
HE'D *DEMAND* TO KNOW.
-DEET-DIT-DEET-DIT-DOOT-DEET-DOOT-DEET-DIT-DOOT-
BUT AFTER ALL HE'S BEEN THROUGH...
...TO TELL HIM NOW THAT HIS *MOTHER* HAS DIED.
DEET-DEET
MOTHER..?

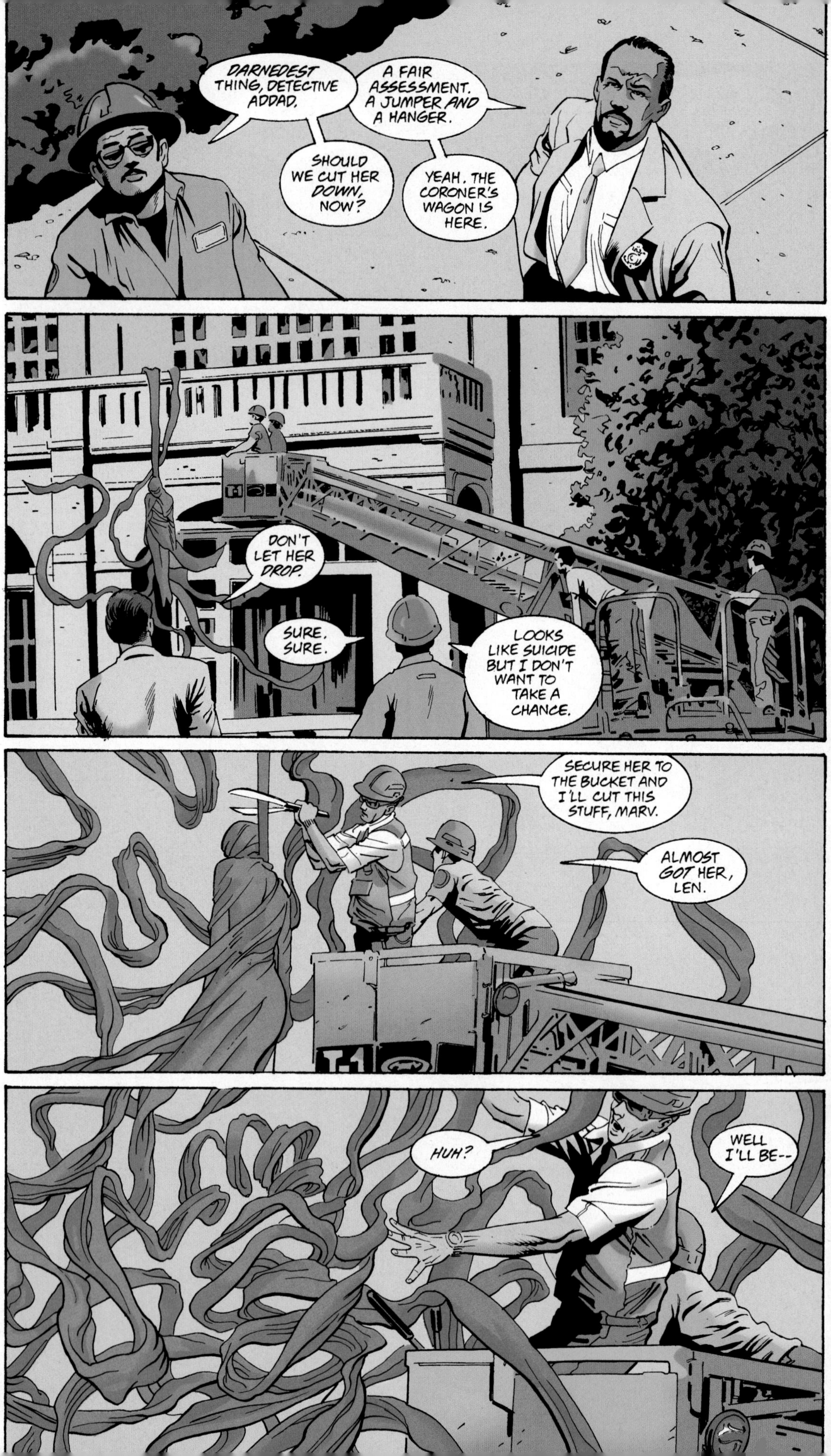
DARNEDEST THING, DETECTIVE ADDAD.
A FAIR ASSESSMENT. A JUMPER AND A HANGER.
SHOULD WE CUT HER DOWN, NOW?
YEAH. THE CORONER'S WAGON IS HERE.
DON'T LET HER DROP.
SURE. SURE.
LOOKS LIKE SUICIDE BUT I DON'T WANT TO TAKE A CHANCE.
SECURE HER TO THE BUCKET AND I'LL CUT THIS STUFF, MARV.
ALMOST GOT HER, LEN.
T-1
HUH?
WELL I'LL BE--

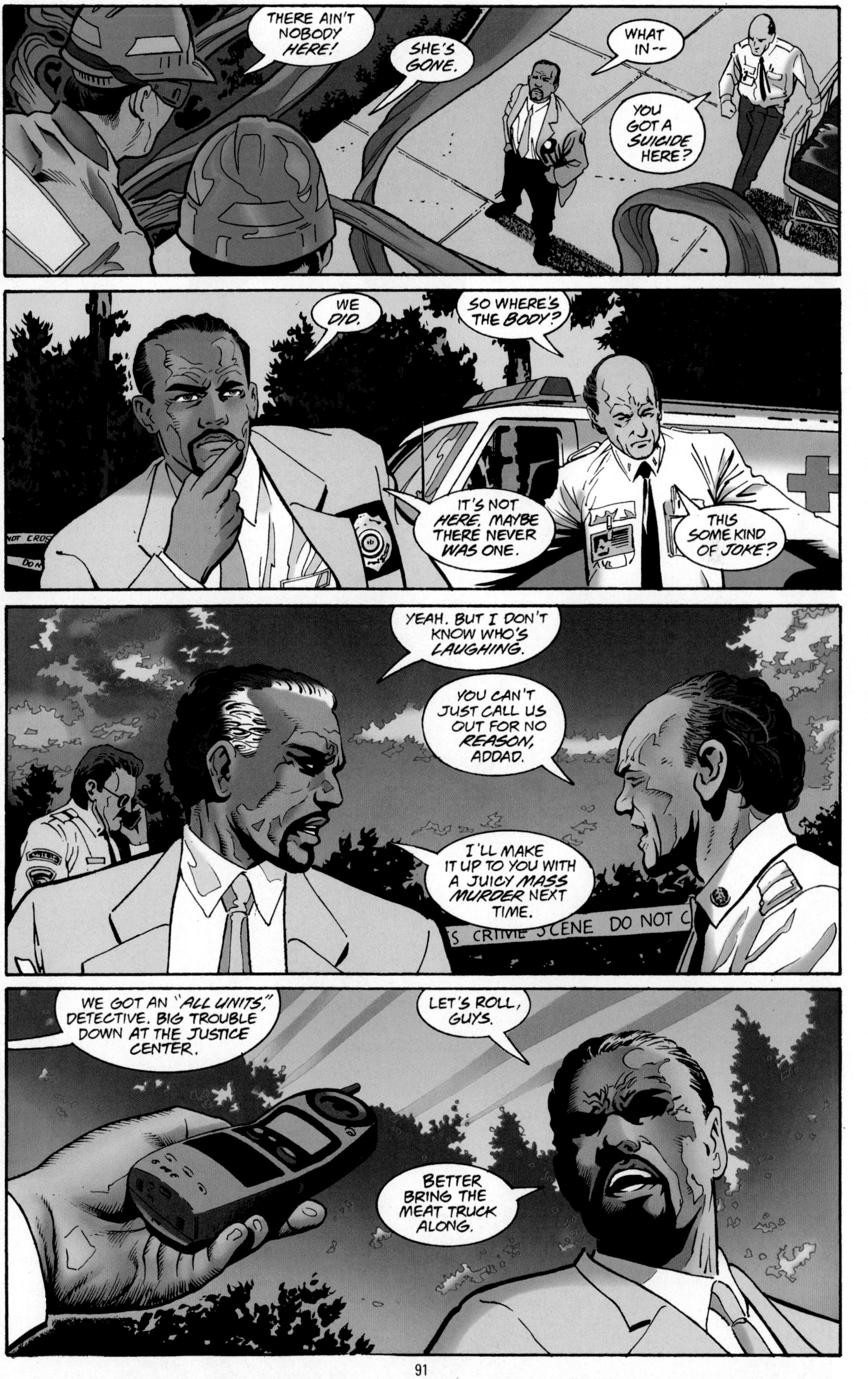
THERE AIN'T NOBODY HERE!
SHE'S GONE.
WHAT IN--
YOU GOT A SUICIDE HERE?
WE DID.
SO WHERE'S THE BODY?
IT'S NOT HERE. MAYBE THERE NEVER WAS ONE.
THIS SOME KIND OF JOKE?
YEAH. BUT I DON'T KNOW WHO'S LAUGHING.
YOU CAN'T JUST CALL US OUT FOR NO REASON, ADDAD.
I'LL MAKE IT UP TO YOU WITH A JUICY MASS MURDER NEXT TIME.
CRIME SCENE DO NOT C
WE GOT AN "ALL UNITS," DETECTIVE. BIG TROUBLE DOWN AT THE JUSTICE CENTER.
LET'S ROLL, GUYS.
BETTER BRING THE MEAT TRUCK ALONG.

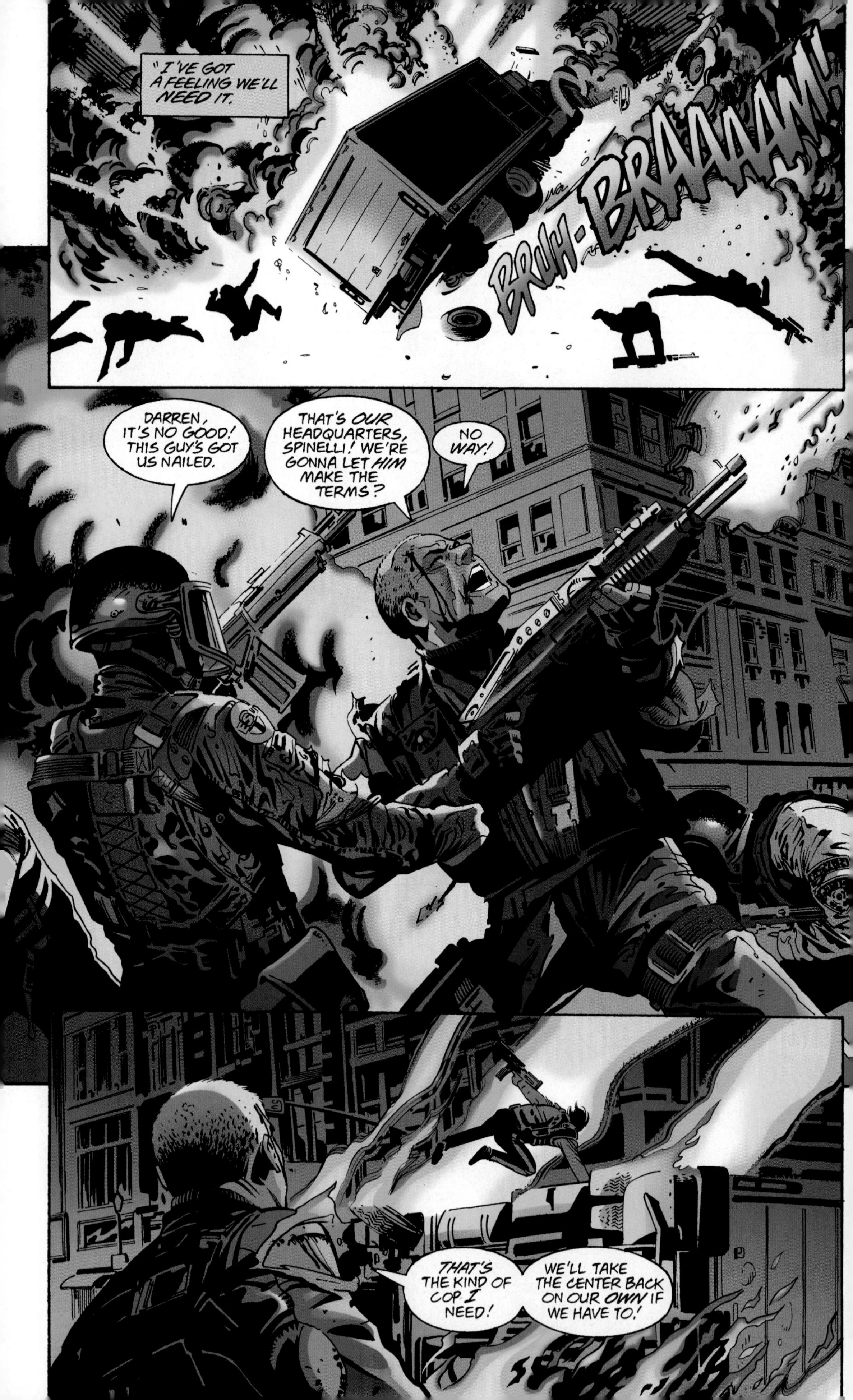
"I'VE GOT A FEELING WE'LL NEED IT.
BRUH-BRAAAAM!
DARREN, IT'S NO GOOD! THIS GUY'S GOT US NAILED.
THAT'S OUR HEADQUARTERS, SPINELLI! WE'RE GONNA LET HIM MAKE THE TERMS?
NO WAY!
THAT'S THE KIND OF COP I NEED!
WE'LL TAKE THE CENTER BACK ON OUR OWN IF WE HAVE TO!

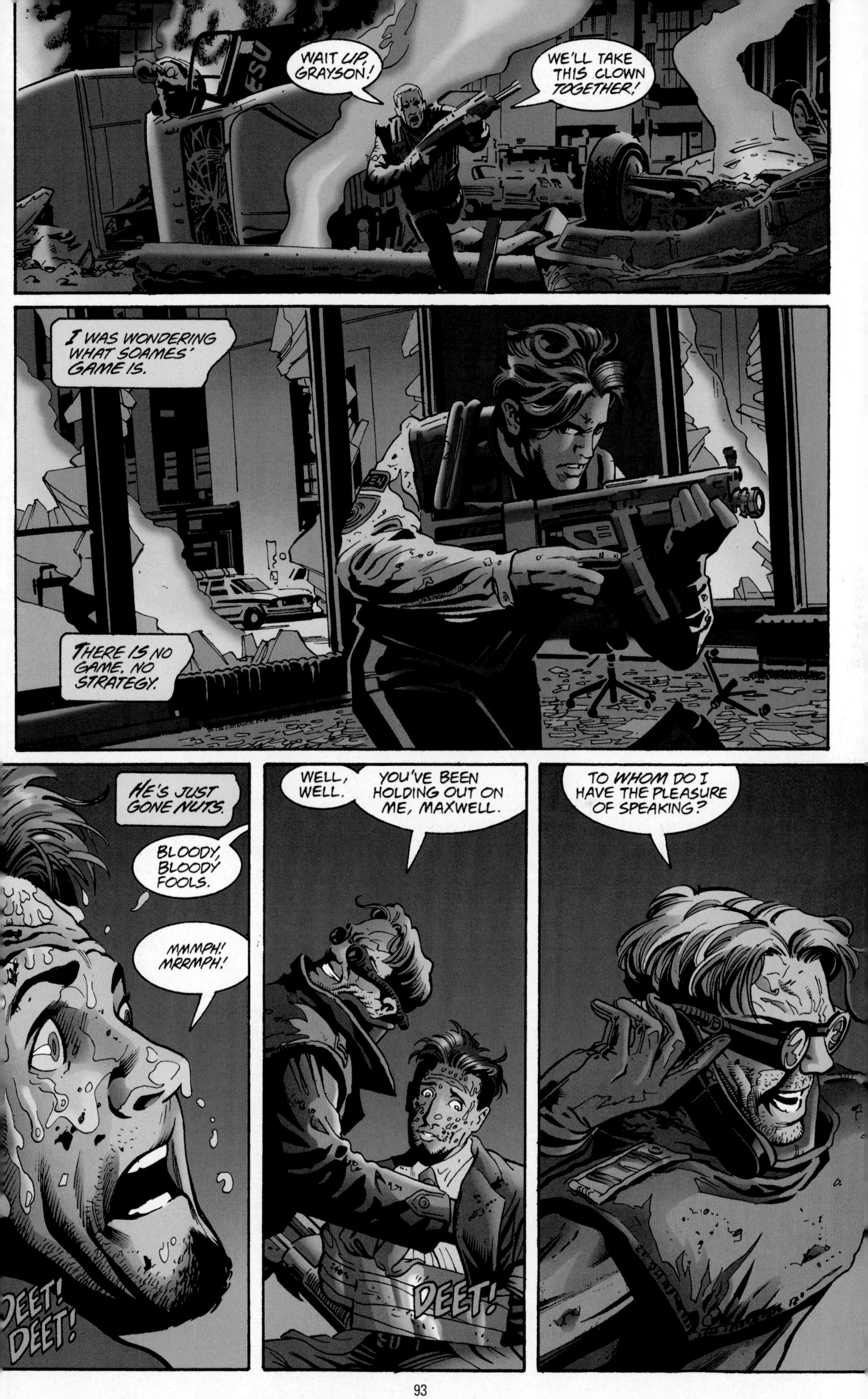
WAIT UP, GRAYSON!
WE'LL TAKE THIS CLOWN TOGETHER!
I WAS WONDERING WHAT SOAMES' GAME IS.
THERE IS NO GAME. NO STRATEGY.
HE'S JUST GONE NUTS.
BLOODY, BLOODY FOOLS.
MMMPH! MRRMPH!
DEET! DEET!
WELL, WELL.
YOU'VE BEEN HOLDING OUT ON ME, MAXWELL.
DEET!
TO WHOM DO I HAVE THE PLEASURE OF SPEAKING?

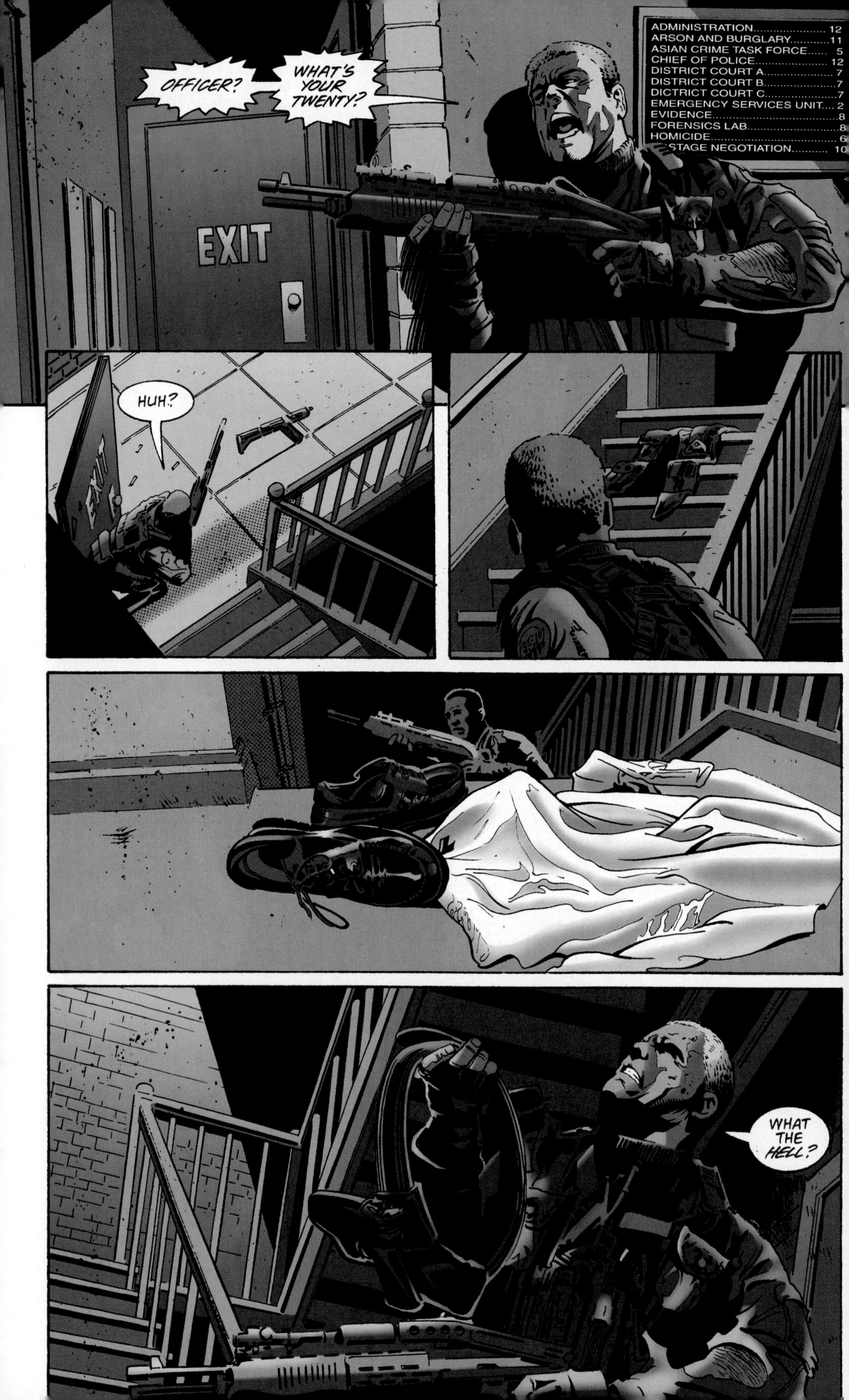
OFFICER?
WHAT'S YOUR TWENTY?
ADMINISTRATION 12
ARSON AND BURGLARY 11
ASIAN CRIME TASK FORCE 5
CHIEF OF POLICE 12
DISTRICT COURT A 7
DISTRICT COURT B 7
DICTRICT COURT C 7
EMERGENCY SERVICES UNIT 2
EVIDENCE 8
FORENSICS LAB 8
HOMICIDE 6
STAGE NEGOTIATION 10
EXIT
HUH?
EXIT
WHAT THE HELL?

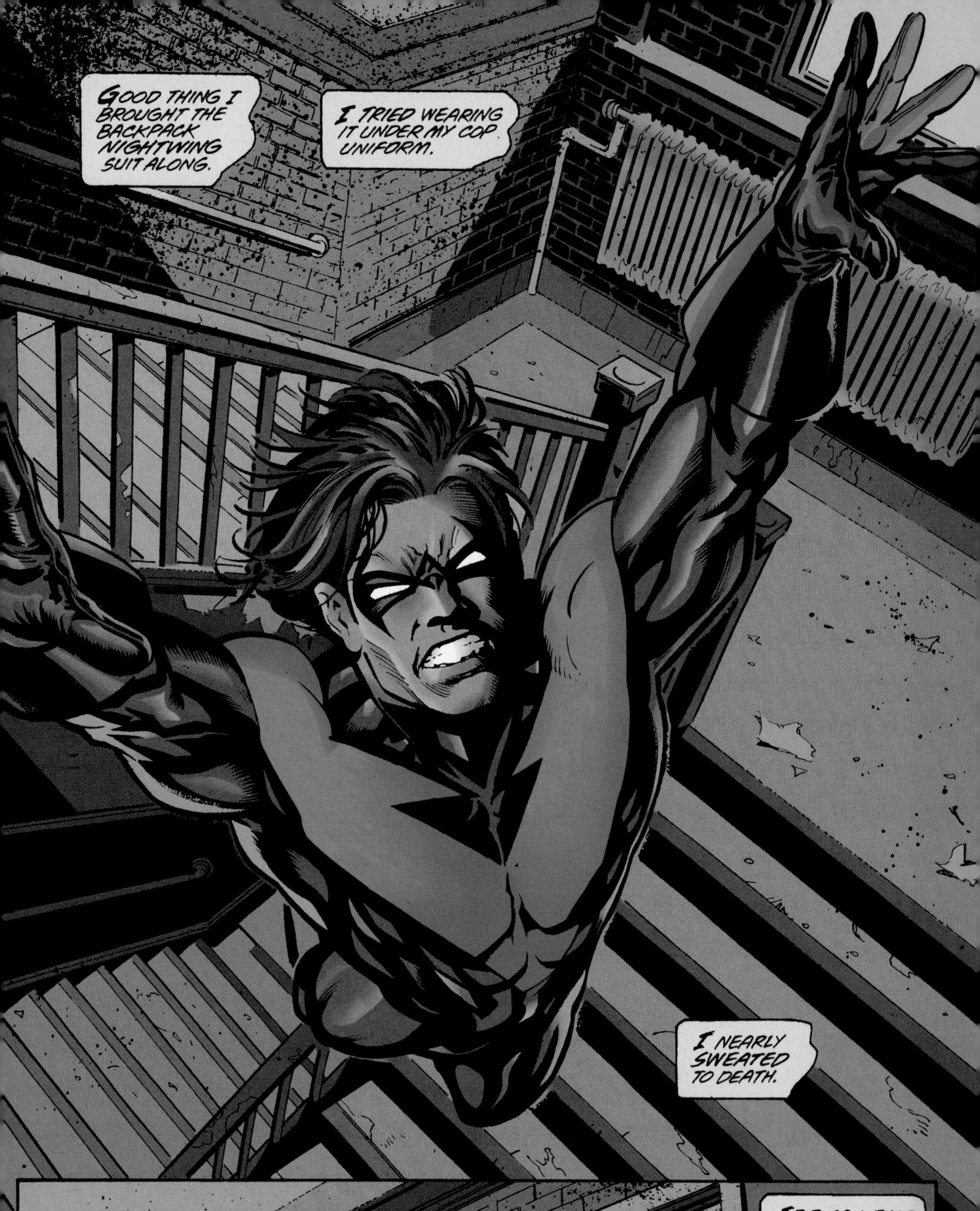
GOOD THING I BROUGHT THE BACKPACK NIGHTWING SUIT ALONG.
I TRIED WEARING IT UNDER MY COP UNIFORM.
I NEARLY SWEATED TO DEATH.

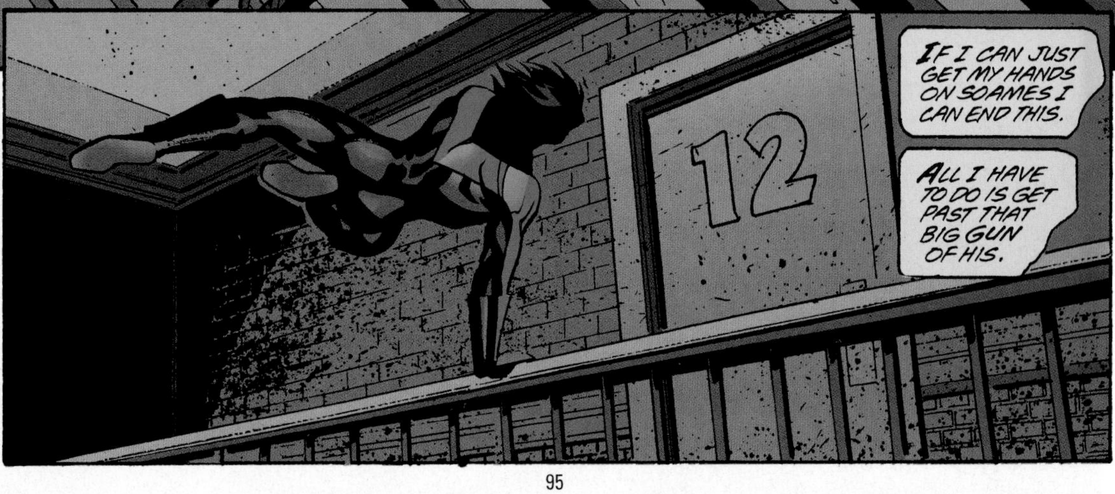
IF I CAN JUST GET MY HANDS ON SOAMES I CAN END THIS.
ALL I HAVE TO DO IS GET PAST THAT BIG GUN OF HIS.
12

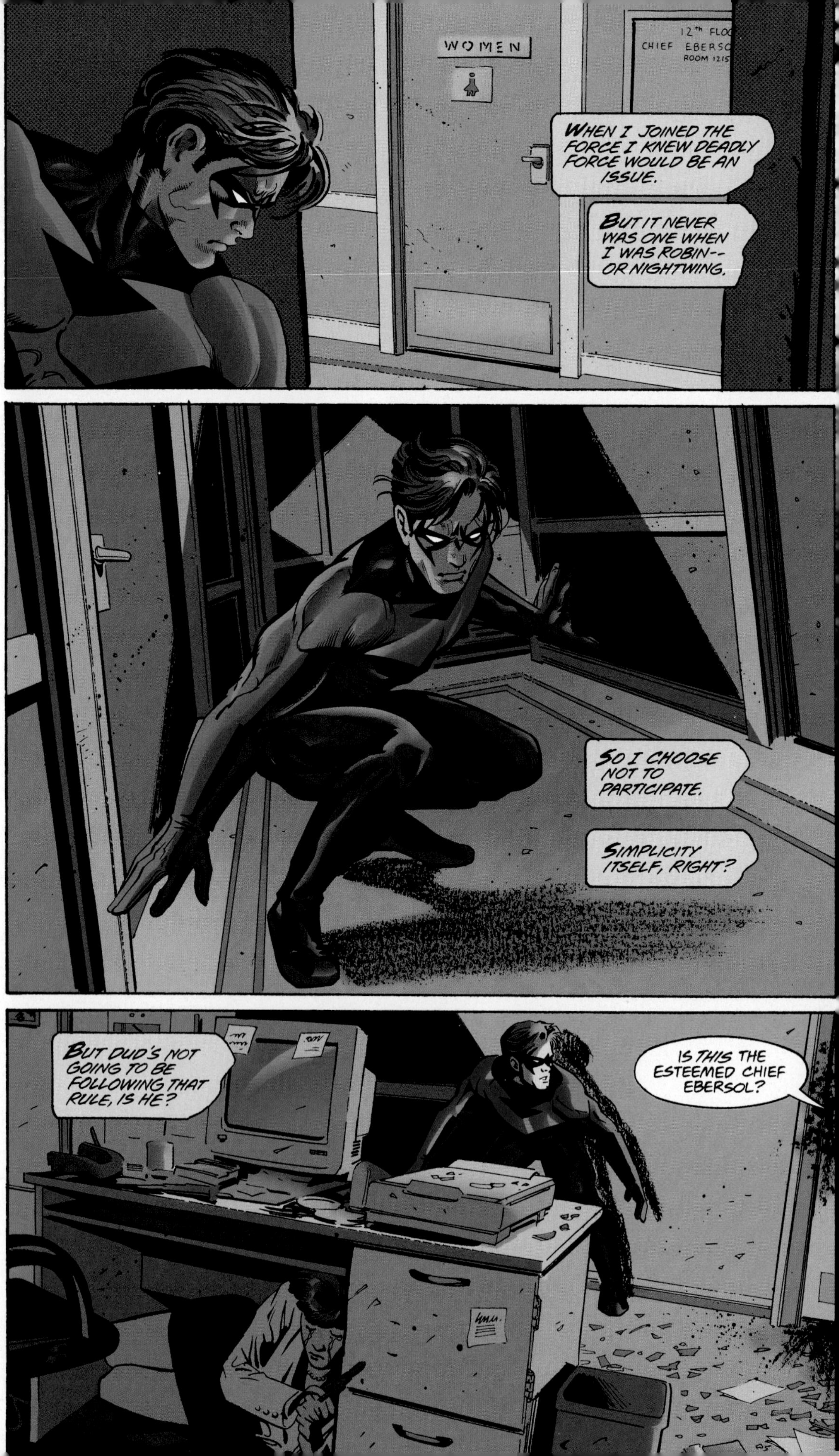
12th FLOO
CHIEF EBERSO
ROOM 1215
WOMEN
WHEN I JOINED THE FORCE I KNEW DEADLY FORCE WOULD BE AN ISSUE.
BUT IT NEVER WAS ONE WHEN I WAS ROBIN-- OR NIGHTWING.
SO I CHOOSE NOT TO PARTICIPATE.
SIMPLICITY ITSELF, RIGHT?
BUT DUD'S NOT GOING TO BE FOLLOWING THAT RULE, IS HE?
IS THIS THE ESTEEMED CHIEF EBERSOL?

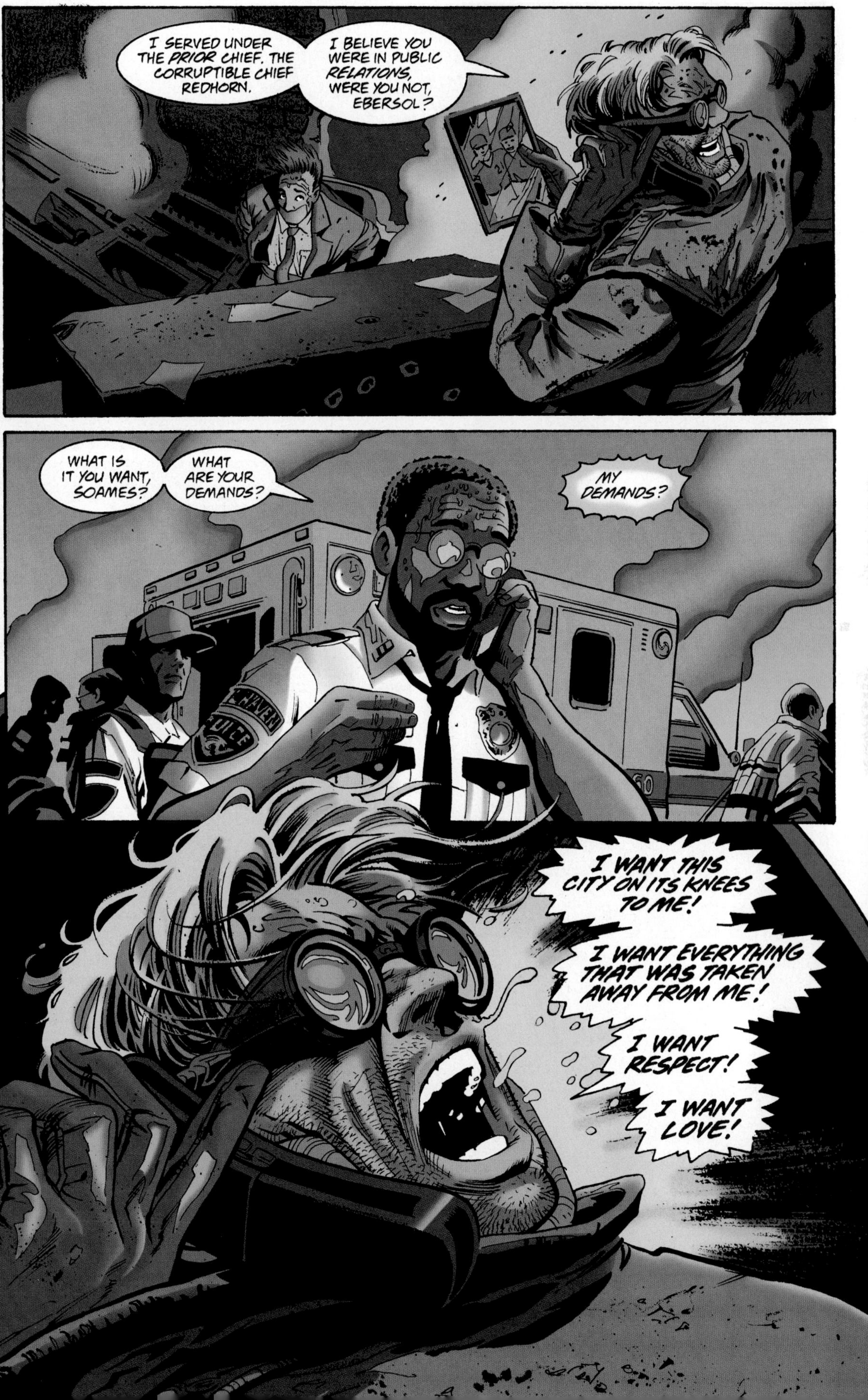
I SERVED UNDER THE PRIOR CHIEF. THE CORRUPTIBLE CHIEF REDHORN.
I BELIEVE YOU WERE IN PUBLIC RELATIONS, WERE YOU NOT, EBERSOL?
WHAT IS IT YOU WANT, SOAMES?
WHAT ARE YOUR DEMANDS?
MY DEMANDS?
I WANT THIS CITY ON ITS KNEES TO ME!
I WANT EVERYTHING THAT WAS TAKEN AWAY FROM ME!
I WANT RESPECT!
I WANT LOVE!

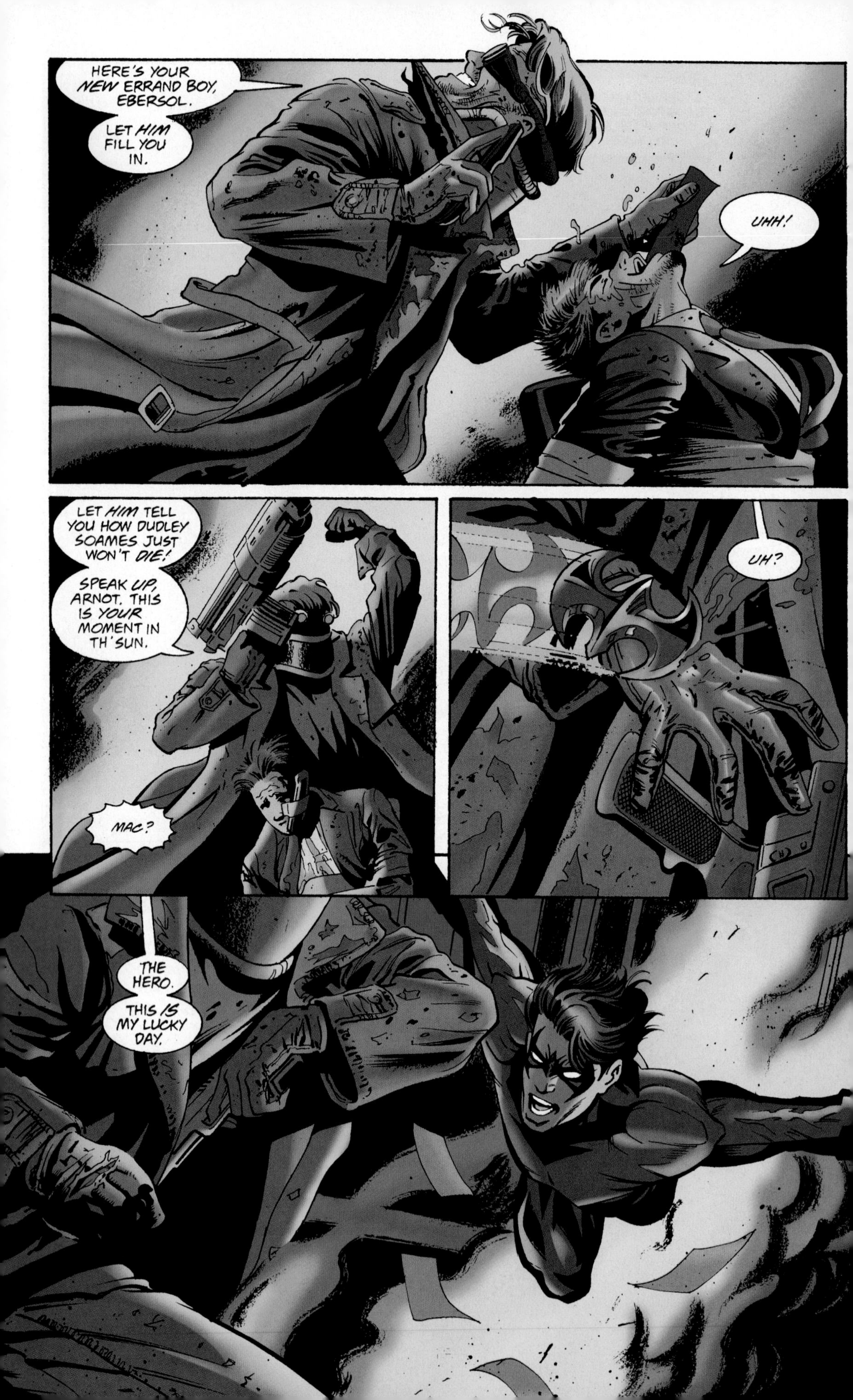
HERE'S YOUR NEW ERRAND BOY, EBERSOL.
LET HIM FILL YOU IN.
UHH!
LET HIM TELL YOU HOW DUDLEY SOAMES JUST WON'T DIE!
SPEAK UP, ARNOT. THIS IS YOUR MOMENT IN TH' SUN.
MAC?
UH?
THE HERO.
THIS IS MY LUCKY DAY.

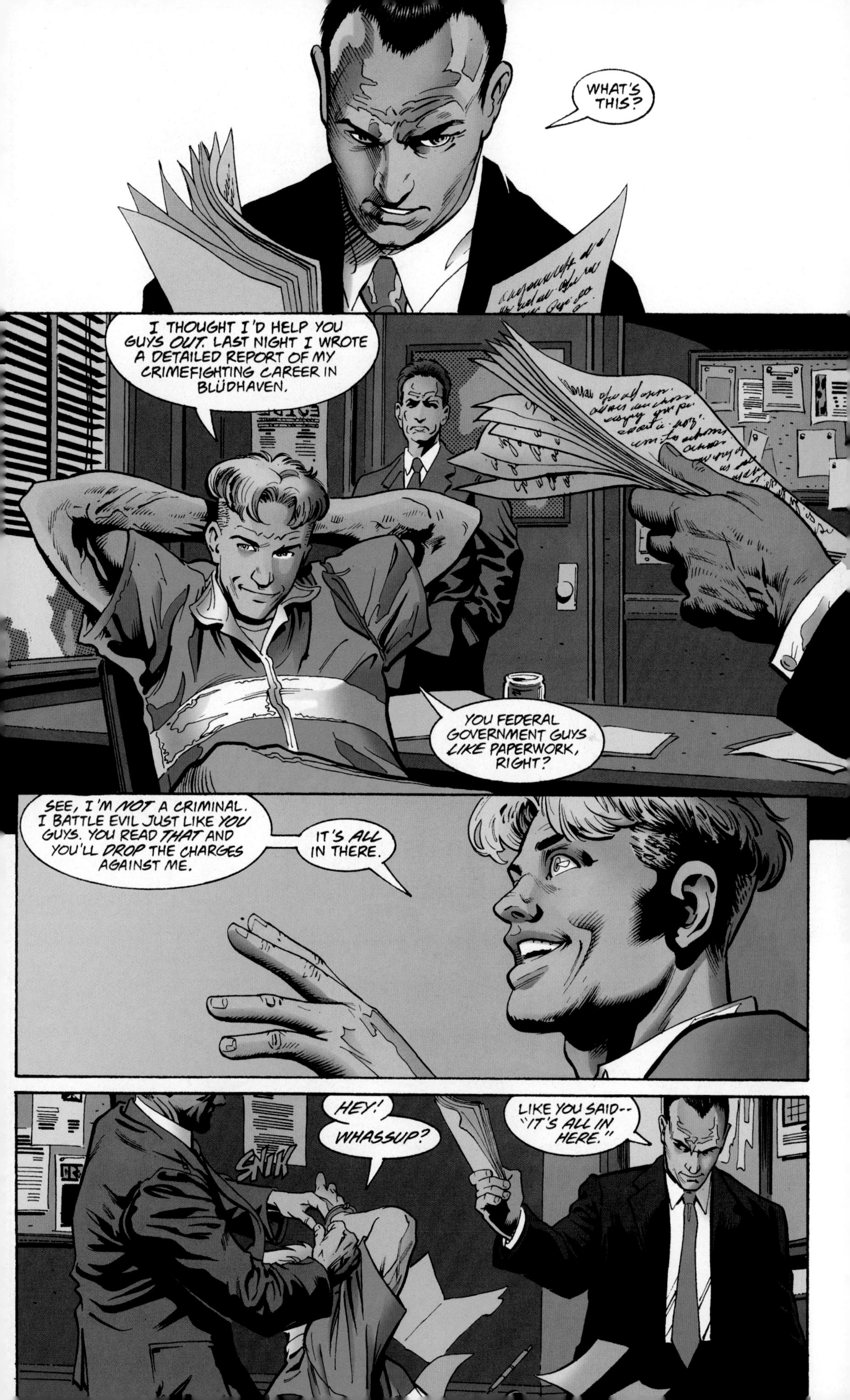
WHAT'S THIS?
I THOUGHT I'D HELP YOU GUYS OUT. LAST NIGHT I WROTE A DETAILED REPORT OF MY CRIMEFIGHTING CAREER IN BLÜDHAVEN.
YOU FEDERAL GOVERNMENT GUYS LIKE PAPERWORK, RIGHT?
SEE, I'M NOT A CRIMINAL. I BATTLE EVIL JUST LIKE YOU GUYS. YOU READ THAT AND YOU'LL DROP THE CHARGES AGAINST ME.
IT'S ALL IN THERE.
HEY! WHASSUP?
SNIK
LIKE YOU SAID-- "IT'S ALL IN HERE."

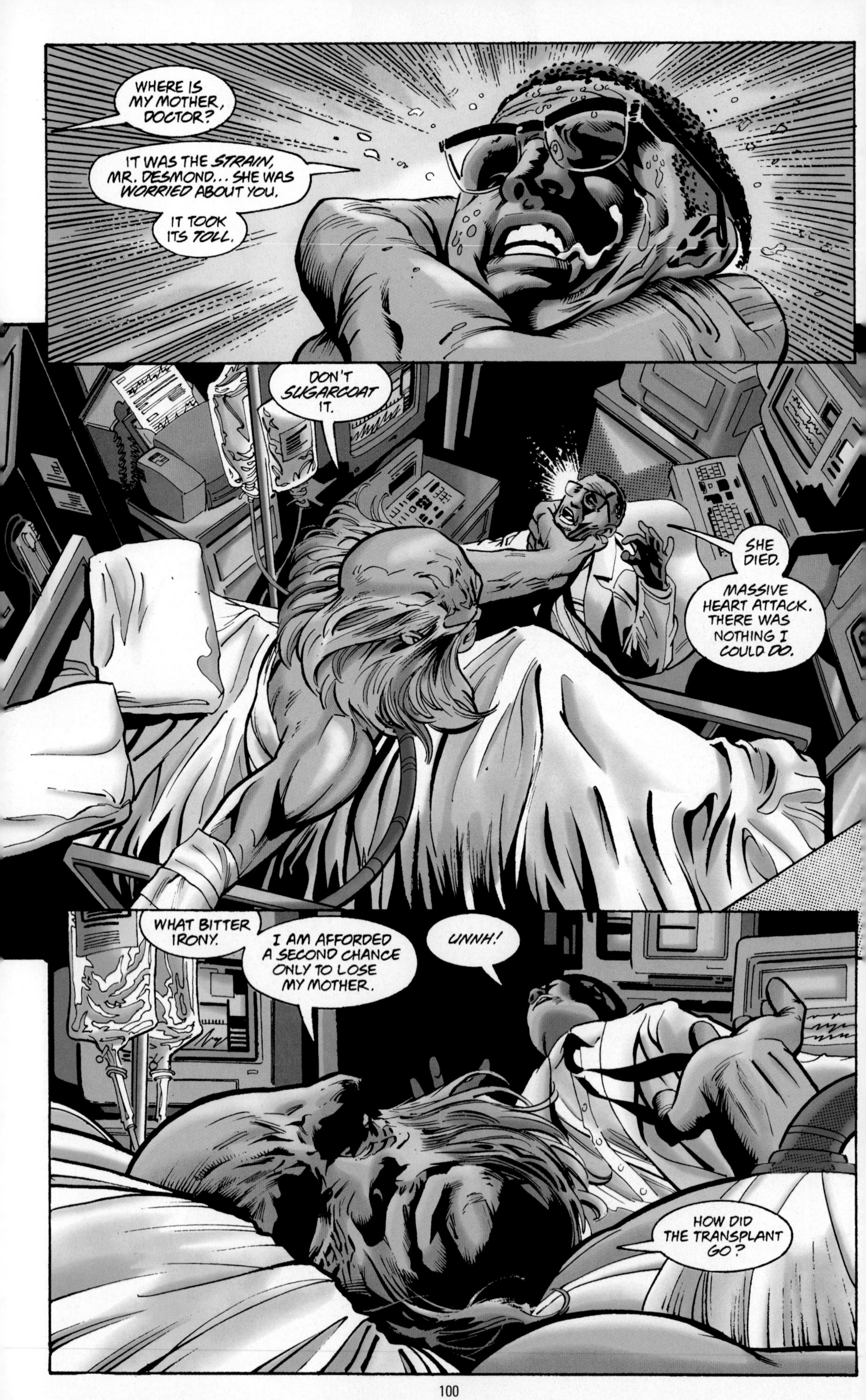
WHERE IS MY MOTHER, DOCTOR?
IT WAS THE STRAIN, MR. DESMOND... SHE WAS WORRIED ABOUT YOU.
IT TOOK ITS TOLL.
DON'T SUGARCOAT IT.
SHE DIED.
MASSIVE HEART ATTACK. THERE WAS NOTHING I COULD DO.
WHAT BITTER IRONY.
I AM AFFORDED A SECOND CHANCE ONLY TO LOSE MY MOTHER.
UNNH!
HOW DID THE TRANSPLANT GO?

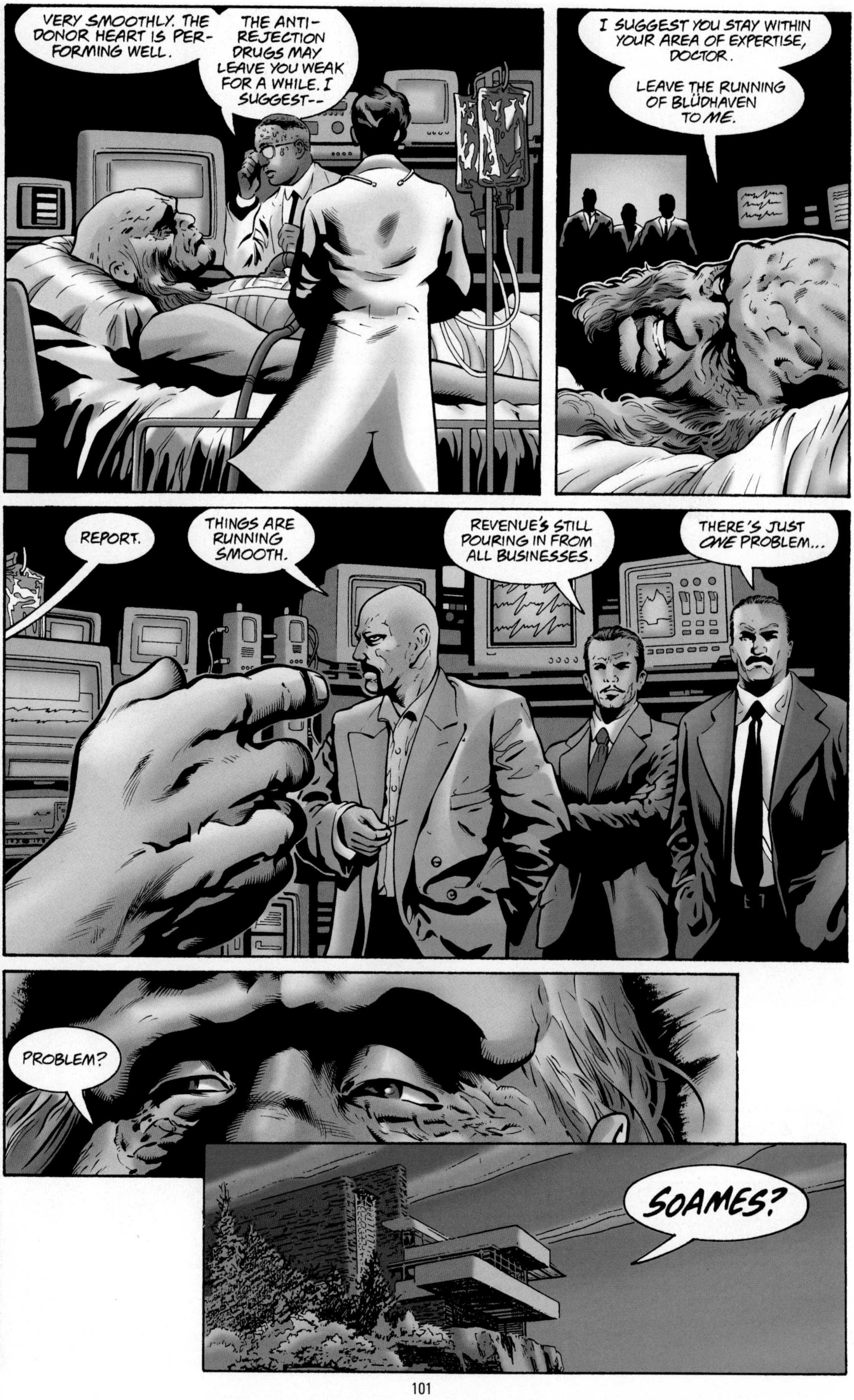
VERY SMOOTHLY. THE DONOR HEART IS PERFORMING WELL.
THE ANTI-REJECTION DRUGS MAY LEAVE YOU WEAK FOR A WHILE. I SUGGEST--
I SUGGEST YOU STAY WITHIN YOUR AREA OF EXPERTISE, DOCTOR.
LEAVE THE RUNNING OF BLÜDHAVEN TO *ME*.
REPORT.
THINGS ARE RUNNING SMOOTH.
REVENUE'S STILL POURING IN FROM ALL BUSINESSES.
THERE'S JUST *ONE* PROBLEM...
PROBLEM?
SOAMES?

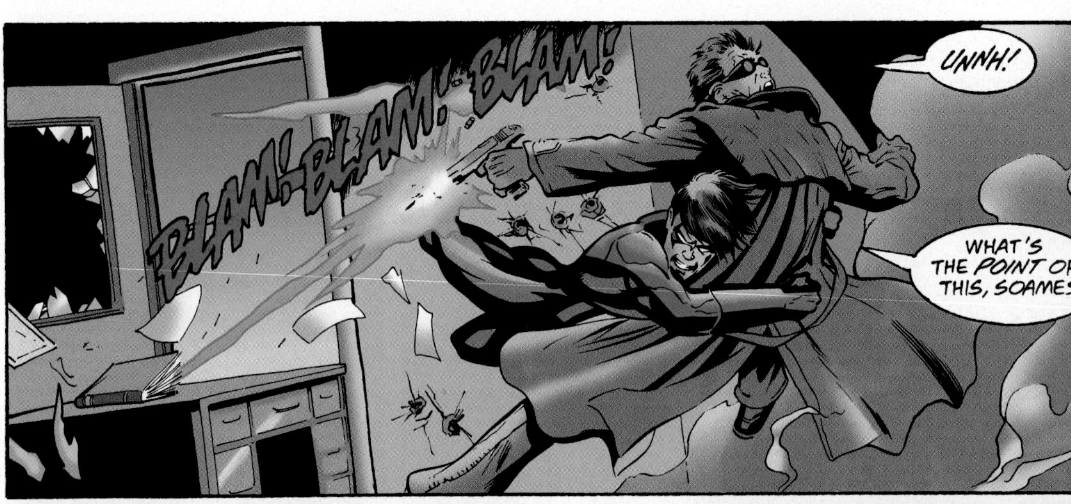
BLAM! BLAM! BLAM!
UNNH!
WHAT'S THE POINT OF THIS, SOAMES?

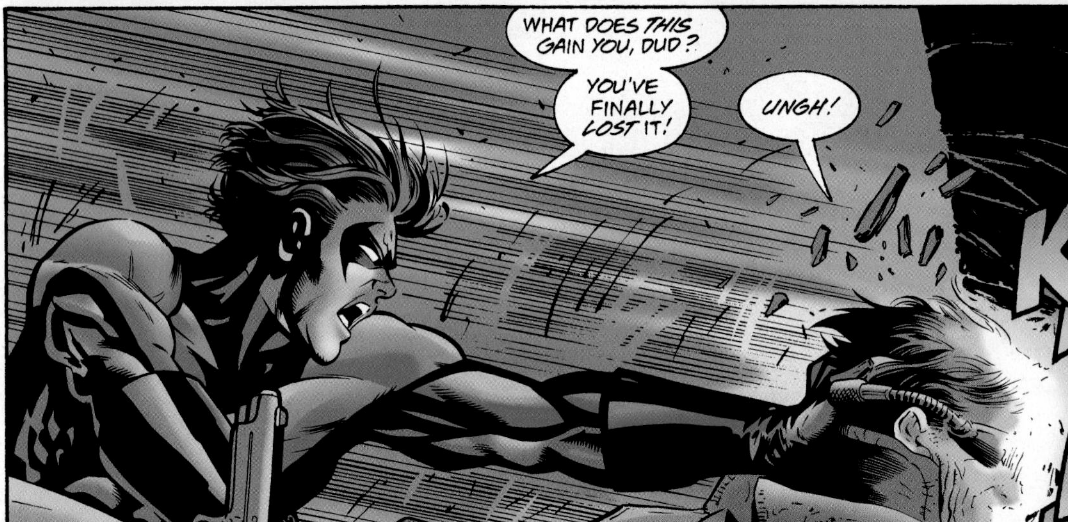
WHAT DOES THIS GAIN YOU, DUD?
YOU'VE FINALLY LOST IT!
UNGH!

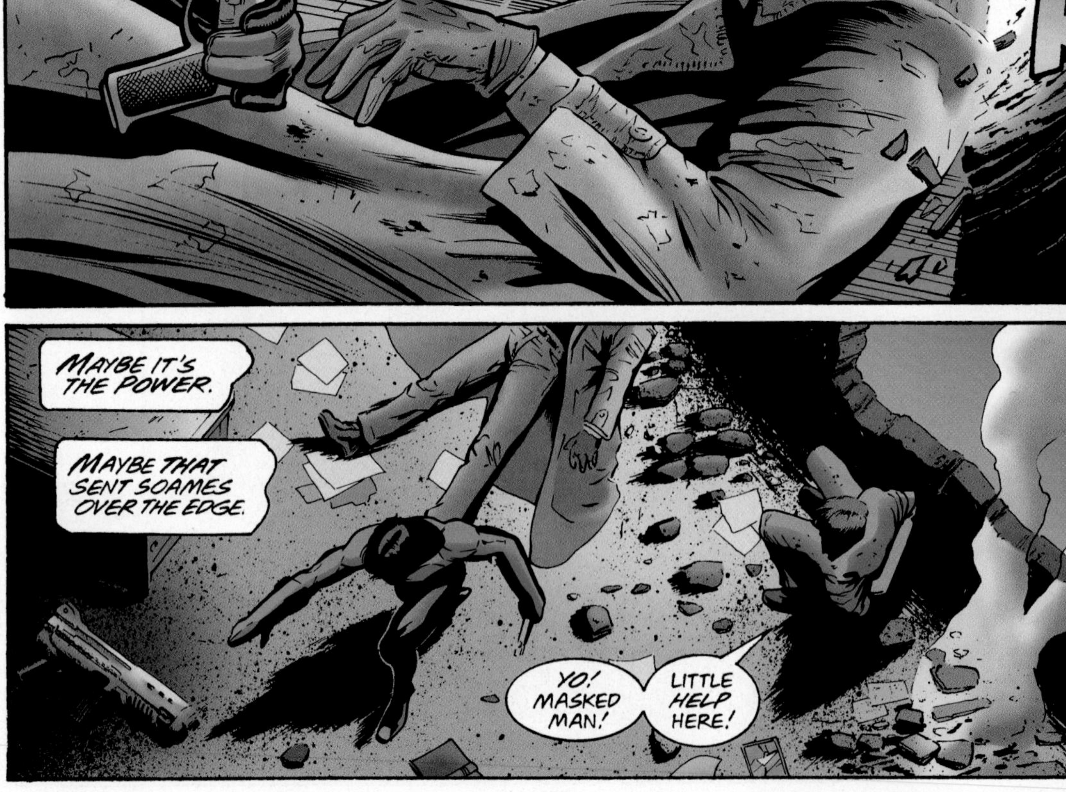
MAYBE IT'S THE POWER.
MAYBE THAT SENT SOAMES OVER THE EDGE.
YO! MASKED MAN!
LITTLE HELP HERE!

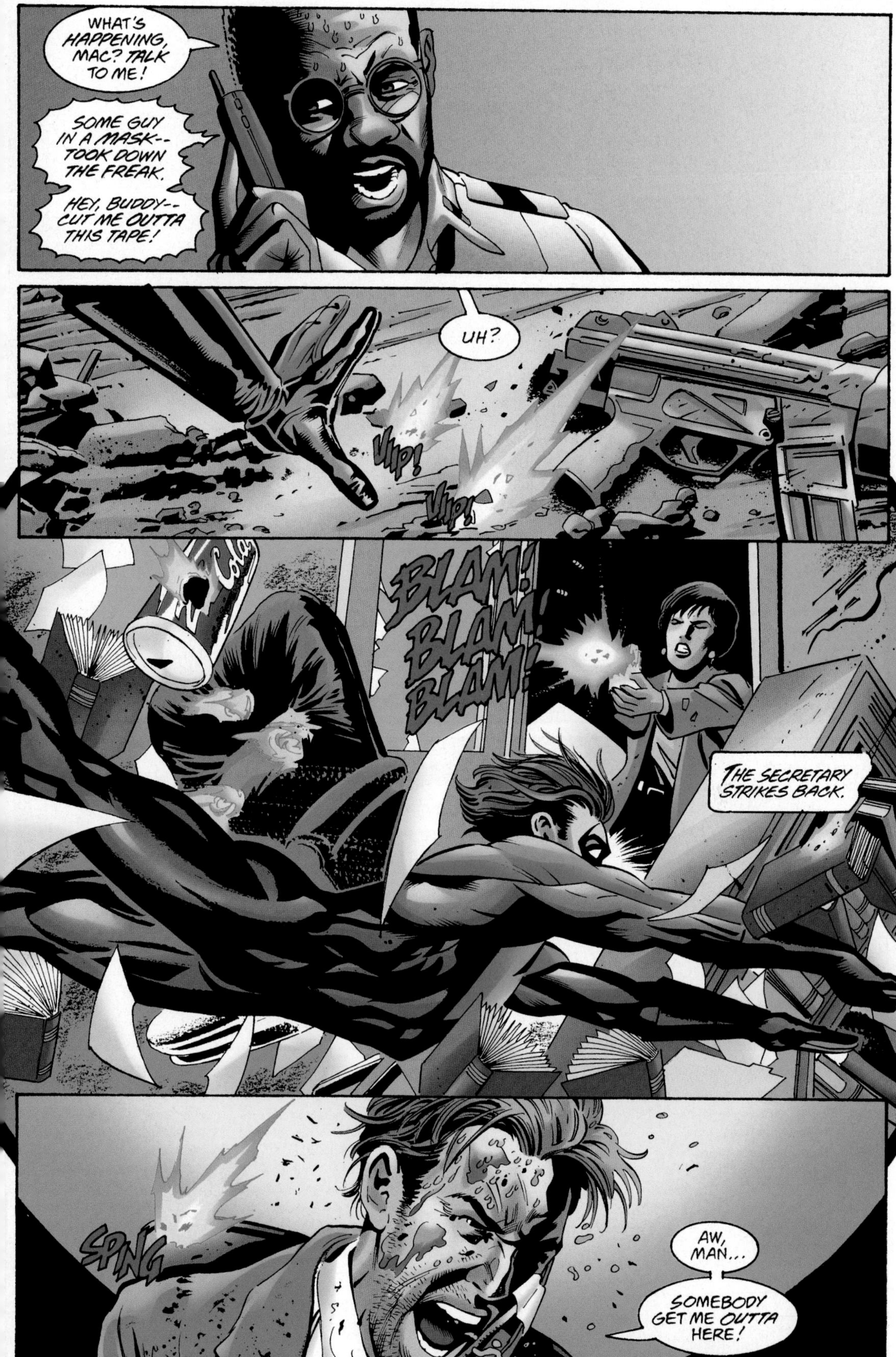
WHAT'S HAPPENING, MAC? TALK TO ME!
SOME GUY IN A MASK-- TOOK DOWN THE FREAK.
HEY, BUDDY-- CUT ME OUTTA THIS TAPE!
UH?
VIIP!
VIIP!
BLAM! BLAM! BLAM!
THE SECRETARY STRIKES BACK.
SPING
AW, MAN...
SOMEBODY GET ME OUTTA HERE!

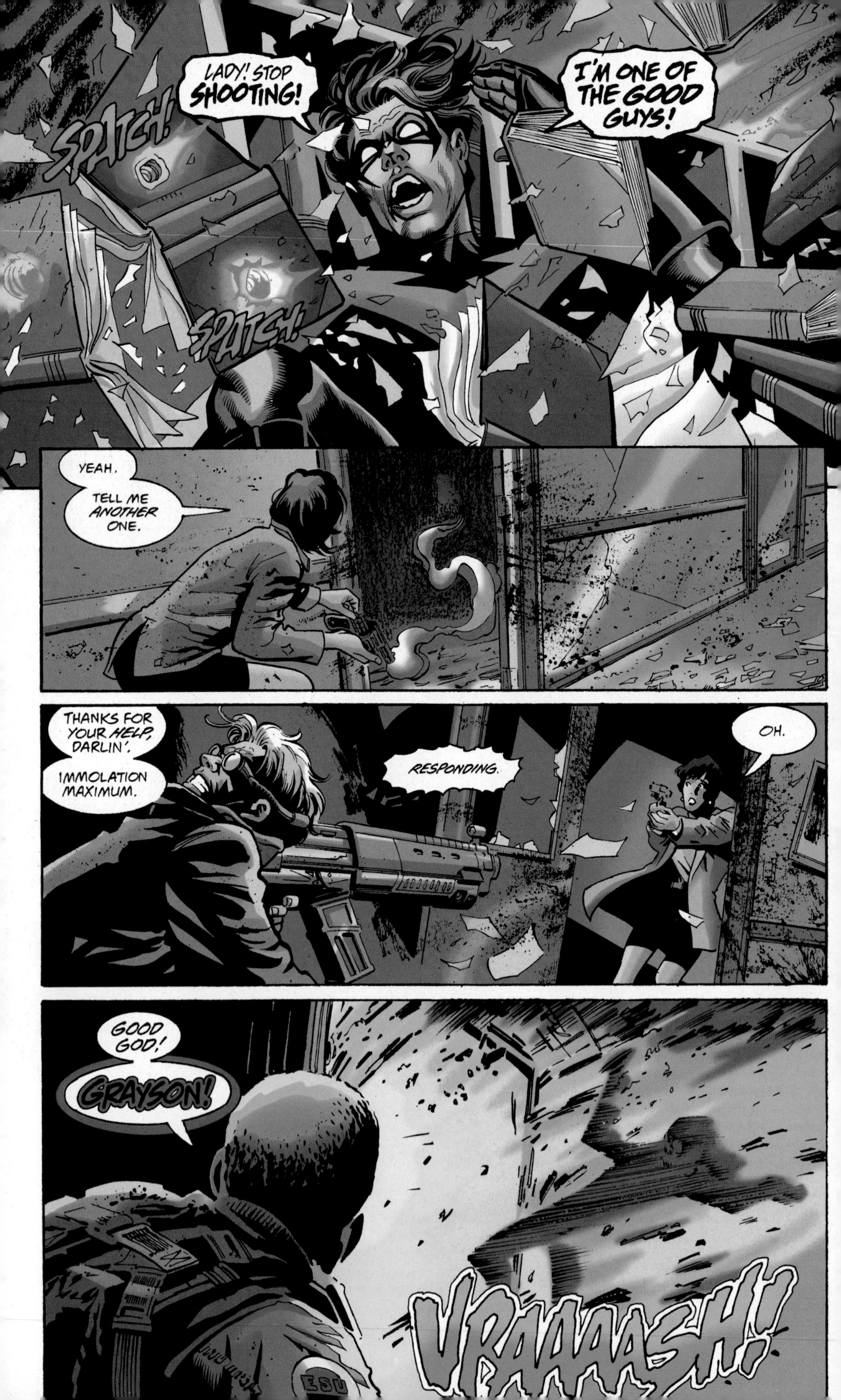
SPATCH!
LADY! STOP SHOOTING!
I'M ONE OF THE GOOD GUYS!
SPATCH!
YEAH.
TELL ME ANOTHER ONE.
THANKS FOR YOUR HELP, DARLIN'.
IMMOLATION MAXIMUM.
RESPONDING.
OH.
GOOD GOD!
GRAYSON!
VRAAAASH!
ESU

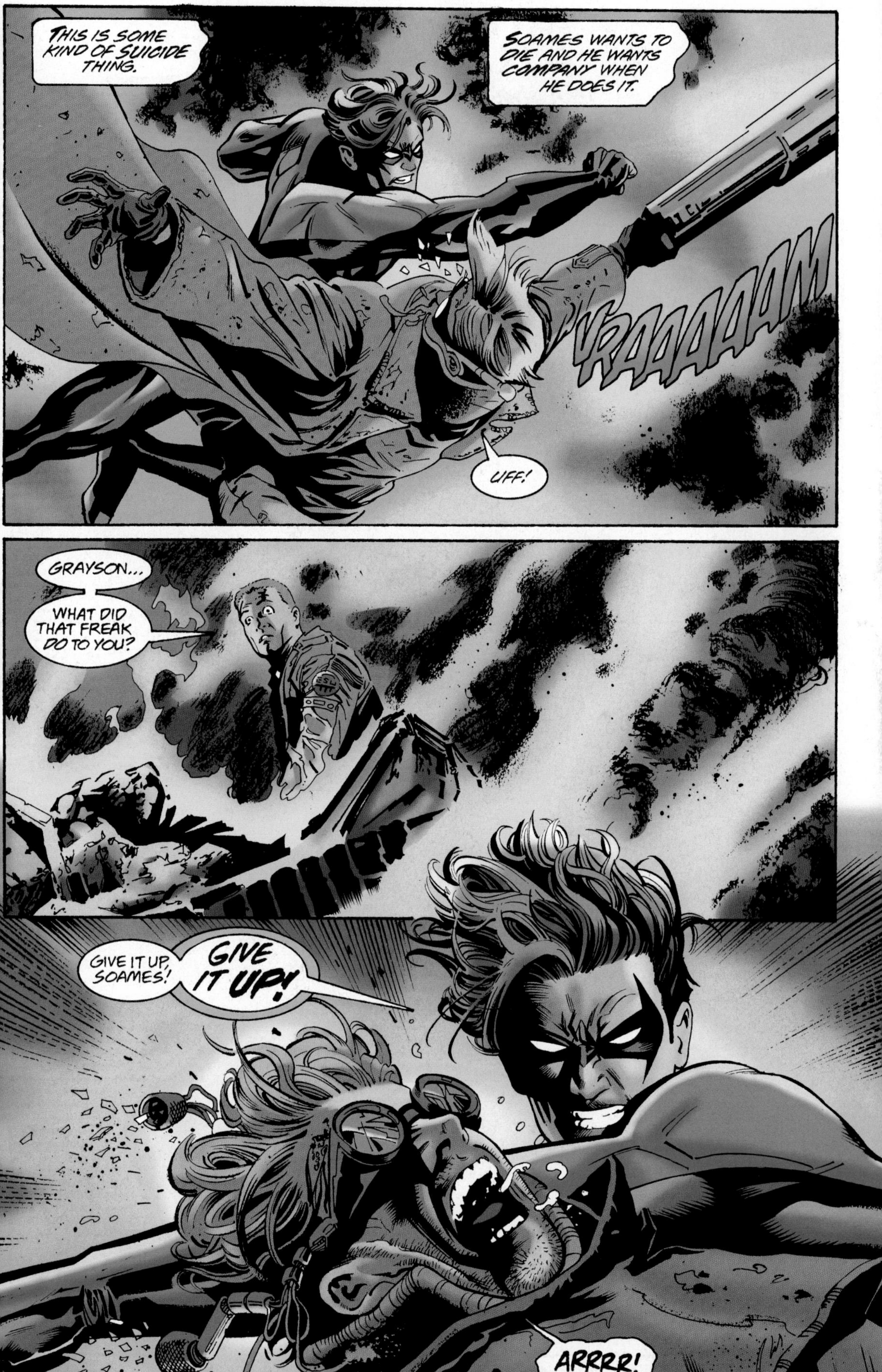
THIS IS SOME KIND OF SUICIDE THING.
SOAMES WANTS TO DIE AND HE WANTS COMPANY WHEN HE DOES IT.
VRAAAAAAM
UFF!
GRAYSON...
WHAT DID THAT FREAK DO TO YOU?
GIVE IT UP, SOAMES!
GIVE IT UP!
ARRRR!

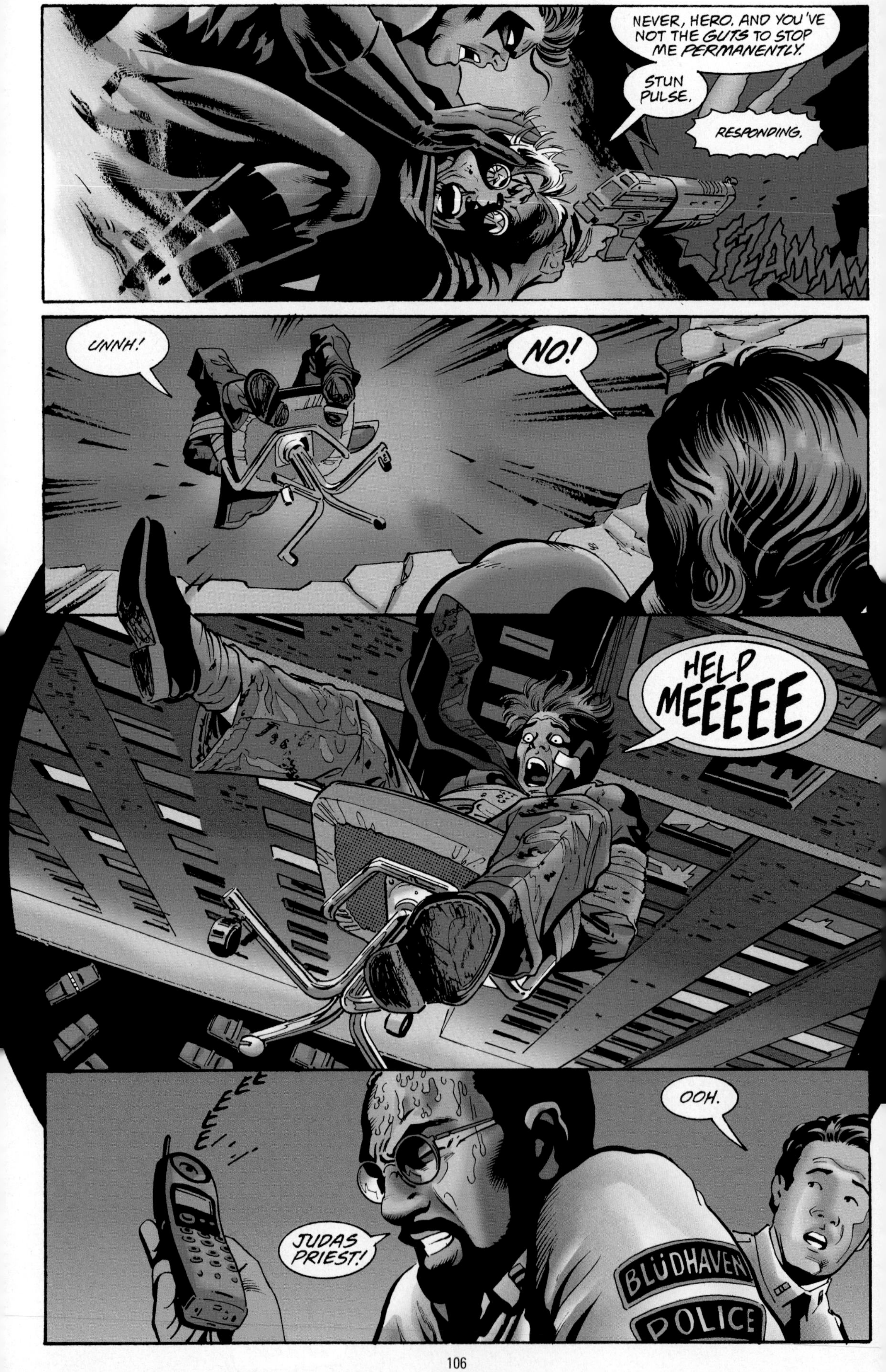
NEVER, HERO, AND YOU'VE NOT THE GUTS TO STOP ME PERMANENTLY.
STUN PULSE.
RESPONDING.
FLAMMM
UNNH!
NO!
HELP MEEEEE
EEEEE
OOH.
JUDAS PRIEST!
BLÜDHAVEN POLICE

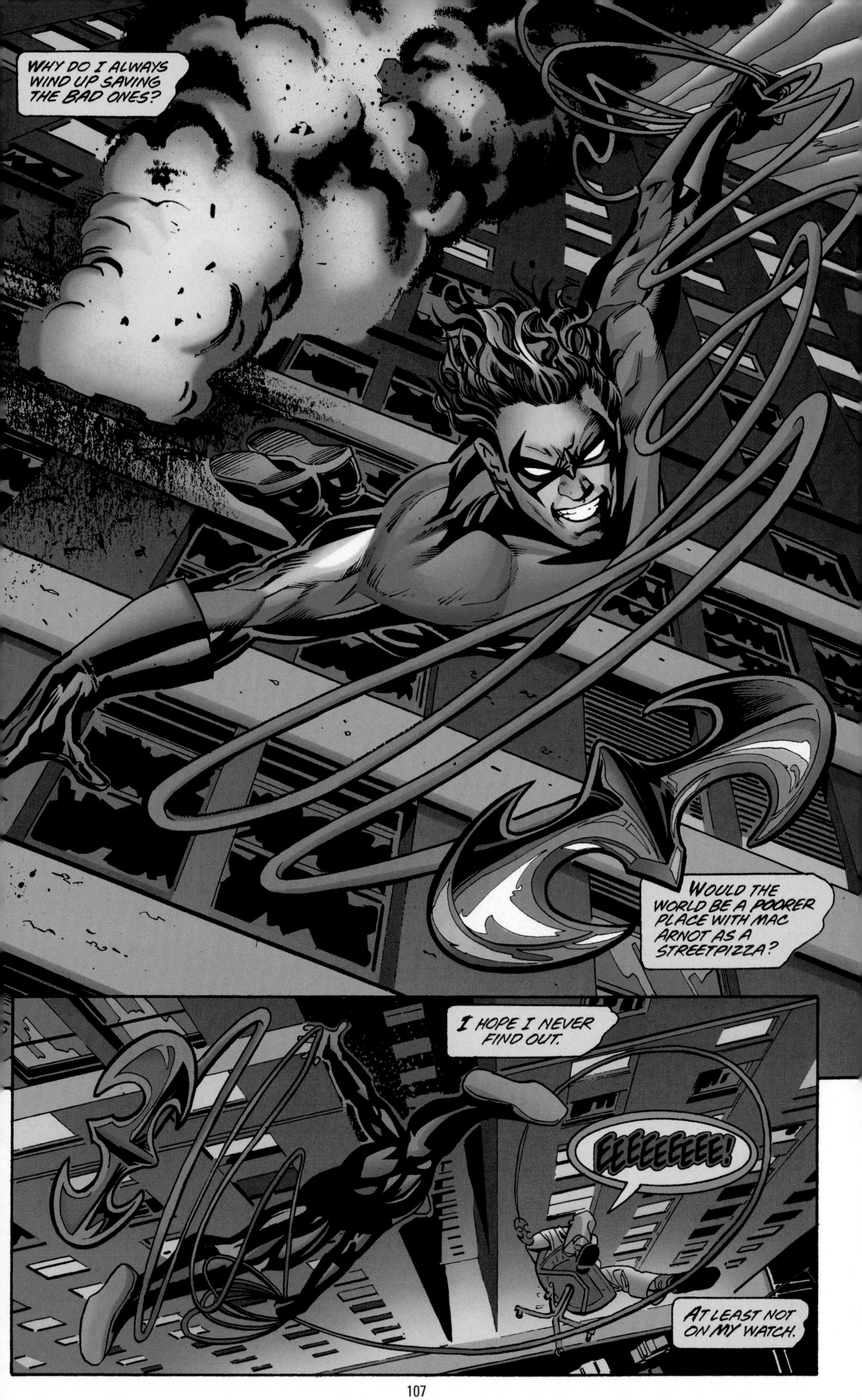
WHY DO I ALWAYS WIND UP SAVING THE BAD ONES?
WOULD THE WORLD BE A POORER PLACE WITH MAC ARNOT AS A STREETPIZZA?
I HOPE I NEVER FIND OUT.
EEEEEEEEE!
AT LEAST NOT ON MY WATCH.

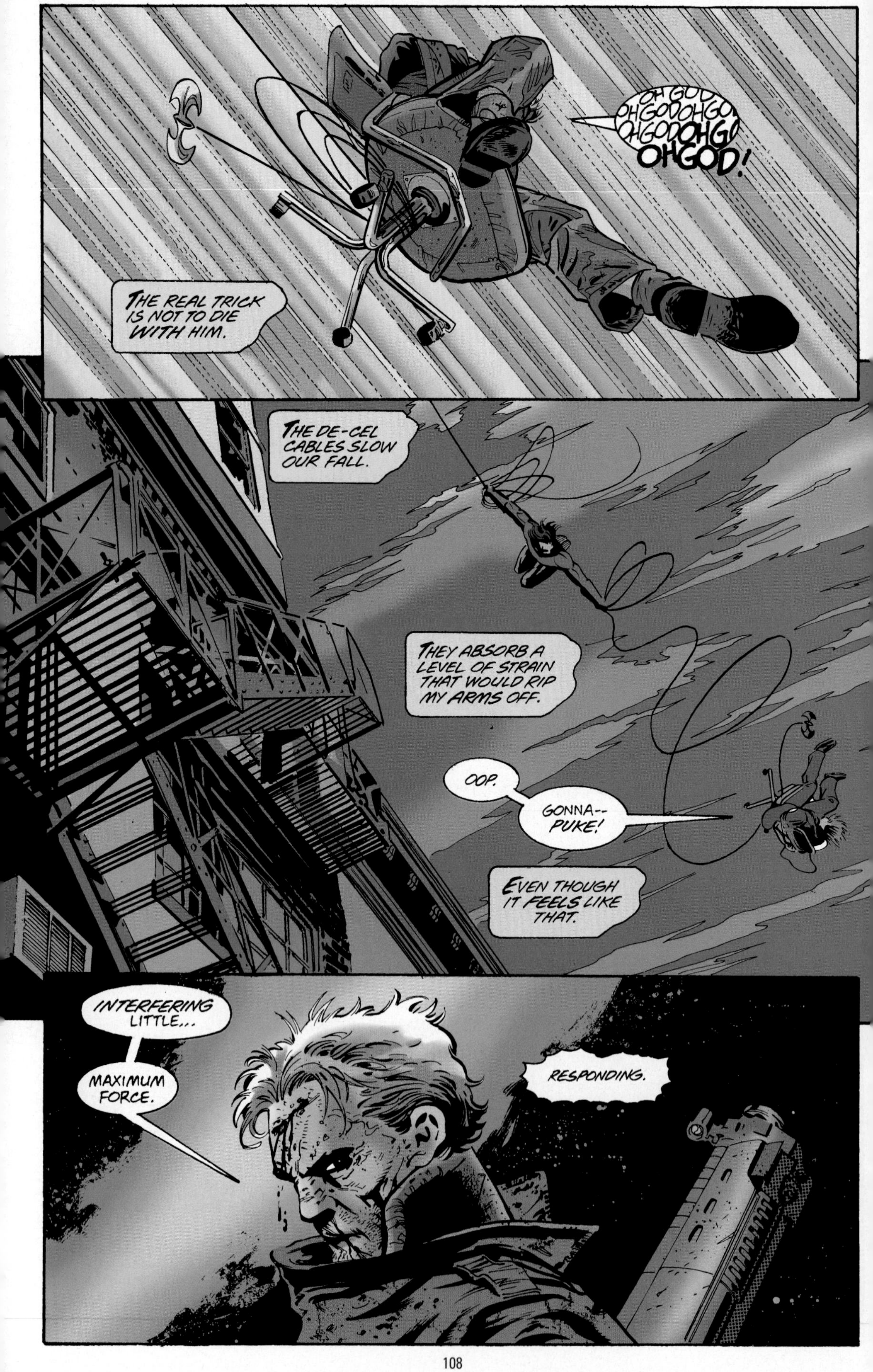
OHGOD OHGODOHGOD OHGODOHG! OHGOD!
THE REAL TRICK IS NOT TO DIE WITH HIM.
THE DE-CEL CABLES SLOW OUR FALL.
THEY ABSORB A LEVEL OF STRAIN THAT WOULD RIP MY ARMS OFF.
OOP.
GONNA-- PUKE!
EVEN THOUGH IT FEELS LIKE THAT.
INTERFERING LITTLE...
MAXIMUM FORCE.
RESPONDING.

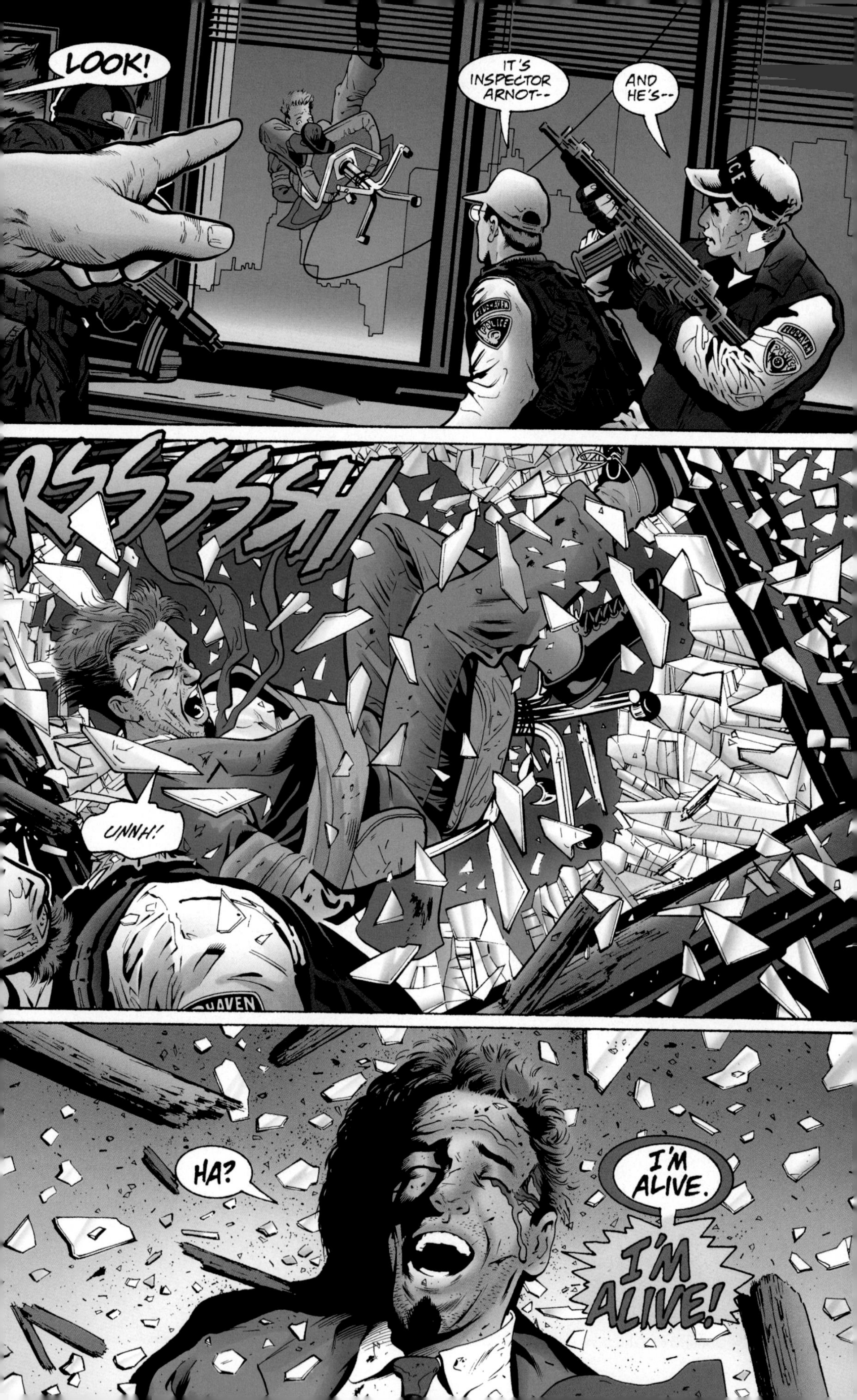
LOOK!
IT'S INSPECTOR ARNOT--
AND HE'S--
RSSSSSH
UNNH!
HA?
I'M ALIVE.
I'M ALIVE!

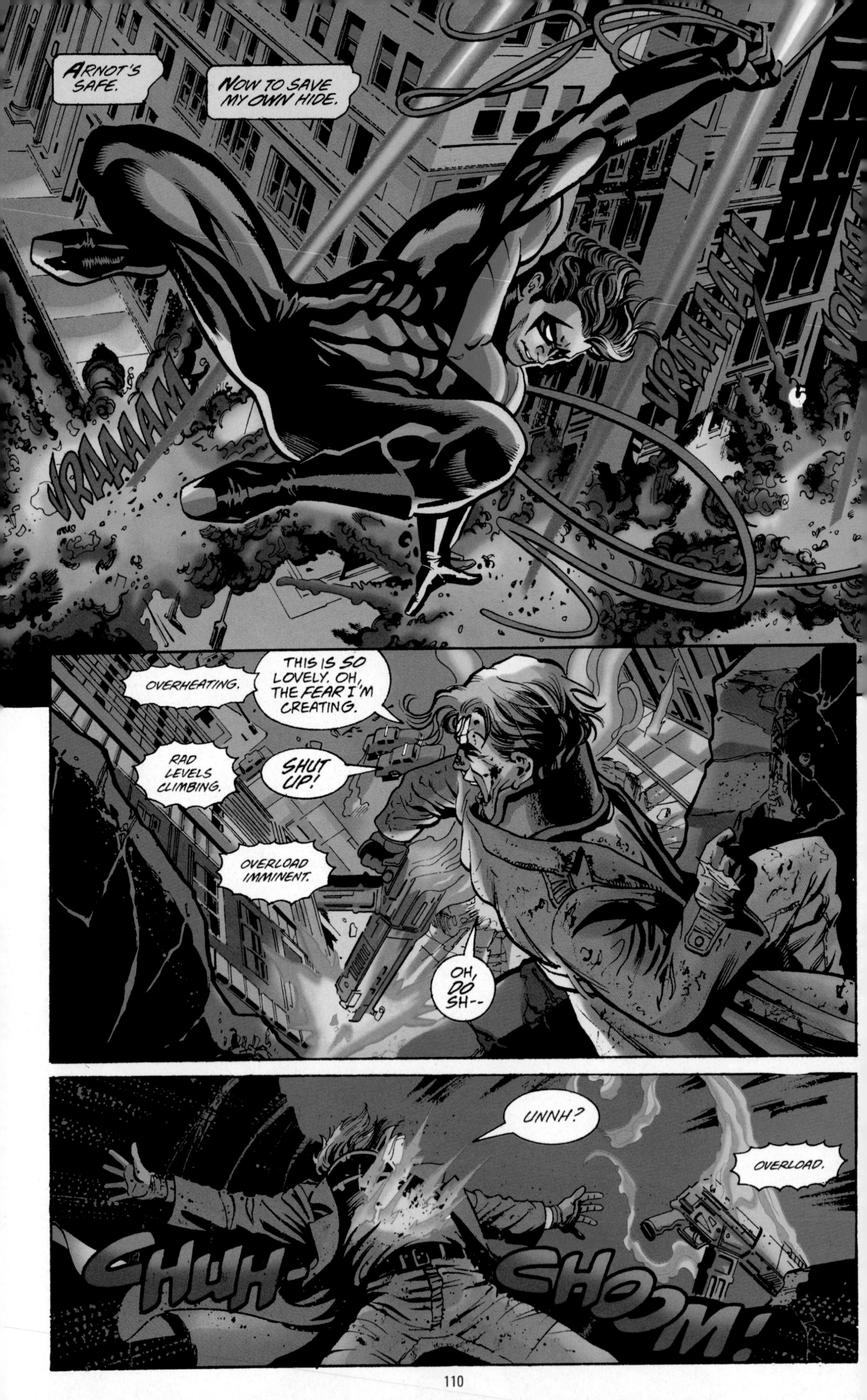
ARNOT'S SAFE.
NOW TO SAVE MY OWN HIDE.
VRAAAAM
OVERHEATING.
THIS IS SO LOVELY. OH, THE FEAR I'M CREATING.
RAD LEVELS CLIMBING.
SHUT UP!
OVERLOAD IMMINENT.
OH, DO SH--
UNNH?
OVERLOAD.
CHUH-CHOOM!

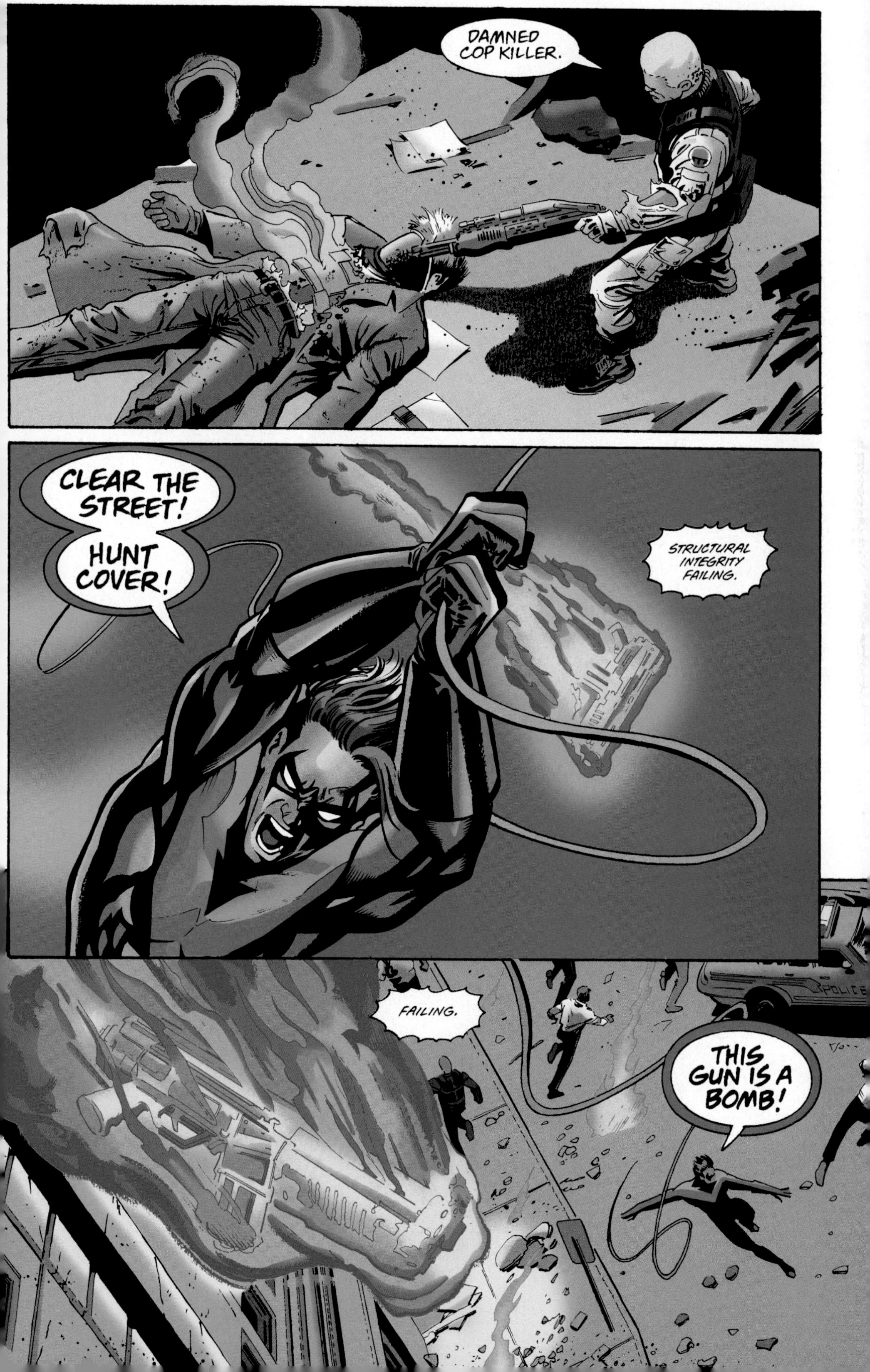
DAMNED COP KILLER.
CLEAR THE STREET!
HUNT COVER!
STRUCTURAL INTEGRITY FAILING.
FAILING.
THIS GUN IS A BOMB!
POLICE

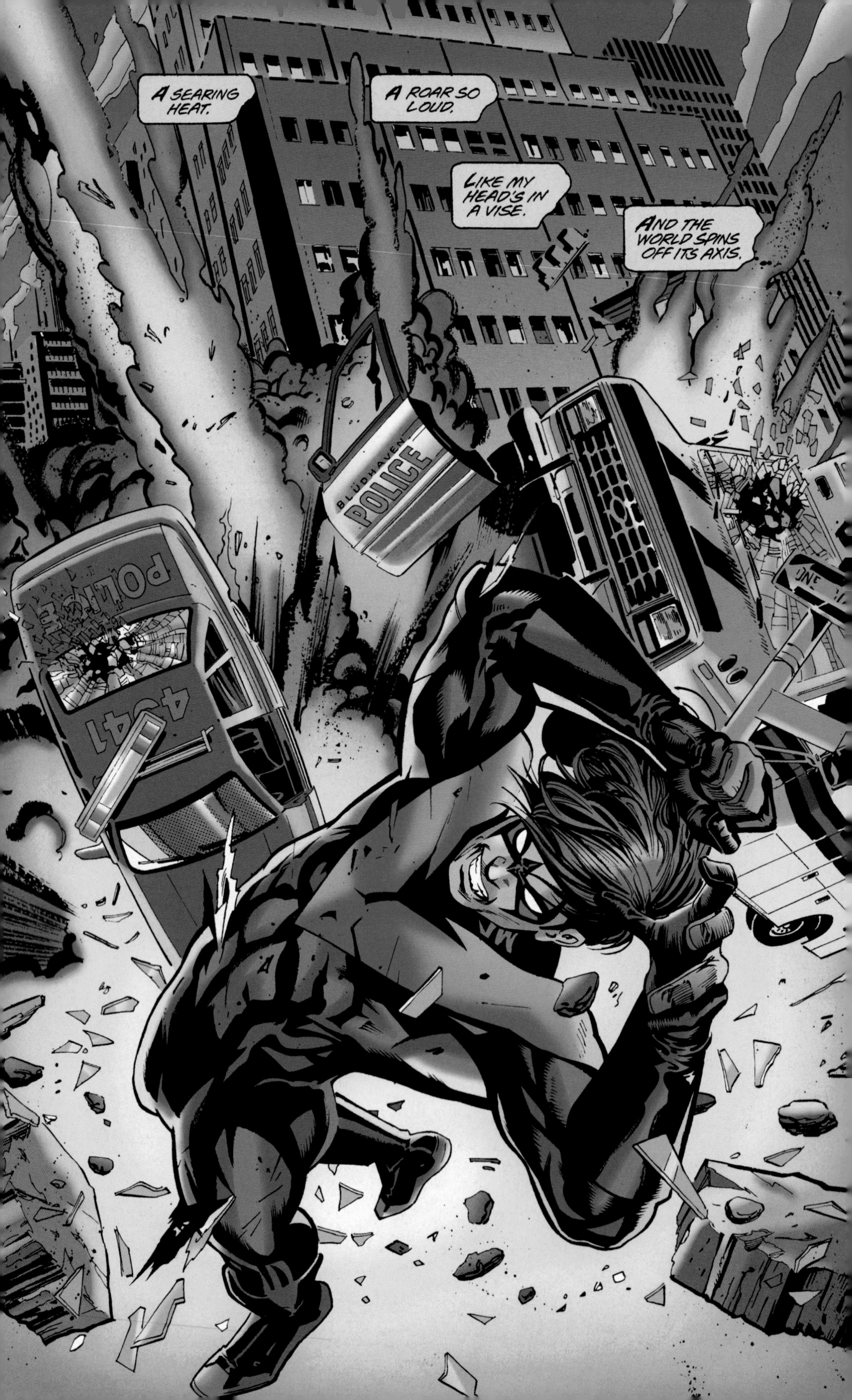
A SEARING HEAT.
A ROAR SO LOUD.
LIKE MY HEAD'S IN A VISE.
AND THE WORLD SPINS OFF ITS AXIS.
BLÜDHAVEN POLICE
POLICE
4041

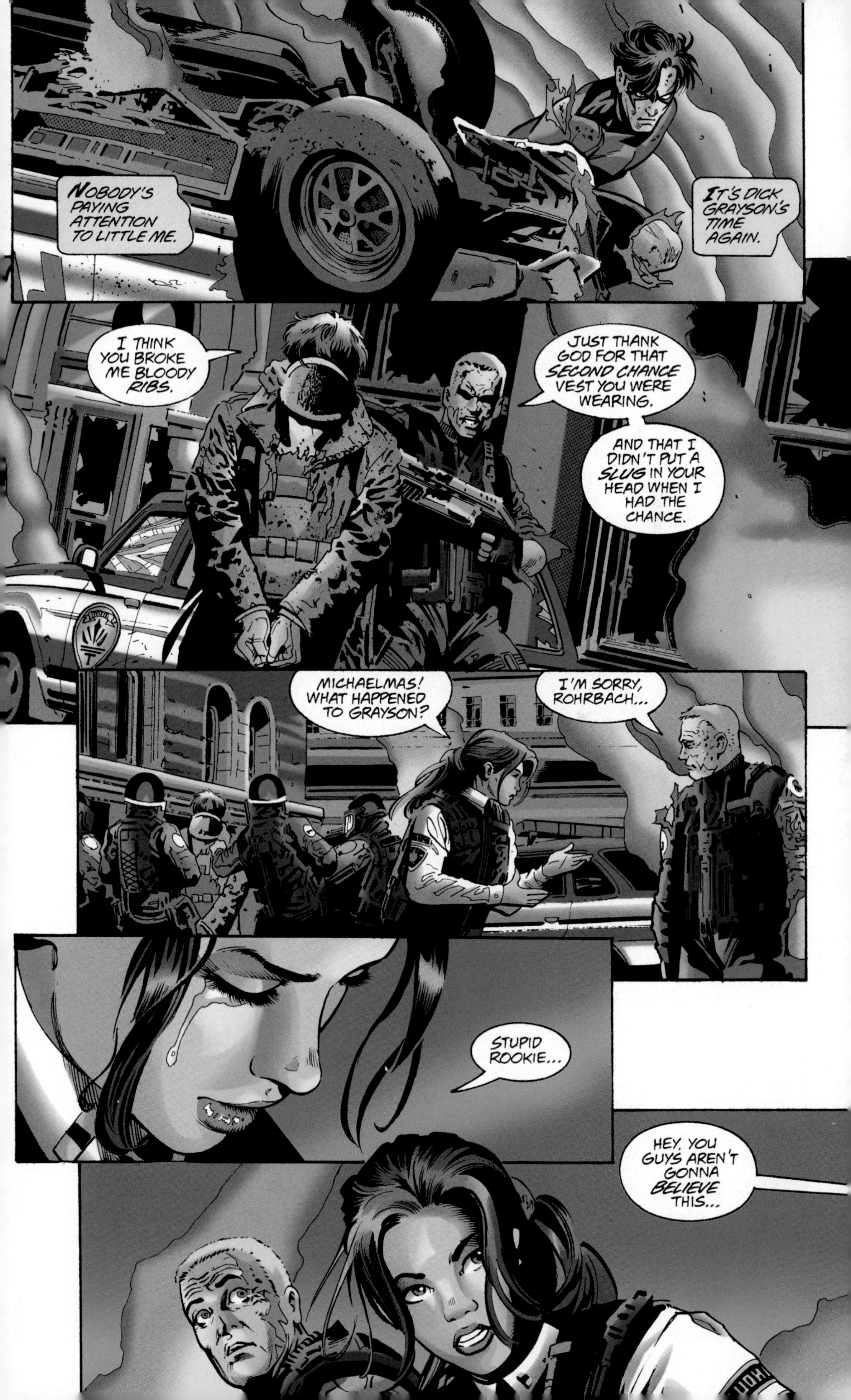
NOBODY'S PAYING ATTENTION TO LITTLE ME.
IT'S DICK GRAYSON'S TIME AGAIN.
I THINK YOU BROKE ME BLOODY RIBS.
JUST THANK GOD FOR THAT SECOND CHANCE VEST YOU WERE WEARING.
AND THAT I DIDN'T PUT A SLUG IN YOUR HEAD WHEN I HAD THE CHANCE.
MICHAELMAS! WHAT HAPPENED TO GRAYSON?
I'M SORRY, ROHRBACH...
STUPID ROOKIE...
HEY, YOU GUYS AREN'T GONNA BELIEVE THIS...

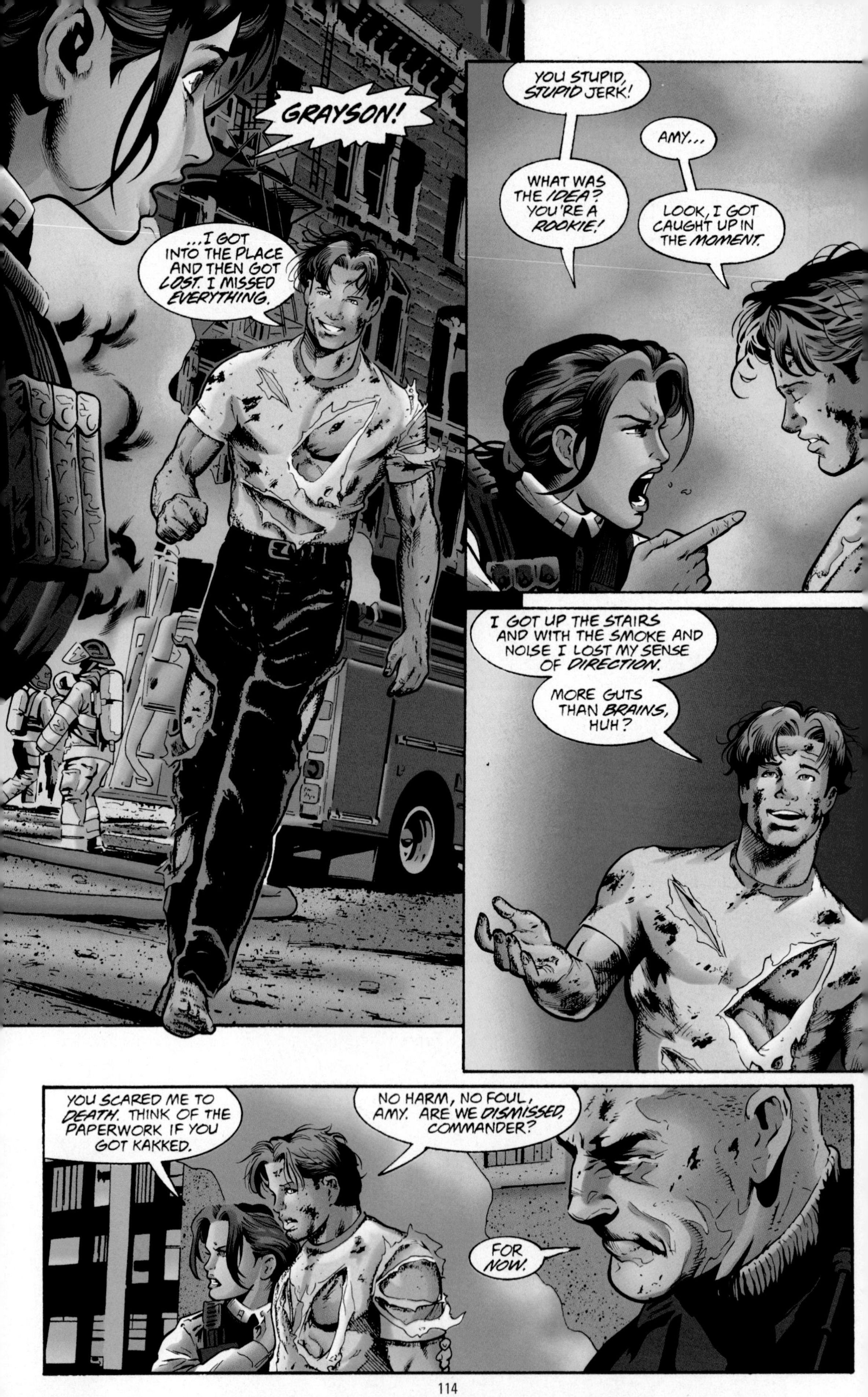
GRAYSON!
...I GOT INTO THE PLACE AND THEN GOT LOST. I MISSED EVERYTHING.
YOU STUPID, STUPID JERK!
WHAT WAS THE IDEA? YOU'RE A ROOKIE!
AMY...
LOOK, I GOT CAUGHT UP IN THE MOMENT.
I GOT UP THE STAIRS AND WITH THE SMOKE AND NOISE I LOST MY SENSE OF DIRECTION.
MORE GUTS THAN BRAINS, HUH?
YOU SCARED ME TO DEATH. THINK OF THE PAPERWORK IF YOU GOT KAKKED.
NO HARM, NO FOUL, AMY. ARE WE DISMISSED, COMMANDER?
FOR NOW.

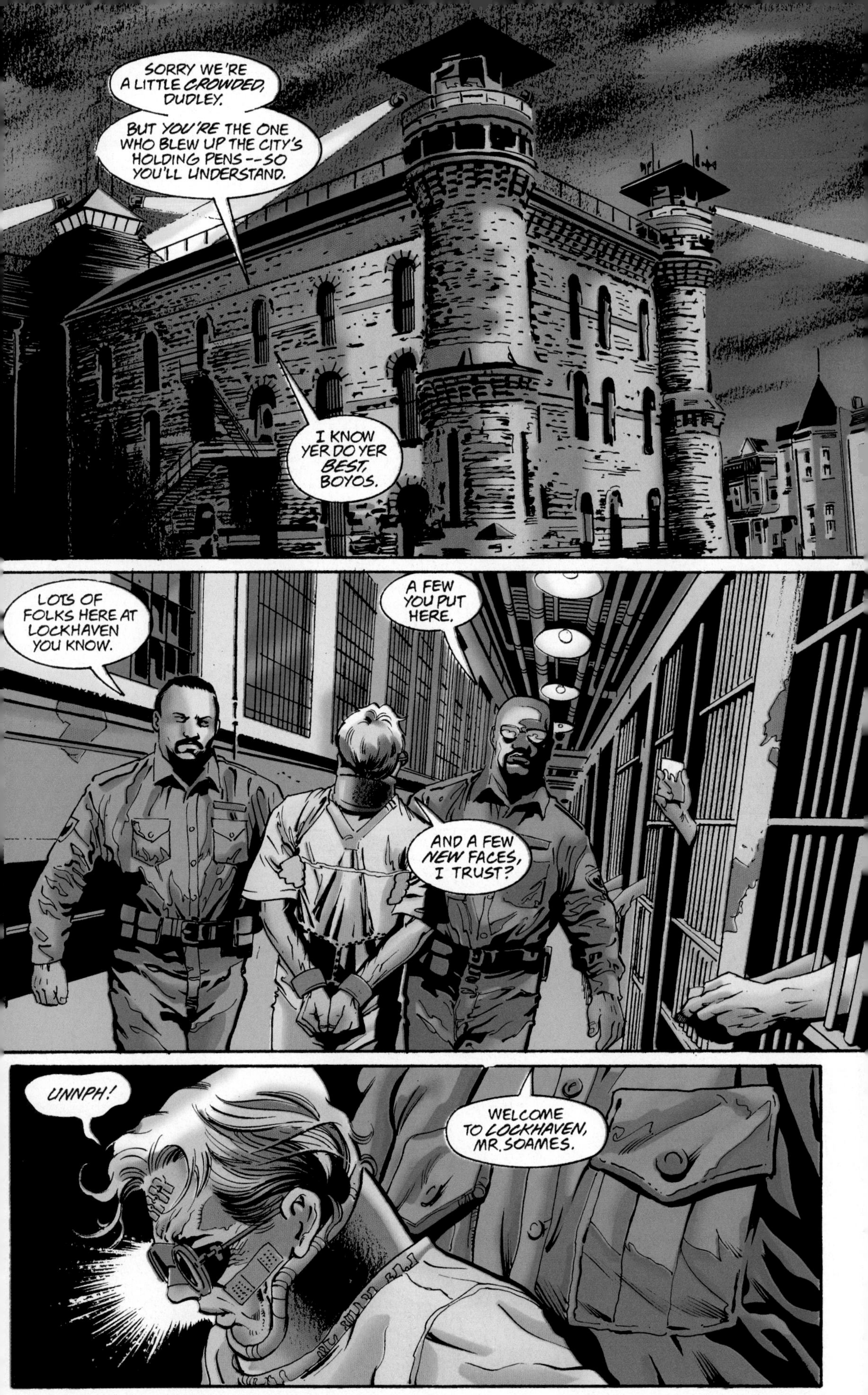
SORRY WE'RE A LITTLE CROWDED, DUDLEY.
BUT YOU'RE THE ONE WHO BLEW UP THE CITY'S HOLDING PENS--SO YOU'LL UNDERSTAND.
I KNOW YER DO YER BEST, BOYOS.
LOTS OF FOLKS HERE AT LOCKHAVEN YOU KNOW.
A FEW YOU PUT HERE.
AND A FEW NEW FACES, I TRUST?
UNNPH!
WELCOME TO LOCKHAVEN, MR. SOAMES.

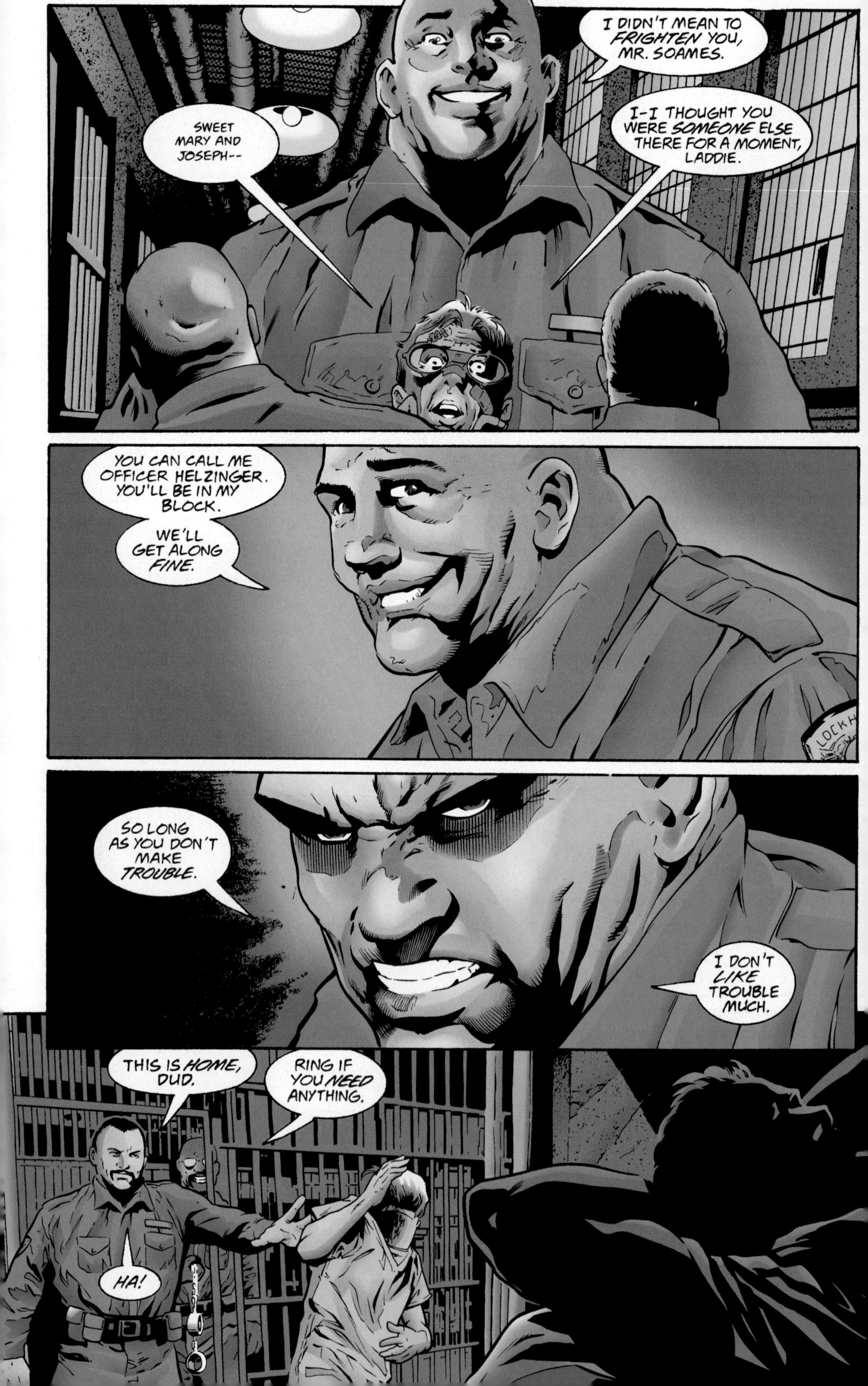
SWEET MARY AND JOSEPH--
I DIDN'T MEAN TO FRIGHTEN YOU, MR. SOAMES.
I-I THOUGHT YOU WERE SOMEONE ELSE THERE FOR A MOMENT, LADDIE.
YOU CAN CALL ME OFFICER HELZINGER. YOU'LL BE IN MY BLOCK.
WE'LL GET ALONG FINE.
SO LONG AS YOU DON'T MAKE TROUBLE.
I DON'T LIKE TROUBLE MUCH.
THIS IS HOME, DUD.
RING IF YOU NEED ANYTHING.
HA!

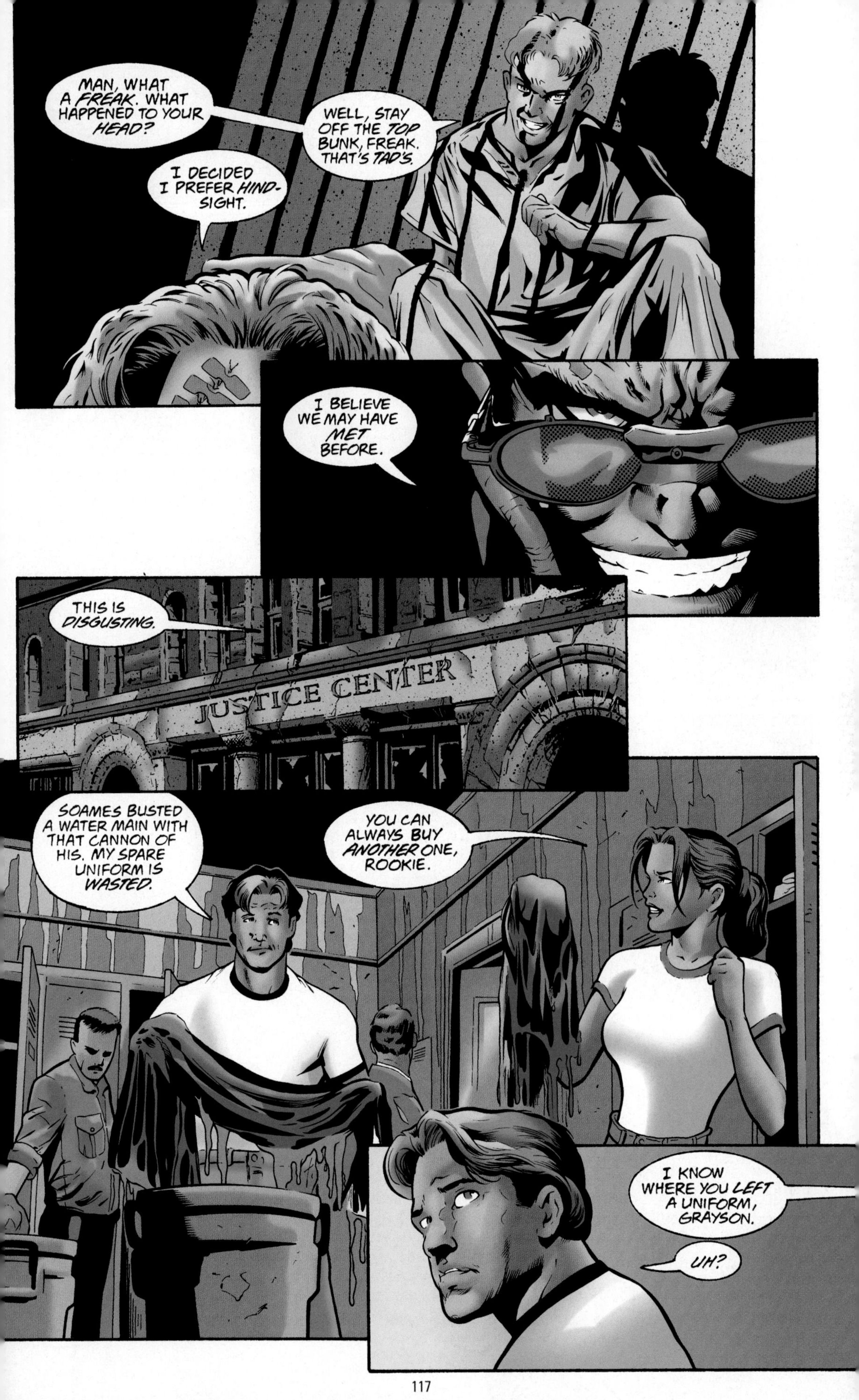

MAN, WHAT A FREAK. WHAT HAPPENED TO YOUR HEAD?
I DECIDED I PREFER HIND-SIGHT.
WELL, STAY OFF THE TOP BUNK, FREAK. THAT'S TAD'S.
I BELIEVE WE MAY HAVE MET BEFORE.
THIS IS DISGUSTING.
JUSTICE CENTER
SOAMES BUSTED A WATER MAIN WITH THAT CANNON OF HIS. MY SPARE UNIFORM IS WASTED.
YOU CAN ALWAYS BUY ANOTHER ONE, ROOKIE.
I KNOW WHERE YOU LEFT A UNIFORM, GRAYSON.
UH?

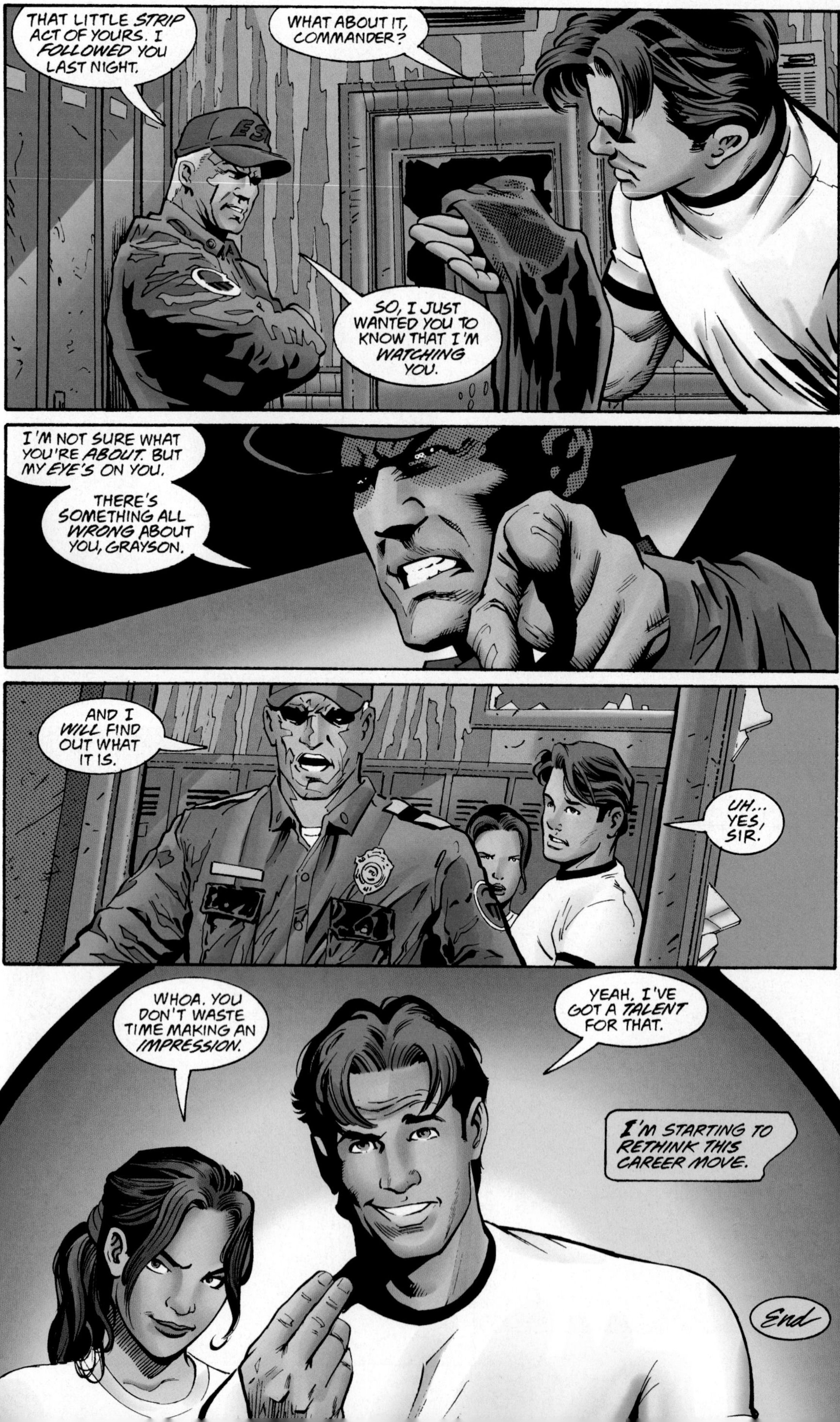
THAT LITTLE STRIP ACT OF YOURS. I FOLLOWED YOU LAST NIGHT.
WHAT ABOUT IT, COMMANDER?
SO, I JUST WANTED YOU TO KNOW THAT I'M WATCHING YOU.
I'M NOT SURE WHAT YOU'RE ABOUT. BUT MY EYE'S ON YOU.
THERE'S SOMETHING ALL WRONG ABOUT YOU, GRAYSON.
AND I WILL FIND OUT WHAT IT IS.
UH... YES, SIR.
WHOA. YOU DON'T WASTE TIME MAKING AN IMPRESSION.
YEAH. I'VE GOT A TALENT FOR THAT.
I'M STARTING TO RETHINK THIS CAREER MOVE.
End

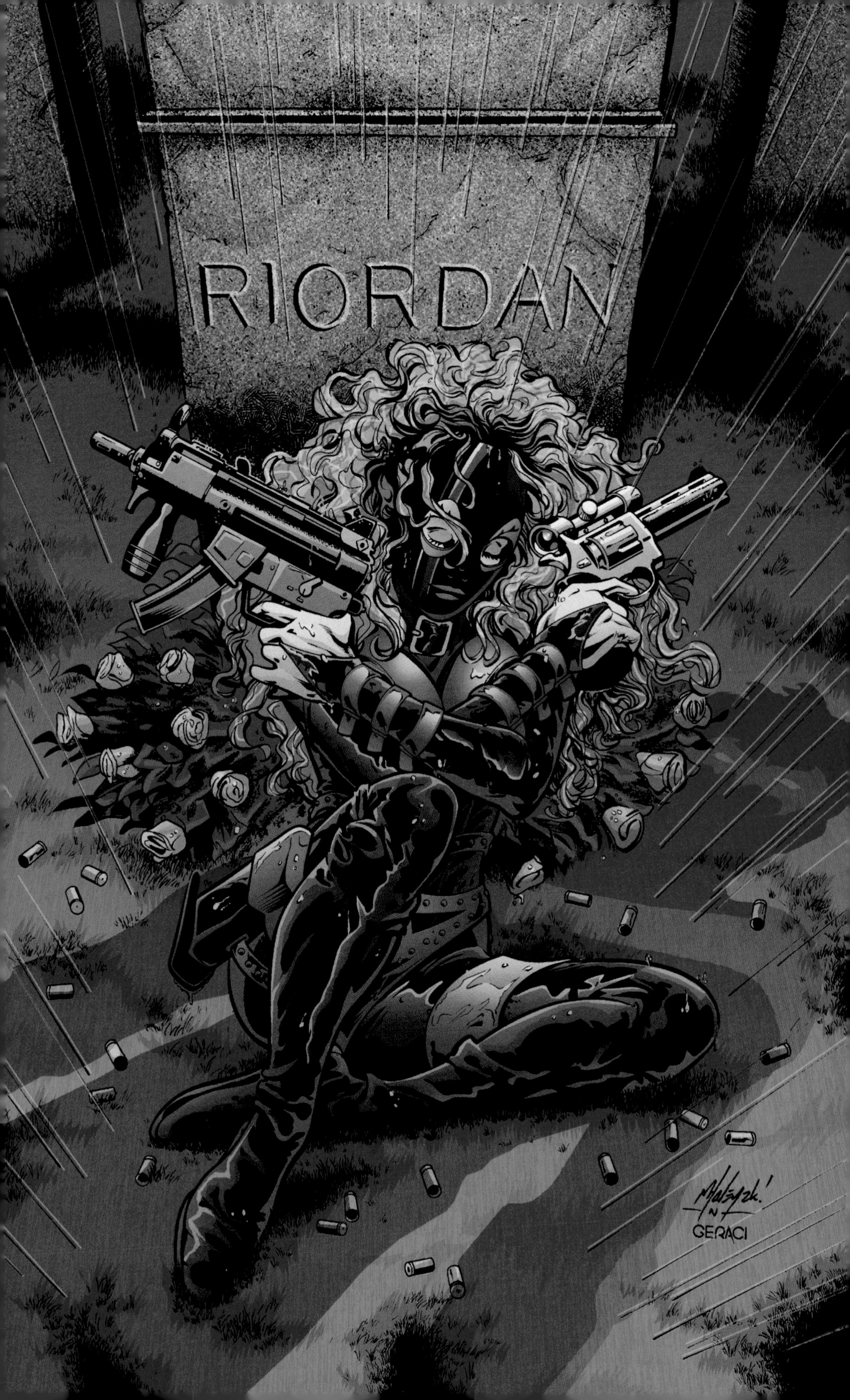
RIORDAN
GERACI

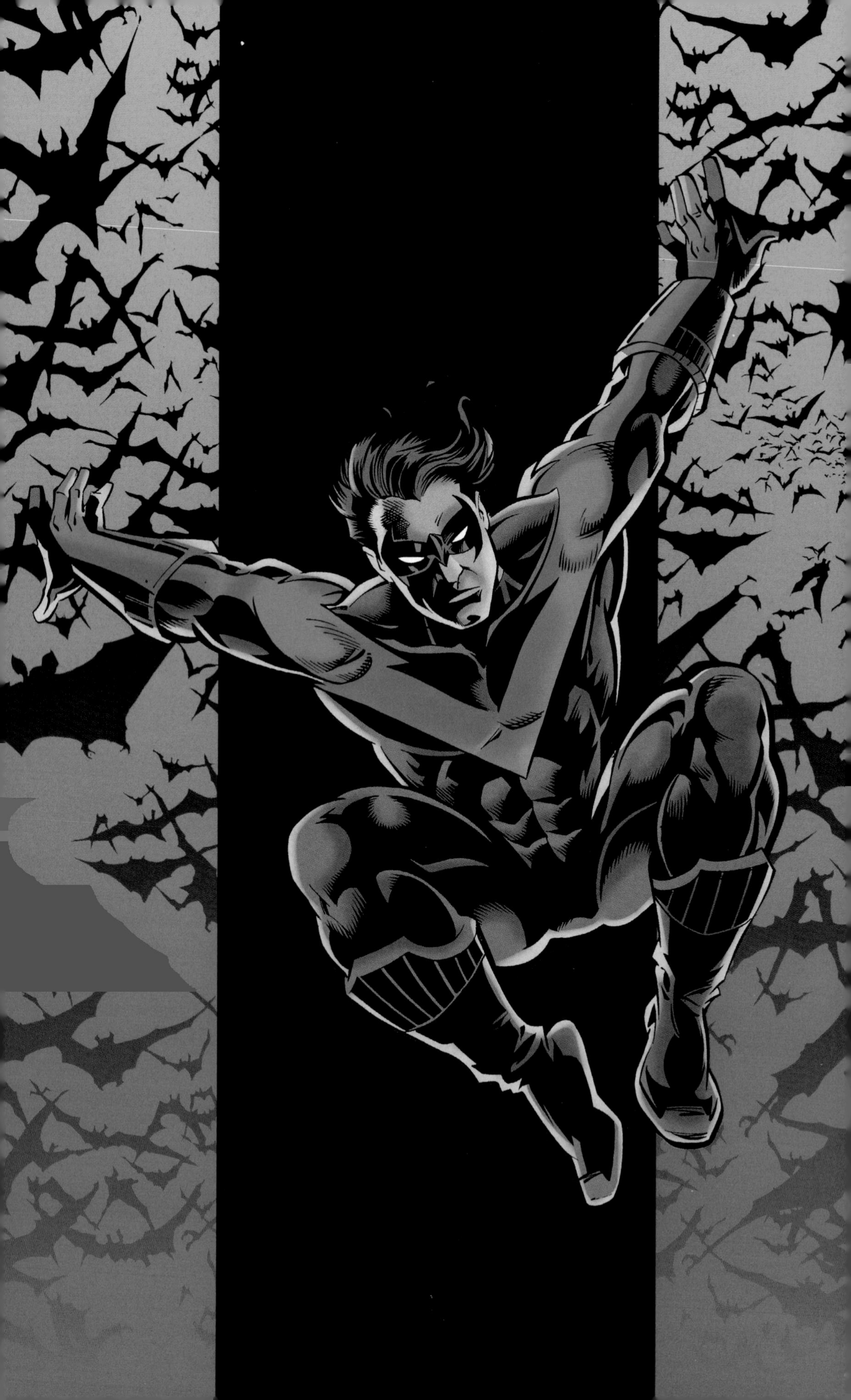

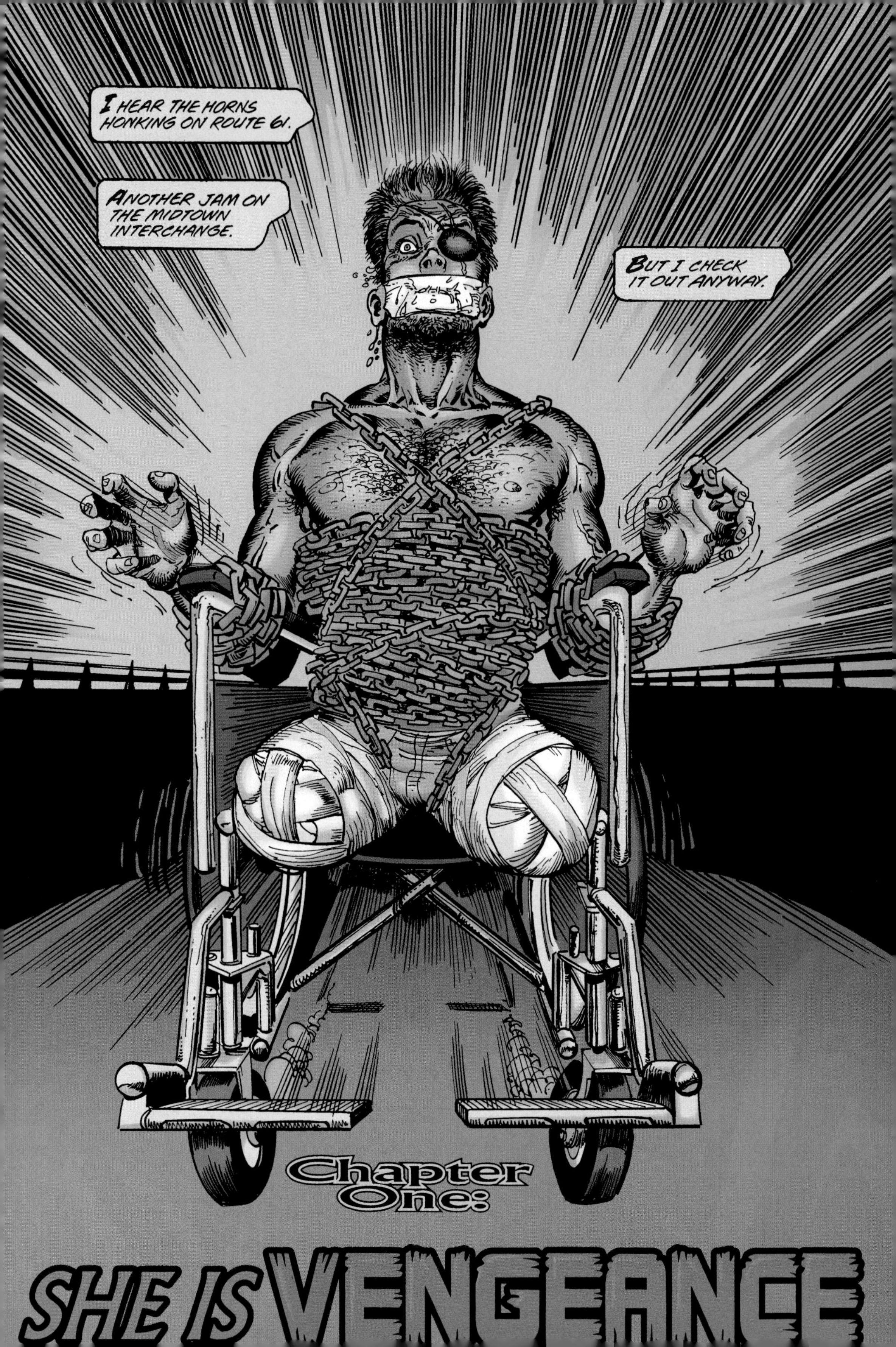
I HEAR THE HORNS HONKING ON ROUTE 61.
ANOTHER JAM ON THE MIDTOWN INTERCHANGE.
BUT I CHECK IT OUT ANYWAY.
Chapter One:
SHE IS VENGEANCE

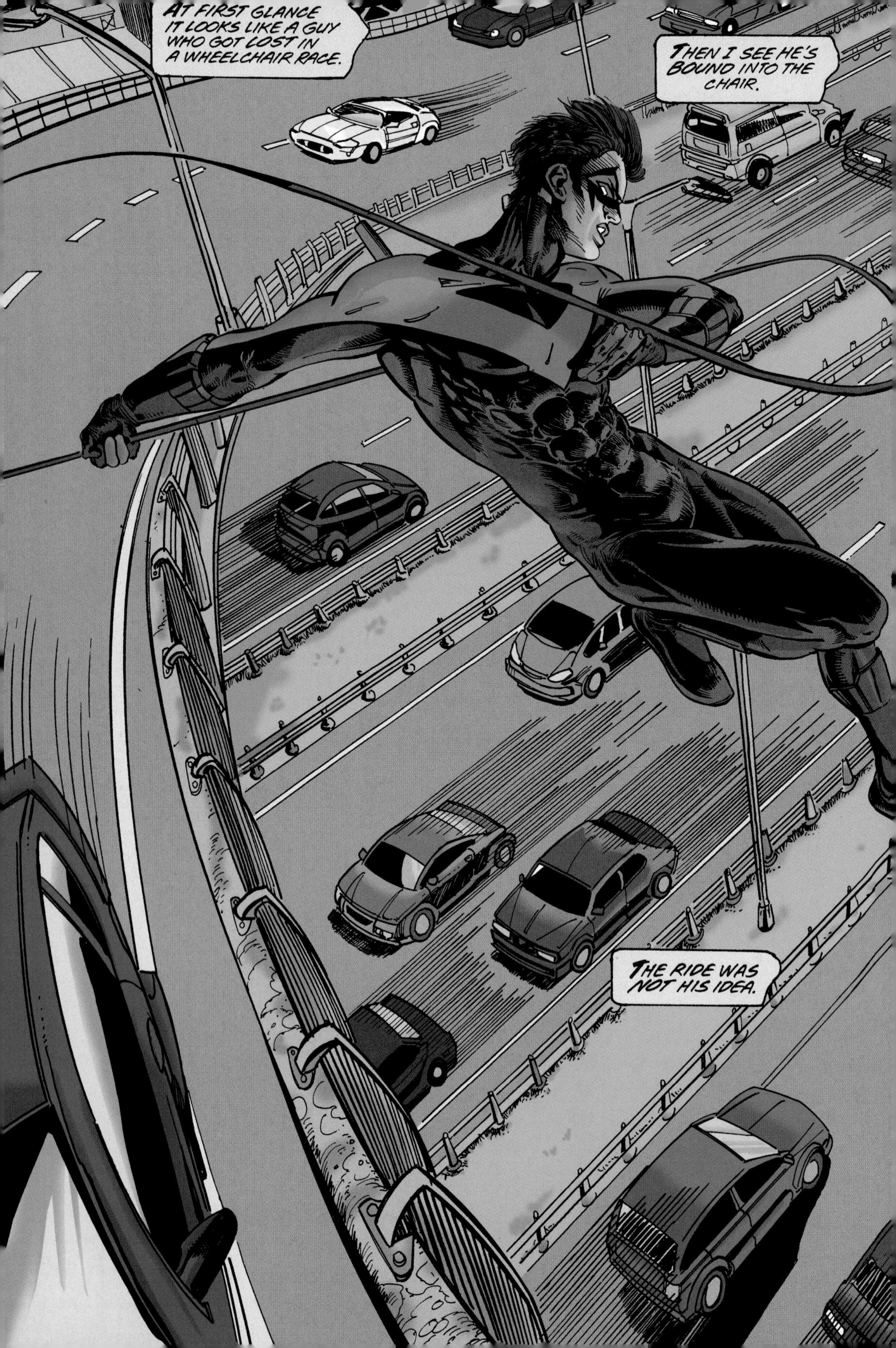
AT FIRST GLANCE IT LOOKS LIKE A GUY WHO GOT LOST IN A WHEELCHAIR RACE.
THEN I SEE HE'S BOUND INTO THE CHAIR.
THE RIDE WAS NOT HIS IDEA.

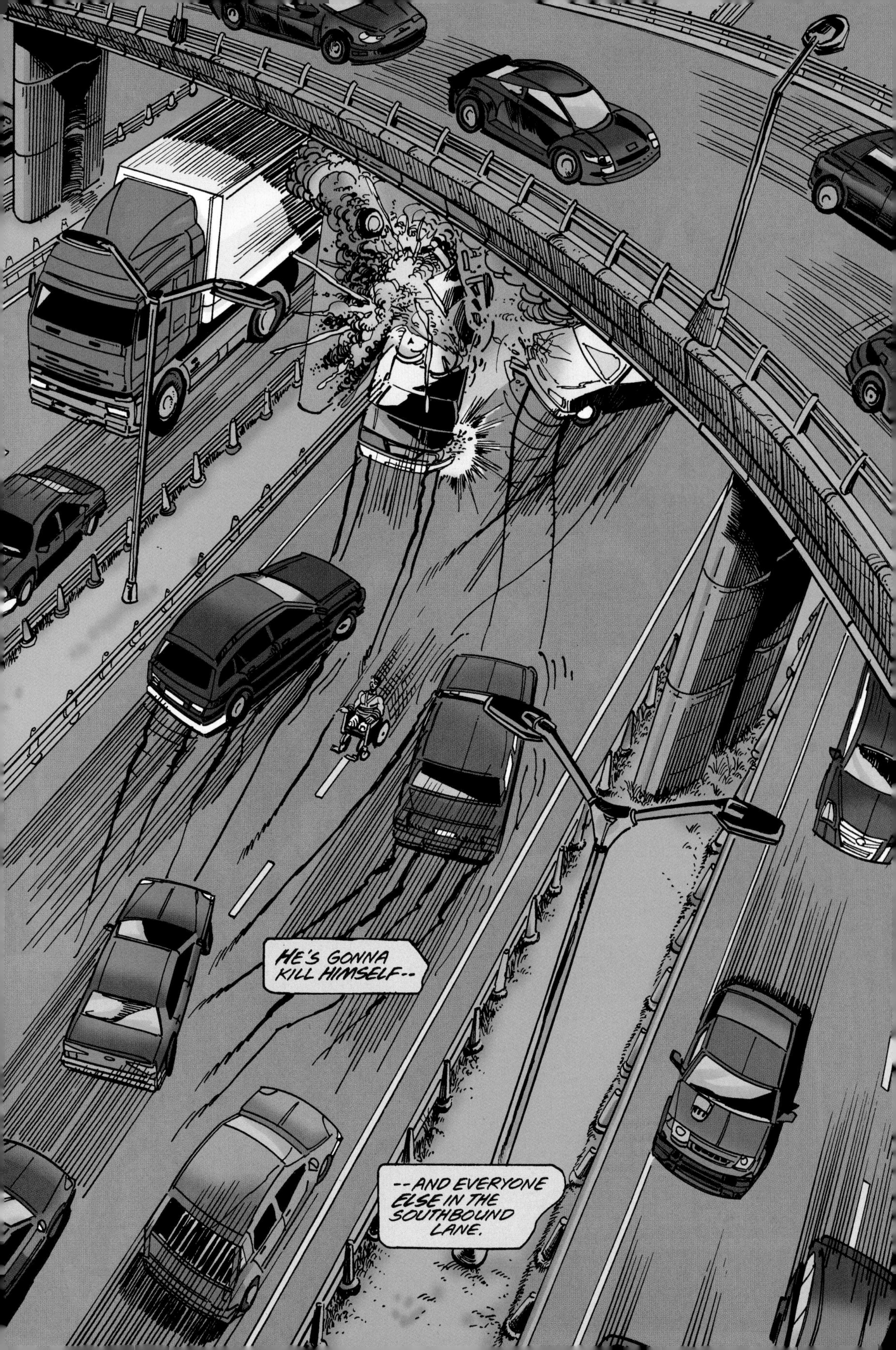
HE'S GONNA KILL HIMSELF--
--AND EVERYONE ELSE IN THE SOUTHBOUND LANE.

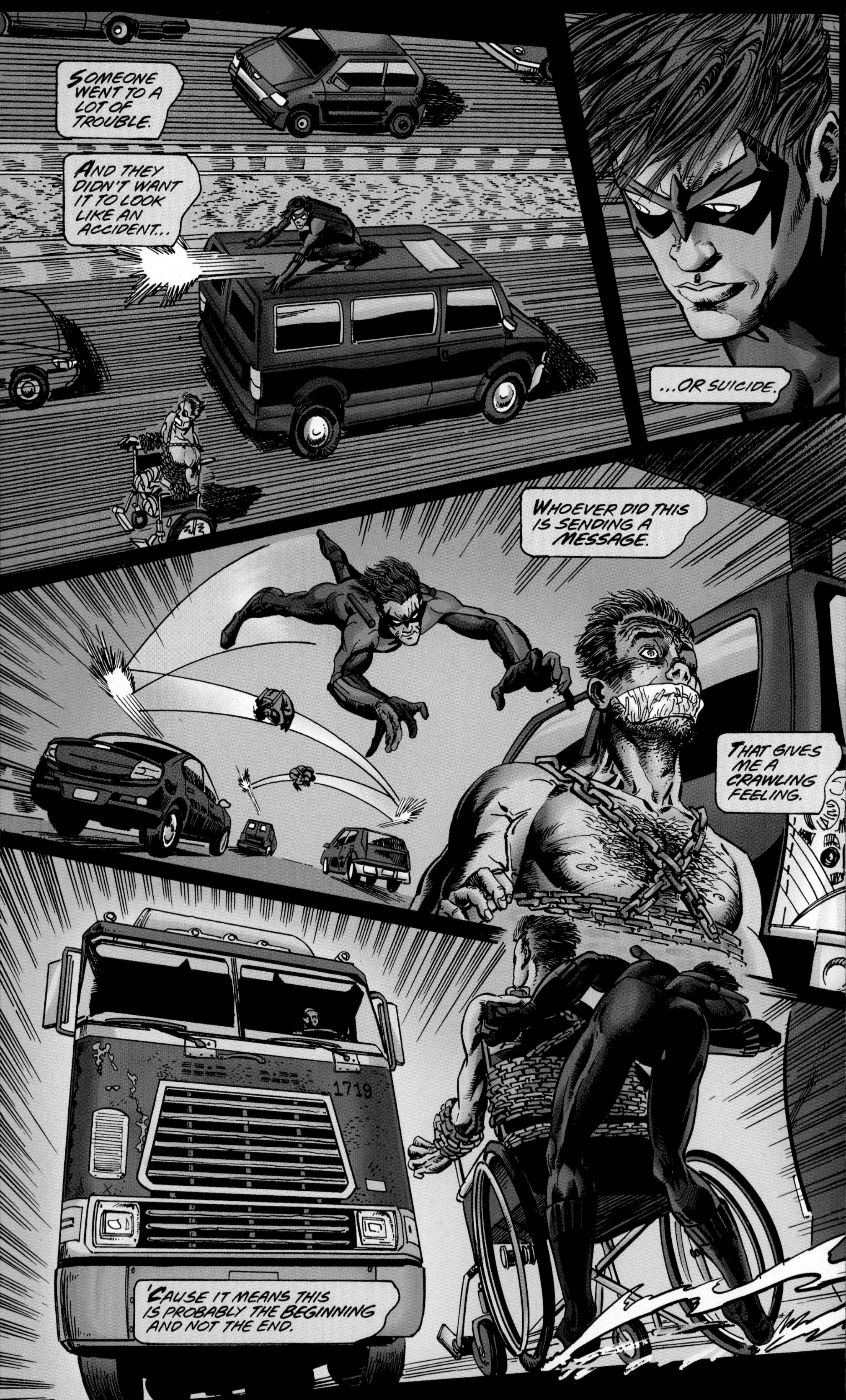

SOMEONE WENT TO A LOT OF TROUBLE.
AND THEY DIDN'T WANT IT TO LOOK LIKE AN ACCIDENT...
...OR SUICIDE.
WHOEVER DID THIS IS SENDING A MESSAGE.
THAT GIVES ME A CRAWLING FEELING.
'CAUSE IT MEANS THIS IS PROBABLY THE BEGINNING AND NOT THE END.

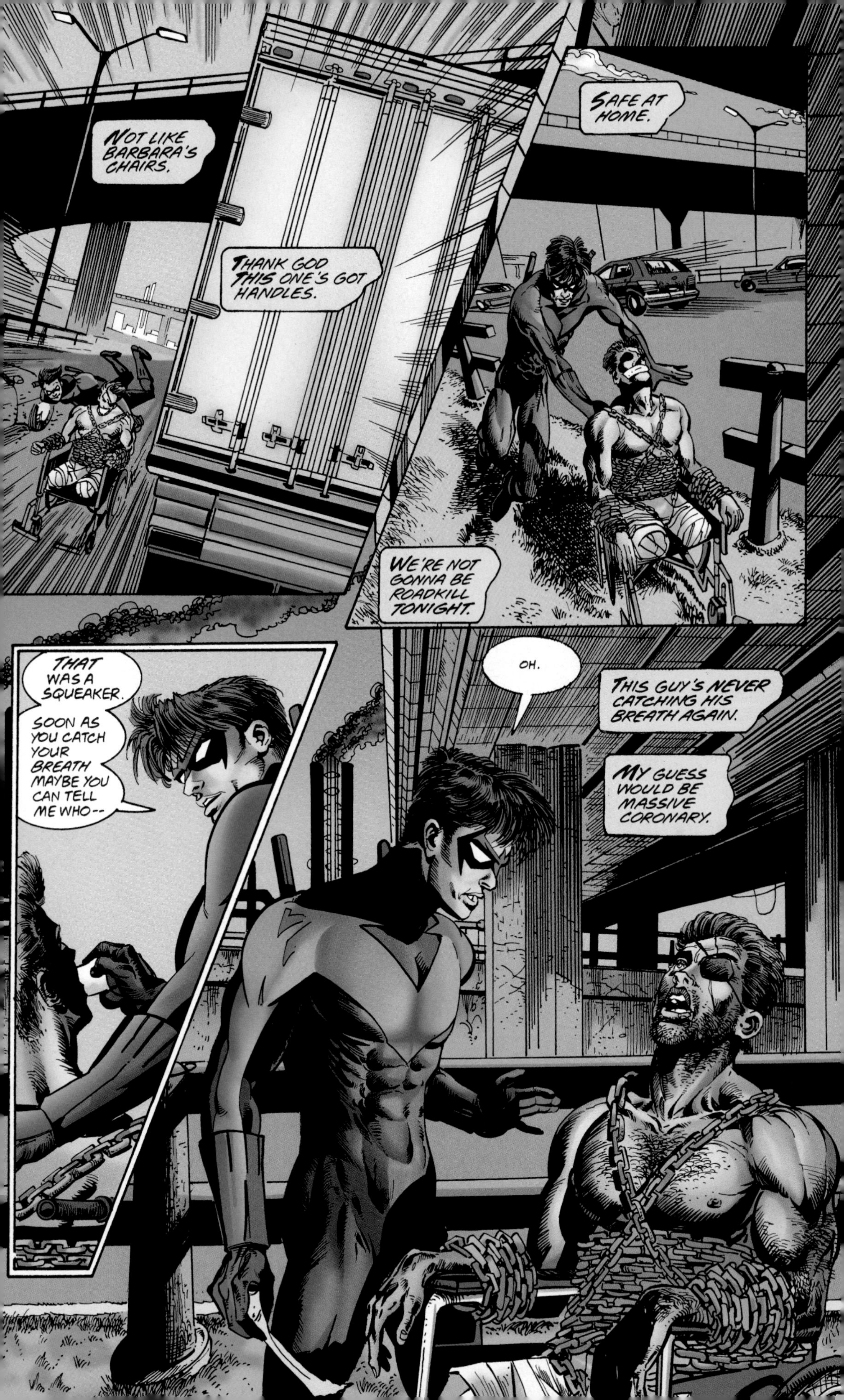
NOT LIKE BARBARA'S CHAIRS.
THANK GOD THIS ONE'S GOT HANDLES.
SAFE AT HOME.
WE'RE NOT GONNA BE ROADKILL TONIGHT.
THAT WAS A SQUEAKER.
SOON AS YOU CATCH YOUR BREATH MAYBE YOU CAN TELL ME WHO--
OH.
THIS GUY'S NEVER CATCHING HIS BREATH AGAIN.
MY GUESS WOULD BE MASSIVE CORONARY.

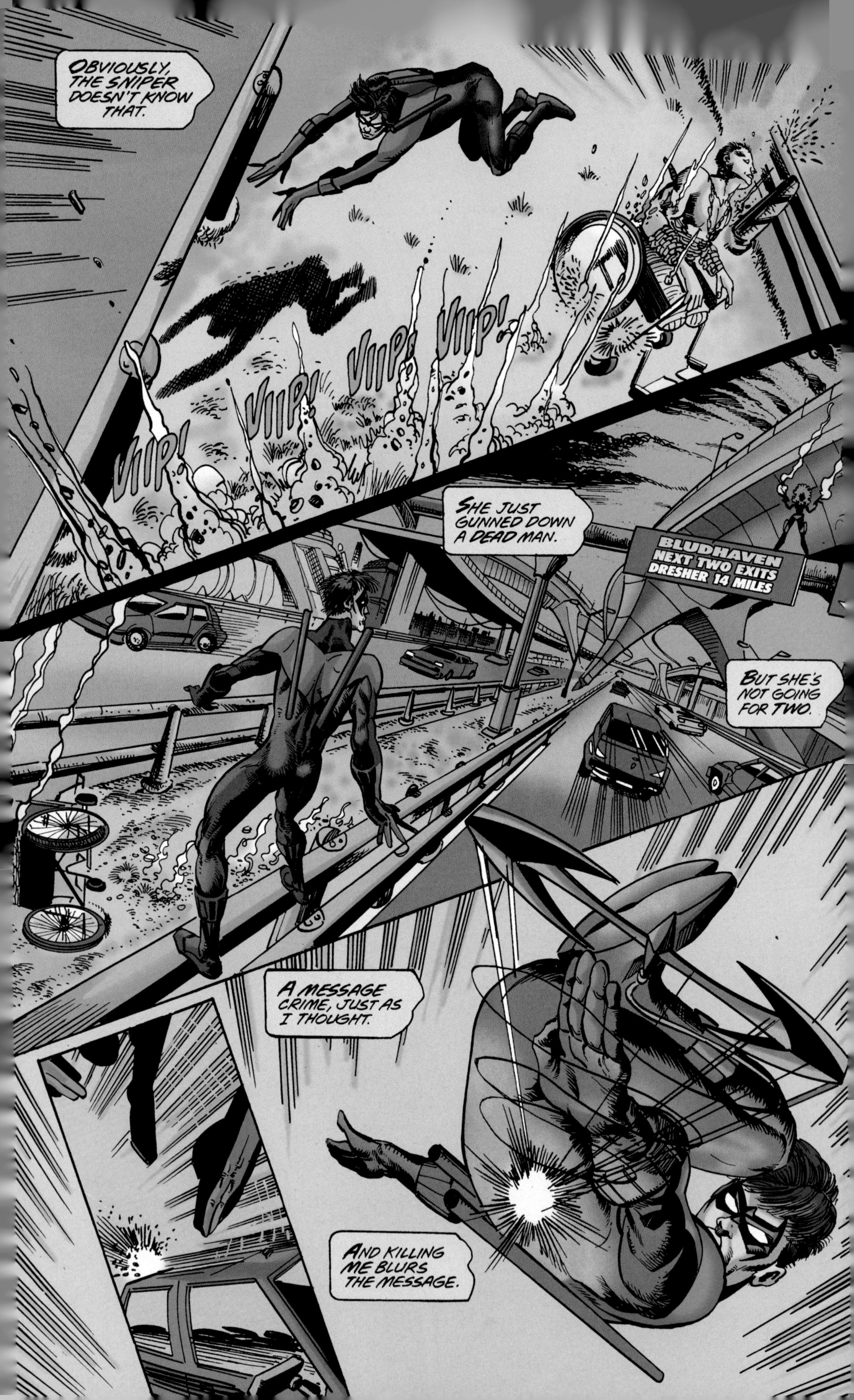
OBVIOUSLY, THE SNIPER DOESN'T KNOW THAT.
VIIP! VIIP! VIIP! VIIP! VIIP!
SHE JUST GUNNED DOWN A DEAD MAN.
BLUDHAVEN NEXT TWO EXITS DRESHER 14 MILES
BUT SHE'S NOT GOING FOR TWO.
A MESSAGE CRIME, JUST AS I THOUGHT.
AND KILLING ME BLURS THE MESSAGE.

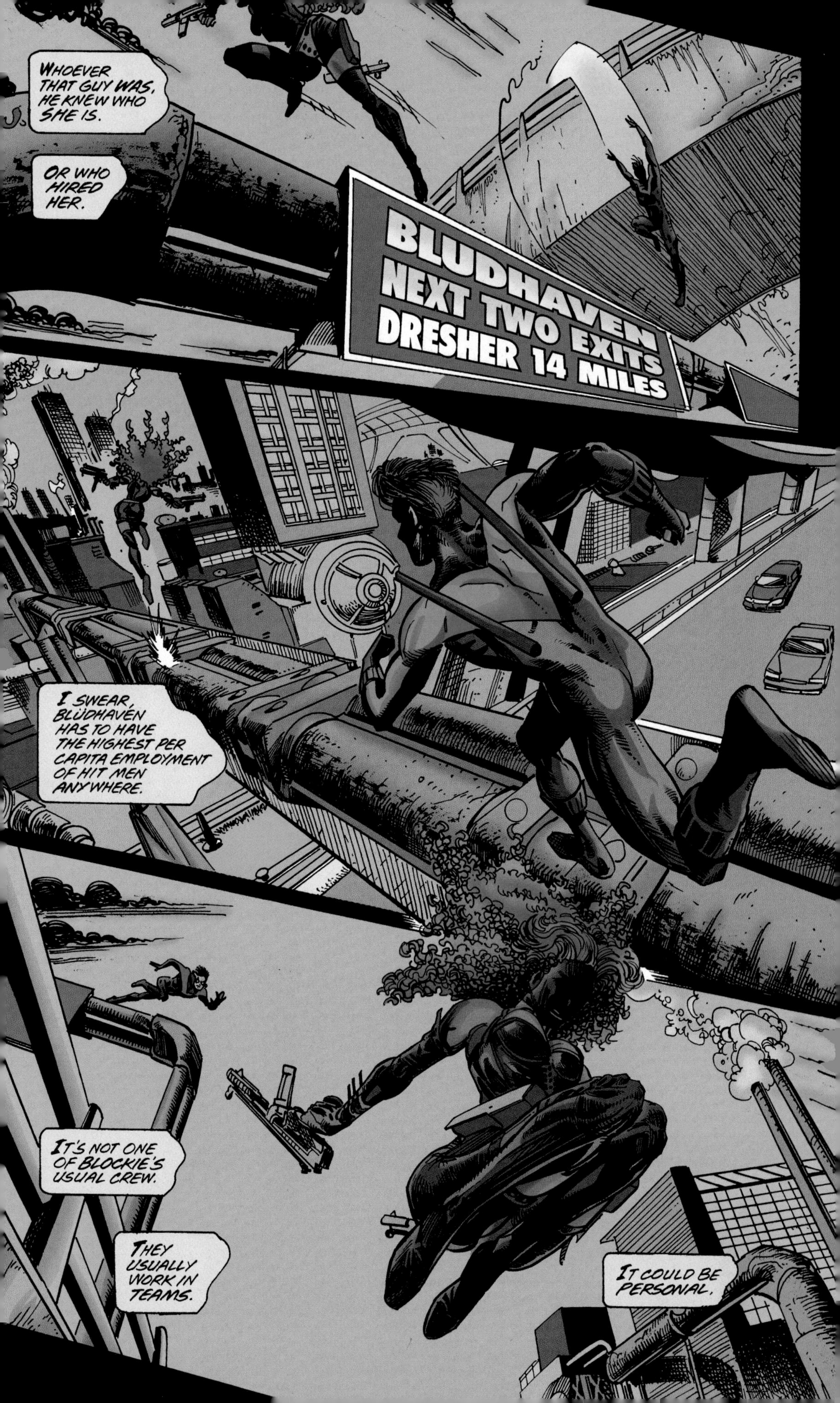
WHOEVER THAT GUY WAS, HE KNEW WHO SHE IS.
OR WHO HIRED HER.
BLUDHAVEN NEXT TWO EXITS DRESHER 14 MILES
I SWEAR, BLÜDHAVEN HAS TO HAVE THE HIGHEST PER CAPITA EMPLOYMENT OF HIT MEN ANYWHERE.
IT'S NOT ONE OF BLOCKIE'S USUAL CREW.
THEY USUALLY WORK IN TEAMS.
IT COULD BE PERSONAL.

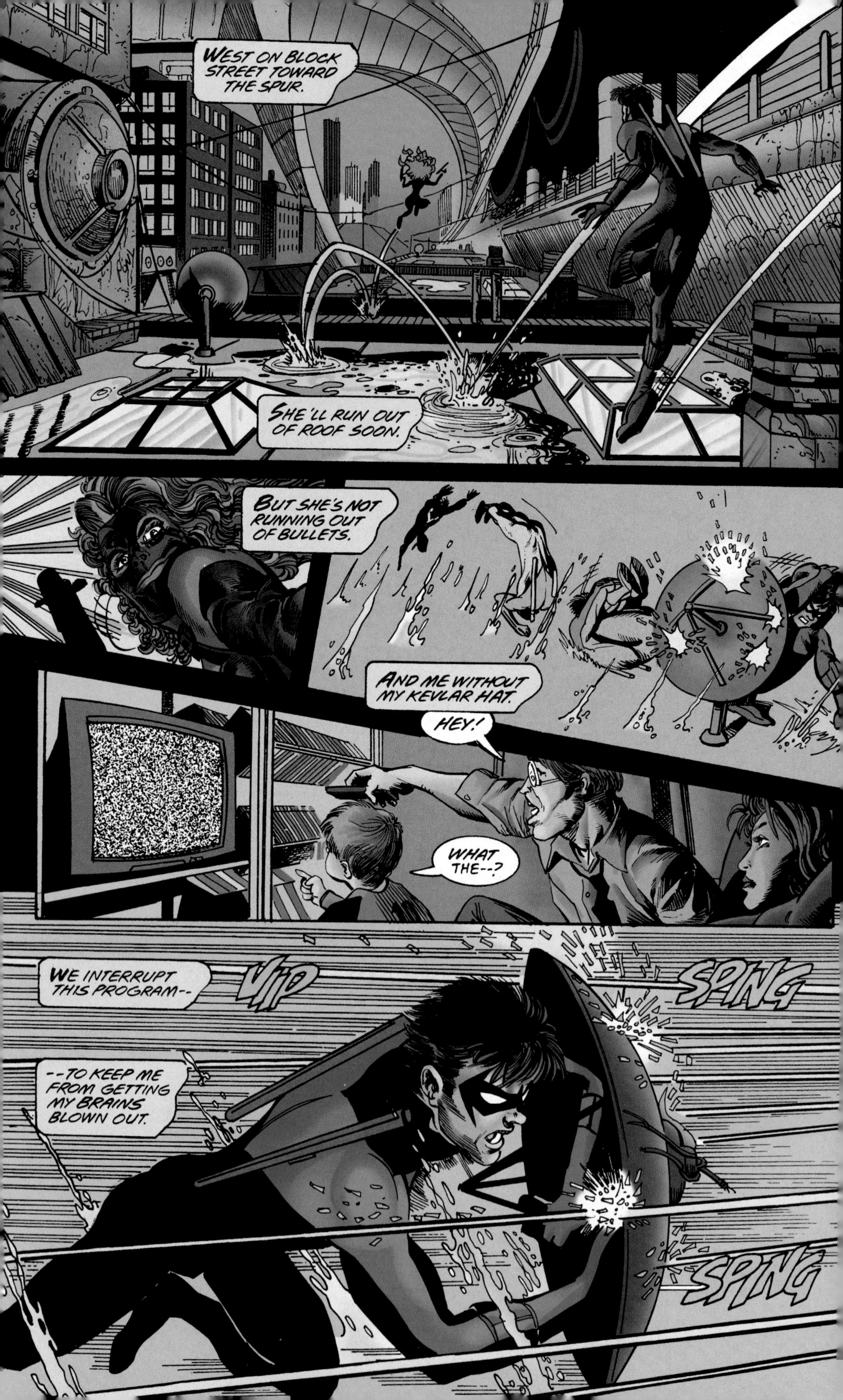
WEST ON BLOCK STREET TOWARD THE SPUR.
SHE'LL RUN OUT OF ROOF SOON.
BUT SHE'S NOT RUNNING OUT OF BULLETS.
AND ME WITHOUT MY KEVLAR HAT.
HEY!
WHAT THE--?
WE INTERRUPT THIS PROGRAM--
VIP
SPING
--TO KEEP ME FROM GETTING MY BRAINS BLOWN OUT.
SPING

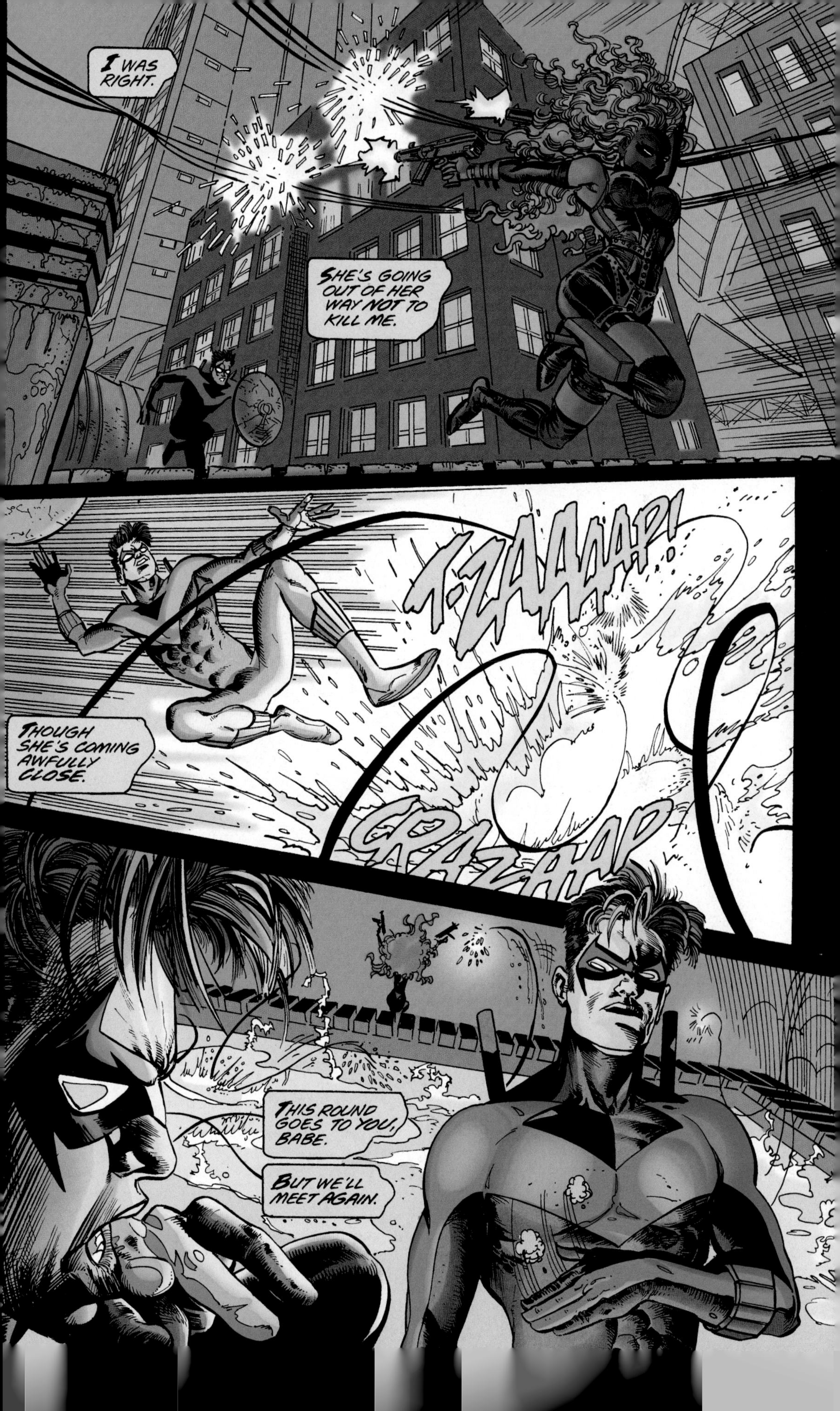
I WAS RIGHT.
SHE'S GOING OUT OF HER WAY NOT TO KILL ME.
T-ZAAAAP!
THOUGH SHE'S COMING AWFULLY CLOSE.
CRAZAAAP
THIS ROUND GOES TO YOU, BABE.
BUT WE'LL MEET AGAIN.

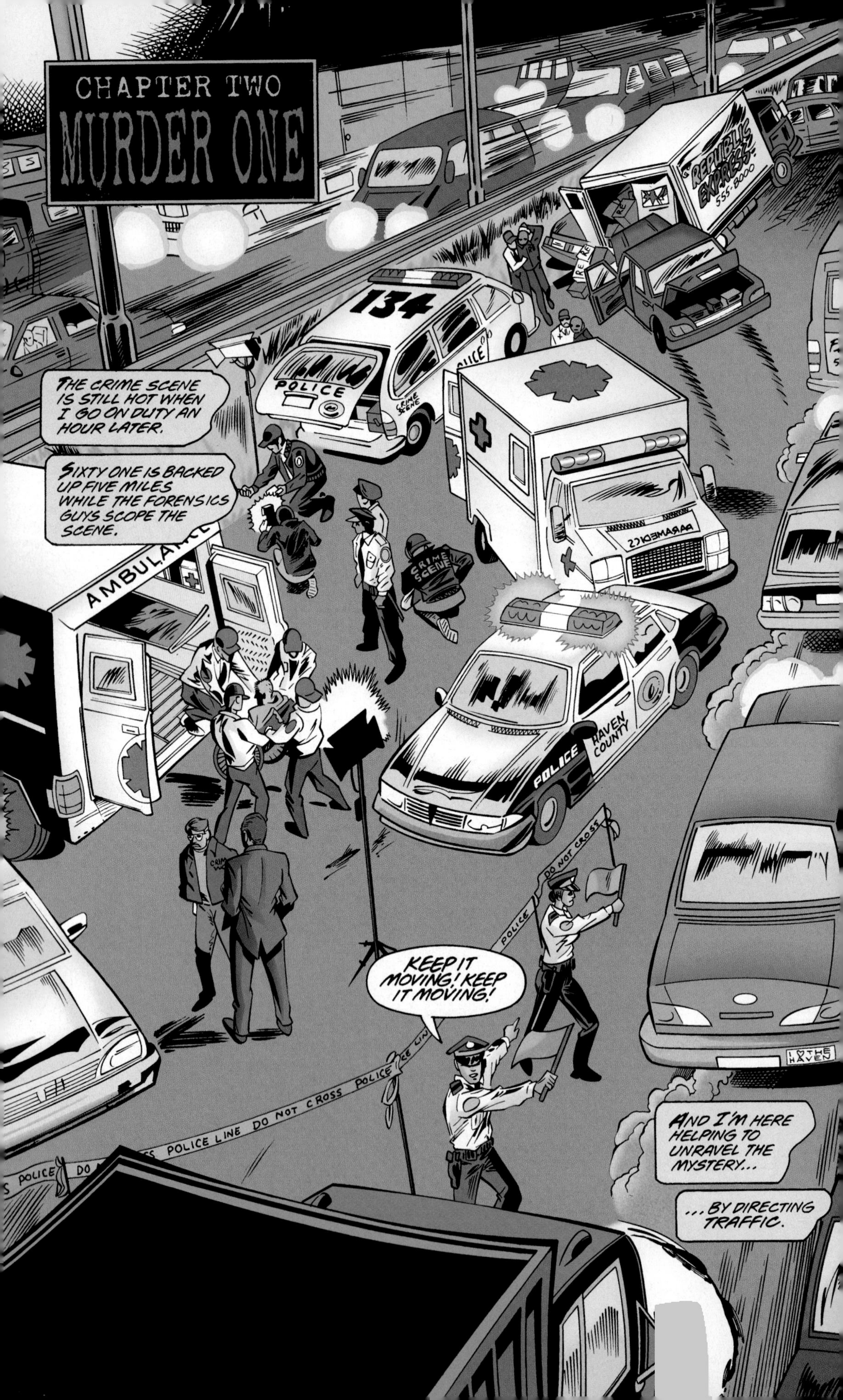
CHAPTER TWO
MURDER ONE
REPUBLIC EXPRESS
555-8000
134
POLICE
CRIME SCENE
THE CRIME SCENE IS STILL HOT WHEN I GO ON DUTY AN HOUR LATER.
SIXTY ONE IS BACKED UP FIVE MILES WHILE THE FORENSICS GUYS SCOPE THE SCENE.
AMBULANCE
PARAMEDICS
HAVEN COUNTY
POLICE
DO NOT CROSS
KEEP IT MOVING! KEEP IT MOVING!
POLICE LINE DO NOT CROSS POLICE
AND I'M HERE HELPING TO UNRAVEL THE MYSTERY...
...BY DIRECTING TRAFFIC.

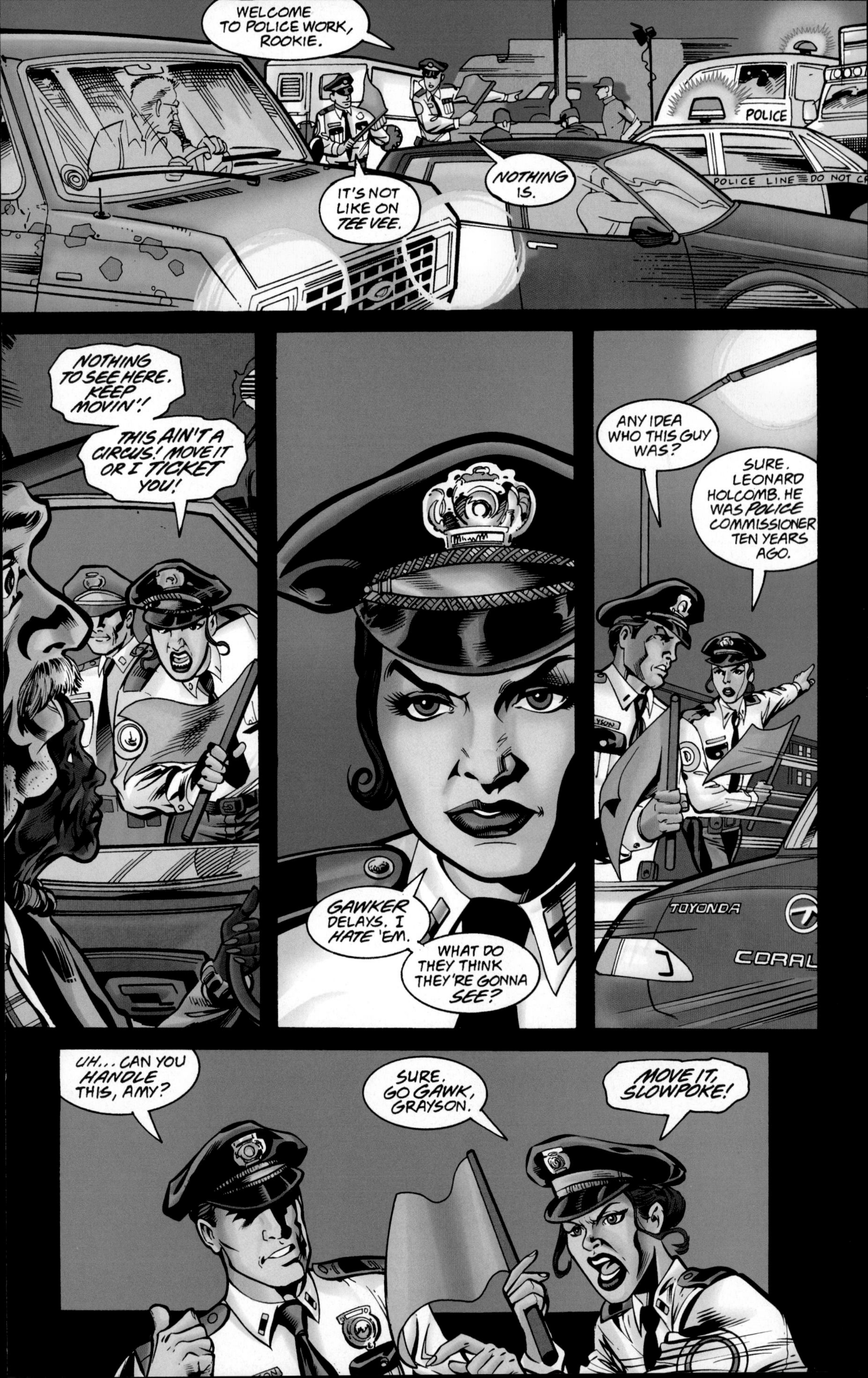
WELCOME TO POLICE WORK, ROOKIE.
IT'S NOT LIKE ON TEE VEE.
NOTHING IS.
POLICE
POLICE LINE DO NOT CR
NOTHING TO SEE HERE. KEEP MOVIN'!
THIS AIN'T A CIRCUS! MOVE IT OR I TICKET YOU!
GAWKER DELAYS. I HATE 'EM.
WHAT DO THEY THINK THEY'RE GONNA SEE?
ANY IDEA WHO THIS GUY WAS?
SURE. LEONARD HOLCOMB. HE WAS POLICE COMMISSIONER TEN YEARS AGO.
TOYONDA
CORAL
UH... CAN YOU HANDLE THIS, AMY?
SURE. GO GAWK, GRAYSON.
MOVE IT, SLOWPOKE!

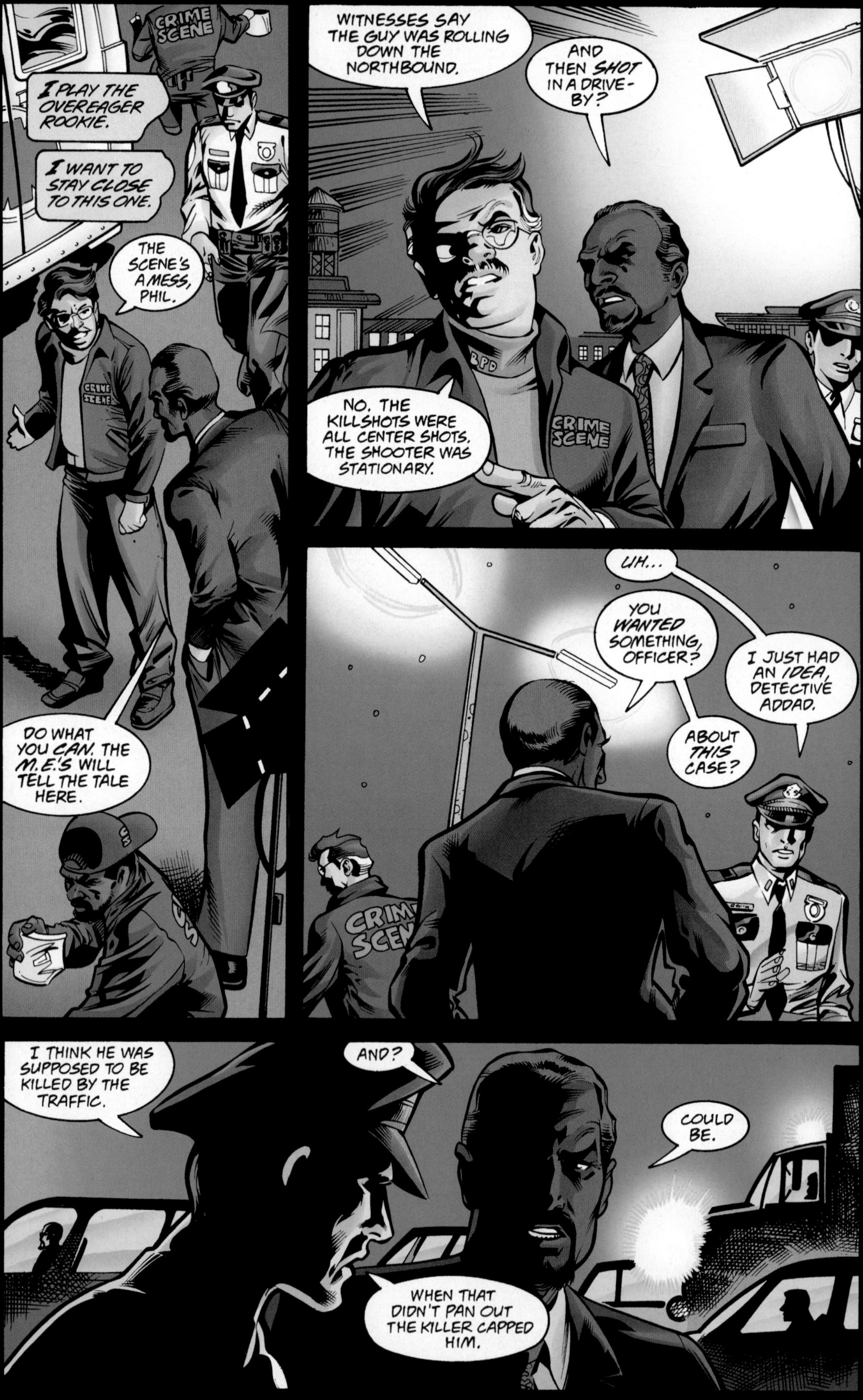
I PLAY THE OVEREAGER ROOKIE.
I WANT TO STAY CLOSE TO THIS ONE.
CRIME SCENE
THE SCENE'S A MESS, PHIL.
DO WHAT YOU CAN. THE M.E.'S WILL TELL THE TALE HERE.
WITNESSES SAY THE GUY WAS ROLLING DOWN THE NORTHBOUND.
AND THEN SHOT IN A DRIVE-BY?
NO. THE KILLSHOTS WERE ALL CENTER SHOTS. THE SHOOTER WAS STATIONARY.
UH...
YOU WANTED SOMETHING, OFFICER?
I JUST HAD AN IDEA, DETECTIVE ADDAD.
ABOUT THIS CASE?
I THINK HE WAS SUPPOSED TO BE KILLED BY THE TRAFFIC.
AND?
COULD BE.
WHEN THAT DIDN'T PAN OUT THE KILLER CAPPED HIM.

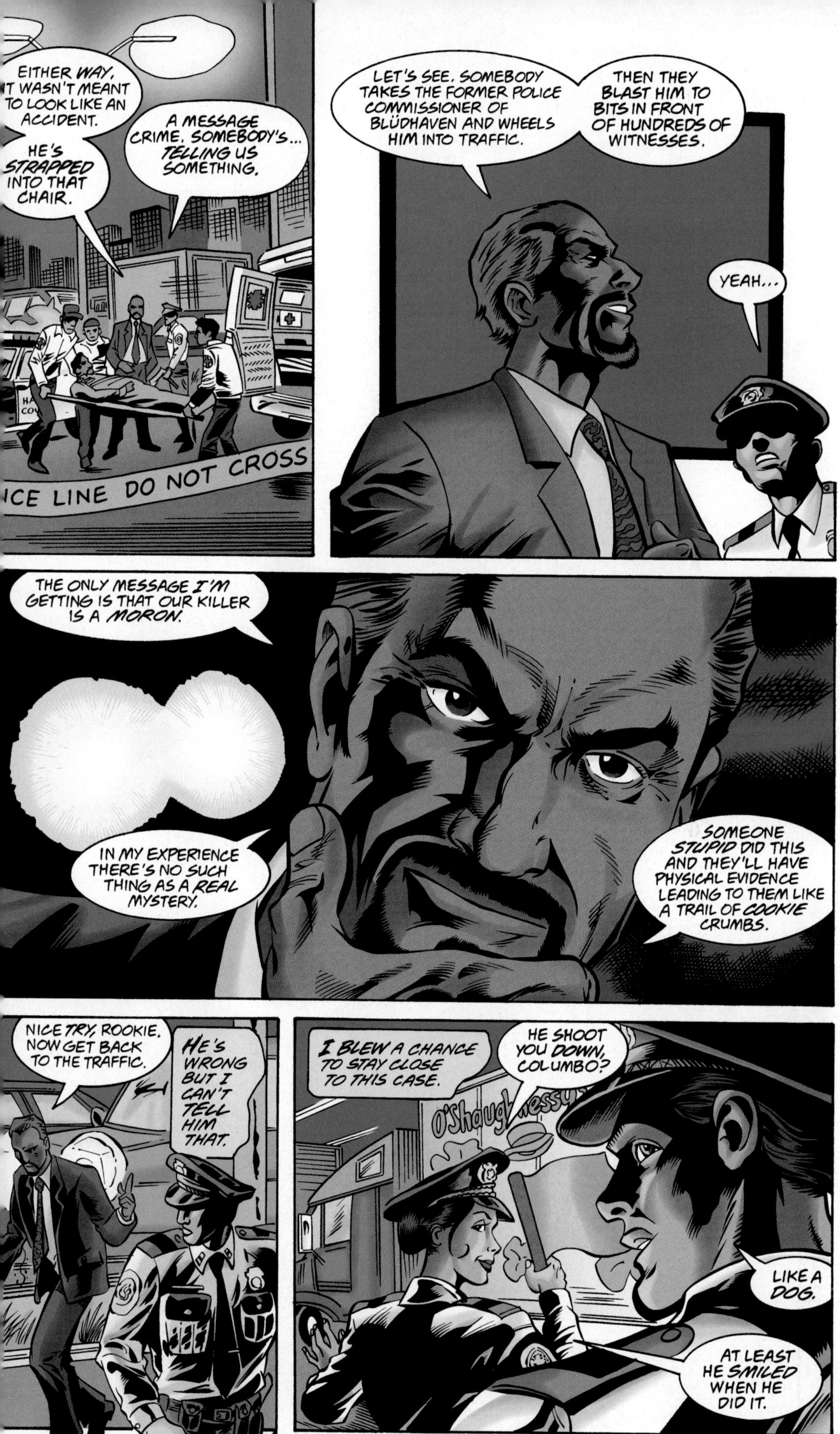

EITHER WAY, IT WASN'T MEANT TO LOOK LIKE AN ACCIDENT.
HE'S STRAPPED INTO THAT CHAIR.
A MESSAGE CRIME. SOMEBODY'S... TELLING US SOMETHING.
ICE LINE DO NOT CROSS
LET'S SEE. SOMEBODY TAKES THE FORMER POLICE COMMISSIONER OF BLÜDHAVEN AND WHEELS HIM INTO TRAFFIC.
THEN THEY BLAST HIM TO BITS IN FRONT OF HUNDREDS OF WITNESSES.
YEAH...
THE ONLY MESSAGE I'M GETTING IS THAT OUR KILLER IS A MORON.
IN MY EXPERIENCE THERE'S NO SUCH THING AS A REAL MYSTERY.
SOMEONE STUPID DID THIS AND THEY'LL HAVE PHYSICAL EVIDENCE LEADING TO THEM LIKE A TRAIL OF COOKIE CRUMBS.
NICE TRY, ROOKIE. NOW GET BACK TO THE TRAFFIC.
HE'S WRONG BUT I CAN'T TELL HIM THAT.
I BLEW A CHANCE TO STAY CLOSE TO THIS CASE.
HE SHOOT YOU DOWN, COLUMBO?
LIKE A DOG.
AT LEAST HE SMILED WHEN HE DID IT.

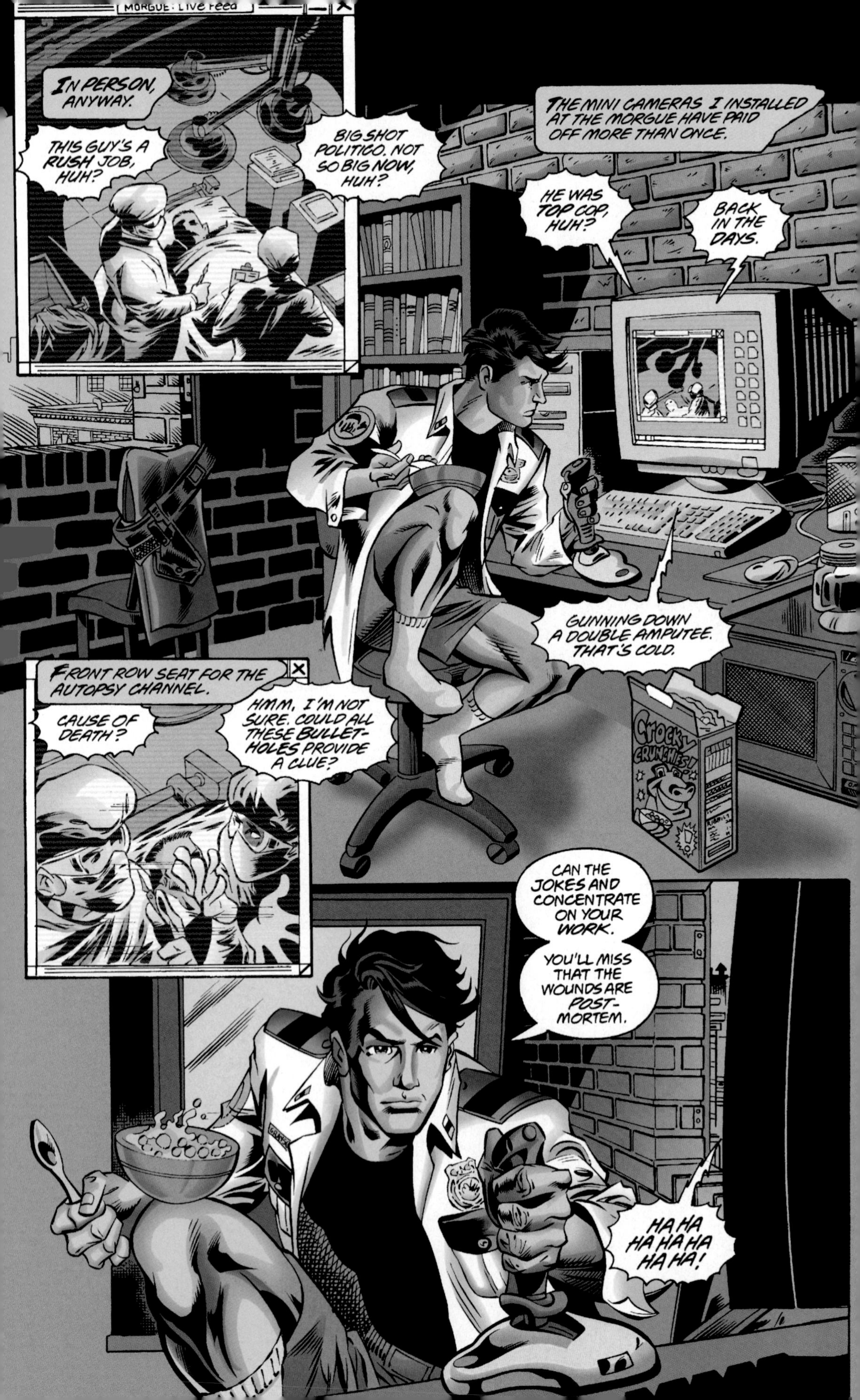
MORGUE: Live Feed
IN PERSON, ANYWAY.
THIS GUY'S A RUSH JOB, HUH?
BIG SHOT POLITICO. NOT SO BIG NOW, HUH?
THE MINI CAMERAS I INSTALLED AT THE MORGUE HAVE PAID OFF MORE THAN ONCE.
HE WAS TOP COP, HUH?
BACK IN THE DAYS.
GUNNING DOWN A DOUBLE AMPUTEE. THAT'S COLD.
FRONT ROW SEAT FOR THE AUTOPSY CHANNEL.
CAUSE OF DEATH?
HMM, I'M NOT SURE. COULD ALL THESE BULLET-HOLES PROVIDE A CLUE?
CROCKY CRUNCHIES!
CAN THE JOKES AND CONCENTRATE ON YOUR WORK.
YOU'LL MISS THAT THE WOUNDS ARE POST-MORTEM.
HA HA HA HA HA HA HA!

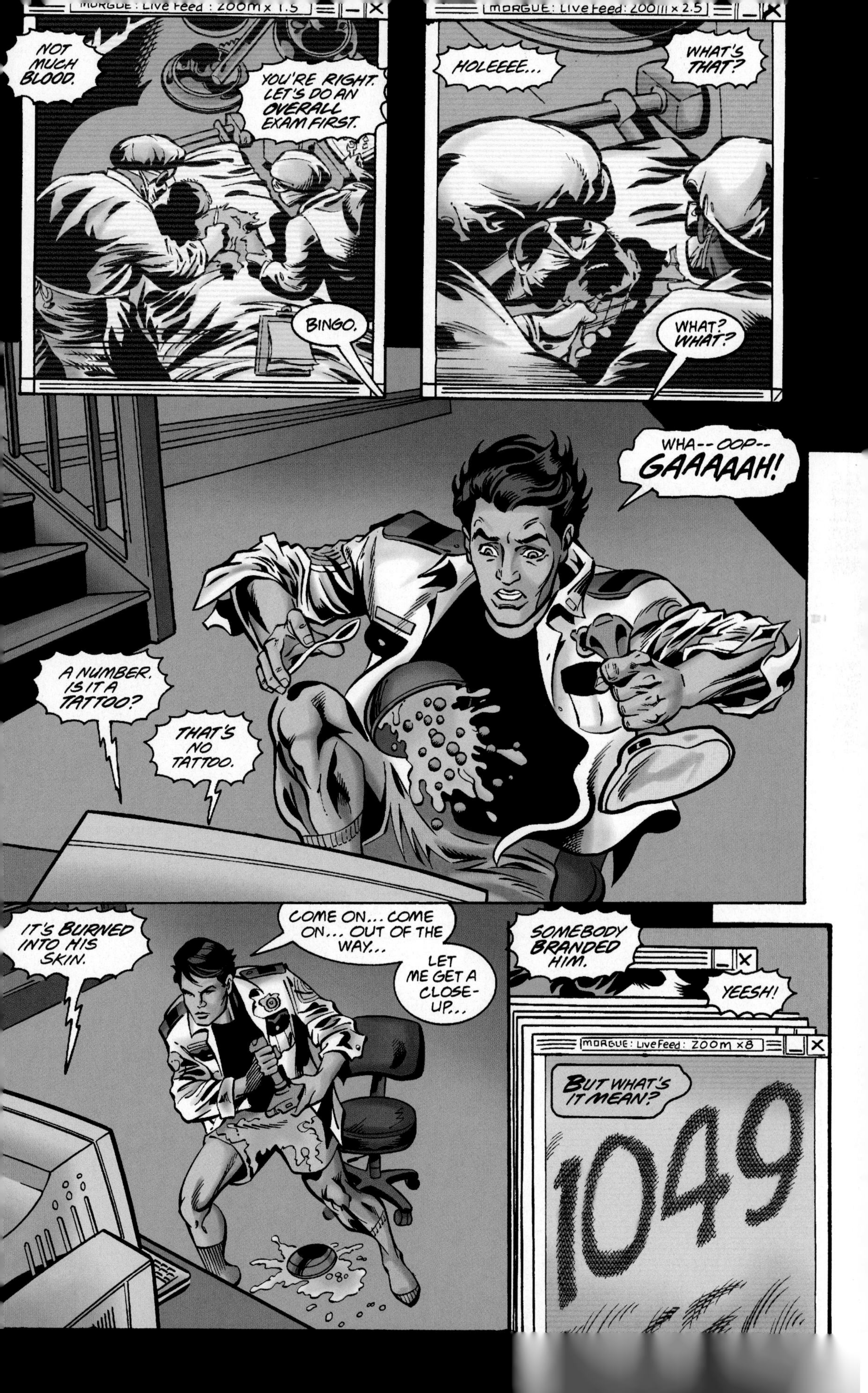
MORGUE : Live Feed : ZOOM x 1.5
NOT MUCH BLOOD.
YOU'RE RIGHT. LET'S DO AN OVERALL EXAM FIRST.
BINGO.
MORGUE : Live Feed : ZOOM x 2.5
HOLEEEE...
WHAT'S THAT?
WHAT? WHAT?
WHA--OOP-- GAAAAAH!
A NUMBER. IS IT A TATTOO?
THAT'S NO TATTOO.
IT'S BURNED INTO HIS SKIN.
COME ON... COME ON... OUT OF THE WAY...
LET ME GET A CLOSE-UP...
SOMEBODY BRANDED HIM.
YEESH!
MORGUE : Live Feed : ZOOM x8
BUT WHAT'S IT MEAN?
1049

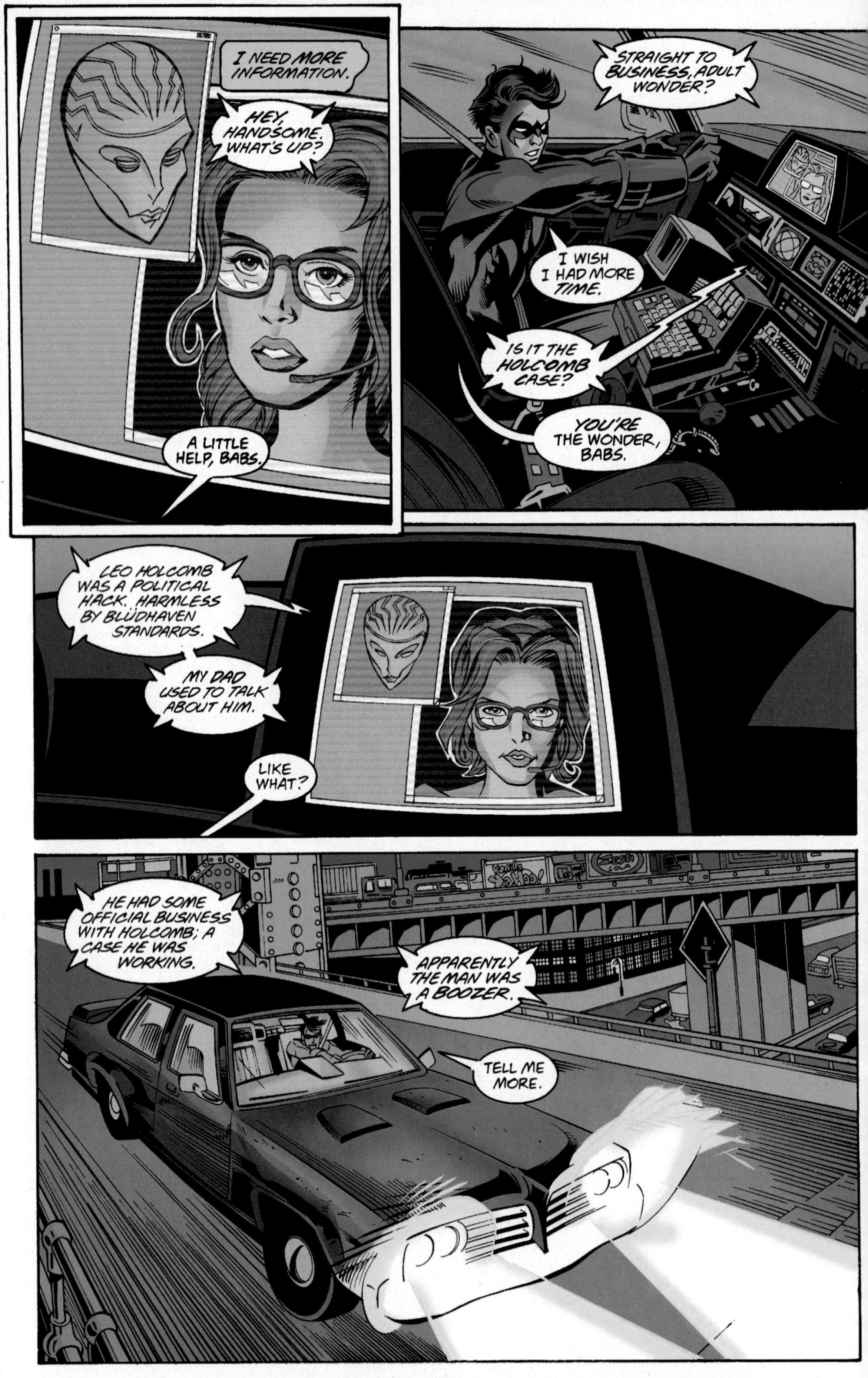
I NEED MORE INFORMATION.
HEY, HANDSOME. WHAT'S UP?
A LITTLE HELP, BABS.
STRAIGHT TO BUSINESS, ADULT WONDER?
I WISH I HAD MORE TIME.
IS IT THE HOLCOMB CASE?
YOU'RE THE WONDER, BABS.
LEO HOLCOMB WAS A POLITICAL HACK. HARMLESS BY BLÜDHAVEN STANDARDS.
MY DAD USED TO TALK ABOUT HIM.
LIKE WHAT?
HE HAD SOME OFFICIAL BUSINESS WITH HOLCOMB; A CASE HE WAS WORKING.
APPARENTLY THE MAN WAS A BOOZER.
TELL ME MORE.

WELL, HOLCOMB HAD RUMORED TIES TO THE MARIN MOB.

THE ONE BLOCKBUSTER RUNS NOW.

YEP. HE WAS UP FOR A FEDERAL INDICTMENT. THEN THE EXPLOSION.

THE BAYSIDE PARK BLAST.

A WHOLE FAMILY OF DECORATED COPS WAS KILLED ALONG WITH A BUNCH OF REPORTERS.

HOLCOMB LOST HIS LEGS AND ONE EYE.

OLD LIBRARIANS NEVER DIE... They just get MIS-FILED!

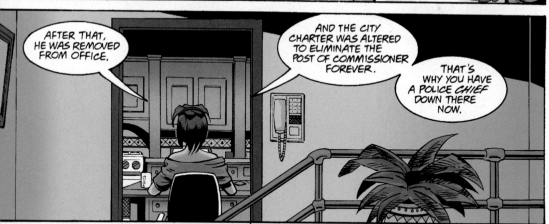

AFTER THAT, HE WAS REMOVED FROM OFFICE.

AND THE CITY CHARTER WAS ALTERED TO ELIMINATE THE POST OF COMMISSIONER FOREVER.

THAT'S WHY YOU HAVE A POLICE CHIEF DOWN THERE NOW.

DID I EVER TELL YOU--

OH.

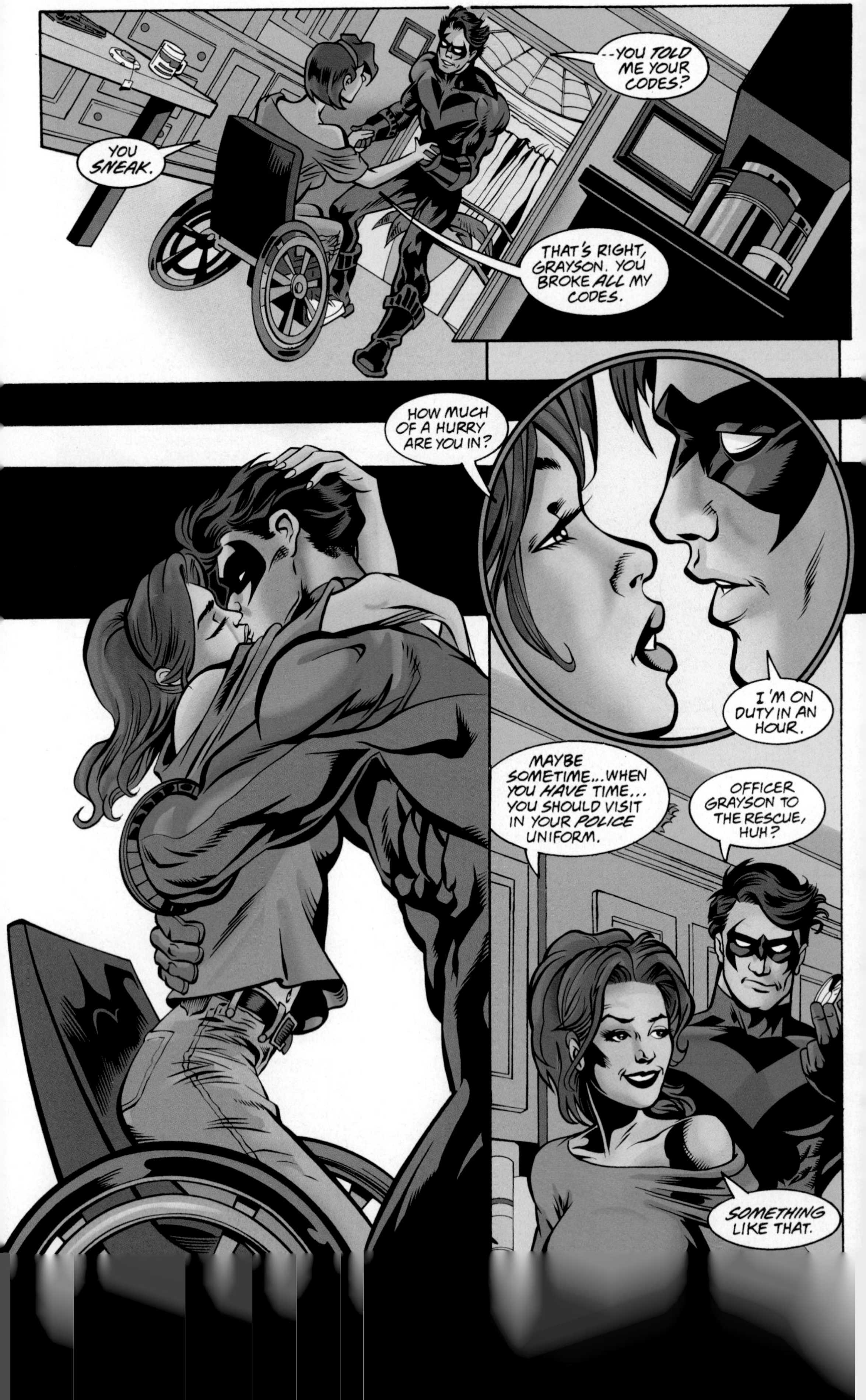
--YOU TOLD ME YOUR CODES?
YOU SNEAK.
THAT'S RIGHT, GRAYSON. YOU BROKE ALL MY CODES.
HOW MUCH OF A HURRY ARE YOU IN?
I'M ON DUTY IN AN HOUR.
MAYBE SOMETIME...WHEN YOU HAVE TIME... YOU SHOULD VISIT IN YOUR POLICE UNIFORM.
OFFICER GRAYSON TO THE RESCUE, HUH?
SOMETHING LIKE THAT.

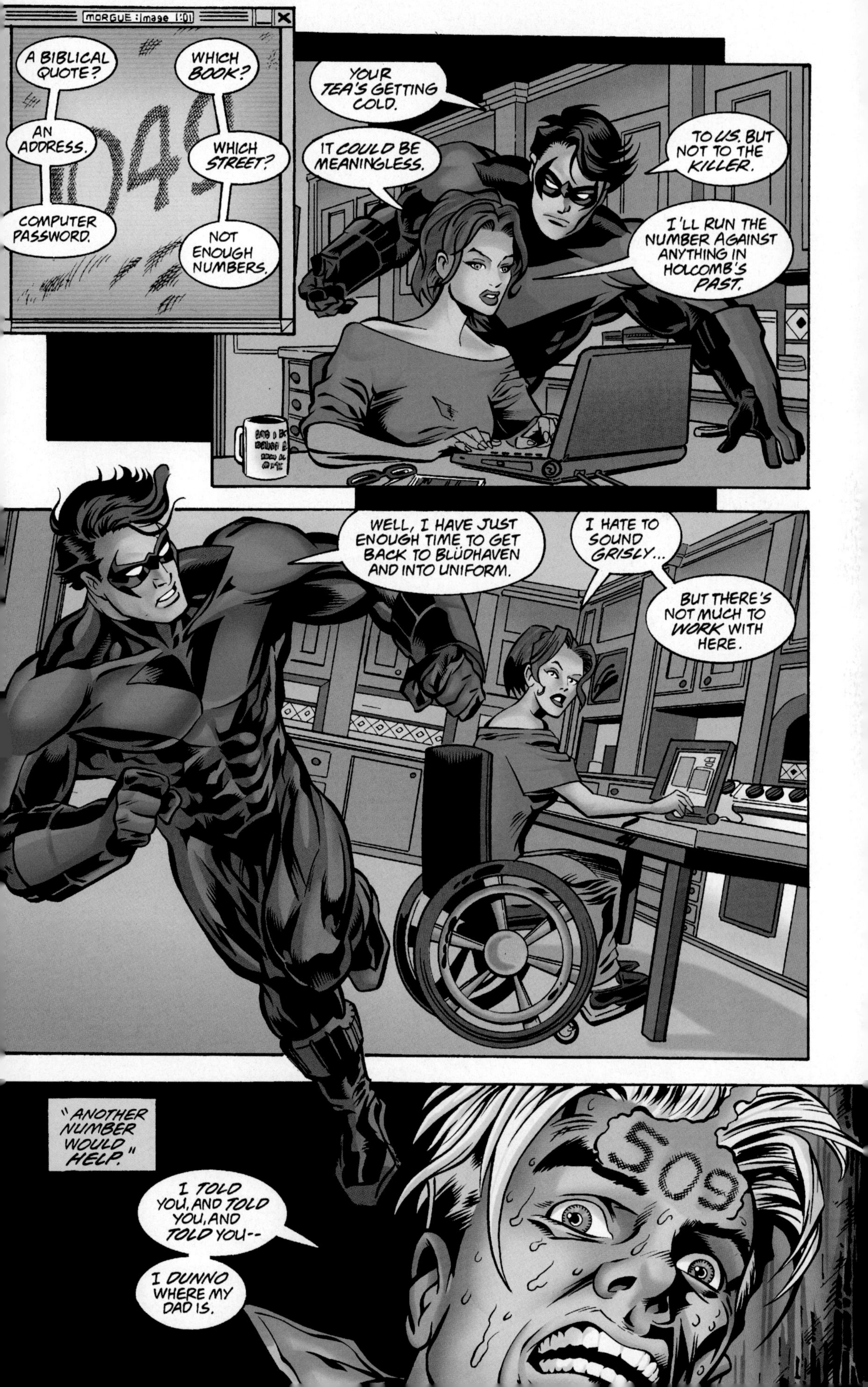
MORGUE :image 1:01
A BIBLICAL QUOTE?
AN ADDRESS.
COMPUTER PASSWORD.
WHICH BOOK?
WHICH STREET?
NOT ENOUGH NUMBERS.
YOUR TEA'S GETTING COLD.
IT COULD BE MEANINGLESS.
TO US. BUT NOT TO THE KILLER.
I'LL RUN THE NUMBER AGAINST ANYTHING IN HOLCOMB'S PAST.
WELL, I HAVE JUST ENOUGH TIME TO GET BACK TO BLÜDHAVEN AND INTO UNIFORM.
I HATE TO SOUND GRISLY...
BUT THERE'S NOT MUCH TO WORK WITH HERE.
"ANOTHER NUMBER WOULD HELP."
I TOLD YOU, AND TOLD YOU, AND TOLD YOU--
I DUNNO WHERE MY DAD IS.

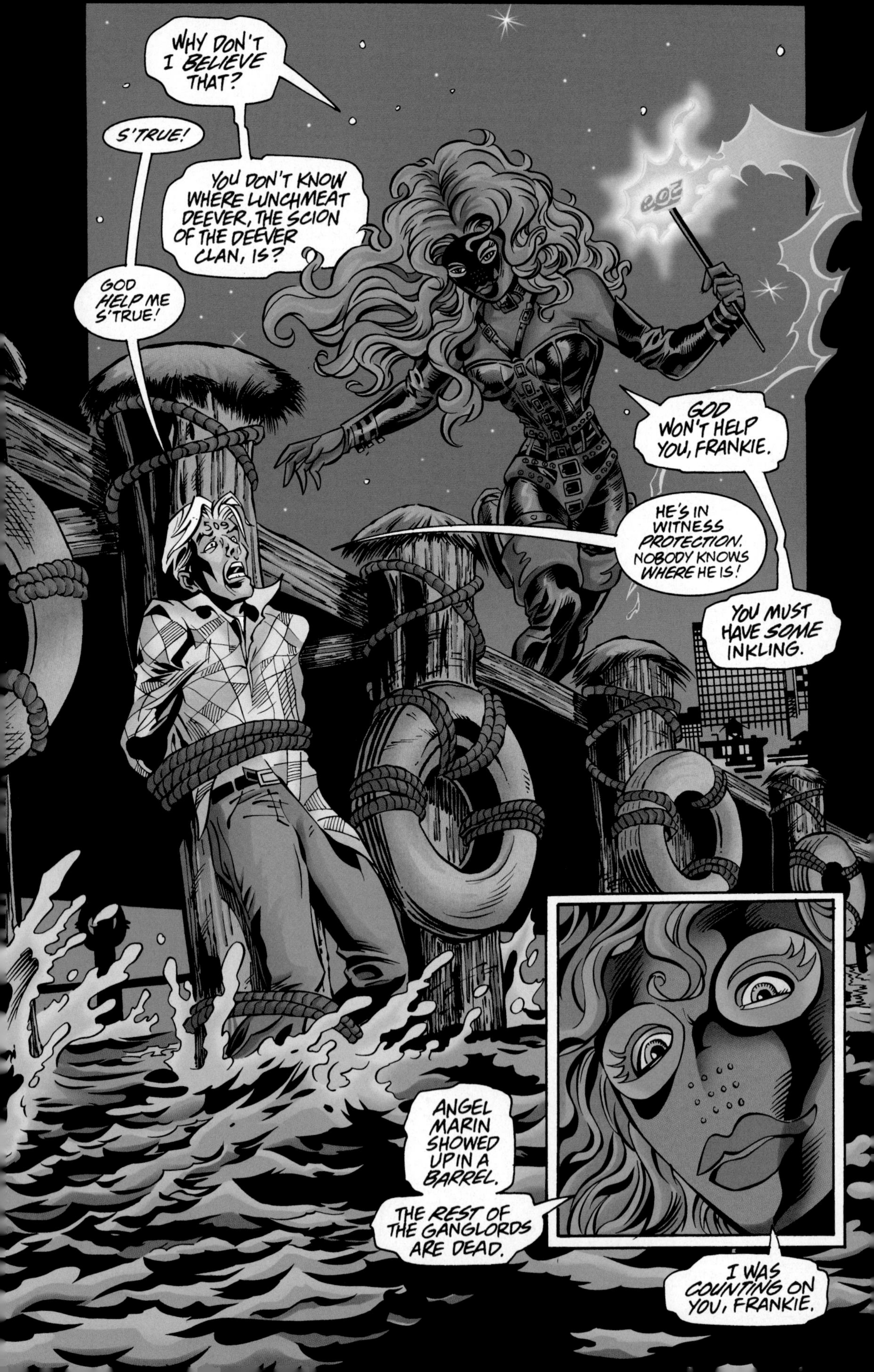
WHY DON'T I *BELIEVE* THAT?
YOU DON'T KNOW WHERE LUNCHMEAT DEEVER, THE SCION OF THE DEEVER CLAN, IS?
S'TRUE!
GOD *HELP* ME S'TRUE!
GOD WON'T HELP YOU, FRANKIE.
HE'S IN WITNESS *PROTECTION.* NOBODY KNOWS *WHERE* HE IS!
YOU MUST HAVE *SOME* INKLING.
ANGEL MARIN SHOWED UP IN A *BARREL.*
THE *REST* OF THE GANGLORDS ARE DEAD.
I WAS *COUNTING* ON YOU, FRANKIE.

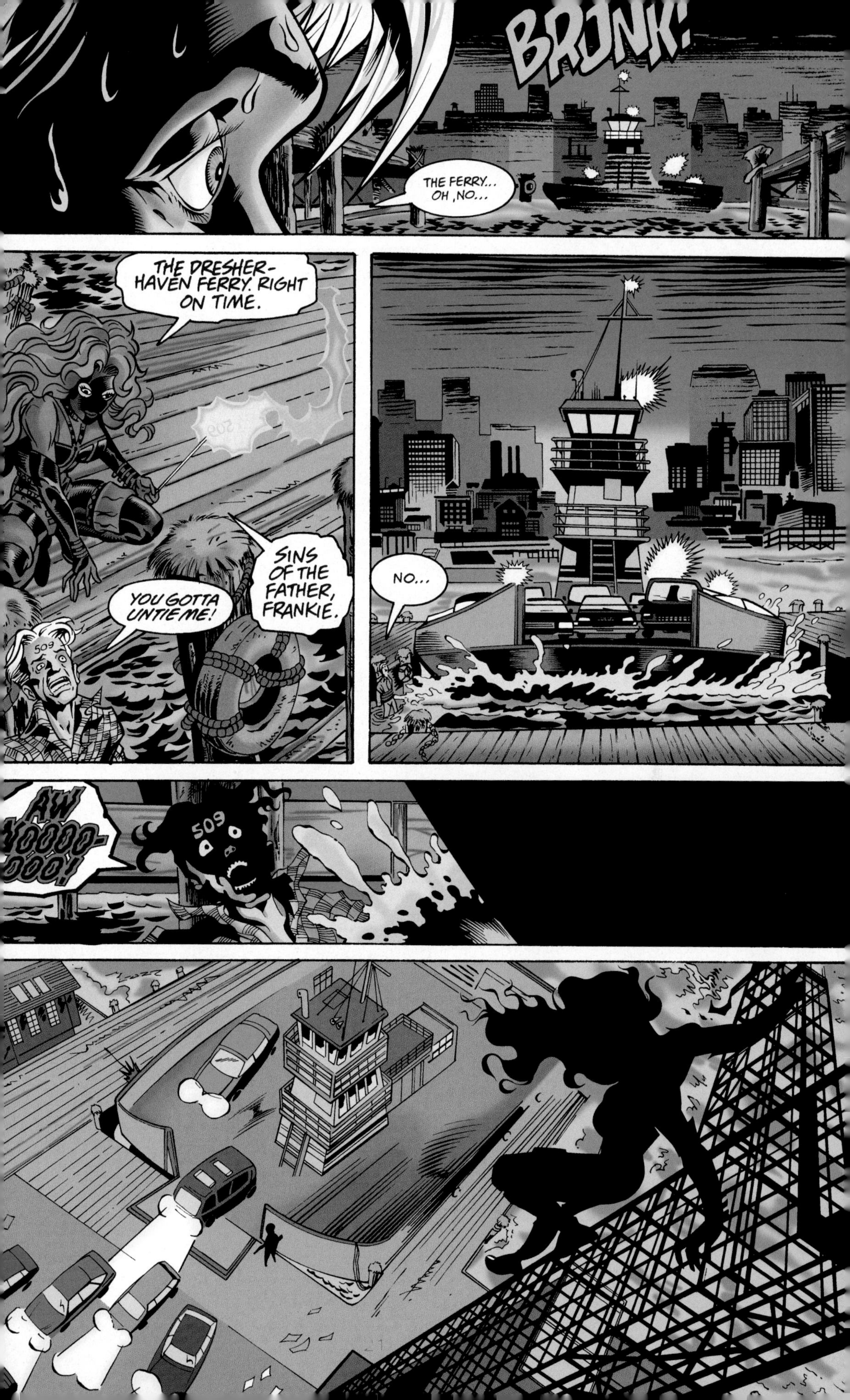
BRONK!
THE FERRY... OH, NO...
THE DRESHER-HAVEN FERRY. RIGHT ON TIME.
SINS OF THE FATHER, FRANKIE.
YOU GOTTA UNTIE ME!
NO...
AW NOOOO-OOO!

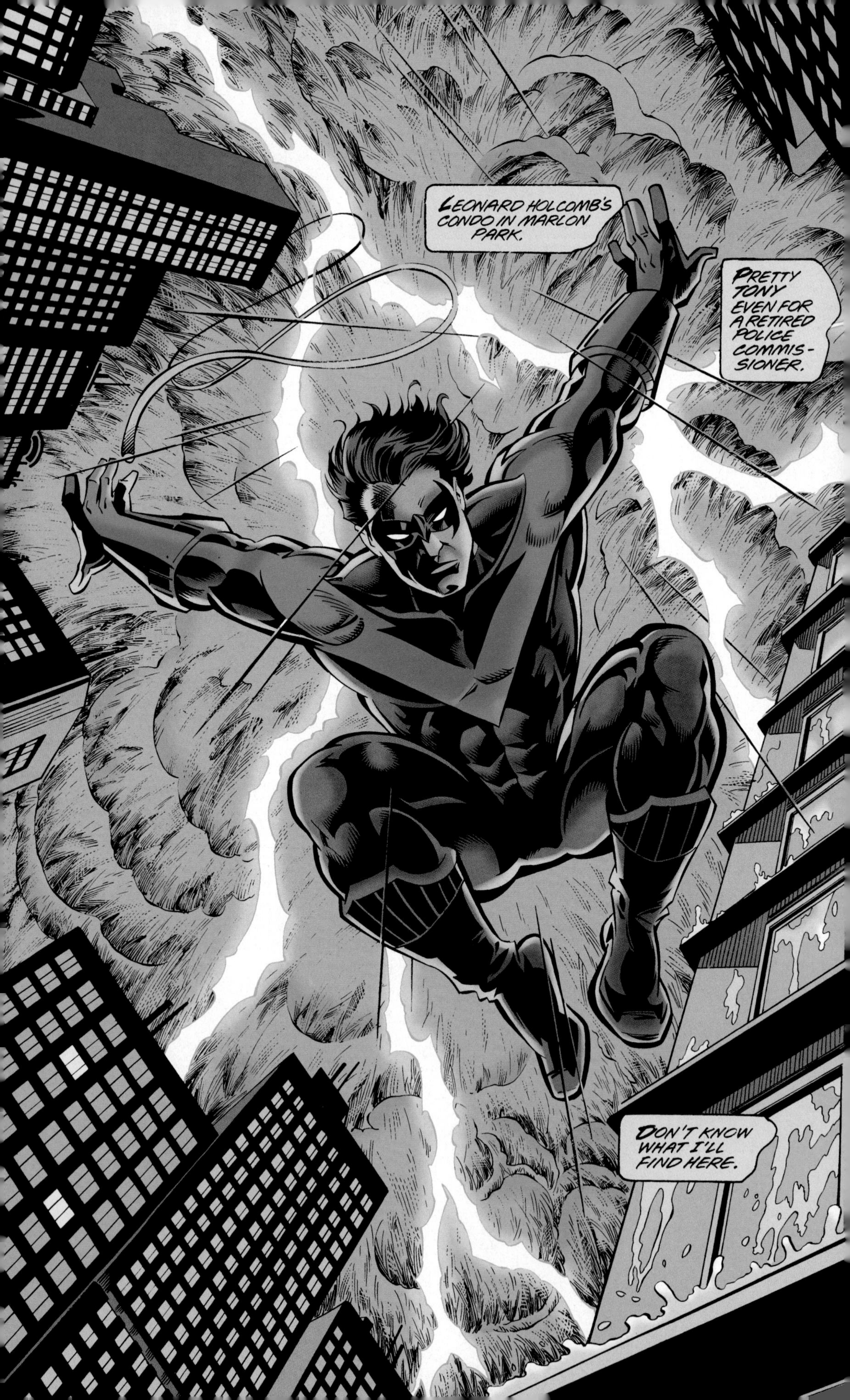
LEONARD HOLCOMB'S CONDO IN MARLON PARK.
PRETTY TONY EVEN FOR A RETIRED POLICE COMMIS-SIONER.
DON'T KNOW WHAT I'LL FIND HERE.

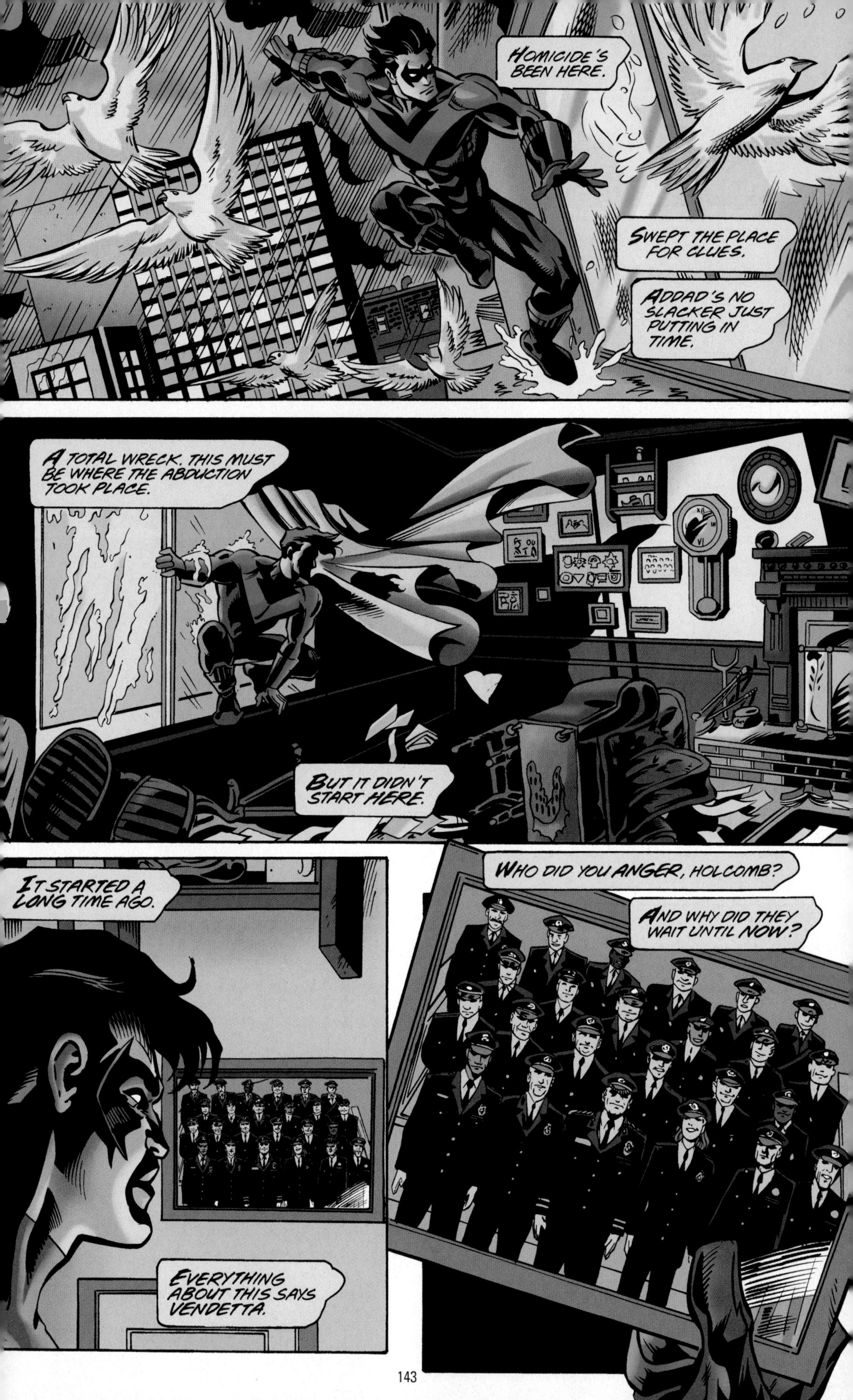
HOMICIDE'S BEEN HERE.
SWEPT THE PLACE FOR CLUES.
ADDAD'S NO SLACKER JUST PUTTING IN TIME.
A TOTAL WRECK. THIS MUST BE WHERE THE ABDUCTION TOOK PLACE.
BUT IT DIDN'T START HERE.
IT STARTED A LONG TIME AGO.
EVERYTHING ABOUT THIS SAYS VENDETTA.
WHO DID YOU ANGER, HOLCOMB?
AND WHY DID THEY WAIT UNTIL NOW?

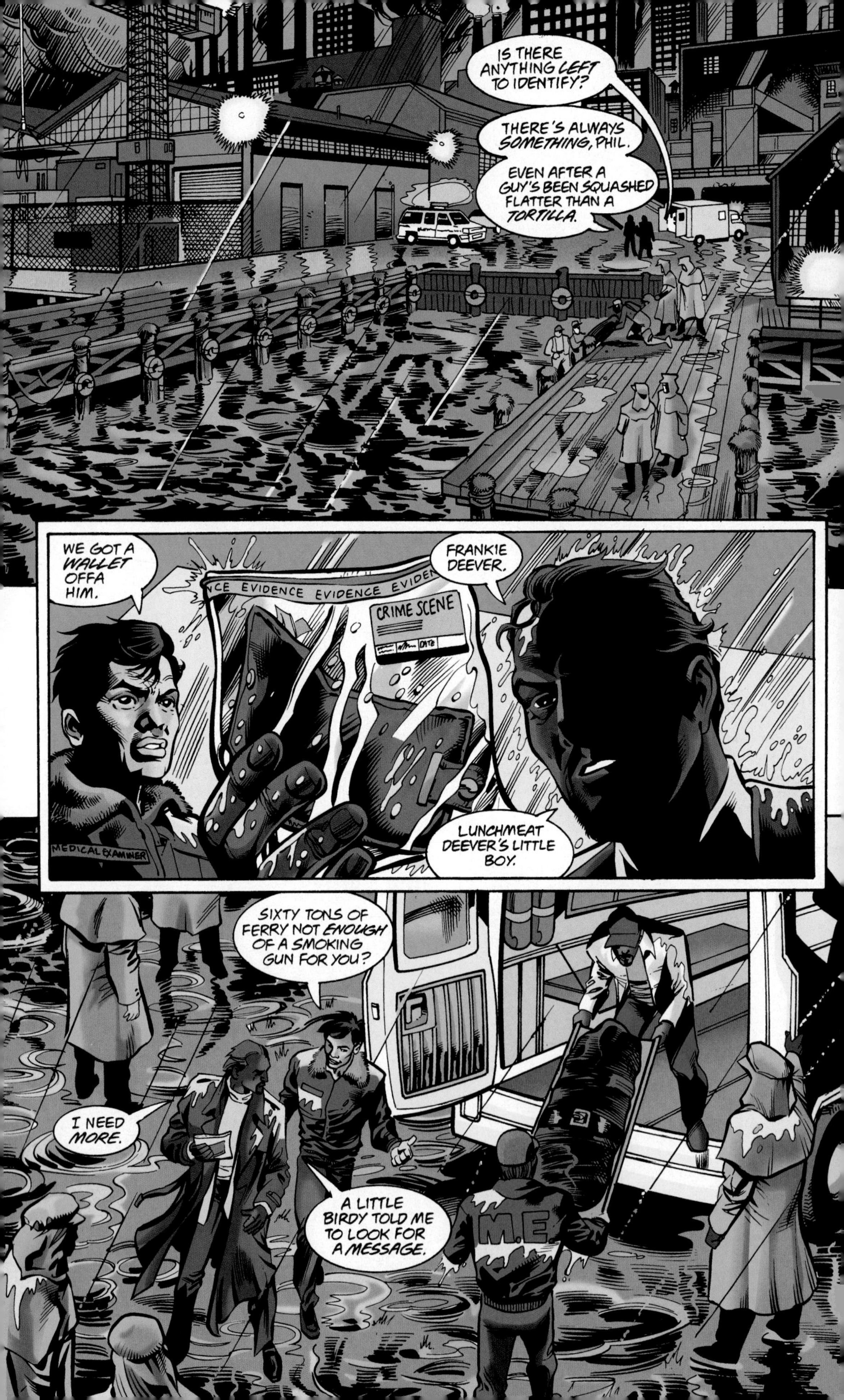
IS THERE ANYTHING LEFT TO IDENTIFY?
THERE'S ALWAYS SOMETHING, PHIL.
EVEN AFTER A GUY'S BEEN SQUASHED FLATTER THAN A TORTILLA.
WE GOT A WALLET OFFA HIM.
EVIDENCE EVIDENCE EVIDEN
CRIME SCENE
FRANKIE DEEVER.
MEDICAL EXAMINER
LUNCHMEAT DEEVER'S LITTLE BOY.
SIXTY TONS OF FERRY NOT ENOUGH OF A SMOKING GUN FOR YOU?
I NEED MORE.
A LITTLE BIRDY TOLD ME TO LOOK FOR A MESSAGE.
M.E.

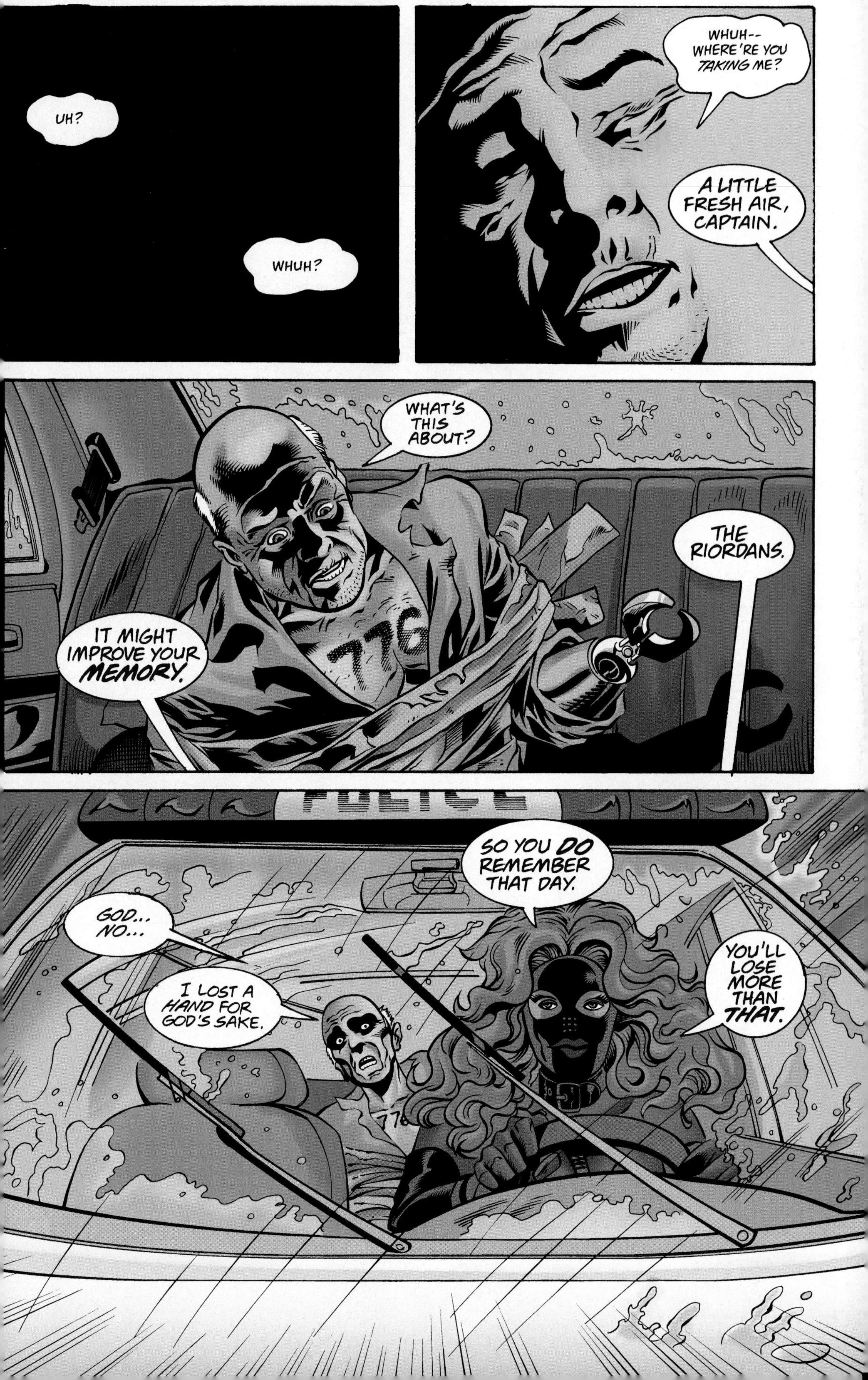
UH?
WHUH?
WHUH-- WHERE'RE YOU TAKING ME?
A LITTLE FRESH AIR, CAPTAIN.
WHAT'S THIS ABOUT?
THE RIORDANS.
IT MIGHT IMPROVE YOUR MEMORY.
776
POLICE
SO YOU DO REMEMBER THAT DAY.
GOD... NO...
I LOST A HAND FOR GOD'S SAKE.
YOU'LL LOSE MORE THAN THAT.

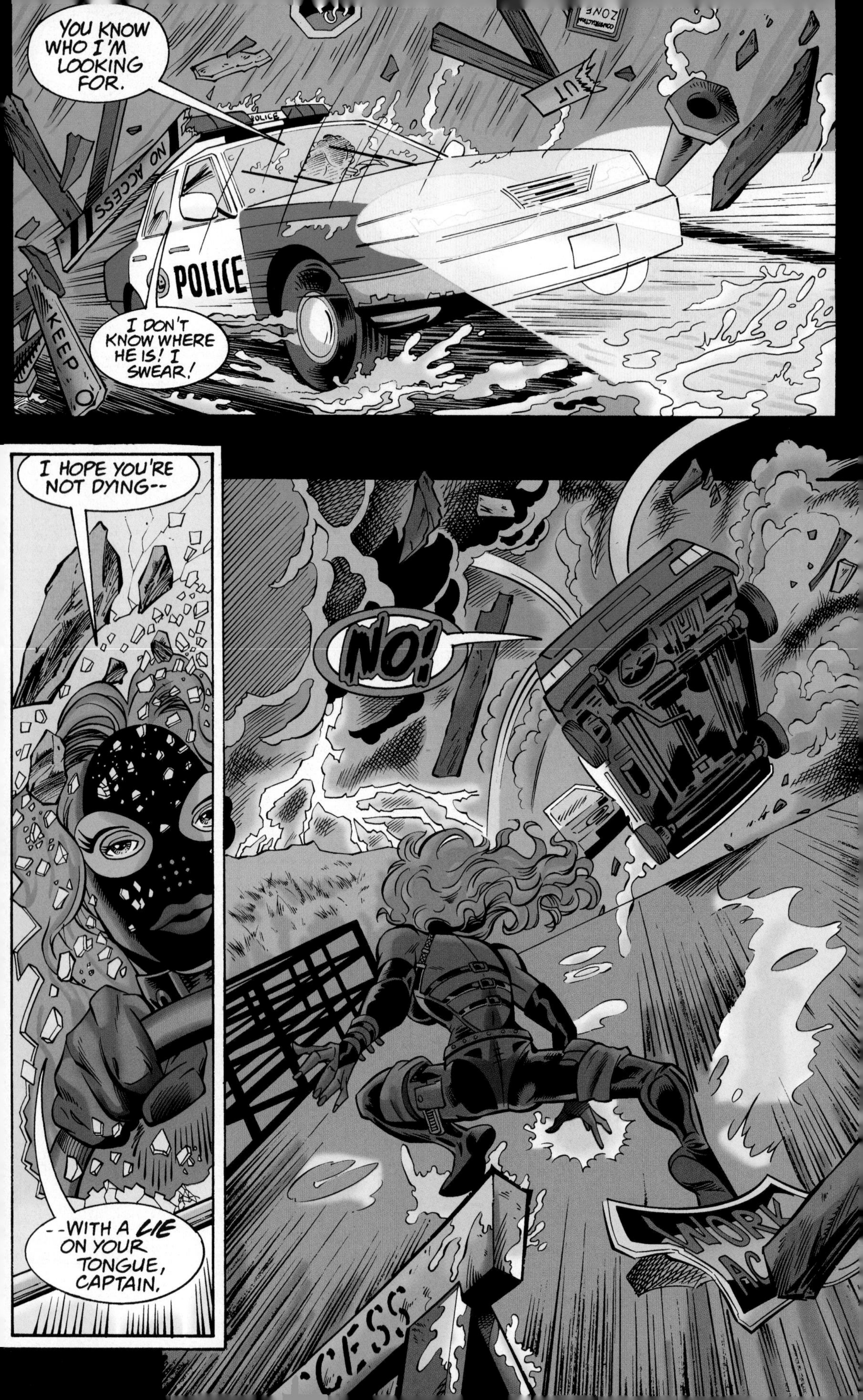

YOU KNOW WHO I'M LOOKING FOR.
I DON'T KNOW WHERE HE IS! I SWEAR!
I HOPE YOU'RE NOT DYING--
NO!
--WITH A LIE ON YOUR TONGUE, CAPTAIN.

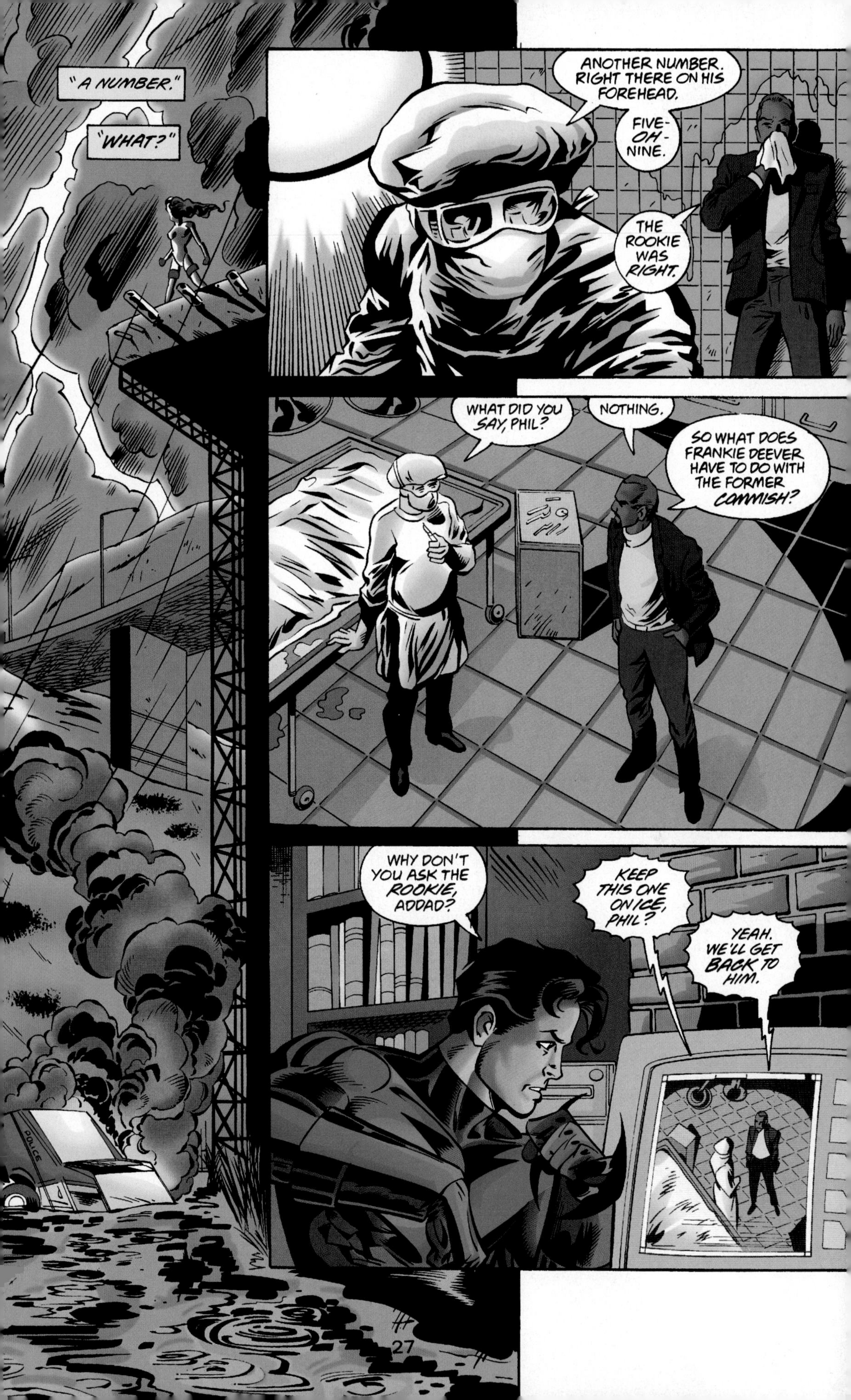
"A NUMBER."
"WHAT?"
ANOTHER NUMBER. RIGHT THERE ON HIS FOREHEAD.
FIVE-OH-NINE.
THE ROOKIE WAS RIGHT.
WHAT DID YOU SAY, PHIL?
NOTHING.
SO WHAT DOES FRANKIE DEEVER HAVE TO DO WITH THE FORMER COMMISH?
WHY DON'T YOU ASK THE ROOKIE, ADDAD?
KEEP THIS ONE ON ICE, PHIL?
YEAH. WE'LL GET BACK TO HIM.
POLICE

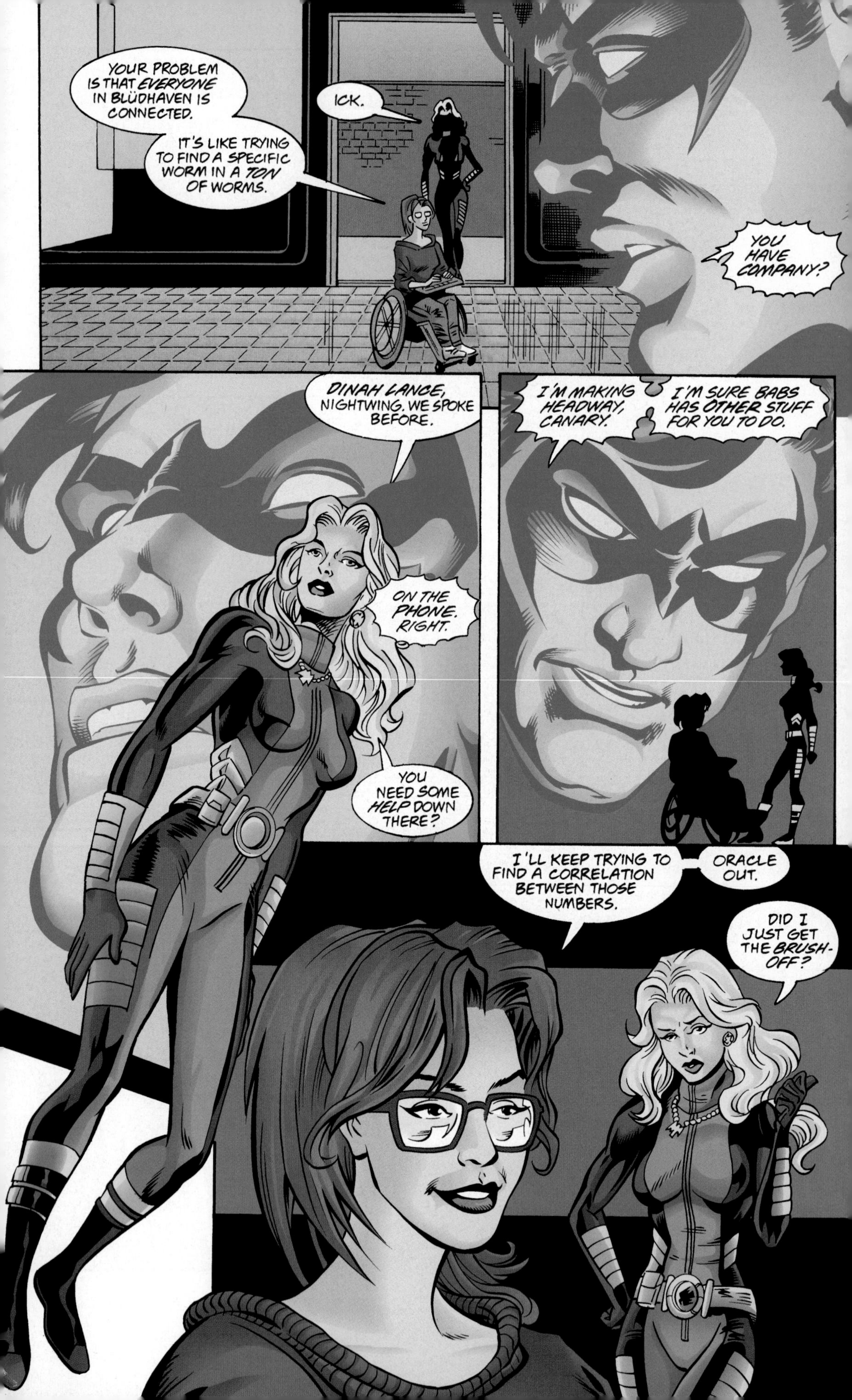
YOUR PROBLEM IS THAT EVERYONE IN BLÜDHAVEN IS CONNECTED.
ICK.
IT'S LIKE TRYING TO FIND A SPECIFIC WORM IN A TON OF WORMS.
YOU HAVE COMPANY?
DINAH LANCE, NIGHTWING. WE SPOKE BEFORE.
ON THE PHONE. RIGHT.
YOU NEED SOME HELP DOWN THERE?
I'M MAKING HEADWAY, CANARY.
I'M SURE BABS HAS OTHER STUFF FOR YOU TO DO.
I'LL KEEP TRYING TO FIND A CORRELATION BETWEEN THOSE NUMBERS.
ORACLE OUT.
DID I JUST GET THE BRUSH-OFF?

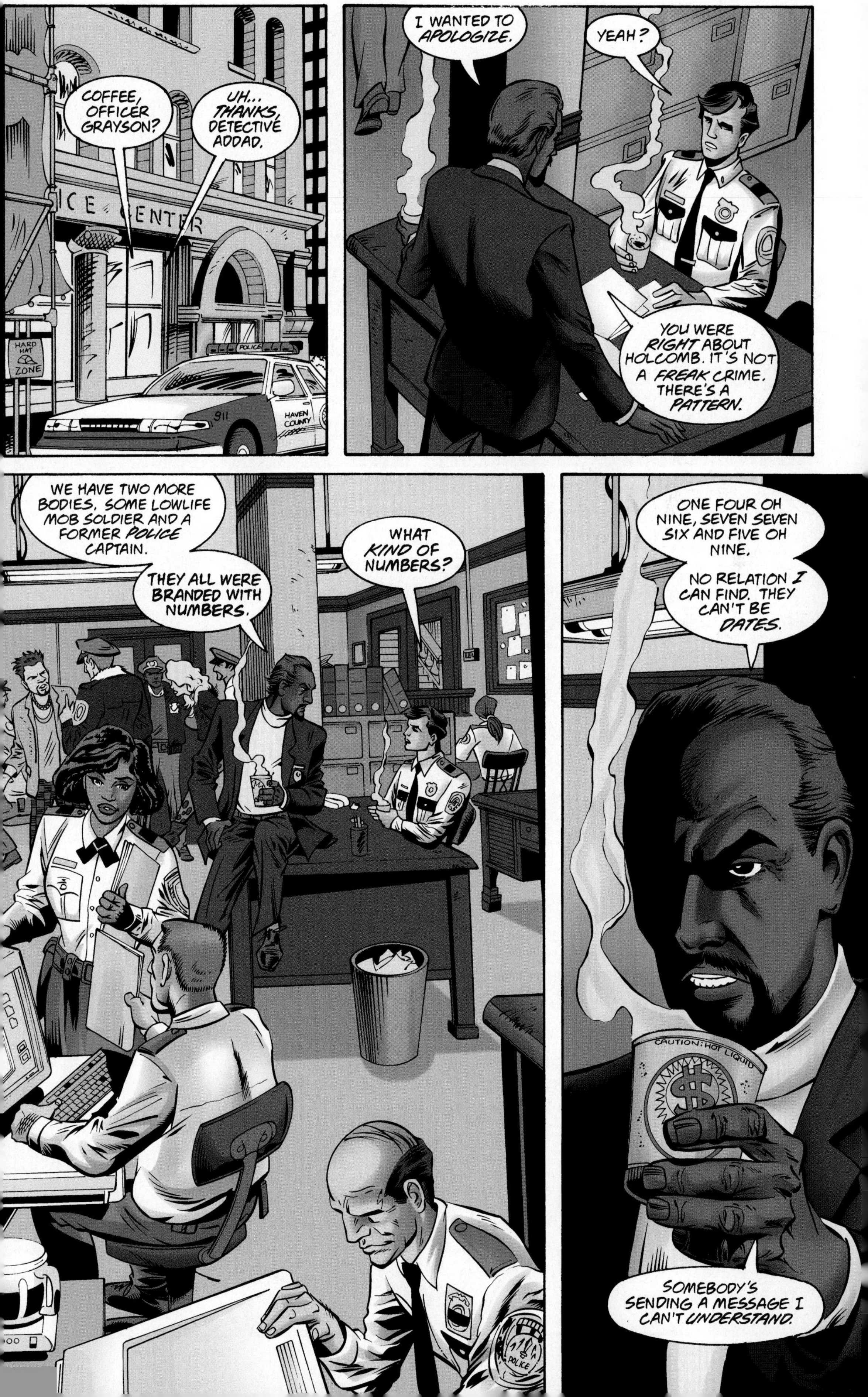

ICE CENTER
HARD HAT ZONE
COFFEE, OFFICER GRAYSON?
UH... THANKS, DETECTIVE ADDAD.
POLICE
911
HAVEN COUNTY
I WANTED TO APOLOGIZE.
YEAH?
YOU WERE RIGHT ABOUT HOLCOMB. IT'S NOT A FREAK CRIME. THERE'S A PATTERN.
WE HAVE TWO MORE BODIES. SOME LOWLIFE MOB SOLDIER AND A FORMER POLICE CAPTAIN.
THEY ALL WERE BRANDED WITH NUMBERS.
WHAT KIND OF NUMBERS?
ONE FOUR OH NINE, SEVEN SEVEN SIX AND FIVE OH NINE.
NO RELATION I CAN FIND. THEY CAN'T BE DATES.
CAUTION: HOT LIQUID
SOMEBODY'S SENDING A MESSAGE I CAN'T UNDERSTAND.

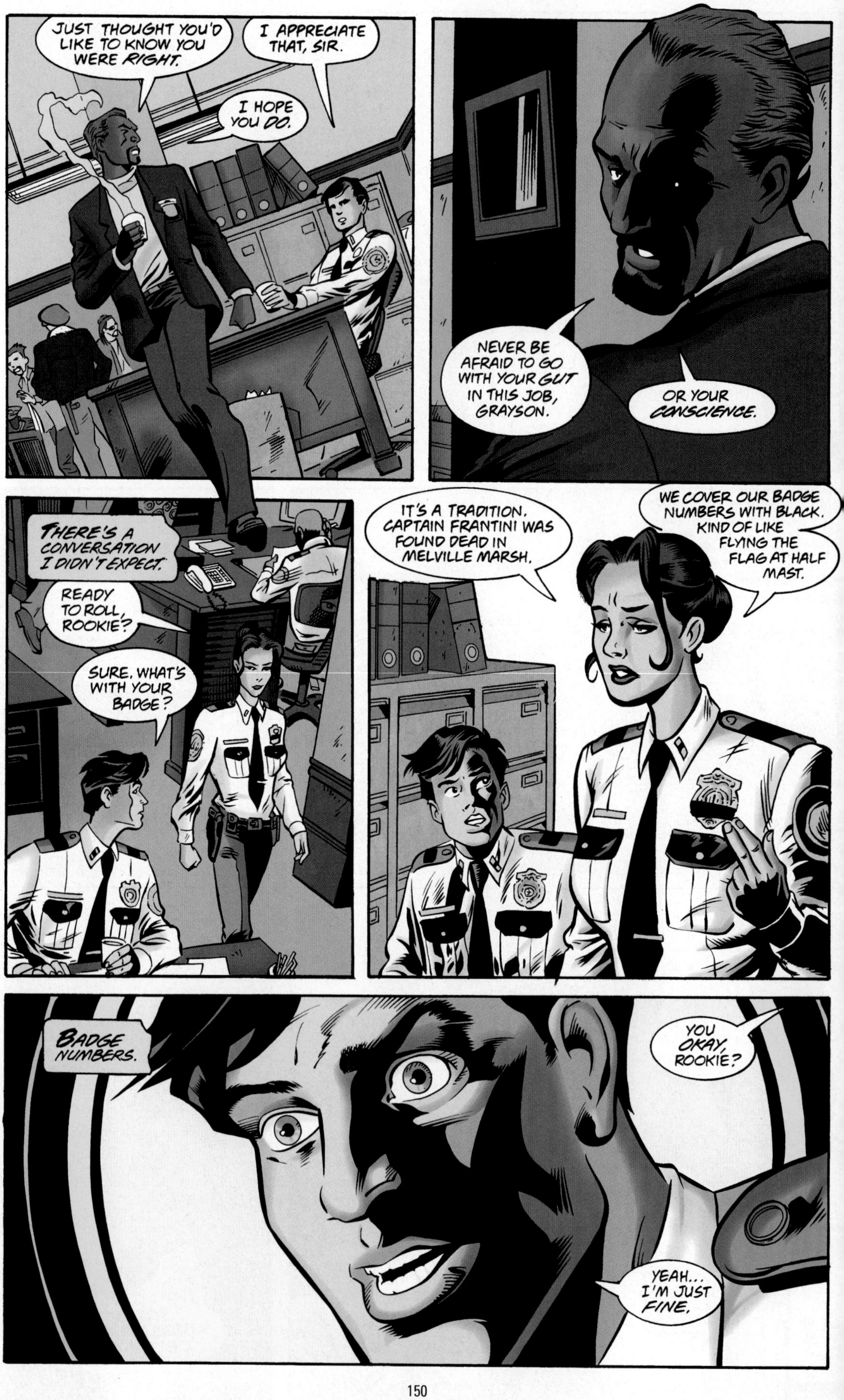
JUST THOUGHT YOU'D LIKE TO KNOW YOU WERE RIGHT.
I APPRECIATE THAT, SIR.
I HOPE YOU DO.
NEVER BE AFRAID TO GO WITH YOUR GUT IN THIS JOB, GRAYSON.
OR YOUR CONSCIENCE.
THERE'S A CONVERSATION I DIDN'T EXPECT.
READY TO ROLL, ROOKIE?
SURE. WHAT'S WITH YOUR BADGE?
IT'S A TRADITION. CAPTAIN FRANTINI WAS FOUND DEAD IN MELVILLE MARSH.
WE COVER OUR BADGE NUMBERS WITH BLACK. KIND OF LIKE FLYING THE FLAG AT HALF MAST.
BADGE NUMBERS.
YOU OKAY, ROOKIE?
YEAH... I'M JUST FINE.

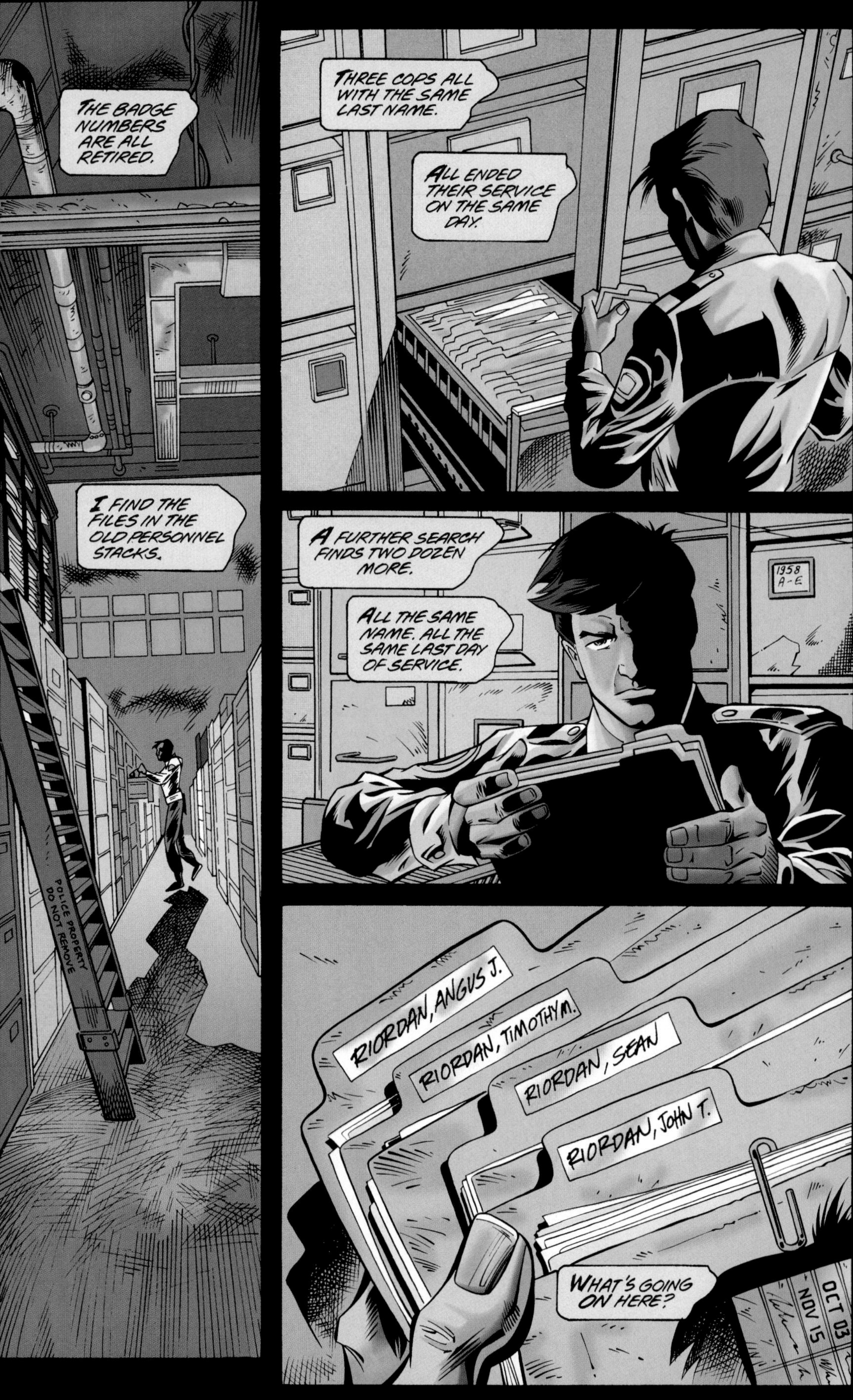
THE BADGE NUMBERS ARE ALL RETIRED.
I FIND THE FILES IN THE OLD PERSONNEL STACKS.
POLICE PROPERTY DO NOT REMOVE
THREE COPS ALL WITH THE SAME LAST NAME.
ALL ENDED THEIR SERVICE ON THE SAME DAY.
A FURTHER SEARCH FINDS TWO DOZEN MORE.
1958 A-E
ALL THE SAME NAME. ALL THE SAME LAST DAY OF SERVICE.
RIORDAN, ANGUS J.
RIORDAN, TIMOTHY M.
RIORDAN, SEAN
RIORDAN, JOHN T.
WHAT'S GOING ON HERE?
OCT 03
NOV 15

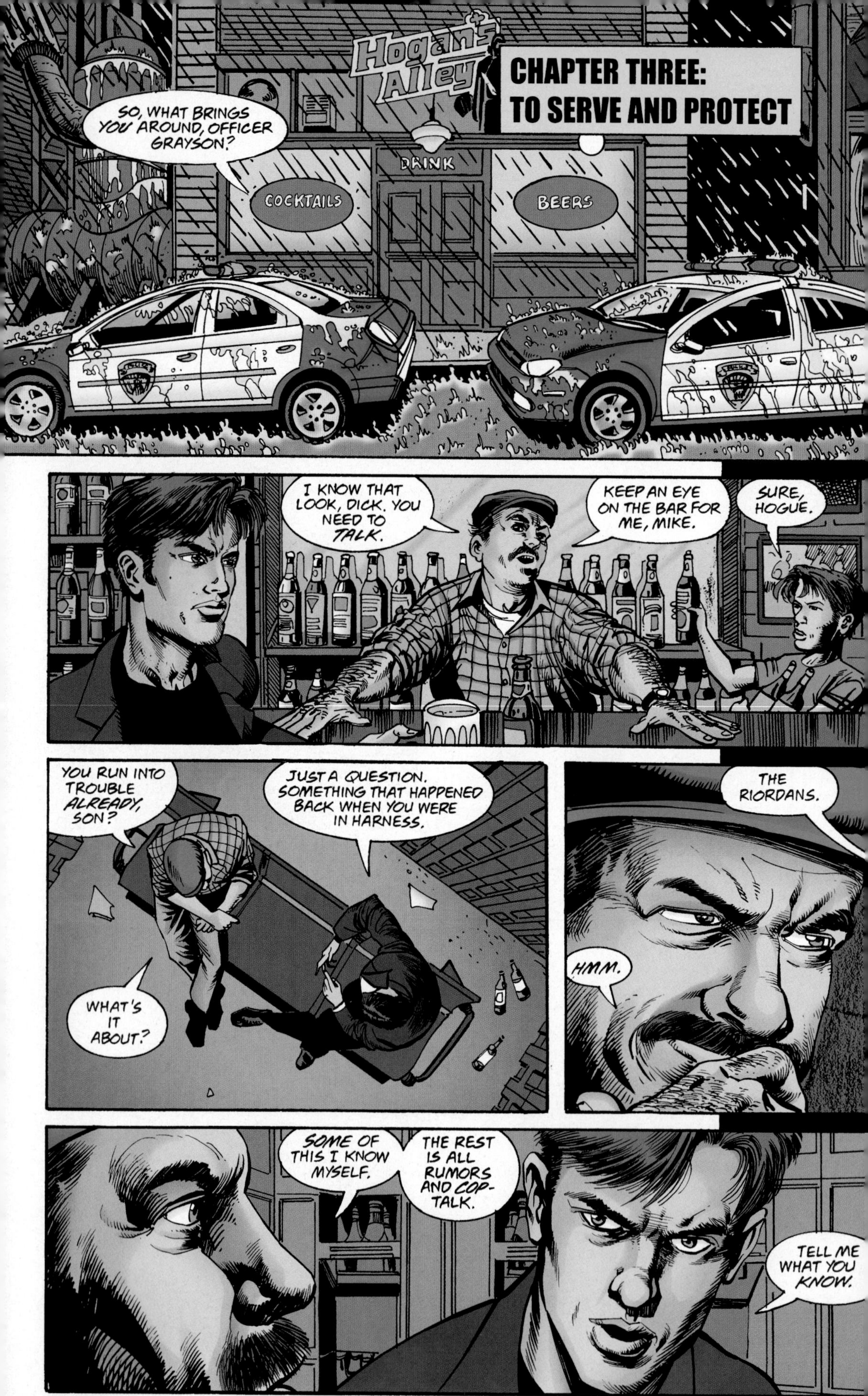
Hogan's Alley
CHAPTER THREE:
TO SERVE AND PROTECT
SO, WHAT BRINGS YOU AROUND, OFFICER GRAYSON?
DRINK
COCKTAILS
BEERS
I KNOW THAT LOOK, DICK. YOU NEED TO TALK.
KEEP AN EYE ON THE BAR FOR ME, MIKE.
SURE, HOGUE.
YOU RUN INTO TROUBLE ALREADY, SON?
JUST A QUESTION. SOMETHING THAT HAPPENED BACK WHEN YOU WERE IN HARNESS.
WHAT'S IT ABOUT?
THE RIORDANS.
HMM.
SOME OF THIS I KNOW MYSELF.
THE REST IS ALL RUMORS AND COP-TALK.
TELL ME WHAT YOU KNOW.

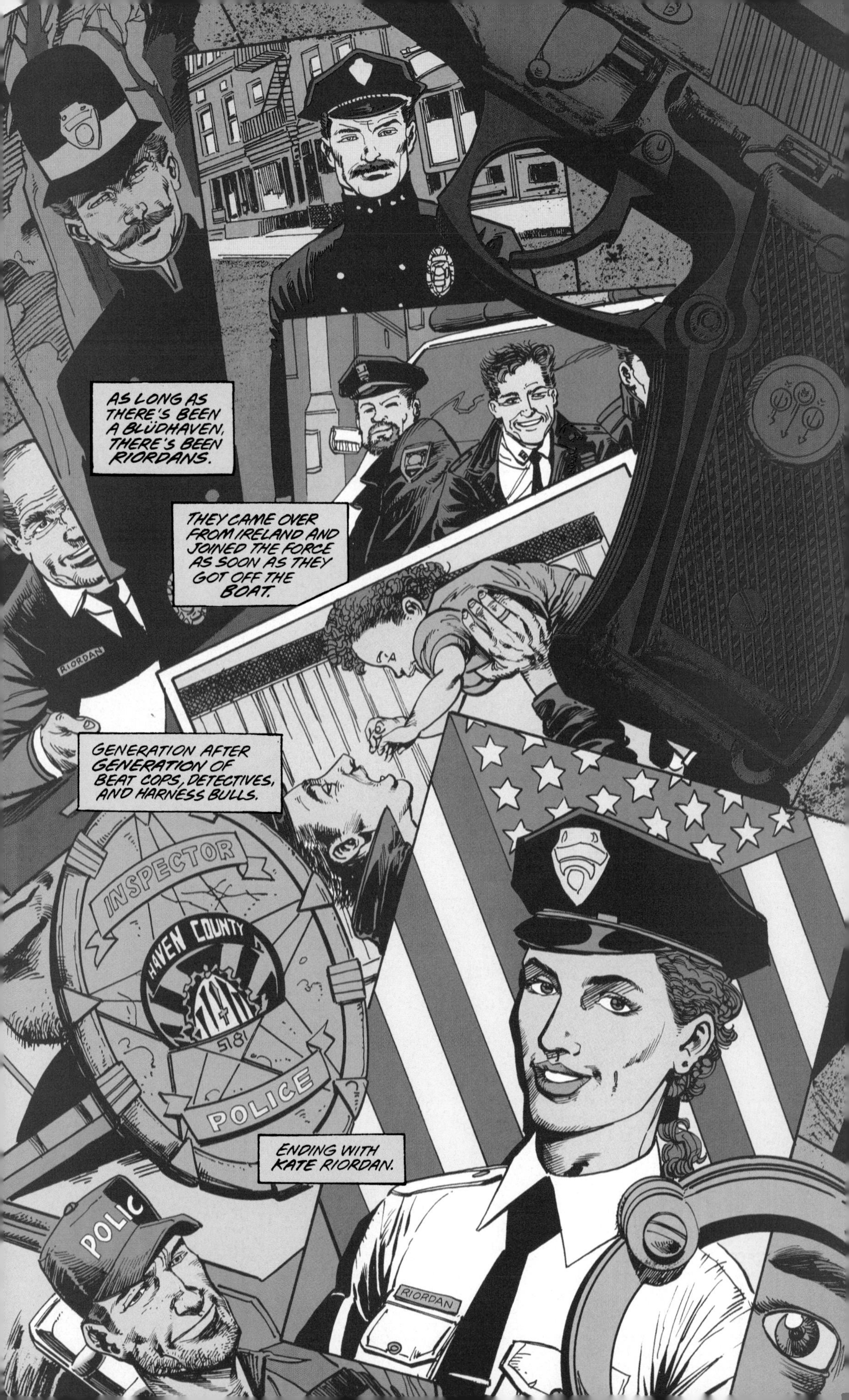
AS LONG AS THERE'S BEEN A BLÜDHAVEN, THERE'S BEEN RIORDANS.
THEY CAME OVER FROM IRELAND AND JOINED THE FORCE AS SOON AS THEY GOT OFF THE BOAT.
RIORDAN
GENERATION AFTER GENERATION OF BEAT COPS, DETECTIVES, AND HARNESS BULLS.
INSPECTOR
HAVEN COUNTY
5181
POLICE
ENDING WITH KATE RIORDAN.
POLIC
RIORDAN

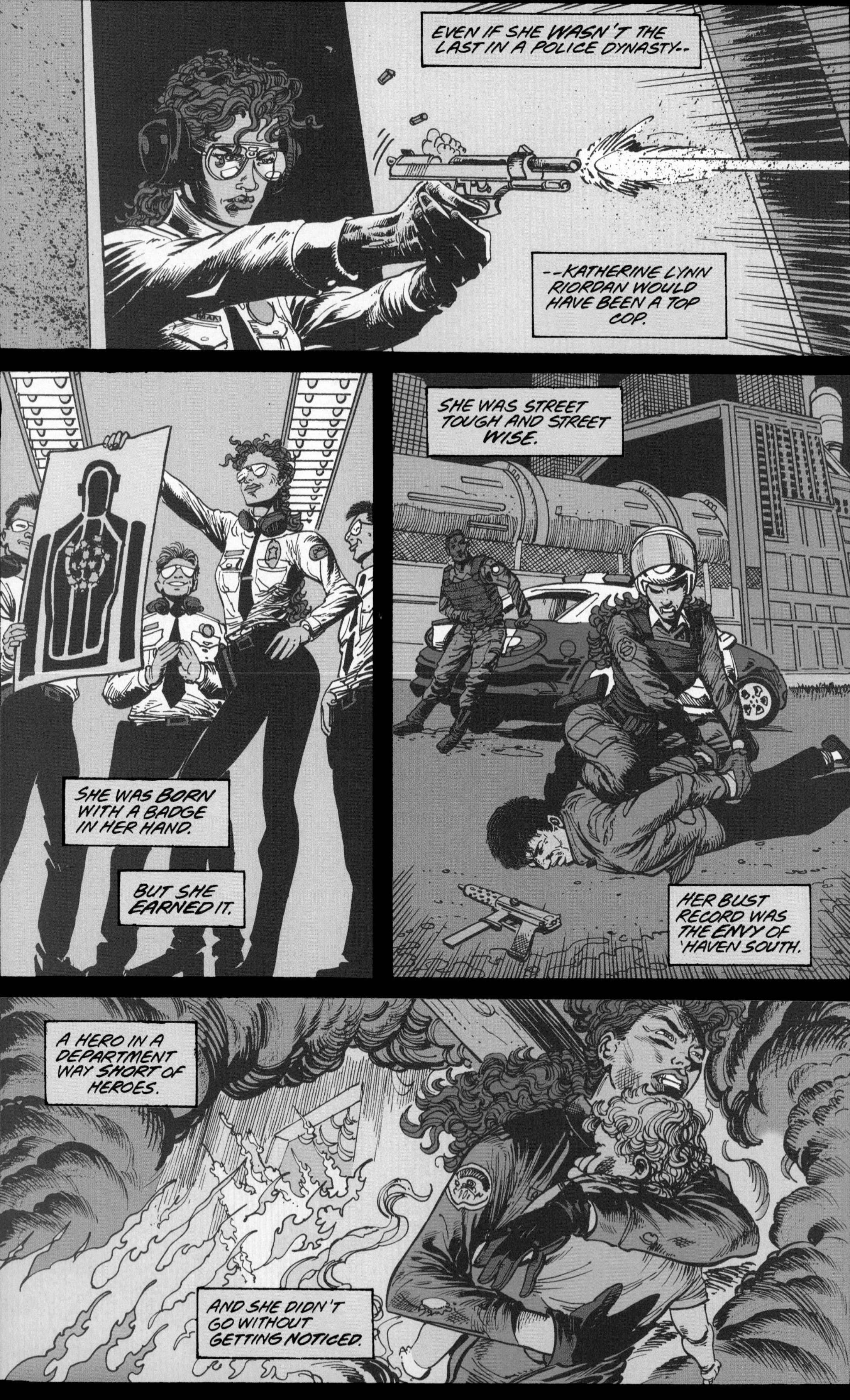

EVEN IF SHE WASN'T THE LAST IN A POLICE DYNASTY--
--KATHERINE LYNN RIORDAN WOULD HAVE BEEN A TOP COP.
SHE WAS BORN WITH A BADGE IN HER HAND.
BUT SHE EARNED IT.
SHE WAS STREET TOUGH AND STREET WISE.
HER BUST RECORD WAS THE ENVY OF 'HAVEN SOUTH.
A HERO IN A DEPARTMENT WAY SHORT OF HEROES.
AND SHE DIDN'T GO WITHOUT GETTING NOTICED.

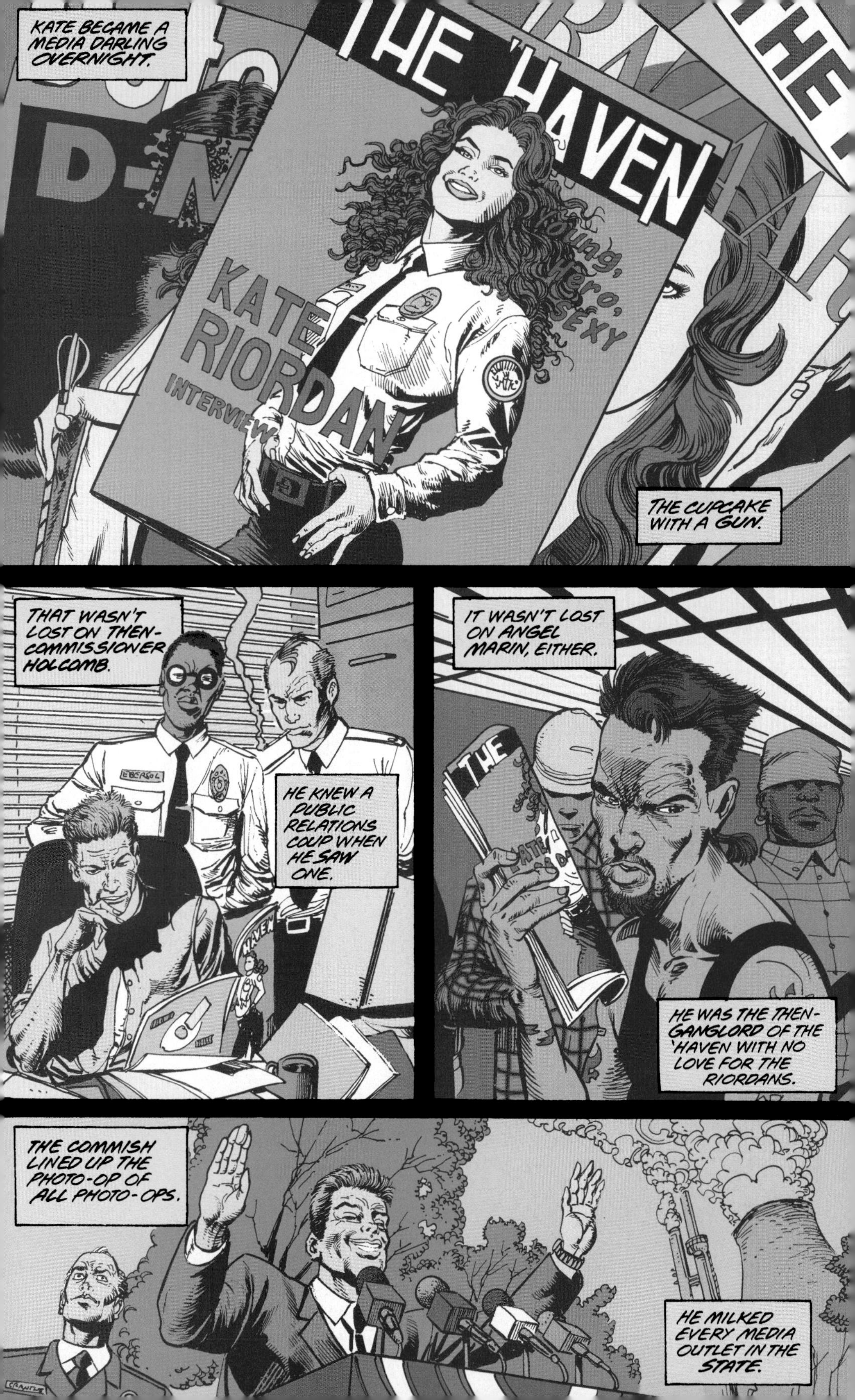
KATE BECAME A MEDIA DARLING OVERNIGHT.
THE 'HAVEN
KATE RIORDAN INTERVIEW
Young, Hero, SEXY
THE CUPCAKE WITH A GUN.
THAT WASN'T LOST ON THEN-COMMISSIONER HOLCOMB.
HE KNEW A PUBLIC RELATIONS COUP WHEN HE SAW ONE.
IT WASN'T LOST ON ANGEL MARIN, EITHER.
HE WAS THE THEN-GANGLORD OF THE 'HAVEN WITH NO LOVE FOR THE RIORDANS.
THE COMMISH LINED UP THE PHOTO-OP OF ALL PHOTO-OPS.
HE MILKED EVERY MEDIA OUTLET IN THE STATE.

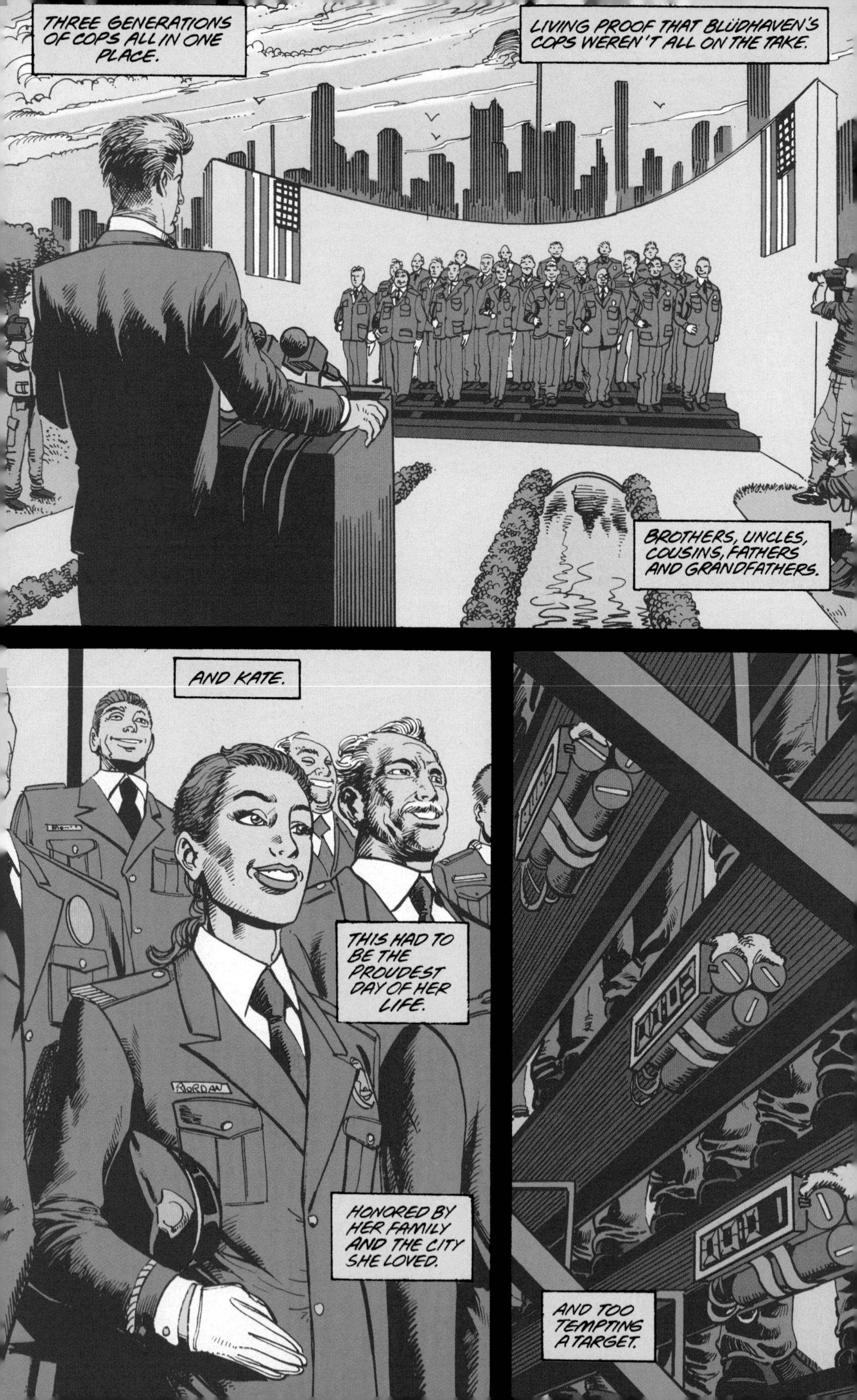
THREE GENERATIONS OF COPS ALL IN ONE PLACE.
LIVING PROOF THAT BLÜDHAVEN'S COPS WEREN'T ALL ON THE TAKE.
BROTHERS, UNCLES, COUSINS, FATHERS AND GRANDFATHERS.
AND KATE.
THIS HAD TO BE THE PROUDEST DAY OF HER LIFE.
HONORED BY HER FAMILY AND THE CITY SHE LOVED.
AND TOO TEMPTING A TARGET.

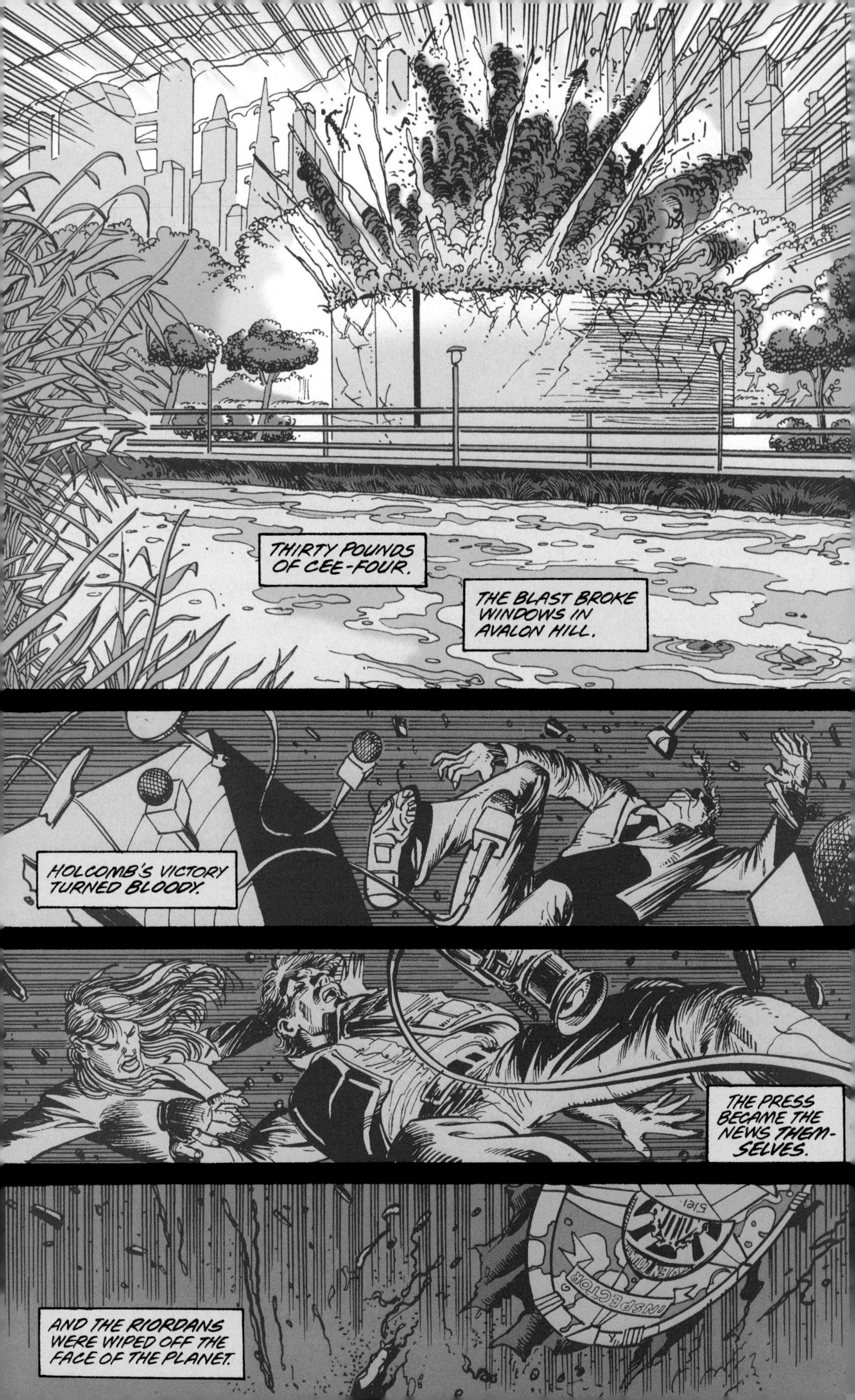
THIRTY POUNDS OF CEE-FOUR.
THE BLAST BROKE WINDOWS IN AVALON HILL.
HOLCOMB'S VICTORY TURNED BLOODY.
THE PRESS BECAME THE NEWS THEM-SELVES.
AND THE RIORDANS WERE WIPED OFF THE FACE OF THE PLANET.
INSPECTOR

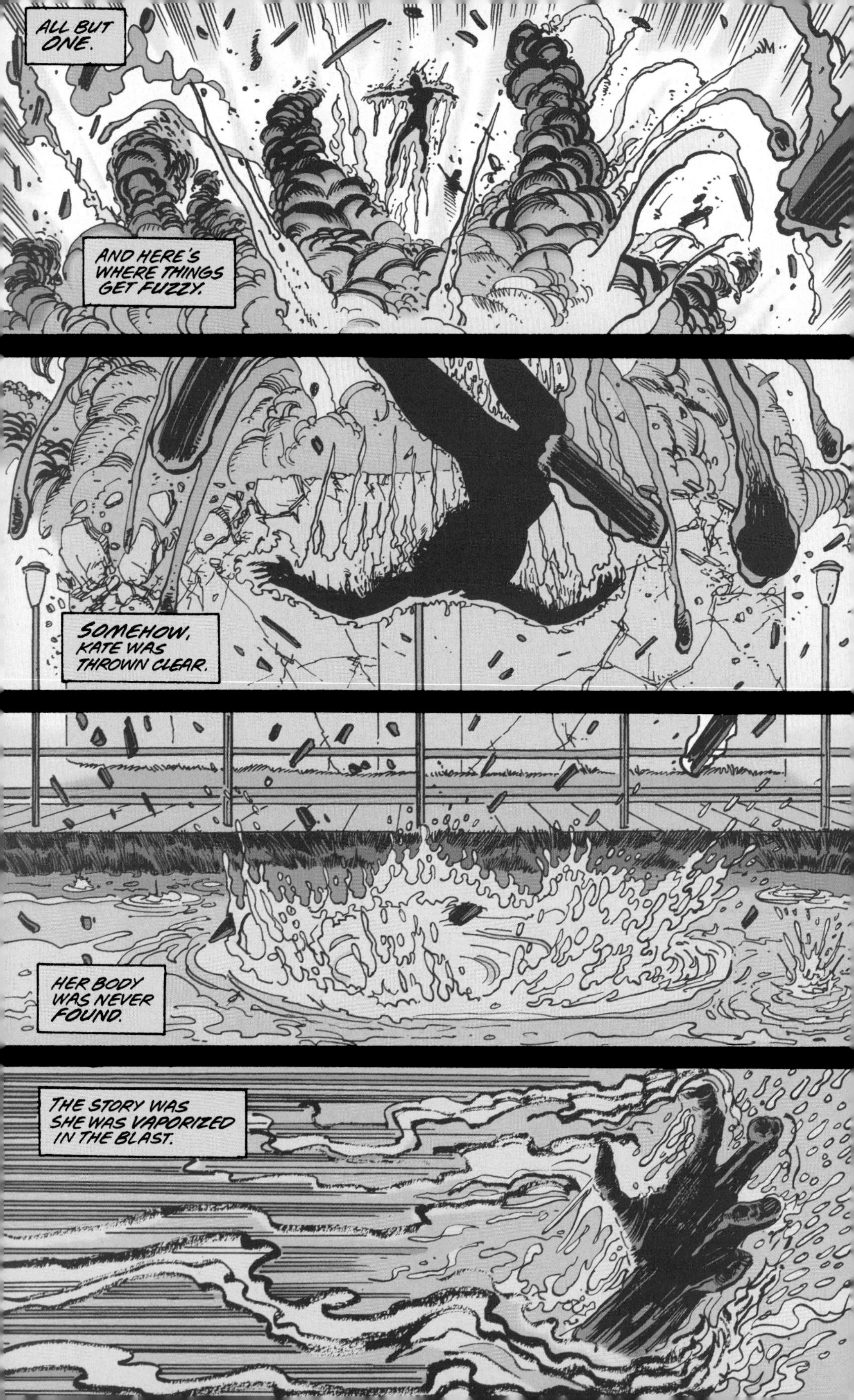
ALL BUT ONE.
AND HERE'S WHERE THINGS GET FUZZY.
SOMEHOW, KATE WAS THROWN CLEAR.
HER BODY WAS NEVER FOUND.
THE STORY WAS SHE WAS VAPORIZED IN THE BLAST.

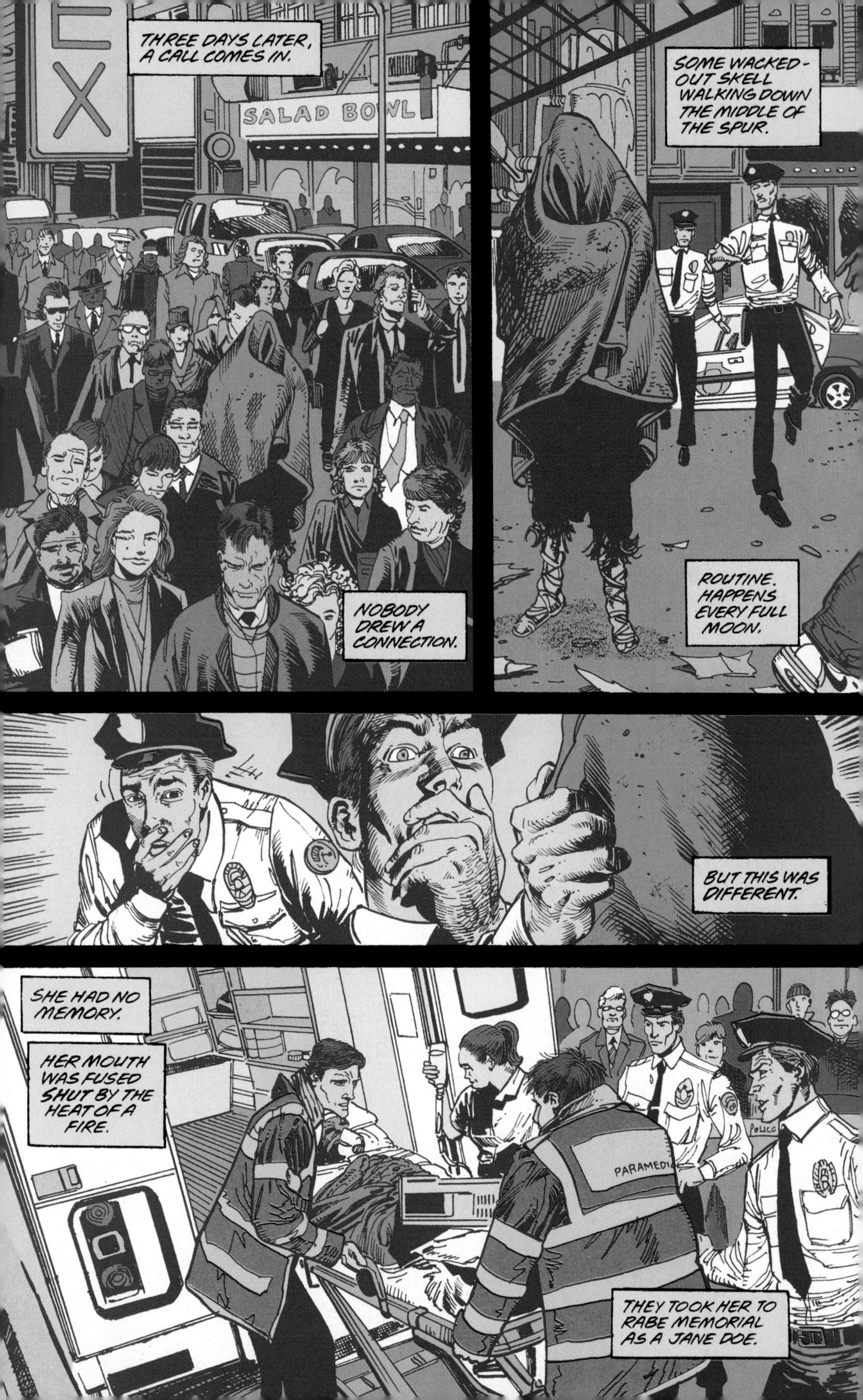
THREE DAYS LATER, A CALL COMES IN.
SALAD BOWL
NOBODY DREW A CONNECTION.
SOME WACKED-OUT SKELL WALKING DOWN THE MIDDLE OF THE SPUR.
ROUTINE. HAPPENS EVERY FULL MOON.
BUT THIS WAS DIFFERENT.
SHE HAD NO MEMORY.
HER MOUTH WAS FUSED SHUT BY THE HEAT OF A FIRE.
PARAMEDIC
POLICE
THEY TOOK HER TO RABE MEMORIAL AS A JANE DOE.

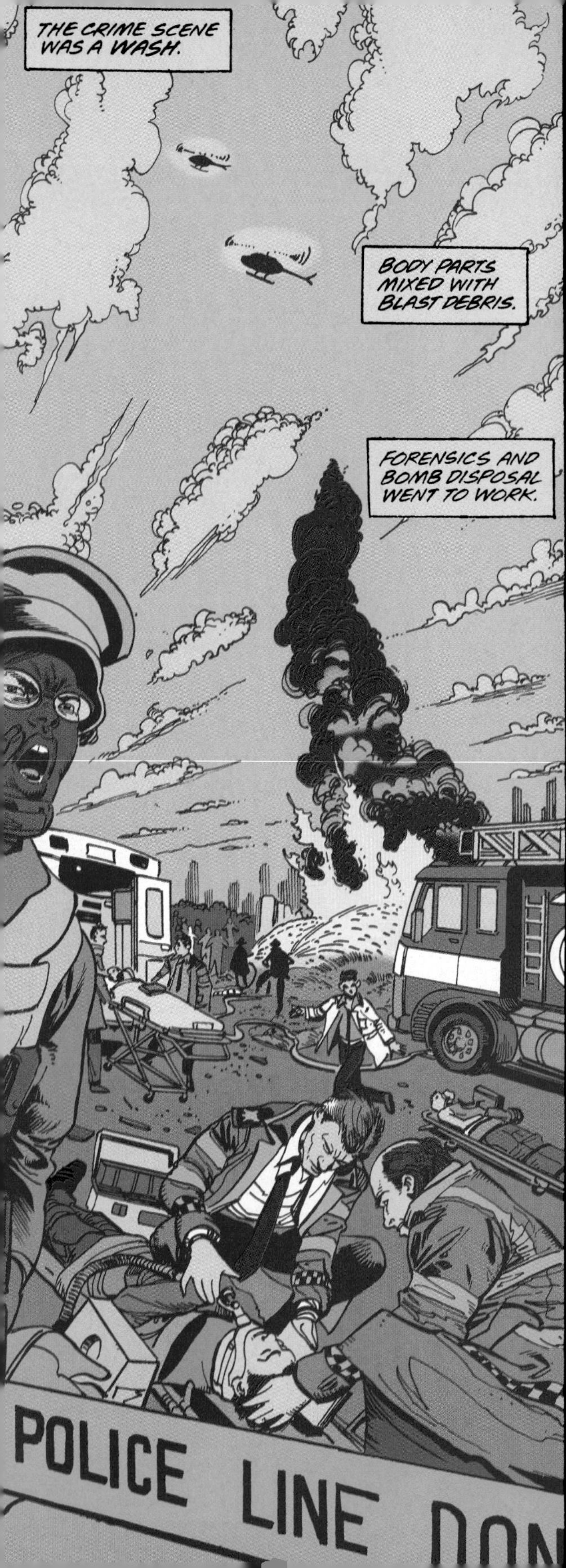
THE CRIME SCENE WAS A WASH.
BODY PARTS MIXED WITH BLAST DEBRIS.
FORENSICS AND BOMB DISPOSAL WENT TO WORK.
POLICE LINE DON

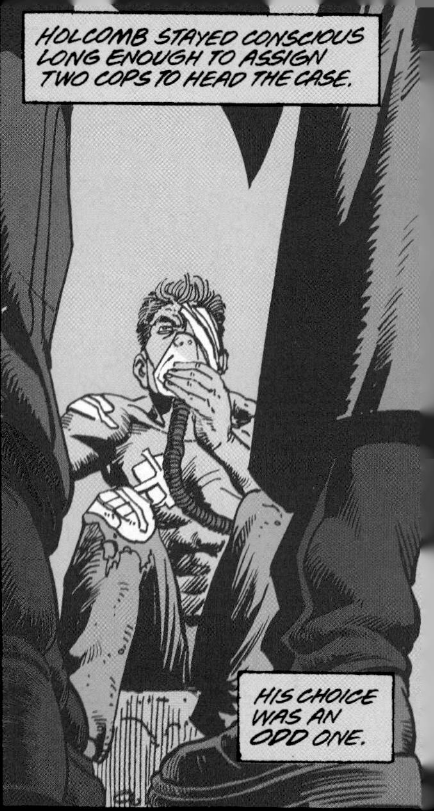
HOLCOMB STAYED CONSCIOUS LONG ENOUGH TO ASSIGN TWO COPS TO HEAD THE CASE.
HIS CHOICE WAS AN ODD ONE.

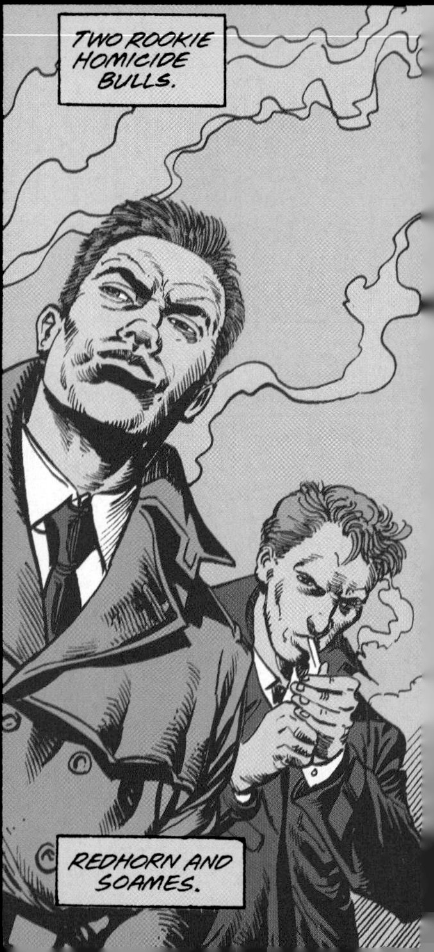
TWO ROOKIE HOMICIDE BULLS.
REDHORN AND SOAMES.

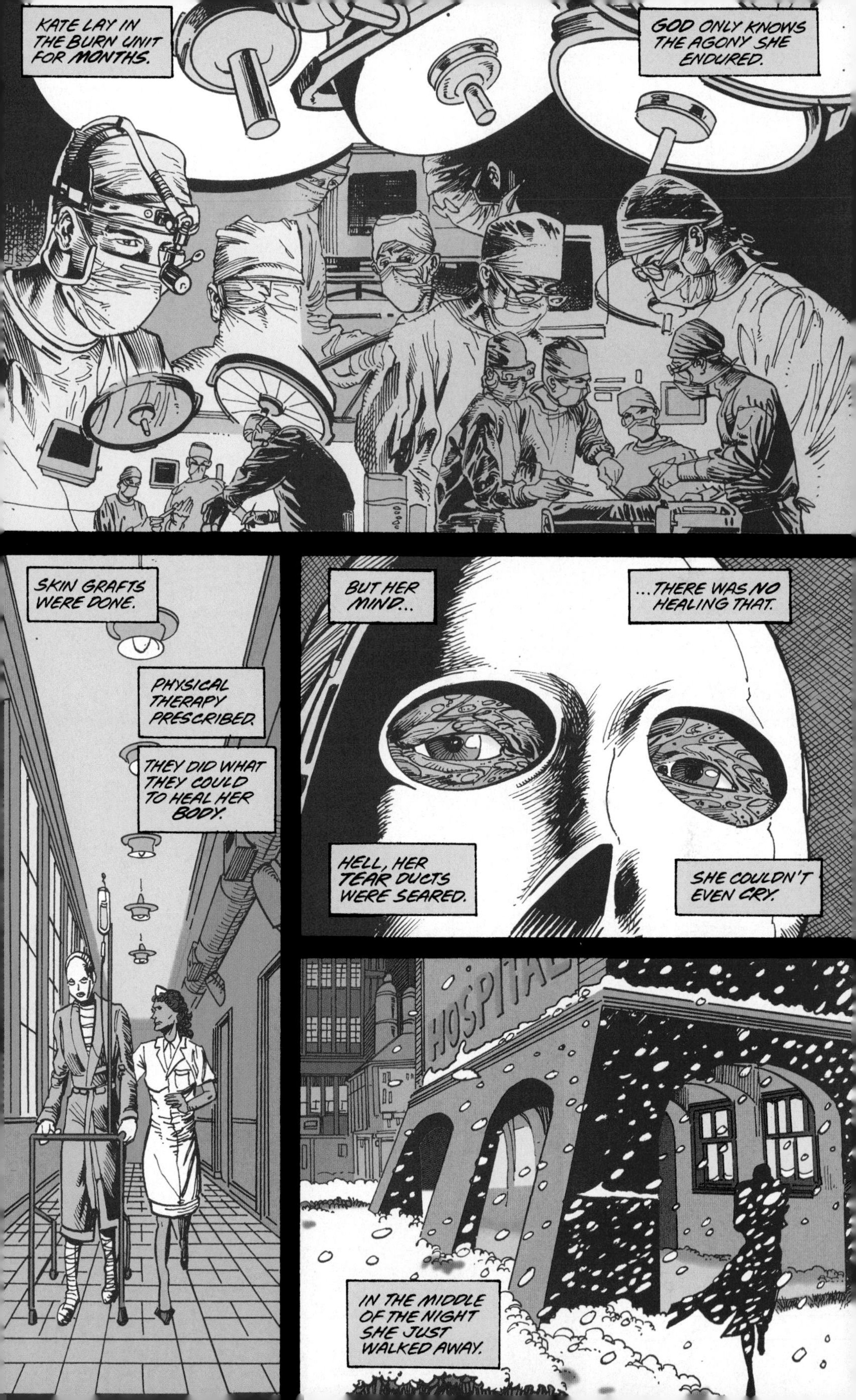
KATE LAY IN THE BURN UNIT FOR MONTHS.
GOD ONLY KNOWS THE AGONY SHE ENDURED.
SKIN GRAFTS WERE DONE.
PHYSICAL THERAPY PRESCRIBED.
THEY DID WHAT THEY COULD TO HEAL HER BODY.
BUT HER MIND...
...THERE WAS NO HEALING THAT.
HELL, HER TEAR DUCTS WERE SEARED.
SHE COULDN'T EVEN CRY.
HOSPITAL
IN THE MIDDLE OF THE NIGHT SHE JUST WALKED AWAY.

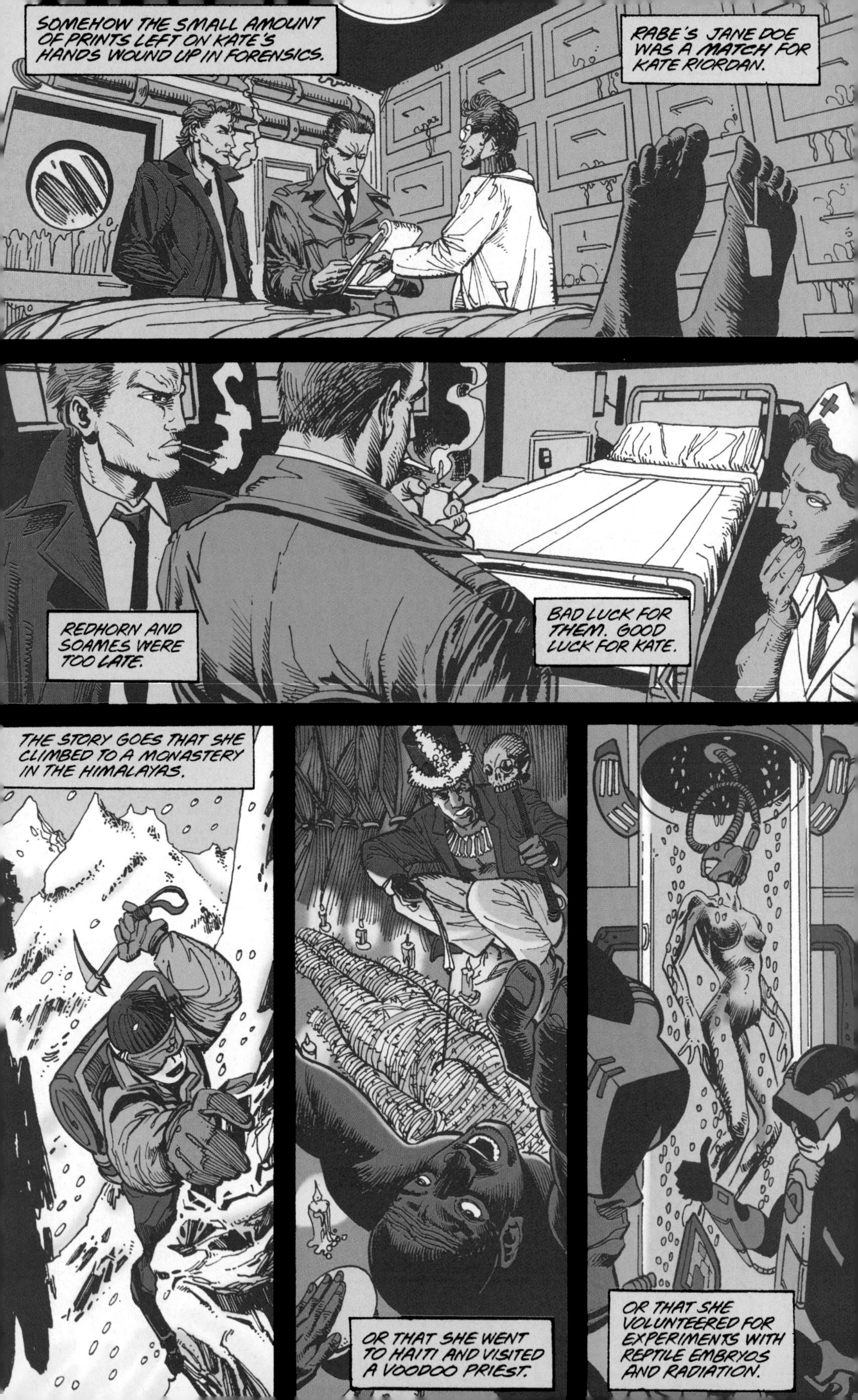
SOMEHOW THE SMALL AMOUNT OF PRINTS LEFT ON KATE'S HANDS WOUND UP IN FORENSICS.
RABE'S JANE DOE WAS A MATCH FOR KATE RIORDAN.
REDHORN AND SOAMES WERE TOO LATE.
BAD LUCK FOR THEM. GOOD LUCK FOR KATE.
THE STORY GOES THAT SHE CLIMBED TO A MONASTERY IN THE HIMALAYAS.
OR THAT SHE WENT TO HAITI AND VISITED A VOODOO PRIEST.
OR THAT SHE VOLUNTEERED FOR EXPERIMENTS WITH REPTILE EMBRYOS AND RADIATION.

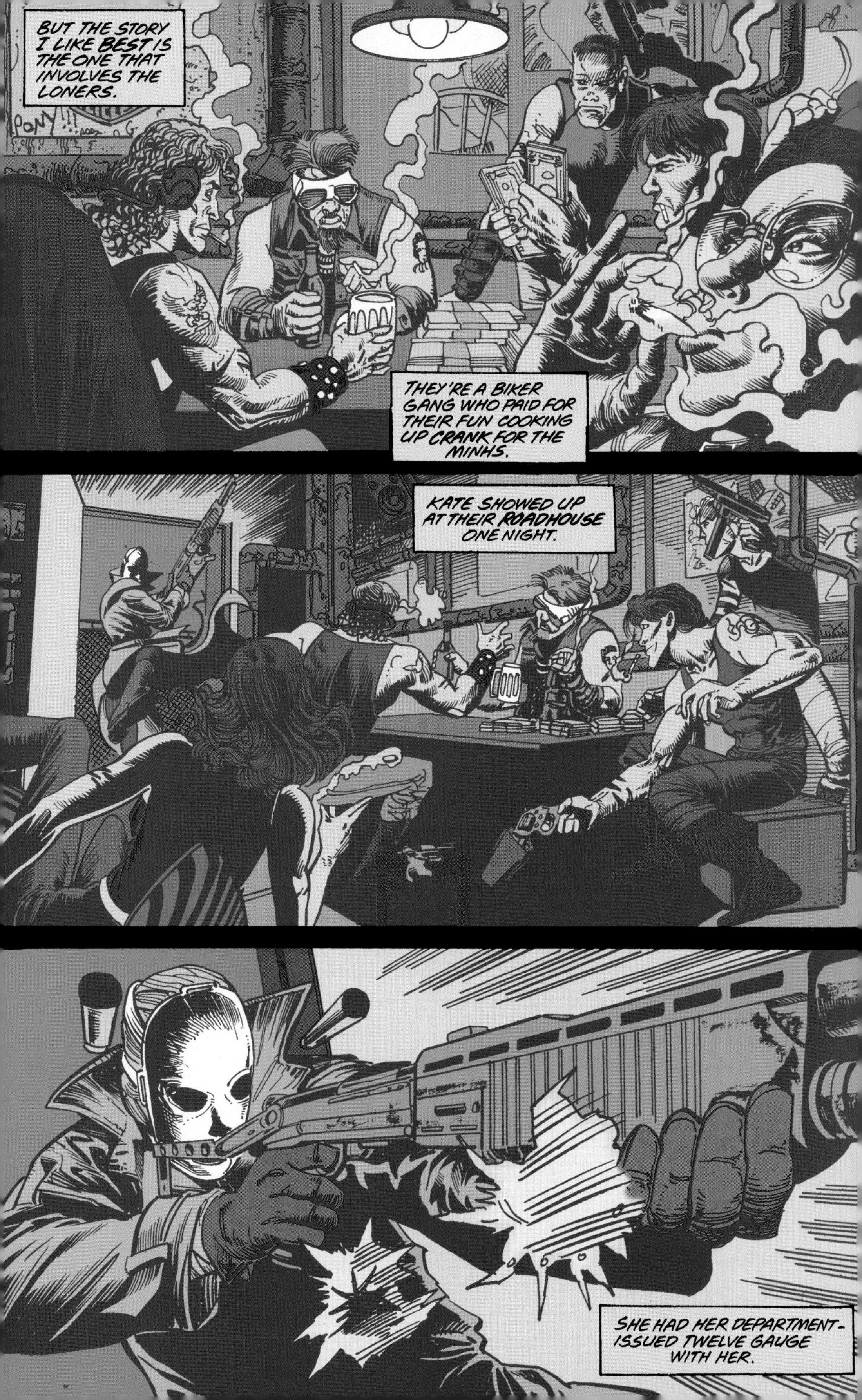
BUT THE STORY I LIKE BEST IS THE ONE THAT INVOLVES THE LONERS.
THEY'RE A BIKER GANG WHO PAID FOR THEIR FUN COOKING UP CRANK FOR THE MINHS.
KATE SHOWED UP AT THEIR ROADHOUSE ONE NIGHT.
SHE HAD HER DEPARTMENT-ISSUED TWELVE GAUGE WITH HER.

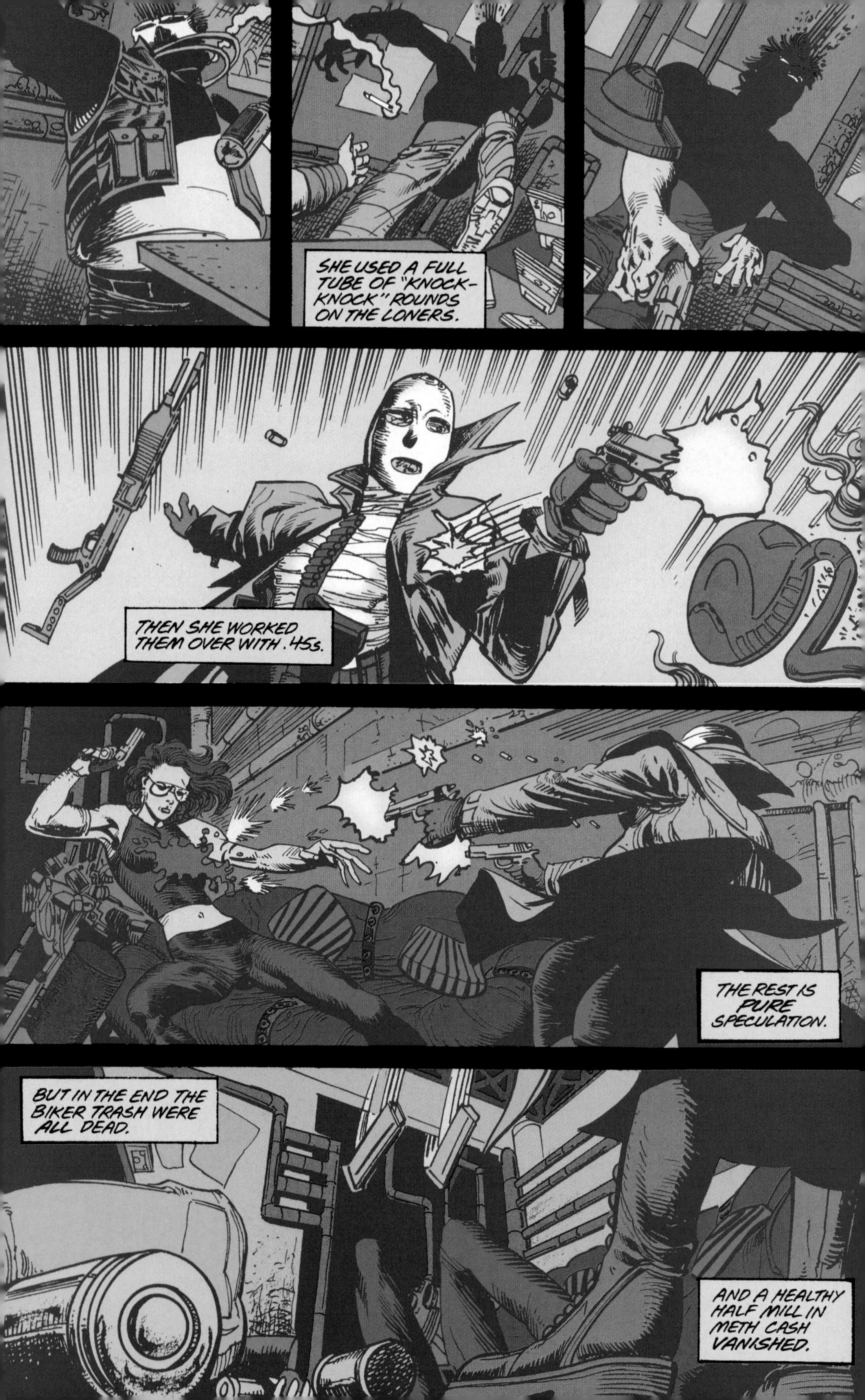
SHE USED A FULL TUBE OF "KNOCK-KNOCK" ROUNDS ON THE LONERS.
THEN SHE WORKED THEM OVER WITH .45s.
THE REST IS PURE SPECULATION.
BUT IN THE END THE BIKER TRASH WERE ALL DEAD.
AND A HEALTHY HALF MILL IN METH CASH VANISHED.

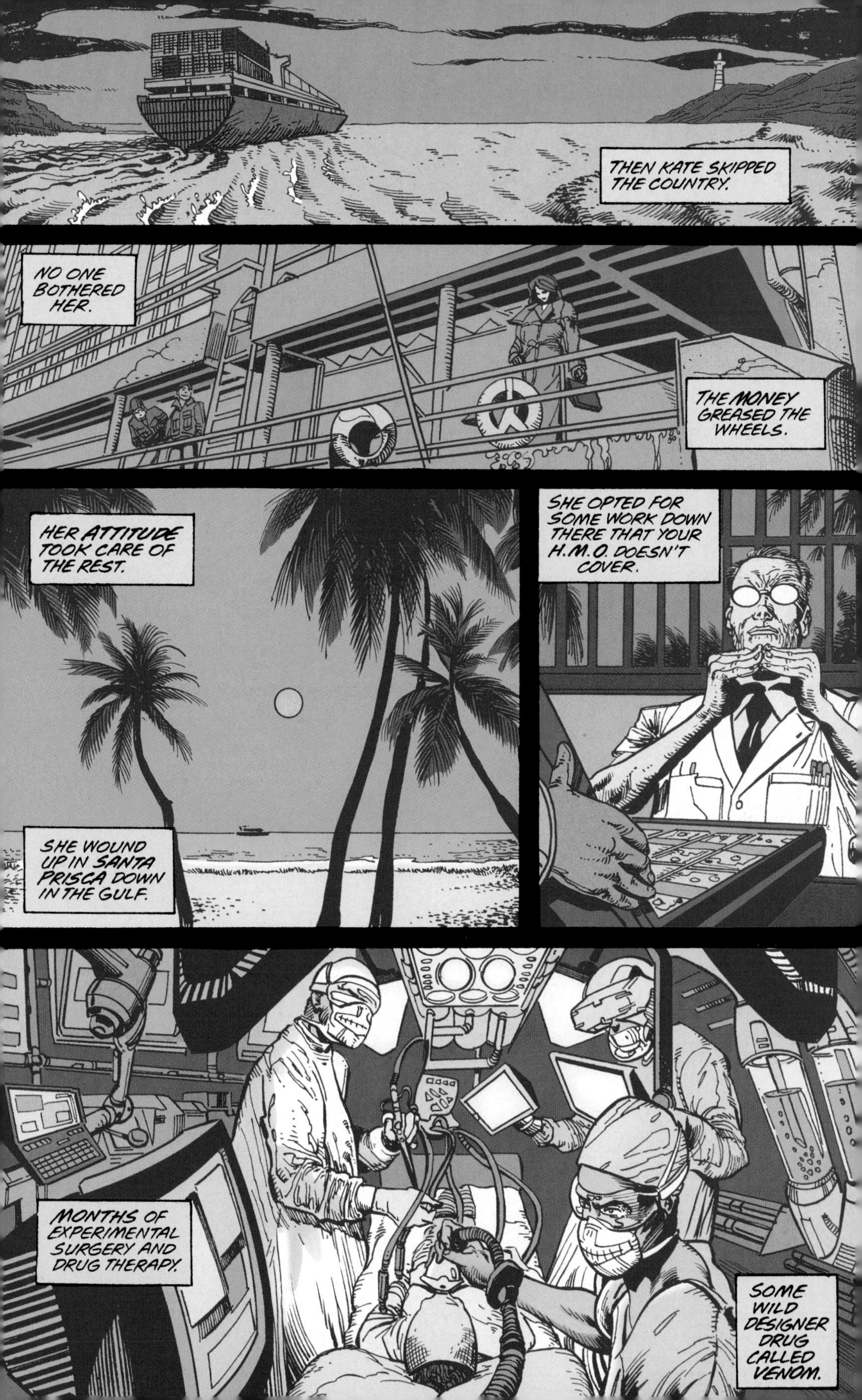
THEN KATE SKIPPED THE COUNTRY.
NO ONE BOTHERED HER.
THE MONEY GREASED THE WHEELS.
HER ATTITUDE TOOK CARE OF THE REST.
SHE WOUND UP IN SANTA PRISCA DOWN IN THE GULF.
SHE OPTED FOR SOME WORK DOWN THERE THAT YOUR H.M.O. DOESN'T COVER.
MONTHS OF EXPERIMENTAL SURGERY AND DRUG THERAPY.
SOME WILD DESIGNER DRUG CALLED VENOM.

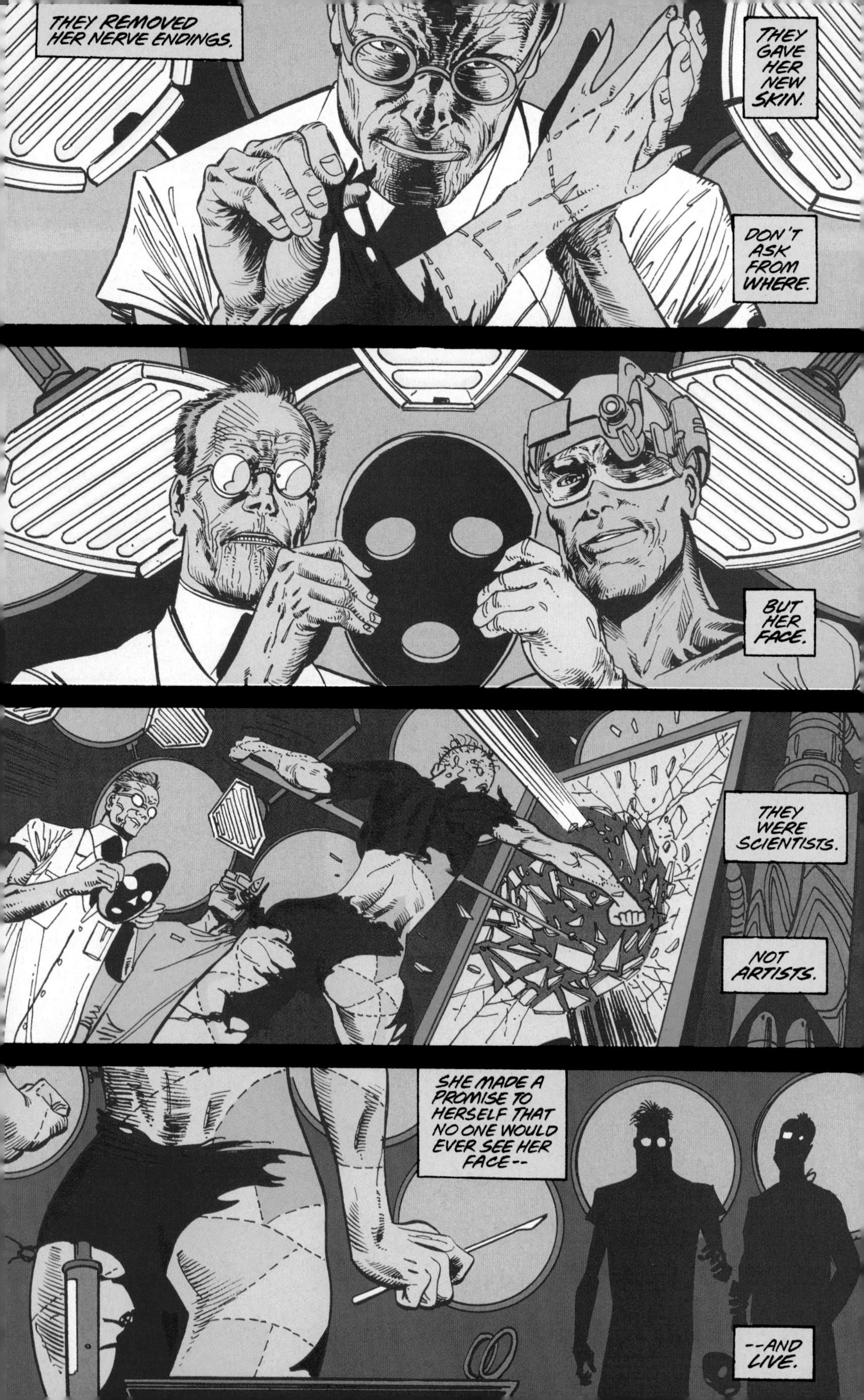
THEY REMOVED HER NERVE ENDINGS.
THEY GAVE HER NEW SKIN.
DON'T ASK FROM WHERE.
BUT HER FACE.
THEY WERE SCIENTISTS.
NOT ARTISTS.
SHE MADE A PROMISE TO HERSELF THAT NO ONE WOULD EVER SEE HER FACE--
--AND LIVE.

RIORDAN

SHE CAME BACK TO THE 'HAVEN TO FIND HER FAMILY FORGOTTEN.

NOTHING BUT THEIR *NAME* ON A FILTHY STONE IN A WEED-CHOKED CORNER OF POTTER'S FIELD.

RODRIGO BUENO

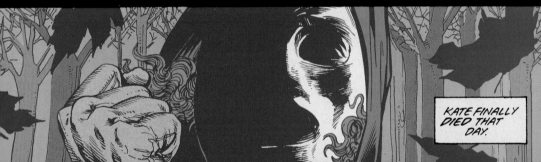

KATE FINALLY DIED THAT DAY.

AND SOMETHING MEAN WAS BORN.

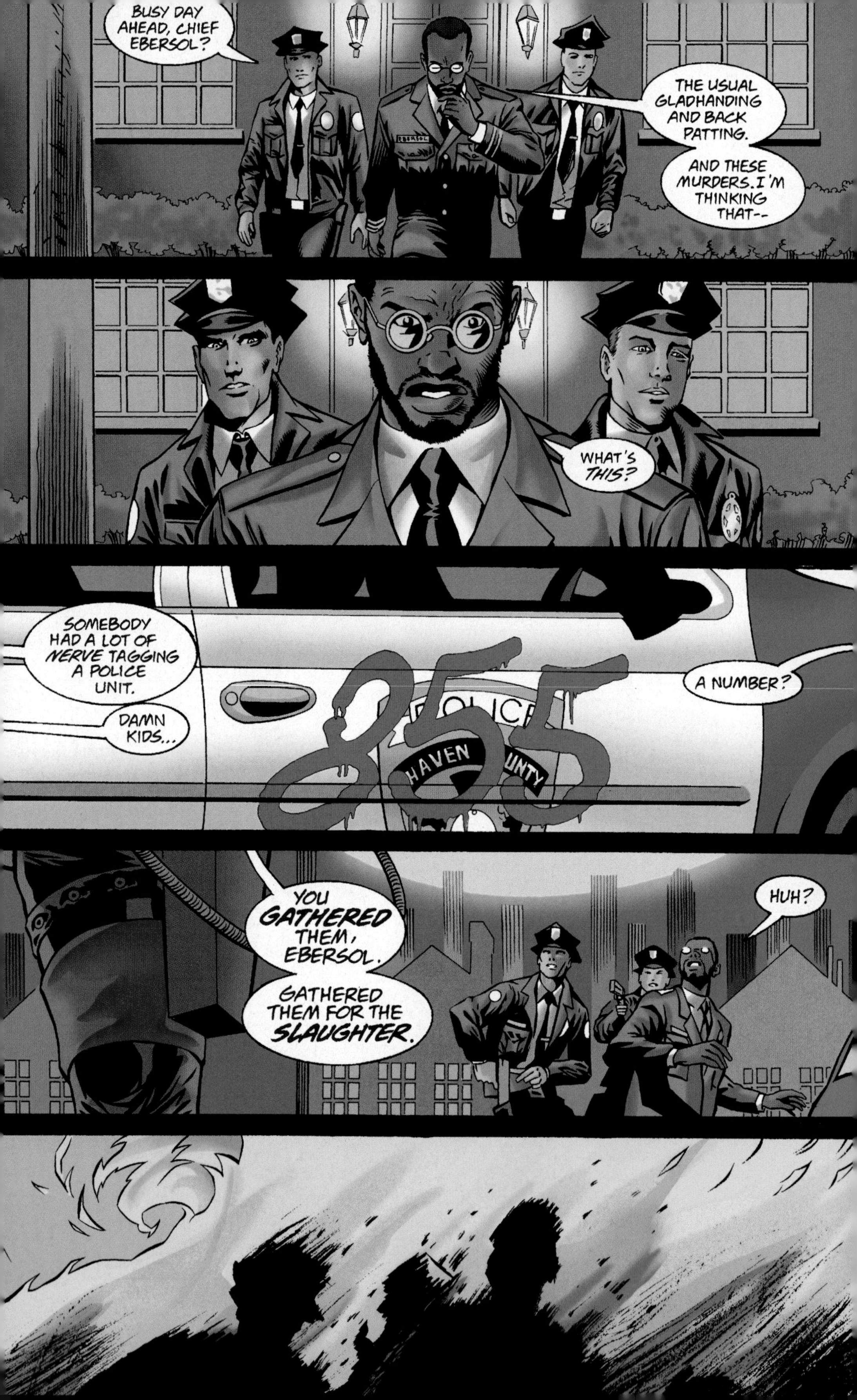
BUSY DAY AHEAD, CHIEF EBERSOL?
THE USUAL GLADHANDING AND BACK PATTING.
AND THESE MURDERS. I'M THINKING THAT--
WHAT'S THIS?
SOMEBODY HAD A LOT OF NERVE TAGGING A POLICE UNIT.
DAMN KIDS...
A NUMBER?
855
POLICE
HAVEN
UNTY
YOU GATHERED THEM, EBERSOL.
GATHERED THEM FOR THE SLAUGHTER.
HUH?

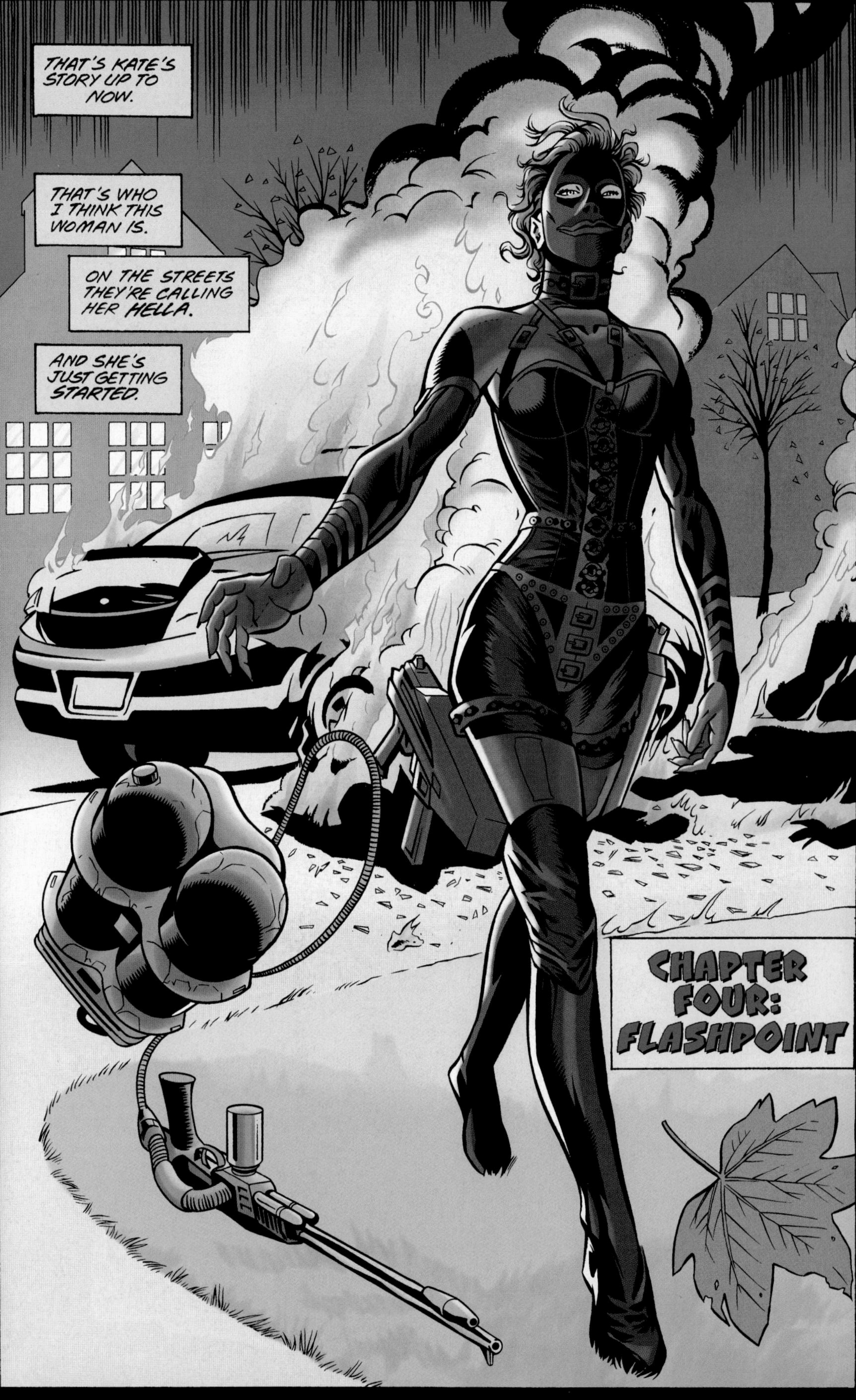
THAT'S KATE'S STORY UP TO NOW.
THAT'S WHO I THINK THIS WOMAN IS.
ON THE STREETS THEY'RE CALLING HER HELLA.
AND SHE'S JUST GETTING STARTED.
CHAPTER FOUR: FLASHPOINT

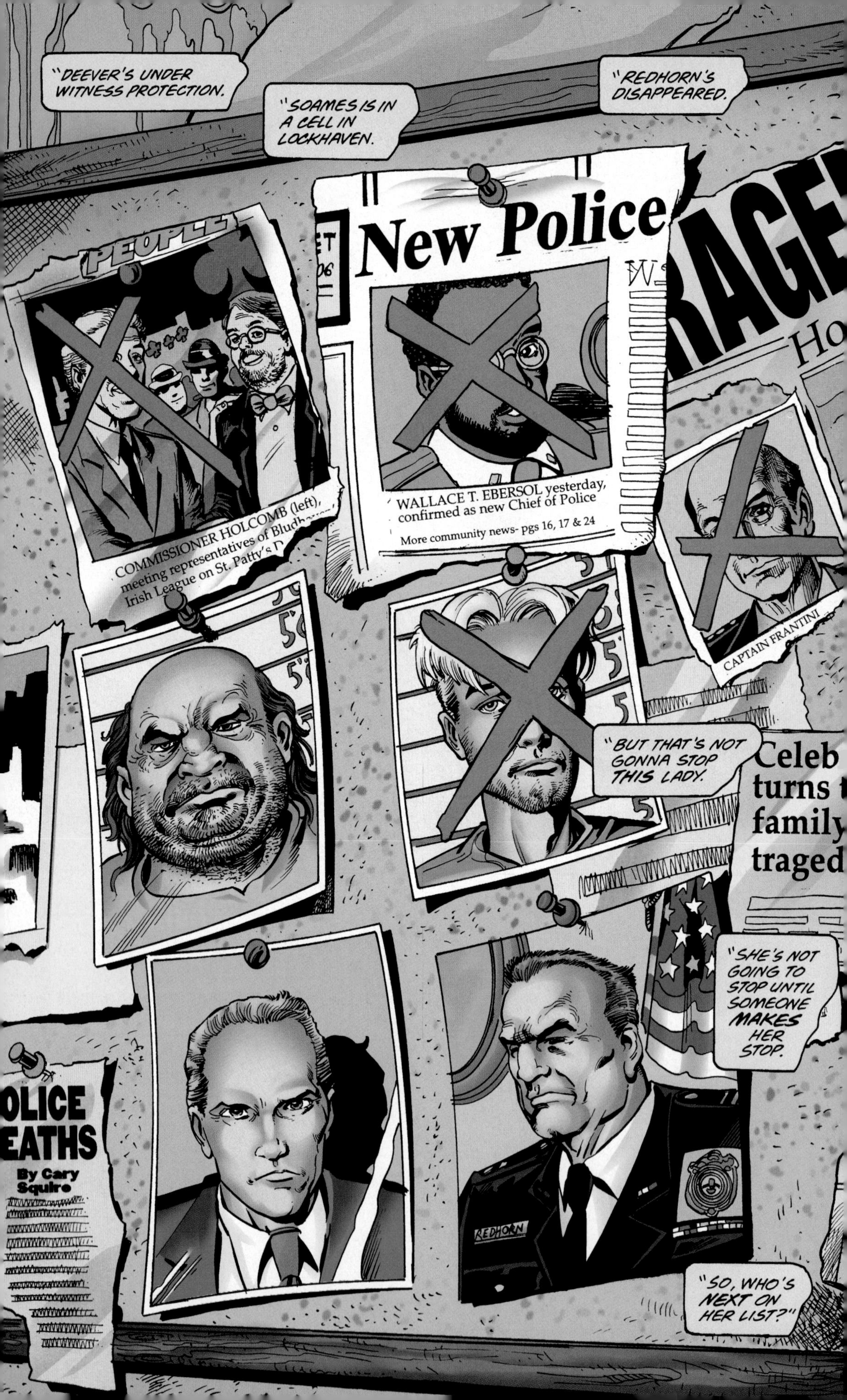
"DEEVER'S UNDER WITNESS PROTECTION.
"SOAMES IS IN A CELL IN LOCKHAVEN.
"REDHORN'S DISAPPEARED.
PEOPLE
New Police
WALLACE T. EBERSOL yesterday, confirmed as new Chief of Police
More community news- pgs 16, 17 & 24
COMMISSIONER HOLCOMB (left), meeting representatives of Bludh... Irish League on St. Patty's D...
CAPTAIN FRANTINI
"BUT THAT'S NOT GONNA STOP THIS LADY.
Celeb turns t family traged
"SHE'S NOT GOING TO STOP UNTIL SOMEONE MAKES HER STOP.
OLICE EATHS
By Cary Squire
REDHORN
"SO, WHO'S NEXT ON HER LIST?"

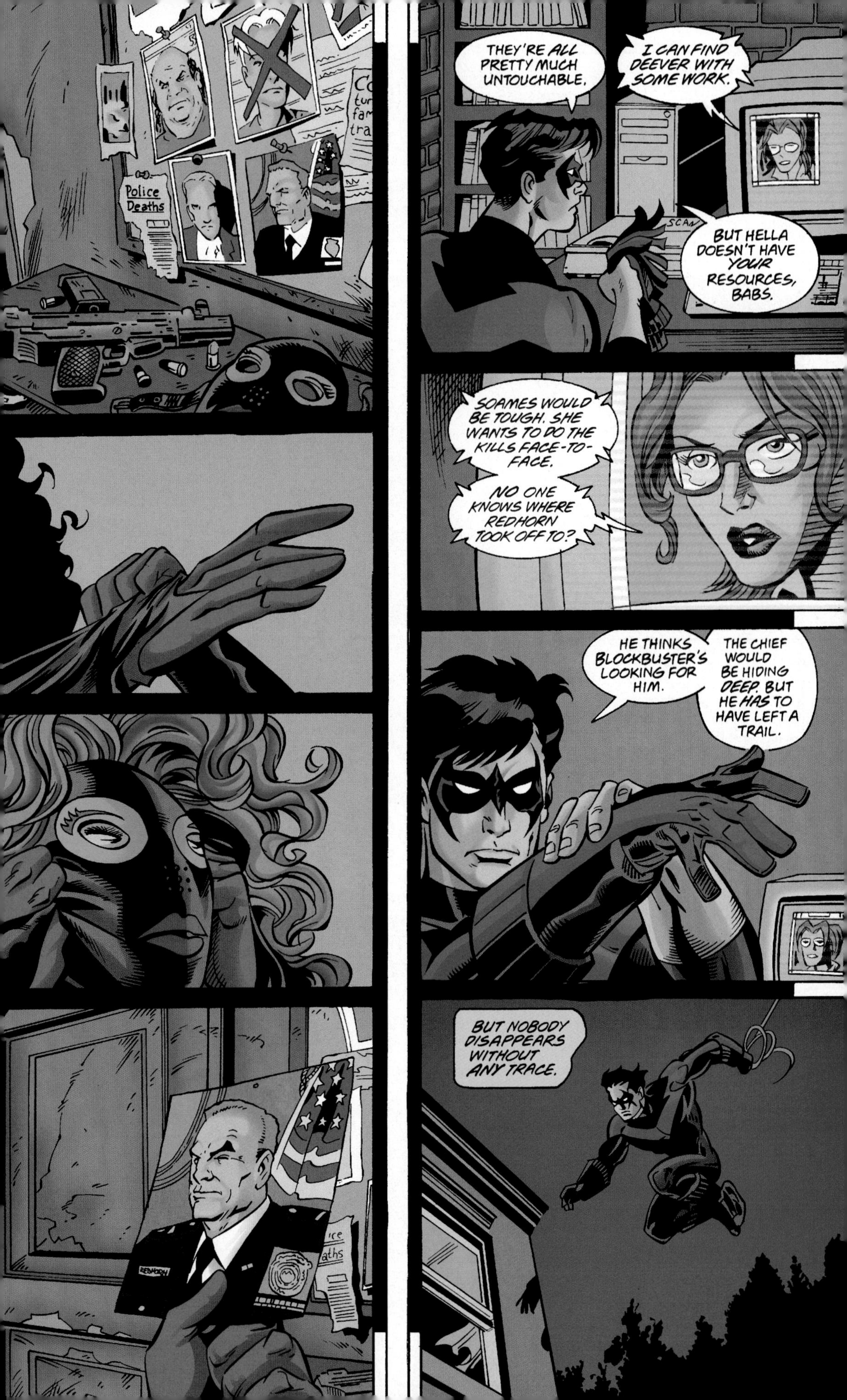
Police Deaths
THEY'RE ALL PRETTY MUCH UNTOUCHABLE.
I CAN FIND DEEVER WITH SOME WORK.
SCAN
BUT HELLA DOESN'T HAVE YOUR RESOURCES, BABS.
SOAMES WOULD BE TOUGH. SHE WANTS TO DO THE KILLS FACE-TO-FACE.
NO ONE KNOWS WHERE REDHORN TOOK OFF TO?
HE THINKS BLOCKBUSTER'S LOOKING FOR HIM.
THE CHIEF WOULD BE HIDING DEEP. BUT HE HAS TO HAVE LEFT A TRAIL.
REDHORN
BUT NOBODY DISAPPEARS WITHOUT ANY TRACE.

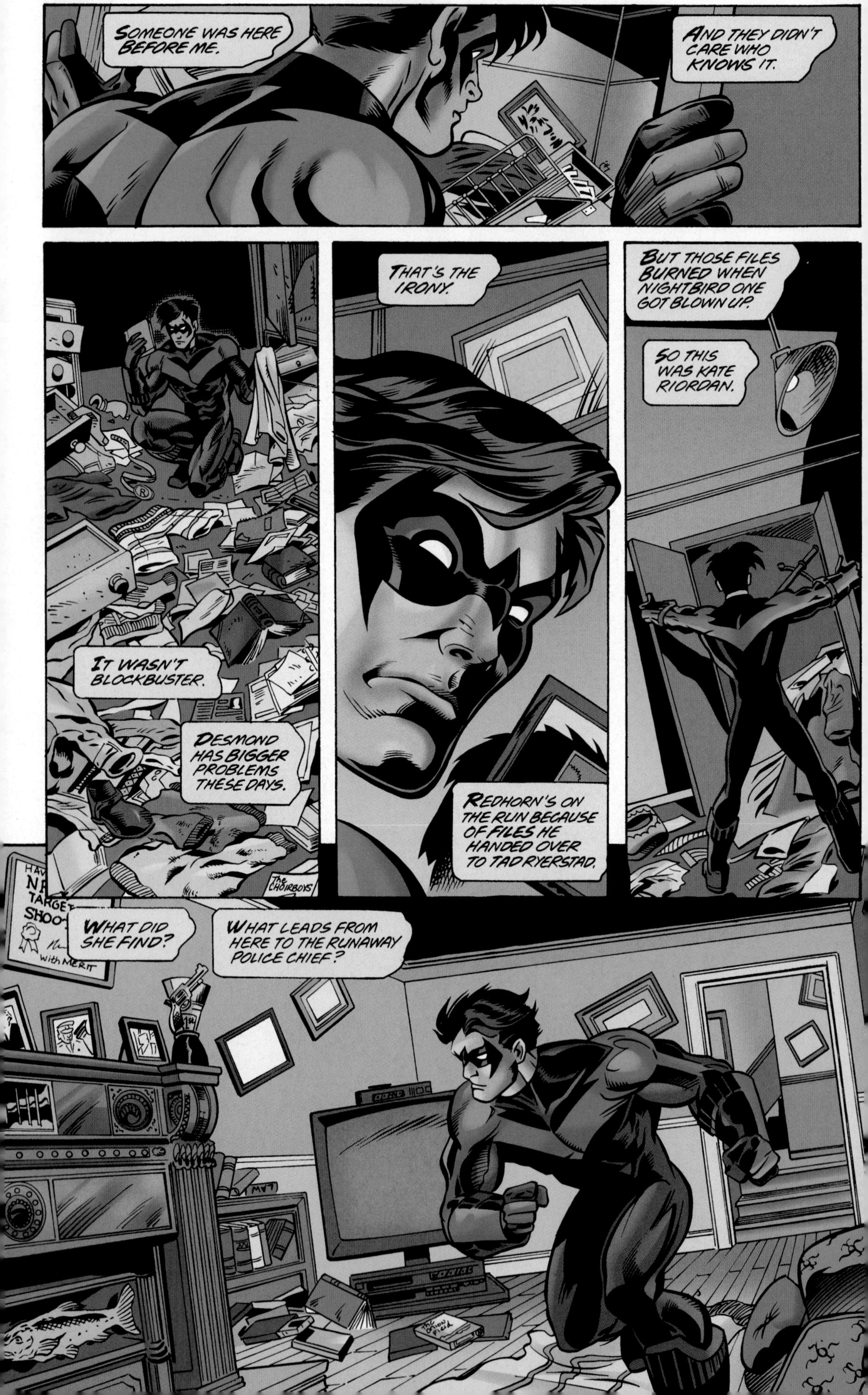
SOMEONE WAS HERE BEFORE ME.
AND THEY DIDN'T CARE WHO KNOWS IT.
IT WASN'T BLOCKBUSTER.
DESMOND HAS BIGGER PROBLEMS THESE DAYS.
THAT'S THE IRONY.
REDHORN'S ON THE RUN BECAUSE OF FILES HE HANDED OVER TO TAD RYERSTAD.
BUT THOSE FILES BURNED WHEN NIGHTBIRD ONE GOT BLOWN UP.
SO THIS WAS KATE RIORDAN.
WHAT DID SHE FIND?
WHAT LEADS FROM HERE TO THE RUNAWAY POLICE CHIEF?

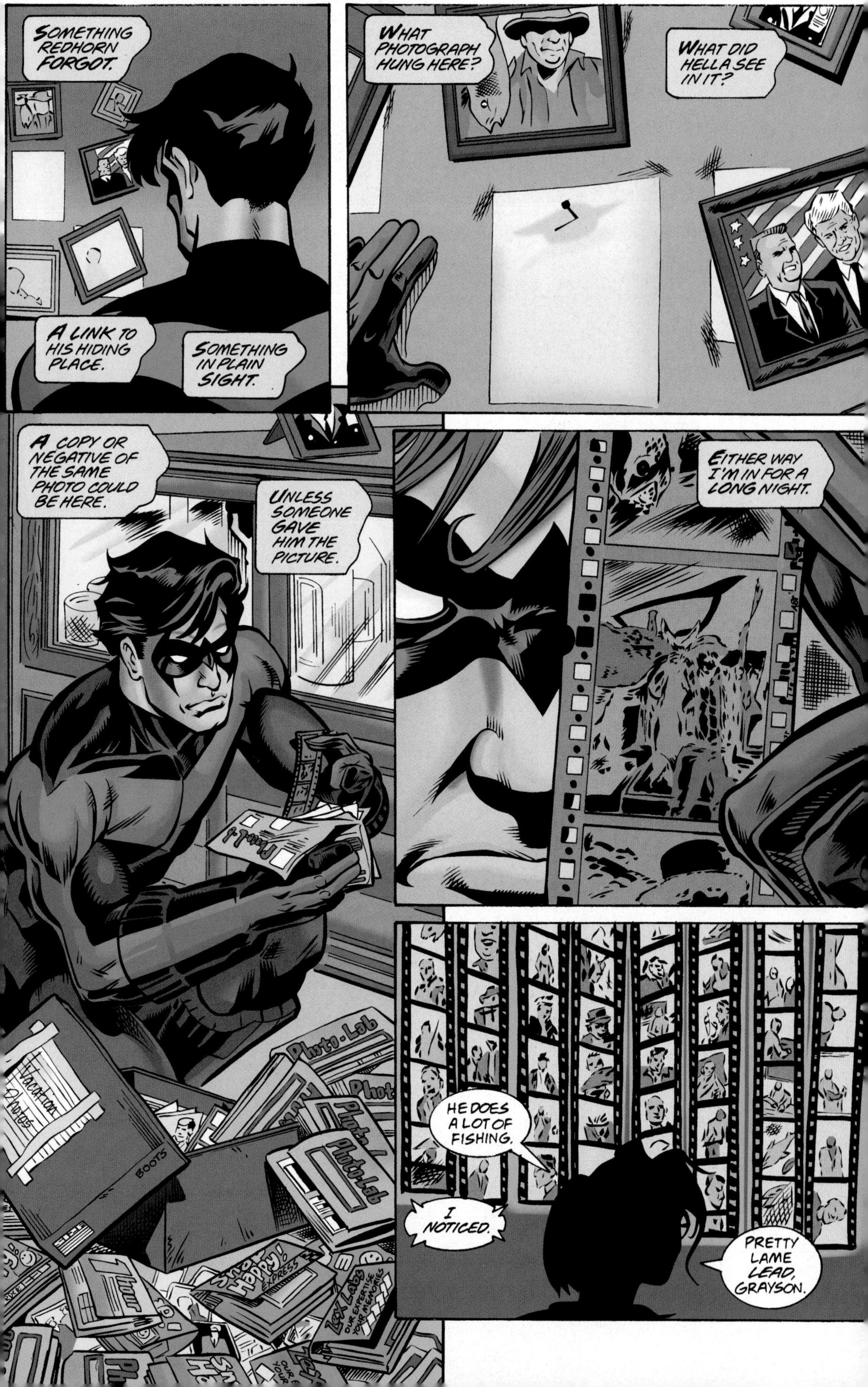
SOMETHING REDHORN FORGOT.
A LINK TO HIS HIDING PLACE.
SOMETHING IN PLAIN SIGHT.
WHAT PHOTOGRAPH HUNG HERE?
WHAT DID HELLA SEE IN IT?
A COPY OR NEGATIVE OF THE SAME PHOTO COULD BE HERE.
UNLESS SOMEONE GAVE HIM THE PICTURE.
EITHER WAY I'M IN FOR A LONG NIGHT.
HE DOES A LOT OF FISHING.
I NOTICED.
PRETTY LAME LEAD, GRAYSON.
Vacation Photos
BOOTS
Photo-Lab

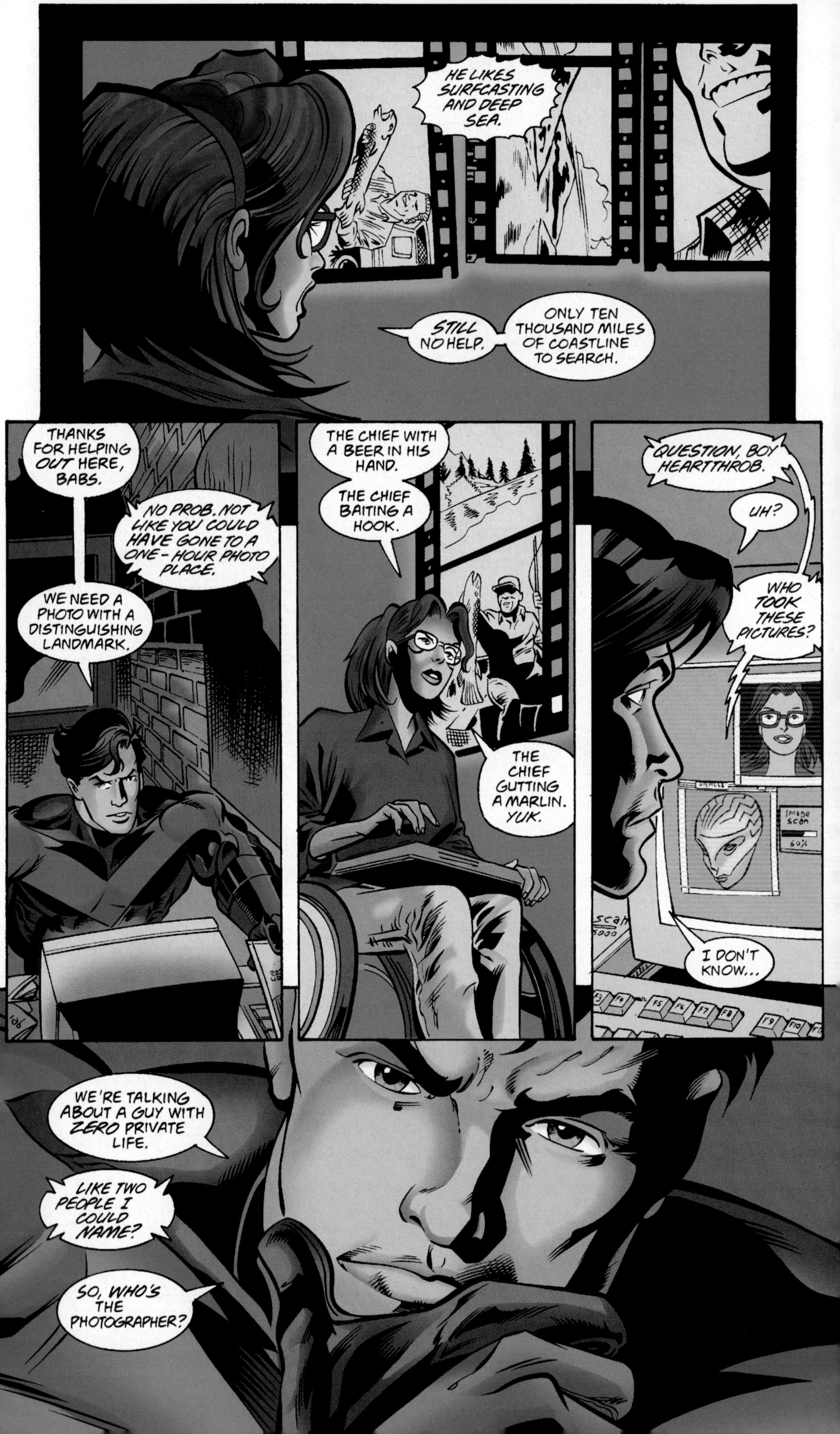
HE LIKES SURFCASTING AND DEEP SEA.
STILL NO HELP.
ONLY TEN THOUSAND MILES OF COASTLINE TO SEARCH.
THANKS FOR HELPING OUT HERE, BABS.
NO PROB. NOT LIKE YOU COULD HAVE GONE TO A ONE-HOUR PHOTO PLACE.
WE NEED A PHOTO WITH A DISTINGUISHING LANDMARK.
THE CHIEF WITH A BEER IN HIS HAND.
THE CHIEF BAITING A HOOK.
THE CHIEF GUTTING A MARLIN. YUK.
QUESTION, BOY HEARTTHROB.
UH?
WHO TOOK THESE PICTURES?
Image scan
60%
I DON'T KNOW...
WE'RE TALKING ABOUT A GUY WITH ZERO PRIVATE LIFE.
LIKE TWO PEOPLE I COULD NAME?
SO, WHO'S THE PHOTOGRAPHER?

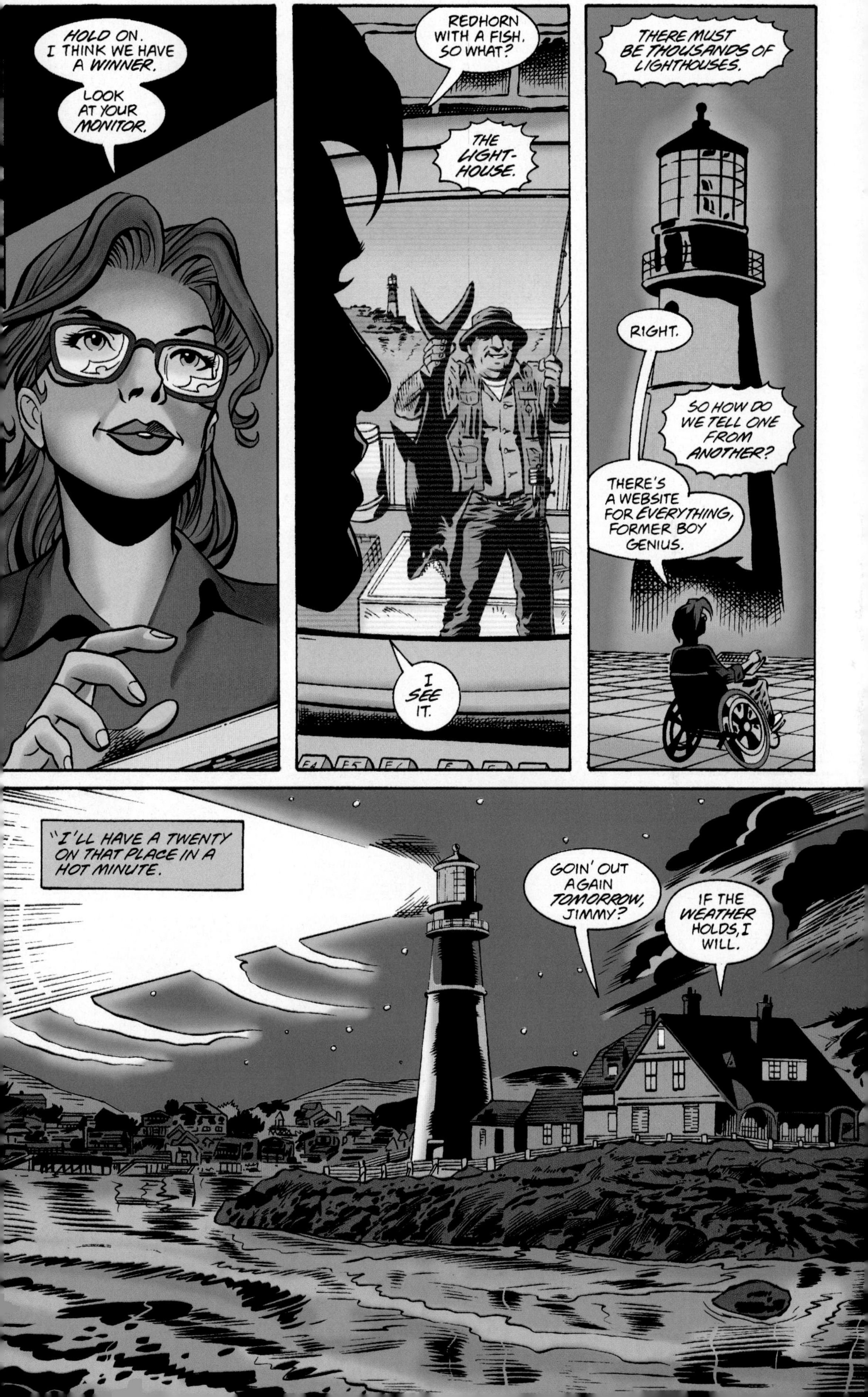

HOLD ON. I THINK WE HAVE A WINNER.
LOOK AT YOUR MONITOR.
REDHORN WITH A FISH. SO WHAT?
THE LIGHT-HOUSE.
I SEE IT.
THERE MUST BE THOUSANDS OF LIGHTHOUSES.
RIGHT.
SO HOW DO WE TELL ONE FROM ANOTHER?
THERE'S A WEBSITE FOR EVERYTHING, FORMER BOY GENIUS.
"I'LL HAVE A TWENTY ON THAT PLACE IN A HOT MINUTE.
GOIN' OUT AGAIN TOMORROW, JIMMY?
IF THE WEATHER HOLDS, I WILL.

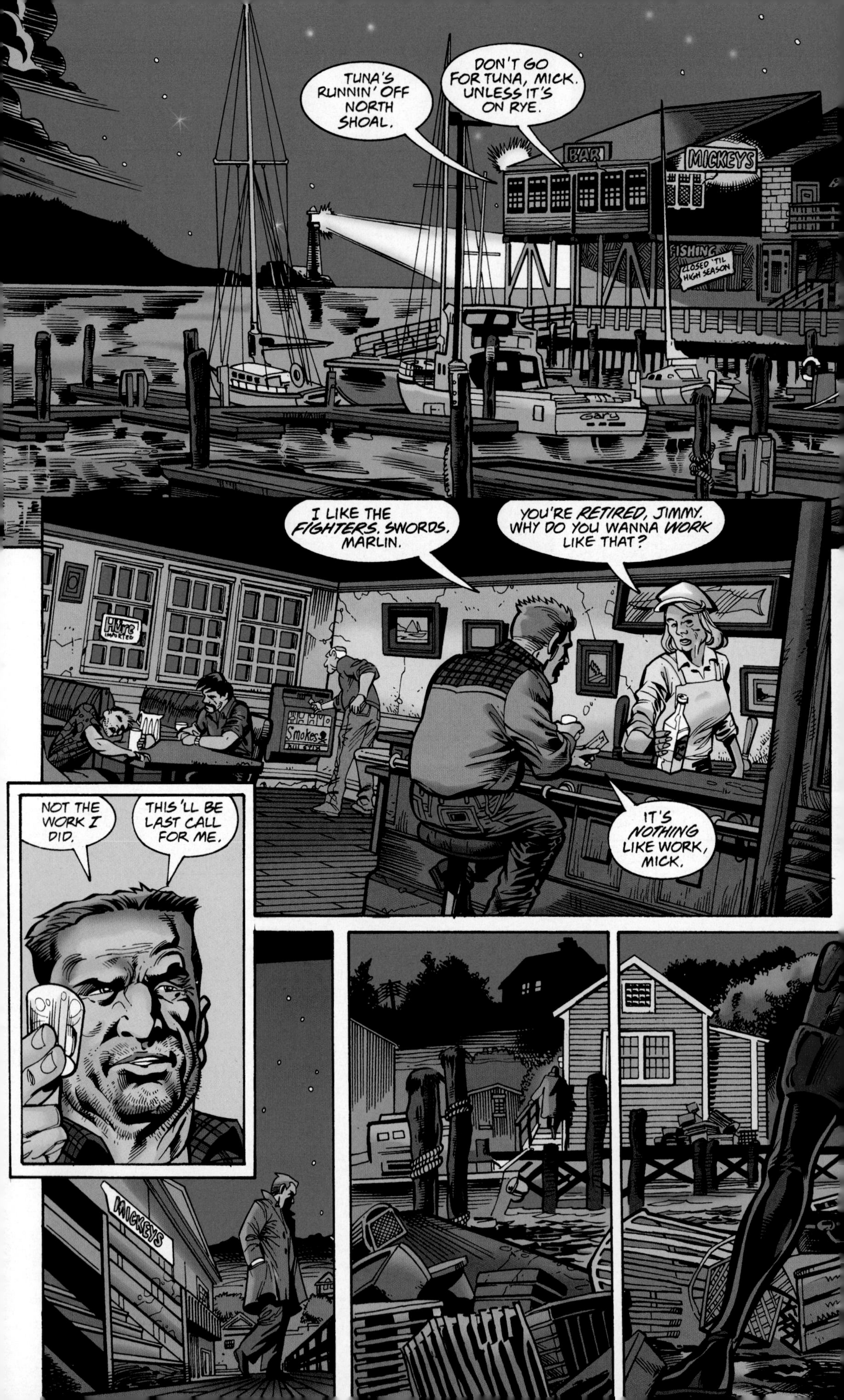
TUNA'S RUNNIN' OFF NORTH SHOAL.
DON'T GO FOR TUNA, MICK. UNLESS IT'S ON RYE.
BAR
MICKEYS
FISHING
CLOSED 'TIL HIGH SEASON
Gary
I LIKE THE *FIGHTERS*. SWORDS. MARLIN.
YOU'RE *RETIRED*, JIMMY. WHY DO YOU WANNA *WORK* LIKE THAT?
Smokes
IT'S *NOTHING* LIKE WORK, MICK.
NOT THE WORK *I* DID.
THIS'LL BE LAST CALL FOR ME.
MICKEYS

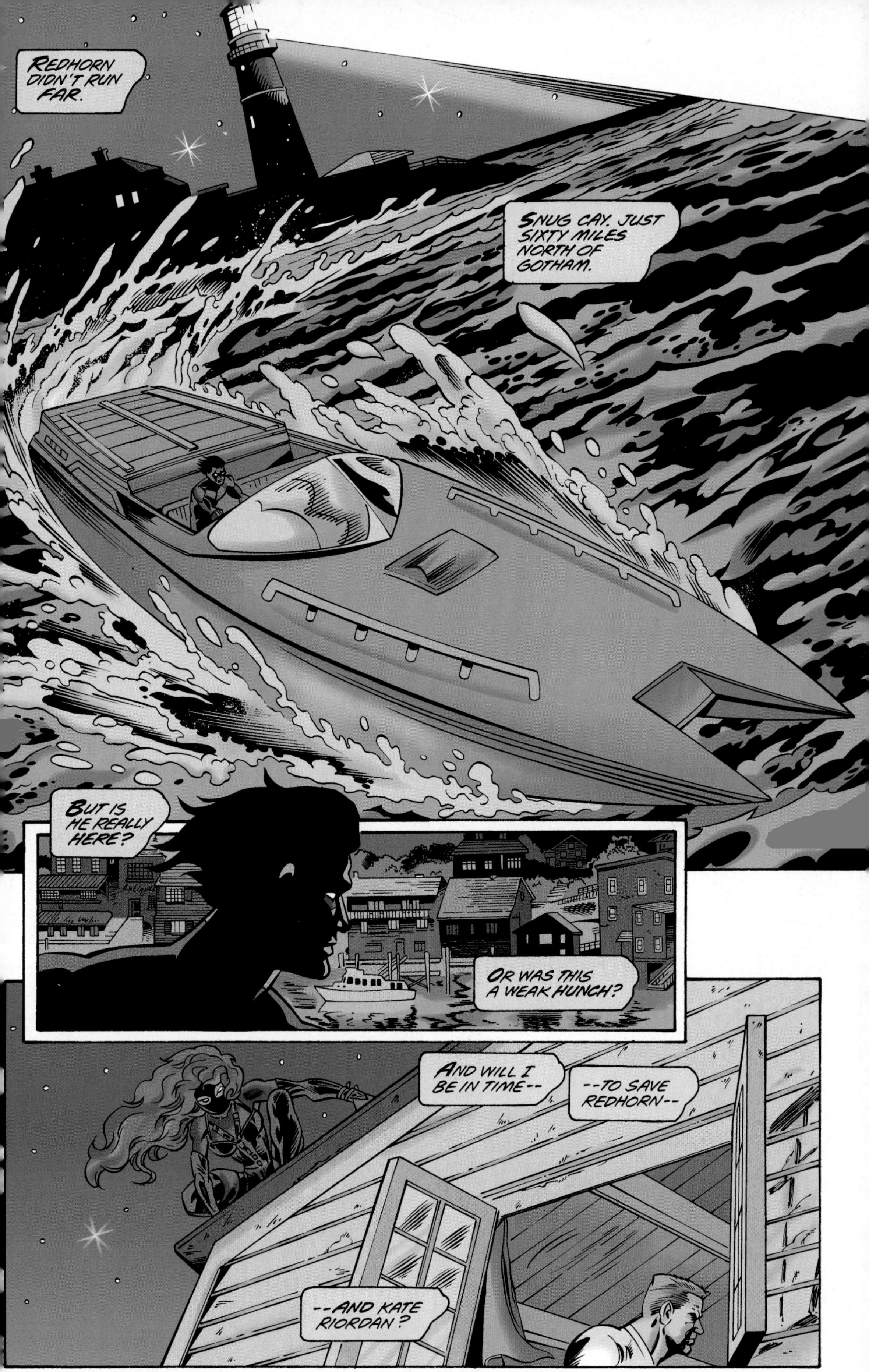
REDHORN DIDN'T RUN FAR.
SNUG CAY. JUST SIXTY MILES NORTH OF GOTHAM.
BUT IS HE REALLY HERE?
OR WAS THIS A WEAK HUNCH?
AND WILL I BE IN TIME--
--TO SAVE REDHORN--
--AND KATE RIORDAN?

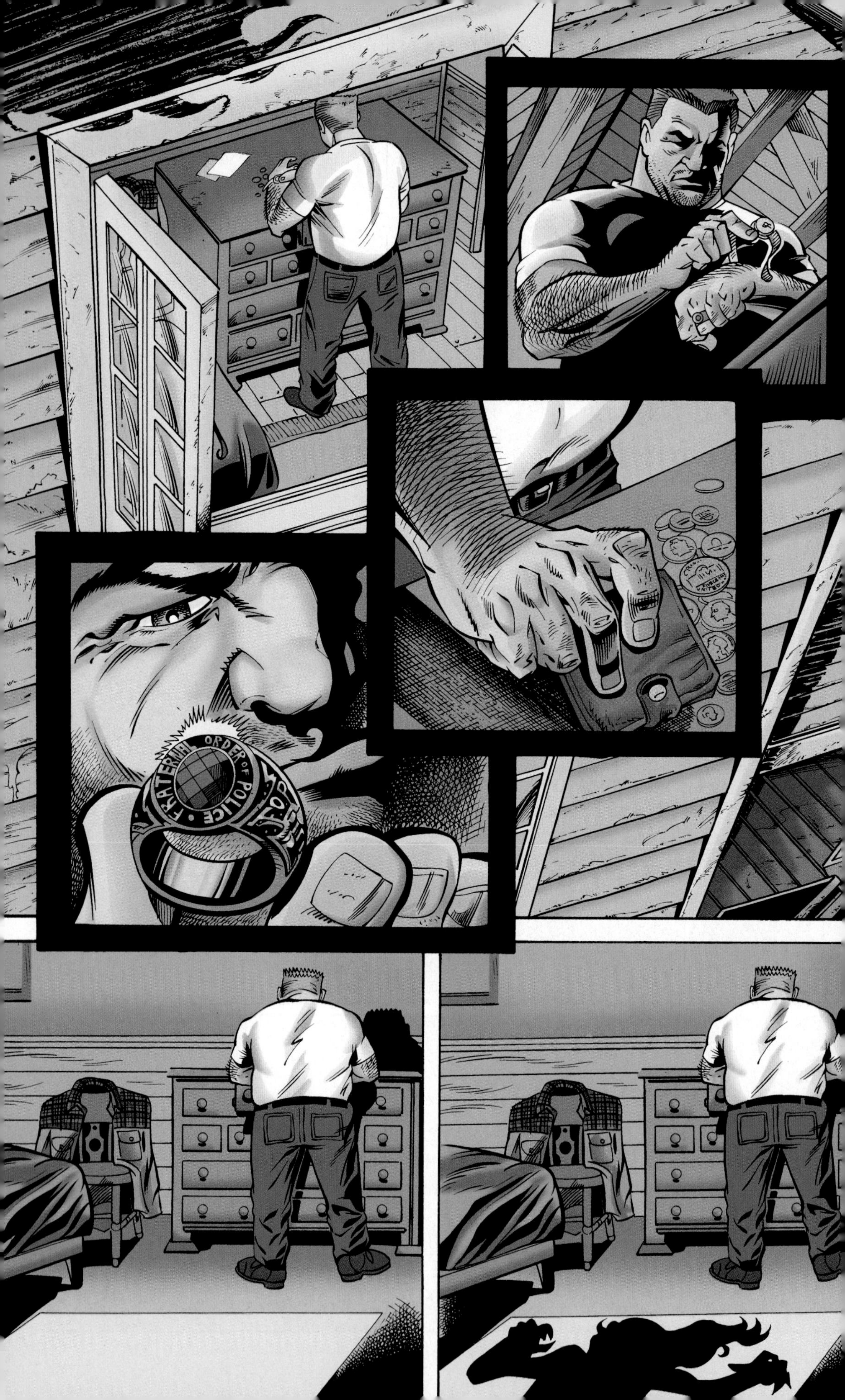
FRATERNAL ORDER OF POLICE

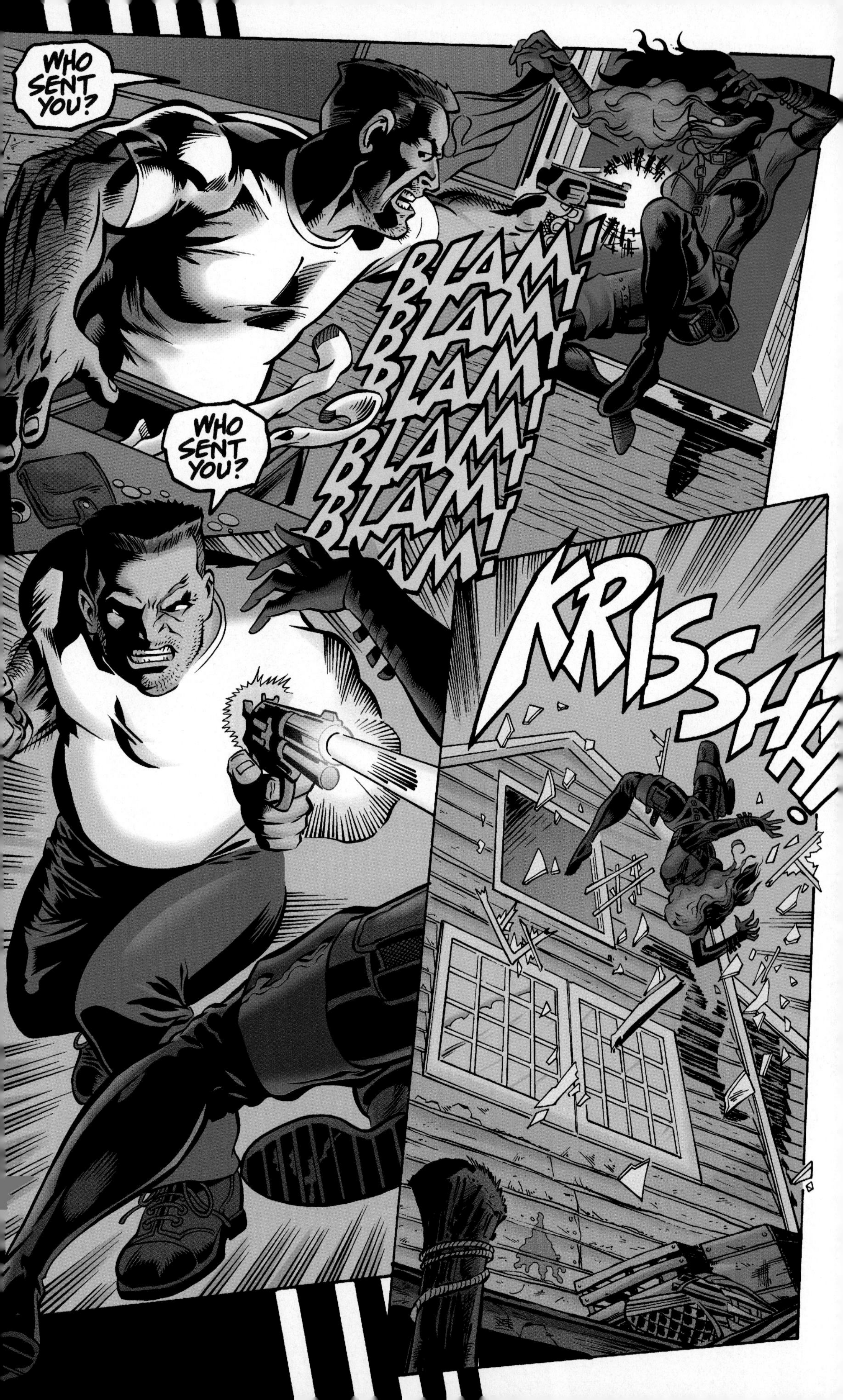
WHO SENT YOU?
BLAM! BLAM! BLAM! BLAM! BLAM! BLAM!
WHO SENT YOU?
KRISSSHH!

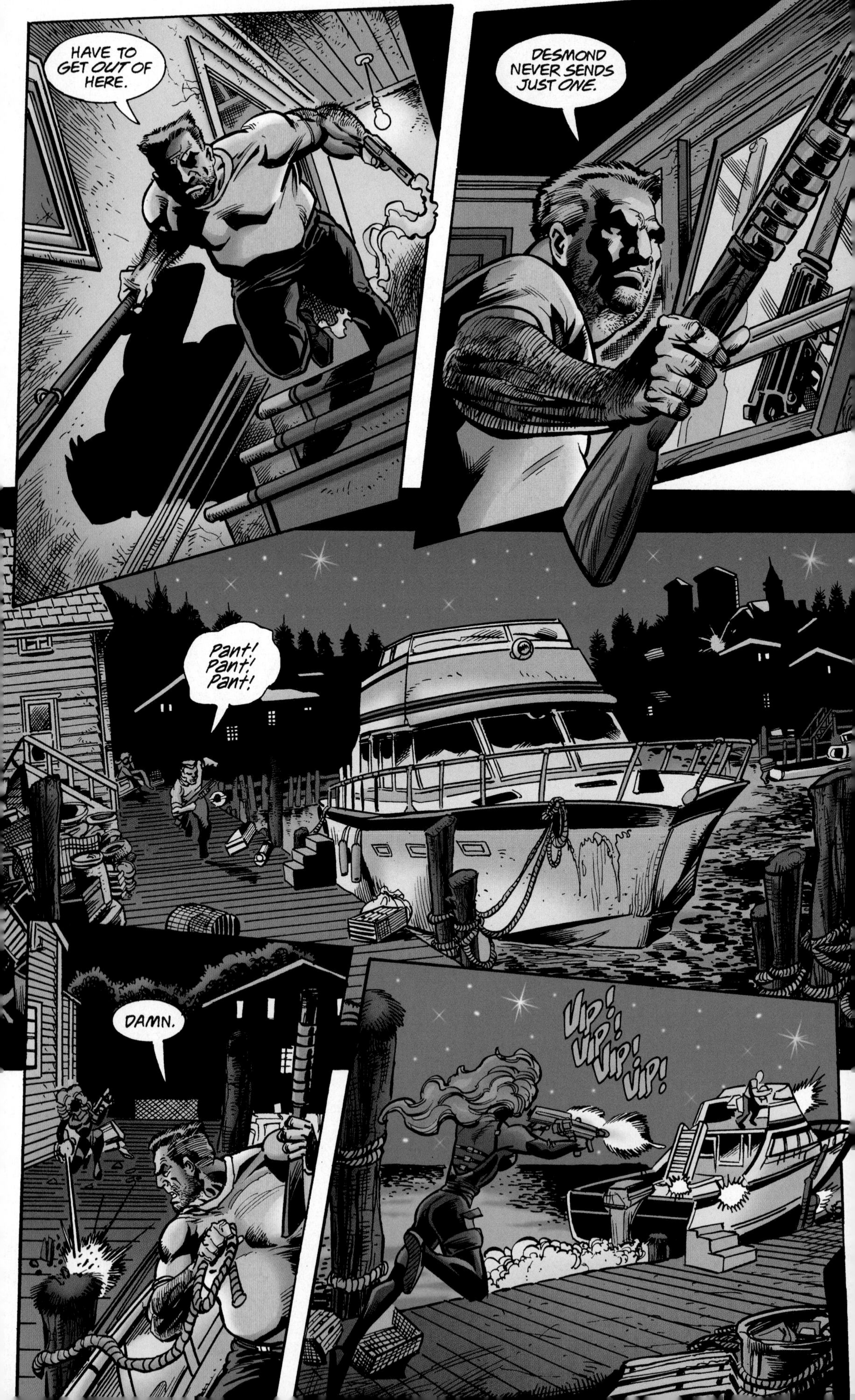
HAVE TO GET OUT OF HERE.
DESMOND NEVER SENDS JUST ONE.
Pant! Pant! Pant!
DAMN.
UIP! UIP! UIP! UIP!

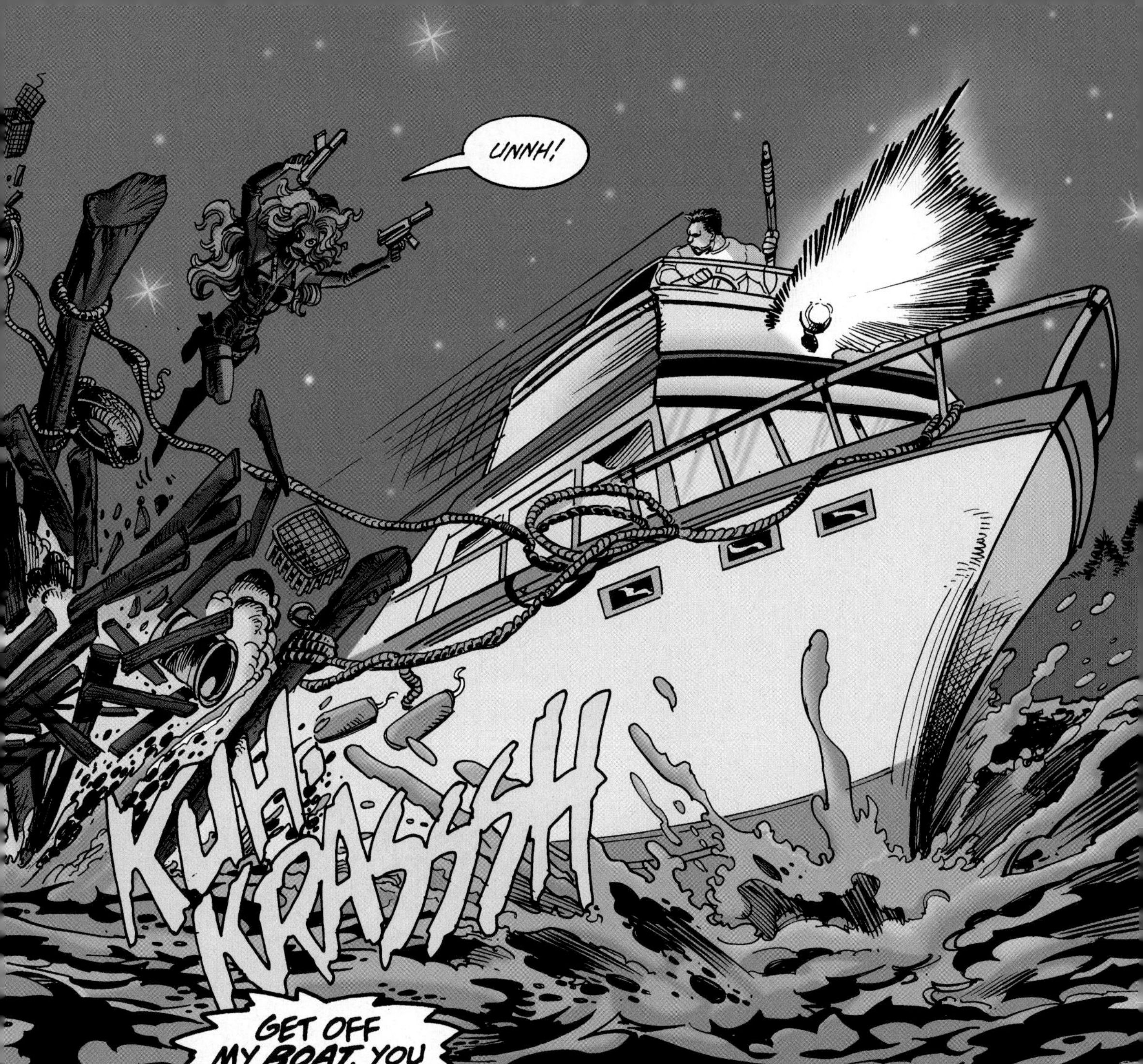
UNNH!
KUH-KRASSHH
GET OFF MY BOAT, YOU WITCH!

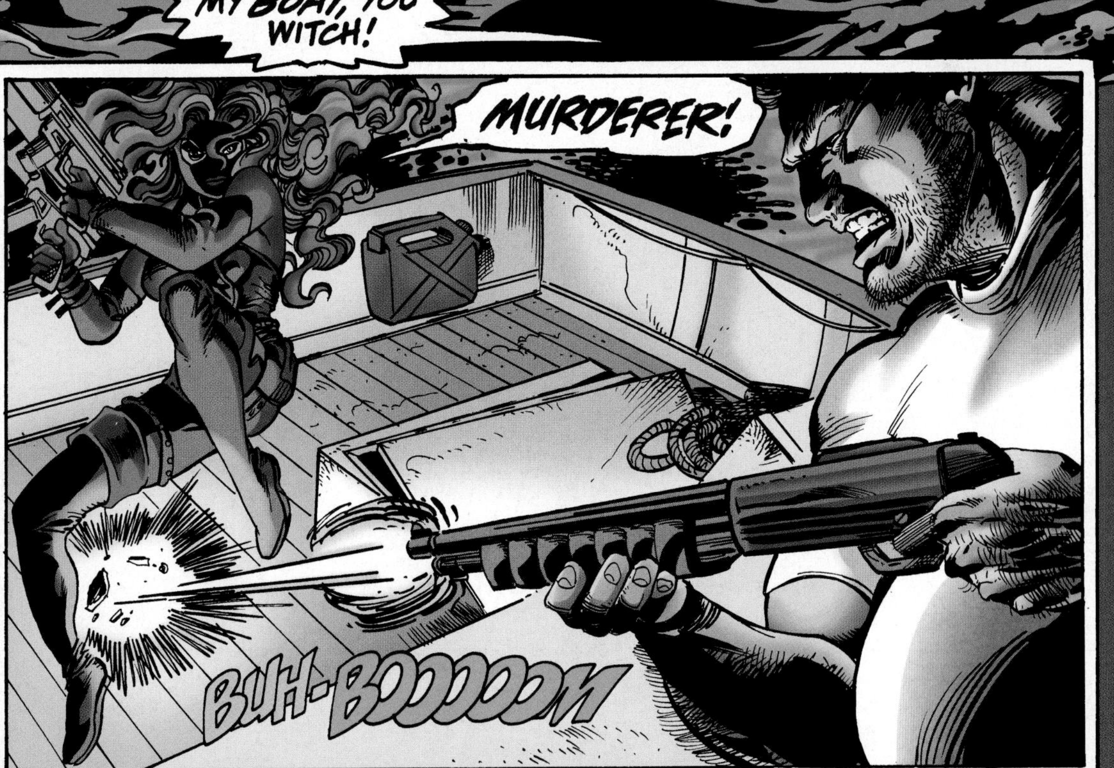
MURDERER!
BUH-BOOOOOOM

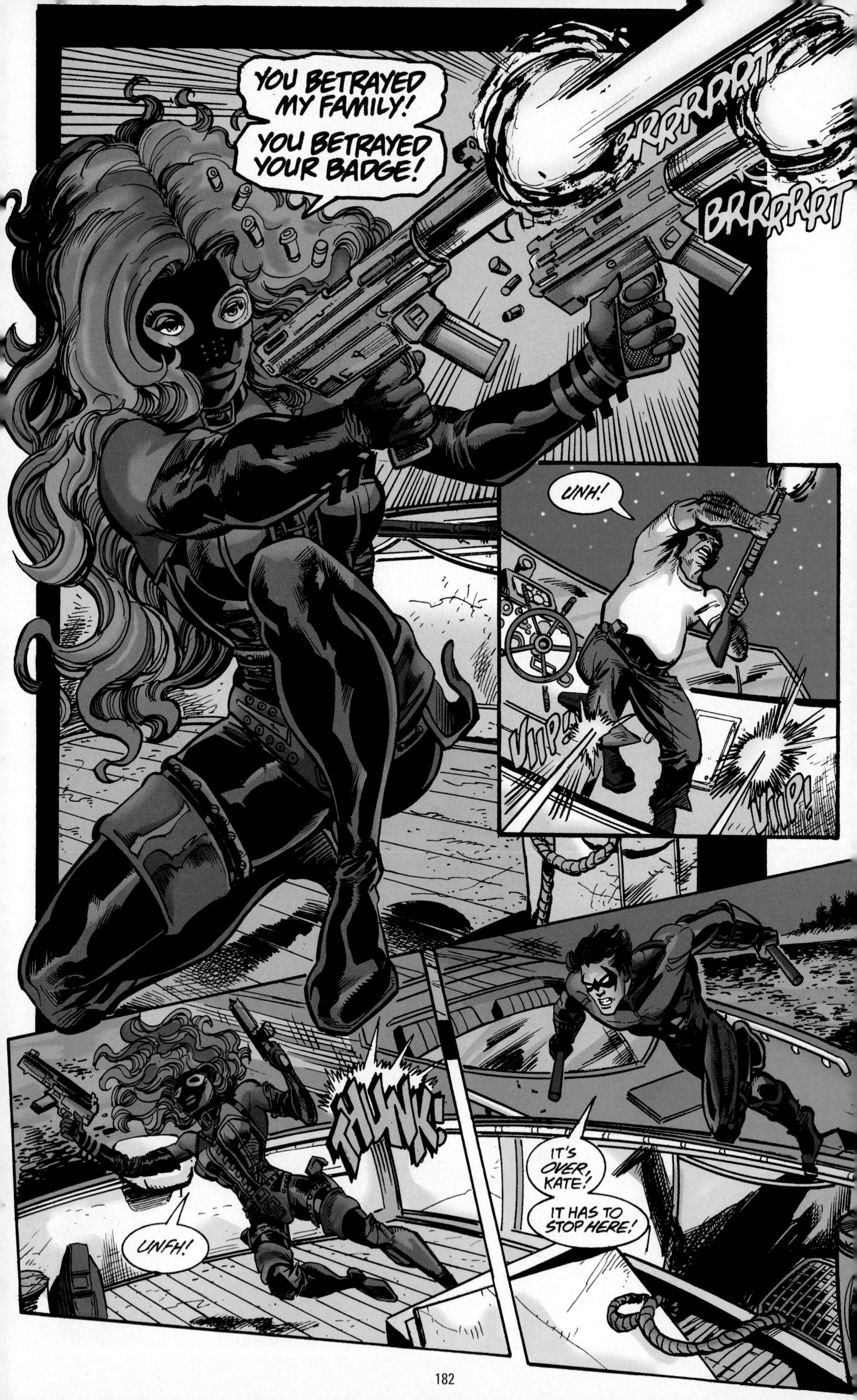
YOU BETRAYED MY FAMILY!
YOU BETRAYED YOUR BADGE!
BRRRRRT
BRRRRRT
UNH!
VIIP!
VIIP!
THUNK!
UNFH!
IT'S OVER, KATE!
IT HAS TO STOP HERE!

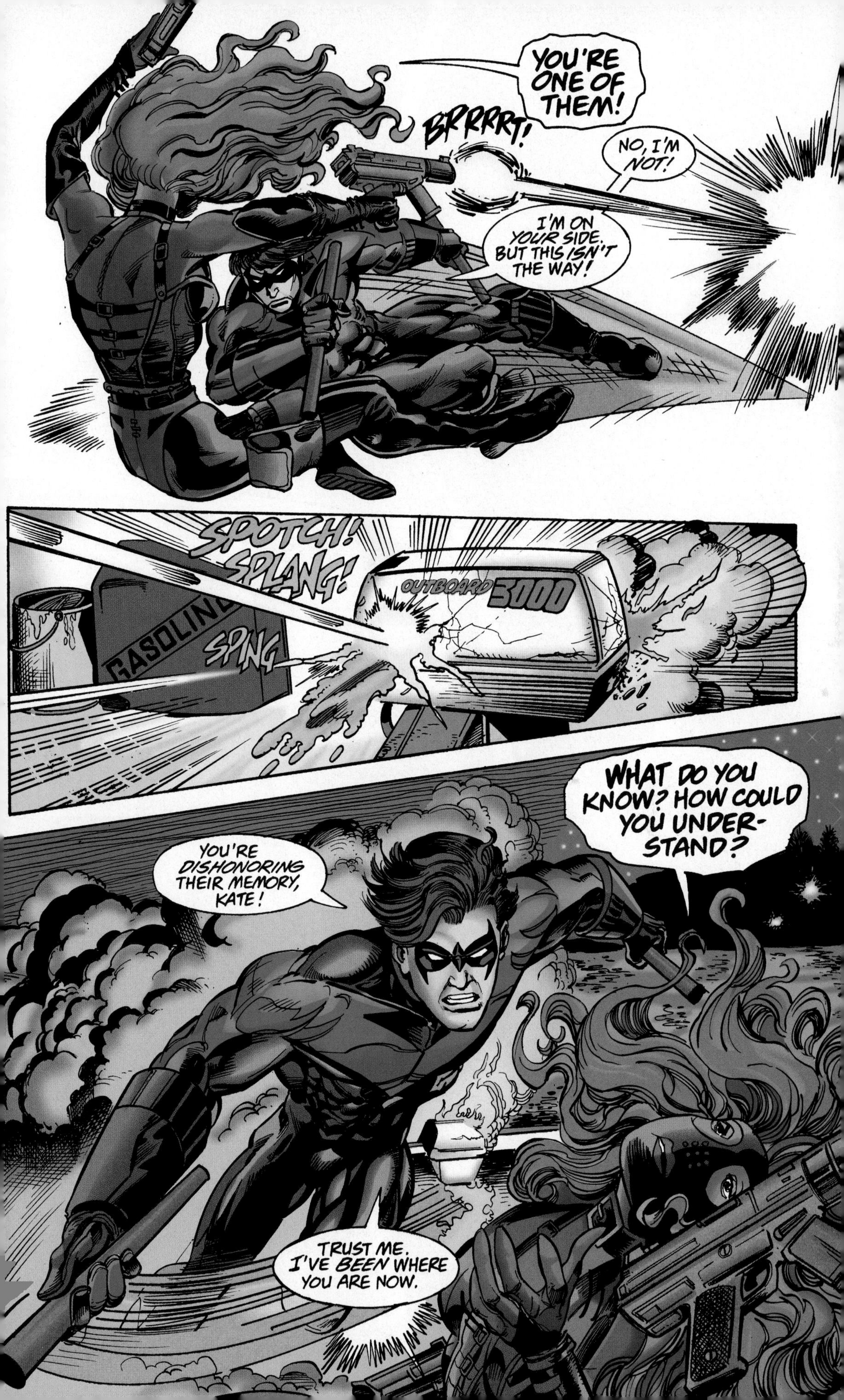
YOU'RE ONE OF THEM!
BRRRRT!
NO, I'M NOT!
I'M ON YOUR SIDE. BUT THIS ISN'T THE WAY!
SPOTCH!
SPLANG!
OUTBOARD 3000
GASOLINE
SPING
YOU'RE DISHONORING THEIR MEMORY, KATE!
WHAT DO YOU KNOW? HOW COULD YOU UNDER-STAND?
TRUST ME. I'VE BEEN WHERE YOU ARE NOW.

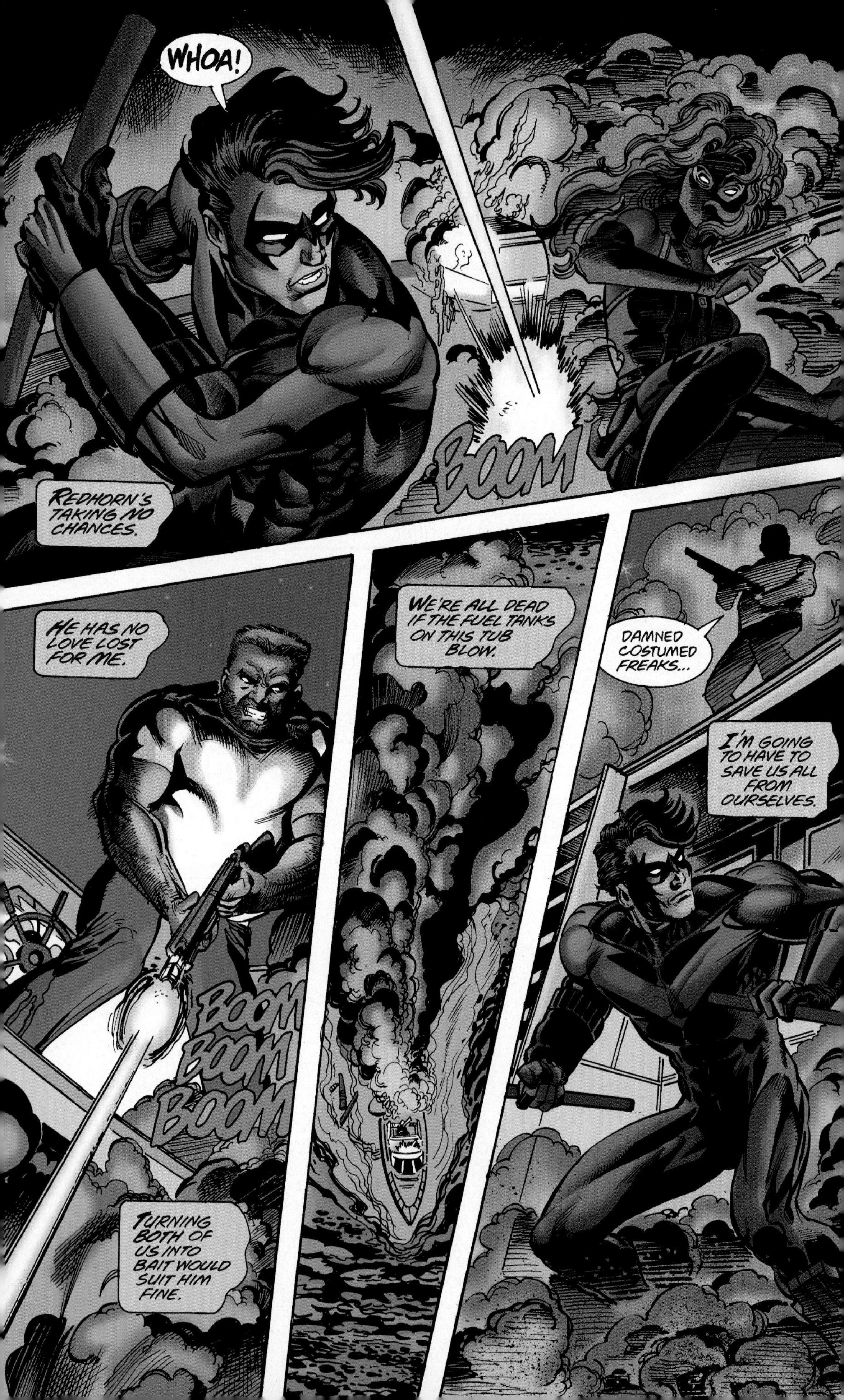
WHOA!
BOOM
REDHORN'S TAKING NO CHANCES.
HE HAS NO LOVE LOST FOR ME.
BOOM BOOM BOOM
TURNING BOTH OF US INTO BAIT WOULD SUIT HIM FINE.
WE'RE ALL DEAD IF THE FUEL TANKS ON THIS TUB BLOW.
DAMNED COSTUMED FREAKS...
I'M GOING TO HAVE TO SAVE US ALL FROM OURSELVES.

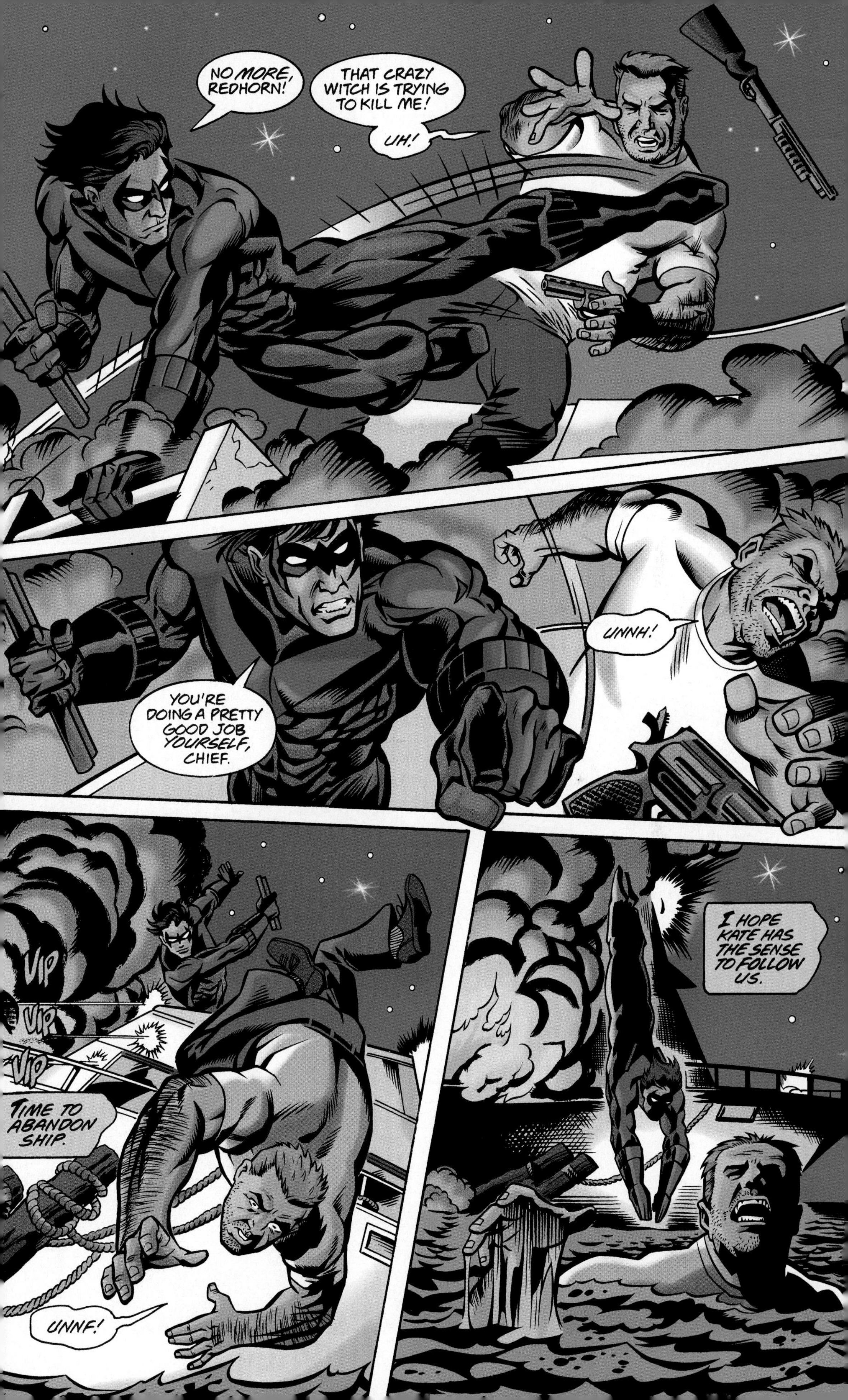
NO MORE, REDHORN!
THAT CRAZY WITCH IS TRYING TO KILL ME!
UH!
UNNH!
YOU'RE DOING A PRETTY GOOD JOB YOURSELF, CHIEF.
VIP
VIP
VIP
TIME TO ABANDON SHIP.
UNNF!
I HOPE KATE HAS THE SENSE TO FOLLOW US.

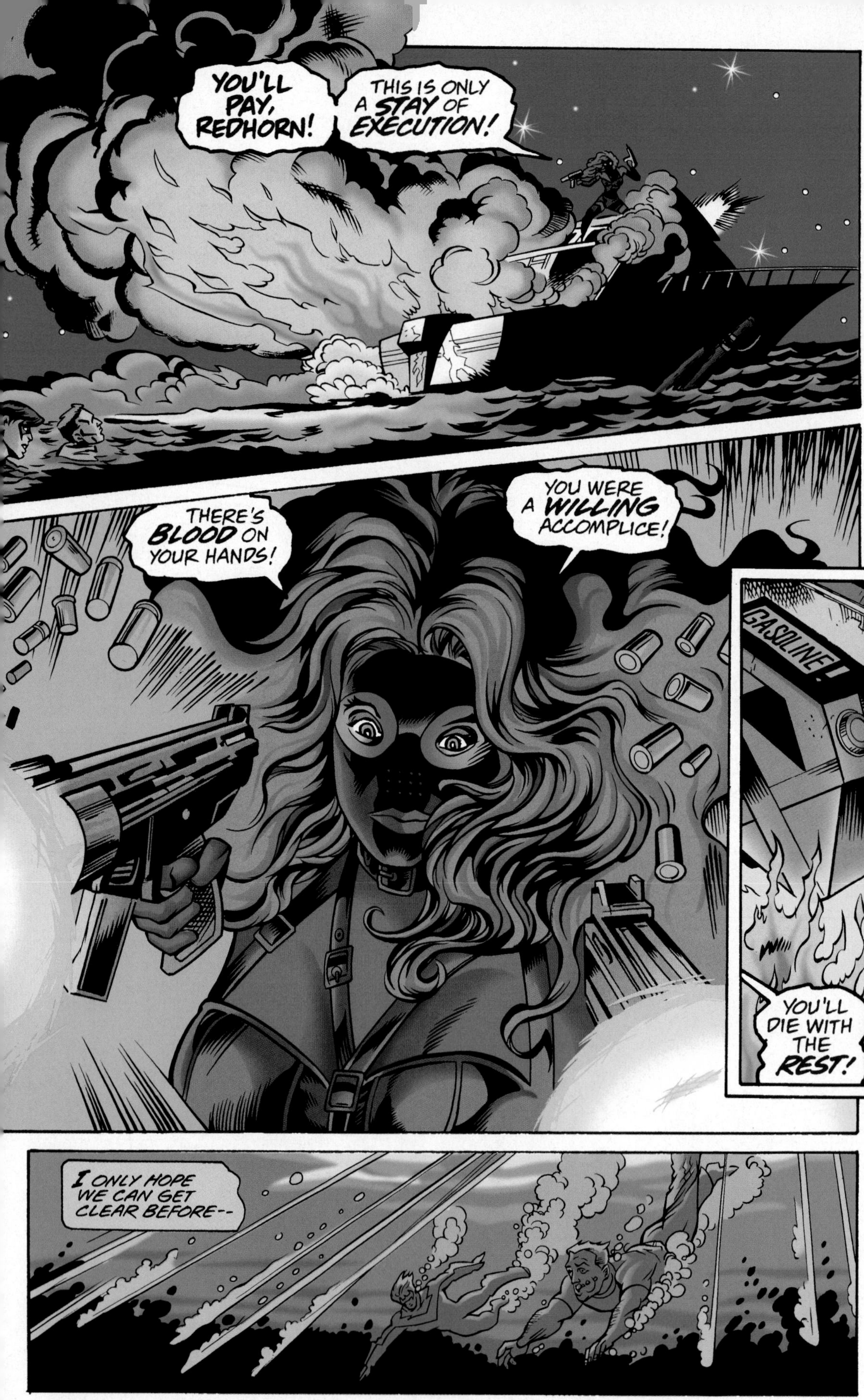
YOU'LL PAY, REDHORN!
THIS IS ONLY A STAY OF EXECUTION!
THERE'S BLOOD ON YOUR HANDS!
YOU WERE A WILLING ACCOMPLICE!
GASOLINE!
YOU'LL DIE WITH THE REST!
I ONLY HOPE WE CAN GET CLEAR BEFORE--

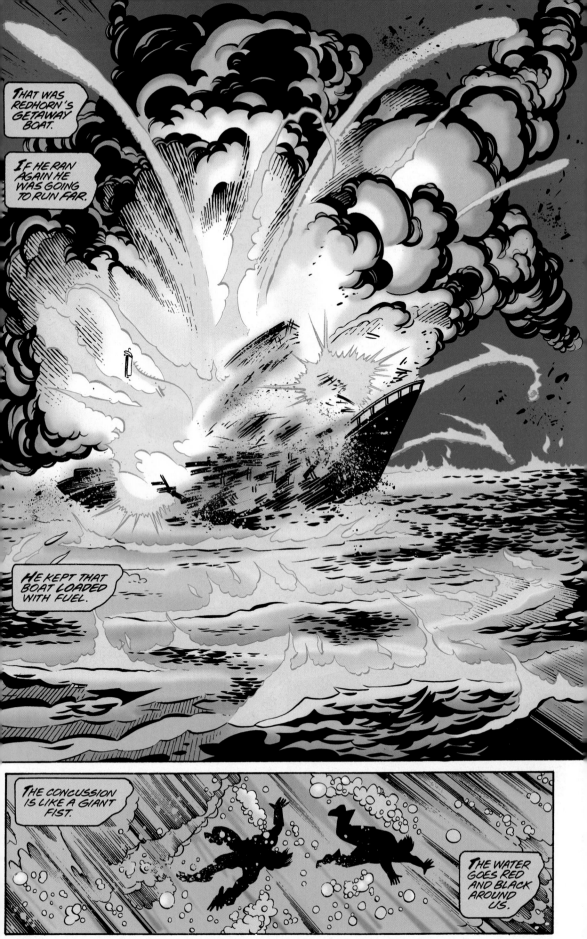

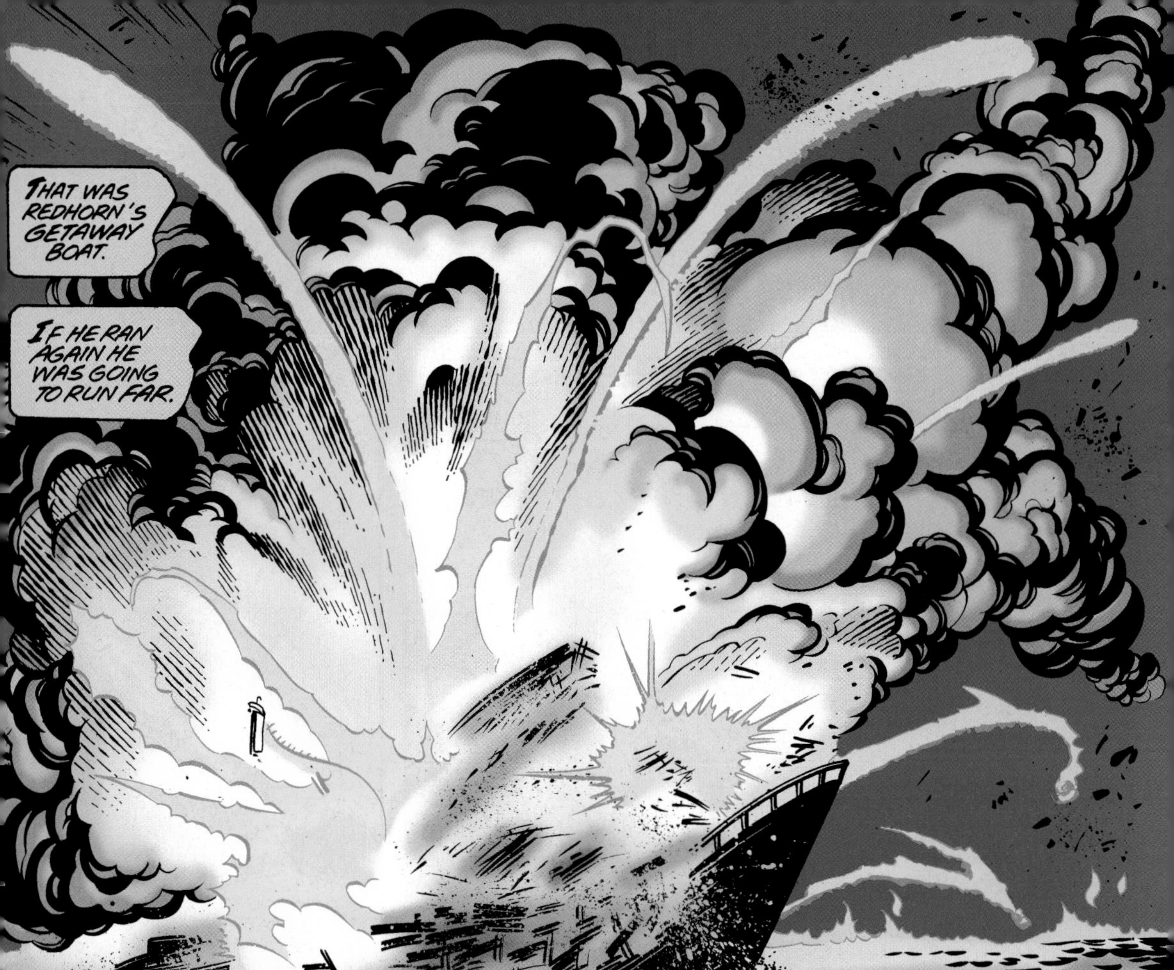
THAT WAS REDHORN'S GETAWAY BOAT.
IF HE RAN AGAIN HE WAS GOING TO RUN FAR.
HE KEPT THAT BOAT LOADED WITH FUEL.

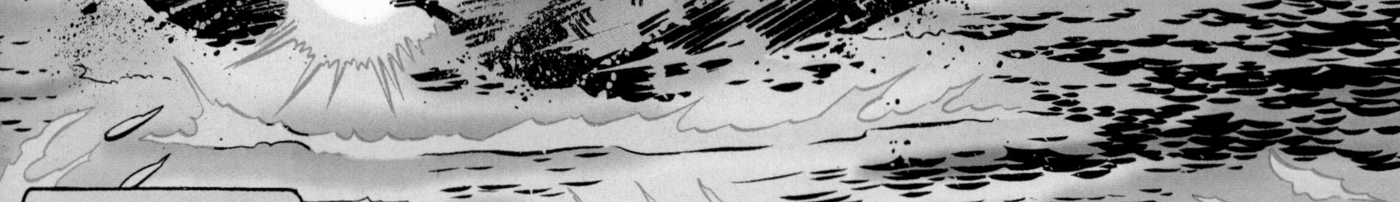
THE CONCUSSION IS LIKE A GIANT FIST.
THE WATER GOES RED AND BLACK AROUND US.

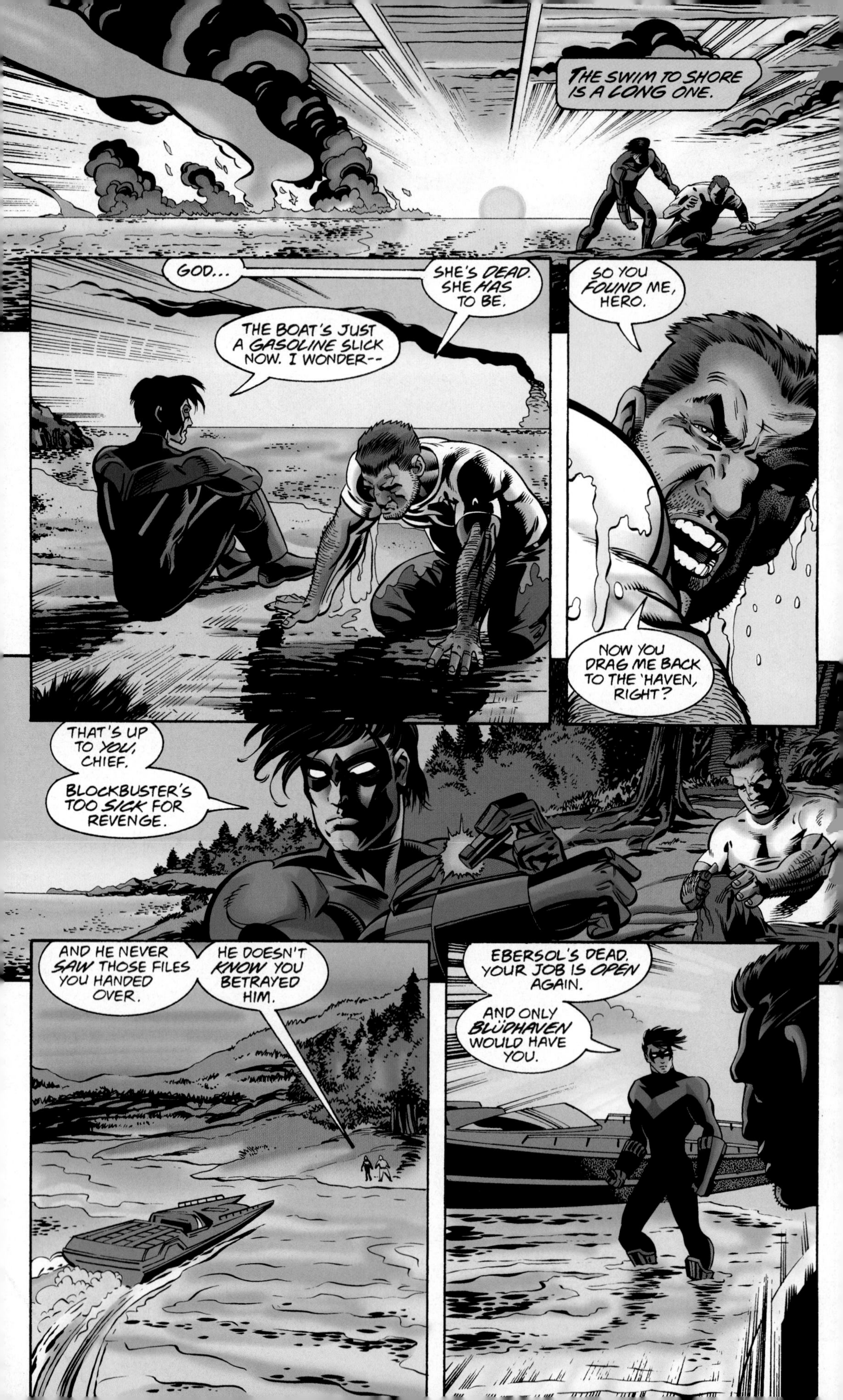

THE SWIM TO SHORE IS A LONG ONE.
GOD...
SHE'S DEAD. SHE HAS TO BE.
THE BOAT'S JUST A GASOLINE SLICK NOW. I WONDER--
SO YOU FOUND ME, HERO.
NOW YOU DRAG ME BACK TO THE 'HAVEN, RIGHT?
THAT'S UP TO YOU, CHIEF.
BLOCKBUSTER'S TOO SICK FOR REVENGE.
AND HE NEVER SAW THOSE FILES YOU HANDED OVER.
HE DOESN'T KNOW YOU BETRAYED HIM.
EBERSOL'S DEAD. YOUR JOB IS OPEN AGAIN.
AND ONLY BLÜDHAVEN WOULD HAVE YOU.

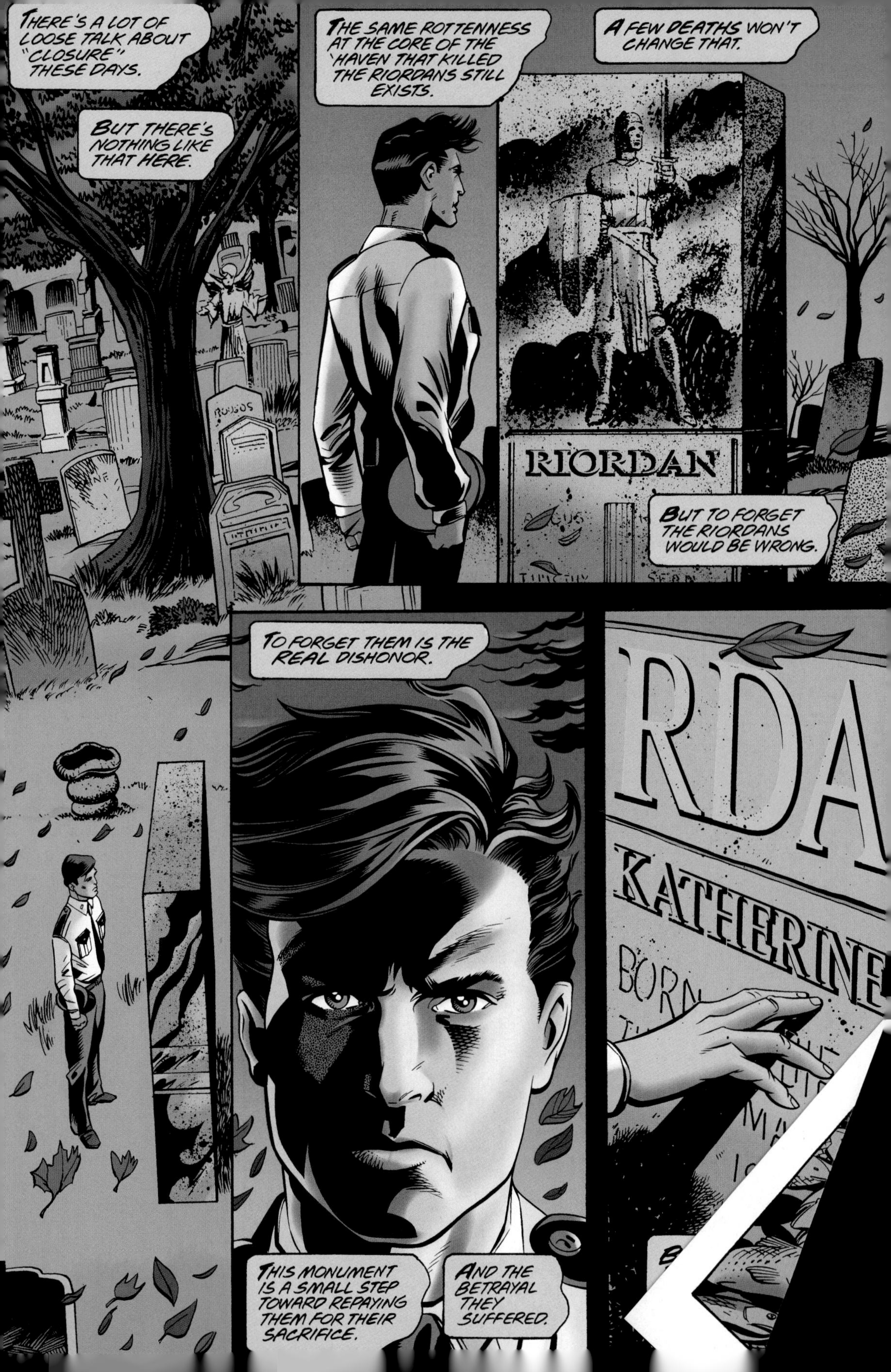
THERE'S A LOT OF LOOSE TALK ABOUT "CLOSURE" THESE DAYS.
BUT THERE'S NOTHING LIKE THAT HERE.
THE SAME ROTTENNESS AT THE CORE OF THE 'HAVEN THAT KILLED THE RIORDANS STILL EXISTS.
A FEW DEATHS WON'T CHANGE THAT.
RIORDAN
BUT TO FORGET THE RIORDANS WOULD BE WRONG.
TO FORGET THEM IS THE REAL DISHONOR.
RDA
KATHERINE
BORN
THIS MONUMENT IS A SMALL STEP TOWARD REPAYING THEM FOR THEIR SACRIFICE.
AND THE BETRAYAL THEY SUFFERED.

NO BODY WAS FOUND.

THERE'S NO REASON TO BELIEVE SHE'S ALIVE.

THERE'S ONLY A SLIM CHANCE SHE SURVIVED.

BUT THAT NEVER STOPPED HER BEFORE.

THE END

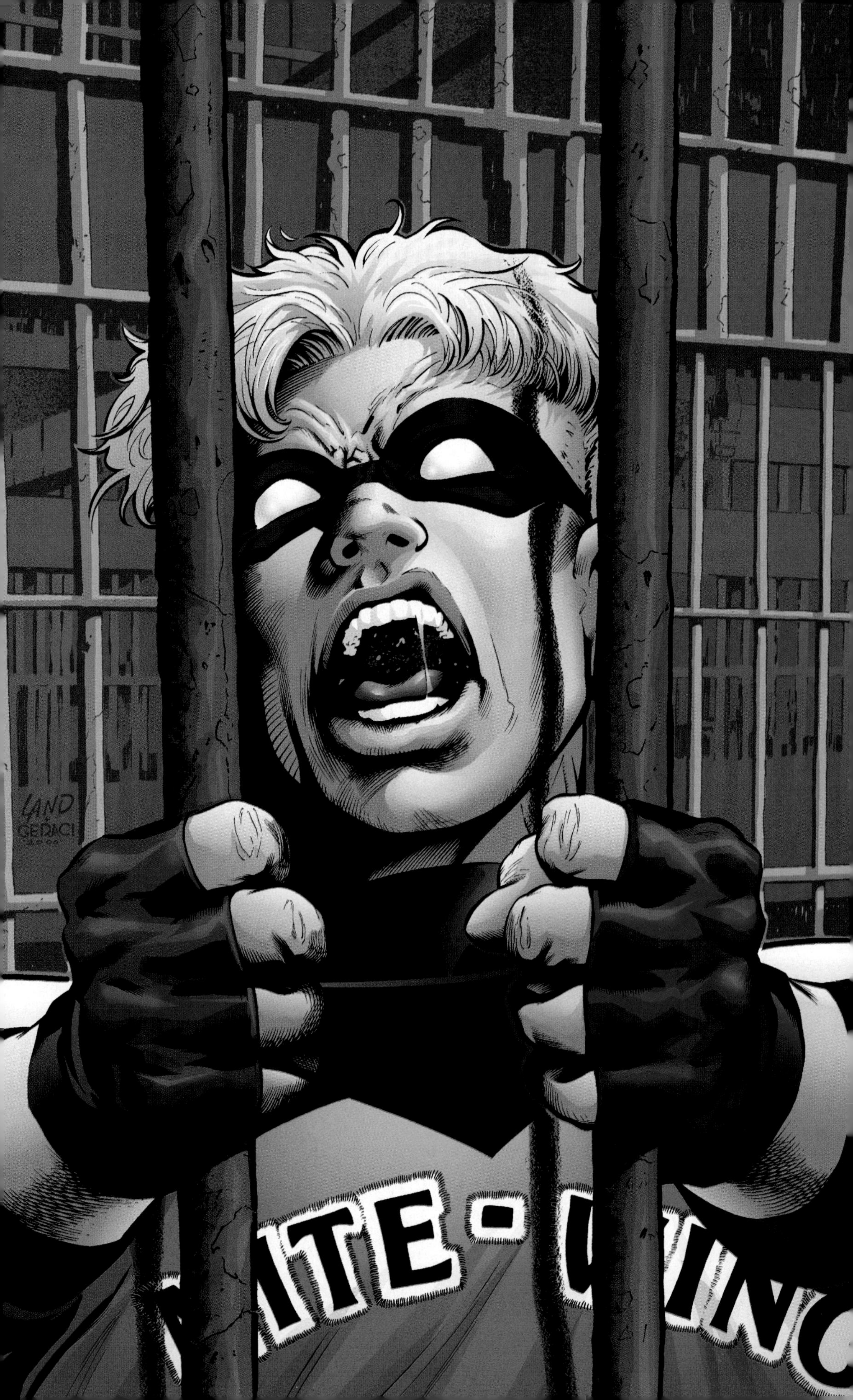
LAND
GERACI
2000

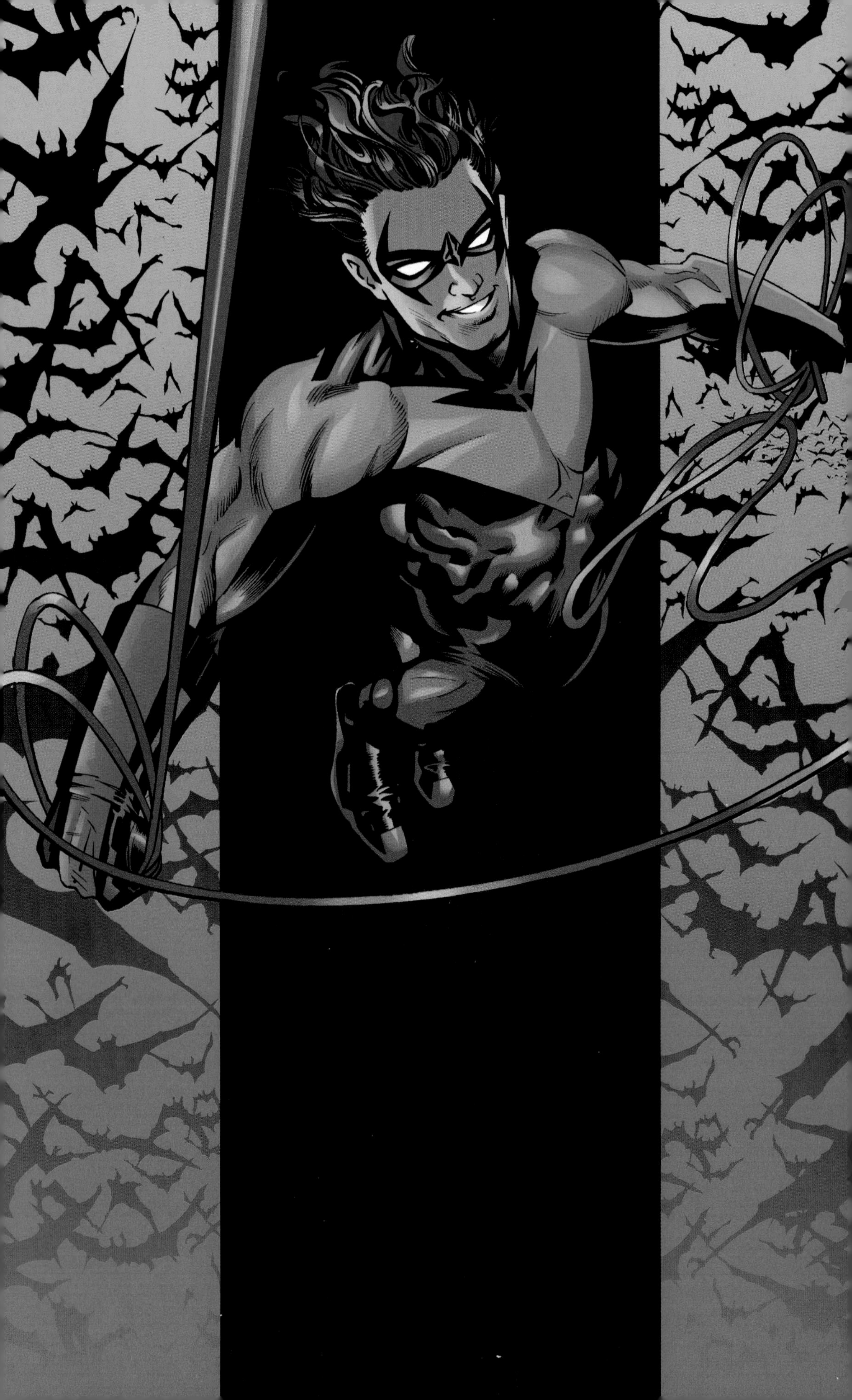

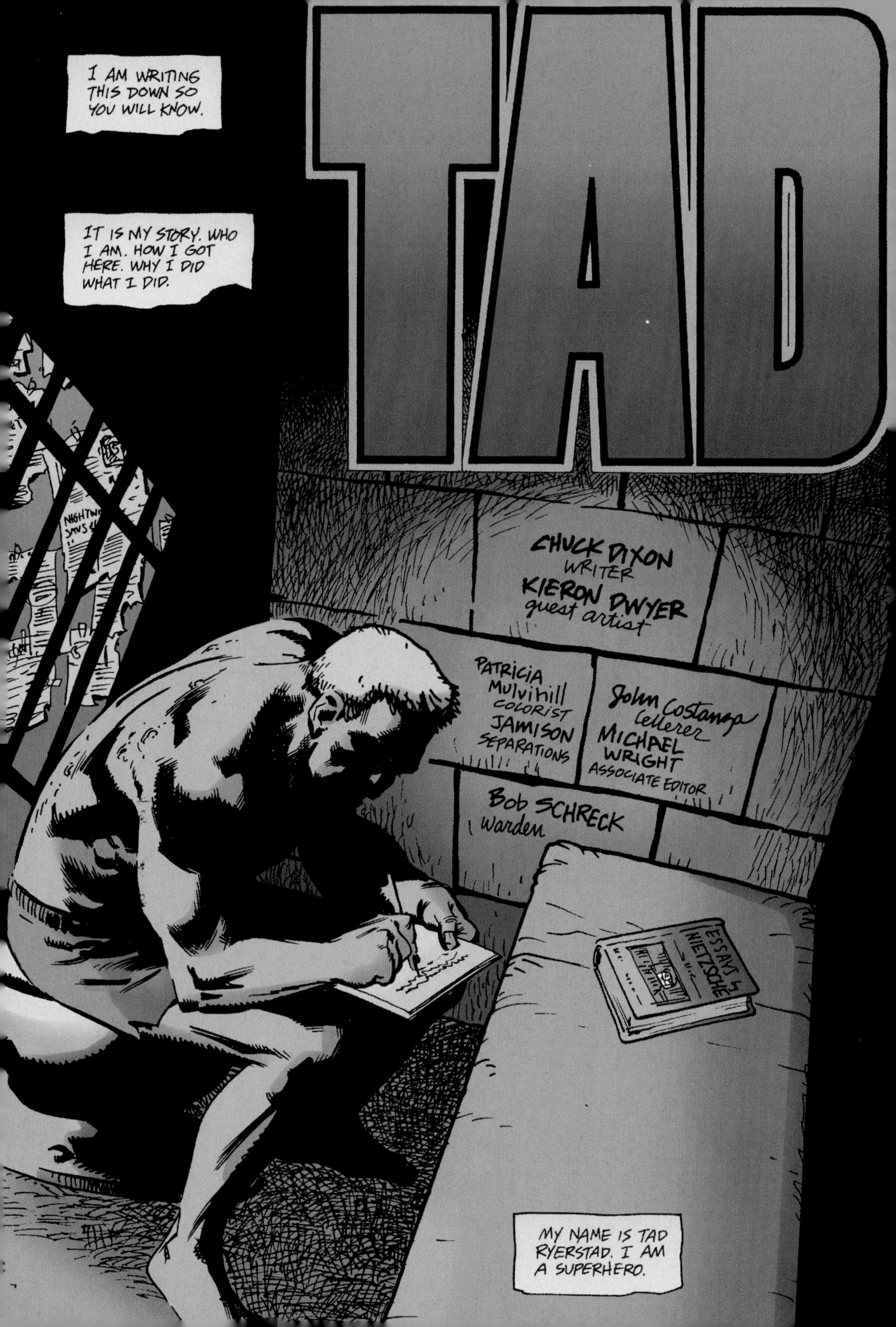
I AM WRITING THIS DOWN SO YOU WILL KNOW.
IT IS MY STORY. WHO I AM. HOW I GOT HERE. WHY I DID WHAT I DID.
TAD
CHUCK DIXON WRITER
KIERON DWYER guest artist
PATRICIA Mulvihill COLORIST
JAMISON SEPARATIONS
John Costanza Letterer
MICHAEL WRIGHT ASSOCIATE EDITOR
Bob SCHRECK warden
ESSAYS by NIETZSCHE
MY NAME IS TAD RYERSTAD. I AM A SUPERHERO.

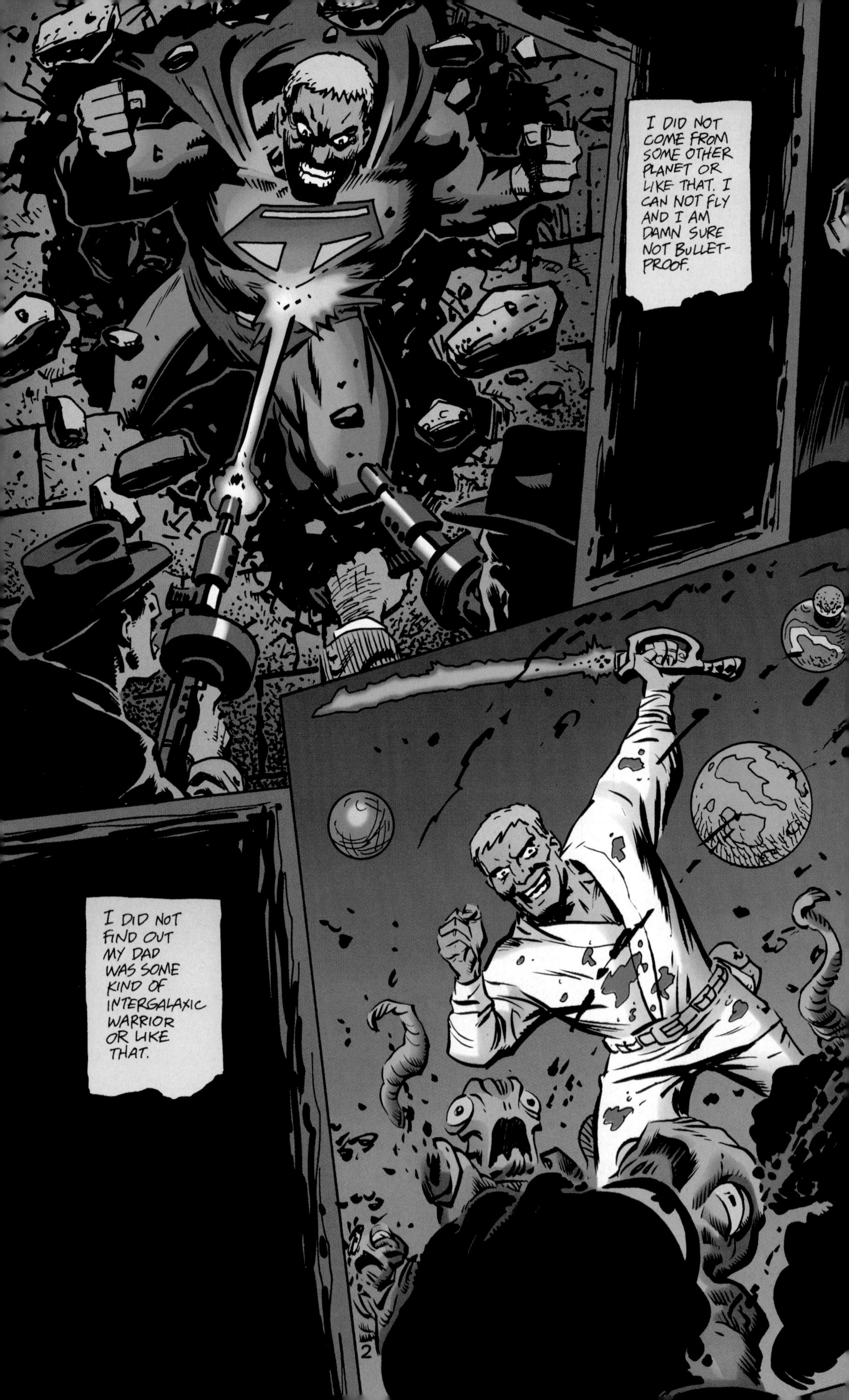
I DID NOT COME FROM SOME OTHER PLANET OR LIKE THAT. I CAN NOT FLY AND I AM DAMN SURE NOT BULLET-PROOF.
I DID NOT FIND OUT MY DAD WAS SOME KIND OF INTERGALAXIC WARRIOR OR LIKE THAT.

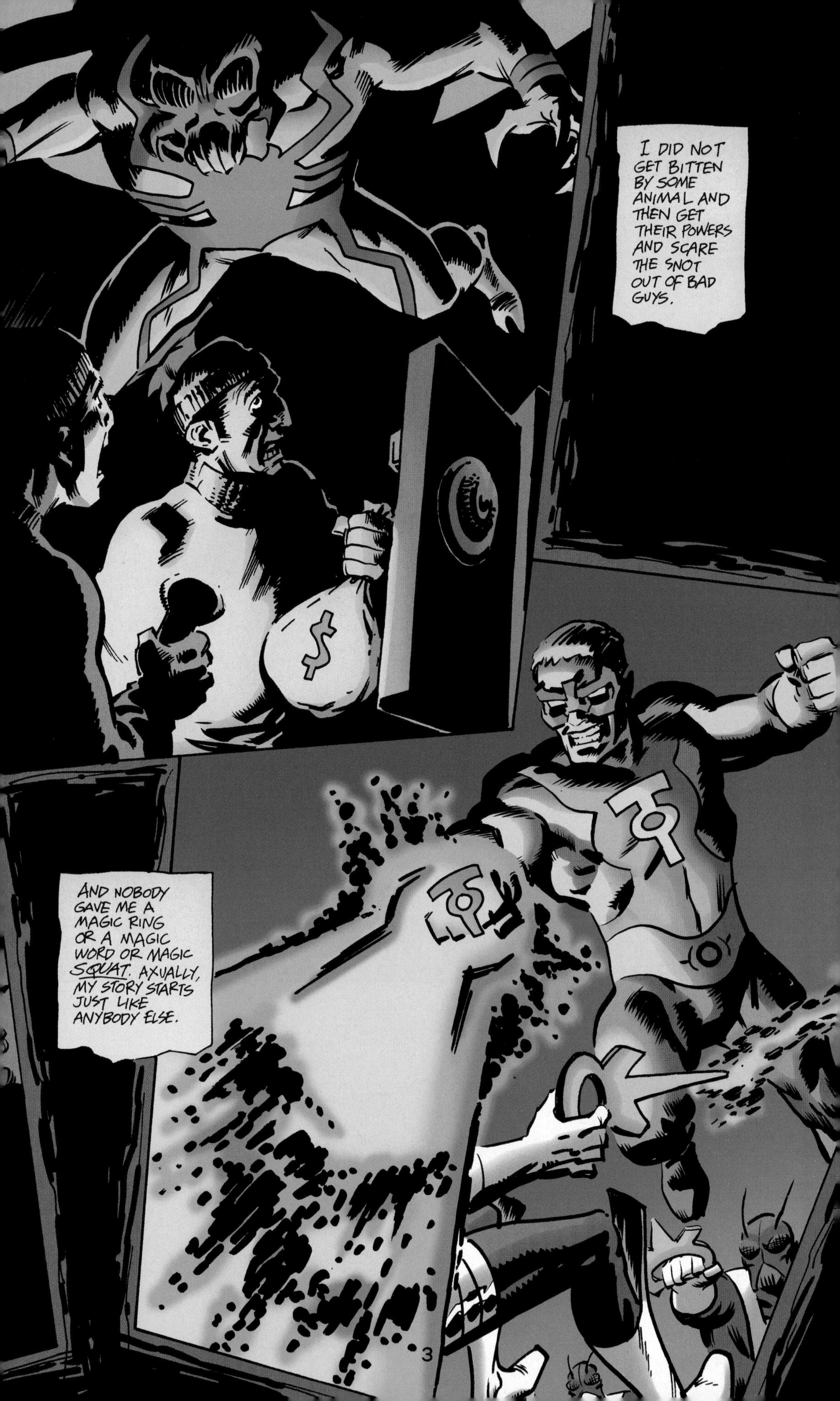
I DID NOT GET BITTEN BY SOME ANIMAL AND THEN GET THEIR POWERS AND SCARE THE SNOT OUT OF BAD GUYS.
AND NOBODY GAVE ME A MAGIC RING OR A MAGIC WORD OR MAGIC SQUAT. AXUALLY, MY STORY STARTS JUST LIKE ANYBODY ELSE.

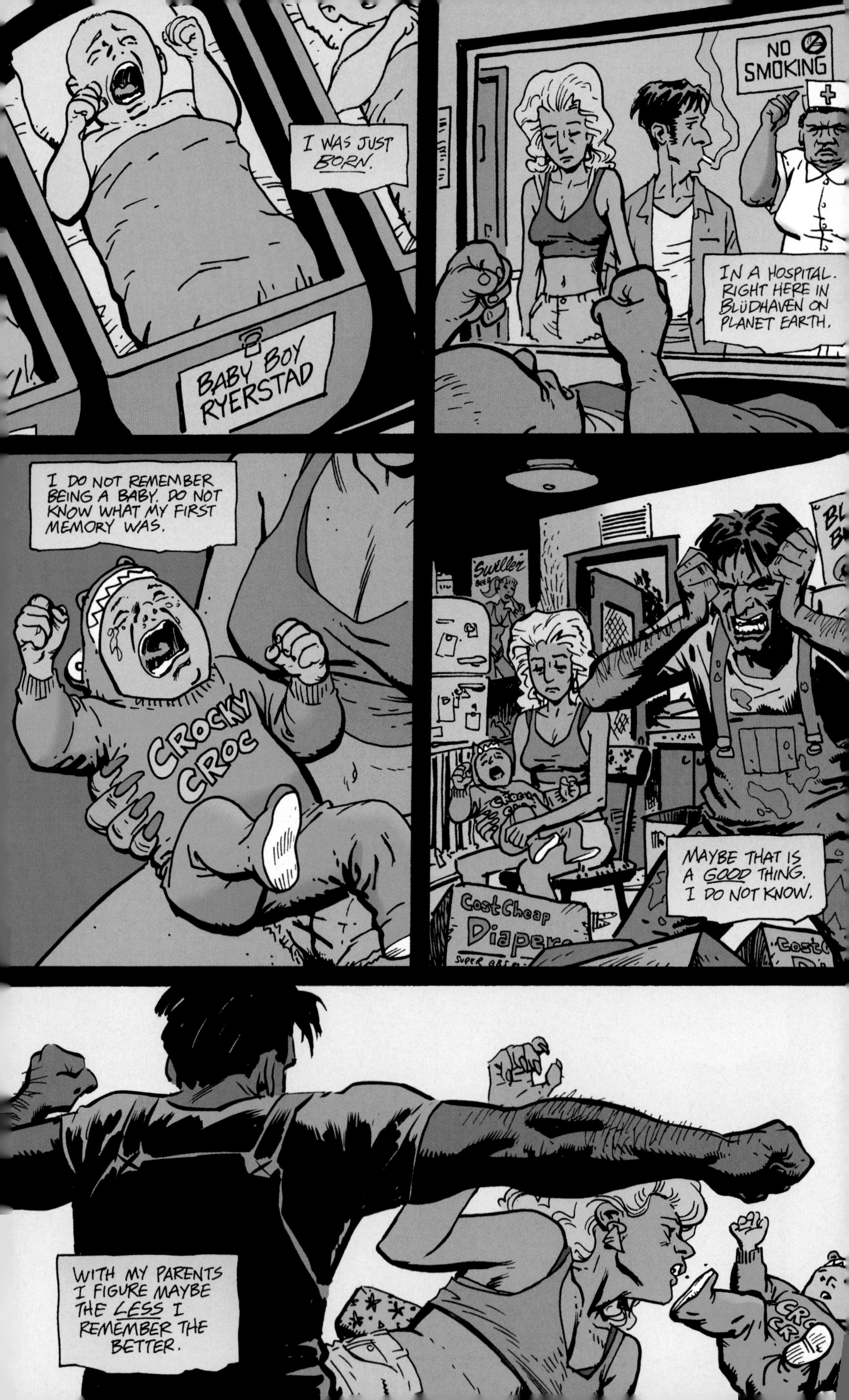
I WAS JUST BORN.
BABY BOY RYERSTAD
NO SMOKING
IN A HOSPITAL. RIGHT HERE IN BLÜDHAVEN ON PLANET EARTH.
I DO NOT REMEMBER BEING A BABY. DO NOT KNOW WHAT MY FIRST MEMORY WAS.
CROCKY CROC
Swiller
MAYBE THAT IS A GOOD THING. I DO NOT KNOW.
CostCheap Diapers
WITH MY PARENTS I FIGURE MAYBE THE LESS I REMEMBER THE BETTER.

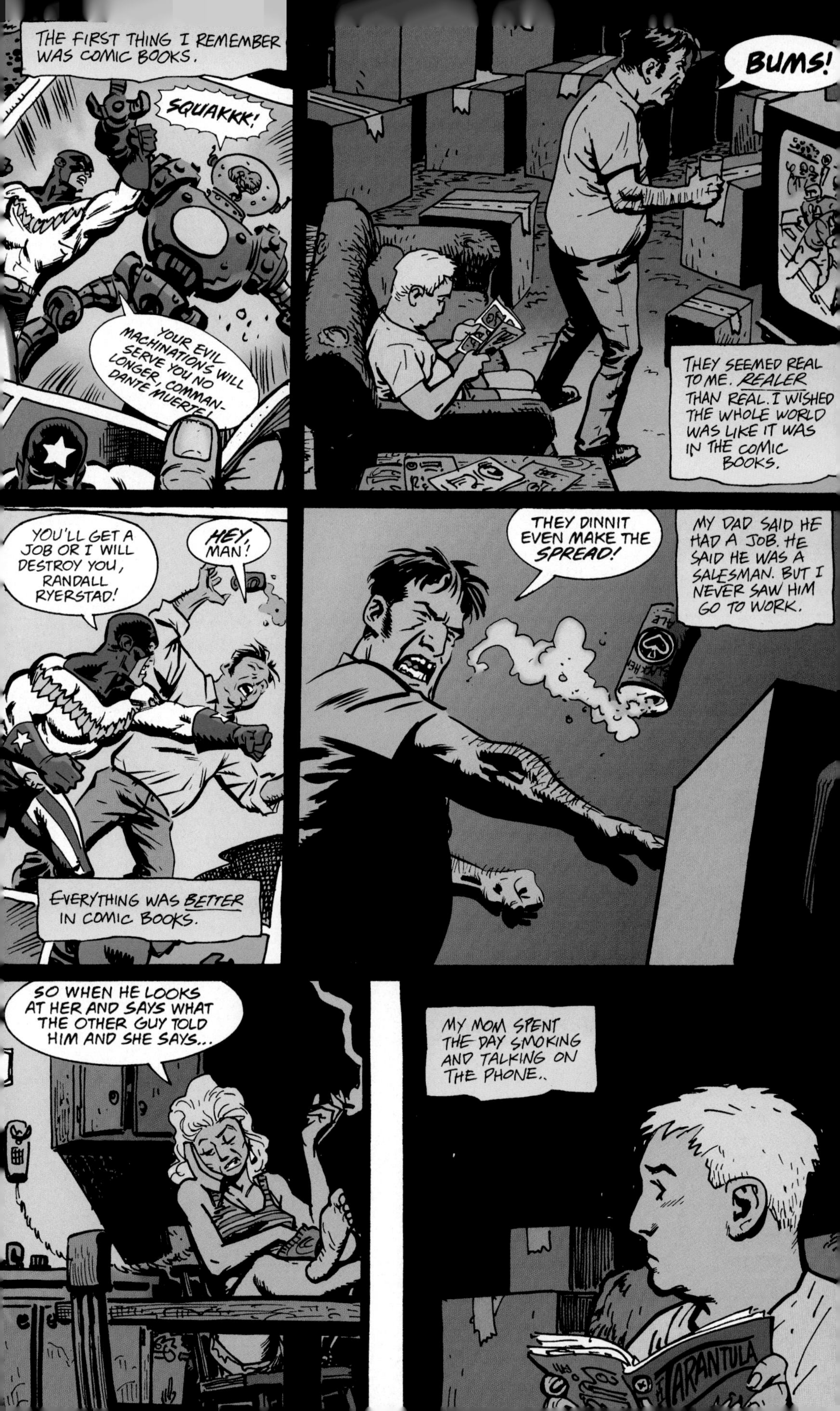
THE FIRST THING I REMEMBER WAS COMIC BOOKS.
SQUAKKK!
YOUR EVIL MACHINATIONS WILL SERVE YOU NO LONGER, COMMANDANTE MUERTE!
BUMS!
THEY SEEMED REAL TO ME. REALER THAN REAL. I WISHED THE WHOLE WORLD WAS LIKE IT WAS IN THE COMIC BOOKS.
YOU'LL GET A JOB OR I WILL DESTROY YOU, RANDALL RYERSTAD!
HEY, MAN!
EVERYTHING WAS BETTER IN COMIC BOOKS.
THEY DINNIT EVEN MAKE THE SPREAD!
MY DAD SAID HE HAD A JOB. HE SAID HE WAS A SALESMAN. BUT I NEVER SAW HIM GO TO WORK.
SO WHEN HE LOOKS AT HER AND SAYS WHAT THE OTHER GUY TOLD HIM AND SHE SAYS...
MY MOM SPENT THE DAY SMOKING AND TALKING ON THE PHONE..
TARANTULA

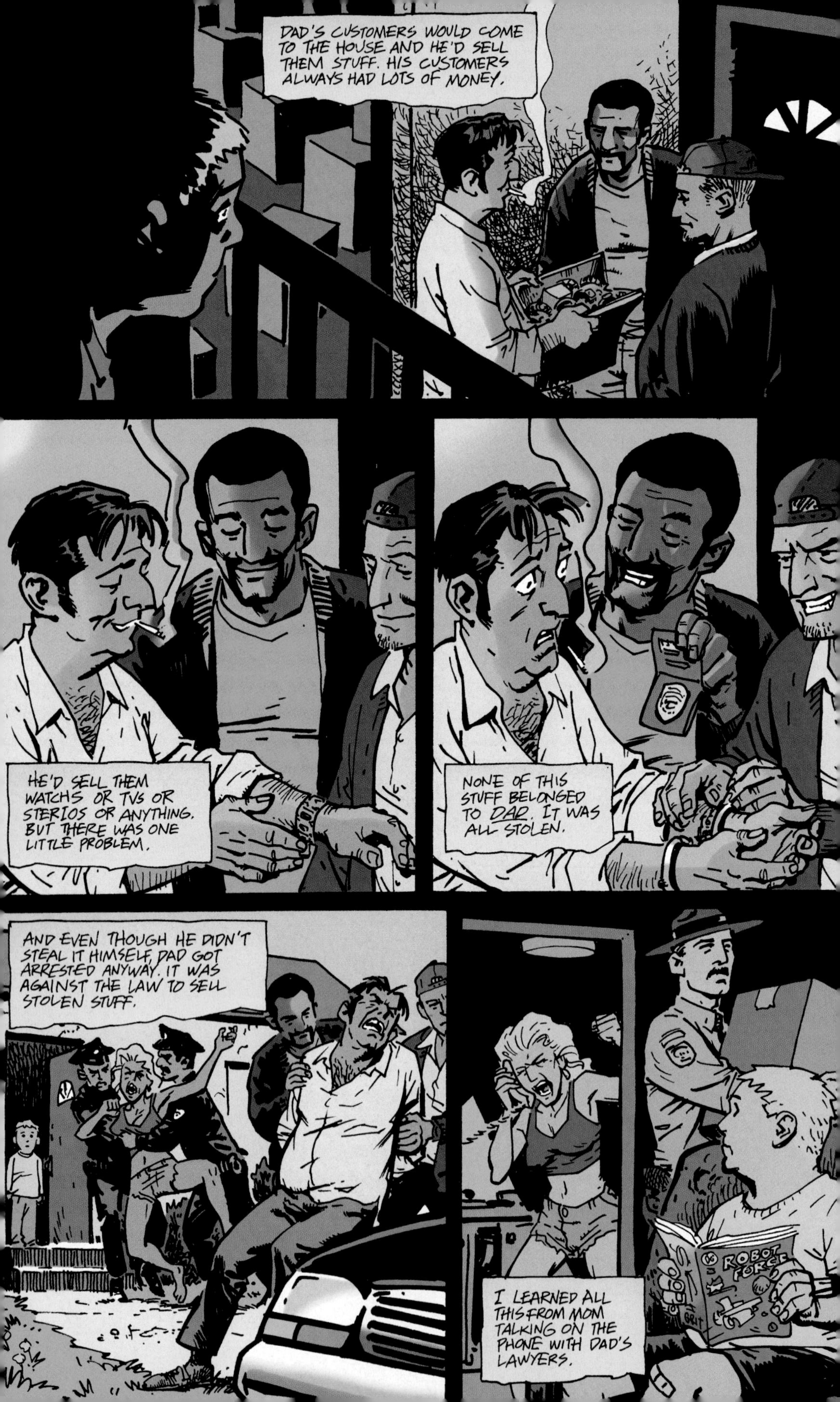
DAD'S CUSTOMERS WOULD COME TO THE HOUSE AND HE'D SELL THEM STUFF. HIS CUSTOMERS ALWAYS HAD LOTS OF MONEY.
HE'D SELL THEM WATCHS OR TVS OR STERIOS OR ANYTHING. BUT THERE WAS ONE LITTLE PROBLEM.
NONE OF THIS STUFF BELONGED TO DAD. IT WAS ALL STOLEN.
AND EVEN THOUGH HE DIDN'T STEAL IT HIMSELF, DAD GOT ARRESTED ANYWAY. IT WAS AGAINST THE LAW TO SELL STOLEN STUFF.
ROBOT FORCE
I LEARNED ALL THIS FROM MOM TALKING ON THE PHONE WITH DAD'S LAWYERS.

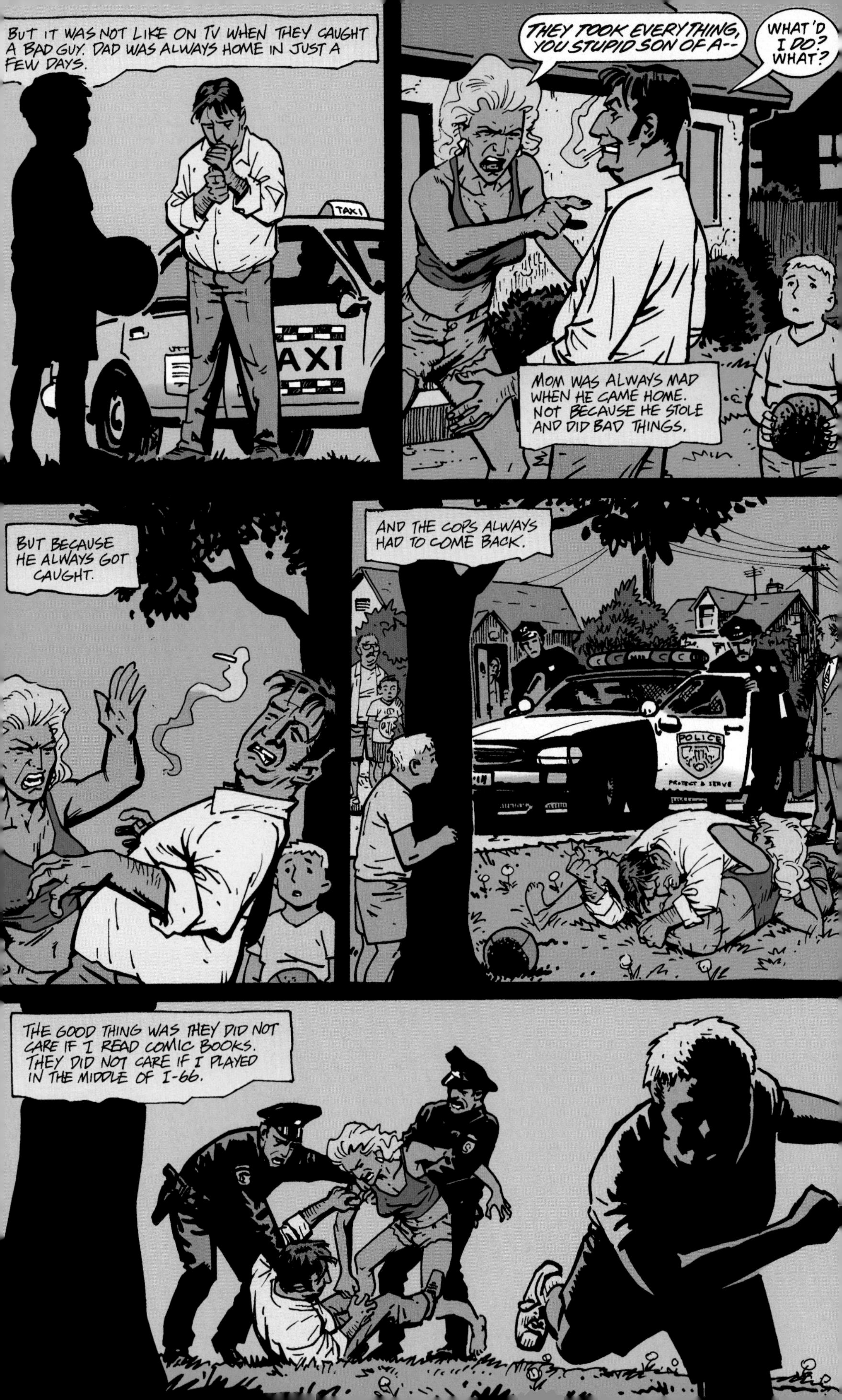
BUT IT WAS NOT LIKE ON TV WHEN THEY CAUGHT A BAD GUY. DAD WAS ALWAYS HOME IN JUST A FEW DAYS.
THEY TOOK EVERYTHING, YOU STUPID SON OF A--
WHAT'D I DO? WHAT?
MOM WAS ALWAYS MAD WHEN HE CAME HOME. NOT BECAUSE HE STOLE AND DID BAD THINGS.
BUT BECAUSE HE ALWAYS GOT CAUGHT.
AND THE COPS ALWAYS HAD TO COME BACK.
POLICE
PROTECT & SERVE
THE GOOD THING WAS THEY DID NOT CARE IF I READ COMIC BOOKS. THEY DID NOT CARE IF I PLAYED IN THE MIDDLE OF I-66.

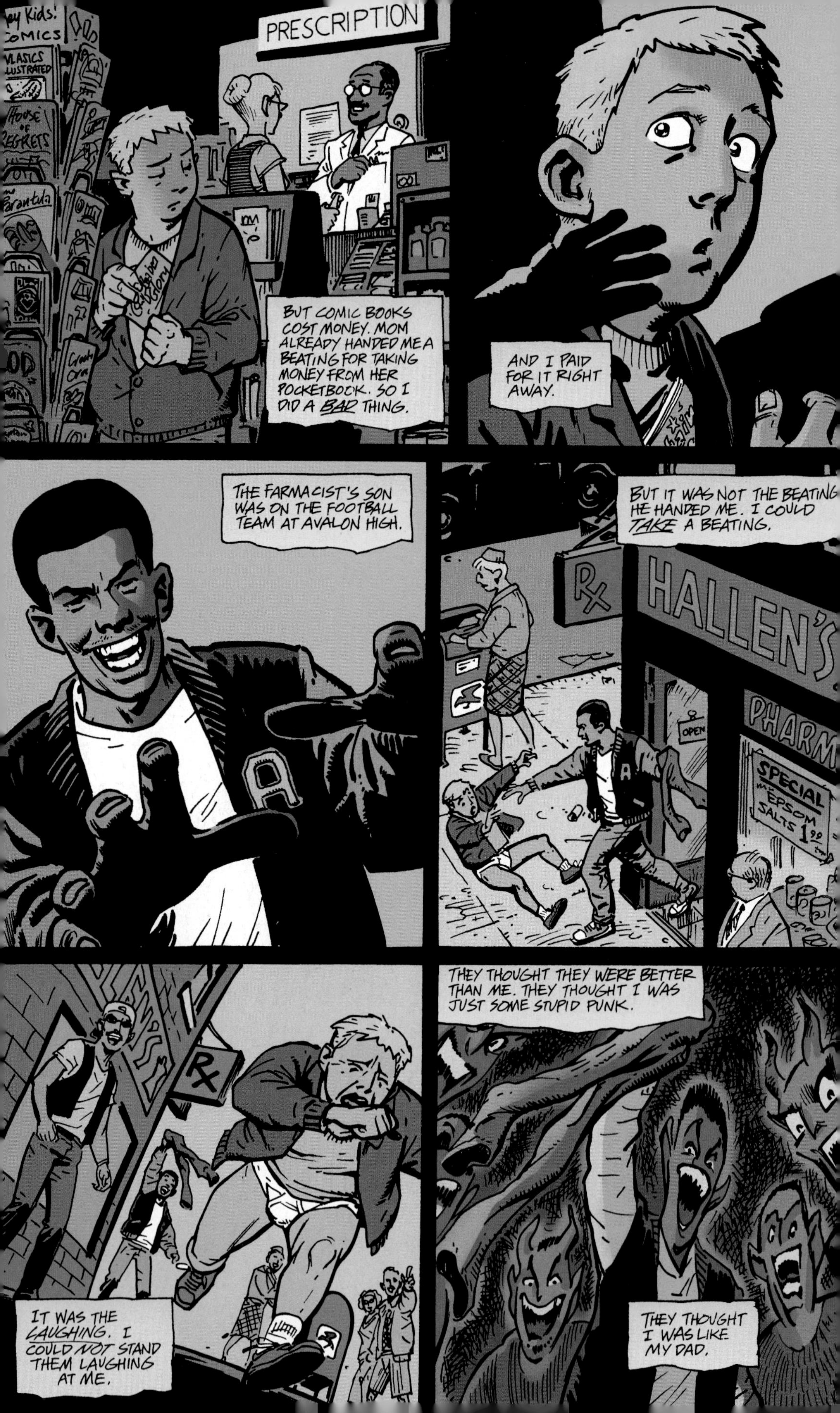
PRESCRIPTION
BUT COMIC BOOKS COST MONEY. MOM ALREADY HANDED ME A BEATING FOR TAKING MONEY FROM HER POCKETBOOK. SO I DID A BAD THING.
AND I PAID FOR IT RIGHT AWAY.
THE FARMACIST'S SON WAS ON THE FOOTBALL TEAM AT AVALON HIGH.
BUT IT WAS NOT THE BEATING HE HANDED ME. I COULD TAKE A BEATING.
HALLEN'S
PHARM
OPEN
SPECIAL
EPSOM SALTS 1.99
IT WAS THE LAUGHING. I COULD NOT STAND THEM LAUGHING AT ME.
THEY THOUGHT THEY WERE BETTER THAN ME. THEY THOUGHT I WAS JUST SOME STUPID PUNK.
THEY THOUGHT I WAS LIKE MY DAD.

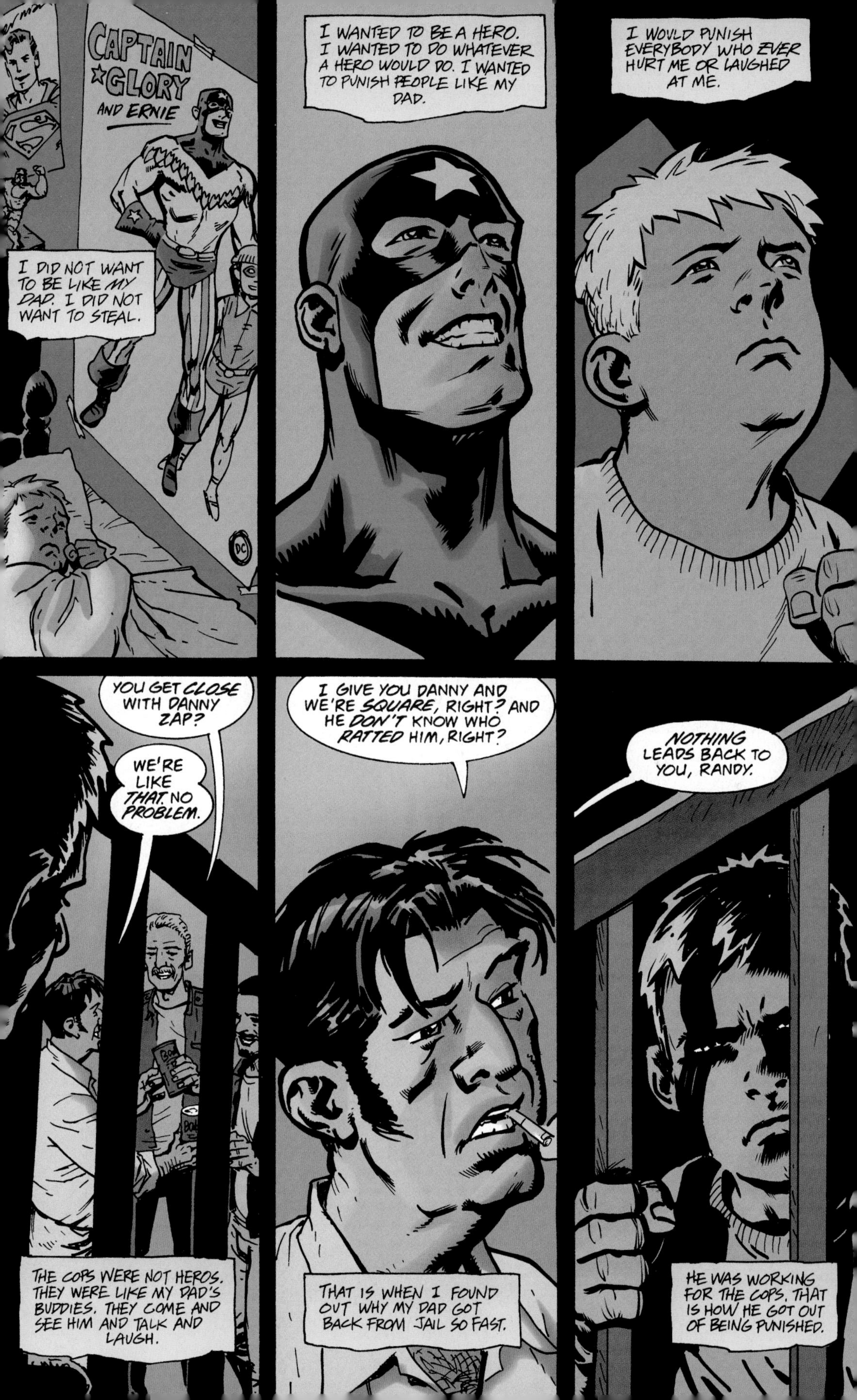
CAPTAIN GLORY AND ERNIE
I DID NOT WANT TO BE LIKE MY DAD. I DID NOT WANT TO STEAL.
I WANTED TO BE A HERO. I WANTED TO DO WHATEVER A HERO WOULD DO. I WANTED TO PUNISH PEOPLE LIKE MY DAD.
I WOULD PUNISH EVERYBODY WHO EVER HURT ME OR LAUGHED AT ME.
YOU GET CLOSE WITH DANNY ZAP?
WE'RE LIKE THAT. NO PROBLEM.
THE COPS WERE NOT HEROS. THEY WERE LIKE MY DAD'S BUDDIES. THEY COME AND SEE HIM AND TALK AND LAUGH.
I GIVE YOU DANNY AND WE'RE SQUARE, RIGHT? AND HE DON'T KNOW WHO RATTED HIM, RIGHT?
THAT IS WHEN I FOUND OUT WHY MY DAD GOT BACK FROM JAIL SO FAST.
NOTHING LEADS BACK TO YOU, RANDY.
HE WAS WORKING FOR THE COPS. THAT IS HOW HE GOT OUT OF BEING PUNISHED.

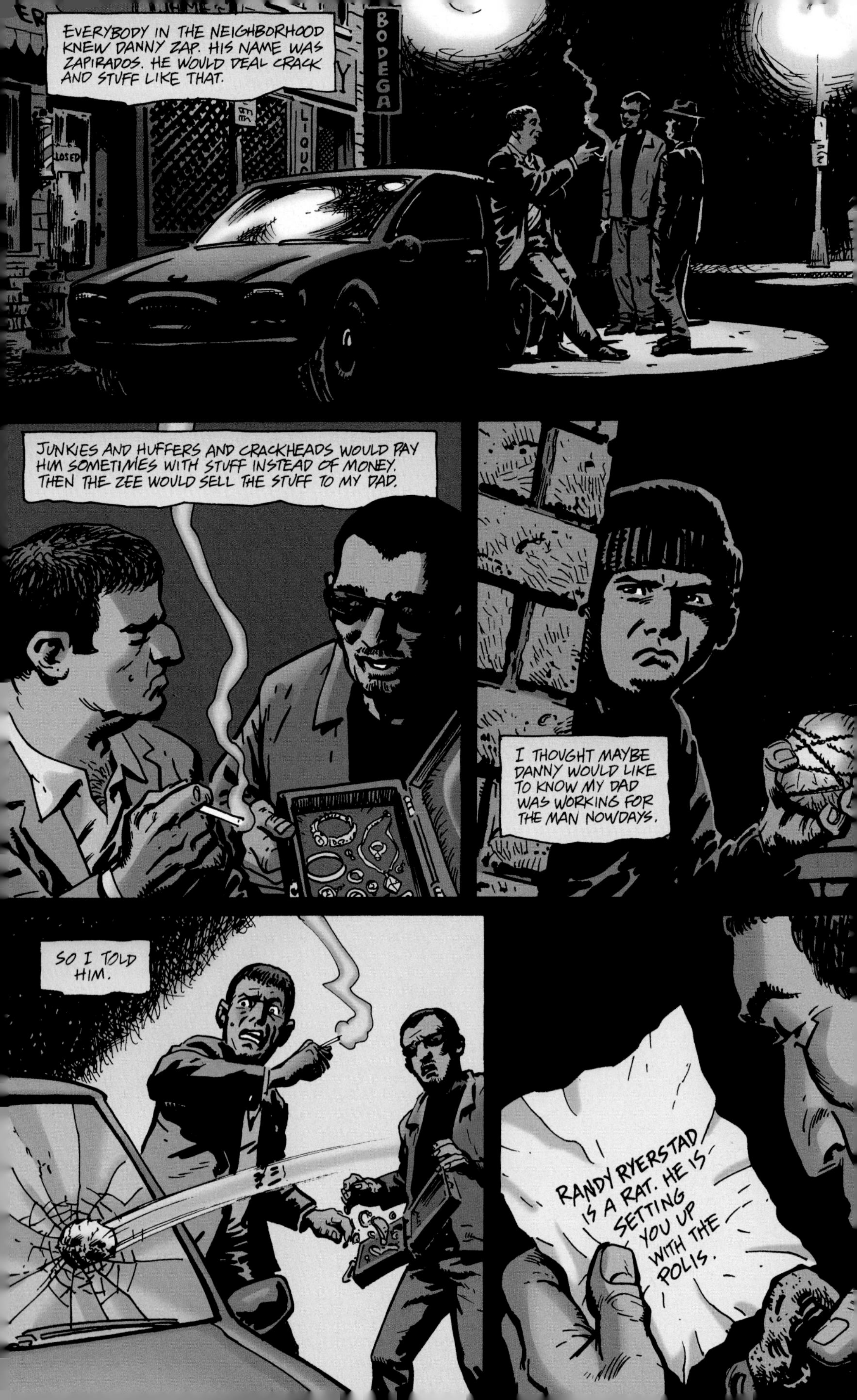
EVERYBODY IN THE NEIGHBORHOOD KNEW DANNY ZAP. HIS NAME WAS ZAPIRADOS. HE WOULD DEAL CRACK AND STUFF LIKE THAT.
BODEGA
JUNKIES AND HUFFERS AND CRACKHEADS WOULD PAY HIM SOMETIMES WITH STUFF INSTEAD OF MONEY. THEN THE ZEE WOULD SELL THE STUFF TO MY DAD.
I THOUGHT MAYBE DANNY WOULD LIKE TO KNOW MY DAD WAS WORKING FOR THE MAN NOWDAYS.
SO I TOLD HIM.
RANDY RYERSTAD IS A RAT. HE IS SETTING YOU UP WITH THE POLIS.

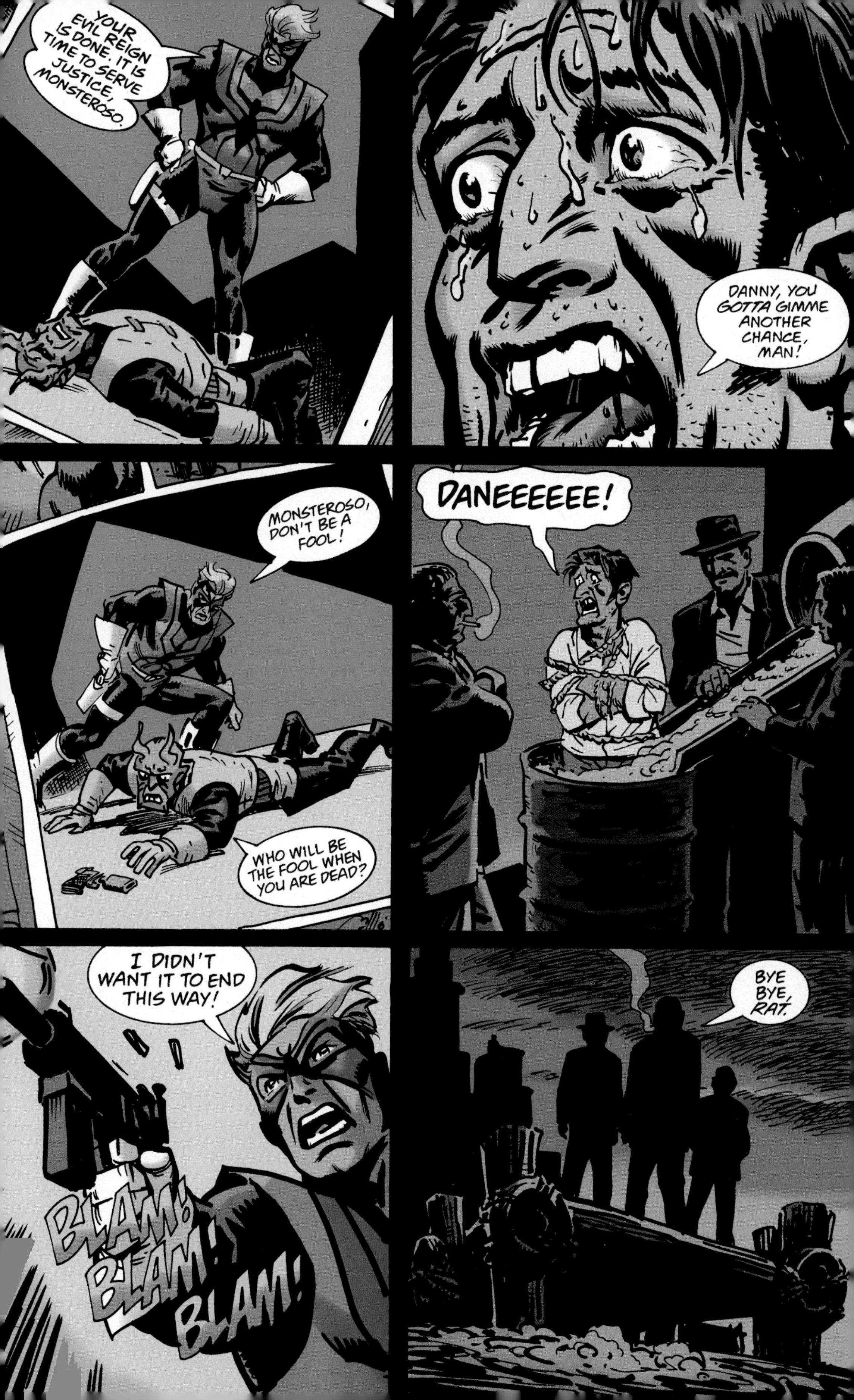
YOUR EVIL REIGN IS DONE. IT IS TIME TO SERVE JUSTICE, MONSTEROSO.
DANNY, YOU GOTTA GIMME ANOTHER CHANCE, MAN!
MONSTEROSO, DON'T BE A FOOL!
WHO WILL BE THE FOOL WHEN YOU ARE DEAD?
DANEEEEEEE!
I DIDN'T WANT IT TO END THIS WAY!
BLAM! BLAM! BLAM!
BYE BYE, RAT.

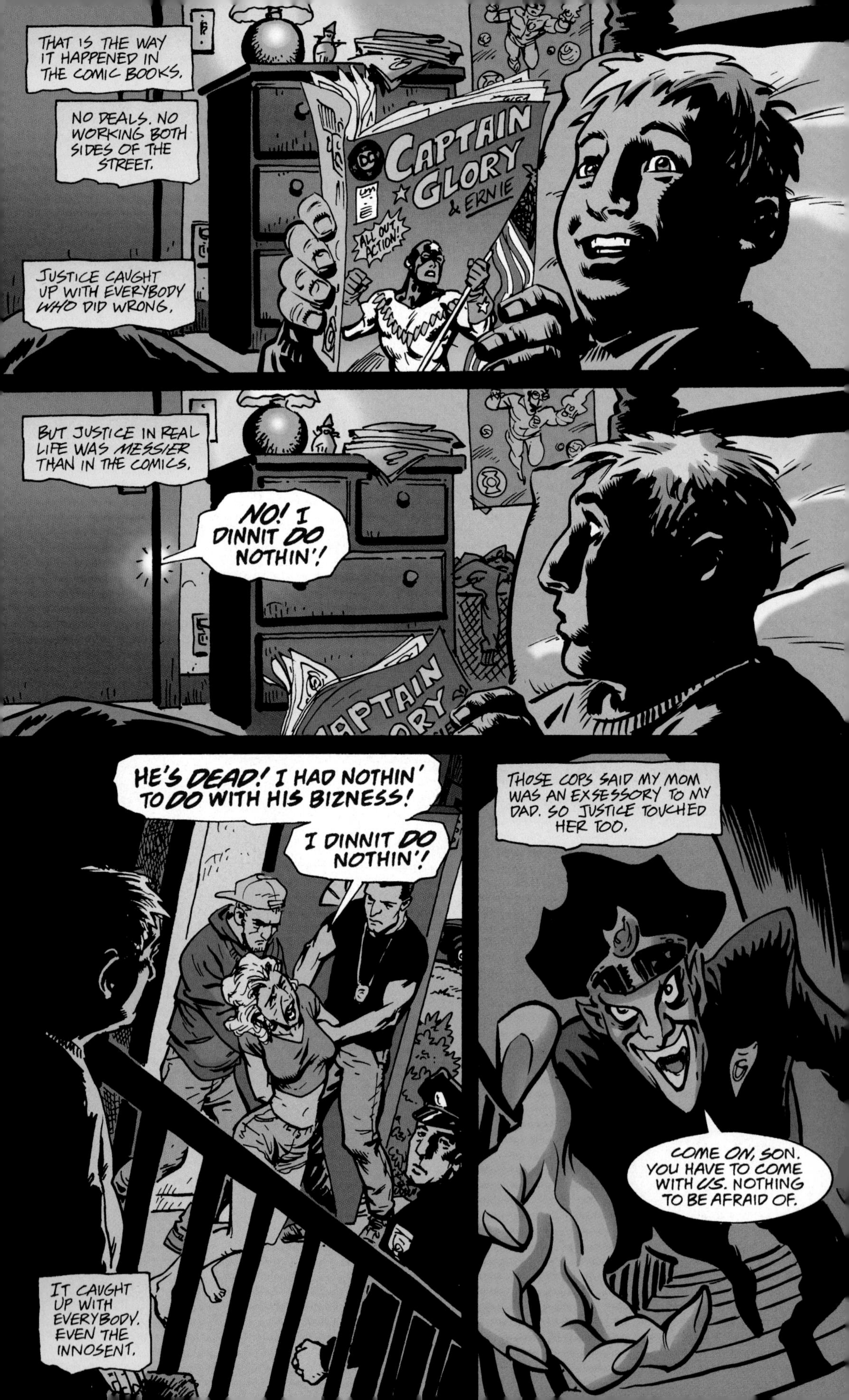
THAT IS THE WAY IT HAPPENED IN THE COMIC BOOKS.
NO DEALS. NO WORKING BOTH SIDES OF THE STREET.
JUSTICE CAUGHT UP WITH EVERYBODY WHO DID WRONG.
CAPTAIN GLORY & ERNIE
ALL OUT ACTION!
BUT JUSTICE IN REAL LIFE WAS MESSIER THAN IN THE COMICS.
NO! I DINNIT DO NOTHIN'!
HE'S DEAD! I HAD NOTHIN' TO DO WITH HIS BIZNESS!
I DINNIT DO NOTHIN'!
IT CAUGHT UP WITH EVERYBODY. EVEN THE INNOSENT.
THOSE COPS SAID MY MOM WAS AN EXSESSORY TO MY DAD. SO JUSTICE TOUCHED HER TOO.
COME ON, SON. YOU HAVE TO COME WITH US. NOTHING TO BE AFRAID OF.

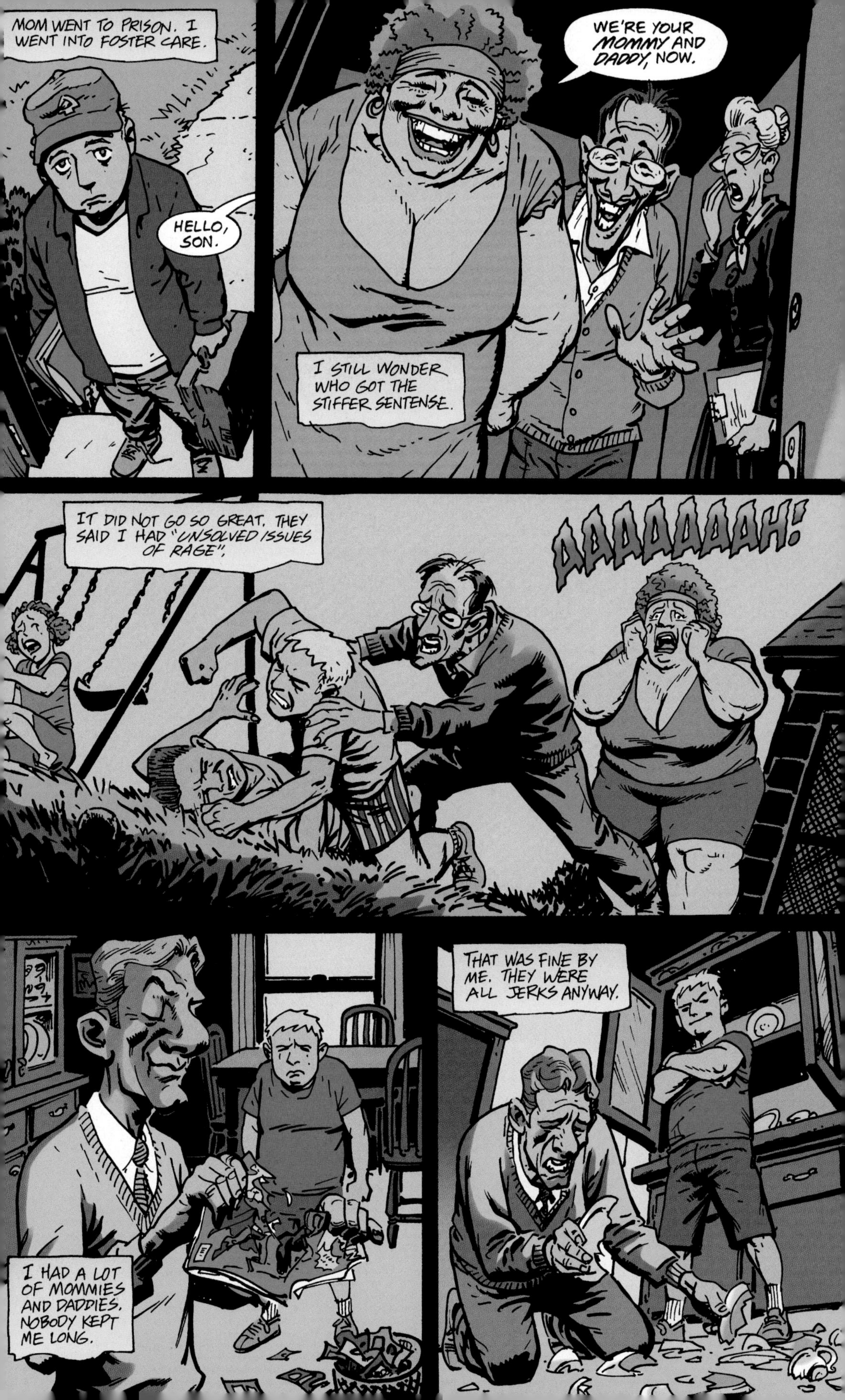
MOM WENT TO PRISON. I WENT INTO FOSTER CARE.
HELLO, SON.
WE'RE YOUR MOMMY AND DADDY, NOW.
I STILL WONDER WHO GOT THE STIFFER SENTENSE.
IT DID NOT GO SO GREAT. THEY SAID I HAD "UNSOLVED ISSUES OF RAGE".
AAAAAAAH!
I HAD A LOT OF MOMMIES AND DADDIES. NOBODY KEPT ME LONG.
THAT WAS FINE BY ME. THEY WERE ALL JERKS ANYWAY.

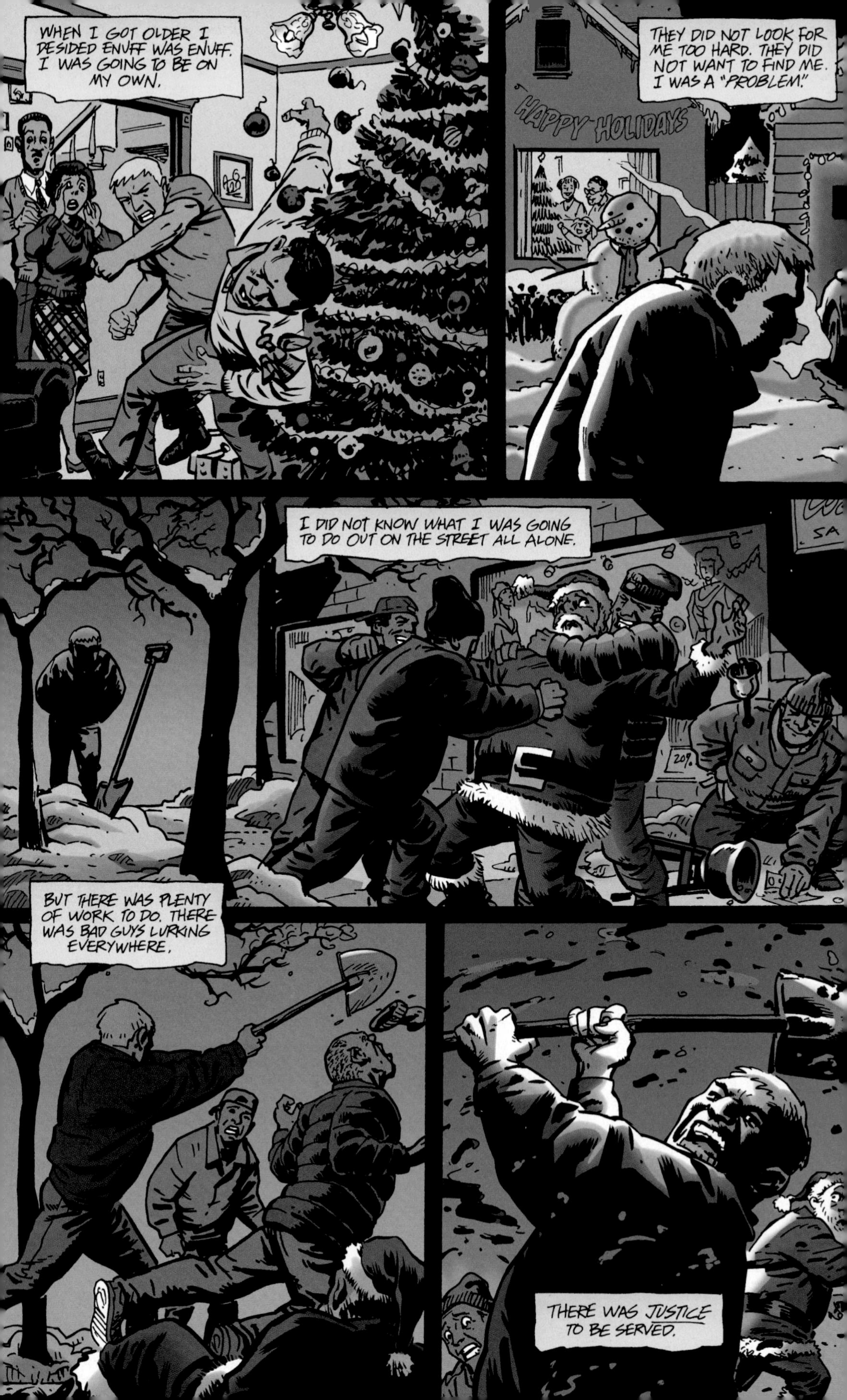
WHEN I GOT OLDER I DESIDED ENUFF WAS ENUFF. I WAS GOING TO BE ON MY OWN.
THEY DID NOT LOOK FOR ME TOO HARD. THEY DID NOT WANT TO FIND ME. I WAS A "PROBLEM."
HAPPY HOLIDAYS
I DID NOT KNOW WHAT I WAS GOING TO DO OUT ON THE STREET ALL ALONE.
BUT THERE WAS PLENTY OF WORK TO DO. THERE WAS BAD GUYS LURKING EVERYWHERE.
THERE WAS JUSTICE TO BE SERVED.

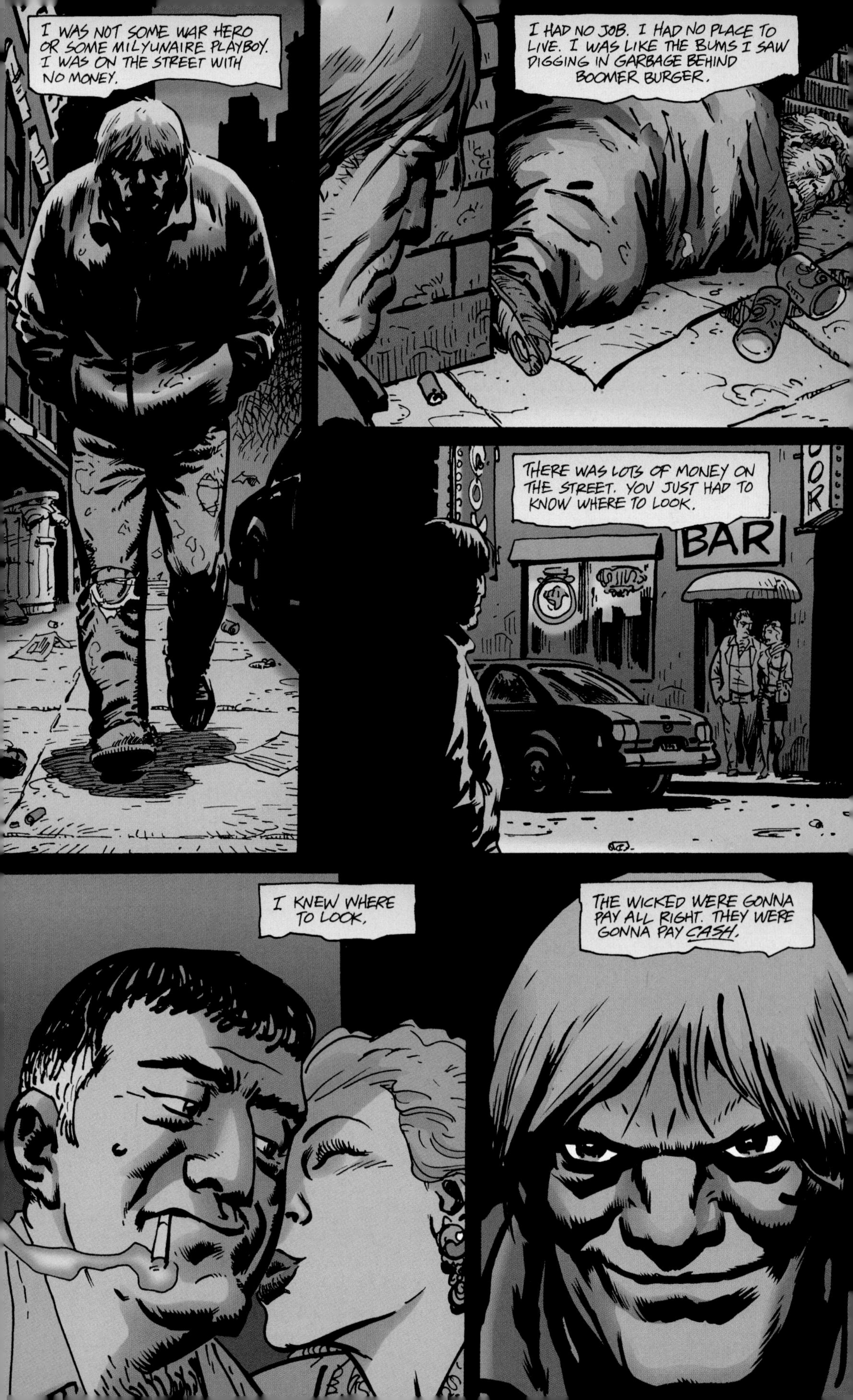
I WAS NOT SOME WAR HERO OR SOME MILYUNAIRE PLAYBOY. I WAS ON THE STREET WITH NO MONEY.
I HAD NO JOB. I HAD NO PLACE TO LIVE. I WAS LIKE THE BUMS I SAW DIGGING IN GARBAGE BEHIND BOOMER BURGER.
THERE WAS LOTS OF MONEY ON THE STREET. YOU JUST HAD TO KNOW WHERE TO LOOK.
BAR
I KNEW WHERE TO LOOK.
THE WICKED WERE GONNA PAY ALL RIGHT. THEY WERE GONNA PAY CASH.

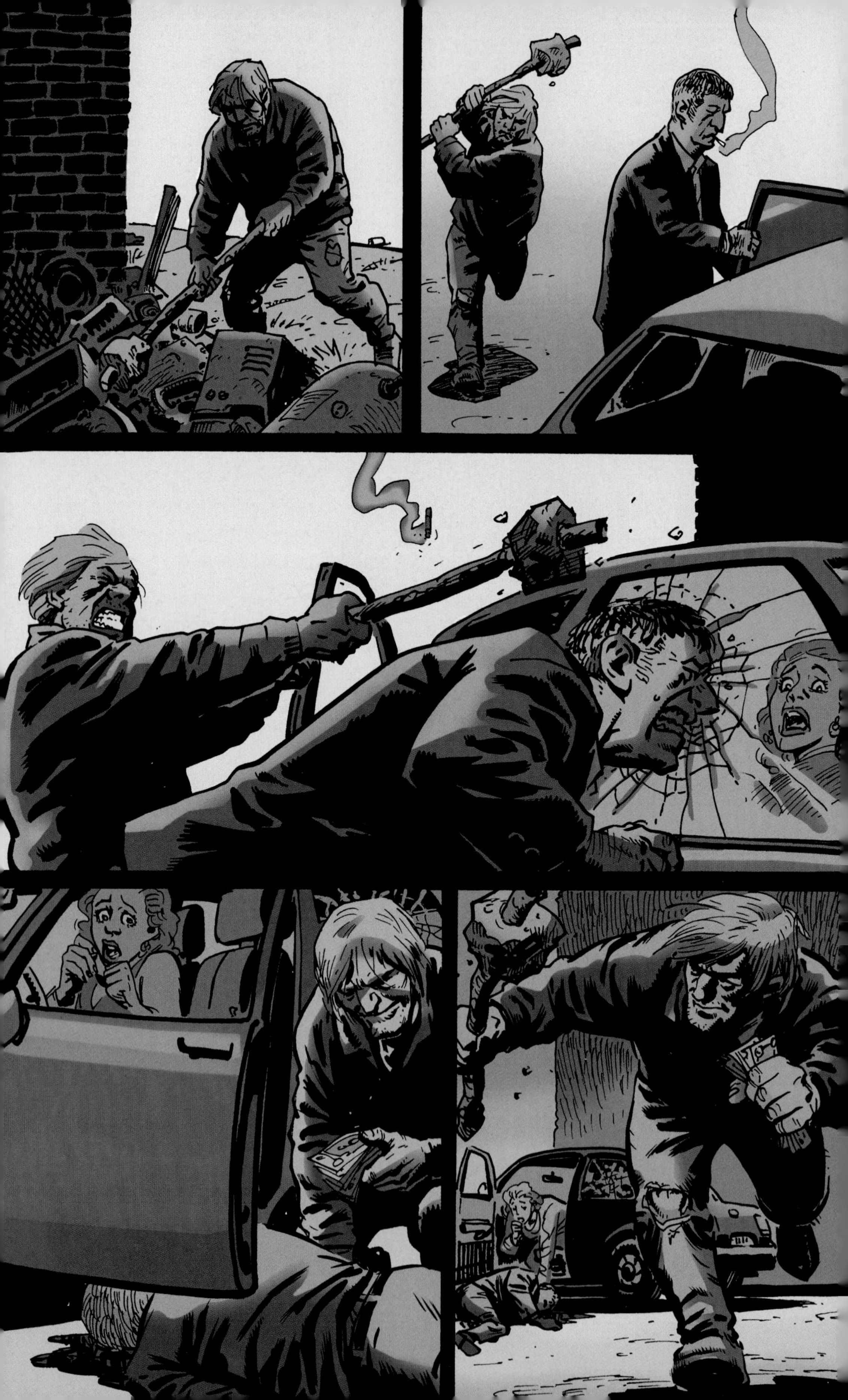

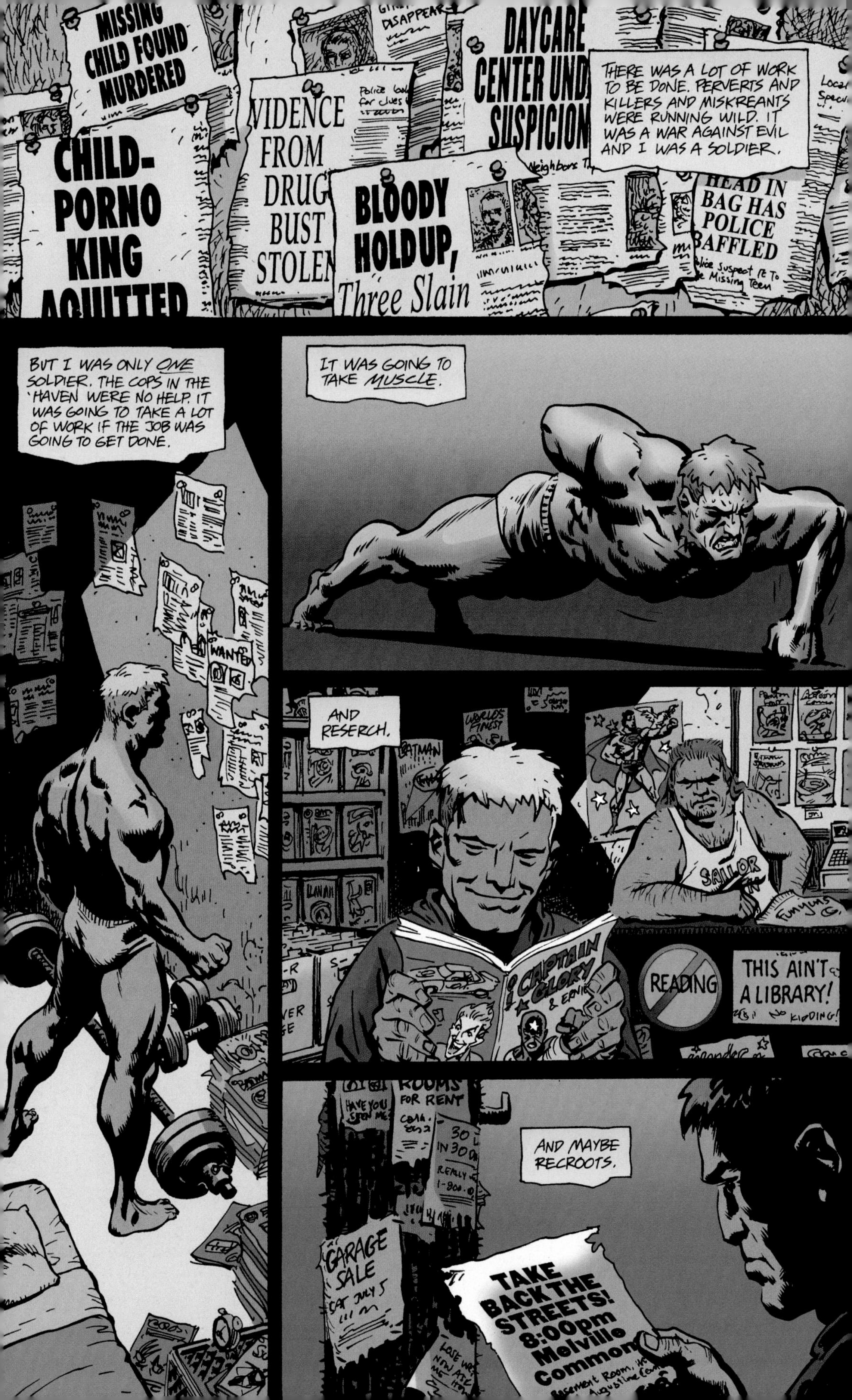
MISSING CHILD FOUND MURDERED
DAYCARE CENTER UND SUSPICION
THERE WAS A LOT OF WORK TO BE DONE. PERVERTS AND KILLERS AND MISKREANTS WERE RUNNING WILD. IT WAS A WAR AGAINST EVIL AND I WAS A SOLDIER.
CHILD-PORNO KING
VIDENCE FROM DRUG BUST STOLEN
BLOODY HOLDUP, Three Slain
HEAD IN BAG HAS POLICE BAFFLED
BUT I WAS ONLY ONE SOLDIER. THE COPS IN THE 'HAVEN WERE NO HELP. IT WAS GOING TO TAKE A LOT OF WORK IF THE JOB WAS GOING TO GET DONE.
IT WAS GOING TO TAKE MUSCLE.
WANTED
AND RESERCH.
CAPTAIN GLORY & ERNIE
SAILOR
READING
THIS AIN'T A LIBRARY!
NO KIDDING!
AND MAYBE RECROOTS.
ROOMS FOR RENT
HAVE YOU SEEN ME?
GARAGE SALE
TAKE BACK THE STREETS! 8:00pm Melville Common

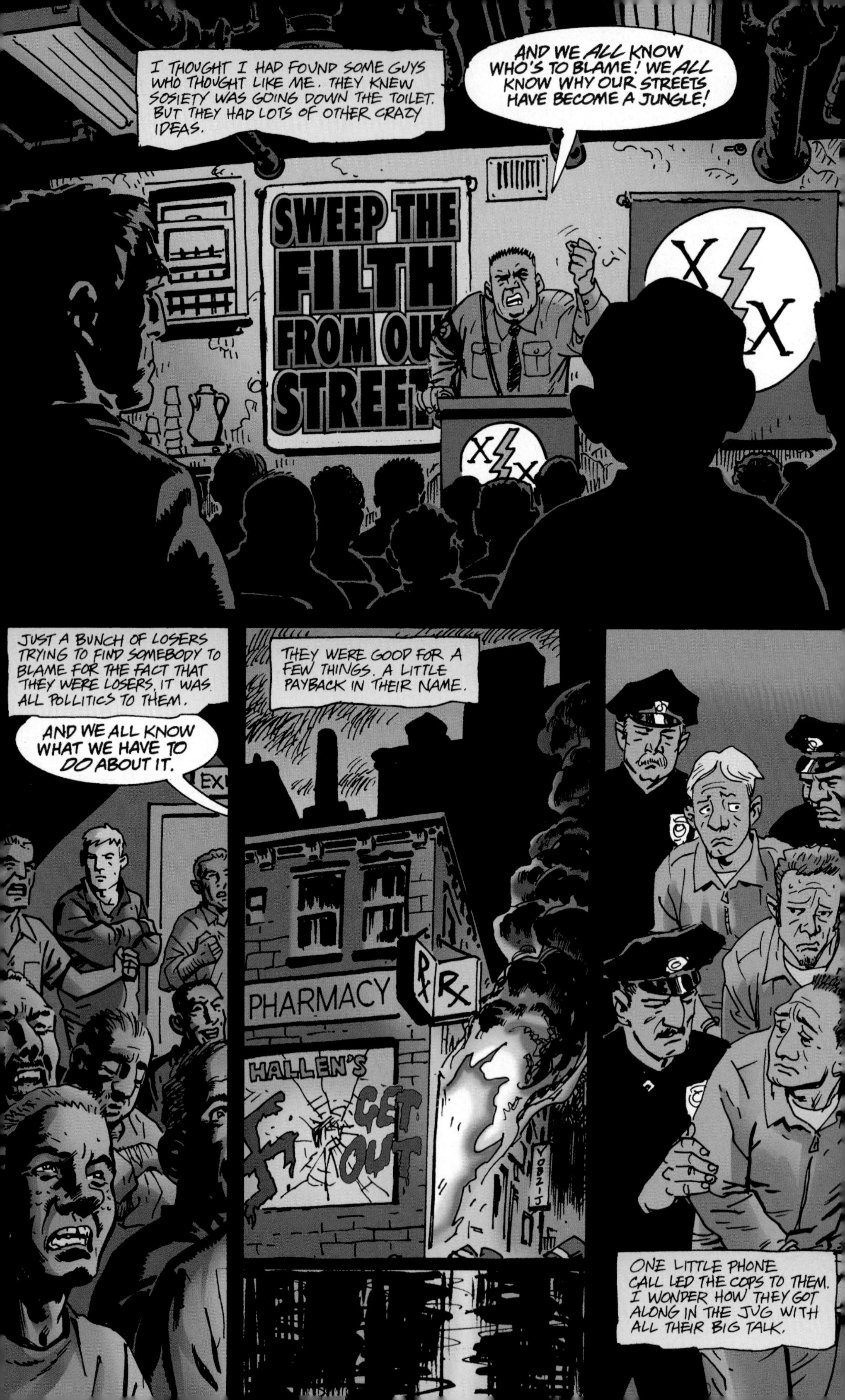
I THOUGHT I HAD FOUND SOME GUYS WHO THOUGHT LIKE ME. THEY KNEW SOSIETY WAS GOING DOWN THE TOILET. BUT THEY HAD LOTS OF OTHER CRAZY IDEAS.
AND WE ALL KNOW WHO'S TO BLAME! WE ALL KNOW WHY OUR STREETS HAVE BECOME A JUNGLE!
SWEEP THE FILTH FROM OU STREET
JUST A BUNCH OF LOSERS TRYING TO FIND SOMEBODY TO BLAME FOR THE FACT THAT THEY WERE LOSERS. IT WAS ALL POLLITICS TO THEM.
AND WE ALL KNOW WHAT WE HAVE TO DO ABOUT IT.
THEY WERE GOOD FOR A FEW THINGS. A LITTLE PAYBACK IN THEIR NAME.
PHARMACY
Rx
HALLEN'S
GET OUT
ONE LITTLE PHONE CALL LED THE COPS TO THEM. I WONDER HOW THEY GOT ALONG IN THE JUG WITH ALL THEIR BIG TALK.

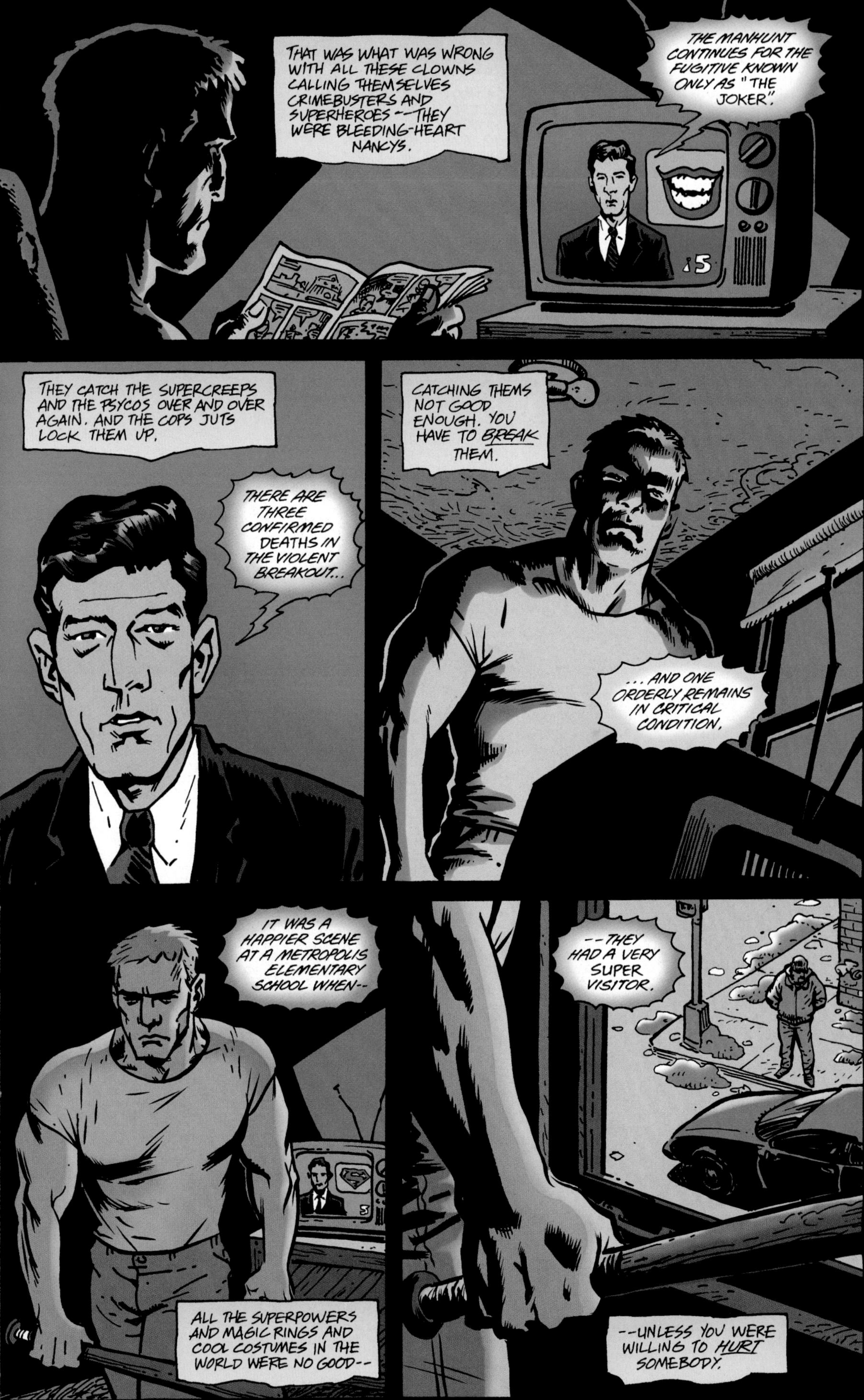
THAT WAS WHAT WAS WRONG WITH ALL THESE CLOWNS CALLING THEMSELVES CRIMEBUSTERS AND SUPERHEROES--THEY WERE BLEEDING-HEART NANCYS.
THE MANHUNT CONTINUES FOR THE FUGITIVE KNOWN ONLY AS "THE JOKER".
THEY CATCH THE SUPERCREEPS AND THE PSYCOS OVER AND OVER AGAIN. AND THE COPS JUTS LOCK THEM UP.
THERE ARE THREE CONFIRMED DEATHS IN THE VIOLENT BREAKOUT...
CATCHING THEMS NOT GOOD ENOUGH. YOU HAVE TO BREAK THEM.
...AND ONE ORDERLY REMAINS IN CRITICAL CONDITION.
IT WAS A HAPPIER SCENE AT A METROPOLIS ELEMENTARY SCHOOL WHEN--
--THEY HAD A VERY SUPER VISITOR.
ALL THE SUPERPOWERS AND MAGIC RINGS AND COOL COSTUMES IN THE WORLD WERE NO GOOD--
--UNLESS YOU WERE WILLING TO HURT SOMEBODY.

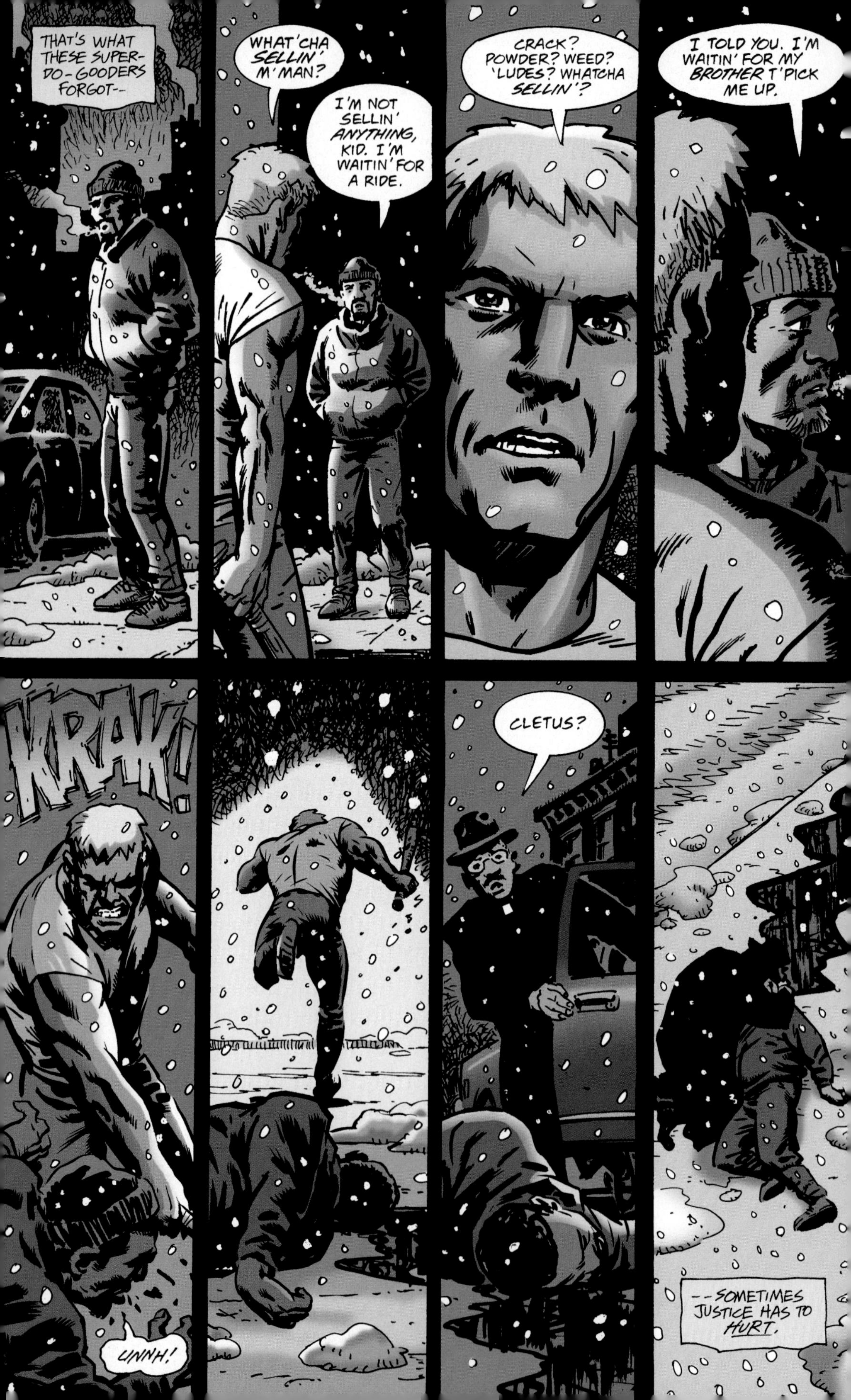
THAT'S WHAT THESE SUPER-DO-GOODERS FORGOT--
WHAT'CHA SELLIN' M'MAN?
I'M NOT SELLIN' ANYTHING, KID. I'M WAITIN' FOR A RIDE.
CRACK? POWDER? WEED? 'LUDES? WHATCHA SELLIN'?
I TOLD YOU. I'M WAITIN' FOR MY BROTHER T'PICK ME UP.
KRAK!
UNNH!
CLETUS?
--SOMETIMES JUSTICE HAS TO HURT.

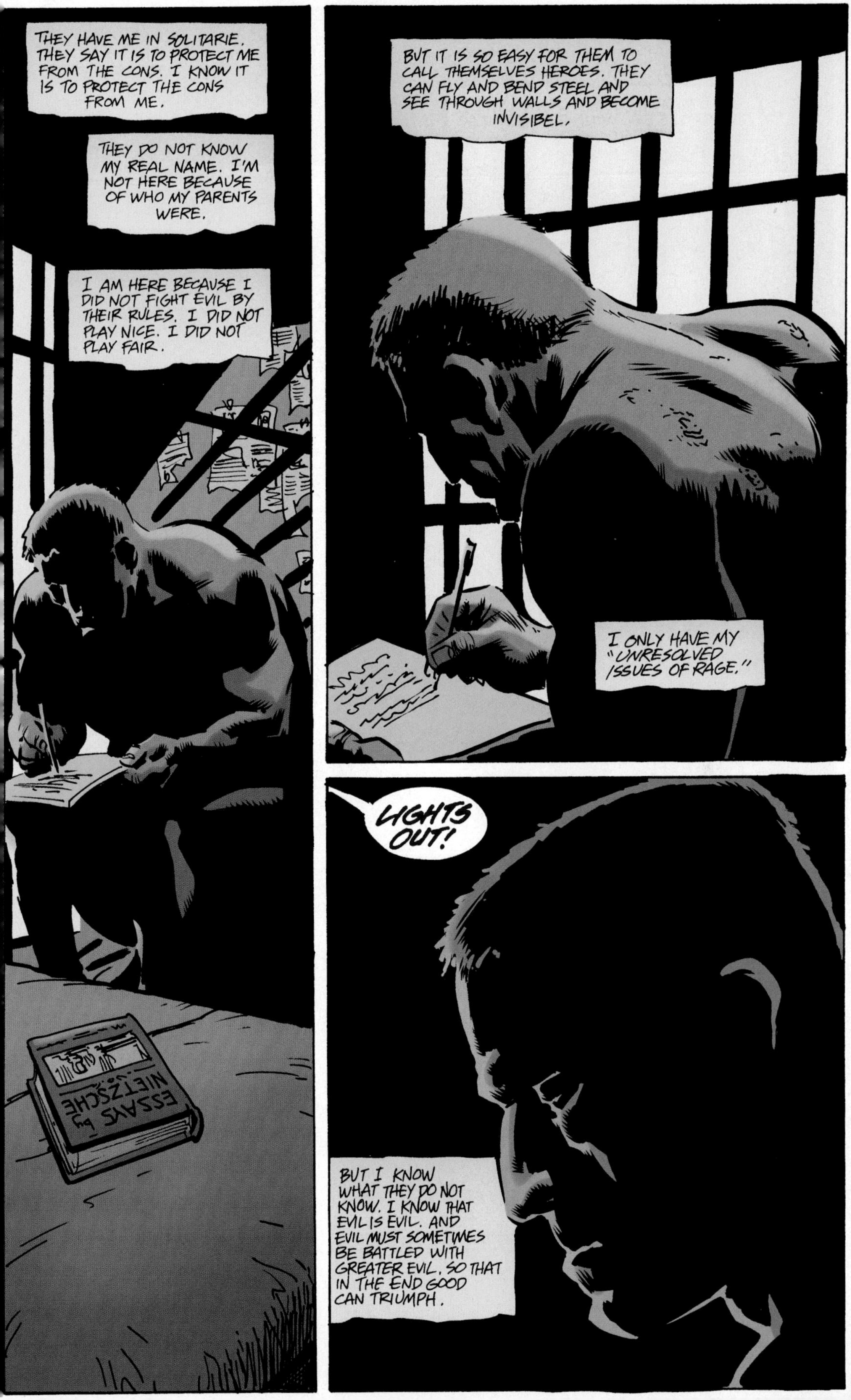
THEY HAVE ME IN SOLITARIE. THEY SAY IT IS TO PROTECT ME FROM THE CONS. I KNOW IT IS TO PROTECT THE CONS FROM ME.
THEY DO NOT KNOW MY REAL NAME. I'M NOT HERE BECAUSE OF WHO MY PARENTS WERE.
I AM HERE BECAUSE I DID NOT FIGHT EVIL BY THEIR RULES. I DID NOT PLAY NICE. I DID NOT PLAY FAIR.
ESSAYS by NIETZSCHE
BUT IT IS SO EASY FOR THEM TO CALL THEMSELVES HEROES. THEY CAN FLY AND BEND STEEL AND SEE THROUGH WALLS AND BECOME INVISIBEL.
I ONLY HAVE MY "UNRESOLVED ISSUES OF RAGE."
LIGHTS OUT!
BUT I KNOW WHAT THEY DO NOT KNOW. I KNOW THAT EVIL IS EVIL. AND EVIL MUST SOMETIMES BE BATTLED WITH GREATER EVIL. SO THAT IN THE END GOOD CAN TRIUMPH.

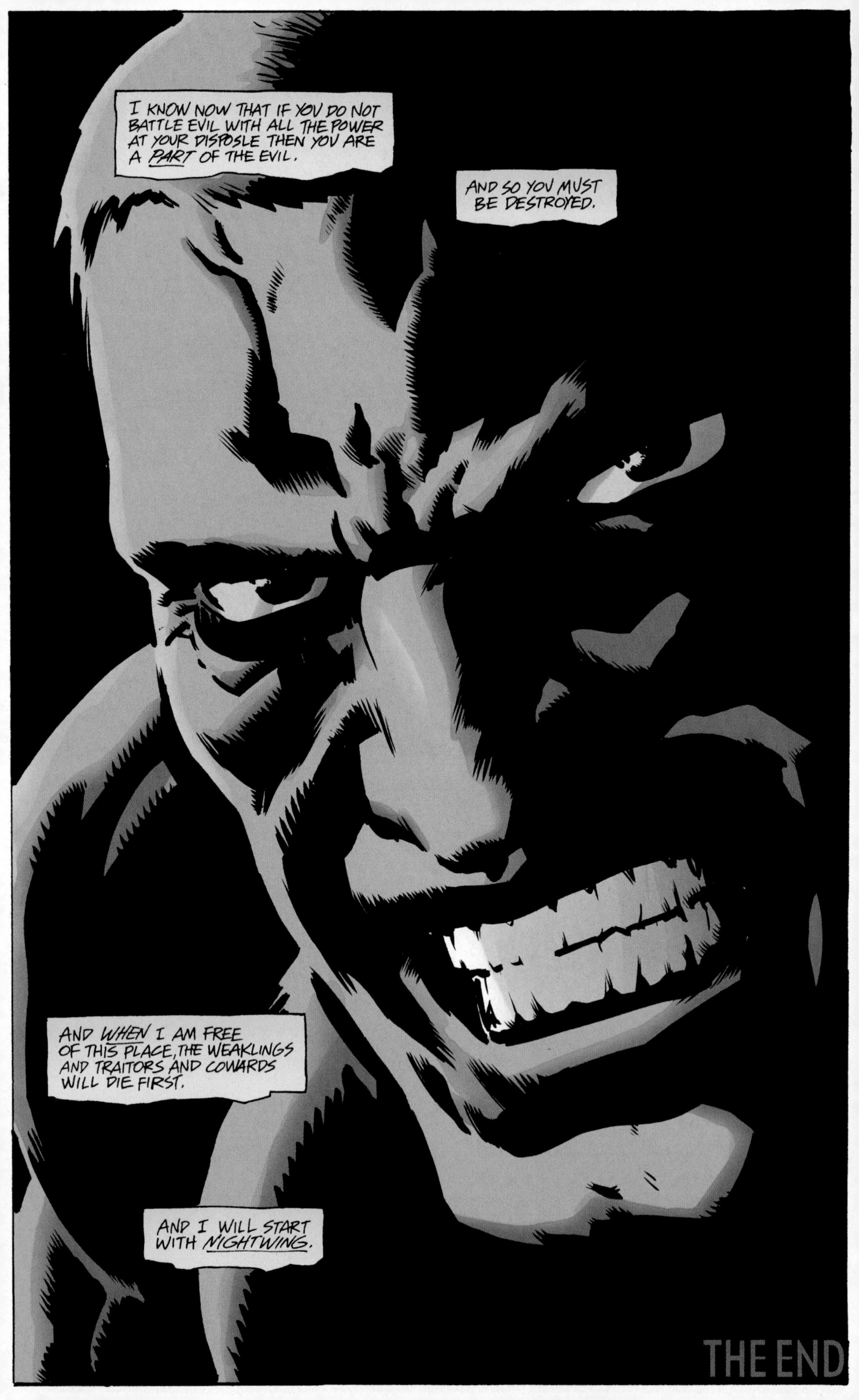
I KNOW NOW THAT IF YOU DO NOT BATTLE EVIL WITH ALL THE POWER AT YOUR DISPOSLE THEN YOU ARE A PART OF THE EVIL.
AND SO YOU MUST BE DESTROYED.
AND WHEN I AM FREE OF THIS PLACE, THE WEAKLINGS AND TRAITORS AND COWARDS WILL DIE FIRST.
AND I WILL START WITH NIGHTWING.
THE END

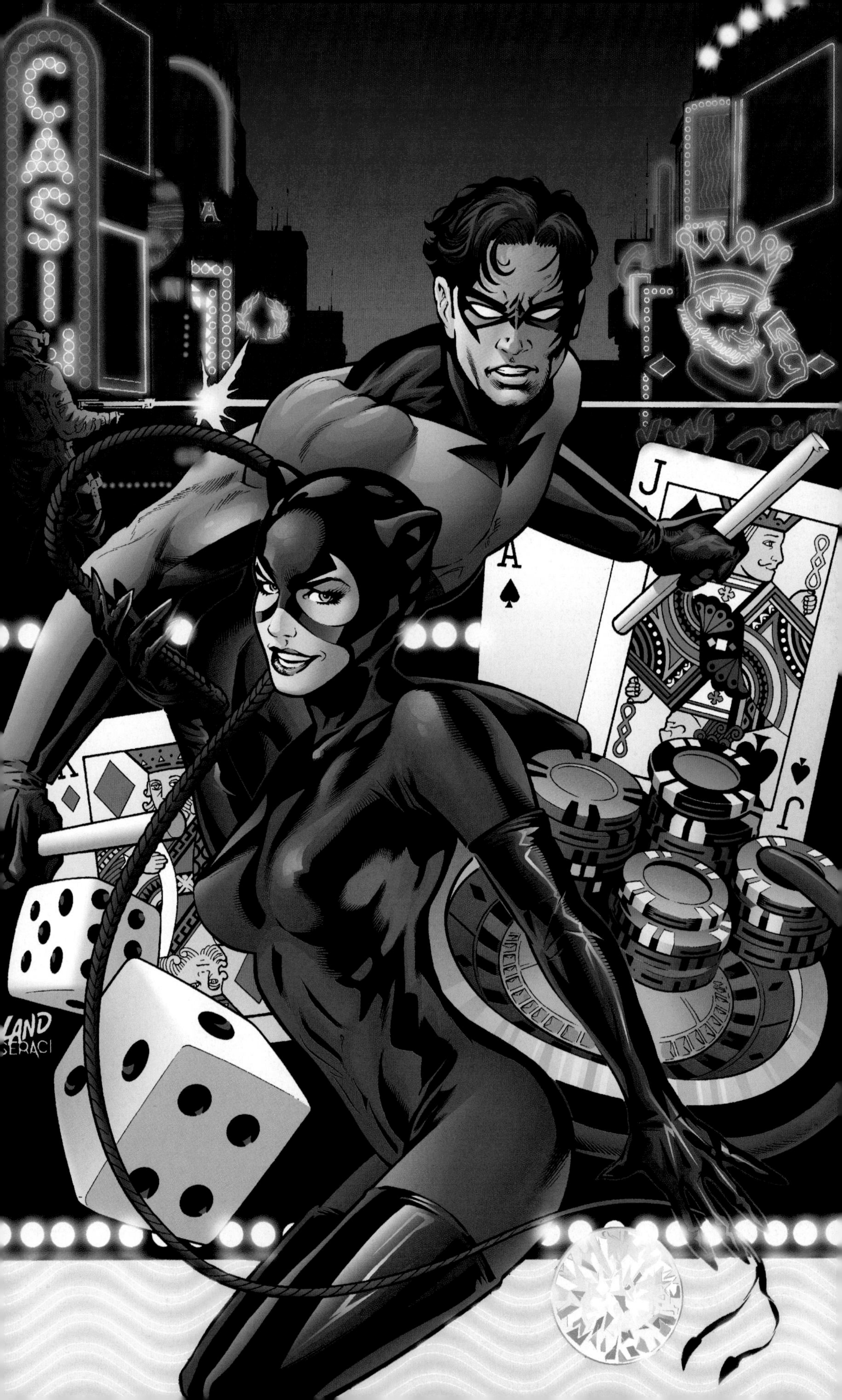
CASI

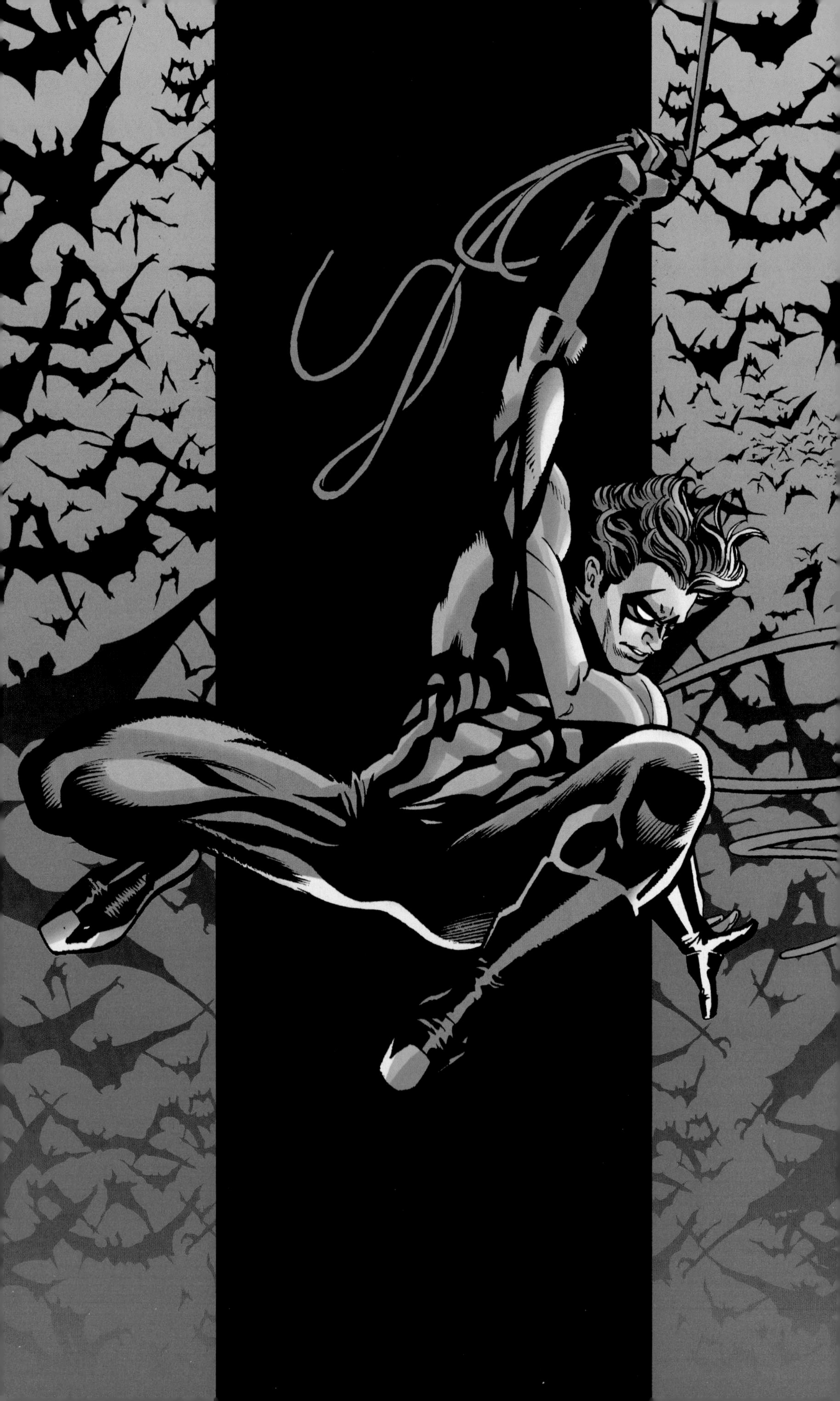

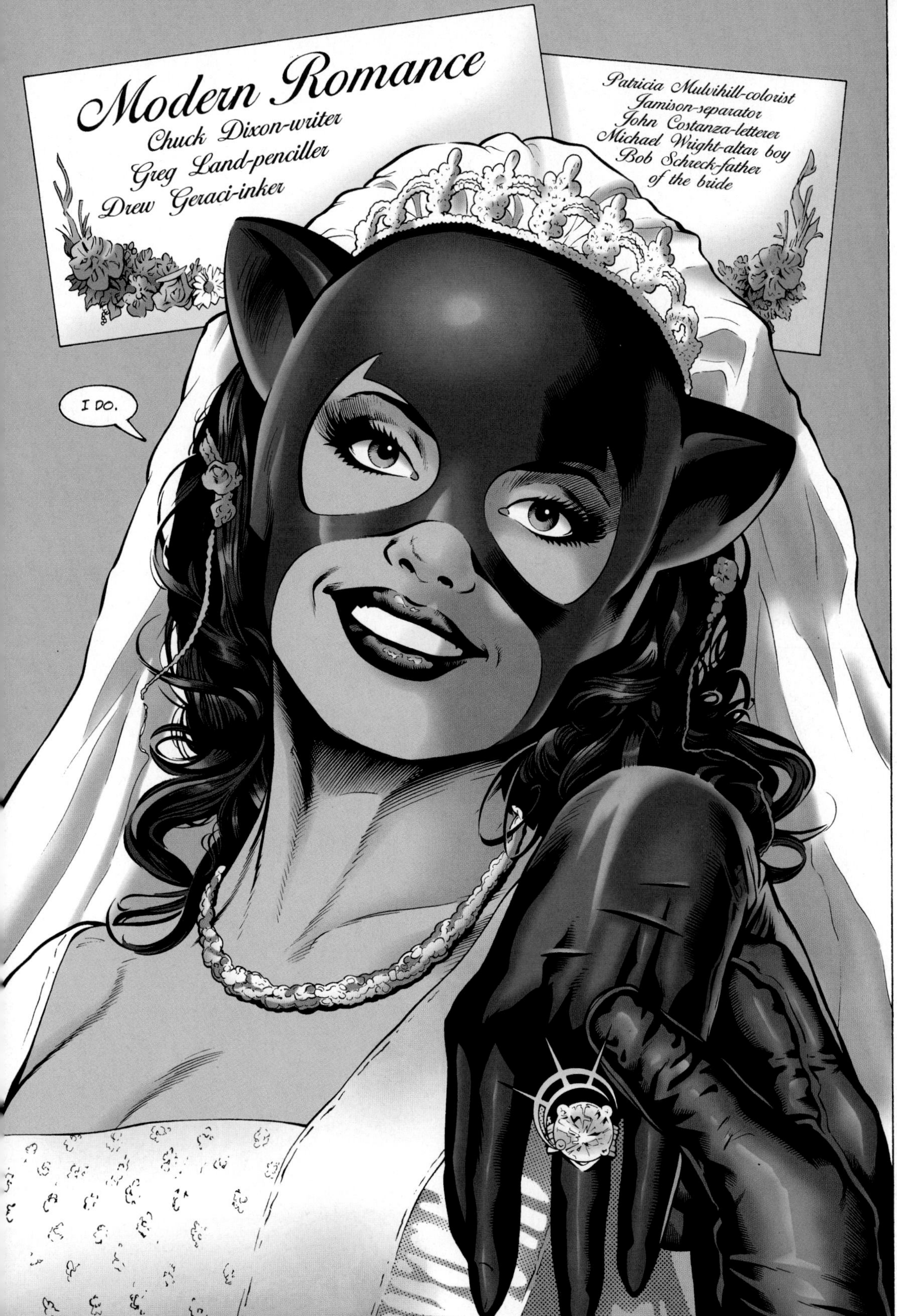
Modern Romance
Chuck Dixon-writer
Greg Land-penciller
Drew Geraci-inker
Patricia Mulvihill-colorist
Jamison-separator
John Costanza-letterer
Michael Wright-altar boy
Bob Schreck-father of the bride
I DO.

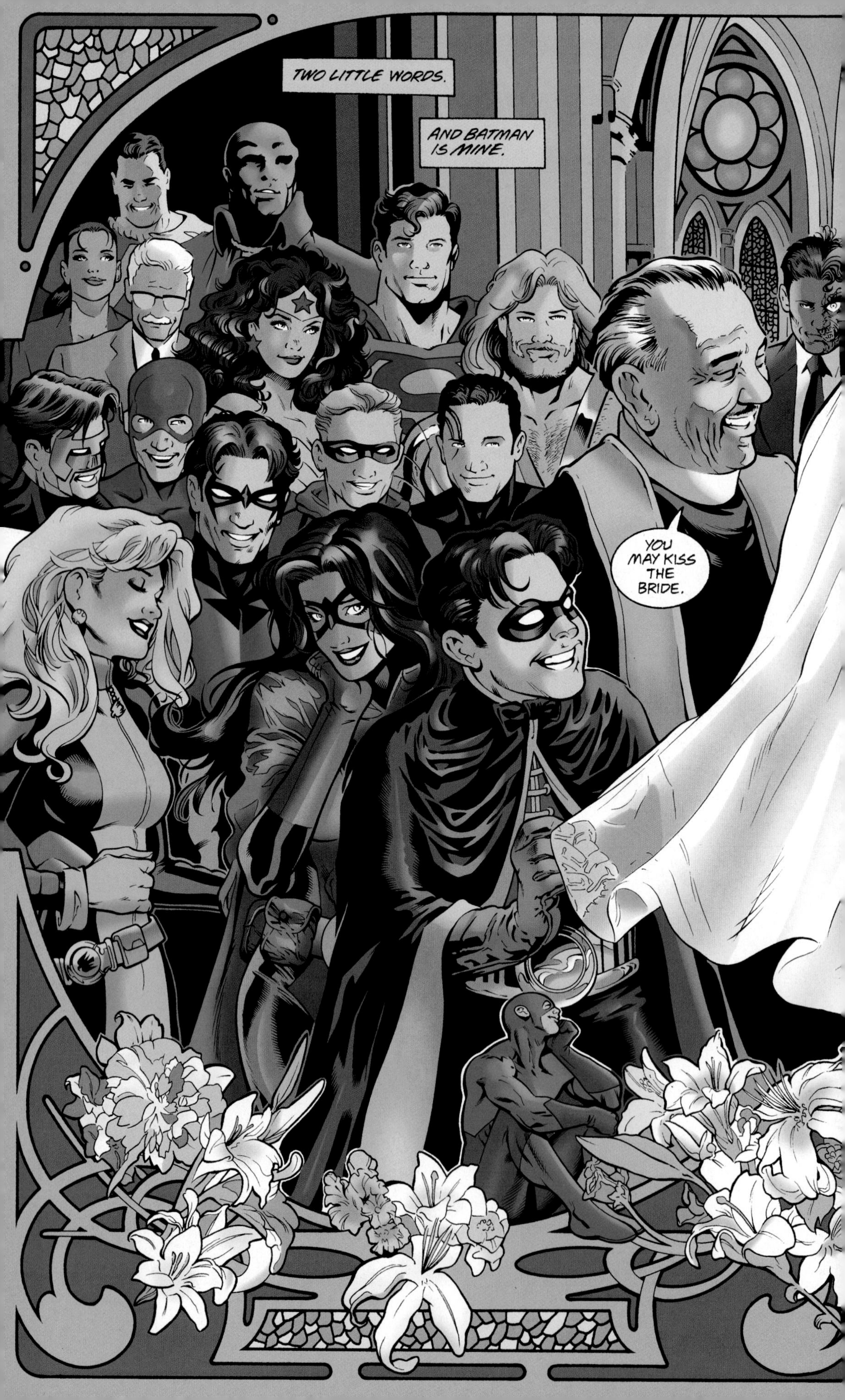
TWO LITTLE WORDS.
AND BATMAN IS MINE.
YOU MAY KISS THE BRIDE.

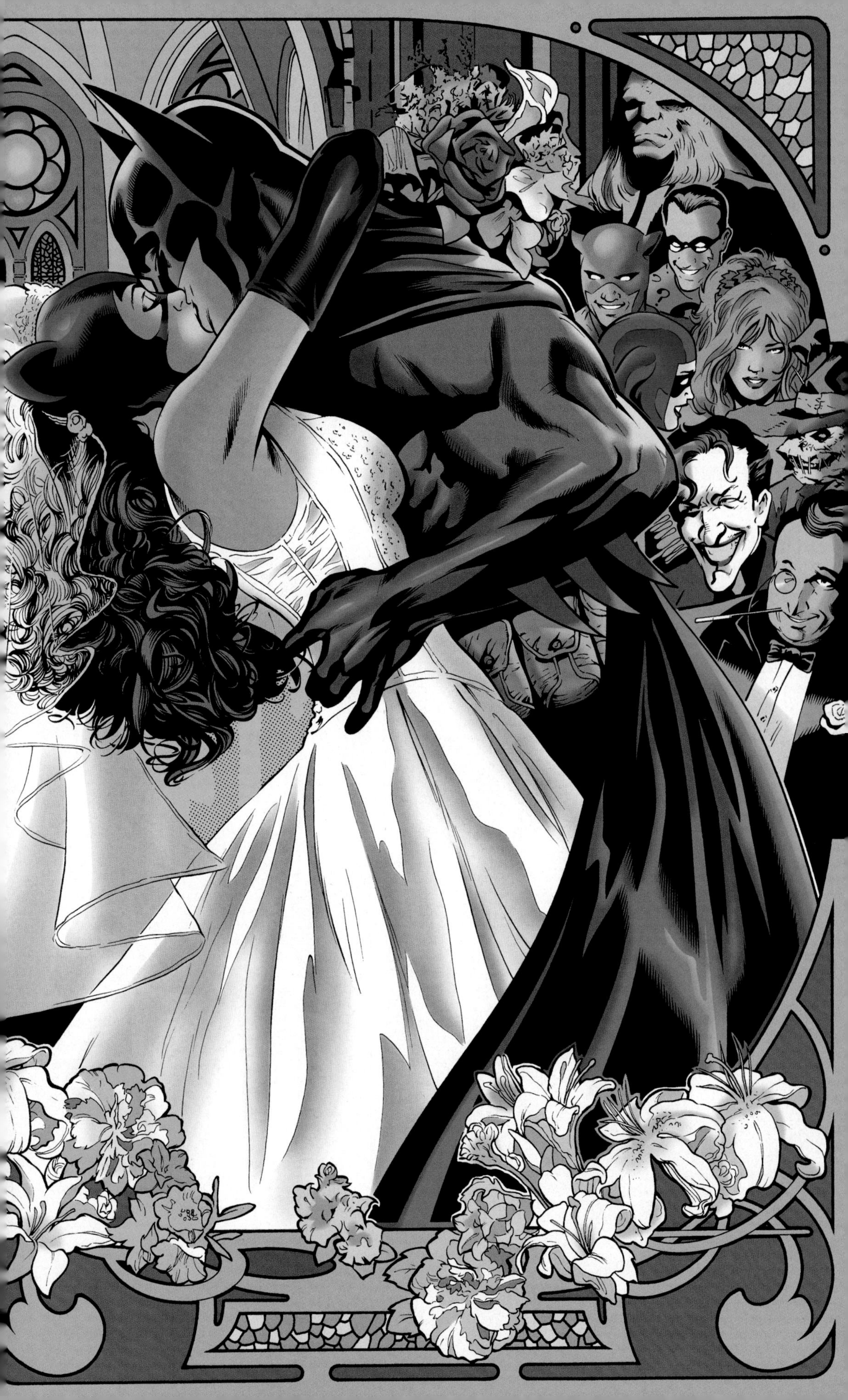

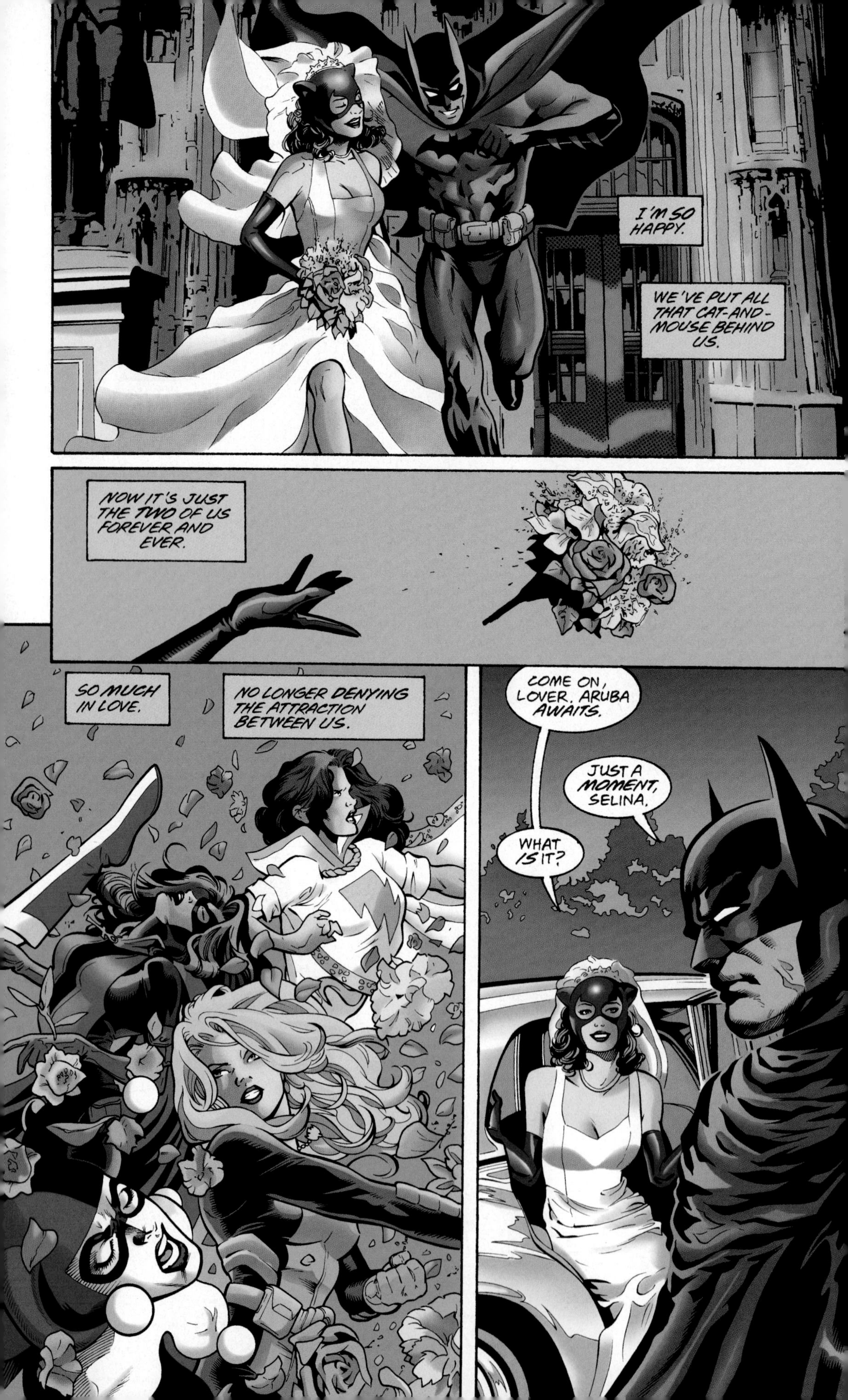
I'M SO HAPPY.
WE'VE PUT ALL THAT CAT-AND-MOUSE BEHIND US.
NOW IT'S JUST THE TWO OF US FOREVER AND EVER.
SO MUCH IN LOVE.
NO LONGER DENYING THE ATTRACTION BETWEEN US.
COME ON, LOVER. ARUBA AWAITS.
JUST A MOMENT, SELINA.
WHAT IS IT?

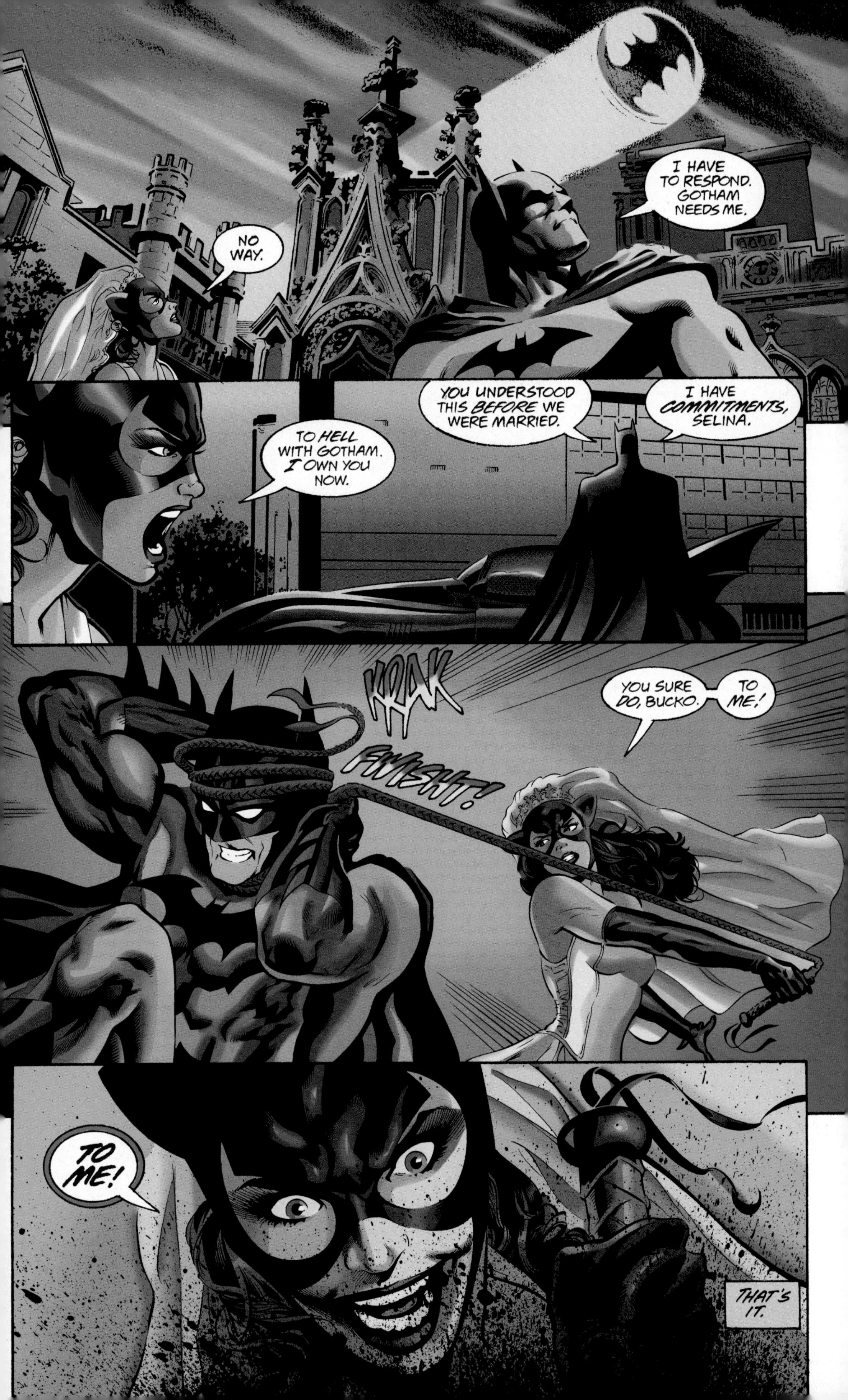
NO WAY.
I HAVE TO RESPOND. GOTHAM NEEDS ME.
TO HELL WITH GOTHAM. I OWN YOU NOW.
YOU UNDERSTOOD THIS BEFORE WE WERE MARRIED.
I HAVE COMMITMENTS, SELINA.
KRAK
FWISHT!
YOU SURE DO, BUCKO.
TO ME!
TO ME!
THAT'S IT.

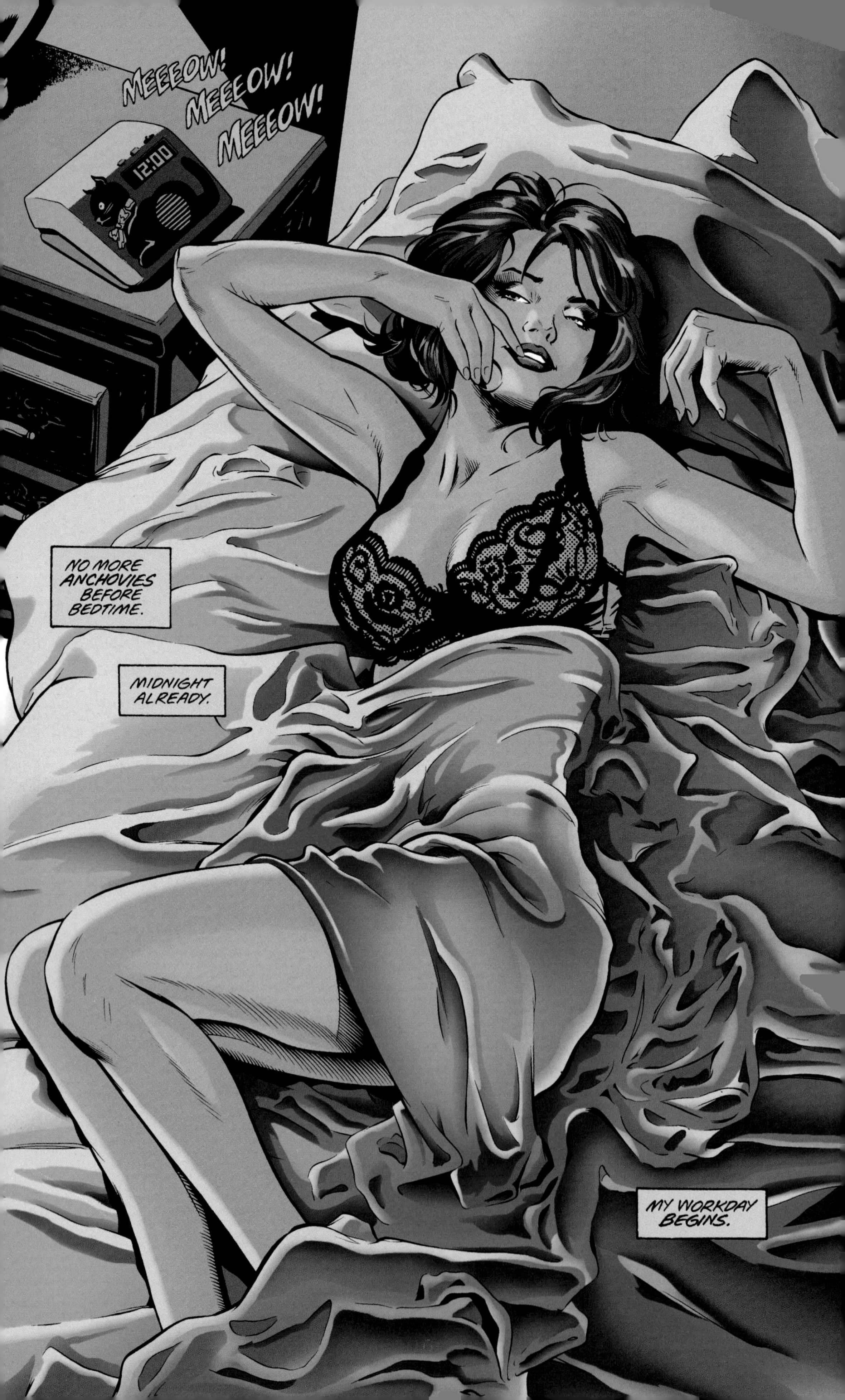
MEEEOW! MEEEOW! MEEEOW!
12:00
NO MORE ANCHOVIES BEFORE BEDTIME.
MIDNIGHT ALREADY.
MY WORKDAY BEGINS.

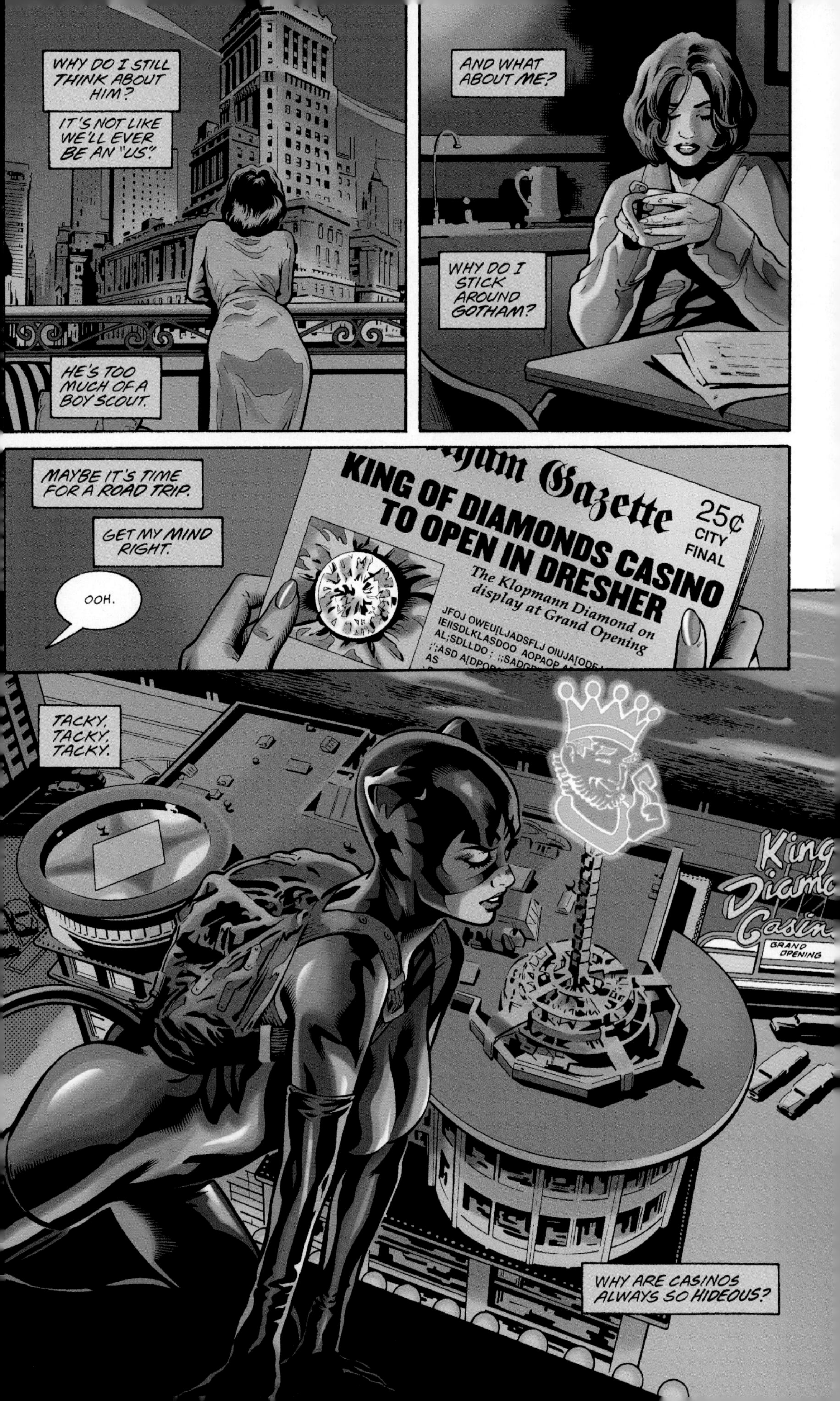
WHY DO I STILL THINK ABOUT HIM?
IT'S NOT LIKE WE'LL EVER BE AN "US."
HE'S TOO MUCH OF A BOY SCOUT.
AND WHAT ABOUT ME?
WHY DO I STICK AROUND GOTHAM?
MAYBE IT'S TIME FOR A ROAD TRIP.
GET MY MIND RIGHT.
OOH.
Gazette
KING OF DIAMONDS CASINO TO OPEN IN DRESHER
25¢ CITY FINAL
The Klopmann Diamond on display at Grand Opening
TACKY, TACKY, TACKY.
GRAND OPENING
WHY ARE CASINOS ALWAYS SO HIDEOUS?

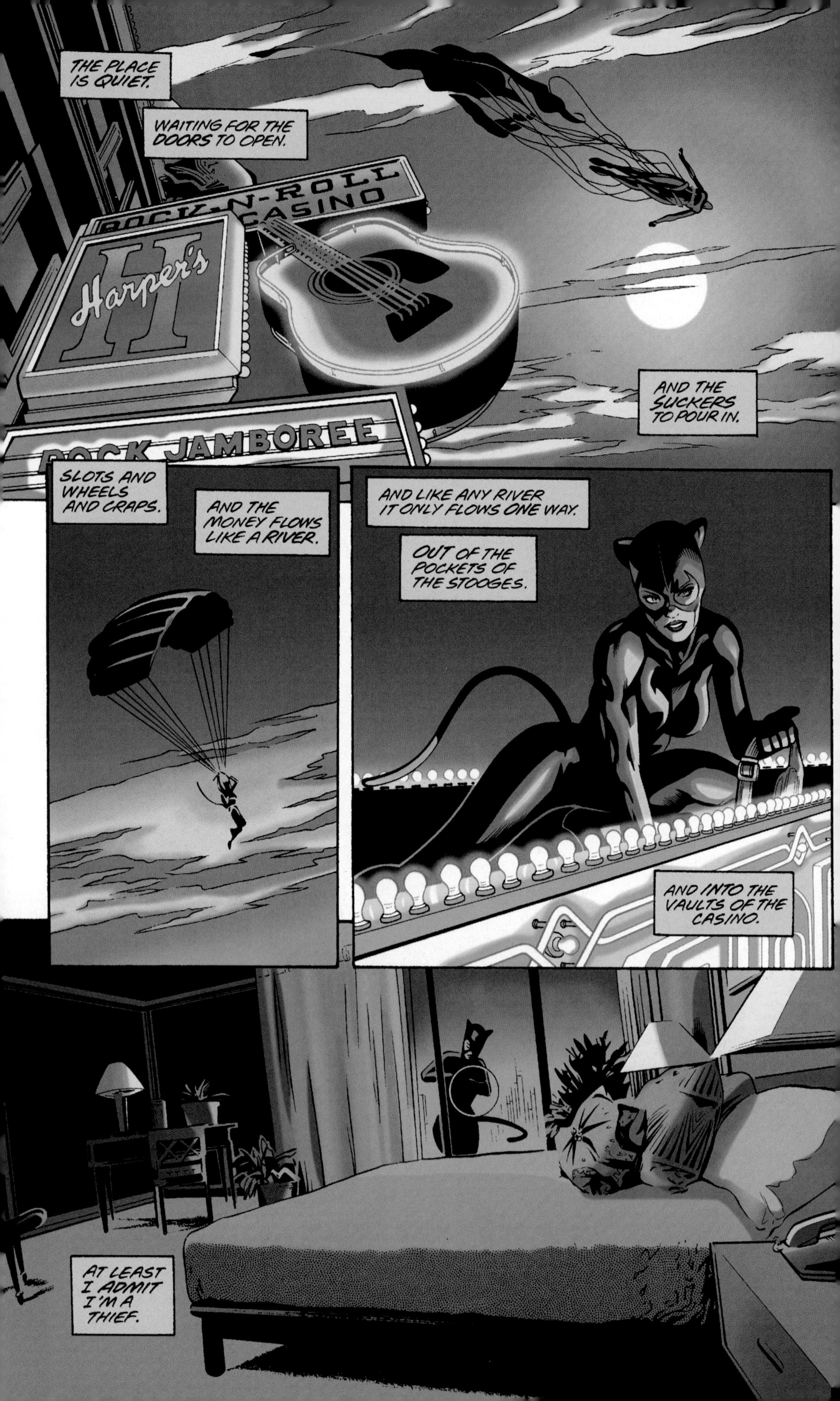
THE PLACE IS QUIET.
WAITING FOR THE DOORS TO OPEN.
ROCK-N-ROLL CASINO
Harper's
ROCK JAMBOREE
AND THE SUCKERS TO POUR IN.
SLOTS AND WHEELS AND CRAPS.
AND THE MONEY FLOWS LIKE A RIVER.
AND LIKE ANY RIVER IT ONLY FLOWS ONE WAY.
OUT OF THE POCKETS OF THE STOOGES.
AND INTO THE VAULTS OF THE CASINO.
AT LEAST I ADMIT I'M A THIEF.

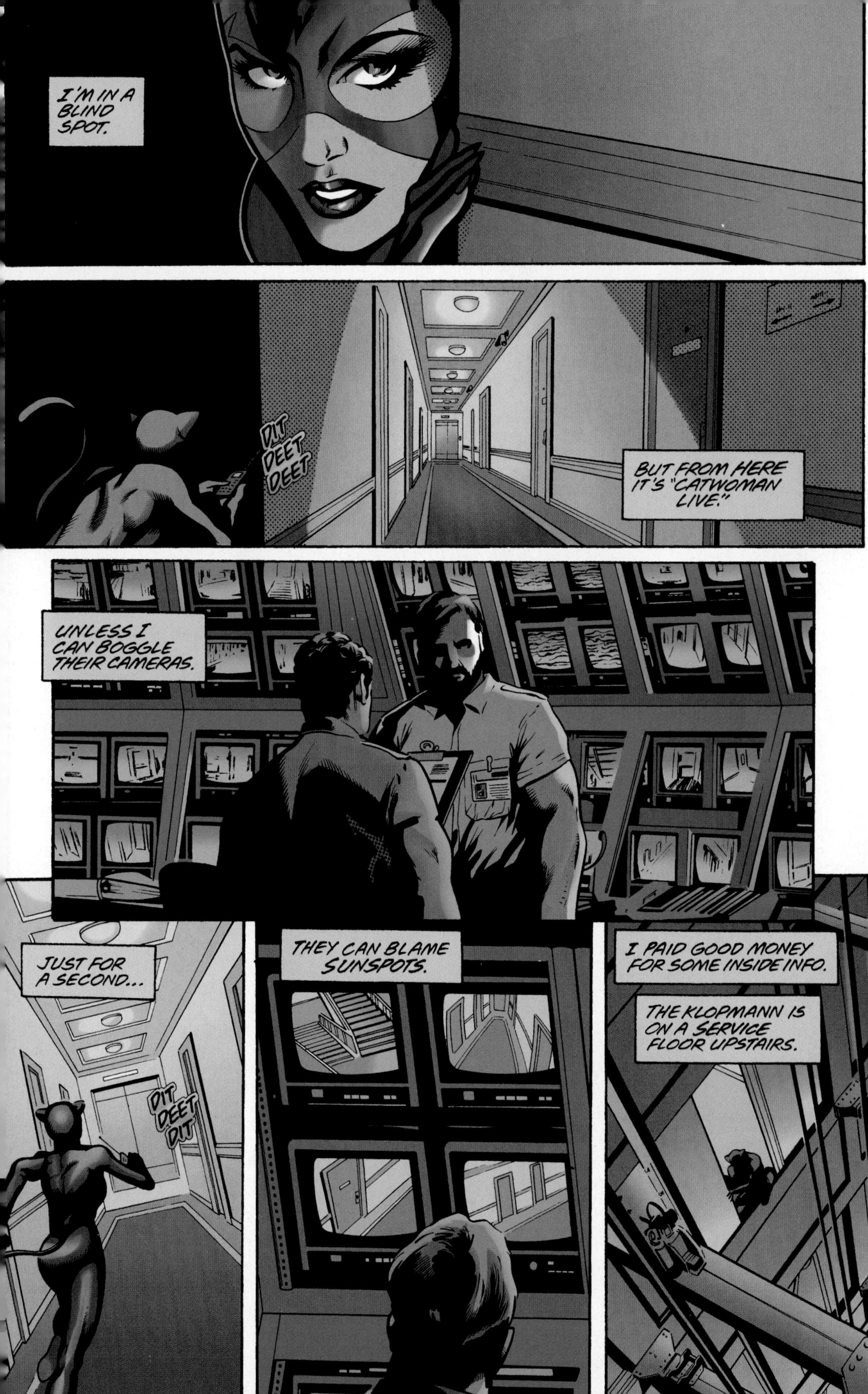
I'M IN A BLIND SPOT.
DIT DEET DEET
BUT FROM HERE IT'S "CATWOMAN LIVE."
UNLESS I CAN BOGGLE THEIR CAMERAS.
JUST FOR A SECOND...
DIT DEET DIT
THEY CAN BLAME SUNSPOTS.
I PAID GOOD MONEY FOR SOME INSIDE INFO.
THE KLOPMANN IS ON A SERVICE FLOOR UPSTAIRS.

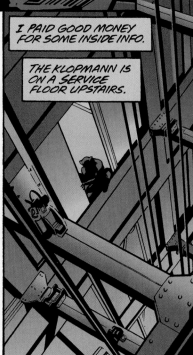

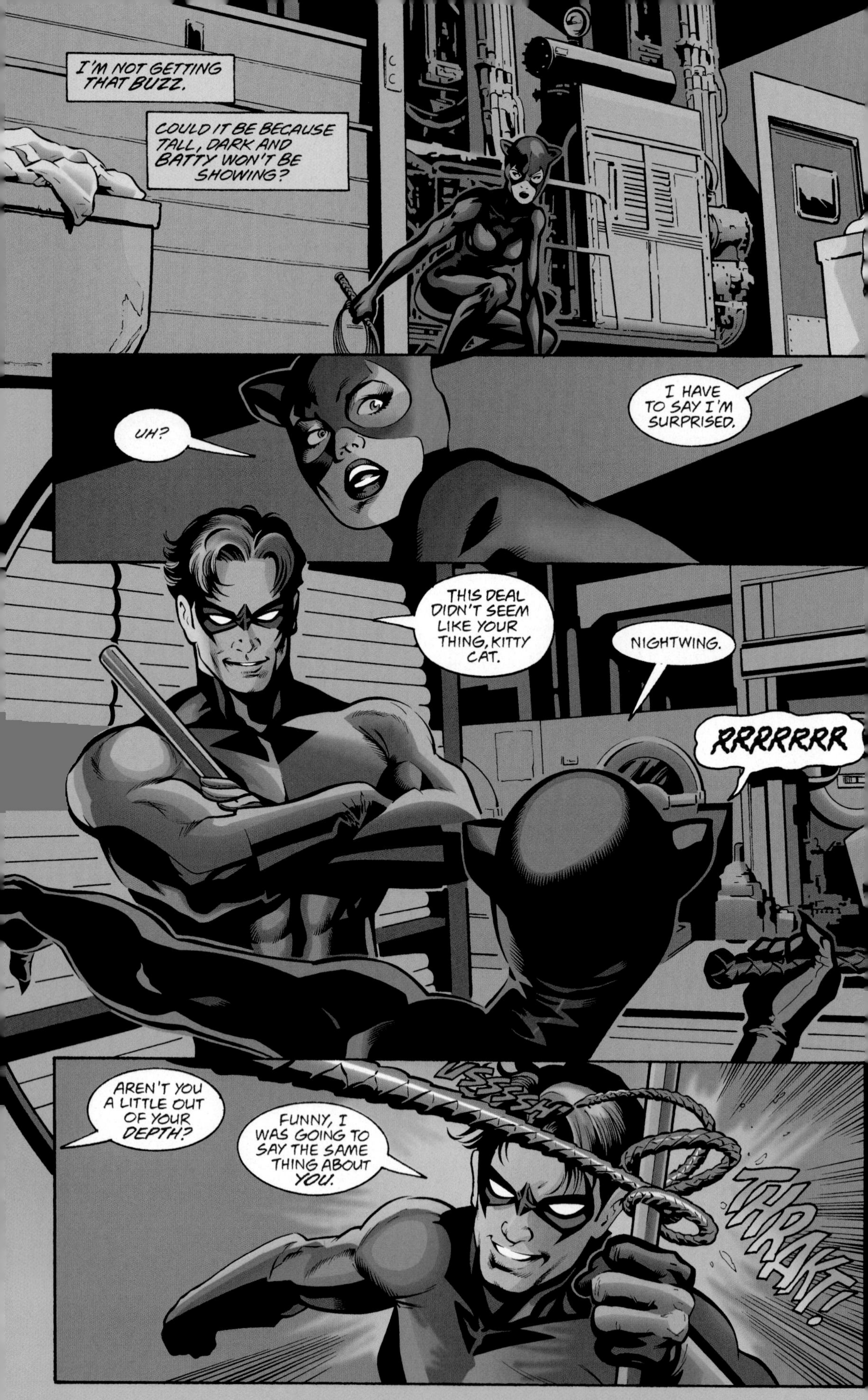
I'M NOT GETTING THAT BUZZ.
COULD IT BE BECAUSE TALL, DARK AND BATTY WON'T BE SHOWING?
UH?
I HAVE TO SAY I'M SURPRISED.
THIS DEAL DIDN'T SEEM LIKE YOUR THING, KITTY CAT.
NIGHTWING.
RRRRRRR
AREN'T YOU A LITTLE OUT OF YOUR DEPTH?
FUNNY, I WAS GOING TO SAY THE SAME THING ABOUT YOU.
THRAK!!

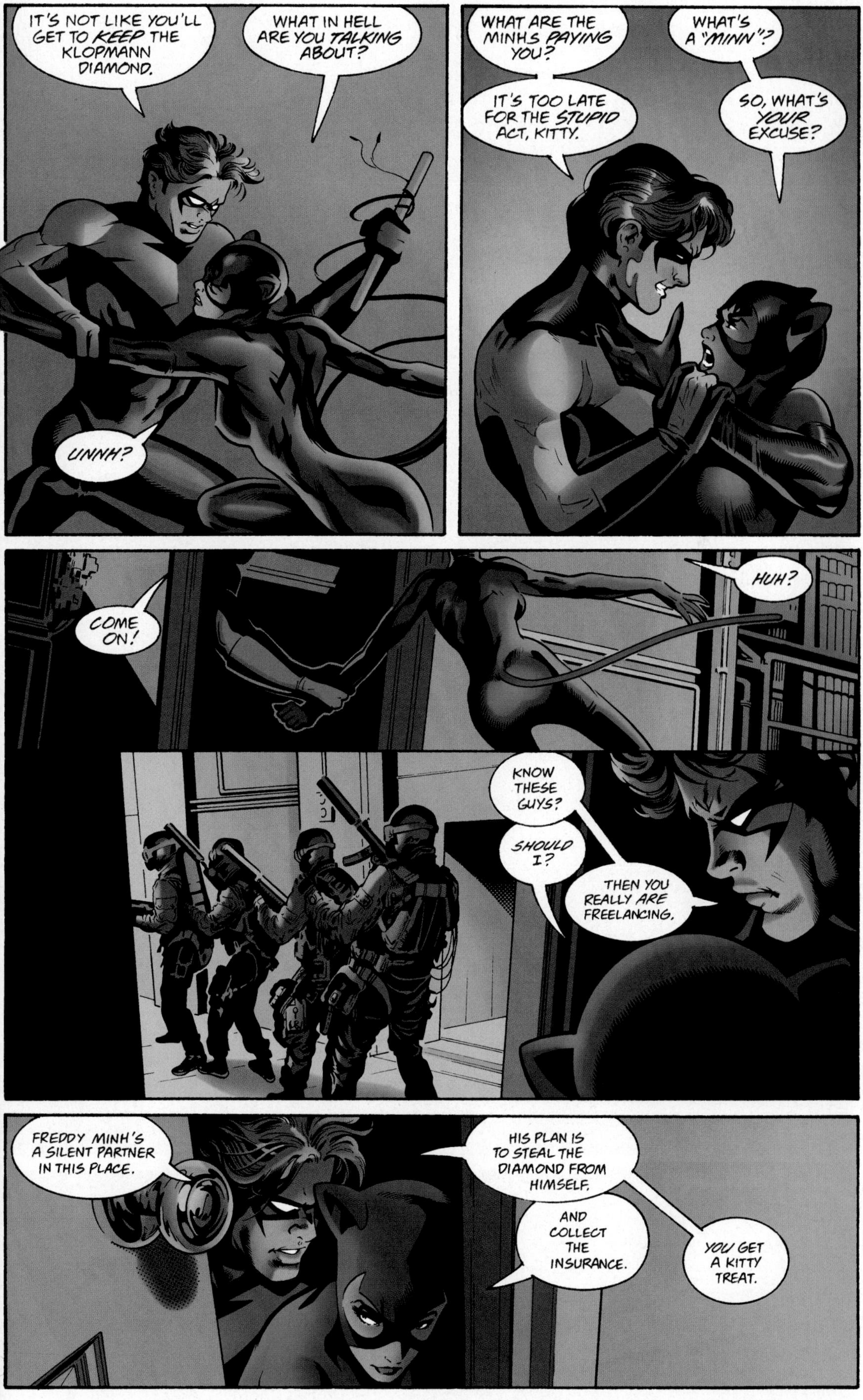
IT'S NOT LIKE YOU'LL GET TO KEEP THE KLOPMANN DIAMOND.
WHAT IN HELL ARE YOU TALKING ABOUT?
UNNH?
WHAT ARE THE MINHS PAYING YOU?
WHAT'S A "MINN"?
IT'S TOO LATE FOR THE STUPID ACT, KITTY.
SO, WHAT'S YOUR EXCUSE?
COME ON!
HUH?
KNOW THESE GUYS?
SHOULD I?
THEN YOU REALLY ARE FREELANCING.
FREDDY MINH'S A SILENT PARTNER IN THIS PLACE.
HIS PLAN IS TO STEAL THE DIAMOND FROM HIMSELF.
AND COLLECT THE INSURANCE.
YOU GET A KITTY TREAT.

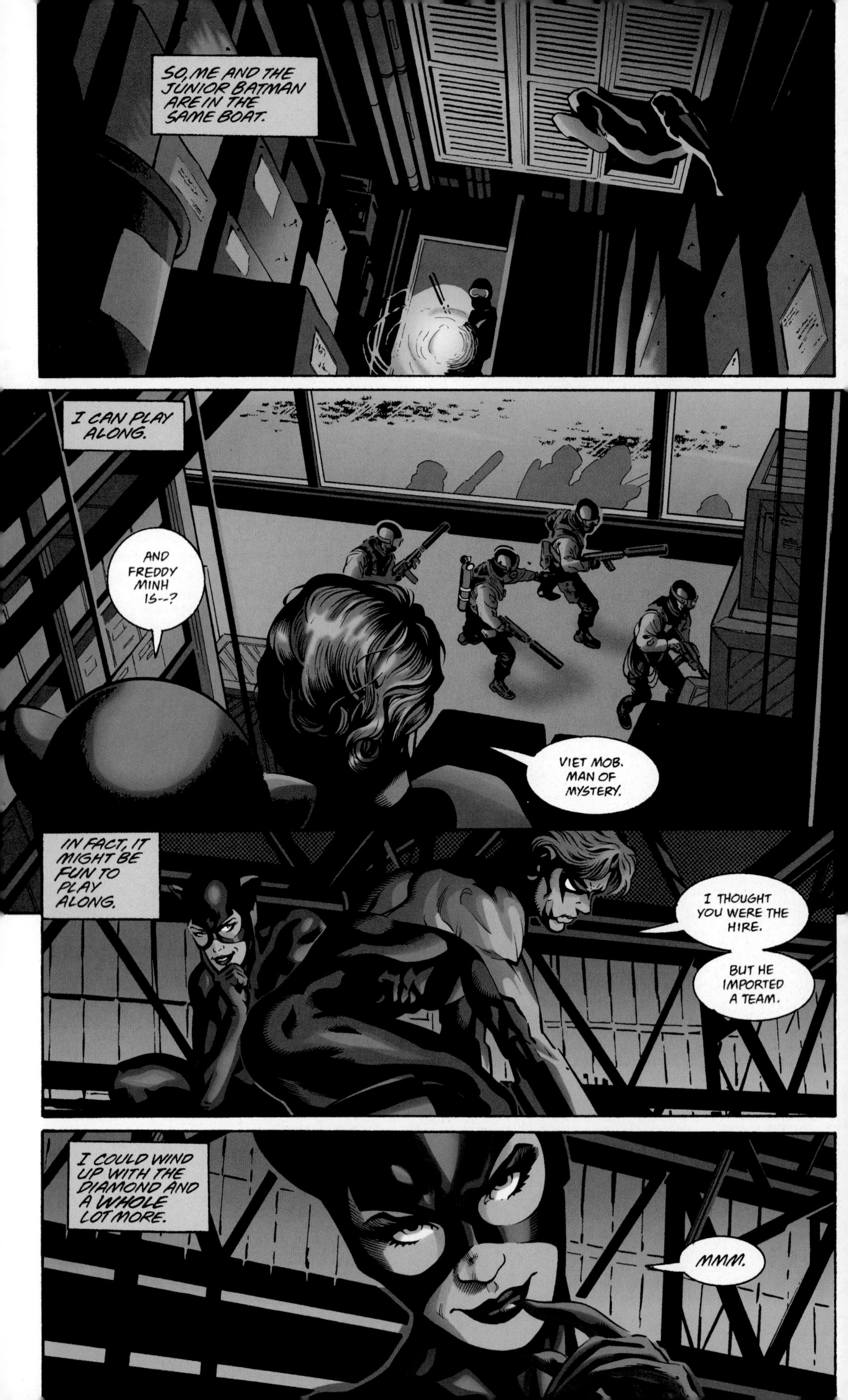
SO, ME AND THE JUNIOR BATMAN ARE IN THE SAME BOAT.
I CAN PLAY ALONG.
AND FREDDY MINH IS--?
VIET MOB. MAN OF MYSTERY.
IN FACT, IT MIGHT BE FUN TO PLAY ALONG.
I THOUGHT YOU WERE THE HIRE.
BUT HE IMPORTED A TEAM.
I COULD WIND UP WITH THE DIAMOND AND A WHOLE LOT MORE.
MMM.

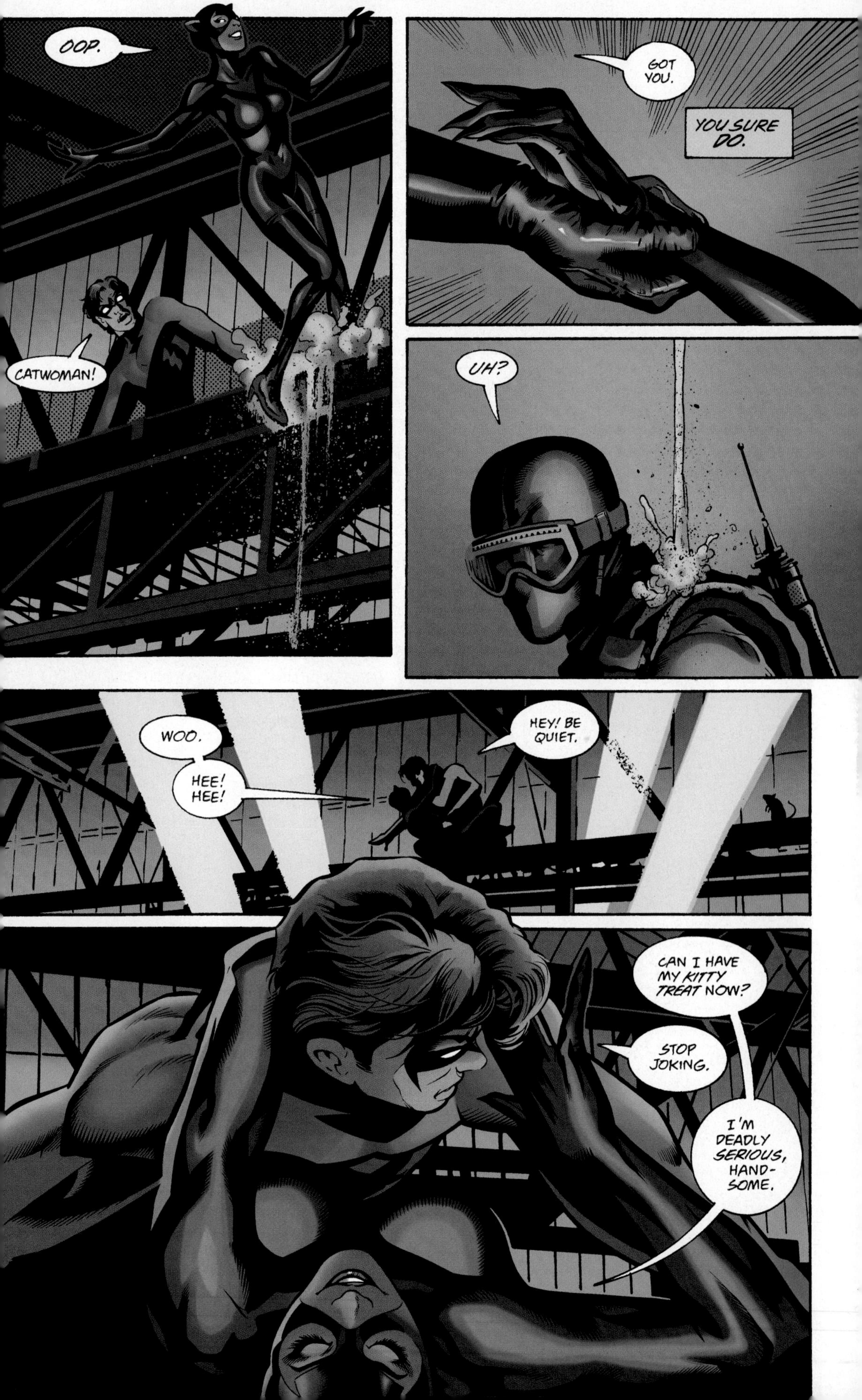
OOP.
CATWOMAN!
GOT YOU.
YOU SURE DO.
UH?
WOO.
HEE! HEE!
HEY! BE QUIET.
CAN I HAVE MY KITTY TREAT NOW?
STOP JOKING.
I'M DEADLY SERIOUS, HAND- SOME.

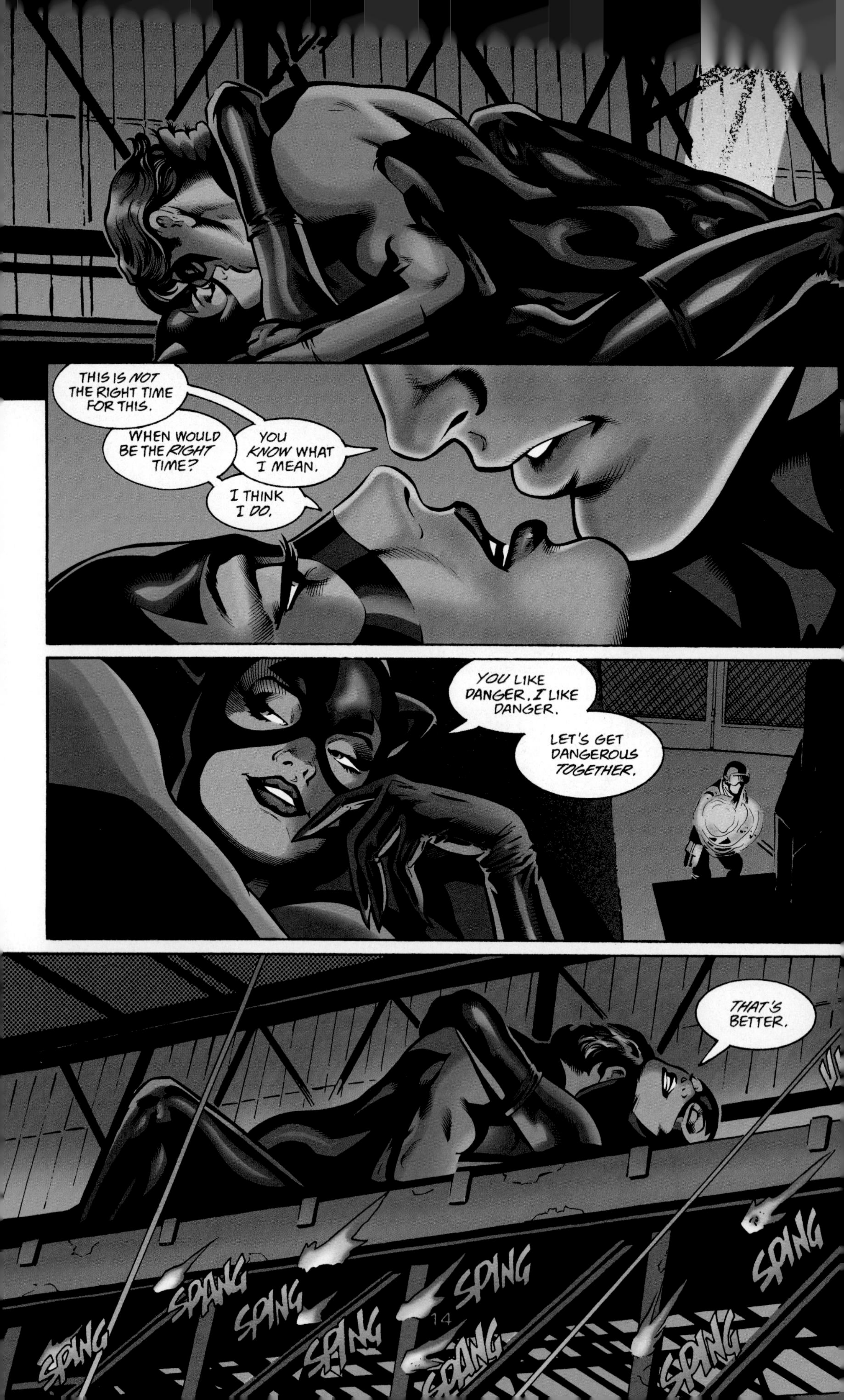
THIS IS NOT THE RIGHT TIME FOR THIS.
WHEN WOULD BE THE RIGHT TIME?
YOU KNOW WHAT I MEAN.
I THINK I DO.
YOU LIKE DANGER. I LIKE DANGER.
LET'S GET DANGEROUS TOGETHER.
THAT'S BETTER.
SPING
SPING
SPING
SPING
SPING
SPING
SPING
SPING
SPING

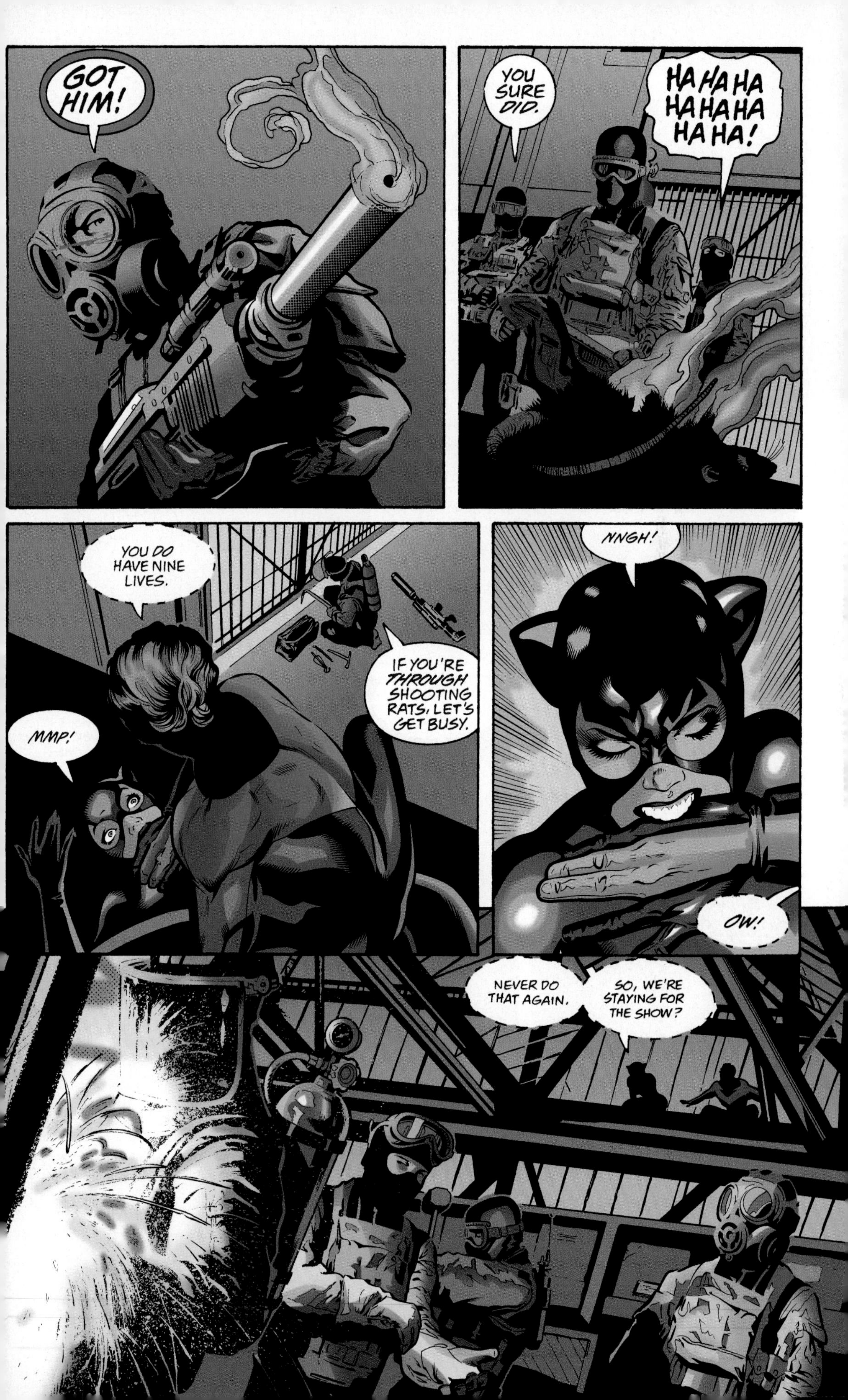
GOT HIM!
YOU SURE DID.
HA HA HA HA HA HA HA HA!
YOU DO HAVE NINE LIVES.
IF YOU'RE THROUGH SHOOTING RATS, LET'S GET BUSY.
MMP!
NNGH!
OW!
NEVER DO THAT AGAIN.
SO, WE'RE STAYING FOR THE SHOW?

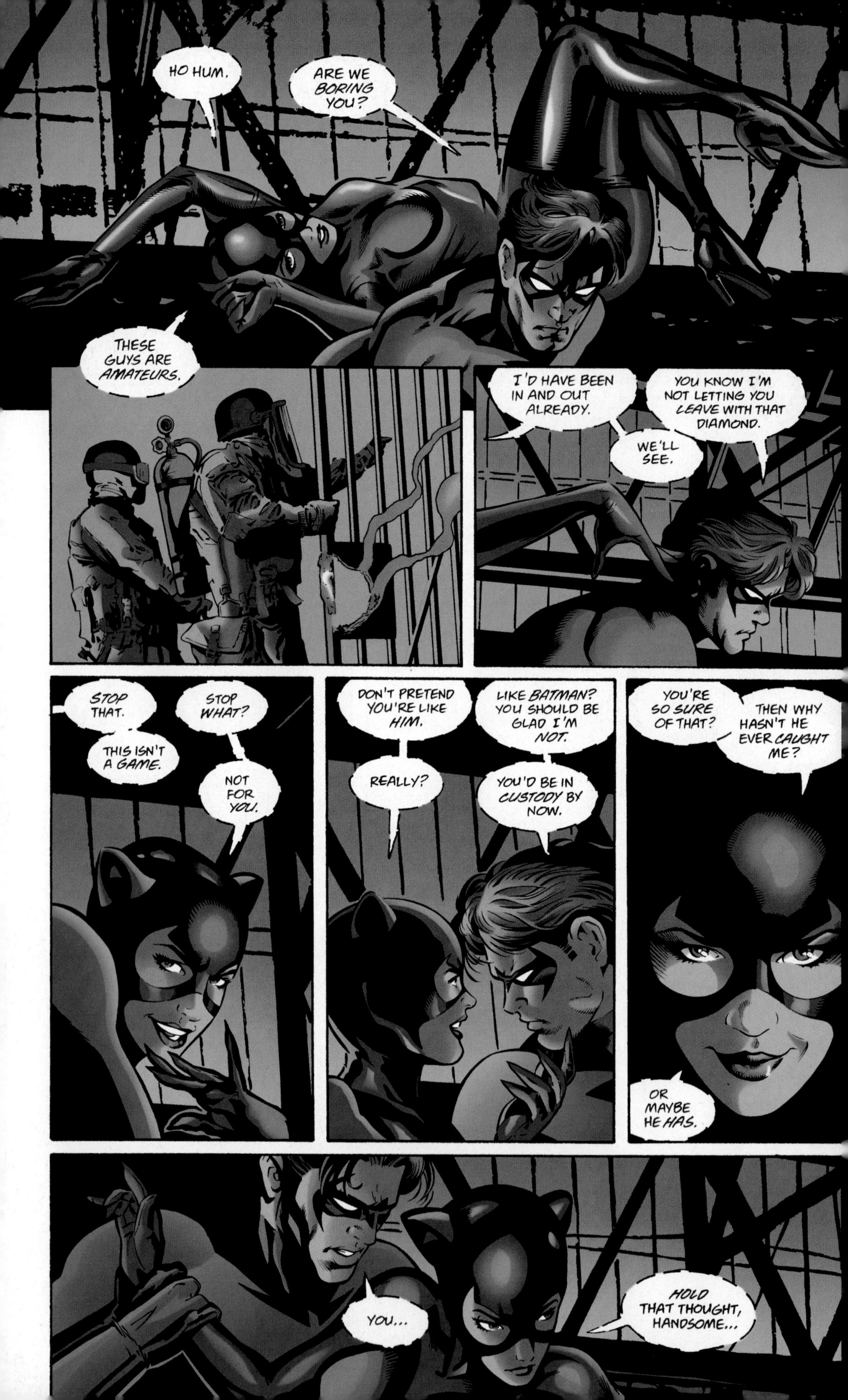
HO HUM.
ARE WE BORING YOU?
THESE GUYS ARE AMATEURS.
I'D HAVE BEEN IN AND OUT ALREADY.
YOU KNOW I'M NOT LETTING YOU LEAVE WITH THAT DIAMOND.
WE'LL SEE.
STOP THAT.
STOP WHAT?
THIS ISN'T A GAME.
NOT FOR YOU.
DON'T PRETEND YOU'RE LIKE HIM.
LIKE BATMAN? YOU SHOULD BE GLAD I'M NOT.
REALLY?
YOU'D BE IN CUSTODY BY NOW.
YOU'RE SO SURE OF THAT?
THEN WHY HASN'T HE EVER CAUGHT ME?
OR MAYBE HE HAS.
YOU...
HOLD THAT THOUGHT, HANDSOME...

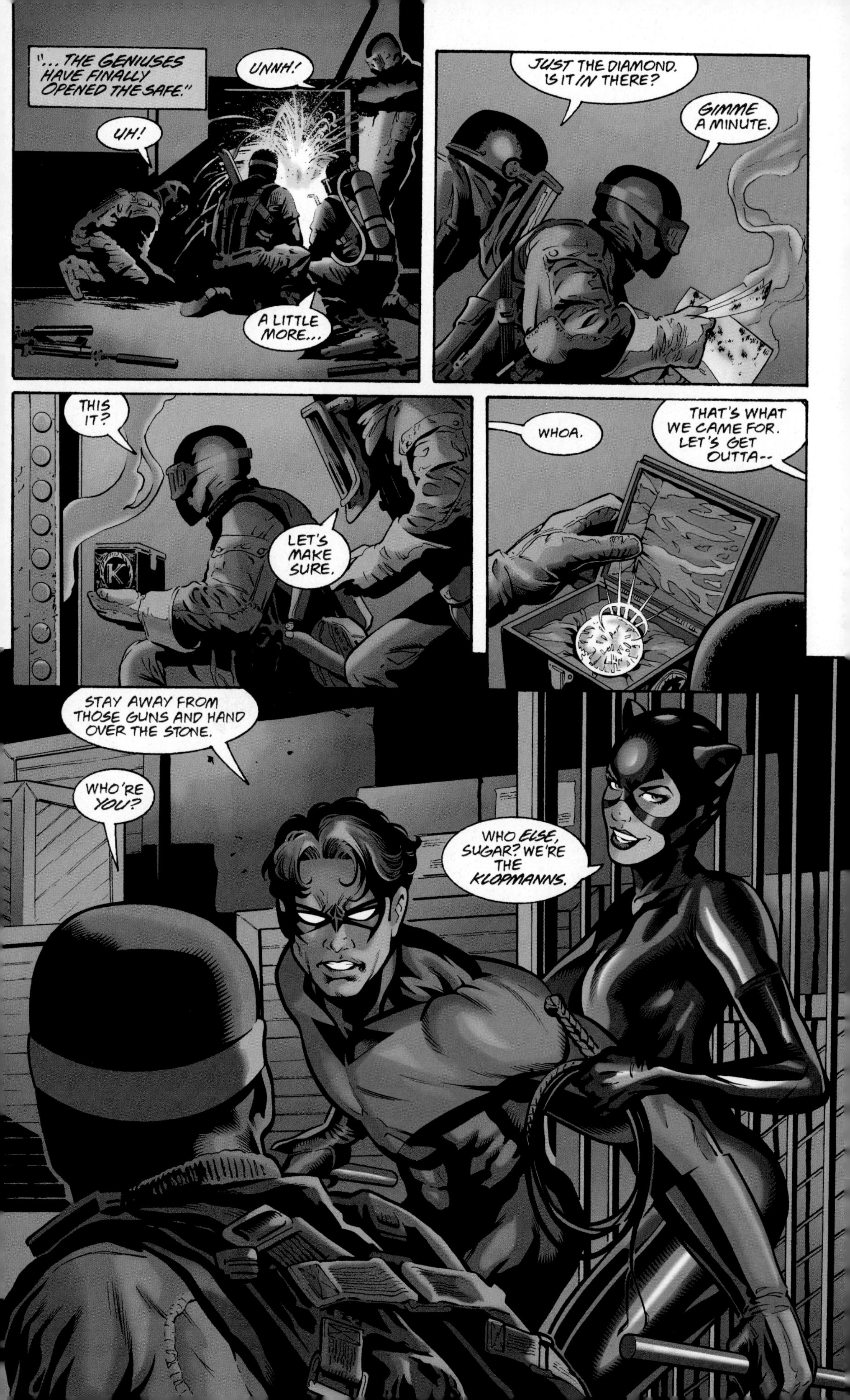
"... THE GENIUSES HAVE FINALLY OPENED THE SAFE."
UNNH!
UH!
A LITTLE MORE...
JUST THE DIAMOND. IS IT IN THERE?
GIMME A MINUTE.
THIS IT?
LET'S MAKE SURE.
WHOA.
THAT'S WHAT WE CAME FOR. LET'S GET OUTTA--
STAY AWAY FROM THOSE GUNS AND HAND OVER THE STONE.
WHO'RE YOU?
WHO ELSE, SUGAR? WE'RE THE KLOPMANNS.

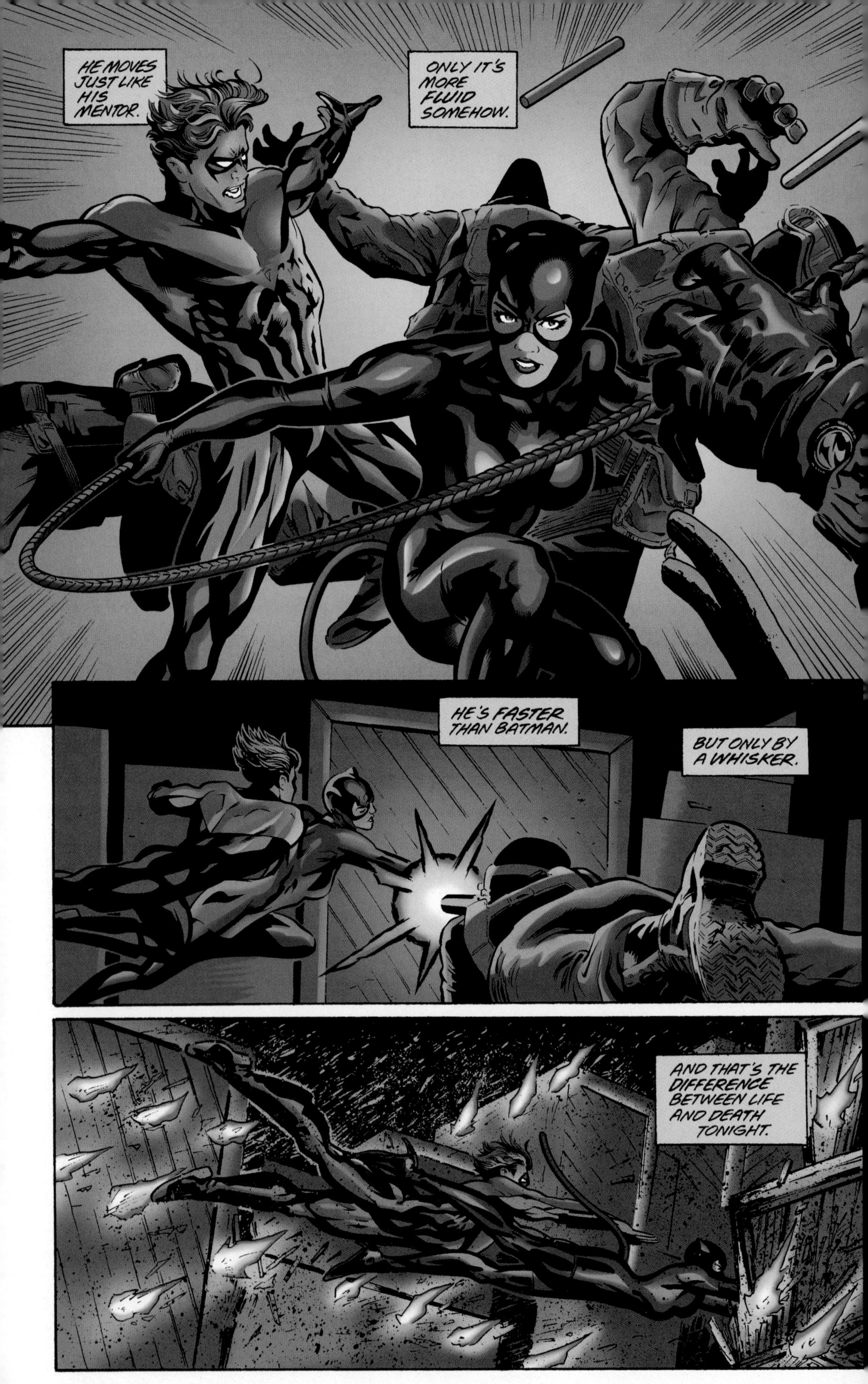
HE MOVES JUST LIKE HIS MENTOR.
ONLY IT'S MORE FLUID SOMEHOW.
HE'S FASTER THAN BATMAN.
BUT ONLY BY A WHISKER.
AND THAT'S THE DIFFERENCE BETWEEN LIFE AND DEATH TONIGHT.

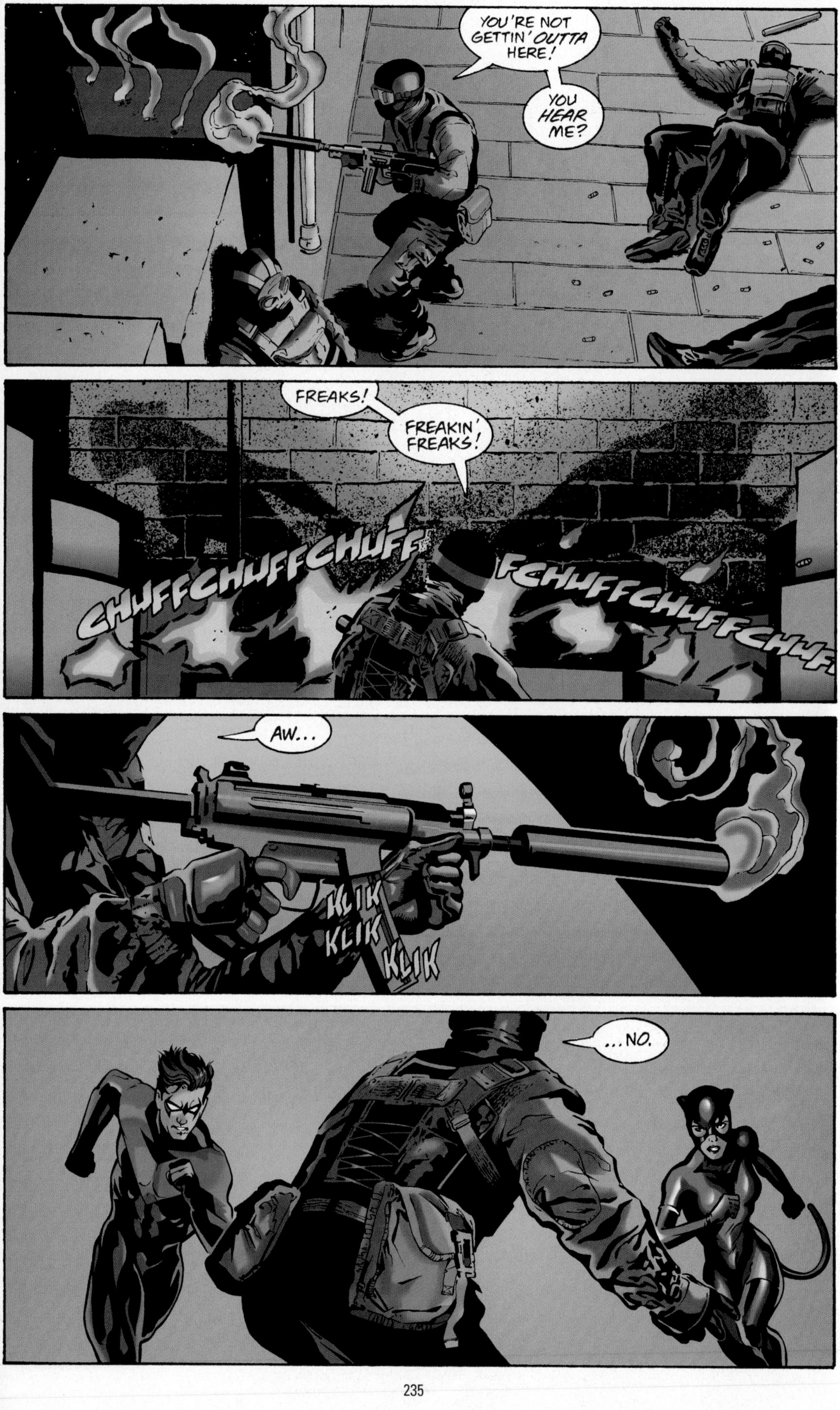
YOU'RE NOT GETTIN' OUTTA HERE!
YOU HEAR ME?
FREAKS!
FREAKIN' FREAKS!
CHUFFCHUFFCHUFF
FCHUFFCHUFFCHUF
AW...
KLIK
KLIK
KLIK
...NO.

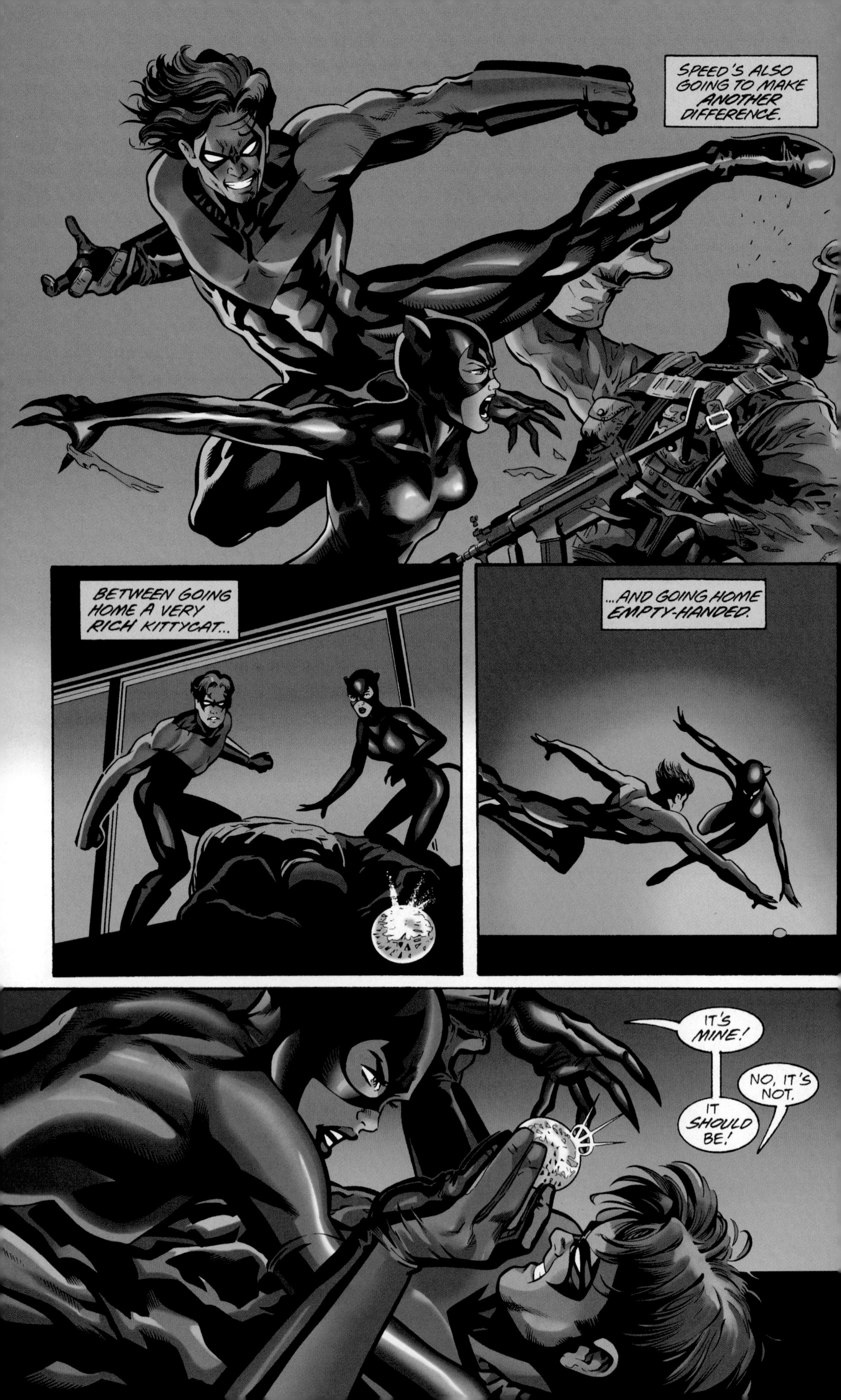
SPEED'S ALSO GOING TO MAKE ANOTHER DIFFERENCE.
BETWEEN GOING HOME A VERY RICH KITTYCAT...
...AND GOING HOME EMPTY-HANDED.
IT'S MINE!
IT SHOULD BE!
NO, IT'S NOT.

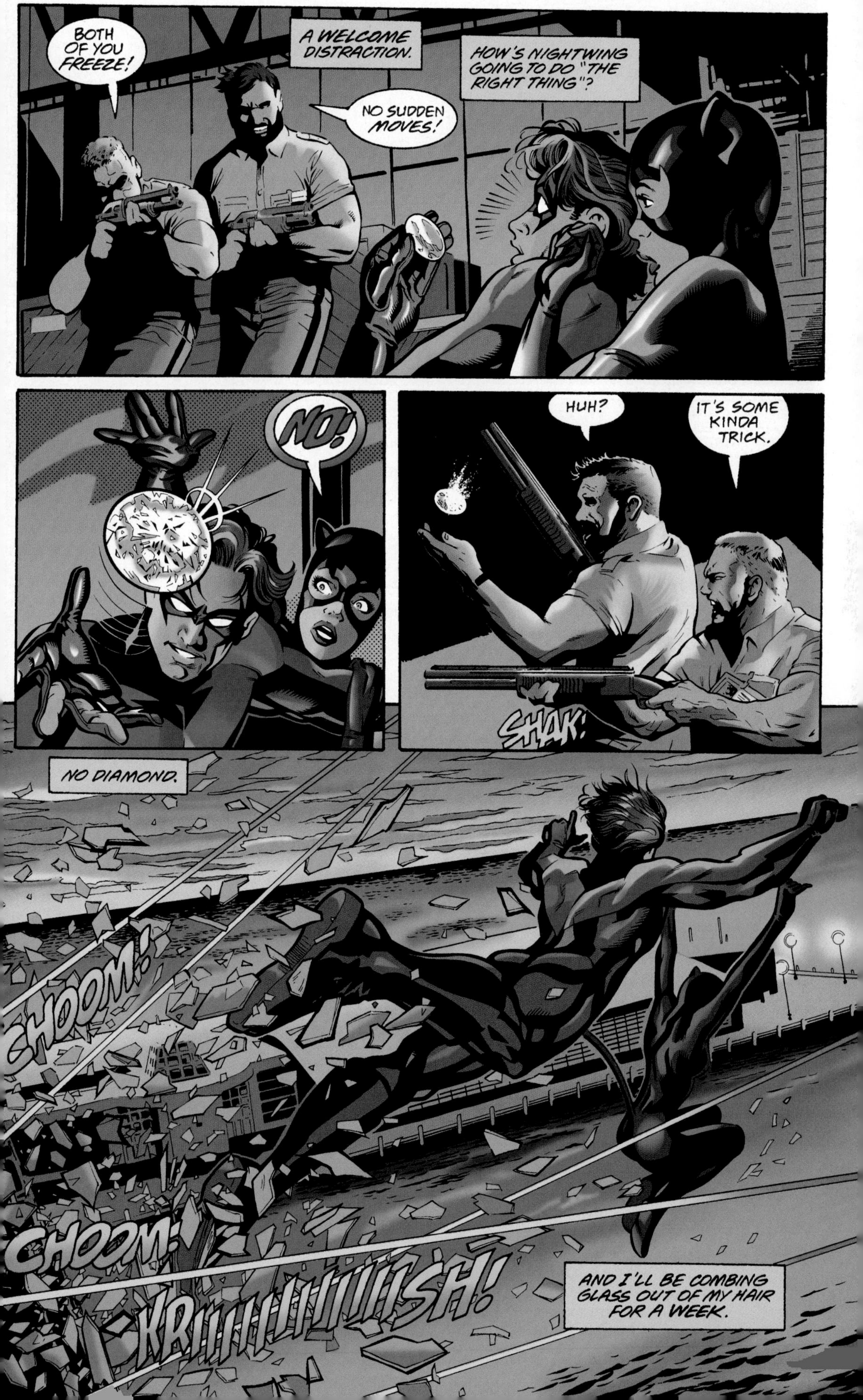

BOTH OF YOU FREEZE!
A WELCOME DISTRACTION.
HOW'S NIGHTWING GOING TO DO "THE RIGHT THING"?
NO SUDDEN MOVES!
NO!
HUH?
IT'S SOME KINDA TRICK.
SHAK!
NO DIAMOND.
CHOOM!
CHOOM!
KRIIIIIIIIIISH!
AND I'LL BE COMBING GLASS OUT OF MY HAIR FOR A WEEK.

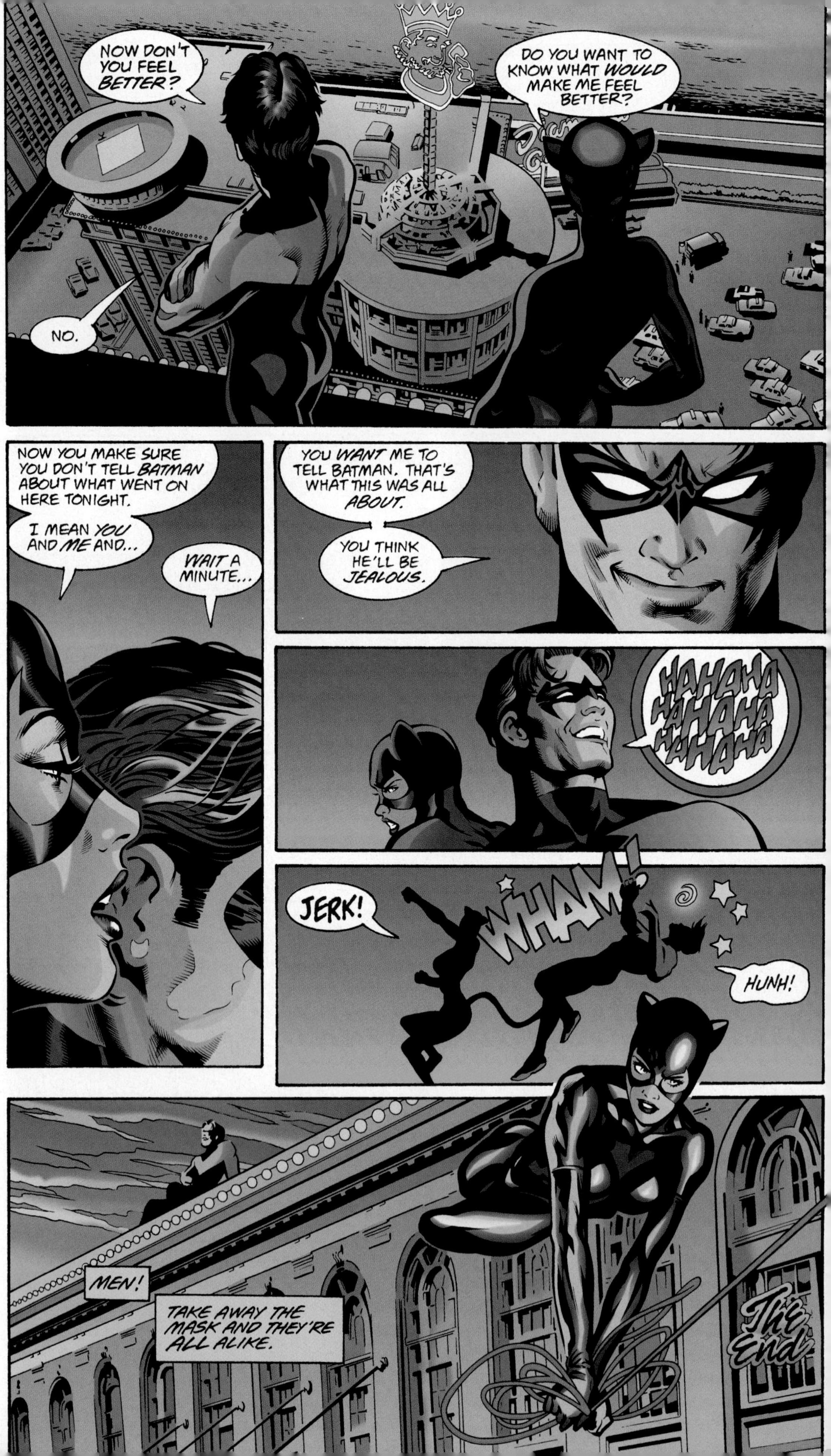

NOW DON'T YOU FEEL BETTER?
DO YOU WANT TO KNOW WHAT WOULD MAKE ME FEEL BETTER?
NO.
NOW YOU MAKE SURE YOU DON'T TELL BATMAN ABOUT WHAT WENT ON HERE TONIGHT.
I MEAN YOU AND ME AND...
WAIT A MINUTE...
YOU WANT ME TO TELL BATMAN. THAT'S WHAT THIS WAS ALL ABOUT.
YOU THINK HE'LL BE JEALOUS.
HAHAHA HAHAHA HAHAHA
JERK!
WHAM!
HUNH!
MEN!
TAKE AWAY THE MASK AND THEY'RE ALL ALIKE.
The End

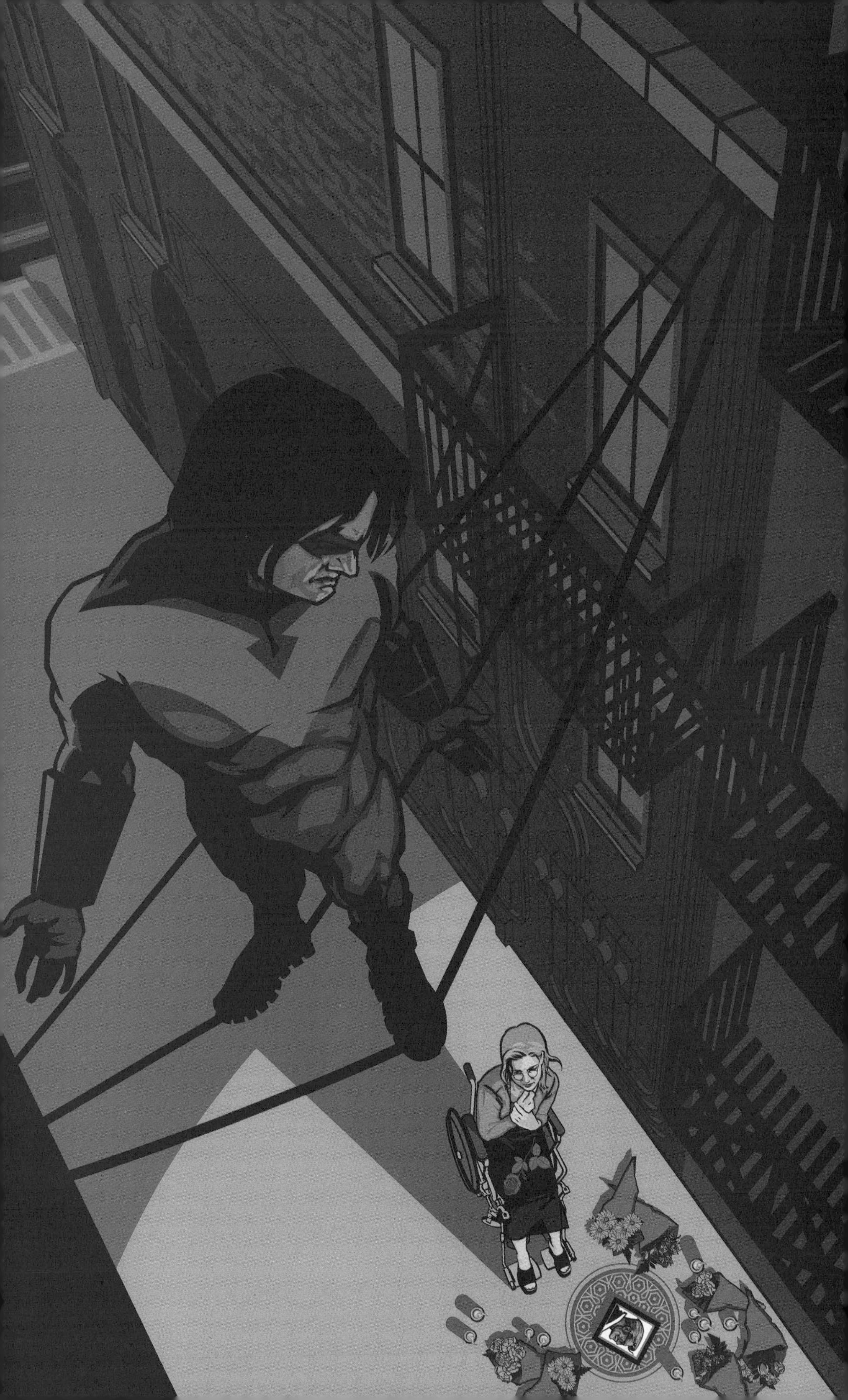

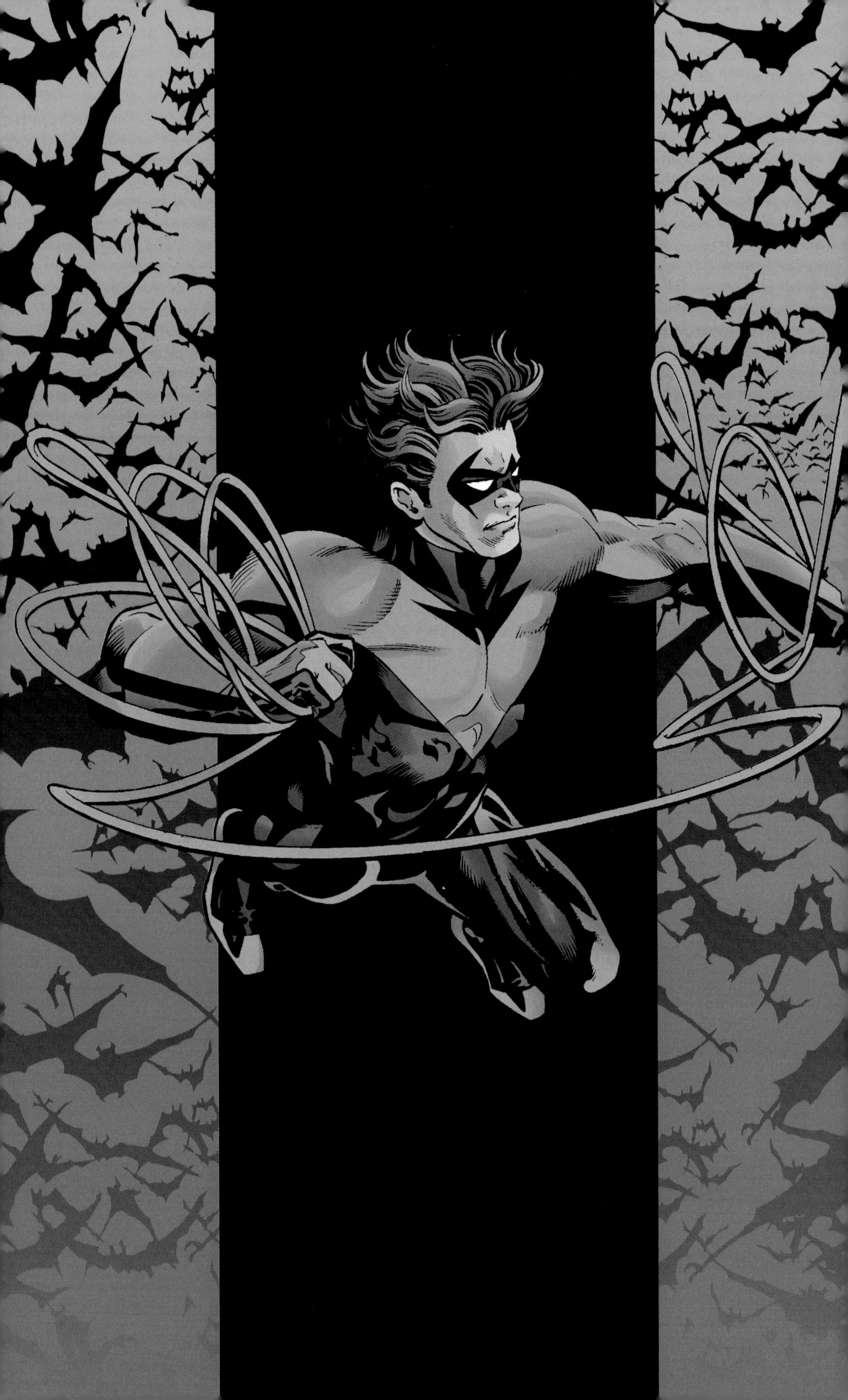

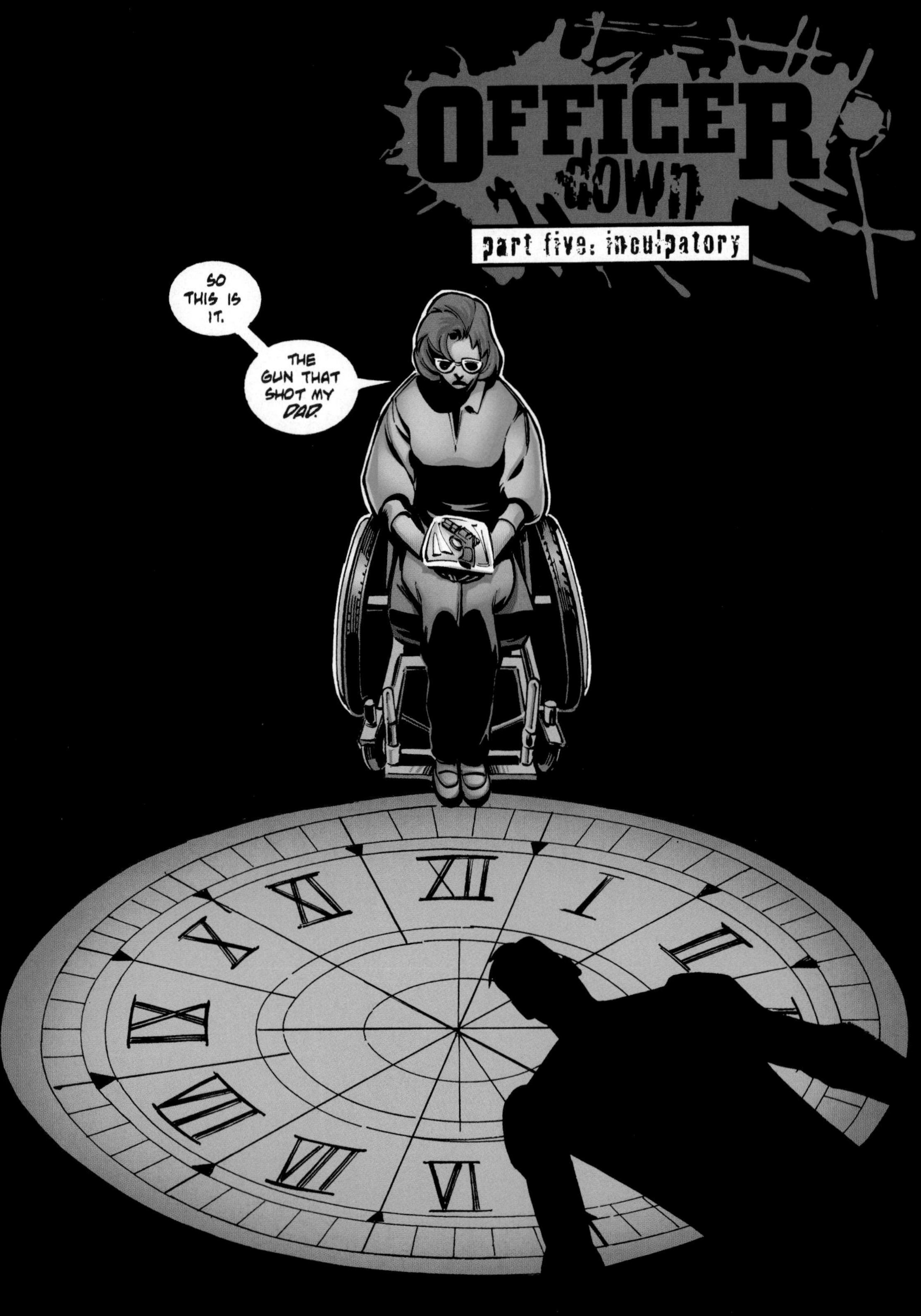
OFFICER down
part five: inculpatory
SO THIS IS IT.
THE GUN THAT SHOT MY DAD.

devin grayson/writer rick burchett/pencils rodney ramos/inks willie schubert/letterer
tom mccraw/colorist digital chameleon/separations idelson & schreck/editors
batman created by bob kane

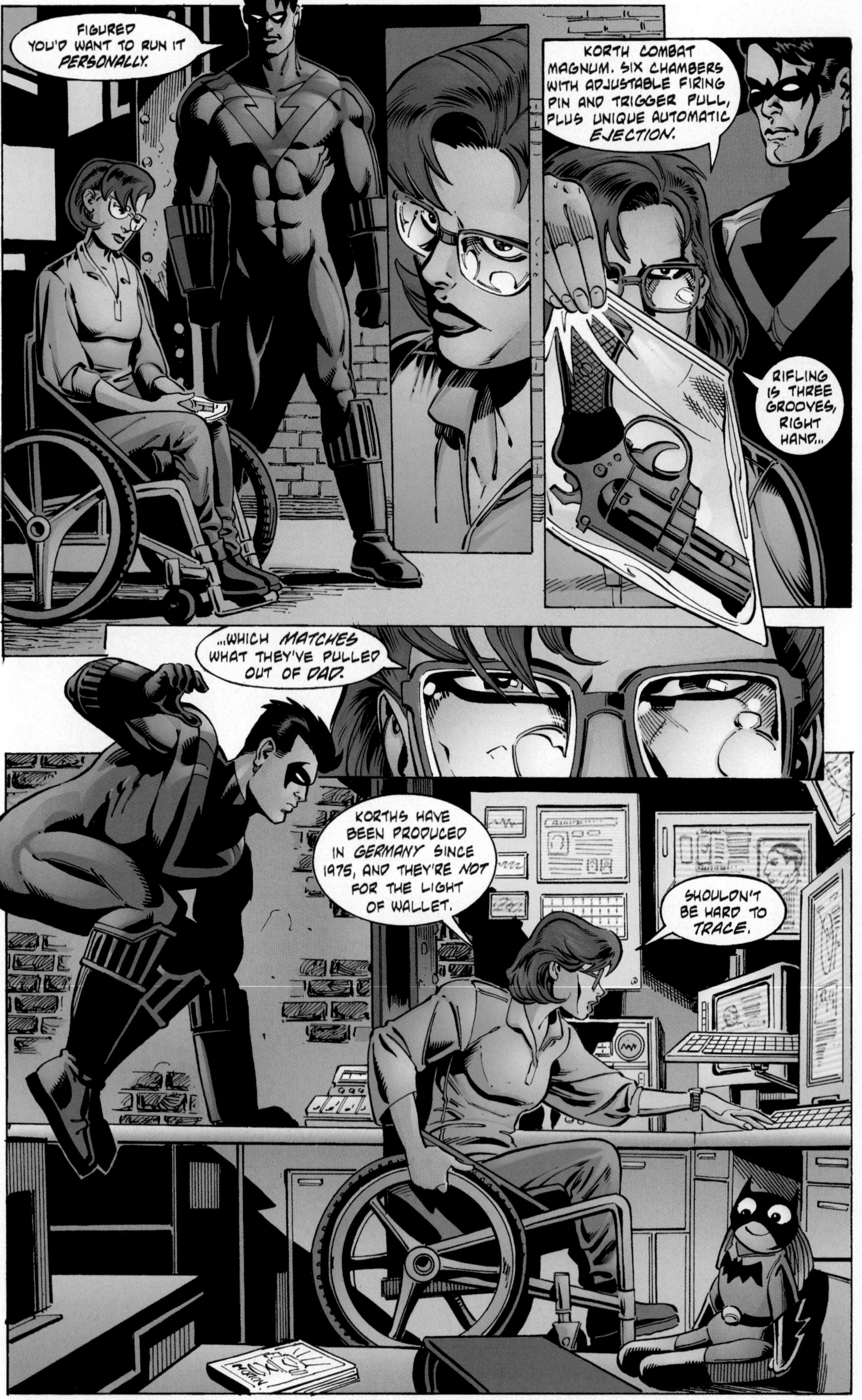
FIGURED YOU'D WANT TO RUN IT PERSONALLY.
KORTH COMBAT MAGNUM. SIX CHAMBERS WITH ADJUSTABLE FIRING PIN AND TRIGGER PULL, PLUS UNIQUE AUTOMATIC EJECTION.
RIFLING IS THREE GROOVES, RIGHT HAND...
...WHICH MATCHES WHAT THEY'VE PULLED OUT OF DAD.
KORTHS HAVE BEEN PRODUCED IN GERMANY SINCE 1975, AND THEY'RE NOT FOR THE LIGHT OF WALLET.
SHOULDN'T BE HARD TO TRACE.

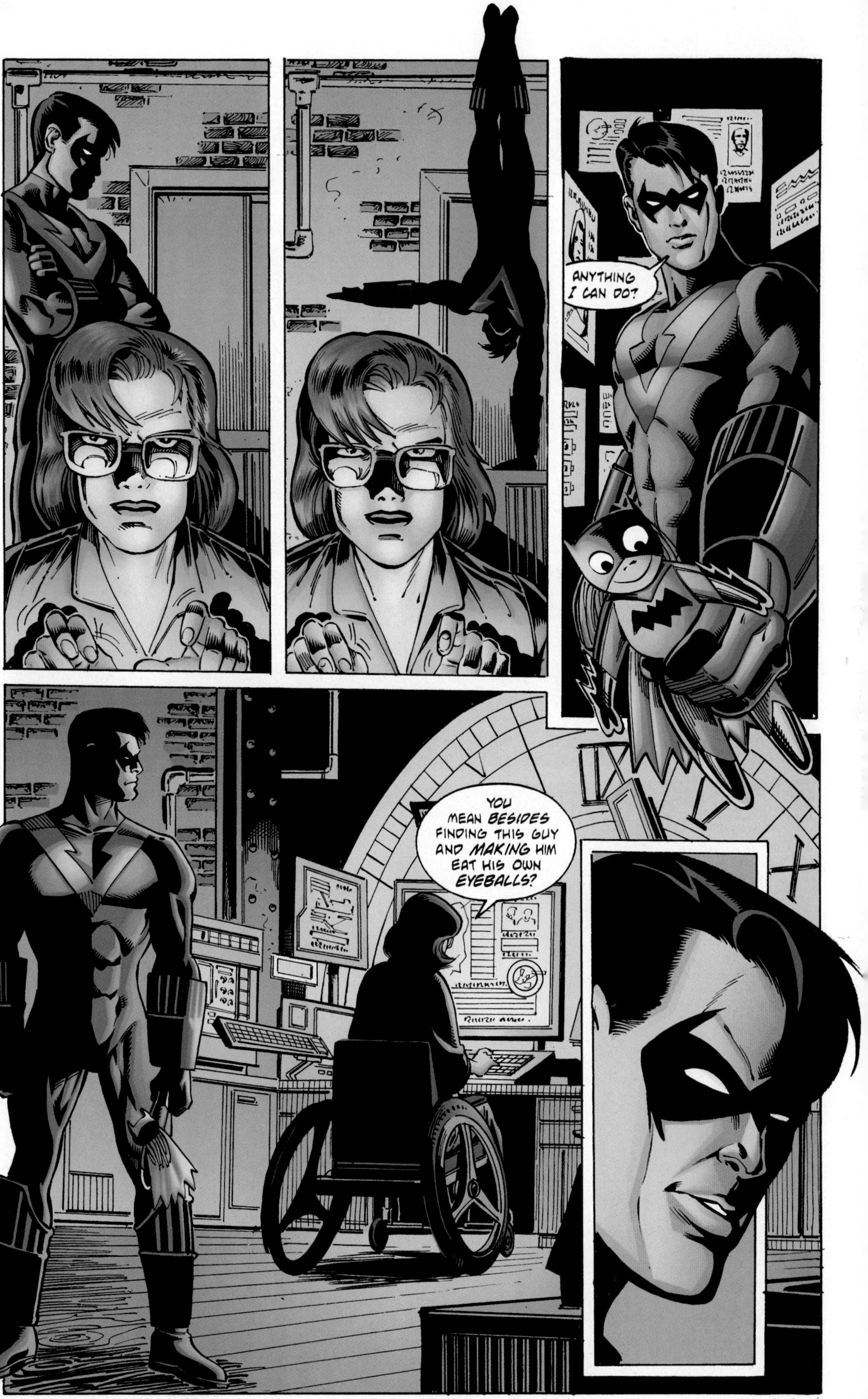
ANYTHING I CAN DO?
YOU MEAN BESIDES FINDING THIS GUY AND MAKING HIM EAT HIS OWN EYEBALLS?

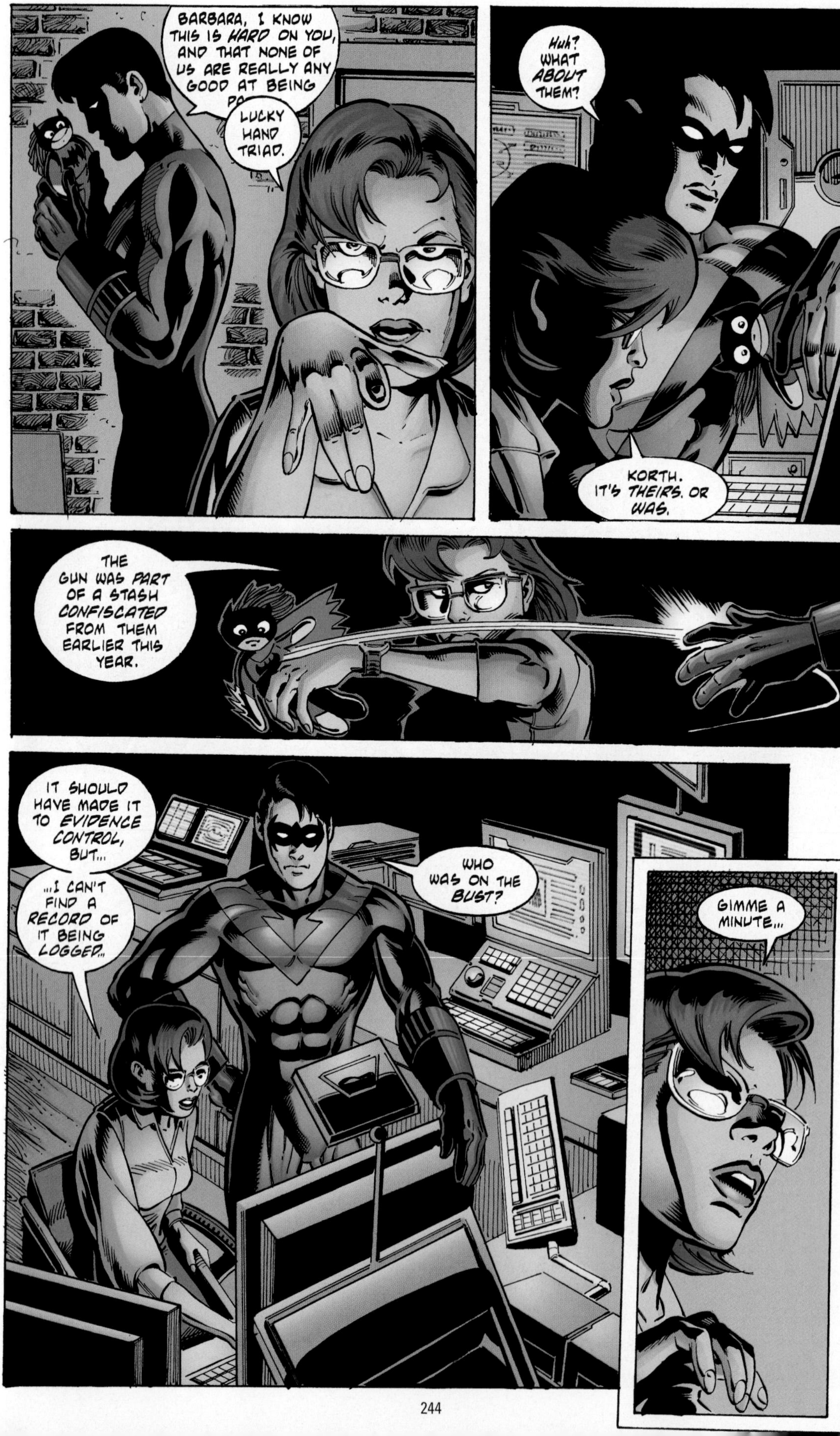
BARBARA, I KNOW THIS IS HARD ON YOU, AND THAT NONE OF US ARE REALLY ANY GOOD AT BEING PA...
LUCKY HAND TRIAD.
Huh? WHAT ABOUT THEM?
KORTH. IT'S THEIRS. OR WAS.
THE GUN WAS PART OF A STASH CONFISCATED FROM THEM EARLIER THIS YEAR.
IT SHOULD HAVE MADE IT TO EVIDENCE CONTROL, BUT...
...I CAN'T FIND A RECORD OF IT BEING LOGGED...
WHO WAS ON THE BUST?
GIMME A MINUTE...

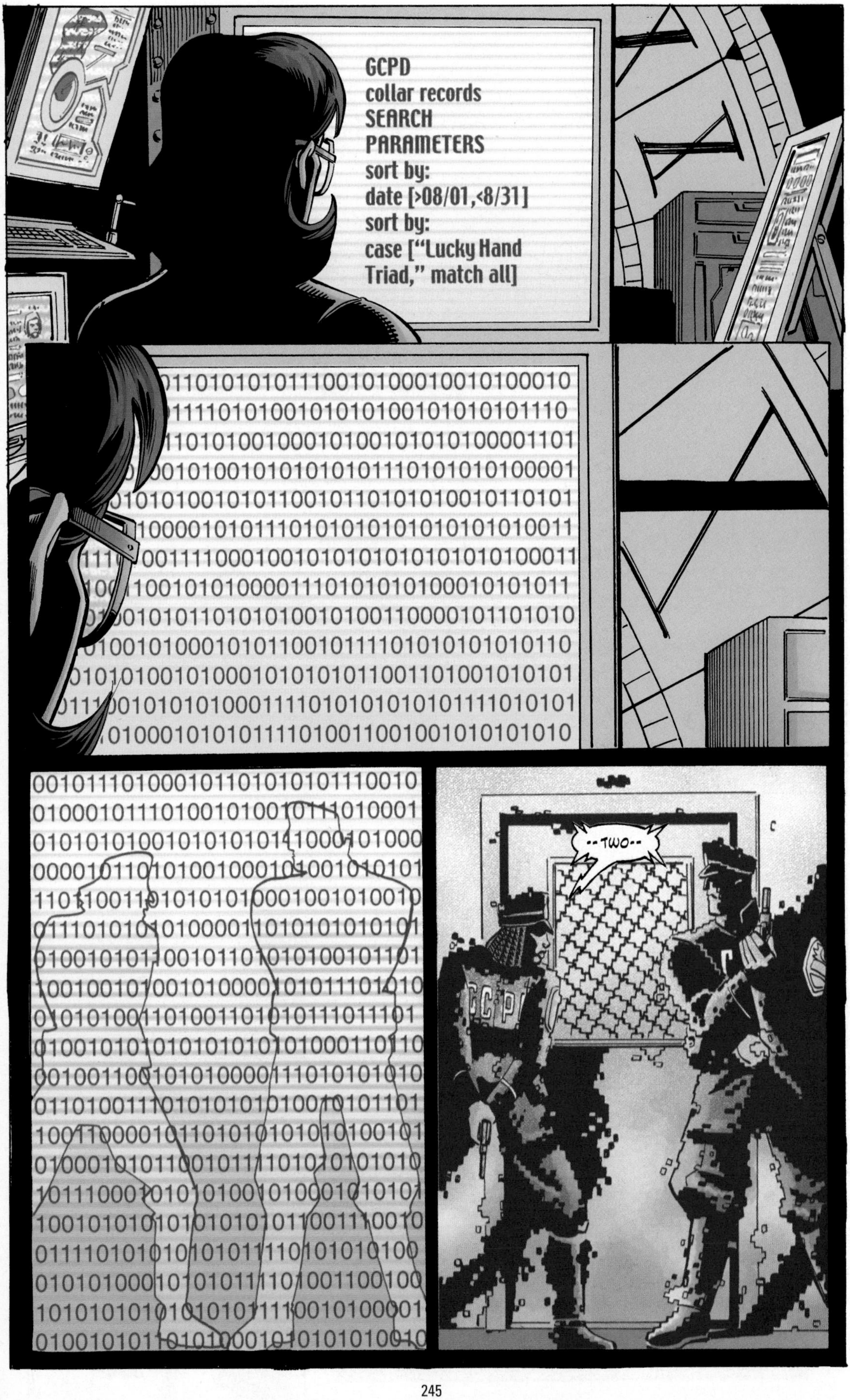
GCPD
collar records
SEARCH
PARAMETERS
sort by:
date [>08/01,<8/31]
sort by:
case ["Lucky Hand
Triad," match all]
--TWO--

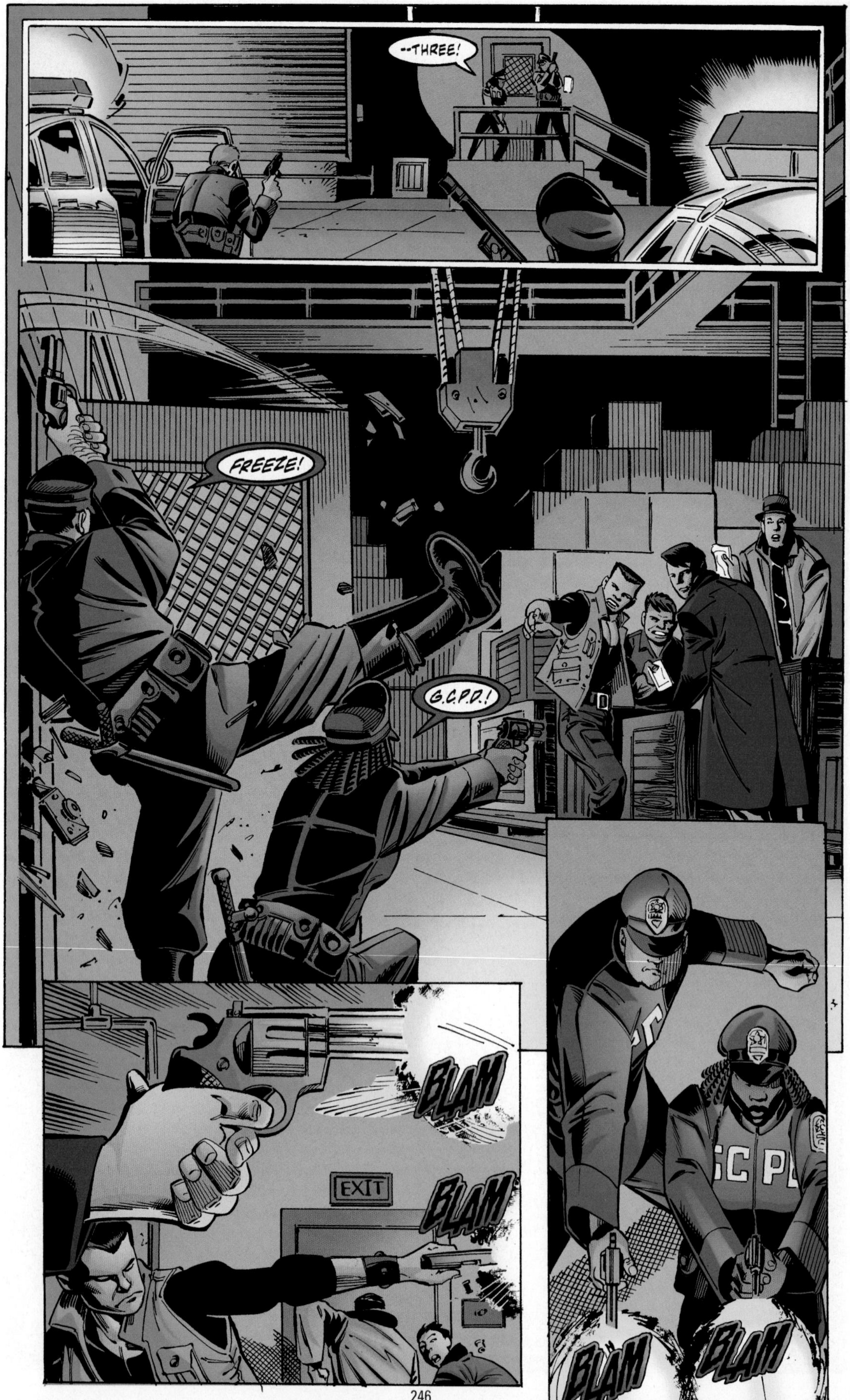

--THREE!
FREEZE!
G.C.P.D.!
EXIT
BLAM
BLAM
GCPD
BLAM
BLAM

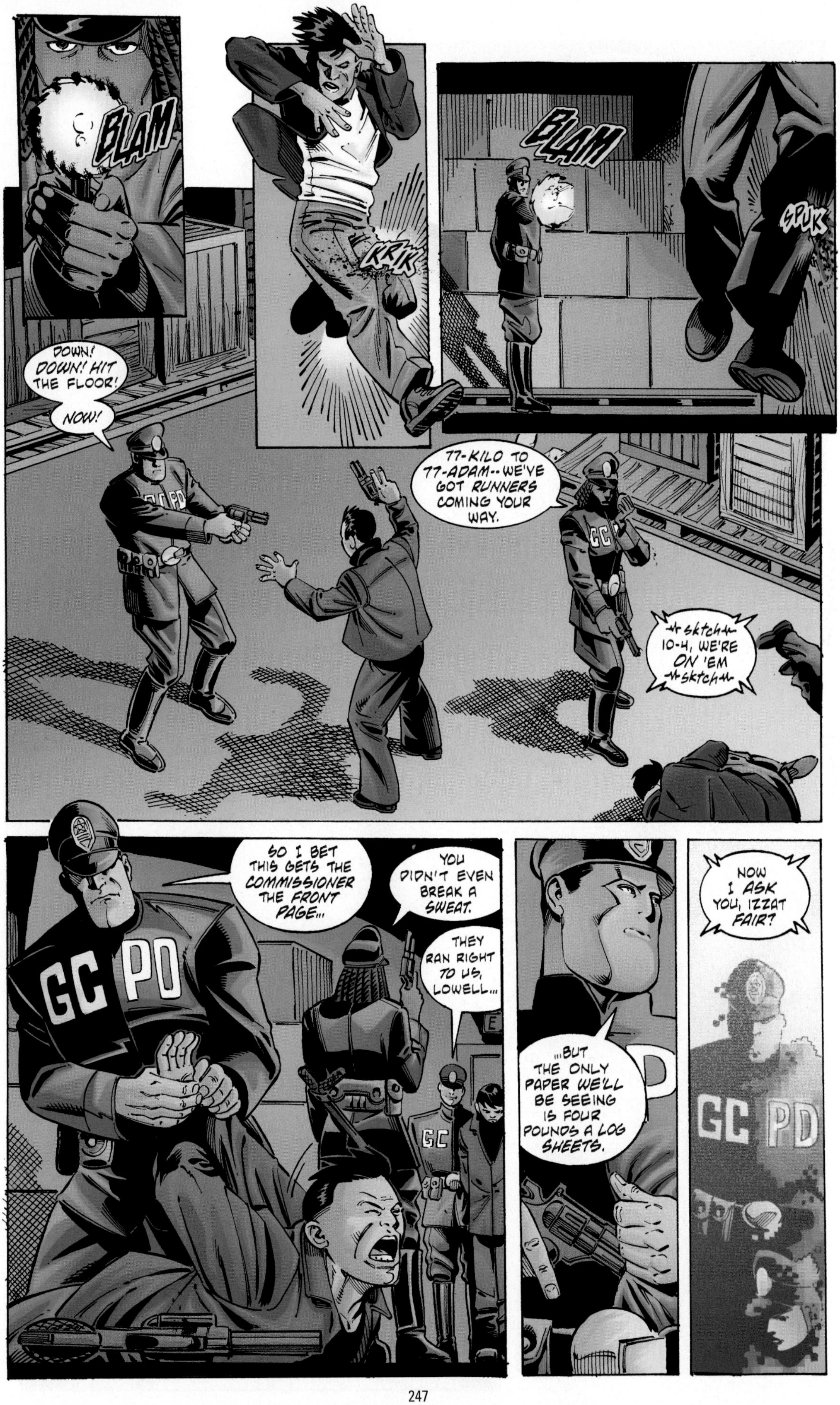
BLAM
KRIK
BLAM
SPUK
DOWN! DOWN! HIT THE FLOOR!
NOW!
77-KILO TO 77-ADAM--WE'VE GOT RUNNERS COMING YOUR WAY.
sktch 10-4, WE'RE ON 'EM sktch
SO I BET THIS GETS THE COMMISSIONER THE FRONT PAGE...
YOU DIDN'T EVEN BREAK A SWEAT.
THEY RAN RIGHT TO US, LOWELL...
...BUT THE ONLY PAPER WE'LL BE SEEING IS FOUR POUNDS A LOG SHEETS.
NOW I ASK YOU, IZZAT FAIR?

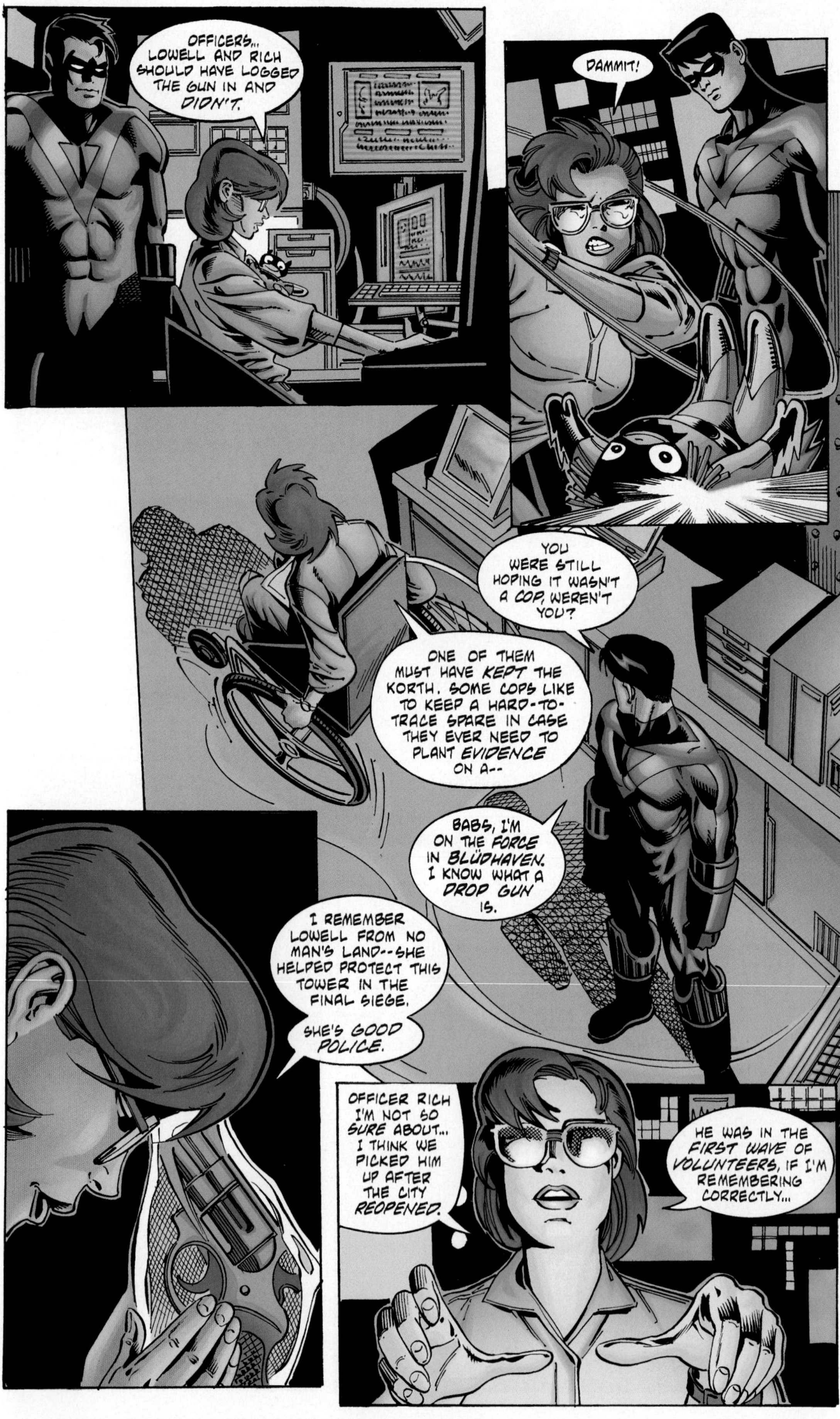
OFFICERS... LOWELL AND RICH SHOULD HAVE LOGGED THE GUN IN AND *DIDN'T.*
DAMMIT!
YOU WERE STILL HOPING IT WASN'T A *COP,* WEREN'T YOU?
ONE OF THEM MUST HAVE *KEPT* THE KORTH. SOME COPS LIKE TO KEEP A HARD-TO-TRACE SPARE IN CASE THEY EVER NEED TO PLANT *EVIDENCE* ON A--
BABS, I'M ON THE *FORCE* IN *BLÜDHAVEN.* I KNOW WHAT A *DROP GUN* IS.
I REMEMBER LOWELL FROM NO MAN'S LAND--SHE HELPED PROTECT THIS TOWER IN THE FINAL SIEGE.
SHE'S *GOOD POLICE.*
OFFICER RICH I'M NOT SO *SURE* ABOUT... I THINK WE PICKED HIM UP AFTER THE CITY *REOPENED.*
HE WAS IN THE *FIRST WAVE* OF *VOLUNTEERS,* IF I'M REMEMBERING CORRECTLY...

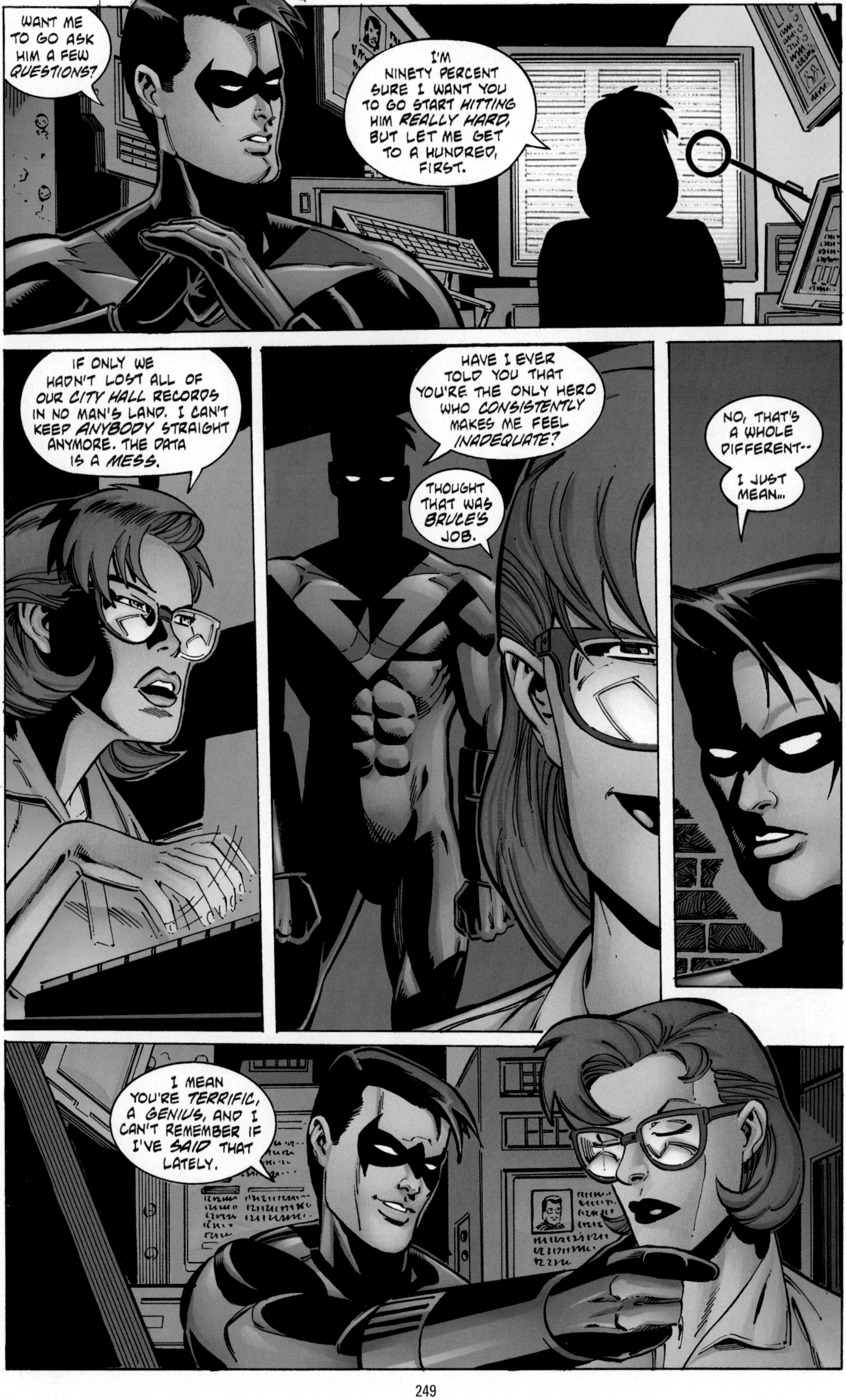
WANT ME TO GO ASK HIM A FEW QUESTIONS?
I'M NINETY PERCENT SURE I WANT YOU TO GO START HITTING HIM REALLY HARD, BUT LET ME GET TO A HUNDRED, FIRST.
IF ONLY WE HADN'T LOST ALL OF OUR CITY HALL RECORDS IN NO MAN'S LAND. I CAN'T KEEP ANYBODY STRAIGHT ANYMORE. THE DATA IS A MESS.
HAVE I EVER TOLD YOU THAT YOU'RE THE ONLY HERO WHO CONSISTENTLY MAKES ME FEEL INADEQUATE?
THOUGHT THAT WAS BRUCE'S JOB.
NO, THAT'S A WHOLE DIFFERENT--
I JUST MEAN...
I MEAN YOU'RE TERRIFIC, A GENIUS, AND I CAN'T REMEMBER IF I'VE SAID THAT LATELY.

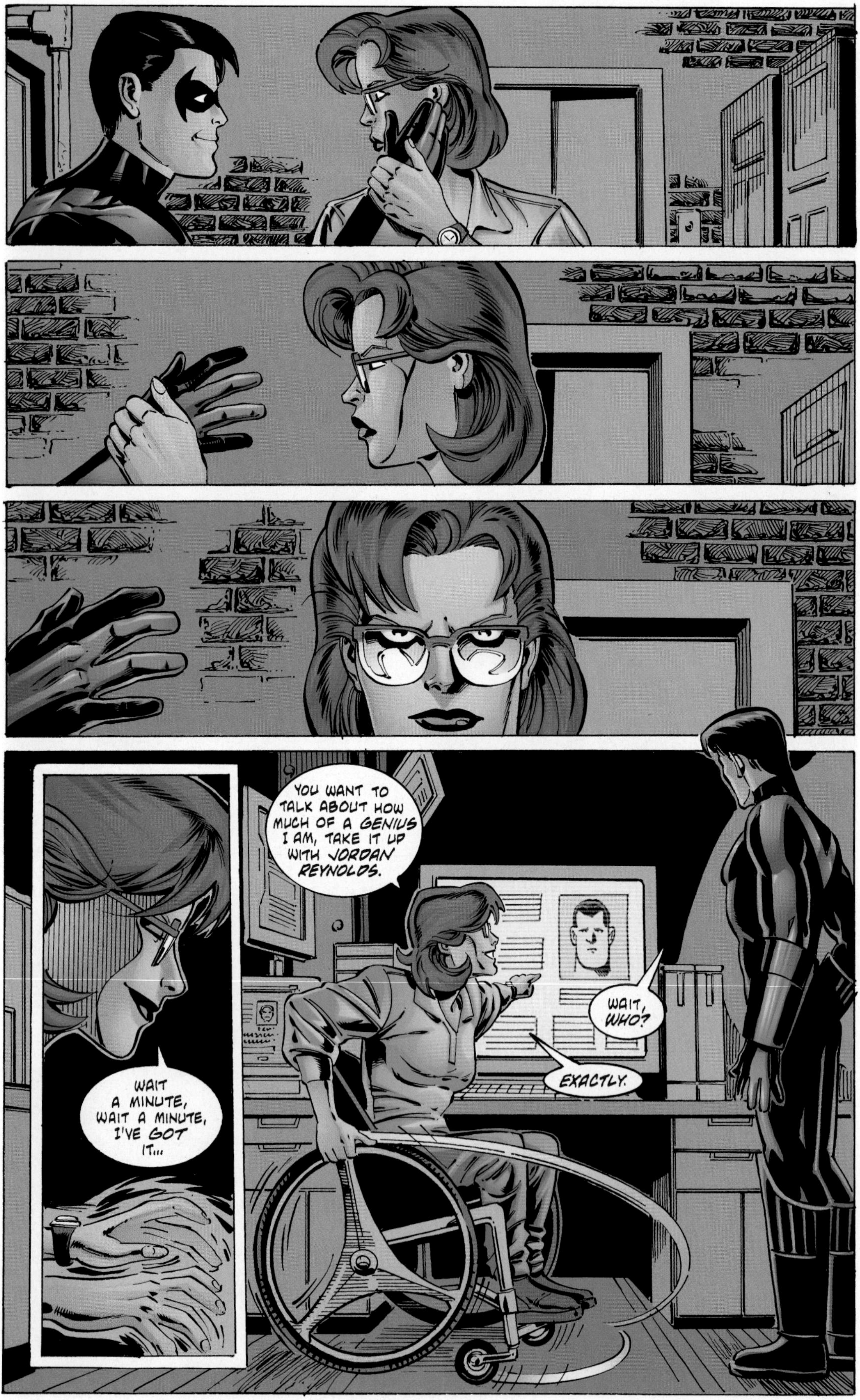
YOU WANT TO TALK ABOUT HOW MUCH OF A GENIUS I AM, TAKE IT UP WITH JORDAN REYNOLDS.
WAIT, WHO?
EXACTLY.
WAIT A MINUTE, WAIT A MINUTE, I'VE GOT IT...

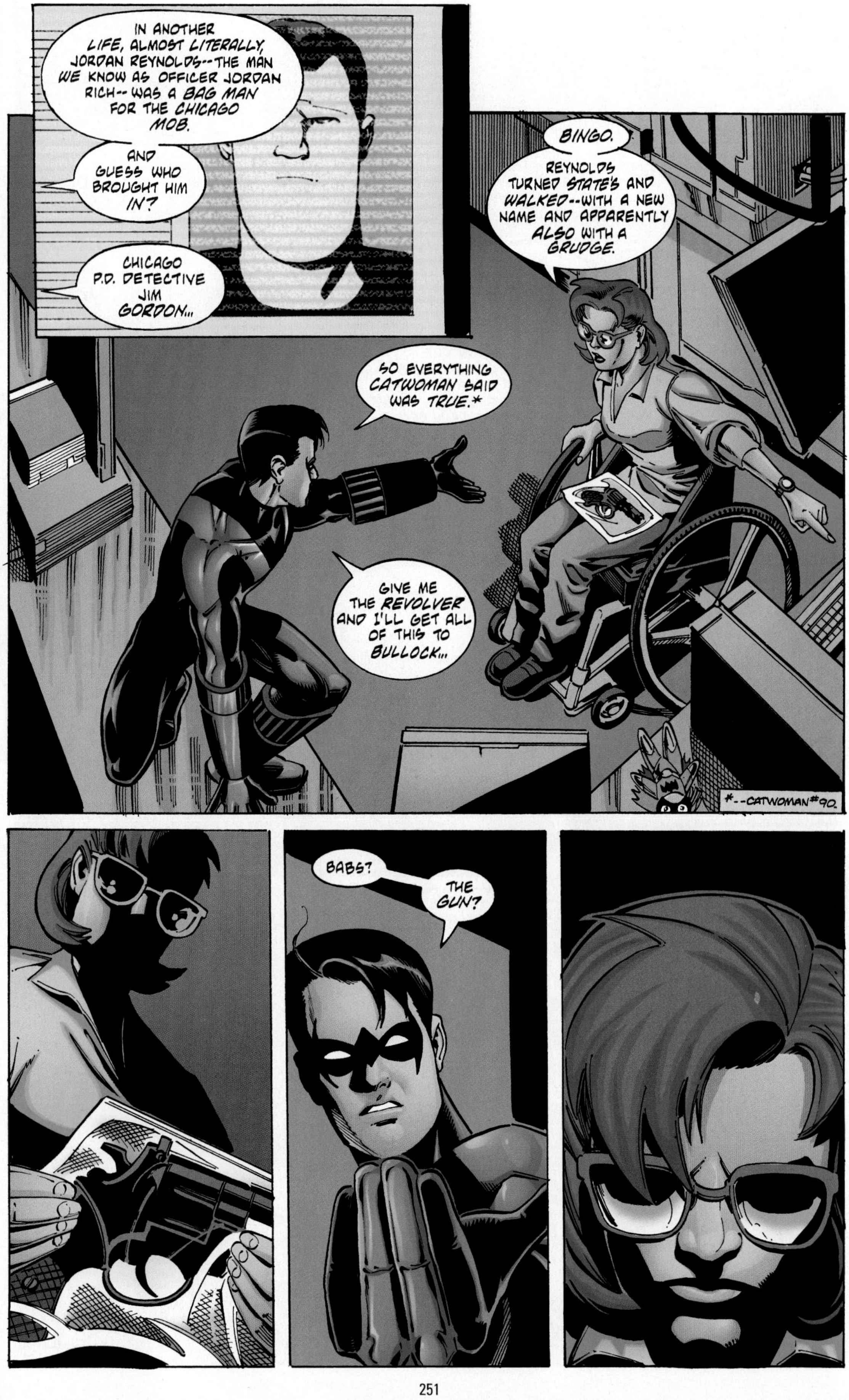
IN ANOTHER LIFE, ALMOST LITERALLY, JORDAN REYNOLDS--THE MAN WE KNOW AS OFFICER JORDAN RICH--WAS A BAG MAN FOR THE CHICAGO MOB.
AND GUESS WHO BROUGHT HIM IN?
CHICAGO P.D. DETECTIVE JIM GORDON...
BINGO.
REYNOLDS TURNED STATE'S AND WALKED--WITH A NEW NAME AND APPARENTLY ALSO WITH A GRUDGE.
SO EVERYTHING CATWOMAN SAID WAS TRUE.*
GIVE ME THE REVOLVER AND I'LL GET ALL OF THIS TO BULLOCK...
*--CATWOMAN #90.
BABS?
THE GUN?

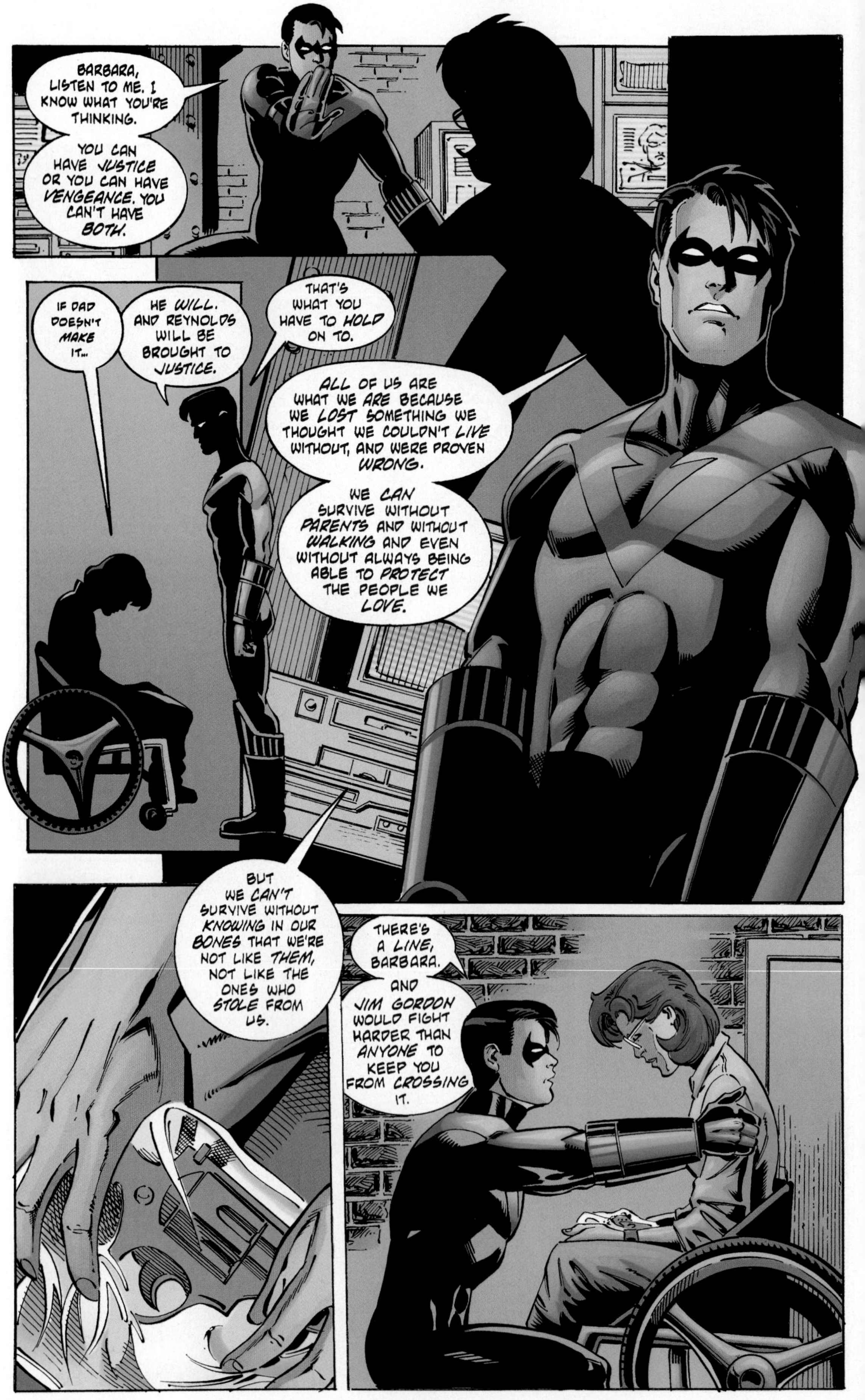
BARBARA, LISTEN TO ME. I KNOW WHAT YOU'RE THINKING.
YOU CAN HAVE JUSTICE OR YOU CAN HAVE VENGEANCE. YOU CAN'T HAVE BOTH.
IF DAD DOESN'T MAKE IT...
HE WILL. AND REYNOLDS WILL BE BROUGHT TO JUSTICE.
THAT'S WHAT YOU HAVE TO HOLD ON TO.
ALL OF US ARE WHAT WE ARE BECAUSE WE LOST SOMETHING WE THOUGHT WE COULDN'T LIVE WITHOUT, AND WERE PROVEN WRONG.
WE CAN SURVIVE WITHOUT PARENTS AND WITHOUT WALKING AND EVEN WITHOUT ALWAYS BEING ABLE TO PROTECT THE PEOPLE WE LOVE.
BUT WE CAN'T SURVIVE WITHOUT KNOWING IN OUR BONES THAT WE'RE NOT LIKE THEM, NOT LIKE THE ONES WHO STOLE FROM US.
THERE'S A LINE, BARBARA.
AND JIM GORDON WOULD FIGHT HARDER THAN ANYONE TO KEEP YOU FROM CROSSING IT.

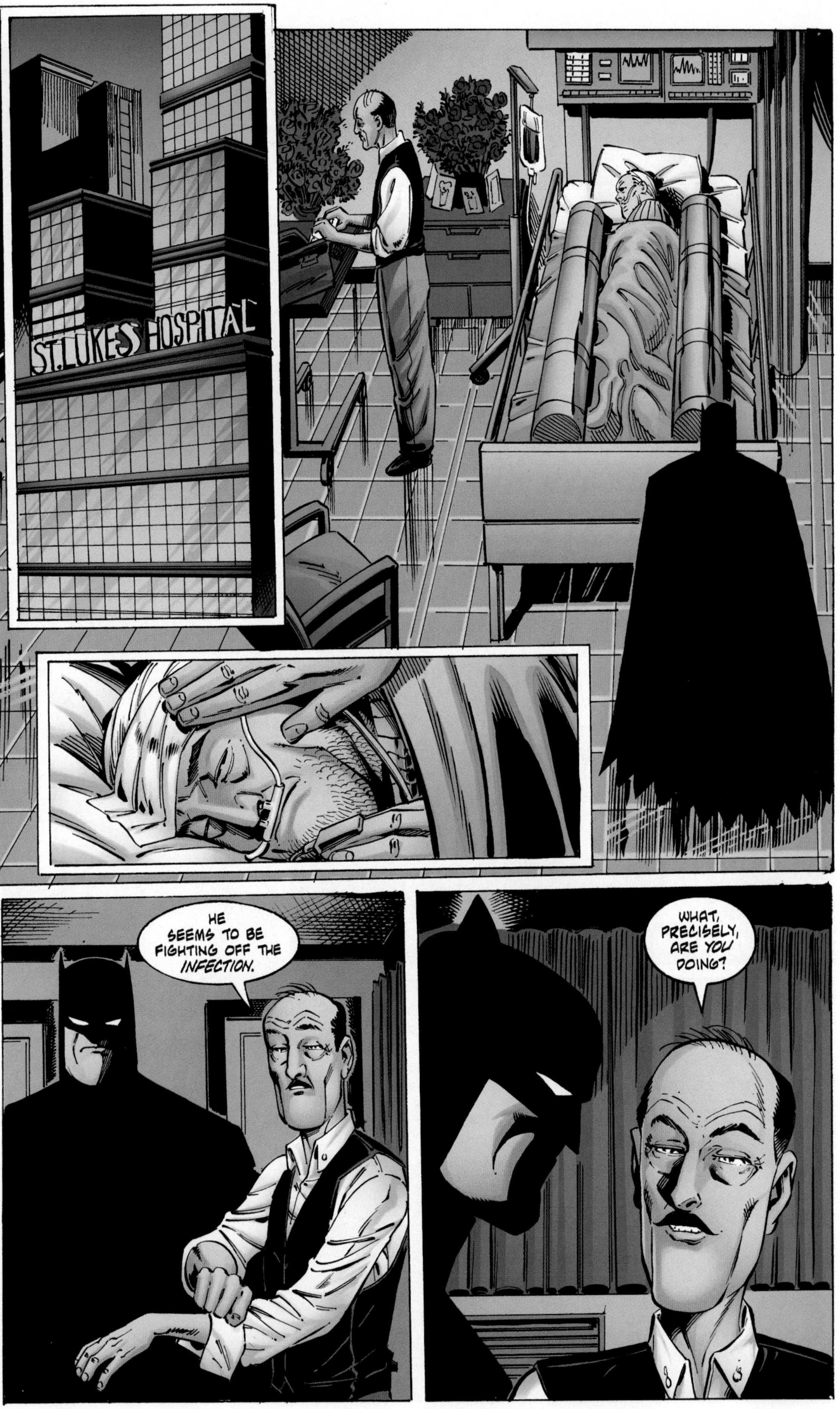
ST. LUKES HOSPITAL
HE SEEMS TO BE FIGHTING OFF THE *INFECTION.*
WHAT, PRECISELY, ARE YOU DOING?

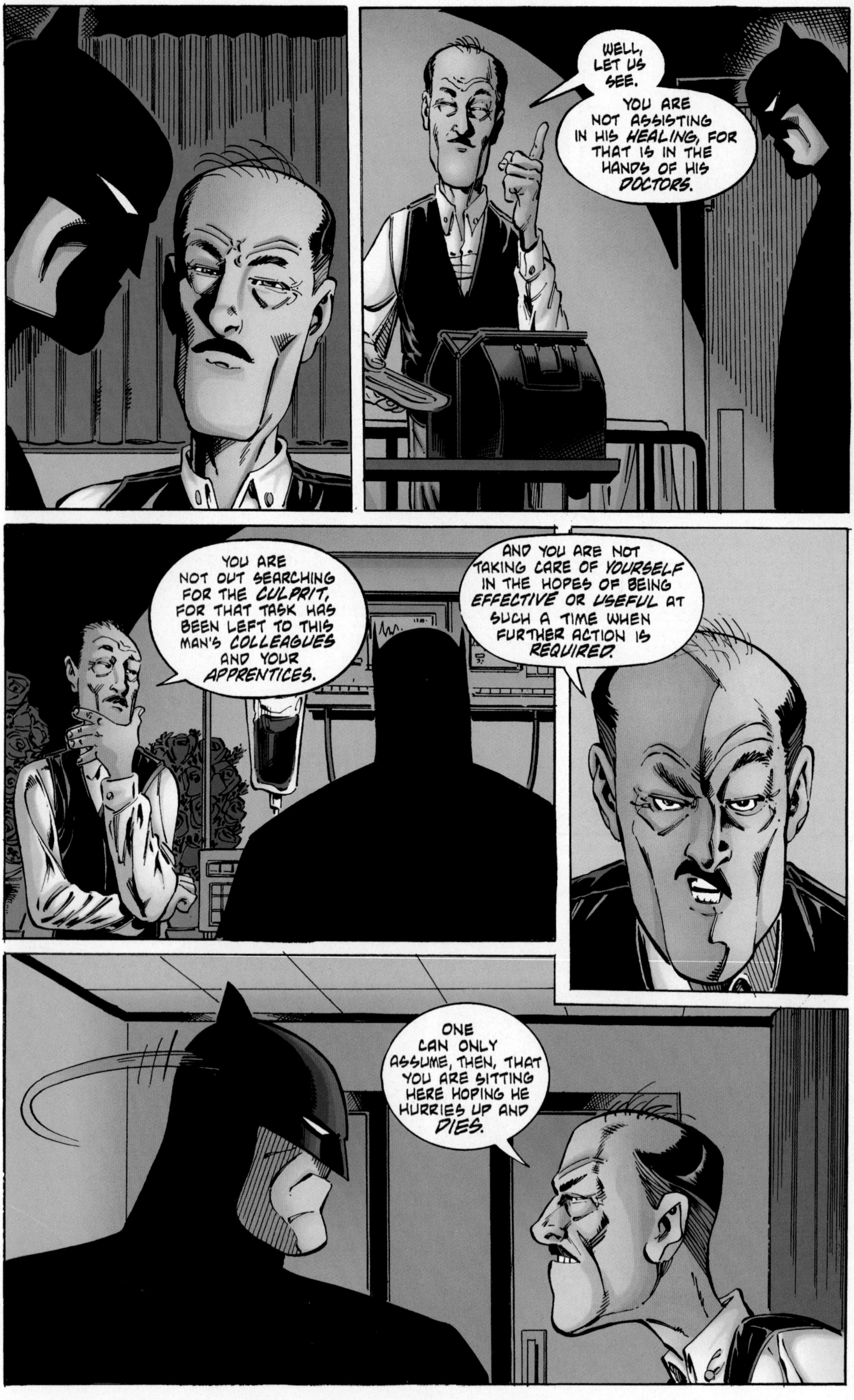
WELL, LET US SEE.
YOU ARE NOT ASSISTING IN HIS HEALING, FOR THAT IS IN THE HANDS OF HIS DOCTORS.
YOU ARE NOT OUT SEARCHING FOR THE CULPRIT, FOR THAT TASK HAS BEEN LEFT TO THIS MAN'S COLLEAGUES AND YOUR APPRENTICES.
AND YOU ARE NOT TAKING CARE OF YOURSELF IN THE HOPES OF BEING EFFECTIVE OR USEFUL AT SUCH A TIME WHEN FURTHER ACTION IS REQUIRED.
ONE CAN ONLY ASSUME, THEN, THAT YOU ARE SITTING HERE HOPING HE HURRIES UP AND DIES.

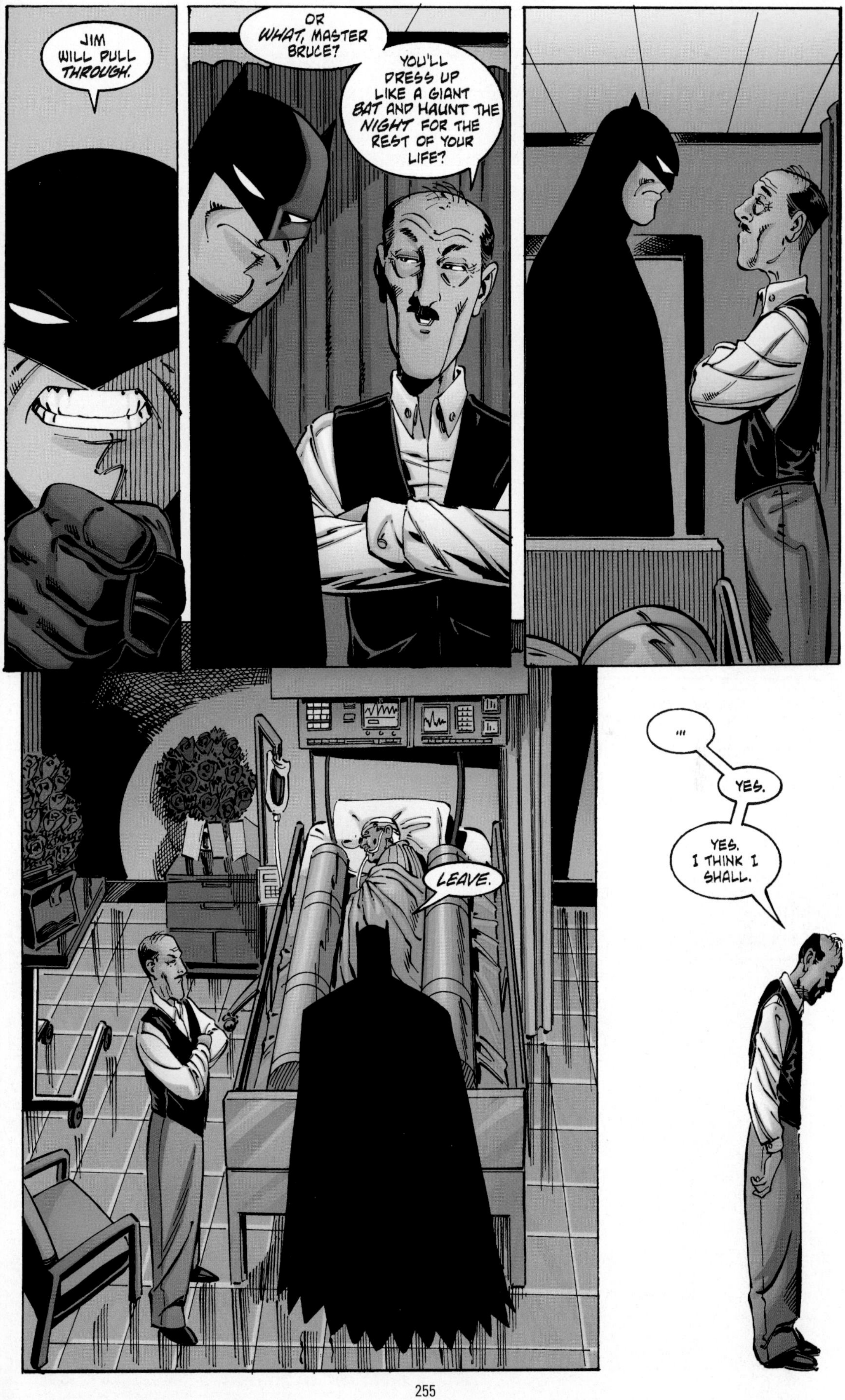
JIM WILL PULL THROUGH.
OR WHAT, MASTER BRUCE?
YOU'LL DRESS UP LIKE A GIANT BAT AND HAUNT THE NIGHT FOR THE REST OF YOUR LIFE?
LEAVE.
...
YES.
YES. I THINK I SHALL.

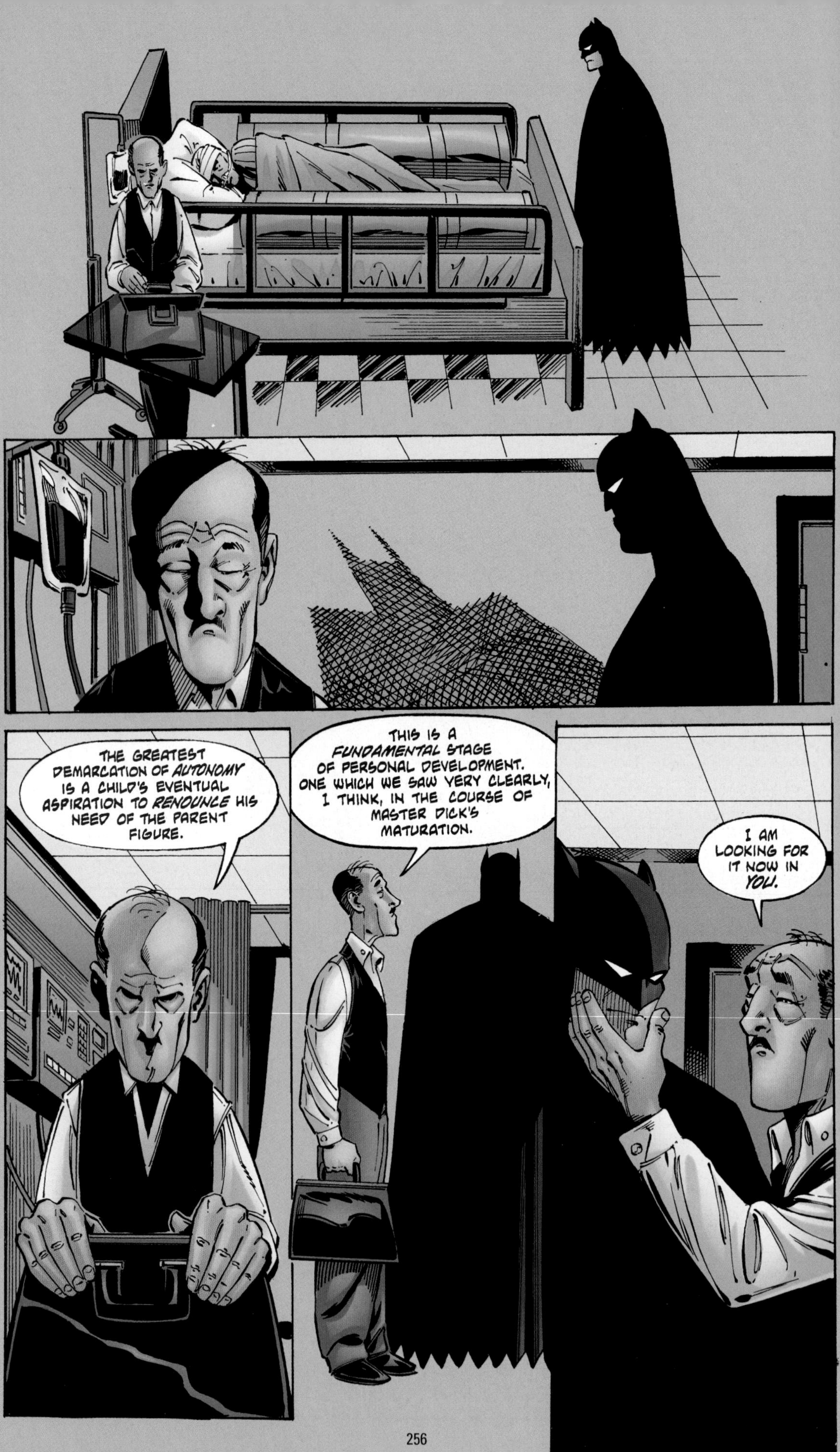
THE GREATEST DEMARCATION OF AUTONOMY IS A CHILD'S EVENTUAL ASPIRATION TO RENOUNCE HIS NEED OF THE PARENT FIGURE.
THIS IS A FUNDAMENTAL STAGE OF PERSONAL DEVELOPMENT. ONE WHICH WE SAW VERY CLEARLY, I THINK, IN THE COURSE OF MASTER DICK'S MATURATION.
I AM LOOKING FOR IT NOW IN YOU.

AND BECAUSE I DO NOT *SEE* IT, BRUCE, I AM LEFT HOPING THAT ITS EFFECT WILL NONETHELESS BE *REVEALED* IF ITS PATTERN IS *REVERSED.*

YOU ARE NOT A *CHILD* AND IT IS TIME YOU CEASED *ACTING* LIKE ONE...

...WHICH MEANS THAT IT IS TIME I STOPPED *ABETTING* YOU.

WHERE ARE YOU *GOING?*

I AM NOT CERTAIN.

I AM *LEAVING* YOUR *EMPLOY.*

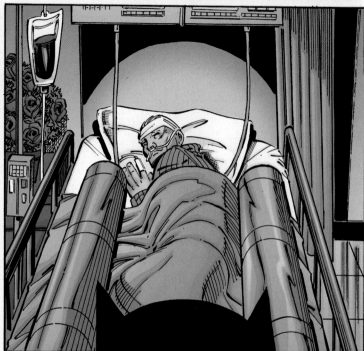

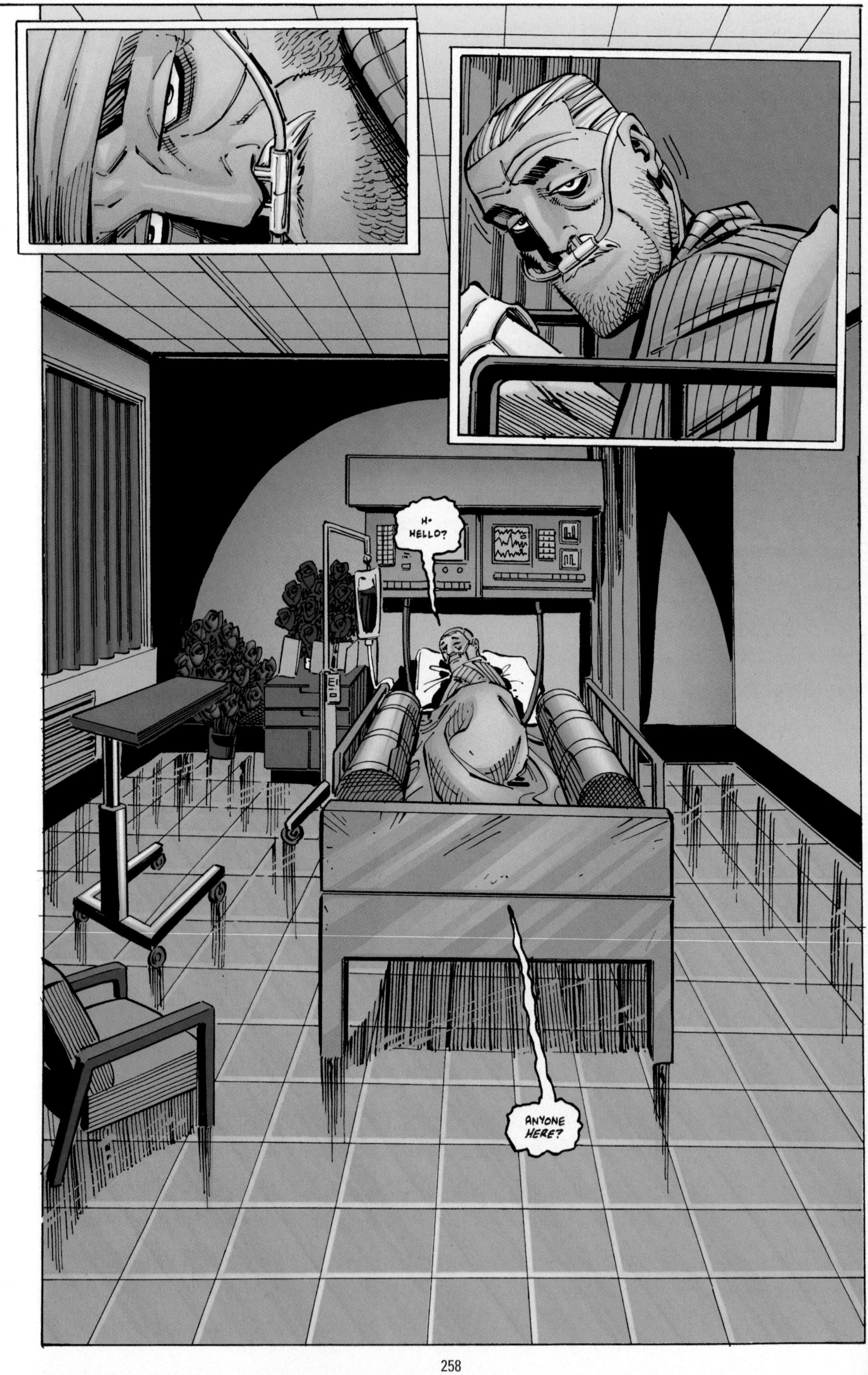
H-
HELLO?
ANYONE
HERE?

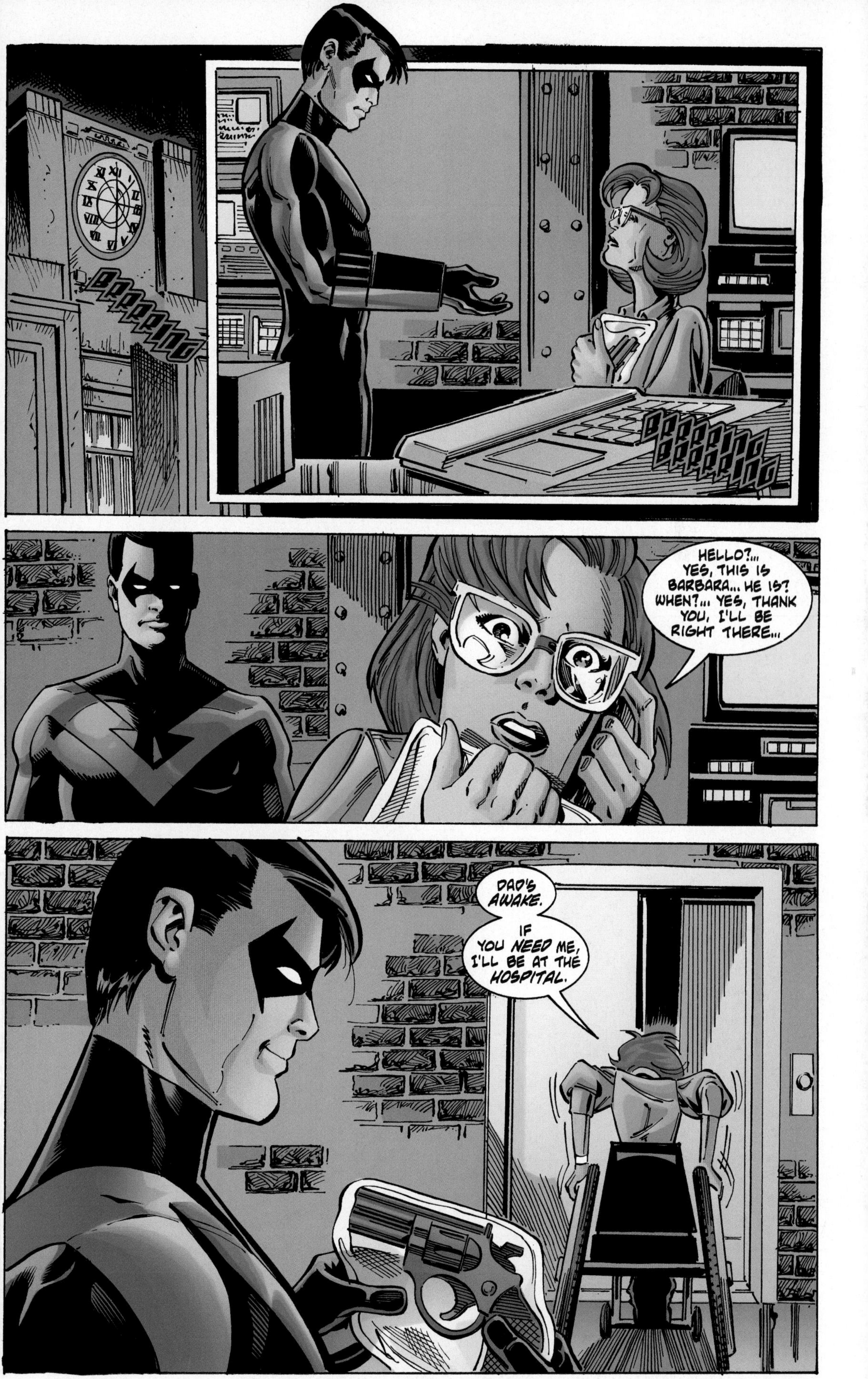
BRRRING
BRRRING
BRRRING
HELLO?... YES, THIS IS BARBARA... HE IS? WHEN?... YES, THANK YOU, I'LL BE RIGHT THERE...
DAD'S AWAKE.
IF YOU NEED ME, I'LL BE AT THE HOSPITAL.

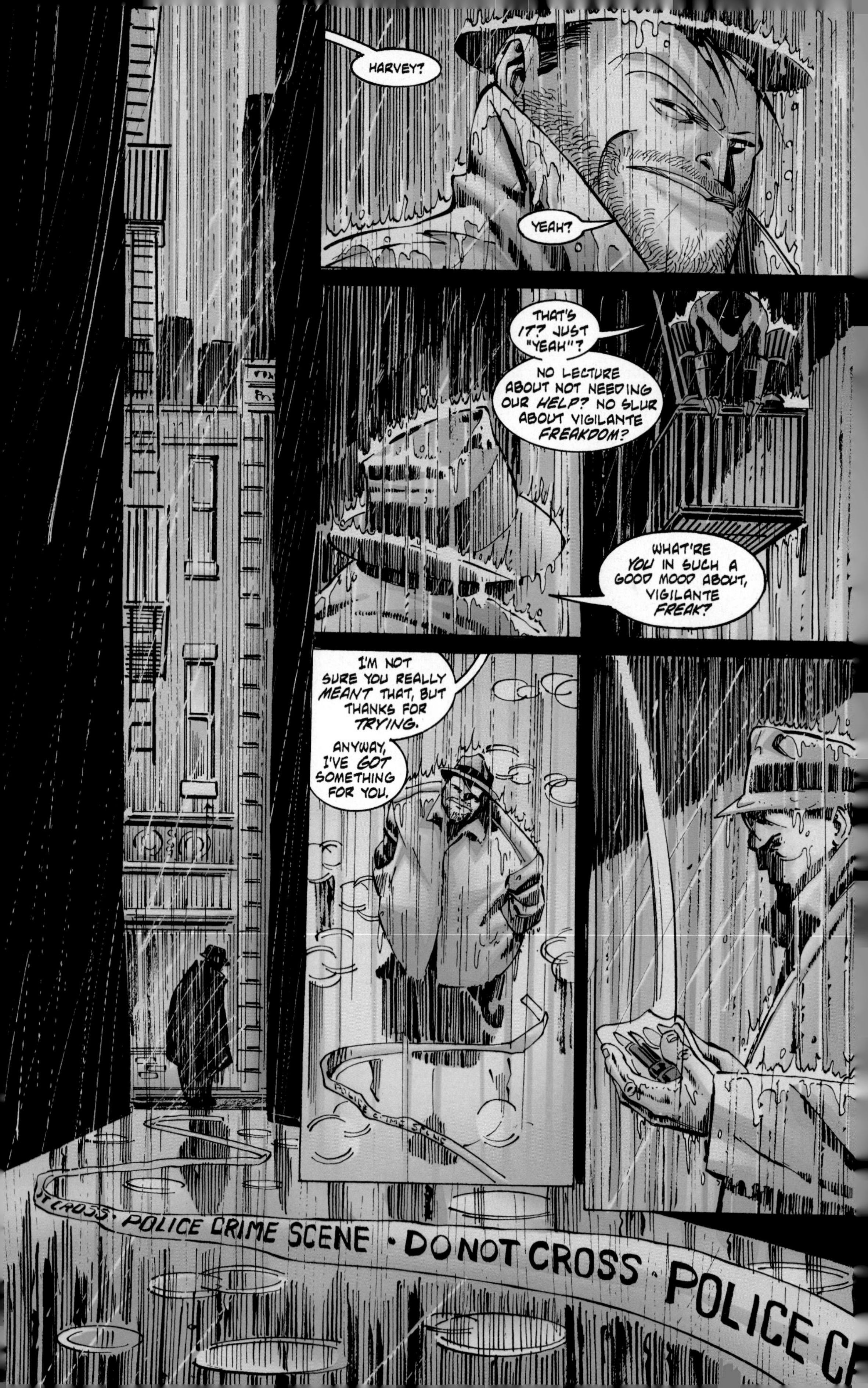
HARVEY?
YEAH?
THAT'S IT? JUST "YEAH"?
NO LECTURE ABOUT NOT NEEDING OUR HELP? NO SLUR ABOUT VIGILANTE FREAKDOM?
WHAT'RE YOU IN SUCH A GOOD MOOD ABOUT, VIGILANTE FREAK?
I'M NOT SURE YOU REALLY MEANT THAT, BUT THANKS FOR TRYING.
ANYWAY, I'VE GOT SOMETHING FOR YOU.
POLICE CRIME SCENE · DO NOT CROSS · POLICE C

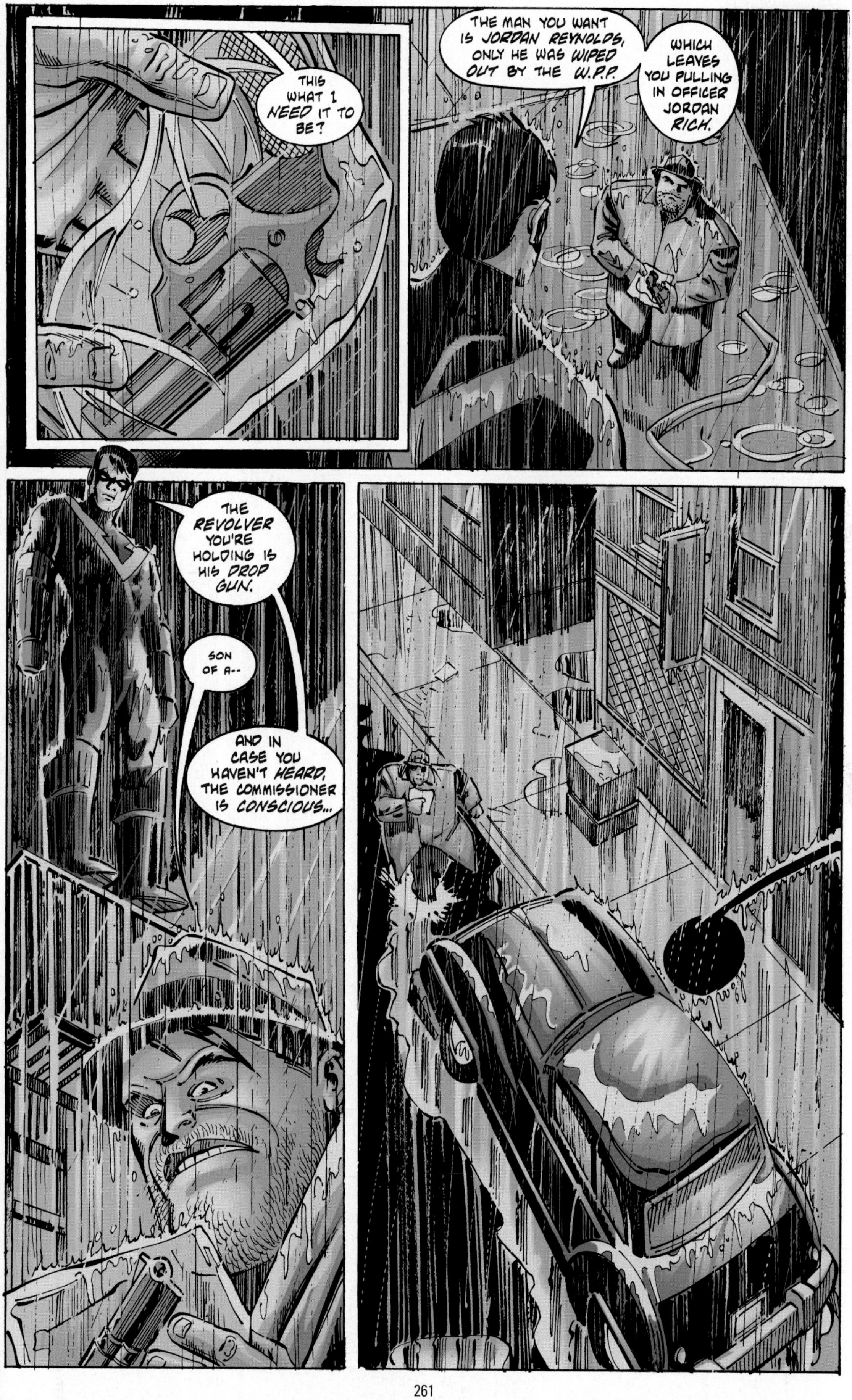
THIS WHAT I NEED IT TO BE?
THE MAN YOU WANT IS JORDAN REYNOLDS, ONLY HE WAS WIPED OUT BY THE W.P.P.
WHICH LEAVES YOU PULLING IN OFFICER JORDAN RICH.
THE REVOLVER YOU'RE HOLDING IS HIS DROP GUN.
SON OF A--
AND IN CASE YOU HAVEN'T HEARD, THE COMMISSIONER IS CONSCIOUS...

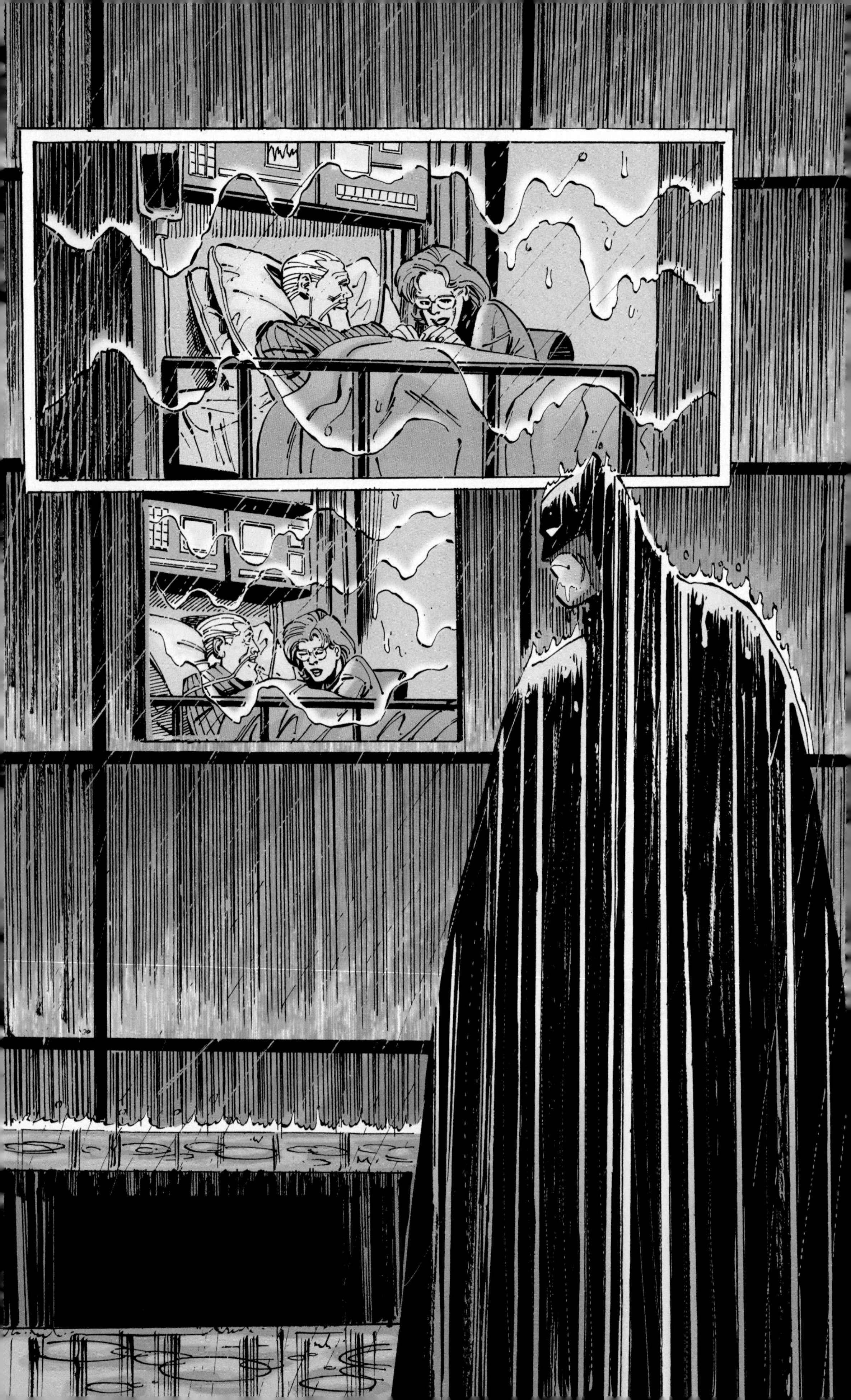

"Stellar. A solid yarn that roots itself in Grayson's past, with gorgeous artwork by Barrows."
— **IGN**

"Dynamic."
— **THE NEW YORK TIMES**

NIGHTWING
VOL. 1: TRAPS AND TRAPEZES
KYLE HIGGINS
with EDDY BARROWS

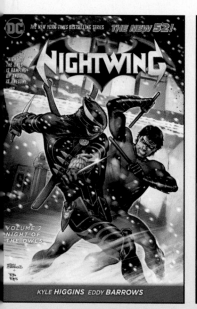

NIGHTWING
VOL. 2: NIGHT OF THE OWLS

NIGHTWING
VOL. 3: DEATH OF THE FAMILY

READ THE ENTIRE EPIC!

NIGHTWING VOL. 4:
SECOND CITY

NIGHTWING VOL. 5:
SETTING SON

"A new generation is going to fall in love with Nightwing."
— **MTV GEEK**

"Batman is getting a brand-new voice."
– USA TODAY

"A great showcase for the new team as well as offering a taste of the new flavor they'll be bringing to Gotham City." **– IGN**

DC UNIVERSE REBIRTH

BATMAN

VOL. 1: I AM GOTHAM

TOM KING
with DAVID FINCH

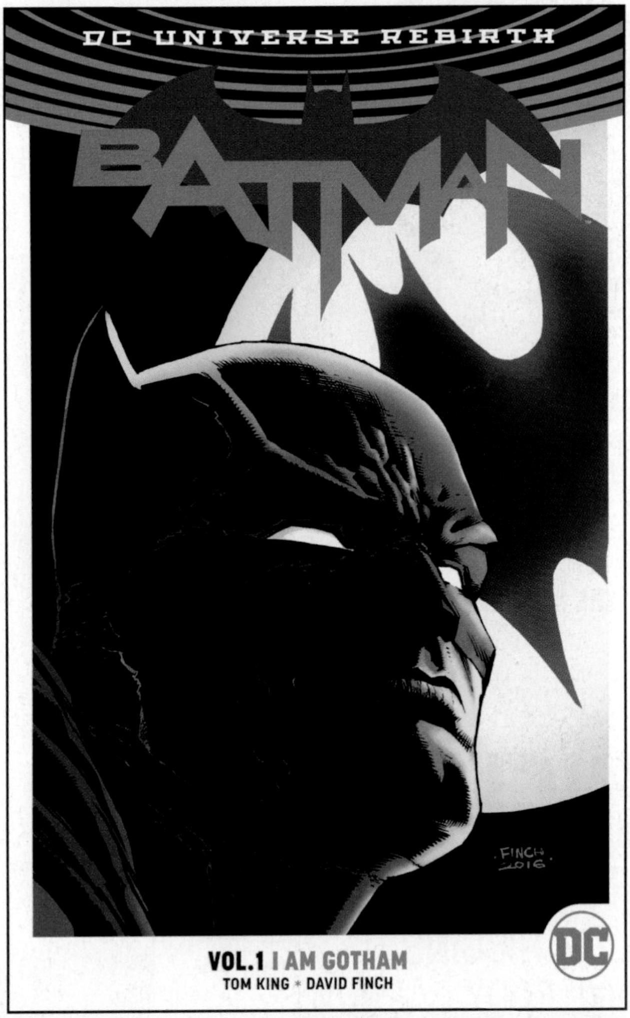
DC UNIVERSE REBIRTH
BATMAN
VOL.1 I AM GOTHAM
TOM KING * DAVID FINCH

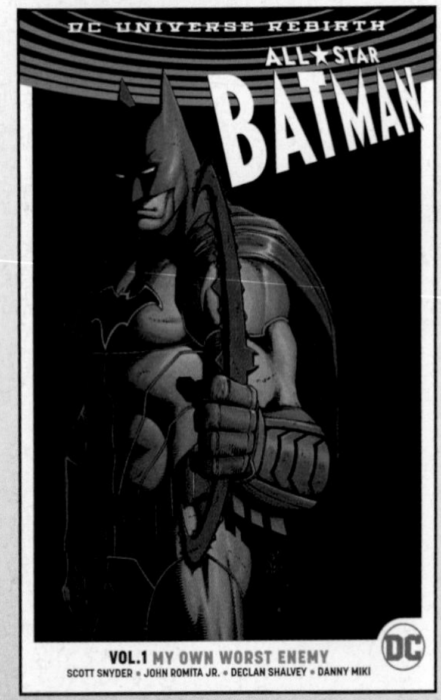
DC UNIVERSE REBIRTH
ALL★STAR
BATMAN
VOL.1 MY OWN WORST ENEMY
SCOTT SNYDER • JOHN ROMITA JR. • DECLAN SHALVEY • DANNY MIKI

ALL-STAR BATMAN VOL. 1:
MY OWN WORST ENEMY

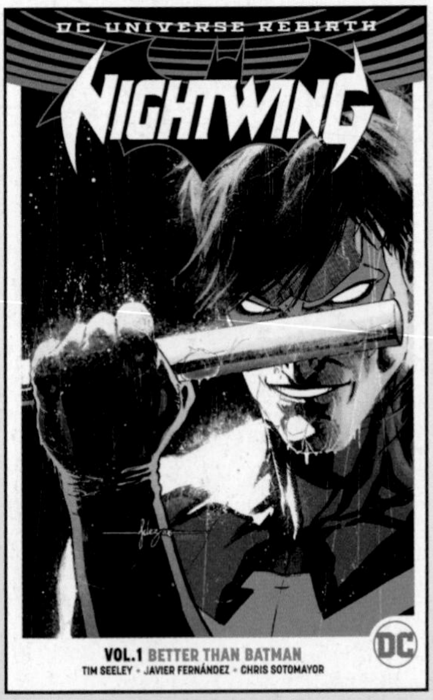
DC UNIVERSE REBIRTH
NIGHTWING
VOL.1 BETTER THAN BATMAN
TIM SEELEY • JAVIER FERNÁNDEZ • CHRIS SOTOMAYOR

NIGHTWING VOL. 1:
BETTER THAN BATMAN

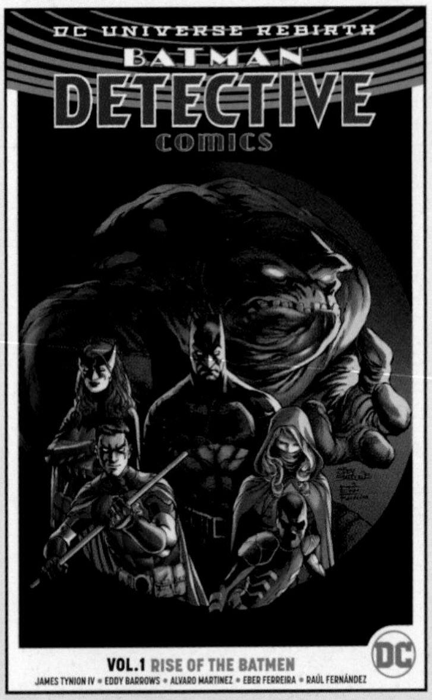
DC UNIVERSE REBIRTH
BATMAN
DETECTIVE
COMICS
VOL.1 RISE OF THE BATMEN
JAMES TYNION IV • EDDY BARROWS • ALVARO MARTINEZ • EBER FERREIRA • RAÚL FERNÁNDEZ

DETECTIVE COMICS VOL. 1:
RISE OF THE BATMEN

Get more DC graphic novels wherever comics and books are sold!

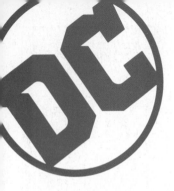